REAL-WORLD JAVA®

Real-World Java®

Real-World Java®

HELPING YOU NAVIGATE THE JAVA ECOSYSTEM

Victor Grazi
Jeanne Boyarsky

WILEY

Published by John Wiley & Sons, Inc., Hoboken, New Jersey.
Published simultaneously in Canada and the United Kingdom.

ISBNs: 9781394275724 (Paperback), 9781394275748 (ePDF), 9781394275731 (ePub)

For general information on our other products and services, please contact our Customer Care Department within the United States at (800) 762- 2974, outside the United States at (317) 572- 3993. For product technical support, you can find answers to frequently asked questions or reach us via live chat at https://support.wiley.com.

If you believe you've found a mistake in this book, please bring it to our attention by emailing our reader support team at wileysupport@wiley.com with the subject line "Possible Book Errata Submission."

Wiley also publishes its books in a variety of electronic formats. Some content that appears in print may not be available in electronic formats. For more information about Wiley products, visit our web site at www.wiley.com.

Library of Congress Control Number: 2024934523

Cover image: © CSA-Printstock/Getty Images
Cover design: Wiley

SKY10093828_121324

To the Java community for being so open to helping people learn.

—Victor & Jeanne

ABOUT THE AUTHORS

VICTOR GRAZI is a voracious learner who back in 1996 heard about this new technology called "the Internet" and a new technology called Java that made the Internet blaze! Inducted as a Java champion in 2012, he serves on the Java Community Process Executive Committee, leads a JSR, served as Java Lead Editor on InfoQ magazine, and has traveled the world evangelizing Java. He is the author of Java Concurrent Animated, an application that has helped thousands of developers visualize Java concurrency.

JEANNE BOYARSKY is excited to be publishing this, her 10th book. She was selected as a Java Champion in 2019 and is a leader of the NYJavaSIG. She has worked as a Java developer for more than 22 years at a bank in New York City where she develops, mentors, and conducts training. Besides being a senior moderator at `CodeRanch.com` in her free time, she works on the forum code base. Jeanne also mentors the programming division of a FIRST robotics team, where she works with students just getting started with Java. She also speaks at several conferences each year. Jeanne is also a Distinguished Toastmaster and a Scrum Master. You can find out more about Jeanne at `https://www.jeanneboyarsky.com`.

ABOUT THE AUTHORS

ABOUT THE TECHNICAL EDITOR

RODRIGO GRACIANO is a seasoned software engineer, Java advocate, and technology leader. He has a BSc in computer science from UNILASALLE, Brazil, and has been working with Java since 2006. In 2011, Rodrigo moved to the United States, where he now lives with his wife, Manuela, and their two sons, Lucas and Theodore.

Rodrigo is a senior member and leader of the NYJavaSIG, the New York Java User Group, where he actively contributes to organizing monthly events to promote the Java language and its community. A frequent speaker at tech conferences across South America, the United States, and Europe, Rodrigo shares his passion for software development and Java best practices.

Currently, he serves as a director of engineering at BNY. In recognition of his contributions to the Java community, Rodrigo was nominated as a Java Champion in 2022.

ABOUT THE TECHNICAL PROOFREADER

BARRY BURD is a professor in the Department of Mathematics and Computer Science at Drew University in Madison, New Jersey. He's a director of the Garden State Java User Group and, along with Jeanne, a leader of the NYJavaSIG. He's the author of several Java books, including *Java For Dummies*, soon to be in its 9th edition. His most recent book is *Quantum Computing Algorithms* published by Packt. In 2020, he was honored to be named a Java Champion.

ACKNOWLEDGMENTS

We would like to thank numerous individuals for their contributions to this book. Thank you to Patrick Walsh and Archana Pragash for guiding us through the process and making the book better in many ways. Thank you to Rodrigo Graciano for being our technical editor and Barry Burd for being our technical proofreader. They made the book better in so many ways. And a special thank-you to our copy editor Kim Wimpsett for finding subtle errors that everyone (including us!) missed. This book also wouldn't be possible without many people at Wiley, including Kenyon Brown, Pete Gaughan, Ashirvad Moses, and many others.

Victor would personally like to say thank-you to his wife, Victoria, for all the date nights she sacrificed to let me work on this book. He continues to learn from her and be awed by her vision every single day. He also wants to thank his parents, Jack and Claudie Grazi, for all they have invested in him. Finally, he thanks posthumously Dr. Isadore Glaubiger, his math professor way back when at Brooklyn Tech, who inspired him and taught him to think. And a special thanks to Jeanne for her organizational skills and attention to detail. Were it not for Jeanne, he says he never would have made it past page 1.

Jeanne would personally like to thank Dani, Janeice, Kim, Norm, Scott, and Shweta during a difficult month that overlapped with book writing. She also wants to thank Scott for his patience as Jeanne worked on two books simultaneously (this one and *Oracle Certified Professional Java 21 Developer Study Guide*). A big thank-you to Victor for coming up with the idea for the book and being a great co-author in bringing it to life. Finally, Jeanne would like to thank all of the new programmers at `CodeRanch.com` and FIRST robotics teams FRC 694 and FTC 310/479 for the constant reminders of how new programmers think.

CONTENTS

INTRODUCTION

CONGRATULATIONS ON MASTERING THE BASICS OF JAVA! You've journeyed through loops, switches, and exception handling, you've made sense of lambdas and streams, and you're starting to get comfortable with the core Java APIs. You've built a solid foundation, and that's no small accomplishment—You are ready to start your elite career as a Java engineer!

But Java is more than a language; it's a vast ecosystem filled with tools, platforms, libraries, and APIs that empower you to extend Java's capabilities into every corner of enterprise development.

This book is your guide to navigating that ecosystem. While numerous tomes delve into specialized areas of Java, few provide an accessible roadmap across the broader landscape. Here, you'll find clear explanations and practical coding examples of the technologies you can expect to encounter most often in enterprise Java environments. The knowledge you gain here will prepare you to delve deeper into additional resources and broaden your skills in this dynamic ecosystem.

WHAT DOES THIS BOOK COVER?

This book begins with a brief coverage through Java's history, offering insights that will deepen your understanding of the language's evolution and its current direction. From there, we dive into essential tools: you'll get acquainted with IDEs, version control, and build tools, that form the backbone of any Java developer's toolkit.

Next, we explore a range of foundational libraries and frameworks—logging, Spring, testing tools, and Project Lombok—that enhance your productivity and code quality. The book then navigates more advanced topics like concurrency and regular expressions, essential for writing efficient, powerful code, and continues with cross-cutting concerns such as aspect-oriented programming and performance optimization.

Finally, we wrap up with a chapter dedicated to additional tools and technologies that every Java developer should have in their arsenal.

Each chapter includes practical code examples and tips to help you work effectively with these technologies. Plus, a "Further References" section at the end of each chapter provides resources to dive deeper into each topic.

WHO SHOULD READ THIS BOOK

This book is intended for anyone who has learned the Java language but is still gaining familiarity with the broader Java ecosystem. It's especially suited to students, IT professionals transitioning to Java, and developers looking to deepen their expertise. For those returning to Java after working on legacy projects, this book is also an excellent way to get up to speed on the latest tools and practices.

READER SUPPORT FOR THIS BOOK

To help you get the most out of this book, here are some additional resources and support links:

Companion Download Files

Throughout the book, you'll find references to code examples and configurations that illustrate key concepts. These files are available for download to save you time and allow you to experiment directly with the material. You can access these companion files at: `https://github.com/realworldjava`.

How to Contact the Author

We appreciate your input, errata reports, and questions about this book! Post in the discussion area of our GitHub organization at `https://github.com/orgs/realworldjava/discussions`. All acknowledged errors will be posted on the `README` page of the repository for the relevant chapter.

1

How We Got Here: History of Java in a Nutshell

WHAT'S IN THIS CHAPTER?

- Understanding the Stewardship of Java
- Differentiating Key Java Versions
- Working with Deprecation and Retirement
- Identifying Renames
- Understanding the Principles of Change

INTRODUCTION

You've learned Java, and you're ready to start using it at work. Or you are already using it in work, but you've discovered the daunting ecosystem that they never taught you in school. This book is for those who have already learned how to code in Java and are looking for the next step. Whether you are a student, career changer, or professional programmer switching languages, this is your opportunity to learn about the Java ecosystem.

This book is not intended to be a comprehensive guide to the Java ecosystem; that would require many thousand-page tomes. If you are just learning Java, we recommend *Head First Java, 3rd Edition* (O'Reilly Media, 2022) or *Java For Dummies* (For Dummies, 2025). Then come back to this book. The goal of this book is to expose the reader to some of the most common frameworks, tools, and techniques used in enterprise Java development shops, with enough background and examples to dive right in.

In this chapter, we will cover some information about Java in general before getting into specialized topics in the later chapters. While chapters can be read out of order, we recommend reading Chapters 1–4 before skipping around.

CODE DOWNLOADS FOR THIS CHAPTER

The source code for this chapter is available on the book page at `www.wiley.com`. Click the Downloads link. The code can also be found at `https://github.com/realworldjava/Ch01-History`. See the `README.md` file in that repository for details.

UNDERSTANDING THE STEWARDSHIP OF JAVA

Java was created by James Gosling at Sun Microsystems and released to the world in 1995.

As legend has it, Java started life as "Oak," a new language for building embedded software in smart devices. The idea was novel: instead of writing software for each embedded operating system, design a "write once, run anywhere," compiled, object-oriented language that produces bytecode, and design a bytecode interpreter for each platform that could execute it.

While they were at it, they would include built-in frameworks that were, in other languages, snap-on additions, such as concurrency or UI designers. Then cap it off with memory management in the form of garbage collection and optimize it using just-in-time (JIT) compiling, and *voilà*, they had everything needed for an embedded language platform.

But alas, it was soon discovered that there was already an "Oak" platform brewing. A long night in a coffee shop over some hot Java brew, and the rest is history.

Many years later, in 2009, Oracle acquired Sun, and ownership of Java transferred to Oracle. To this day, Oracle remains the steward, or caretaker, of Java.

The Java community's commitment to ensuring that Java is backward compatible and its robust series of thousands of Technology Compatibility Kit (TCK) tests that must pass for every feature provide the stability and dependability that have thrust Java into its place as one of the most successful programming languages in history.

Oracle recognizes its stewardship as a critical responsibility, given the sheer number of people and companies heavily using Java. The JCP (Java Community Process) has an Executive Committee (basically Java's board of directors) with many organizations as members to ensure the community is represented. Some past/future members are competitors with their own JDKs (Java Development Kits), for example, Amazon, Azul, and Microsoft. Others are complementary, notably Integrated Development Environment (IDE) providers like Eclipse and JetBrains. Others are simply strong proponents of Java like BellSoft and Fujitsu. Finally, there are community members like SouJava (Brazilian Java User Group) and Ken Fogel (individual member).

One of the changes introduced under Oracle's stewardship was a more frequent and predictable release schedule. Notice in Figure 1.1 that releases have varied in both frequency and month of release. In one case, Java users had to wait more than five years for a new version.

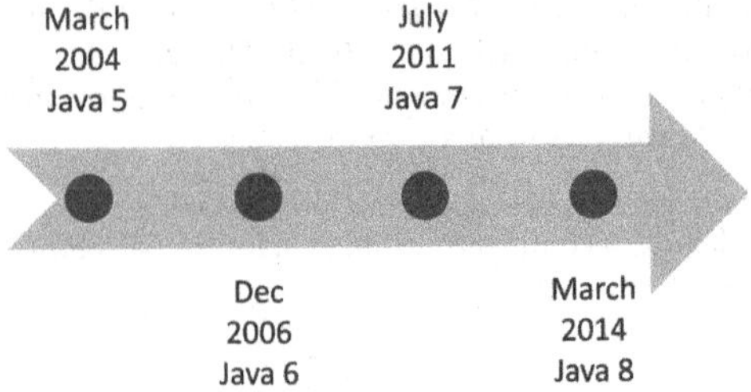

FIGURE 1.1: Java releases

With the new release cadence, a new version of Java comes out every six months. You may be thinking that many companies don't want to upgrade every six months, and you'd be right! There are also less frequent releases called *Long-Term Support* (*LTS*) releases. When the new release cycle started, LTS releases were every three years. They are now every two years.

Table 1.1 shows releases from the start of the new release cadence to the publishing of this book. As you can see, there are now regular, predictable releases. This book uses Java 21, which was the latest LTS at the time of printing.

Figure 1.2 shows the LTS release schedule. You can predict LTS dates into the future now that there is a pattern. This helps companies plan.

Many companies run their Java programs remotely, such as through a website. Until 2020, this was often done through *Spring* or *Java EE* (Enterprise Edition.) See Chapter 6, "Getting to Know the Spring Framework," and Chapter 14, "Getting to Know More of the Ecosystem," for more details. In 2020, Oracle handed over stewardship of Java EE to an open-source foundation. Since "Java" is a trademark, the Java EE framework was renamed to "Jakarta EE" at that point.

TABLE 1.1: Java Releases

YEAR	MARCH RELEASE	SEPTEMBER RELEASE
2017	n/a (cadence started in September)	Java 9
2018	Java 10	**Java 11 (LTS)**
2019	Java 12	Java 13
2020	Java 14	Java 15
2021	Java 16	**Java 17 (LTS)**
2022	Java 18	Java 19
2023	Java 20	**Java 21 (LTS)**
2024	Java 22	Java 23

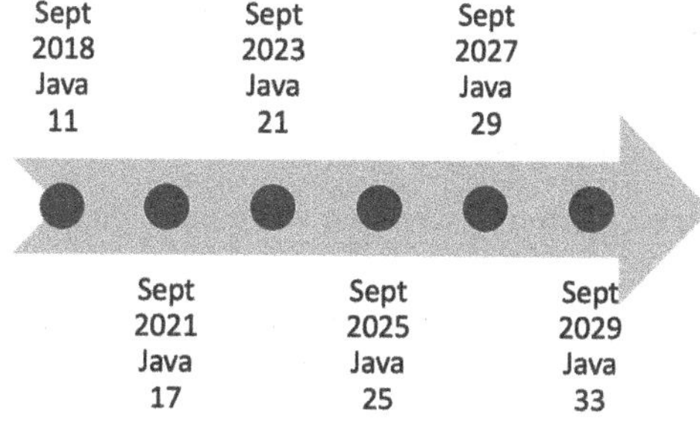

FIGURE 1.2: LTS release schedule, with future predictions

DIFFERENTIATING KEY JAVA VERSIONS

The Java language has evolved quite a bit over time. By looking at key features added over time, you can get a feel for this evolution along with an expectation that the language will continue to improve. Additionally, you will know what to expect if your work project is not on the latest version.

Note that this section is not even close to a full list of features. We picked the most significant feature of each version covered.

You might be wondering why we aren't including type inference with the `var` keyword in this section. While both of this book's authors use `var` in some cases in our work code, we felt it would be clearer in this book to specify what the types are and ensure all imports are represented.

Coding Generics in Java 5

Before Java 5, the compiler had no way of knowing what you intended to put in a list. Java 5 introduced *generics*, which allow you to specify the type, in the case of the following example, a `String`:

```
1:  import java.util.ArrayList;
2:  import java.util.List;
3:
4:  public class Java5Generics {
5:
6:     private static List<String> createList() {
7:        List<String> buildingNames = new ArrayList<String>();
8:        buildingNames.add("Firehouse");
9:        return buildingNames;
10:    }
11:
12:    public static void main(String[] args) {
13:       List<String> buildingNames = createList();
14:
15:       System.out.println(buildingNames);   // [Firehouse]
16:    }
17: }
```

Now that we've informed the compiler about our intent, it is our assistant. The compiler will produce an error if we attempt to add an `Integer` or `LocalDate` or anything else to `buildingNames`.

You might be wondering why the line 7 doesn't say `new ArrayList<>()` and instead uses a longer version. The diamond operator (`<>`) was added in Java 7, and this example is for Java 5. Even this shows the evolution of the language, though!

Coding with Functional Programming from Java 8

Functional programming is a way of writing code more declaratively. You specify what you want to do rather than dealing with the state of objects. You focus more on expressions than loops.

Java 8 introduced lambdas and method references to facilitate writing code with *deferred execution*, also known as "code that runs later." Both let you easily pass executable code to a method. In the following code, you can see two lambdas and a method reference:

```
import java.util.Arrays;
import java.util.List;

public class Java8FunctionalProgramming {

```

```
6:      public static void main(String[] args) {
7:
8:         List<String> computerCompanies = Arrays.asList(
9:            "Dell", "Acer", "Microsoft", "IBM", "Lenovo");
10:        computerCompanies.stream()
11:           .filter(n -> n.length() > 5)
12:           .map(n -> "*" + n)
13:           .sorted()
14:           .forEach(System.out::println);
15:     }
16: }
```

This code outputs these two lines:

```
*Lenovo
*Microsoft
```

Line 10 kicks off the stream pipeline. Lines 11 and 12 use lambdas to specify what should happen at each step. The `->` gives you a clue that you are looking at a lambda. Line 11 only allows names with at least five characters through the pipeline. Line 12 adds an asterisk to the beginning of each line in the pipeline. Notice it does not change the original `computerCompanies` contents.

Then on line 14, you can see the first method reference. The `::` tells you it is a method reference and in this case prints the values. A method reference is a more compact version of a lambda. Writing `n -> System.out.println(n)` would have been equivalent.

You might have noticed that we didn't call `List.of()` instead of `Arrays.asList()` on line 8. `List.of()` was added in Java 9!

Coding Modules from Java 11

The *Java Platform Module System* (JPMS) groups code at a higher level than packages. The main purpose of a module is to provide groups of related packages to offer a particular set of functionality to developers. It's like a JAR file except a developer chooses which packages are accessible outside the module. Many companies choose not to use modules and indeed their use is optional.

Java modules were introduced in Java 9, not Java 11. We are listing them under Java 11 because that was the first LTS release of Java that supported modules. Any projects on a version of Java lower than 8 will upgrade to Java 11, 17, 21, etc. They will not go to 9 since support for Java 9 ended in March 2018 (six months after its release in September 2017).

A module is a Java Archive (JAR) consisting of a `module-info.java` file at the root of the project and one or more Java packages. For example, here is a module with two packages containing one class each:

```
book-module
| -- module-info.class
| -- com
   | -- wiley
      | -- realworldjava
         | -- modulecode
            | -- internal
               | -- PrivateHelper.class
            | -- utils
               | -- BookUtils.class
```

This example shows `.class` files instead of `.java` files because the JAR file contains executable bytecode. But wait. You don't want the callers of your module to reference `PrivateHelper`. That's where the `module-info` file comes into play:

```
module com.wiley.realworldjava.modulecode {
   exports com.wiley.realworldjava.modulecode.utils;
   requires java.sql;
}
```

The `module` keyword lets Java know we are specifying a module here rather than a `class` or `interface` or other Java top-level type. The `exports` directive tells Java that callers can reference the `utils` package directly from their code. Since the `internal` package is not mentioned in the module-info file, callers cannot use it directly, only through `BookUtils`. Finally, the `requires` directive specifies that we use the `java.sql` module, which is provided by Oracle with the JDK. There is another module we use called `java.base`, but that one is provided automatically without having to specify it. It contains common classes such as `String` and `List`.

Coding Text Blocks and Records from Java 17

It was hard to pick one favorite from Java 17, so we picked two. Text blocks are also known as *multiline strings*. Text blocks were added in Java 15. Like modules, we are listing them under the first LTS release that made them available. You can see a text block here surrounded by three double quotes ("):

```
1:  public class Java17TextBlocks {
2:
3:     public static void main(String[] args) {
4:
5:        String data = """
6:           Apple,Fruit
7:            Banana,Fruit
8:           Potato,Vegetable
9:           """;
10:
11:       String formatted = String.format("*%s*", data);
12:       System.out.println(formatted);
13:    }
14: }
```

This outputs these four lines:

```
*Apple,Fruit
 Banana,Fruit
Potato,Vegetable
*
```

Notice that the indentation of our text block is preserved and the incidental whitespace used for IDE formatting is not. Also note that the triple quotes in line 9 will introduce a blank line in the string. If you want to omit the trailing line break, place the three closing double quotes (") at the end of line 8.

Records were introduced in Java 17 and got rid of a ton of boilerplate code when creating an immutable class. A simple record is used in this example:

```
public class Java17Records {

   record Coordinate(double x, double y) {}

   public static void main(String[] args) {

      Coordinate coord = new Coordinate(1.2, 5.9);
      System.out.println(coord.x());
      System.out.println(coord);
   }
}
```

This outputs the following:

```
1.2
Coordinate[x=1.2, y=5.9]
```

Line 3 creates a record with two fields. A record is like an immutable class that includes the following:

- An instance variable for each parameter listed
- Getters (without the `get`/`is` prefix)
- A constructor taking a parameter for each instance variable
- `equals()` and `hashCode()` methods that include the value of each instance variable
- A `toString()` method that prints each field of the record in a convenient, easy-to-read format

Line 8 demonstrates that the getter method is `x()` rather than `getX()`. Finally, line 9 implicitly calls `toString()` showing you can get a useful implementation without writing any code.

Records are convenient when you need a simple immutable class. You can override methods in the record body or add your own methods. When you need more customization power or setters such as for Java Persistence API (JPA) entities, Project Lombok may better match your needs. See Chapter 8, "Annotation-Driven Code Using Project Lombok," for details.

Learning About Virtual Threads from Java 21

A long time ago Java used the raw `Thread` class for concurrency. Although this remains the low-level unit of concurrency, the language then added the `Executors` class and more powerful concurrency techniques such as fork join and `parallelStream()`. However, parallelization is not free; there are setup and coordination costs in addition to the memory resources of the threads themselves.

As computers get more central processing units (CPUs), parallelization becomes more important. Java 21 introduced virtual threads to greatly reduce the cost of concurrency. See Chapter 9, "Parallelizing Your Application Using Java Concurrency," for a more detailed explanation and example of virtual threads.

WORKING WITH DEPRECATION AND RETIREMENT

As more and more gets added to the Java language, you might be wondering how things get removed. First, the developers identify classes or methods as *deprecated*, which means further usage is discouraged but still allowed. Suppose you want users to stop passing a parameter to `magicNumber()`.

```
public class DeprecationExample {
   /**
    * Returns a number
    * @deprecated Use {@link #getNumber()} instead
    * @param num number
    * @return number based on num
   */
   @Deprecated(forRemoval = true)
   public int getNumber(int num) {
      return num % 2;
   }

   public int getNumber() {
      return 42;
   }
}
```

Line 4 uses a Javadoc tag, `@deprecated`, to include in the documentation that using this method is discouraged. The `@link` tag is used to explain that the `magicNumber()` call without a parameter is preferred instead.

Line 8 shows the annotation marking the method as `@Deprecated`. IDEs show the use of deprecated code as a warning to call your attention to it. See Chapter 2, "Getting to Know your IDE: The Secret to Success," for more information on IDEs.

Line 8 also shows the `forRemoval` attribute, which was added in Java 9. This is used to signify whether the intent is to remove the deprecated code in the future or merely encourage alternative application programming interfaces (APIs). This allows developers to make intelligent decisions on whether to migrate code.

Oracle keeps a list of APIs that were removed at `https://docs.oracle.com/en/java/javase/21/migrate/removed-apis.html`. This page shows what was removed in each version between Java 9 and Java 21. For example, in Java 21, this was one of two APIs that were removed:

```
java.lang.ThreadGroup.allowThreadSuspension(boolean)
```

You are unlikely to have used this method. Oracle values backward compatibility and does not remove code in broad use. In fact, some of the methods in `java.util.Date` have been deprecated since Java 1.1!

IDENTIFYING RENAMES

Given the evolution of the Java ecosystem over the years, there are some renames you should be familiar with. This section helps you identify whether old guides/documentation are equivalent or obsolete.

Changing to Jakarta EE

As mentioned, in 2020, Oracle announced the migration of Java EE to Jakarta EE. Since that wasn't so long ago, documentation mentioning Java EE is still relatively useful. After all, a Java EE tutorial on *servlets*, commonly used to serve web pages, is mostly the same as Jakarta EE servlets, and the concepts described in good tutorials will all apply.

The key difference is that Jakarta EE 9 renamed the package name prefix from `javax` to `jakarta` since Java is trademarked by Oracle. Additionally, new features are covered only in the Jakarta EE documentation.

Renaming Certifications

Oracle had a number of certifications including Sun Certified Java Associate (SCJA), Sun Certified Java Professional (SCJP), and Sun Certified Master Java Developer (SCMJD) that you could earn. All of these certifications were renamed to begin with "O," for Oracle, giving us certifications like OCJA, OCJP, and OCMJD. When looking at résumés, remember that these certifications are all equivalent.

Many of these certifications don't exist anymore or have changed significantly since the renaming, so learning from websites with the old Sun cert names is unlikely to be useful.

UNDERSTANDING THE PRINCIPLES OF CHANGE

Change is constant in Java and keeps the language current and useful. Some changes are inspired by other languages. You should expect that the language will continue to evolve as more versions are released. These changes will include enhancements to the language and new APIs.

Changes to the Java ecosystem come from three main places.

- **Bug fixes:** Java provides fixes to bugs that are reported in the bug database. You are unlikely to encounter these changes, but it is important to be aware that Java is committed to fixing reported bugs.

- **Java Enhancement Proposals (JEPs):** For example, virtual threads are JEP 444. Some Java features are released as previews before they get committed to as final. Virtual threads had its first preview in Java 19 as JEP 425 and second preview in Java 20 as JEP 436 before being fully released in Java 21.
- **Java Specification Requests (JSRs):** JSRs are bigger and more impactful than JEPs. For example, lambdas were JSR 335.

While committed to a six-month release cycle, Java heavily values backward combability of both the language itself and APIs. Using a later version of Java shouldn't prevent your code from compiling or running. Backward compatibility isn't always met, but Oracle tries to minimize the change as much as possible.

Preview features assist in this goal since they aren't locked into backward compatibility yet. This is why you shouldn't use preview features in production; they could change in any way. Backward compatibility is why so few deprecated APIs are actually removed.

FURTHER REFERENCES

- `https://docs.oracle.com/en/java/javase/15/text-blocks/index.html`

  Oracle's guide to text blocks
- `https://docs.oracle.com/en/java/javase/14/language/records.html`

  Oracle's guide to records
- *OCP Certified Professional Java SE 17 Developer Study Guide* (Sybex, 2022)

  Jeanne's certification study guide for more details on all features
- *The Java Module System* (Manning, 2019)

  Book on modules with great detail

SUMMARY

The following are the key takeaways from the chapter:

- Java is owned by Oracle, with others helping guide the process.
- New versions of Java are released every six months, with less frequent LTS versions.
- New features are continually being added.
- APIs that are no longer encouraged for use are deprecated and, optionally, tagged for removal.
- Backward compatibility is a central tenet of Java's evolution and ensures that existing Java applications will run smoothly without requiring extensive modifications when a new version of Java is released.

2

Getting to Know your IDE: The Secret to Success

WHAT'S IN THIS CHAPTER?

- Understanding IDE History
- Starting a New Project
- Creating a Run Configuration
- Getting to Know Your Keyboard Shortcuts
- Debugging Your Code
- Refactoring Your Code
- Exploiting the Editor
- Extending the IDE
- Peeking at Eclipse
- Peeking at VS Code
- Comparing IDEs

Whether you're a carpenter or a programmer, the first critical decision you will make is your selection of tools. Choosing your integrated development environment (IDE) and getting to know it well will be one of the most important things you will do in your programming career.

In the early days of Java, you could read a copy of the Java API, a 200-page book that contained everything you needed to know to do great things. Today you would need a dozen 500-page books to get the same. Or you could save some time and rely on your IDE for professional support and guidance.

In this chapter, we'll look at the "big three" IDEs—IntelliJ, Eclipse, and Visual Studio Code—and cover the following topics:

- **Getting to know your keyboard shortcuts:** Your IDE is a productivity tool, and you can often identify coding professionals by their use of keyboard shortcuts. There are many, but in this section, we will discuss some of the most important ones and how to learn them, and we'll show you how to discover more.
- **Professional code refactoring:** If you do as many code reviews as we have, you can easily spot nonprofessionals by how they repeat code snippets throughout their codebase. You will see how your IDE can help you locate and correct "copy-and-paste" code.
- **Other productivity pearls:** You should not forget that the primary purpose of your IDE is *editing*! We will review some powerful, lesser-known editing features.

This chapter is certainly not attempting to be a comprehensive guide to every feature. You can get that from the user manuals. Rather, we will emphasize techniques for leveraging your IDE features to greatly improve your productivity.

CODE DOWNLOADS FOR THIS CHAPTER

The source code for this chapter is available on the book page at `www.wiley.com`. Click the Downloads link. The code can also be found at `https://github.com/realworldjava/Ch02-IDEs`. See the `README.md` file in that repository for details.

UNDERSTANDING IDE HISTORY

There's an old adage that advises never to discuss religion or politics in mixed company. We should add to that discussing your favorite IDE. But in elite circles, the IDE of choice seems to be IntelliJ IDE. "Why?" you may ask.

To answer this, let's cover a bit of history. When Java first arrived on the scene, there were some popular IDEs called Symantec Visual Café (the first Java IDE), Microsoft Visual J++, Borland JBuilder, and a variety of other niche offerings. These IDEs offered features like code completion and a smattering of interesting tidbits designed to help developers cut through the ever-growing weeds.

Visual J++ would have won the IDE battle, were it not for their bigger battle with Java founder Sun Microsystems, ultimately resulting in their own bytecode language C# and the sudden withdrawal of Visual J++ from the planet. But the IDE wars exploded when the free, industry-backed Eclipse project and Sun Micro's own NetBeans (also free) surfaced in turn, followed shortly by the super-slick IntelliJ Idea, a feature-rich paid offering from a company named JetBrains.

Fast-forward 25 years and you will find IntelliJ and Eclipse are still innovating, and Microsoft Visual Studio now offers Java support and has been growing steadily especially among young developers or those who started with other languages like JavaScript or Python. A number of years ago IntelliJ introduced a free "community edition" (CE) to compete with the other free offerings. CE sports most of the features that people use every day, the most notable exception being its lack of special Spring integration; it still works with Spring, of course, but if you want the rich IntelliJ-style Spring experience, they ask you to pay.

In our humble opinion, IntelliJ has one salient feature: it is very focused on developer experience, so the IDE can do almost anything you might imagine. There are many capabilities, as you can see by looking at the menus.

There is a built-in code locator that finds duplicate code across disparate files, even in a large codebase, and refactorings are always intuitive, precise, and reliable! That said, Eclipse is still widely used, and Visual Studio has been growing both in capability and traction.

In this chapter, we will discuss the big three IDEs, starting with an emphasis on IntelliJ and concluding with the important differences between it, Eclipse, and Visual Studio. In the rest of this book, we will mostly be using IntelliJ. Nonetheless, if you are a loyal Eclipse or VS Code user, much of this discussion will translate easily, differing mostly in keyboard shortcuts and menu offerings. IntelliJ provides a keyboard shortcut for all its important functionality, and you can add and modify these as you like. You can also select an Eclipse theme that borrows many of those shortcuts, in case you happen to have extensive Eclipse experience. The other IDEs also provide basic key mappings out of the box and allow you to create your own custom mappings. But if you enjoy the power of keyboard shortcuts, you will find IntelliJ provides the largest selection of these out of the box.

> **TIP** *When you launch IntelliJ, a window will come up offering feature tips. Read them!*

There are versions of the top three IDEs available for Windows, Mac, and Linux. The more powerful your computer, the faster and more responsive your IDE will be. See the "Further References" section to download a new IDE if you'd like to try a different one than you are used to.

Let's start by looking at IntelliJ. Remember to read it even if you plan to use Eclipse or VS Code as those sections assume you have read the entire chapter. It is by far our favorite IDE, and who knows, you might even decide to try IntelliJ once you see what it can do!

STARTING A NEW PROJECT

When you want to start a new project, you can choose from several options, as shown in Figure 2.1.

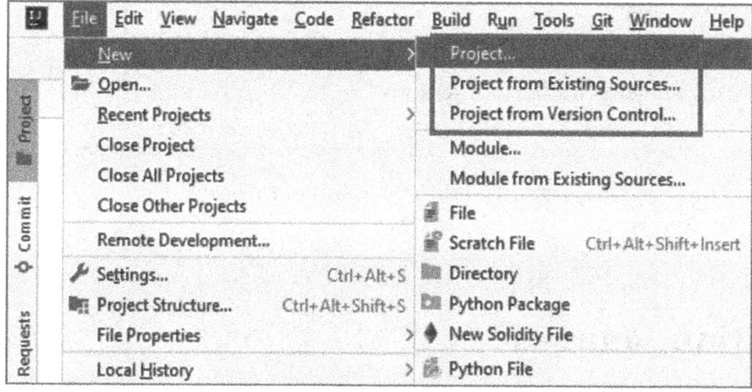

FIGURE 2.1: Creating a new project

Creating a Project from Scratch

To create a project from scratch, choose Project from the menu. A large list of project types is displayed for you to choose from, as shown in Figure 2.2. Make your selection based on your project type. When getting started, you will want to select New Project to create a minimal project with just a main class.

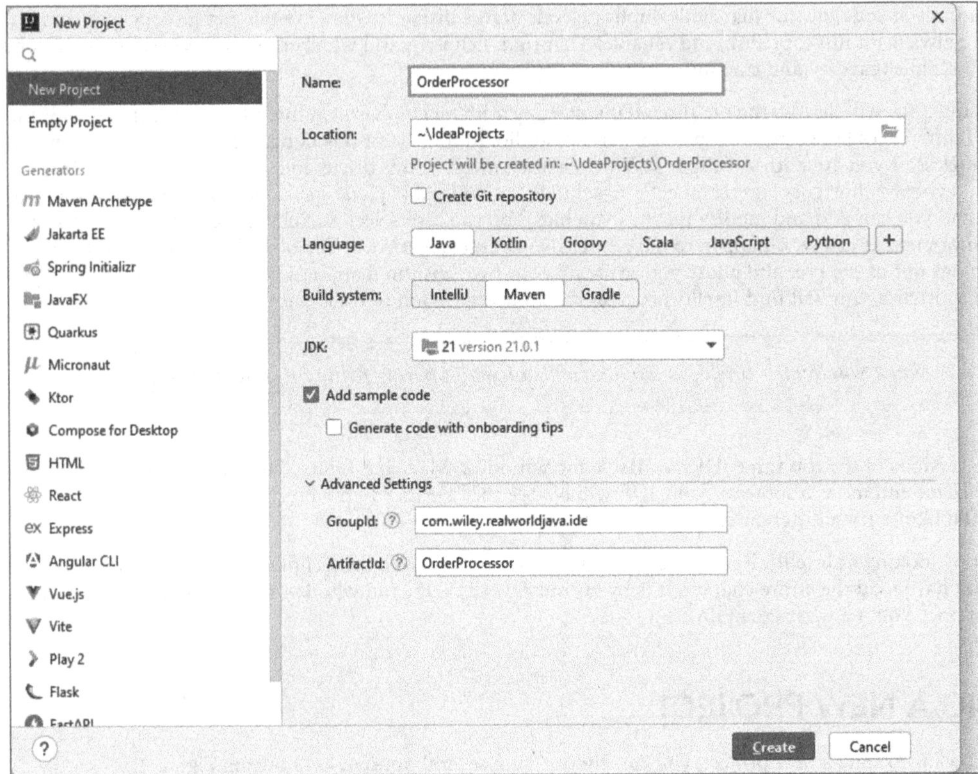

FIGURE 2.2: Creating a new application from scratch

There are many other options including whether you want to use a build tool, which is covered in depth in Chapter 4, "Automating Your CI/CD Builds with Maven, Gradle, and Jenkins."

> **NOTE** *Once you learn about Spring Boot in Chapter 6, "Getting to Know the Spring Framework," you will often choose the Spring Initializer type instead.*

Creating a Project from Existing Sources

You can also import the source from an existing directory into IntelliJ by selecting Project From Existing Sources and pointing to the directory containing the existing project. IntelliJ does a great job locating your build tools, tests, and so on, and staging it all for you to execute.

> **TIP** *Creating a project from existing sources is particularly useful if you are switching over from another IDE like Eclipse or if you are using a build tool and already have the directories on your machine.*

Creating a Project from Version Control

When you are working on a project with a team, you will most often be importing an existing project from version control. To do so, you will *clone* a remote repository. (For more on cloning a repo, see Chapter 3, "Collaborating Across the Enterprise with Git, Jira, and Confluence.")

Adding a Project to Version Control

In most cases you will be cloning an existing project, but every project has a start, and if that is the case, you will need to add your new project to version control after creating it. To do so, perform the following steps. (We are using GitHub, but the process is similar for other repository types. For more on Git, see Chapter 3.)

1. In your browser, create a repository in GitHub, and grab the URL.
2. In IntelliJ, select menu item VCS ➪ Enable Version Control Integration from the drop-down menu.
3. Select a version control system (in our case Git).
4. Add some files to your project and perhaps a `README.md` file.
5. Select the menu item Git ➪ Commit.
6. Now do a push to the remote (select the menu Git ➪ Push, or press Ctrl+Shift+K/Cmd+Shift+K).
7. In the Push Commits window, click the Define Remote button.

You can now navigate to the URL you provided where you will find your code, as shown in Figure 2.3.

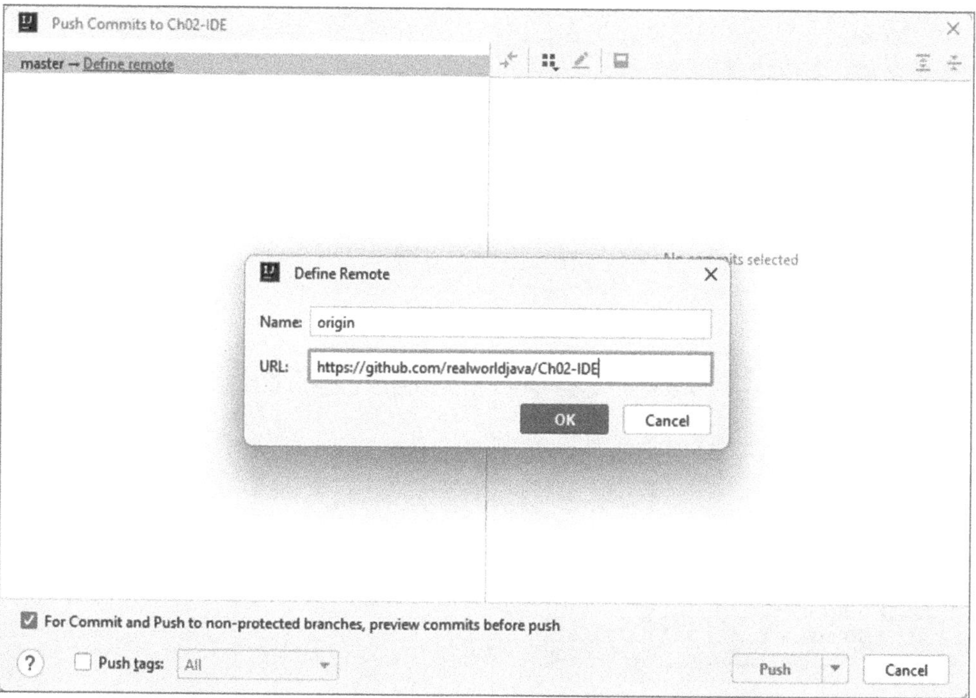

FIGURE 2.3: Defining Git Remote

Adding a Module to an Existing Project

It is common to have multiple services (which are essentially distinct applications) that serve a single application. In such cases you might want to have those services reside in one master project. To accomplish that, you can choose menu item File ➪ New Module or File ➪ New Module From Existing Sources, which provides options that are similar to the menu item File ➪ New Project options.

CREATING A RUN CONFIGURATION

There are many ways to run the `main()` method of a class. While all require a *run configuration* (which contains the main class, runtime arguments, Java version to use, etc.), IntelliJ will create one for you with default values if you simply run the application. To run the application, you can do one of the following:

- Click the green arrow to the left of the class name, as shown in Figure 2.4.
- Click the green arrow to the left of the `main()` method.
- Right-click the class editor.

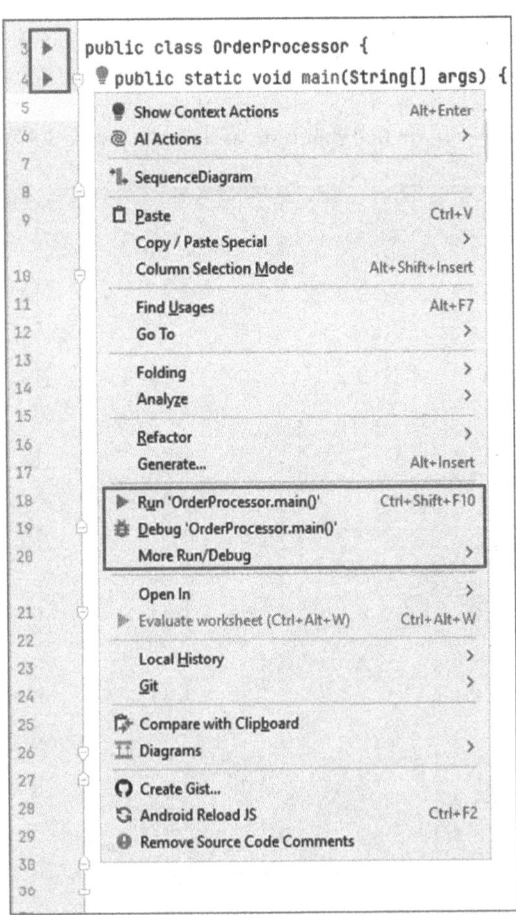

FIGURE 2.4: Running and debugging

All of these give you the option to choose Run from the context menu, which will create a default run configuration. (Debug is also an option. See the "Debugging Your Code" section for more on debugging.) All of these also give you the Modify The Run Configuration option, possibly in a submenu that lets you specify the details of your run configuration.

Alternatively, you can click Current File on top and choose Edit Configurations from the drop-down that appears (Figure 2.5). Despite the name, you have the option to add a new runtime configuration in addition to editing existing ones.

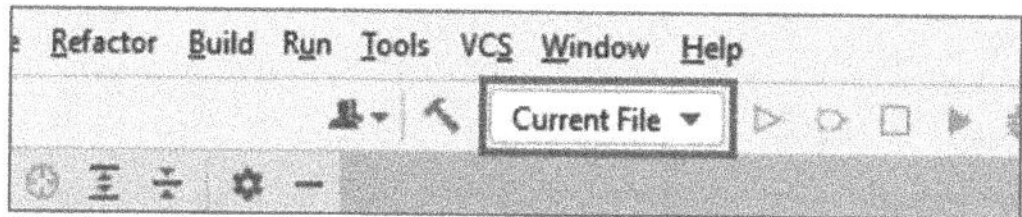

FIGURE 2.5: Editing the configuration

Select an appropriate application type (for example, Application for a vanilla Java application). See Figure 2.6.

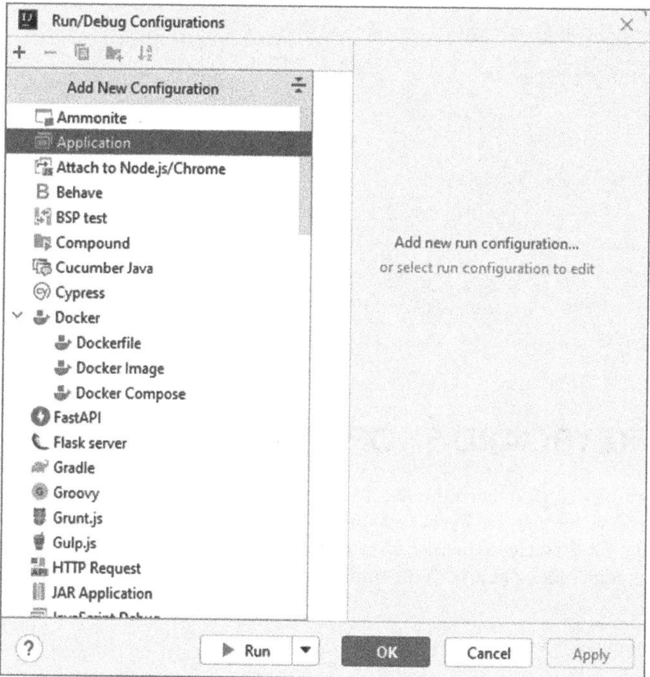

FIGURE 2.6: Adding an application configuration

Then complete the configuration form by entering a main class, Java version, and so on, as in Figure 2.7.

If you are in a test class (annotated with `@Test`; see Chapter 7, "Testing Your Code with Automated Testing Tools"), then you can click the green arrow next to any test method and select the Run option.

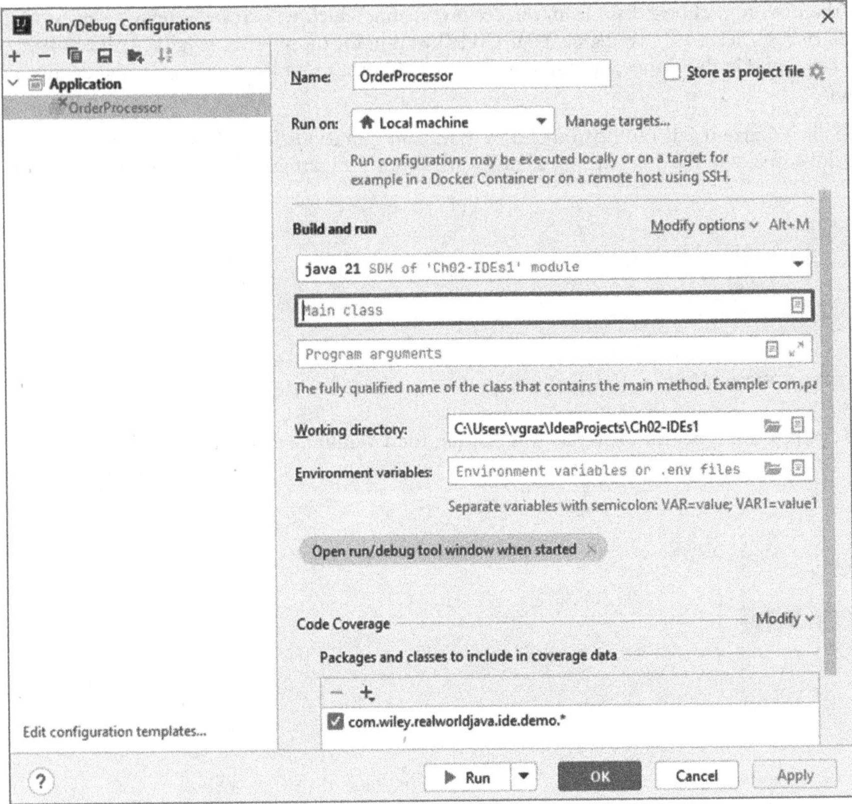

FIGURE 2.7: Adding a `main()` method

GETTING TO KNOW YOUR KEYBOARD SHORTCUTS

Whichever IDE makes you comfortable, our advice is to learn the shortcuts and use them. How do you do that? Every time you look for a function in the menu, look at the keyboard shortcut for that function (listed to the right of the menu item, as shown in Figure 2.8), then close the menu, and use the shortcut! Start with your most frequently used functions until your fingers remember them without thinking.

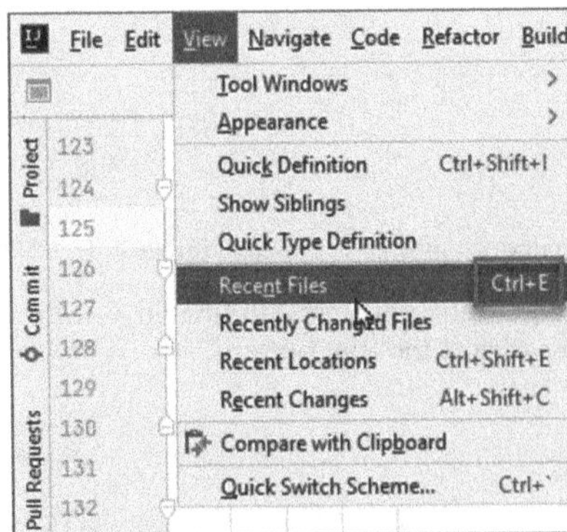

FIGURE 2.8: Using menus to discover keyboard shortcuts

For example, to get a list of files that you recently worked on, press Ctrl+E/Cmd+E. It will take a few times to remember it, so follow this advice:

1. Look it up in the menu.
2. Close the menu.
3. Use the shortcut.

> **TIP** *Many shortcuts differ between Windows and Mac. When that happens, we type the Windows shortcut followed by a slash followed by the Mac version. If you are using Linux, please follow the Windows shortcuts as they are usually the same.*

In the following sections, you'll see many useful shortcuts. There will be others throughout the chapter as we cover specific topics. After a short time, the keyboard shortcuts will be etched in your memory, and you will find your productivity increasing greatly.

Navigating Your Codebase

You want to be able to glide through your codebase without too much mouse clicking. The IDE makes that easy.

To open a class file in IntelliJ, use the shortcut Ctrl+N/Cmd+O. You do not need to type the entire filename, and you can even use camel case to enter prefixes for portions of the name. For example, Figure 2.9 shows how you can look for the beginning of **Or**der**Pro**cessor by typing `OrPro`.

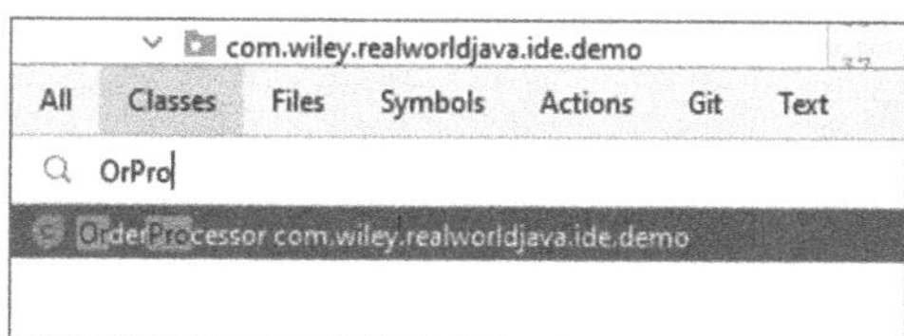

FIGURE 2.9: Navigating to a class

Similarly, you can open a file that is not a class file using the shortcut Ctrl+Shift+N/Cmd+Shift+O. And you can find a method name or class/instance variable name using Ctrl+Alt+Shift+N/Cmd+Option+O. Figure 2.10 uses the camel case technique to search for the **sendEma**il**Con**firmation method by typing `sendEmaCon`.

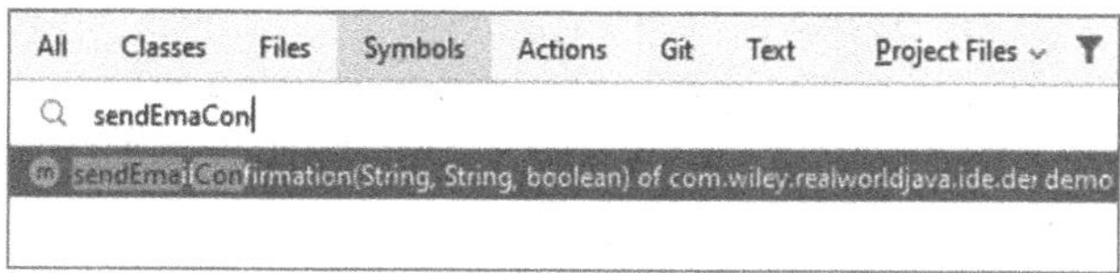

FIGURE 2.10: Navigating to a symbol

You can navigate to the last position that you visited, and then the previous and so on, using Ctrl+Alt+Left Arrow/Cmd+[. Then you can navigate in the forward direction using Ctrl+Alt+Right Arrow/Cmd+].

You can navigate to the last edit position using Ctrl+Shift+Backspace/Cmd+Shift+Backspace. While that moves backwards through recent edits, we have not seen a shortcut to move forward afterward. As a work-around, you can just move the cursor anywhere, and then the next Ctrl+Shift+Backspace/Cmd+Shift+Backspace will start again from the most recent edit position.

If you want to find usages of a certain method, you can Ctrl/Cmd-click the method name to get a quick pop-up with this information. Alternatively, you can use Alt+F7/Option+F7 to see the list in a window at the bottom of your IDE.

You can create your own custom navigation by using bookmarks. In IntelliJ, Ctrl+Shift+1 (or any number from 1 to 9) will set a numbered bookmark at the cursor location. Then you can return to that bookmark using Ctrl+1 (or whichever number you used to create the bookmark). These are some of the few shortcuts that are the same on Windows and Mac!

To get a quick outline of the API of the current file, use Ctrl+F12/Cmd+F12, as shown in Figure 2.11. You can click within the outline to go right to that part of the file.

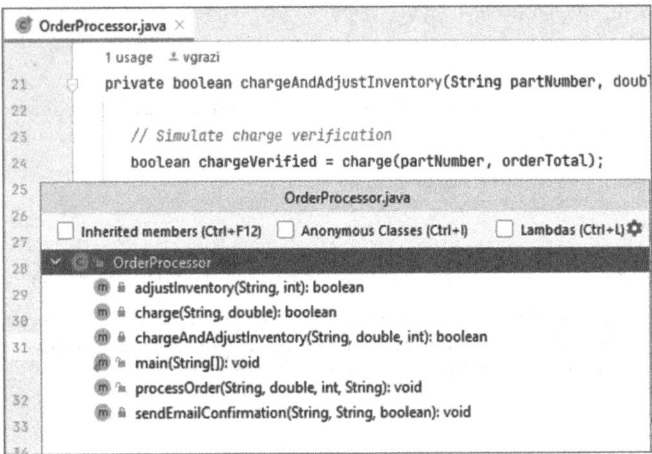

FIGURE 2.11: Outline view

Copying and Pasting Shortcuts

Copy and pasting? You know how to do that already. However, Ctrl+C/Cmd+C works differently from what you are used to with other tools. IntelliJ's philosophy is to not waste time trying to select an entire line; just position your cursor in the line you want to copy, hit Ctrl+C/Cmd+C, and the entire line is copied to the clipboard. Of course, if you want to copy part of a line or multiple lines, you can still select those as usual and hit Ctrl+C/Cmd+C.

Cutting the entire line works similarly using Ctrl+X/Cmd+X. Again, without selecting anything it cuts the entire cursor line to the clipboard.

To retrieve the clipboard, Ctrl+V/Cmd+V works in IntelliJ just like it does in other tools. However, the more useful Ctrl+Shift+V/Cmd+Shift+V displays your clipboard history and lets you select which cut of the clipboard you want to paste, as shown in Figure 2.12.

Reordering Code

Next try the unique Ctrl+W/Option+Up Arrow and Ctrl+Shift+W/Option+Down Arrow. Each press of Ctrl+W/Option+Up Arrow starts at the cursor and selects increasing scope, first a word, then a phrase, then a block, a method, a class, and so on. Ctrl+Shift+W/Option+Down Arrow reverses the order, bringing you back one click at a time to your original selection. If you apply Ctrl+W/ Option+Up Arrow to an arithmetic expression, each Ctrl+W/ Option+Up Arrow selects in the order it will calculate.

FIGURE 2.12: Paste Special context menu

There's a trick to selecting an entire method in two clicks, and that is to position your cursor to any space to the left of the method name and hit Ctrl+W/ Option+Up Arrow twice. Another click will select Javadoc and annotations. That is very useful for reordering the methods in your code, because with the entire method selected, you can then use Ctrl+Shift+Up Arrow/Cmd+Shift+Up Arrow and Ctrl+Shift+Down Arrow/Cmd+Shift+Down Arrow to move the method up or down in the file, past the next method above or below it, and will also move any Javadoc along with it. (Good code is self-documenting; great code has great Javadoc!)

Using Other Helpful Shortcuts

First come three shortcuts when working with lines.

- Ctrl+D/Cmd+D duplicates the current line.
- Ctrl+Y/Cmd+Backspace deletes the current line.
- Ctrl+Alt+Up Arrow/Option+Shift+Up Arrow and Down Arrow move the current line up or down, respectively.

Next, when you want to find errors and warnings in your code, use F2 to find the ones after the cursor, and use Shift+F2 to navigate backwards away from the cursor.

The Alt+Enter/Option+Enter shortcut opens a context-sensitive menu. For example, you can use it to fix a compiler error or generate code for your class.

Each IDE has its own keyboard shortcuts. In this section, we have seen a few examples of some of the more useful keyboard shortcuts, and as we cover more functionality, we will mention the related shortcuts. It is beyond the scope of this book to cover every shortcut, but we encourage you to explore them and get fluent with them. You can get the full listing from within the IDE for your operating system: select menu item Help ➪ Keyboard Shortcuts PDF. Take the plunge with learning shortcuts. Mastery of the keyboard shortcuts will make you a better, faster, and more professional programmer.

META SHORTCUTS

IntelliJ has a "keyboard-first" philosophy making for some very powerful shortcuts. Luckily, there are three more general shortcuts that are good to learn as you master more specific ones.

- Shift+Shift opens a feature called Search Anywhere. It's a quick way to search for files or symbols or even IntelliJ actions themselves.
- Control+Control opens the Run Anything feature, which lets you run things like a main method or a test.
- Ctrl+Shift+A/Cmd+Shift+A opens the ability to find any action. This is a subset of Shift+Shift, but it's useful to go directly to that list.

DEBUGGING YOUR CODE

The real power of your IDE starts to emerge when you use the debugger. The debugger allows you to set *breakpoints* in your code so that when your program reaches a breakpoint, it pauses execution. Launch your program in debug mode, and when the code reaches a breakpoint, it will pause, allowing you to view the current values of variables that are visible in the current scope. You can change values. From there you can move forward one step at a time or have execution continue until the next breakpoint. Or you can step into a method or step over or step out of a method. It also allows you to navigate the *call stack*, which lets you see the variables available to methods that called the one the breakpoint is in. Debugging is valuable not only for chasing down bugs but also for just getting a good understanding of the inner workings of your code. When you are trying to understand code, there is nothing better than setting some strategic breakpoints and letting your debugger take you on a tour of the code.

Debugging a Program

The sample code in the GitHub repository for this chapter is a simulated order processing system, where a customer can order a part, and the system will (simulated) verify the customer's charge account as well as the inventory. If the order is successful, it will send a success email. Otherwise, it will send an order cancellation email. (In our sample, it will just print a message to the console.)

First, you need to import the project. You can use menu item File ➪ New ➪ Project From Version Control and supply the GitHub URL `https://github.com/realworldjava/Ch02-IDEs`.

Before starting a debugging session, take a moment to understand what this code does. The program flow starts by calling the `main` method, which in turn creates a new `OrderProcessor` and then calls the `processOrder` method on it.

To see the debugger in action, set two breakpoints where indicated in the comments, one in the `main` method on line 6 and another in `chargeAndAdjustInventory` on line 28.

Next launch the program by clicking the green arrow in the margin to the left of the `main` method and selecting Debug `OrderProcessor.main()`, or click the debug icon from the menu.

This will bring up the Debug window (see Figure 2.13).

The program will break at line 6. Choose Step Over (or hit F8) and see the execution step forward by one line. Now choose Resume Program (F9), and the execution will continue until it reaches the next breakpoint in the `chargeAndAdjustInventory` method.

When the program breaks, take a look at the variables in the debugger window (see Figure 2.14).

Now click the next frame in the call stack (`processOrder`: line 13), and see the variables in that scope. Then do the same for the `main`:7 frame.

In this way, you can walk the call stack and see and even modify the variables in each scope. To modify a variable, click the variable in the variables window, right-click the variable, and choose Set Value (or hit the F2 key).

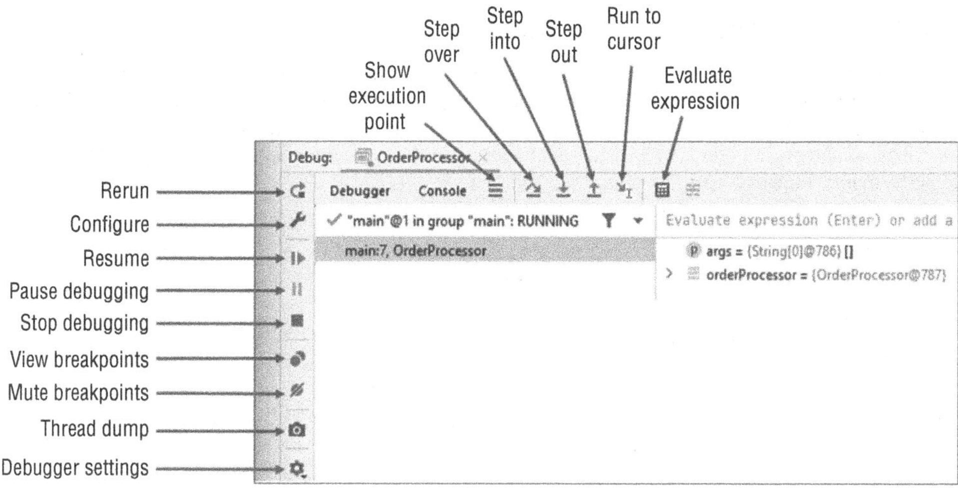

FIGURE 2.13: Debug window overview

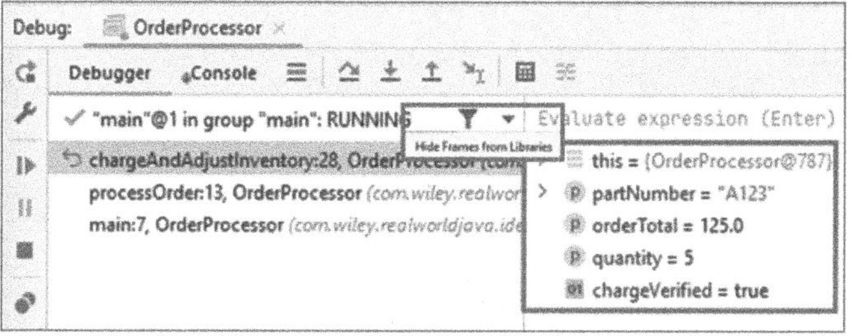

FIGURE 2.14: Debugger Variables

If there are library classes in the call stack, you can choose to ignore them by clicking the funnel Hide Frames From Libraries icon at the top of the debug frames window, as in Figure 2.14.

You can also mouse over a variable in the editor to see its value. String values are also displayed (in an alternate font) next to the variable in the editor. Strings and primitives will be displayed as is. As for other object types, you can click the values to drill into them.

If you navigate away from the execution point by opening other windows or by scrolling around, you can always return to the execution point by hitting the Show Execution Point icon (Alt+F10/Option+F10).

You can mute all breakpoints by hitting the Mute Breakpoints icon and then click Resume Program (F9). The execution will continue uninterrupted, until you unmute.

By right-clicking a breakpoint you can find settings to temporarily disable the breakpoint, set a condition that must be true for it to pause, and enable other settings. If you put a breakpoint on an interface method, then any execution that hits that method will cause the debugger to break.

> **TIP** *Let's say you're stepping through the debugger and you get an unexpected exception that takes you far from where you were. Where was that exception thrown? Press Ctrl+Alt+Left/Cmd+Alt+Left Arrow to get back to the previous location.*

Speeding Up Debugger Performance

If your computer's memory is limited or if your program is very large, you might find that your debugger slows down. You can speed things up considerably by tuning the debugger. To do so, navigate to File ➪ Settings on Windows or the IntelliJ IDEA menu on Mac. Then select Build, Execution, Debugger ➪ Data Views ➪ Java, and turn off the settings, as shown in Figure 2.15. If the debugger is slow, tweak these settings and you will realize a considerable performance improvement.

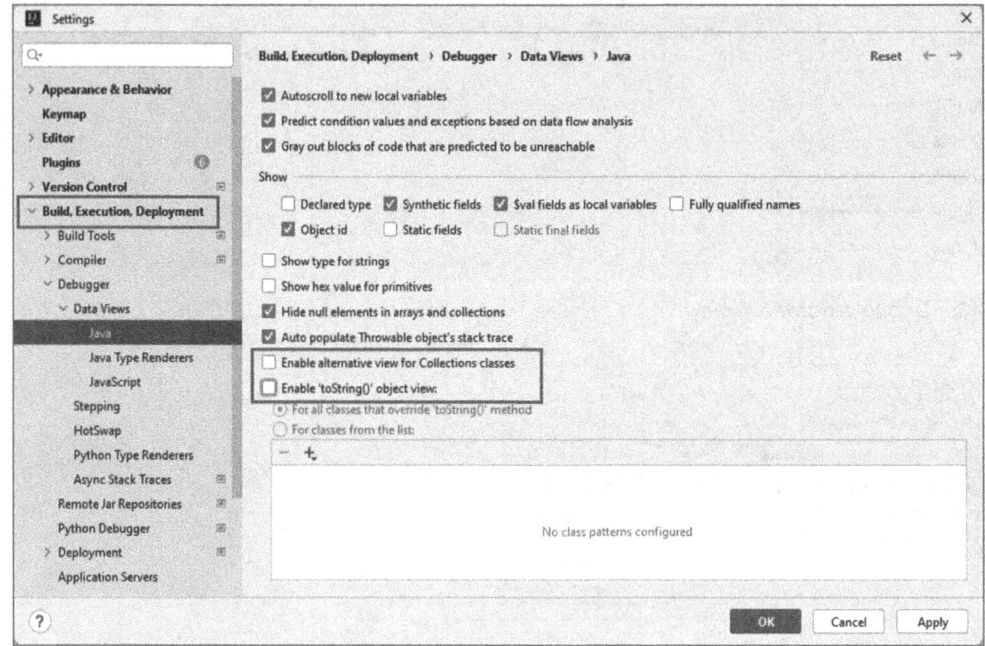

FIGURE 2.15: Tuning debugging settings

You can make further performance improvements by making adjustments to the layout settings, at the top right side of the Debug window. Threads, Memory, and Overhead should be unchecked, as shown in Figure 2.16.

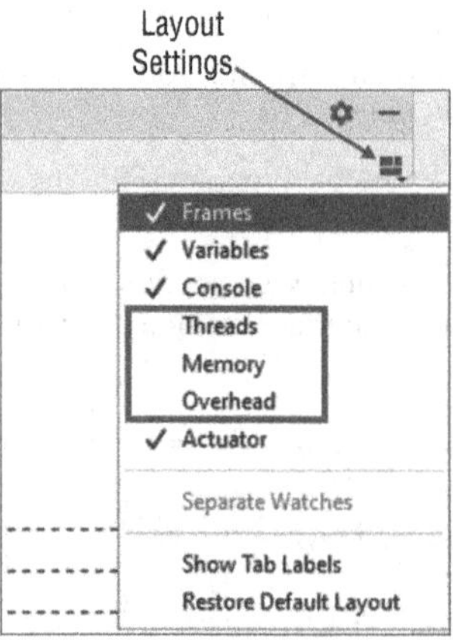

FIGURE 2.16: More debugging optimization settings

Remote Debugging

Debugging is a handy tool when you are writing your application and when you are diagnosing issues that are easily reproducible. However, as Murphy's law states, "Anything that can go wrong will go wrong." This manifests as a problem that can go wrong will go wrong on the server, but you just can't reproduce it locally. In such cases, Java supports remote debugging, which lets you debug code running on a remote server, setting breakpoints, and viewing variables, just as if the application were running locally.

We aren't showing an example here, but to do remote debugging on the job, create a new run configuration and select Remote JVM Debug as the type. Enter the host name, but retain the defaults unless the remote system requires you to change them.

Before you can do remote debugging, you must launch the server using a special remote debugging agent. To do so, copy the command-line arguments `agentlib:jdwp=transport=dt_socket,server=y,suspend=n, address=*:5005` from the runtime configuration, as shown in Figure 2.17, and add those to your application runtime arguments.

Once remote debugging is configured, you can debug the application just as if it were running locally, using the steps we are about to discuss.

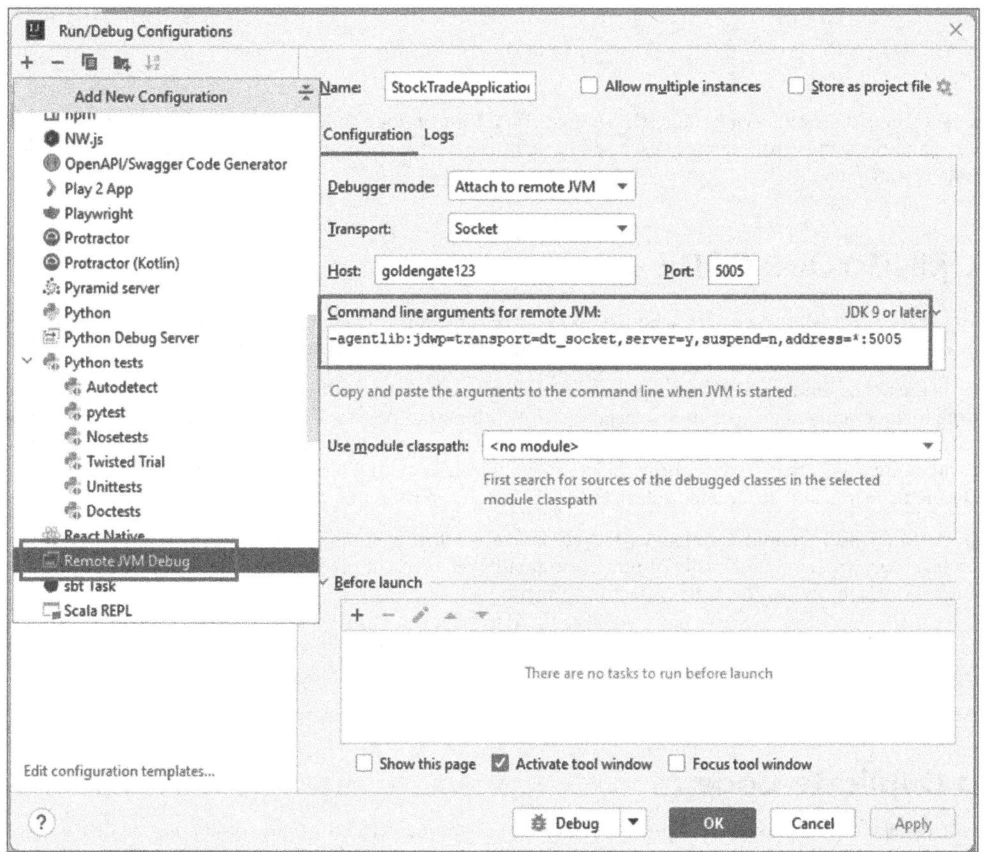

FIGURE 2.17: Command-line arguments

Debugging with Hot Swap

During your debugging, you might find bugs in your program (after all, it is called *debugging*!). Many people think you need to restart the application after every change; however, that is not always the case. If you make simple changes, you do not have to restart your session. Just recompile the class where you made the change (select the menu item Build ➪ Recompile or press Ctrl+Shift+F9/Cmd+Shift+F9), and *voilà*, Java's *Hot Swap* feature will reload the classes, and your program will just work. Some caveats, though: Hot Swap will work only if no class signatures are changed. That means there cannot be any new class variables or instance variables, no new or deleted methods, and no method signature or annotation changes. If you try to apply Hot Swap after any of those bigger changes, the IDE will warn you that the Hot Swap did not work, and you will need to restart the application.

> **LOG SCROLLING**
>
> One final word about debugging: when you are in the debugger tab, if you want to see the logging output, switch to the console tab. If the logging is pouring out to the console very quickly, you can stop it from scrolling by simply clicking into the console window. The log messages will still be appended at the bottom, but the scrolling will stop at the line where you clicked. This click-to-pause feature is also available in the run console, not just the debugging console.

Debugging is a vital skill for allowing your IDE to give you a tour of your code's execution flow. Every IDE has debugging capabilities similar to the ones described here. In the next section, we will discuss another vital skill, which is code refactoring.

REFACTORING YOUR CODE

In the words of the great Martin Fowler, who first popularized the term *refactoring*, "Any fool can write code that a computer can understand. Good programmers write code that a human can understand."

Refactoring is the art of improving existing code by applying known patterns for reorganizing the code. Examples of refactoring include removing superfluous variables and eliminating copy-and-paste code. But keep in mind that refactoring has a risk: when you change existing code, you are exposing opportunities for regression issues; that is, you risk breaking things that were working before. This is where the IDE comes in. You see, the major IDEs all provide a Refactor menu, and automated refactorings are much safer than manual ones.

We strongly recommend becoming familiar with each of the refactoring menu items, especially Extract and Inline ones. Much has been written on the topic of refactoring, but even without reading it all, you can learn quite a bit of commonsense refactoring just from the refactoring menu.

> **TIP** *IntelliJ has by far the most extensive refactor options of the major Java IDEs.*

Avoiding Duplicate Code

Our first rule of refactoring is to never copy and paste code. If you need to introduce some functionality in two or more places, extract that functionality into a method. If any of those methods are contained in different classes, pull them up to a common superclass, or extract them to a utility class. If you are working on a codebase that has repetitive code, take it on yourself to refactor it out.

To extract code into a method, select the code, go to the Refactor menu, and select Extract/Introduce ➪ Method, as shown in Figure 2.18. The shortcut is Ctrl+Alt+M/Cmd+Option+M, and it will be one of your most used shortcuts, so use it until you remember it.

FIGURE 2.18: IntelliJ IDE's refactor menu

In Figure 2.19, we have two methods for sending emails. The first does so weekly, and the second does so every other week. A closer look reveals that the two methods are basically doing the same things, with some slight variations. Why not extract the common functionality into a method and pass in the differences as parameters? Here's the technique: start with one method, say the first one, `processWeeklyReminders()`, in Figure 2.19.

```
public void processWeeklyReminders(LocalDate lastMail, Properties props) {
    LocalDate nextMail = lastMail.plusWeeks( weeksToAdd: 1);
    Consumer<Properties> mailer = this::sendWeeklyMailer;
    LocalDate now = LocalDate.now();
    if (now.isAfter(nextMail)) {
        mailer.accept(props);
    }
}

public void processBiWeeklyReminders(LocalDate lastMail, Properties props) {
    LocalDate nextMail = lastMail.plusWeeks( weeksToAdd: 2);
    Consumer<Properties> mailer = this::sendBiWeeklyMailer;
    LocalDate now = LocalDate.now();
    if (now.isAfter(nextMail)) {
        mailer.accept(props);
    }
}
```

FIGURE 2.19: Extracting common functionality to a method

Step 1 is to factor out the noncommon elements by extracting any differences to variables. In our example, our weekly and biweekly methods are similar, although they do have noncommon elements, specifically the number of weeks and the method to send the email. Select the number 1 (the `weeksToAdd` variable in line 10) and choose menu item Refactor ➪ Extract/Introduce ➪ Variable and assign it to the variable named `numWeeks`. Rearrange the lines if necessary so that `numWeeks` and the `Comsumer` are before the code to extract (see Figure 2.20).

```
9 @     public void processWeeklyReminders(LocalDate lastMail, Properties props)
10          int numWeeks = 1;
11          LocalDate nextMail = lastMail.plusWeeks(numWeeks);
12          Consumer<Properties> mailer = this::sendWeeklyMailer;
13          LocalDate now = LocalDate.now();
14          if (now.isAfter(nextMail)) {
15              mailer.accept(props);
16          }
17      }
18
19 @     public void processBiWeeklyReminders(LocalDate lastMail, Properties props
20          LocalDate nextMail = lastMail.plusWeeks( weeksToAdd: 2);
21          Consumer<Properties> mailer = this::sendBiWeeklyMailer;
22          LocalDate now = LocalDate.now();
23          if (now.isAfter(nextMail)) {
24              mailer.accept(props);
25          }
26      }
```

FIGURE 2.20: Extracting differences into variables

Next select the common functionality to extract, as in Figure 2.21.

```
9 @     public void processWeeklyReminders(LocalDate lastMail, Properties props) {
10          int numWeeks = 1;
11          LocalDate nextMail = lastMail.plusWeeks(numWeeks);
12          Consumer<Properties> mailer = this::sendWeeklyMailer;
13          LocalDate now = LocalDate.now();
14          if (now.isAfter(nextMail)) {
15              mailer.accept(props);
16          }
17      }
18
19 @     public void processBiWeeklyReminders(LocalDate lastMail, Properties props) {
20          LocalDate nextMail = lastMail.plusWeeks( weeksToAdd: 2);
21          Consumer<Properties> mailer = this::sendBiWeeklyMailer;
22          LocalDate now = LocalDate.now();
23          if (now.isAfter(nextMail)) {
24              mailer.accept(props);
25          }
26      }
```

FIGURE 2.21: Selecting the common functionality

Choose Ctrl+Alt+M/Cmd+Option+M, the shortcut for extracting a method. The IDE will assign a name, which you want to change to something meaningful, `sendIfTime` in our case, as shown in Figure 2.22.

The IDE will offer to replace other places with the extracted method, as shown in Figure 2.23.

```
public void processWeeklyReminders(LocalDate lastMail, Properties props) {
    int numWeeks = 1;
    LocalDate nextMail = lastMail.plusWeeks(numWeeks);
    Consumer<Properties> mailer = this::sendWeeklyMailer;
    sendIfTime (props, nextMail, mailer);
}

private static void sendIfTime(Properties props, LocalDate nextMail, Consumer<Properties> mailer) {
    LocalDate now = LocalDate.now();
    if (now.isAfter(nextMail)) {
        mailer.accept(props);
    }
}

public void processBiWeeklyReminders(LocalDate lastMail, Properties props) {
    LocalDate nextMail = lastMail.plusWeeks( weeksToAdd: 2);
    Consumer<Properties> mailer = this::sendBiWeeklyMailer;
    LocalDate now = LocalDate.now();
    if (now.isAfter(nextMail)) {
        mailer.accept(props);
    }
}
```

FIGURE 2.22: Extracting the method

```
public void processWeeklyReminders(LocalDate lastMail, Properties props) {
    int numWeeks = 1;
    LocalDate nextMail = lastMail.plusWeeks(numWeeks);
    Consumer<Properties> mailer = this::sendWeeklyMailer;
    sendIfTime (props, nextMail, mailer);
}

private static void sendIfTime(Properties props, LocalDate nextMail, Consumer<Properties> mailer) {
    LocalDate now = LocalDate.now();
    if (now.isAfter(nextMail)) {
        mailer.accept(props);
    }
}

public void processBiWeeklyReminders(LocalDate lastMail, Properties props) {
    LocalDate nextMail = lastMail.plusWeeks( weeksToAdd: 2);
    Consumer<Properties> mailer = this::sendBiWeeklyMailer;
    LocalDate now = LocalDate.now();
    if (now.isAfter(nextMail)) {
        mailer.accept(props);
    }
}
```

Process Duplicates

Do you want to replace this occurrence?

Cancel | Skip | All | Replace

FIGURE 2.23: The IDE helps locate opportunities to apply the new method.

You can place the cursor in the method name and use Ctrl+Shift/Cmd+Shift with the Up or Down Arrow keys to move the methods up and down in the class, as shown in Figure 2.24.

The code would look a lot cleaner if you inline the `mailer` parameters into the code. Just click the variable name and choose Refactor ➪ Inline Variable (Ctrl+Alt+N) to inline the variables, as shown in Figure 2.25. You'll see inlining again shortly.

```
    public void processWeeklyReminders(LocalDate lastMail, Properties props) {
        LocalDate nextMail = lastMail.plusWeeks( weeksToAdd: 1);
        Consumer<Properties> mailer = this::sendWeeklyMailer;
        sendIfTime(props, nextMail, mailer);
    }

    private static void sendIfTime(Properties props, LocalDate nextMail, Consumer<Properties> mailer) {
        LocalDate now = LocalDate.now();
        if (now.isAfter(nextMail)) {
            mailer.accept(props);
        }
    }

    public void processBiWeeklyReminders(LocalDate lastMail, Properties props) {
        LocalDate nextMail = lastMail.plusWeeks( weeksToAdd: 2);
        Consumer<Properties> mailer = this::sendBiWeeklyMailer;
        sendIfTime(props, nextMail, mailer);
    }
```

FIGURE 2.24: The first refactored draft

```
    public void processWeeklyReminders(LocalDate lastMail, Properties props) {
        LocalDate nextMail = lastMail.plusWeeks( weeksToAdd: 1);
        sendIfTime(props, nextMail, this::sendWeeklyMailer);
    }

    public void processBiWeeklyReminders(LocalDate lastMail, Properties props) {
        LocalDate nextMail = lastMail.plusWeeks( weeksToAdd: 2);
        sendIfTime(props, nextMail, this::sendBiWeeklyMailer);
    }

    private static void sendIfTime(Properties props, LocalDate nextMail, Consumer<Properties> mailer) {
        LocalDate now = LocalDate.now();
        if (now.isAfter(nextMail)) {
            mailer.accept(props);
        }
    }
```

FIGURE 2.25: The final refactored version. Compare this to Figure 2.19.

You can see that the code is much neater now, with two smaller methods that delegate to the extracted method containing the main code. Use this technique to safely refactor much more complex real-world code as well.

> **TIP** *You don't need duplicate code for extract method to be valuable. It also helps in dealing with methods that are too long by having smaller methods with clear names to take care of some of the logic.*

Extracting methods is arguably the most important refactoring pattern. But all the refactoring patterns contribute to good clean code. Let's look at another important refactoring: renaming members, that is, renaming methods and variables.

Renaming Members

Our next rule for refactoring is naming your methods and variables with meaningful names. Remember, while renaming, you want to avoid nonstandard abbreviations. This is important for making your code self-documenting. If you are working through legacy code with variable or method names that are too short or confusing, it will be helpful to rename the variables and methods to something meaningful.

To rename a variable, click the variable (no need to select the whole variable; just click anywhere in it), hit Shift+F6, and then type the new name. It will be replaced with the new version throughout your codebase. And guess what? This is another shortcut that is the same on Windows and Mac!

You can also rename methods and classes using the same Shift+F6 shortcut, and you can take it to the bank that your code will still compile and preserve the same semantics.

Renaming members is an important pattern for making code more readable. But sometimes there are variables or methods that are just unnecessary, and in those cases, we will benefit by inlining.

Inlining

The use of variables can often make code clearer, but not always. There will be times where the variable declaration just takes up an extra line without adding any clarity at all. For example, in the following code snippet, the declaration of the variable `rgbInt` is using up an extra line, arguably without adding any clarity at all. In such cases, it would make sense to just inline the expression and remove the variable declaration, as shown in Figure 2.26.

```
5   public static Color parseColor(String rbgString) {
6       int rgbInt = Integer.parseInt(rbgString);
7       Color color = new Color(rgbInt);
8       return color;
9   }
```

FIGURE 2.26: The variable declaration in line 8 adds no clarity; inline it.

You can inline the unwanted variable by clicking any occurrence of the variable in the code (for example, you can see the location of the insert cursor in Figure 2.26, line 6) and then hit Ctrl+Alt+N/Cmd+Option+N. The previous changes to what you can see in Figure 2.27.

```
public static Color parseColor(String rbgString) {
    Color color = new Color(Integer.parseInt(rbgString));
    return color;
}
```

FIGURE 2.27: The variable is inlined.

We won't go through every aspect of refactoring here, but if you want to take your programming skills to the next level, please see the "Further References" section for an excellent book on refactoring.

Once upon a time IDEs had very limited refactoring capabilities, if at all. There were techniques for performing refactoring in as safe a manner as possible. But now that most of the common refactoring patterns are built into the IDEs, make an effort to study them and use them.

But refactoring is not the only thing that IDEs are great at. Let's look at some other interesting tools.

Changing Signatures: Adding and Removing Parameters

You will frequently find methods where arguments are not used or that can be obtained in some other way. Or you might find that method arguments might lend themselves to a more natural ordering in the argument list.

You can easily add, delete, or reorder arguments in a method signature by clicking the method name and pressing Ctrl+F6/Cmd+F6 to launch the Change Signature pop-up. Then you can move things around as you like. You do not have to navigate to the method declaration; the refactoring can be applied anywhere the method name is invoked.

EXPLOITING THE EDITOR

An IDE is first and foremost an editor, and IntelliJ offers a robust set of editing capabilities, which you should become familiar with. In this section, you will learn some important editing capabilities and productivity enhancements. We encourage you to keep your IDE open and follow the examples we describe here.

One important note: this one should go without saying, but if you are not happy with anything, just press Ctrl+Z/Cmd+Z to undo it. We have seen unindoctrinated developers trying to back out a tangle of unhappy edits or refactorings when all they needed to do was hit Ctrl+Z/Cmd+Z to undo.

In IntelliJ, you can add quotes around a string by selecting the string and just hitting the double quote (") key. For example, suppose you have the following line:

```
public static final String TEXT = text;
```

Highlight the letters `text` and press the double quote ("). The code transforms into this:

```
public static final String TEXT = "text";
```

Single quotes, parentheses, and brackets should work similarly, although we have found varying results using different keyboard mappings.

If you have two lines of code that you want to merge into a single line, simply hit Ctrl+J/Ctrl+Shift+J. This is great for reformatting comments or for merging a declaration with an assignment. For example, if you have the following two lines:

```
11: String name = null;
12: name = "Henry";
13: // Assignment was done
```

position the cursor anywhere on line 11 and hit Ctrl+J/Ctrl+Shift+J. That yields the following:

```
11: String name = "Henry";
12: // Assignment was done
```

Automated Reformatting of Code

IntelliJ offers some options for organizing your code more cleanly. This can give a more professional look to your code.

Organizing Imports

Keeping your imports clean is a simple matter; just use the Code ➪ Optimize Imports menu option (Ctrl+Alt+O/Ctrl+Option+O). This option removes unused imports and orders the imports to make them more organized.

Reformatting Code

To reformat your code, you can hit the menu item Code ➪ Reformat (Ctrl+Alt+L/Cmd+Option+L), which will apply the formatting to the entire file. If you select a code snippet, that same command will just reformat the selected bit of code. You can also select a package or directory in the Project Explorer, and that same command will reformat everything in that directory.

The reformatting command understands the file types being reformatted and will apply appropriate formatting for Java, JSON, CSS, XML, and so on.

The reformatting uses standard formats for each file type, but you can tweak things like adding spaces around an equals sign in assignments, or where to place the squiggly bracket at the end of a method declaration. These are found under the File menu item for Windows or IntelliJ menu item for Mac. Then select Settings ➪ Code Style for each file type. For example, Figure 2.28 shows the Java options.

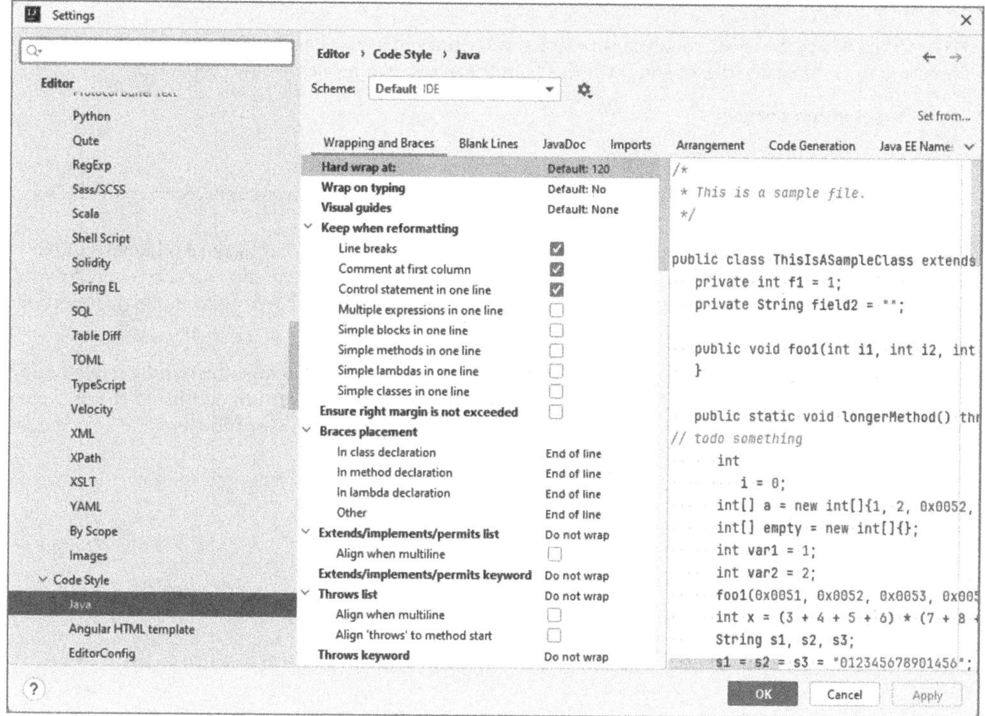

FIGURE 2.28: Reformatting options

Unwrapping

One code smell we find often, even among experienced developers, is around exception handling. We are allergic to any code that says `throw new Exception("some message");`. The proper way to handle exceptions is to handle the exception as early as possible. If you must throw an exception, throw as specific an exception as possible.

One technique we use to discover opportunities for fixing exception handling is to search for instances of `catch(Exception e)`. If there is a `throws Exception` clause in the method signature, just delete it. Then delete a character from the word `Exception` in the `catch` block, which will cause the IDE to believe the exception was not handled and will put a red underline under every exception that must be handled. If there are none, you can unwrap the `try-catch` block using the Unwrap feature. Just position your cursor inside the `try-catch` block and hit Ctrl+Shift+Delete/Cmd+Shift+Delete. You get prompted to unwrap the try. After confirming, it is gone.

> **TIP** *You can also unwrap* `if` *and* `else` *clauses, Strings, etc. Give it a try!*

Comparing Code

We should mention another allergy: duplicated code. If you think there are files that are similar, and which may need to be refactored, you can do a side-by-side comparison by selecting the two or more files in the Project Explorer and choosing the menu item View ⇨ Compare Files (Ctrl+D/Cmd+D). This will open the files in side-by-side windows, where you can edit in either side.

Similarly, you can copy a selection to the clipboard and then make another selection, right-click, and choose Compare With Clipboard.

Using Column Mode

There are situations where you need to edit a series of similar lines in a file, for example, where you need to add a common function in front of a series of similar lines. To turn on column mode, follow these steps:

1. Press Ctrl/Option once.
2. Press again, this time holding it down.
3. Hit the down arrow until you have selected the entire column you want to edit. (See Figure 2.29.)

Now you can paste into that column from the clipboard, or you can edit in place. Hit the End key to move your cursors to the end of the line, and the Home key will bring them the start. You can also use Ctrl+Left Arrow/Cmd+Option+Shift+Left Arrow and Ctrl+Right Arrow/Cmd+Option+Shift+Left Arrow to move them left or right, a word at a time.

In the following snippet, there is a series of RGB triples. Let's say you want to change the middle triple to 255 for each line. Place the cursor anywhere in the top line and select the column you want to edit using the three-key keyboard sequence Ctrl/Option, Ctrl/Option, Down Arrow, until every row you want to change is selected, as shown in Figure 2.29.

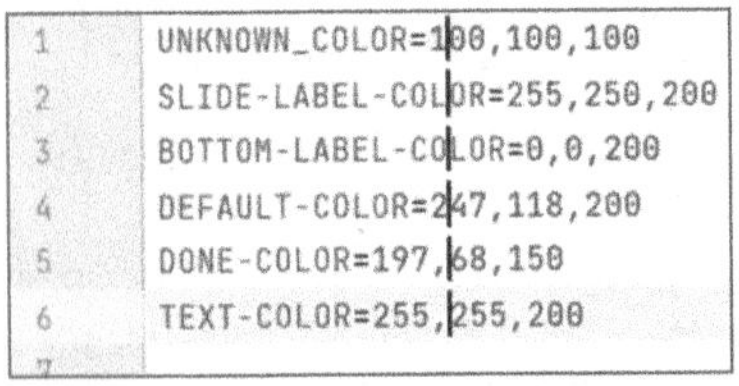

```
UNKNOWN_COLOR=100,100,100
SLIDE-LABEL-COLOR=255,250,200
BOTTOM-LABEL-COLOR=0,0,200
DEFAULT-COLOR=247,118,200
DONE-COLOR=197,68,150
TEXT-COLOR=255,255,200
```

FIGURE 2.29: Selecting column mode

Then hit the End key, and the cursors will move to the end of each line, as shown in Figure 2.30.

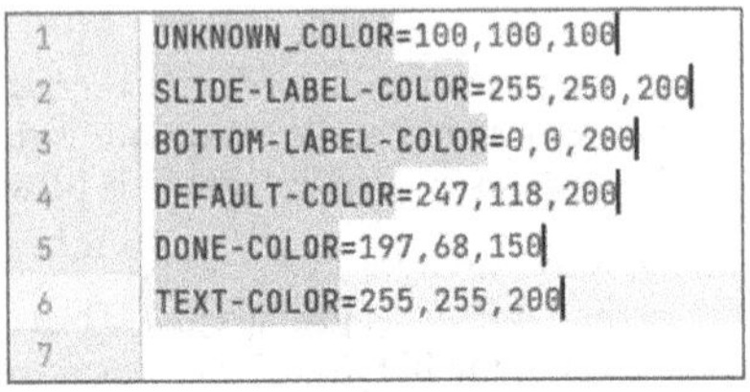

```
UNKNOWN_COLOR=100,100,100
SLIDE-LABEL-COLOR=255,250,200
BOTTOM-LABEL-COLOR=0,0,200
DEFAULT-COLOR=247,118,200
DONE-COLOR=197,68,150
TEXT-COLOR=255,255,200
```

FIGURE 2.30: All cursors at the end of the line

Now hit Ctrl+Left Arrow/Option+Left Arrow to move all the cursors left one word, and press one more Left Arrow to get them to the left of the comma, as shown in Figure 2.31.

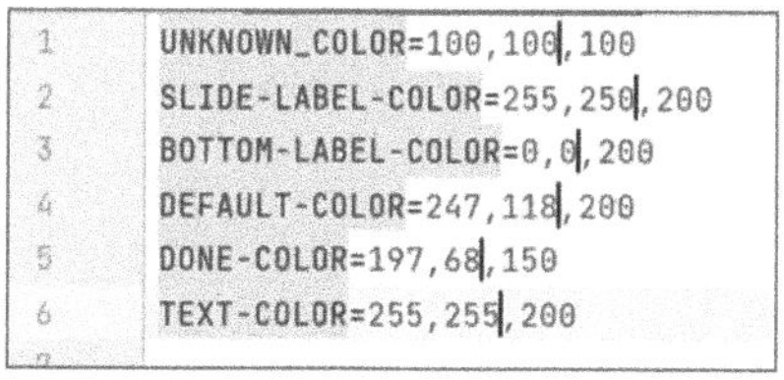

```
UNKNOWN_COLOR=100,100,100
SLIDE-LABEL-COLOR=255,250,200
BOTTOM-LABEL-COLOR=0,0,200
DEFAULT-COLOR=247,118,200
DONE-COLOR=197,68,150
TEXT-COLOR=255,255,200
```

FIGURE 2.31: All cursors moving left

Finally, pressing Ctrl+Backspace/Option+Backspace will delete the entire middle segment, as shown in Figure 2.32.

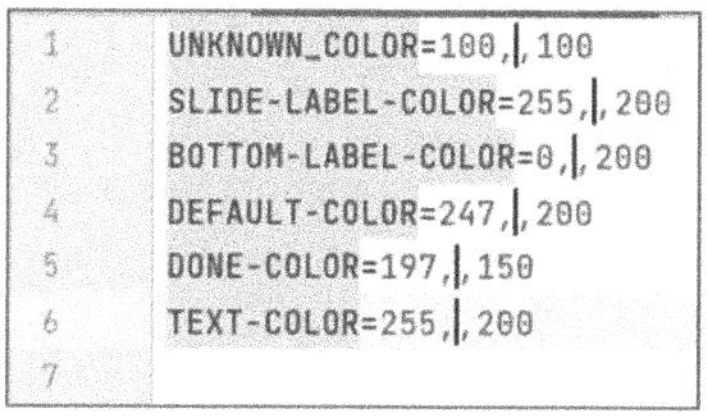

```
UNKNOWN_COLOR=100,,100
SLIDE-LABEL-COLOR=255,,200
BOTTOM-LABEL-COLOR=0,,200
DEFAULT-COLOR=247,,200
DONE-COLOR=197,,150
TEXT-COLOR=255,,200
```

FIGURE 2.32: All lines deleting the middle segment

Now just type in your replacement text, as shown in Figure 2.33.

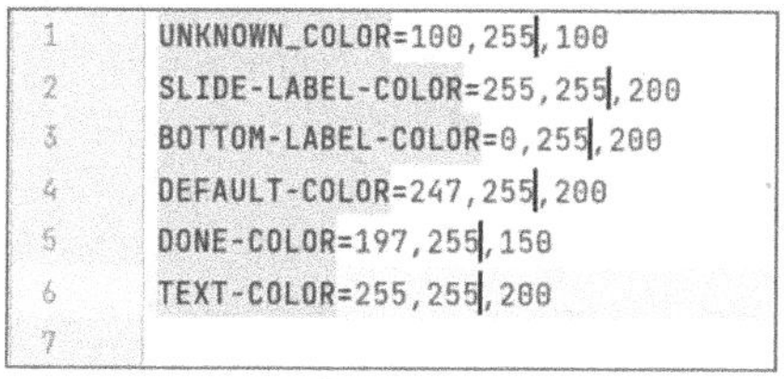

```
UNKNOWN_COLOR=100,255,100
SLIDE-LABEL-COLOR=255,255,200
BOTTOM-LABEL-COLOR=0,255,200
DEFAULT-COLOR=247,255,200
DONE-COLOR=197,255,150
TEXT-COLOR=255,255,200
```

FIGURE 2.33: Replacement text on all lines

You will find this technique useful when changing similar configurations, such as connection strings, text prompts, and even changing adjacent lines of similar code.

EXTENDING THE IDE

While IntelliJ has a lot of built-in functionality, there are many more features available through *plugins*. A plugin is a piece of code that runs in the IDE to add or customize behavior. Many plugins come bundled with IntelliJ. Others are downloaded from a location called the Marketplace.

To install a plugin from the Marketplace, start at the File menu item for Windows or the IntelliJ menu item for Mac. Then choose Settings ➪ Plugins. This brings up the Marketplace where you can choose which plugin you want, as shown in Figure 2.34. For example, Key Promoter is a good one for learning keyboard shortcuts. When you do something with the mouse, a pop-up shows you what shortcut you could have used. Click Install, and the plugin will download. You will then be prompted to restart the IDE, and the plugin will be available.

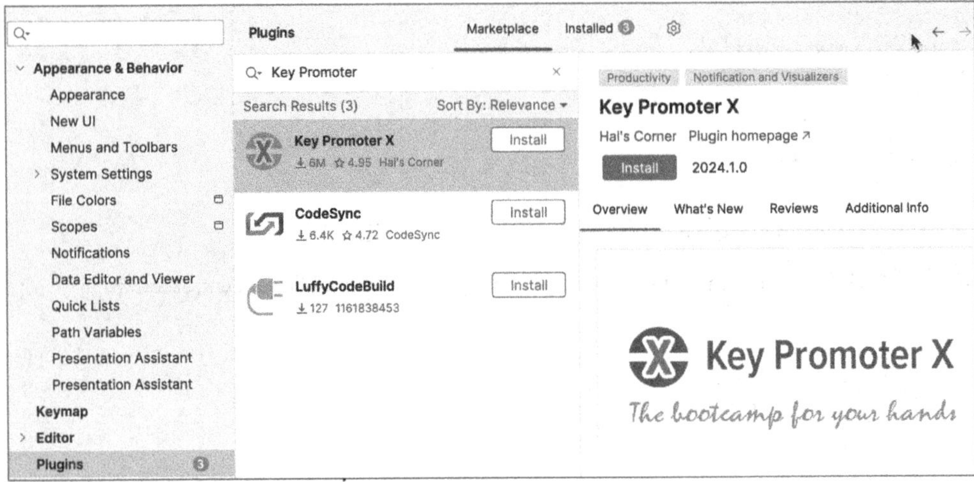

FIGURE 2.34: Installing a plugin in IntelliJ

PEEKING AT ECLIPSE

Now that you understand IntelliJ, it is time to look at Eclipse. First, there are two important vocabulary differences to understand. In IntelliJ, you open a *project*, which consists of one or more *modules*. In Eclipse, you open a *workspace*, which also consists of one or more *modules*. Therefore, *project* means different things across IDEs: in IntelliJ, *project* refers to the top-level entity, and in Eclipse it refers to a buildable artifact. Eclipse is open-source and therefore free to use. It gets contributions from major companies such as IBM and Oracle.

ALWAYS GREEN?

IntelliJ has a guiding principle called "always green." In IntelliJ, the code is expected to compile at all times. If you have a compiler error in any class in the module, you will not be able to run any main methods or tests. By contrast, Eclipse makes a best-effort attempt to run the code. If the code that doesn't compile doesn't need to be executed by your code path, Eclipse will let you run it.

To get started in Eclipse, open a new project by selecting File ➪ New ➪ Java Project, as shown in Figure 2.35.

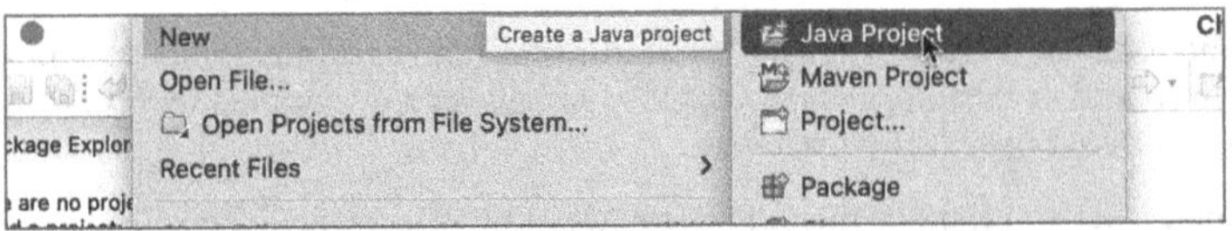

FIGURE 2.35: Creating a project in Eclipse

Like IntelliJ, you get prompted for a project name and the version of Java at a minimum. Alternatively, you can use File ➪ Import ➪ Git ➪ Projects from Git to pull a project from version control, or you can use File ➪ Import ➪ General ➪ Existing Projects Into Workspace to use a project that has already been created.

There are three common ways to run a Java application:

- Choose the drop-down on the green arrow icon and select Run As ➪ Java Application, as shown in Figure 2.36.
- Right-click the Java class name and choose from the run options.
- Choose the Run menu option and then Run As ➪ Java Application.

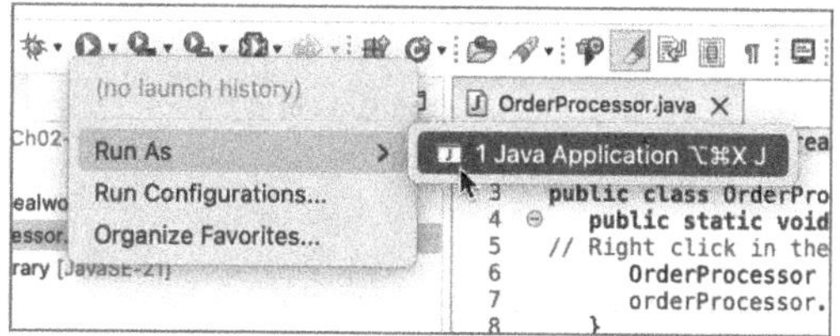

FIGURE 2.36: Running an application in Eclipse

All of these approaches have an option for a run configuration, just like in IntelliJ where you can save settings for running the application. To use the debugger, launch your program using the bug icon instead of the arrow icon. The bug icon puts your program in debug mode.

Like IntelliJ, you can extend IDE behavior through plugins. Go to menu Help ➪ Eclipse Marketplace. Once you chose the plugin you want, install it and restart Eclipse to have it take effect.

If you plan to use Eclipse, we recommend looking at the settings. On Windows, this is under Window ➪ Preferences. On Mac, it is under Eclipse ➪ Settings.

Eclipse has many keyboard shortcuts. We will explore some in the "Comparing IDEs" section. One particularly useful one is Ctrl+3/Cmd+3, which opens a pop-up where you can type the name of any command to run.

PEEKING AT VS CODE

Visual Studio (VS) Code by Microsoft has its own set of vocabulary. Like Eclipse, the top-level entity is a workspace. The lower-level units are simply referred to as *folders*. VS Code is termed an *editor*, rather than an integrated development environment.

Visual Studio is a separate product, not to be confused with VS Code. Both are distributed by Microsoft, but Visual Studio is a commercial IDE typically used by .NET developers, whereas VS Code is a free editor. This distinction between editor and IDE typically shows up in the limited functionality although it has been quickly improving.

> **TIP** *Since VS Code is an editor, it allows you to easily open a single file and edit it.*

Like with IntelliJ and Eclipse, you can download code that extends the functionality of the IDE. VS Code calls those *extensions* rather than plugins. You should install the Java extension before starting to write code in the IDE. The extensions are under File ➪ Preferences ➪ Extensions on Windows and Code ➪ Settings ➪ Extensions on Mac. In the Marketplace, search for "Extension Pack for Java," click Install, and restart VS Code.

WHICH JAVA EXTENSION?

There are at least two extension packs adding Java support to VS Code.

- Extension Pack for Java (from Microsoft)
- Oracle Platform Extension for Visual Studio Code

Since Java support for VS Code is newer, these plugins are rapidly evolving. The Microsoft and Oracle ones are both worth exploring to see which is best at the time you are reading this.

There is also a Language Support for Java from RedHat, but the Microsoft one bundles it in their extension, so there is no need to try it independently.

When you open a new window in VS Code, you have three options. You can open an existing folder on disk, get code from version control, or create a new Java project, as shown in Figure 2.37.

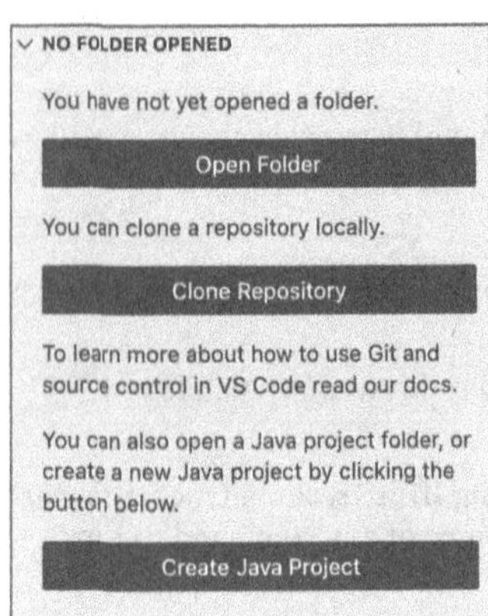

FIGURE 2.37: Creating a project in VS Code

If you chose to create a new project, you are first asked which build tool you would like to use. You can choose no build tool for now. In Chapter 4, you will learn about build tools like Maven and Gradle. Then you are asked to navigate to the directory where you'd like the project stored. Finally, you enter a project name.

There are three common ways to run a Java program.

- Click the Run text in the file, as shown in Figure 2.38.
- Right-click the Java class name and choose Run Java.
- On the Run menu, choose Run Without Debugging.

```
public class App {
    Run | Debug
    public static void main(String[] args) throws Exception {
        System.out.println(x:"Hello, World!");
```

FIGURE 2.38: Running an application in VS Code

The option to run in debug mode is located in the same locations. VS Code calls saved settings for running and debugging a launch configuration. Click the icon in the left navigation (showing an arrow and a bug) to get the option for creating a launch configuration, as shown in Figure 2.39.

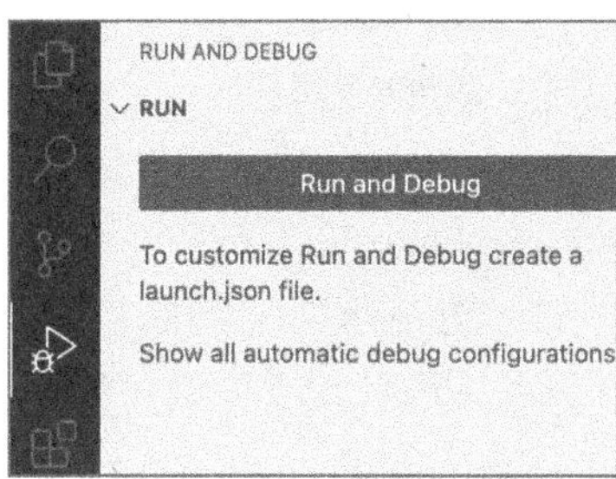

FIGURE 2.39: Creating a launch configuration in VS Code

If you plan to use VS Code, we recommend looking at the settings. On Windows, select File ➪ Preferences ➪ Settings. On Mac, select Code ➪ Settings ➪ Settings.

VS Code has many keyboard shortcuts. We will explore some in the "Comparing IDEs" section. One particularly useful one is the shortcut to open the command palette. Pressing Ctrl+Shift+P/Cmd+Shift+P opens the palette so you can type the name of any VS Code command!

COMPARING IDEs

In some enterprises, everyone uses the same IDE. In others, each developer can use their favorite. Even then, you should be able to understand what people who use a different IDE are talking about. Table 2.1 shows the major vocabulary differences.

All the IDEs offer a wide variety of keyboard shortcuts. Table 2.2 compares some common ones to get a feel for the variety. Note that some IDEs allow you to import keyboard mappings from others. If you are used to one IDE, you may be able to keep those settings in another. However, there is a benefit to learning the default shortcuts so you can more easily work with others who use that IDE.

TABLE 2.1: IDE Terminology

ITEM	INTELLIJ	ECLIPSE	VS CODE
Buildable unit	Module	Workspace	Workspace
Shared settings and home for buildable units	Project	Project	Folder
Optional libraries to customize the behavior of the IDE	Plugin	Plugin	Extension
Saved settings for runs	Run configuration	Run configuration	Launch configuration

TABLE 2.2: Summary of IDE Keyboard Shortcuts

COMMAND	INTELLIJ	ECLIPSE	VS CODE
Run any command	Shift+Shift	Ctrl+3/ Cmd+3	Ctrl+Shift+P/ Cmd+Shift+P
Opening a file	Ctrl+N/ Cmd+O	Ctrl+Shift+T/ Cmd+Shift+R	Ctrl+P/ Cmd+P
Running an application	Shift+F10/ Ctrl+R	Ctrl+Shift+F11/ Cmd+Shift+F11	Ctrl+F5
Extracting a method	Ctrl+Alt+M/ Cmd+Alt+M	Ctrl+Alt+M/ Cmd+Option+M	Ctrl+Shift+R then Ctrl+E
Organizing imports	Ctrl+Alt+O/ Ctrl+Option+O	Ctrl+Shift+O/ Cmd+Shift+O	Option+Shift+O/ Alt+Shift+0
Formatting Code	Ctrl+Alt+L/ Ctrl+Option+L	Ctrl+Shift+F/ Cmd+Shift+F	Ctrl+Shift+I/ Cmd+Shift+I

FURTHER REFERENCES

- `https://www.jetbrains.com/idea`

  Download IntelliJ IDEA
- `https://www.eclipse.org/downloads`

  Download Eclipse
- `https://code.visualstudio.com/download`

  Download VS Code
- *Refactoring: Improving the Design of Existing Code* (Addison-Wesley, 2018)

  Classic refactoring book by Kent Beck and Martin Fowler
- `https://dev.java/learn/debugging`

  Article by Jeanne on using a debugger

SUMMARY

The IDE is arguably the most important item in the Java ecosystem, and your success as a programmer begins when you learn to use the full power of this vital tool. The most important elements of that are mastering the keyboard shortcuts, using the refactoring features, and learning how to use all the subtleties of the editor itself.

- In this chapter, we explored the evolution of the Java IDE, and we learned how familiarity with your IDE can make you an expert programmer. We took a deep dive into some of the most important features of IntelliJ IDEA, including keyboard shortcuts, refactoring, and other important editor capabilities.
- In the rest of the book, our emphasis will be more on programming, but we will discuss other IDE capabilities appropriate to the technologies we cover.

3

Collaborating Across the Enterprise with Git, Jira, and Confluence

WHAT'S IN THIS CHAPTER?

- Collaborating with Git
- Using Jira for Enterprise Process Collaboration
- Working with Confluence, the Enterprise Knowledge Management System

When a team of developers is working on an application, collaboration is absolutely critical lest people step on one another's code. The situation is compounded when teams are distributed globally, from India to the United States, where active development is happening on one continent while developers on another continent are fast asleep. How do you move forward in lockstep? How do you roll back when the need arises? In addition, standards must be published and adhered to. Without good coordination and collaboration, a lot of time would be wasted handing off code and fixing things.

There are many popular tools used in modern enterprises to aid in collaboration. For version control you might find enterprises using Git, Mercurial, SVN, or ClearCase. For requirements management, Jira has become synonymous with issue tracking, although GitHub, Gitlab, and others also provide issue tracking capabilities. For knowledge sharing, Confluence has become very popular, but there are also teams that use Twiki or Jive, among many others.

In this chapter, we focus on some of the most popular tools for code sharing, issue tracking, and knowledge management, namely, Git, Jira, and Confluence. But if your team is using other solutions, the knowledge is readily transferable.

> **CODE DOWNLOADS FOR THIS CHAPTER**
>
> The source code for this chapter is available on the book page at `www.wiley.com`. Click the Downloads link. The code can also be found at `https://github.com/realworldjava/Ch03-Collaboration`. See the `README.md` file in that repository for details.

COLLABORATING WITH GIT

True story: when I (Victor) was a young lad, I was working on a Java three-tier UI application, and I was having a hard time getting some code to work. I was kind of new to programming, and after struggling with it for a few days, I was finally able to squeeze out a working version.

The code needed some cleanup, so I then spent a day tweaking here and extracting methods there, until it finally looked clean.

But to my horror, when I went to execute it, I found my new code had broken. I tried to undo, but in those days, you could only undo a few layers back, and the more I undid and redid, the worse it got. I tried to reproduce what I had done, but it was no use—after days of coding it was broken beyond repair.

The story had a happy ending. I started from scratch, and after a few days, I had a nice, shiny, working version, better than the original. But I quickly learned the hard way to use version control. And here's a sobering thought—this can happen to anyone.

Version control systems (VCSs) today are far more mature than they were back then. In the twentieth century, version control was performed on a middleware server. You would call a lock on a file, check it out, do some work on it, and then check it back in and release the lock.

The process was grindingly slow. You had to wait for the files to arrive; then when you checked it in, you had to wait for the files to get to the server and for the server to do its thing integrating the changes, and finally the lock would be released.

If you went to lunch or left early and forgot to unlock, then your team would be blocked for the day because *you* held the lock.

That was the operating model in the olden days for version control systems such as RCS, CVS, and, to an extent, the ever-popular Subversion (SVN). Then as the twenty-first century settled in, Linus Torvalds (the inventor of Linux) produced Git, with a new, revolutionary operating model.

By contrast, Git is a decentralized version control system. There are no locks, and many version control operations happen on your local computer, so it is blazingly fast.

Introducing Git Basics

Let's take a look at a day in the life of a developer who uses Git. Suppose you want to make a change to some files. First, you *clone* the remote repository, which places a copy of it, including all history, on your computer. Next you make your desired change to the file.

Once you are happy with your changes, you *pull* to update locally any code that others may have changed in the meantime. If a teammate has made any changes, Git will determine if it can automatically reconcile or if you need to manually *merge* your changes. Finally, it is time to *commit* your changes. Do a *push* to make your changes available to your teammates.

Learning Key Concepts

Git maintains three key areas in every installation:

- **Working area:** Where your files live and evolve
- **Staging area:** Where files are staged to be *committed*
- **Repository:** Where commits are saved

In addition, you can access Git repos on other, remote machines (assuming you have the proper permissions). In fact, technically any Git instance can act as a Git remote, although in most enterprises everyone shares a centralized remote server that uses GitHub, GitLab, Bitbucket, or the like.

To pull the files from a remote project onto your local computer, you *clone* the project repository. All the files are then downloaded and automatically included in your working area, where they are tracked by Git.

If you are creating a new project from scratch and you want to add it to Git, you must initialize the project by calling `git init` in the root of the project directory. Then for any files that you want Git to track, you must call `git add <file1> <file2>` specifying the name of each file (or filenaming pattern with `*` wildcards) or call `git add .` to add everything in that directory and below.

Similarly, when you change files, you want to call `git add` to stage the changes. You can stage and commit in a single operation using `git commit -am "some meaningful log message."`.

After you have staged your changes and you are happy with them, you want to save those changes to your repository. The process for that is to commit them.

Differentiating Commits

The word *commit* is both a verb and a noun. As a verb, *commit* refers to the action of moving your changes to your local Git repo. As a noun, a *commit* refers to all the files and context information included in that action of committing. A broad algorithm is applied to the files, their previous commits, the committer's username, the log message, and other information to produce a unique 40-character hexadecimal *commit ID*, also known as a *commit hash*.

Displaying Git Status

The `git status` command is a useful tool for displaying the status of your files. This will show you a list of changed, untracked, and staged files, as well as the current branch, and a list of specific commands you can execute to change status.

If there are files that you absolutely don't want Git to track (such as IDE configuration files or local files that you don't ever want to commit), you can add their names (or directories or a name pattern) to a file called `.gitignore` in the root of your working area (more on this later).

Ignored files are not tracked by Git, they don't show in status, and their changes are not included when checking for modifications. You can change them and use them, but as far as Git is concerned, they do not exist.

Branching

All Git commits reside on a branch. A *branch* is a named pointer to a set of commits; or more accurately, it is a pointer to a particular *HEAD* commit, which happens to include all the historical commits that produced that commit. As you make further commits to that branch, the branch pointer moves forward to point to the latest commit.

You can create a branch from a selected branch, do work on the new branch, then compare that branch to the original branch to review your changes, and finally merge your branch into the original branch. Traditionally, Git would assign a default branch named *master*. But recently they have been transitioning to use the name *main* instead of *master* to promote inclusivity. Depending on your Git provider and version, you will see one or the other.

Tagging

Tags are like branches, except that they are static. Where a branch pointer continuously moves to the latest commit, a tag pointer never moves, and so it captures the state of your codebase at a given moment in time. A tag is like a human-readable name for the commit hash.

> **TIP** *While the commit hash that the tag pointer references is immutable, the tag name itself can be deleted and recreated.*

Merging

Merging refers to the activity of integrating the changes from one branch into another branch. This is one step in a common workflow in Git—you start with an existing branch, usually the common branch used by everyone, which can be called anything, but traditionally it is called *develop*. You create your branch off that existing branch into a new branch of your own naming, for example *feature-123*. You, and perhaps some other members of your team, do some work on *feature-123*, you run your tests, everything passes, and you're ready to release the code. You must merge *feature-123* into develop and then *push* that to the remote server.

> **TIP** *It's common in the enterprise to name the feature branch using the JIRA ticket number to facilitate tracking. We will see an example of this in the "Using Jira for Enterprise Process Collaboration" section, later in this chapter.*

Reading Git Logs

Git gives you the ability to view a *log* of your commit history in configurable levels of detail. `git log` displays a fairly verbose listing of all your commit history.

Here is one entry from a recent `git log` run:

```
commit f162588e53d536dd0738968e952adf7e86740a8f (refactoring1)
Author: vgrazi <vgrazi@gmail.com>
Date:   Mon Feb 19 19:54:05 2024 -0500

    added a display
```

This displays the commit ID, branch, author, commit date, and commit message.

> **TIP** *If you see a colon at the end of the log, that indicates a page break; hit the spacebar to list more, or type* `q` *to quit and get back to your command line.*

Staging Your Changes

As mentioned, Git maintains a local *staging* area; any files that you intend to track must be added to the staging area using the `git add` command. You can stage specific files using the following:

```
git add <file1> <file2> <file3> <etc>
```

or you can stage every changed file using a dot to indicate all of them.

```
git add .
```

The `git add` operation stages any new, modified, and deleted files. When using `git add .`, the staging is recursive, picking up any changed files from the current directory and below. What about moved files? Git will make its best effort to recognize moved files and directories and preserve their version history.

To unstage a file that was already added, use the following:

```
git rm -cached <file>
```

which is essentially the inverse of `add`.

After performing `git add`, your next step will usually be to commit the staging area to the local repo. You will want to add a commit message using the `-m` (for "message") switch.

```
git commit -m "Some meaningful commit message"
```

When you are happy with your changes, you *add* them to the staging area, again using the `git add` command. You then *commit* the staging area (with all its added files) to the Git repository (residing on your local computer) using the command `git commit -m "Some meaningful commit message"`, and eventually you push your repo to a remote server using the `git push` command.

You can both add and commit in a single command by calling `git commit -am`. For example:

```
git commit -am "Some meaningful commit message"
```

To summarize, Git is a critical code collaboration system used in most development shops, and you want to become familiar with it early on.

Let's get some hands-on practice, but first, please install Git, and then follow along.

Installing Git

To install Git, head over to `https://git-scm.com/downloads`. You will find installation instructions for Windows, macOS, and Linux.

Git for Windows will generally work from the normal Windows command shell, but many developers prefer to use Git Bash, which is installed with Git for Windows. Git Bash is a Windows implementation of the popular Unix/Linux *bash* shell, which recognizes all the Linux commands, such as `grep`, `ls`, and `ps`, and is great for developers with a Unix/Linux background.

Once Git is installed, set your email and name.

```
git config --global user.name "Your Name"
git config --global user.email you@example.com
```

The name will be used to annotate all your commits. The email address may be used by the Git provider to communicate with you.

This book uses GitHub, so if you don't already have an account set up, we encourage you to head over to `github.com` and create a free account.

Understanding Git Workflow by Example

Let's dive right in by following the typical command sequence. we recommend that you follow along by typing all the commands; the experience will help you acquire a visceral understanding of the Git workflow.

First, please fork the book repo. Forking is the process of making your own personal copy of an existing repo. In theory you could use the original repo without forking it; however, the repo is read-only, so you won't be able to push changes. A forked copy becomes your own to do as you wish.

Head over to the project repo at `https://github.com/realworldjava/Ch03-Collaboration`. As shown in Figure 3.1, fork the project repo. This creates a new repo under your user ID such as `https://github.com/<your git id>/Ch03-Collaboration`.

Click the Fork button. On the fork screen, keep all the defaults and click the Create Fork button, as in Figure 3.2.

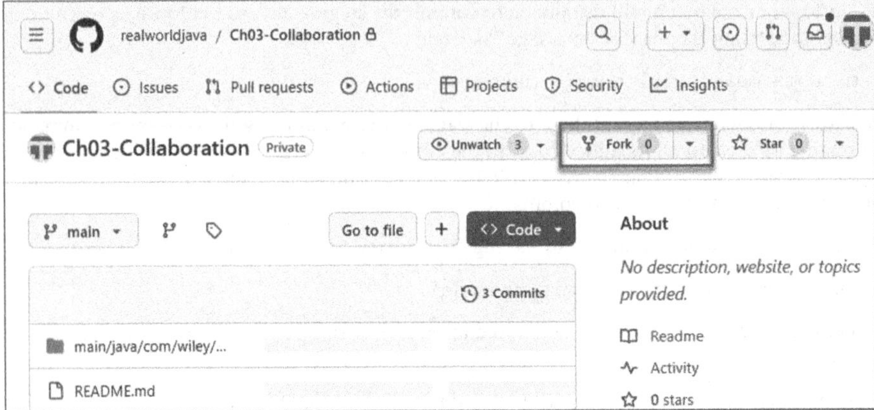

FIGURE 3.1: Forking a GitHub project

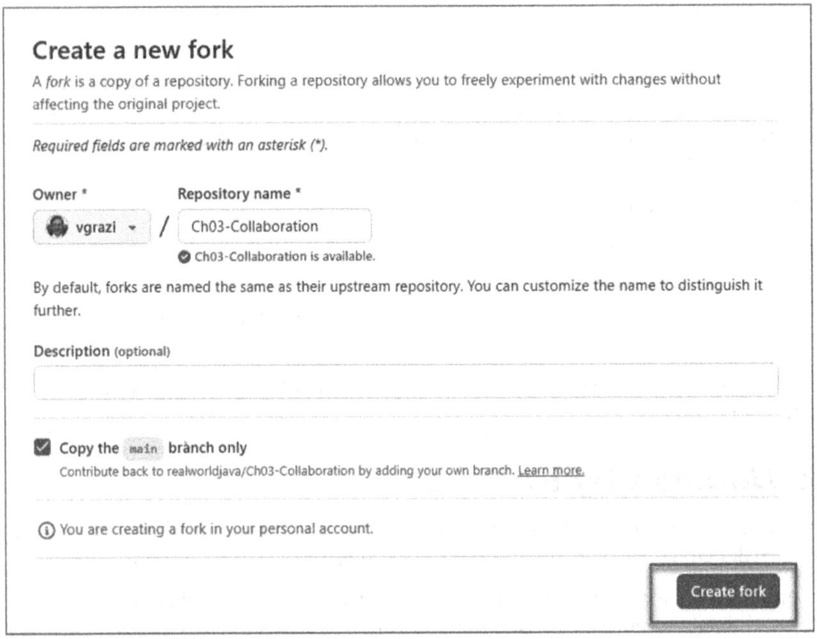

FIGURE 3.2: Completing the fork

Now clone the fork of our project repo. Cloning is the operation of bringing the Git project to your development machine for viewing and editing.

To clone the repo, open a command shell, `cd` to an empty directory, and clone your fork of our book project using the following:

```
git clone https://github.com/<your git id>/Ch03-Collaboration
```

That will clone and initialize the repository in the current directory, enabling you to work on it. (Git clone will move all the files directly into the current directory, so you always want to start from an empty directory.) The clone operation will only bring the default branch and will download the list of remote branches. If you want to check out other branches, you need to check those out explicitly.

CLONING VIA SSH

The Uniform Resource Indicator (URI) we used in the Git clone operation earlier was simply the HTTPS URL of our GitHub repo. This is a common cloning practice for public GitHub repos, and you may continue to use that approach for this book. However, in enterprises they will sometimes require you to use a secure SSH URI, which means you need to generate and add SSH keys to your repo. That is not as scary as it sounds.

From a Linux or macOS shell or from Git Bash, generate the keys using this:

```
ssh-keygen -t rsa -b 4096 -f ~/.ssh/id_rsa -C "github keys"
```

Or from a standard Windows shell, use this:

```
ssh-keygen -t rsa -b 4096 -f %USERPROFILE%\.ssh\id_rsa1 -C
"github keys"
```

You can use the generated key with all your GitHub repos. You will need to send the key to GitHub. Here's how:

1. Copy the contents of the `~/.ssh/id_rsa` file you just generated to the clipboard.
2. Click your profile picture in the top-right corner, and choose the Settings option.
3. In the left navigation, select the entry for SSH and GPG keys, as shown in Figure 3.3.
4. Select SSH Keys and New SSH Key.

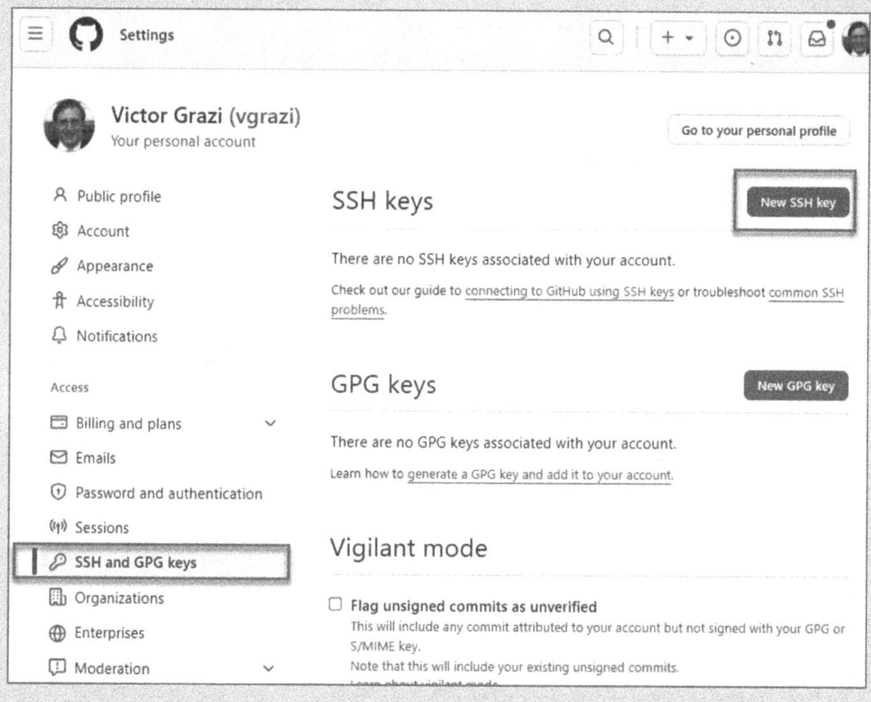

FIGURE 3.3: Adding SSH keys to your GitHub repo

5. Paste in the contents of your `id_rsa` file you copied in step 1, and click Add SSH Key. In a few seconds, you should receive an email announcing that your key has been set up, as in Figure 3.4.

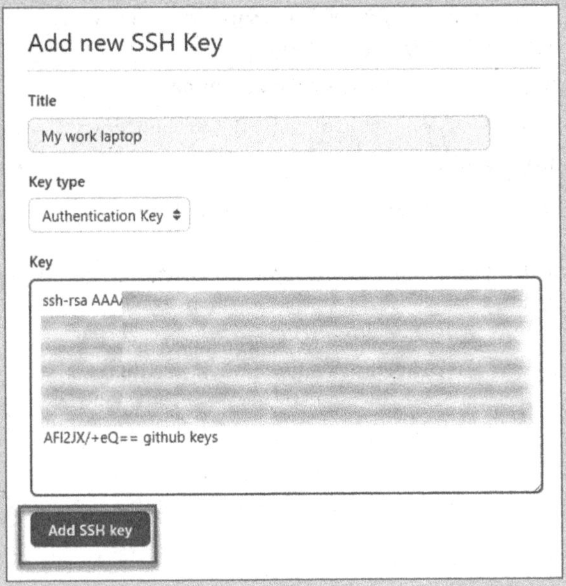

FIGURE 3.4: Adding new SSH keys

We will see an example of the `checkout` and the `switch` commands next.

1. Please `cd` to the directory `main/java/com/wiley/realworldjava/gitplay`.
2. There is one file there (see Listing 3.1).

LISTING 3.1: Original File

```
package com.wiley.realworldjava.gitplay;

public class GitDemo {
   private String description;

   public GitDemo(String description) {
      this.description = description;
   }

   public void displayDescription() {
      System.out.println("Description: " + description);
   }
```

```
    public static void main(String[] args) {
       GitDemo demo = new GitDemo("Hello, Git!");

       // Display the initial description
       demo.displayDescription();
    }
}
```

To make the editing and compilation easier, create a new project in your IDE from version control. Refer to Chapter 2, "Getting to Know Your IDE: The Secret to Success," to learn how to create a project from version control.

The `git status` command will hold your hand, displaying your current status and showing you available options for what to do next.

```
git status
```

For my environment, this displays the following:

```
Your branch is up to date with 'origin/main'.

Untracked files:
  (use "git add <file>..." to include in what will be committed)
        .idea/
```

Now you don't want to check in your `.idea` directory (after all, you don't want to dictate your dynamic .idea state to others or even to your future self), and you certainly don't want to check in your compile output directory; Git is for source, not for compiled output.

Wouldn't it be great if you could tell Git to completely ignore such files? Fortunately, Git provides a facility for ignoring selected files and directories. To do so, create a file named `.gitignore` in the project root, and include the names of files and directories to ignore. You can include the exact filename (`temp.txt`), a wildcard (`temp*.*`), or directories. You can ignore entire directories by specifying the directory names. For example:

- `/logs/` will ignore the `logs` directory at the root.
- `logs/` will ignore any directory named `logs` at any level.
- `logs` without a path separator will match the `logs/` directory and any file named `logs`.

If you want to make the recursion explicit, you can say `**/logs`, which will ignore everything in any directory named `logs`. You can add comments to the `.gitignore` file by starting them with #. Blank lines are ignored.

You cannot ignore files that are already tracked. To untrack a tracked file, you can do this:

```
git rm --cached -r com/wiley/realworldjava/gitplay/
```

In our case, we will use the following `.gitignore` file:

```
# Ignore the entire .idea directory
.idea

# Ignore the output directory.
out/
```

Remember to stage and commit that so Git will track it.

```
git add .gitignore
git commit -m "Added .gitignore"
```

The `add` command is to stage the file. The `commit` command is to check it in. The `-m` flag specifies a log message to be associated with that commit.

Like all good developers, we don't want to commit our code until it is done and tested. Yet we do want to track our code as it evolves. How can we push our changes to the remote repo without impacting other developers? The answer is to create a branch and make your changes on that branch. Then you can make changes to that branch, or even collaborate with others on that branch, without impacting the main branch.

Let's name this branch *refactoring1*. The command for this is shown here:

```
git branch refactoring1
```

That will create a new branch named *refactoring1* from the current commit. If you want to delete a branch, you can do the following (but for now, don't delete it):

```
git branch -d refactoring1
```

Then to check out the branch, do the following:

```
git checkout refactoring1
```

You can both create and check out the branch in a single instruction using this:

```
git checkout -b refactoring1
```

The `-b` flag tells the `checkout` instruction to create the branch and then check it out. Later Git added perhaps a more indicatively named `switch` instruction.

To switch to an existing branch using switch, use the following:

```
git switch refactoring1
```

Using `switch`, the syntax for creating and checking out a new branch is as follows:

```
git switch -c refactoring1
```

To list the names of all the known branches on your computer (the current branch gets a * and a color highlight), use the following:

```
git branch
```

displays:

```
* refactoring1
  main
```

If you want to list the remote branches as well, use this:

```
git branch -a
```

Next you want to do some work and change some files. Let's modify our main method by adding lines 19 to 22 as shown in Listing 3.2.

LISTING 3.2: Modified File

```
14: public static void main(String[] args) {
15:     GitDemo demo = new GitDemo("Hello, Git!");
16:
17:     // Display the initial description
18:     demo.displayDescription();       // Make some changes and commit
19:
20:     // Make more changes and commit
21:     demo.description = "Version control with Git is fun and easy.";
22:     demo.displayDescription();
23: }
```

Now commit those changes. For convenience let's first `cd` to the directory containing the file.

```
cd ./main/java/com/wiley/realworldjava/gitplay
```

Then stage our changes using this:

```
git add GitDemo.java
```

Look at the `git status`, which displays the following:

```
On branch refactoring1

Changes to be committed:
  (use "git restore --staged <file>..." to unstage)
        modified:   GitDemo.java
```

and commit our changes to the current branch:

```
git commit -m "Added a line to GitDemo"
```

Those changes are now committed to your local repo, and you can see the commits, along with the files they contain, and their commit messages, using any variation of the `git log` command (stay tuned!).

Of course, you want to share those changes with the rest of the development team. The process for that is to push to the remote repo. (There can be zero or more named remotes, and by default the remote is named *origin*.)

```
git push origin refactoring1
```

That means *push* any commits from your local repo to the remote machine (*origin* by default) to the *branch* named *main*. (More on branching to come.)

To push the code to the current branch and the origin that you cloned from, you can dispense with the formality and just call the following:

```
git push
```

To see the URL of the origin, use this:

```
git remote get-url origin
```

To set the URL or the origin or to name a new remote, such as `other-machine`, simply use this:

```
git remote add other-machine <url>
```

You can also get a list of the current remotes and associated URLs via this:

```
git remote -v
```

That will display a list of *fetch* and push URLs for each remote repo. Fetch and push URLs can be the same, but they don't have to be. For example, if your network requires different protocols for pushing and fetching, they will differ. Or if you have mirrored repos, where you push to a central "hub" repo but you pull from a "spoke" node in your region, the fetch and push URLs will differ.

Fetching, Merging, and Pulling

The `git fetch` command will fetch the specified branch from the specified remote server. This makes it available on your local machine but does not integrate it with your checked-out code, where origin and the branch name are optional.

```
git fetch origin my-branch
```

The `git merge` command will merge a specified source branch from a specified remote into the currently checked-out branch. This has the effect of combining all the commits from the source branch into the currently checked-out branch. In the following example, you are commanding Git to merge a branch named *my-branch* that is on the remote origin into the currently checked-out branch on your machine.

```
git merge origin my-branch
```

You can omit `origin`, and Git will merge the specified branch from the local repository into the currently checked-out branch.

It is common to have an *integration* aka *develop* branch, which is essentially a catchall branch that is shared by the full development team. This branch is generally used to stage features that are scheduled to be included in the next release. (See the "Using Gitflow for Collaboration" section later in this chapter for a detailed explanation.)

When merging into `develop` and other shared branches, it is a good practice to use the "no fast-forward" (`no-ff`) switch.

```
git checkout develop
git merge -no-ff my-branch
```

By default, merges are *fast-forwarded*. That means Git looks at all commits on your source branch between the time you created that branch and now. If there are no conflicts with the current state of your branch, then those commits will be moved to the end of the target branch. In contrast, if you do a *no-ff* merge, then the branch where you have been making your commits will remain as a separate parallel branch, with a single merge commit to join them. This makes it easy to identify the commits that comprise a given feature. Figure 3.5 illustrates this flow.

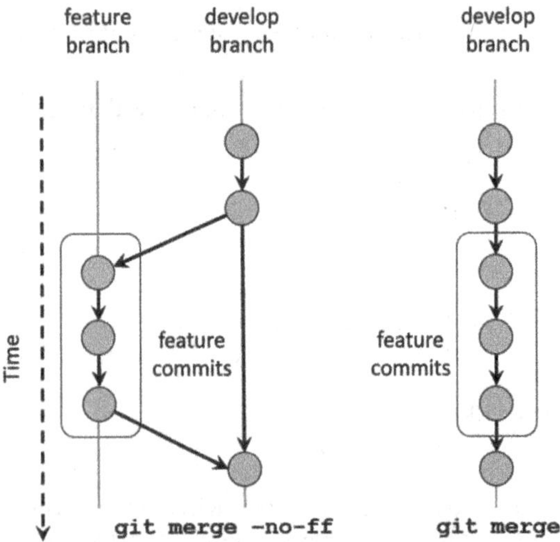

FIGURE 3.5: Git merge without and with fast-forward

The `git pull` command combines `git fetch` and `git merge` into a single command, pulling the branch from the remote server and merging it into the current branch.

```
git pull origin my-branch
```

The `--no-ff` switch cannot directly be used on a pull operation. But you can direct Git to default to `no-ff` on pulls by setting the global variable `pull-ff`.

```
git config --global pull.ff only
```

Playing with Branches

By now you have modified the `GitDemo` class and committed the changes. Now for the Git magic.

Back on the command line, let's switch back to the main branch.

```
git switch main
```

Now look at the `GitDemo` class, but don't panic! The new code that you added earlier is no longer there, because those code changes are in the *refactoring1* branch but you are on the *main* branch.

Let's create a new branch called *refactoring2*.

```
git switch -c refactoring2
```

This is now a replica of *main*. Now modify the `GitDemo` class in a different part of the code, by adding the method `setAndDisplayDescription`.

```
public void displayDescription() {
    System.out.println("Description: " + description);
}

public void setAndDisplayDescription(String description) {
    this.description = description;
    System.out.println("Description: " + description);
}
```

Now commit that.

```
git commit -am "added setAndDisplayDescription"
```

Here is the fun part. What happens when we merge the changes from the first branch into the changes from the second branch? (A Git window may appear with a default commit message; you can leave that message and type **:q** as earlier.)

```
git merge refactoring1
```

Git does a fabulous job of merging branch *refactoring1* into *refactoring2*, producing a hybrid class:

```
package com.wiley.realworldjava.gitplay;

public class GitDemo {
    private String description;

    public GitDemo(String description) {
        this.description = description;
    }

    public void displayDescription() {
        System.out.println("Description: " + description);
    }

    public void setAndDisplayDescription(String description) {
        this.description = description;
        System.out.println("Description: " + description);
    }

    public static void main(String[] args) {
        GitDemo demo = new GitDemo("Hello, Git!");

```

```
        // Display the initial description
        demo.displayDescription();

        // Make more changes and commit
        demo.description = "Version control with Git is fun and easy.";
        demo.displayDescription();
    }
}
```

Resolving Merge Conflicts

That's the happy path, where multiple developers are working on the same set of files, and you make changes in one place in a file, and someone else made changes somewhere else in the same file or even different files. When you try to merge their changes into yours, Git does a great job of producing a hybrid result.

But there will be times (especially when you let many days pass before merging) when you and they made changes in the same general area of the file, and Git is not able to resolve the merge. In such cases, a *merge-conflict* results. When that happens, Git will ask the person who performed the merge to resolve the conflict manually and continue. Resolving a conflict can be done manually, but it is much easier to have the IDE assist. All the major IDEs have great support for manual side-by-side conflict resolution; more on this later.

Let's create a new branch off main, called *refactoring3*.

```
git switch main
git switch -c refactoring3
```

The new *refactoring3* branch contains the original version of `GitDemo` in Listing 3.1. Let's add some new code (lines 19 to 22).

```
14: public static void main(String[] args) {
15:     GitDemo demo = new GitDemo("Hello, Git!");
16:
17:     // Display the initial description
18:     demo.displayDescription();
19:
20:     // Make more changes and commit
21:     demo.description = "Git is powerful.";
22:     demo.displayDescription();
23: }
```

And commit that.

```
git add GitDemo.java
git commit -m "added conflicting code"
```

Now let's try to merge refactoring1 (Listing 3.2) into our newly modified branch *refactoring3*:

```
git merge refactoring1
```

The result is a message:

```
Automatic merge failed; fix conflicts and then commit the result.
```

Looking at the code, we find this ugly concoction:

```
public static void main(String[] args) {
    GitDemo demo = new GitDemo("Hello, Git!");

    // Display the initial description
```

```
    demo.displayDescription();
<<<<<<< HEAD
    // Make more changes and commit
    demo.description = "Git is powerful.";
=======

    // Make more changes and commit
    demo.description = "Version control with Git is fun and easy.";
>>>>>>> refactoring1
    demo.displayDescription();
}
```

You can see that the code following `<<<<<<< HEAD` and up to `=======` is the code from the current branch, and the code following that, up to `>>>>>>> refactoring1`, is from the *refactoring1* branch.

When you get a merge conflict like this, you have two options: either abort or fix it. To abort a merge after a conflict and restore everything to be as it was before the merge, use this:

```
git merge --abort
```

Give that a try, and presto, the original code is restored! On the other hand, you can choose to fix it—remove the lines `<<<<<<< HEAD`, `=======`, and `>>>>>>> refactoring1` and adjust the code to your liking.

```
public static void main(String[] args) {
    GitDemo demo = new GitDemo("Hello, Git!");

    // Display the initial description
    demo.displayDescription();

    // Make more changes and commit
    demo.description = "Git is fun and easy, and very powerful.";
    demo.displayDescription();
}
```

Then call `git add` to mark the conflict as resolved, and call `git commit` to tell Git to continue the merge.

```
git add GitDemo.java
git commit -m "resolved conflict"
```

Yay, peace on earth!

Using Pull/Merge Requests

When you are working in a collaborative environment, especially in a large open-source project, enterprises will assign read-access to the larger team, reserving write-access just to "committers." In such cases, the team might have the ability to create branches but might not have the ability to merge into the main shared branches like *main* and *develop*. Or in more extreme cases, the team would be required to clone the repo and make all changes in the clone.

In such enterprises, when you want to incorporate your changes into the main branches in the main repository, you would need to request that from an administrator in the form of a pull request. To create a pull request, you log onto the provider and choose the option for creating a new pull request (or merge request in GitLab).

> **TIP** *Pull requests and merge requests are just different names for essentially the same thing. The term pull request is used by GitHub and Bitbucket, where merge request is used by GitLab. For the purposes of this book, we will use the term pull request, often abbreviated as PR.*

Using the Git Log

We saw that the `git log` command lists all the commits on the current branch.

You can add various options to the `git log` command to control things like the range of commits, formatting options, graphing options, and so on. We won't go into all that here; refer to the Git documentation at `https://git-scm.com/docs/git-log`.

One option we will mention here is the appropriately named `--oneline`, which displays a concise one-commit-per-line view of the log. When you add the `--graph` option, it also displays a graphical view of your branches.

```
git log --graph --oneline
```

The following displays a commit history for the current branch:

```
*   00cdd10 (HEAD -> refactoring3) Merge branch 'refactoring1' into refactoring3
|\
| * f162588 (refactoring1) added a display
* | b635ca1 Whitespace
* | 51d31a6 added conflicting display message
|/
* 822d223 (main) Formatting
* 55de6c6 (origin/main, origin/HEAD) added detail
* 53753a2 renaming
* ed46f26 Initial commit
```

You can also display commit history for any specific branch by adding the branch name.

```
git log --graph --oneline refactoring1
* f162588 (refactoring1) added a display
* 822d223 (main) Formatting
* 55de6c6 (origin/main, origin/HEAD) added detail
* 53753a2 renaming
* ed46f26 Initial commit
* 283d86f Initial commit
```

To see all branches, use the `--all` option. You can also format the output, as in the following example:

```
git log --graph --oneline --all --pretty=format:'%h %an %ar - %s'
*   00cdd10 vgrazi 2 days ago - Merge branch 'refactoring1' into refactoring3
|\
* | b635ca1 vgrazi 2 days ago - Whitespace
* | 51d31a6 vgrazi 2 days ago - added conflicting display message
| | *   d0f9078 vgrazi 2 days ago - Merge branch 'feature/refactoring1' into
feature/refactoring2
| | |\
| | |/
| |/|
| * | f162588 vgrazi 2 days ago - added a display
|/ /
| * 640faec vgrazi 2 days ago - added method
|/
* 822d223 vgrazi 2 days ago - Formatting
* 55de6c6 vgrazi 2 days ago - added detail
| * 80dbc6d vgrazi 2 days ago - Added .gitignore
| * 22fe224 vgrazi 2 days ago - Typo
|/
* 53753a2 vgrazi 2 days ago - renaming
```

```
* ed46f26 vgrazi 2 days ago - Initial commit
* 283d86f realworldjava 7 days ago - Initial commit
```

These are the placeholder definitions that you can pass to the formatter. They will be replaced by information from each commit.

- `%h`: Abbreviated commit hash
- `%an`: Author name
- `%ar`: Author date, relative
- `%s`: Commit subject

Rebasing

When you merge branches, Git creates an extra "merge" commit that contains the results of the merge. This is useful in situations where you want to emphasize the commits that resulted in this branch. On the other hand, this tends to clutter up the commit history with extra commits.

If you want to bypass that extra merge commit, there is a workaround in some situations, and that is to *rebase* instead of merge. A rebase is like a merge, except that it moves your commits to the end of the target branch, instead of creating a parallel branch and creating a merge commit.

To understand it, you really need to experience it, so let's set up an example. Let's create a feature branch, make some commits, and compare the results of a merge versus a rebase.

1. Create a feature branch from `refactoring3`, and call it `feature`.

   ```
   git switch -c feature
   ```

2. Make some commits to the `feature` branch: by adding lines 23 to 26, and then commit.

   ```
   20: // Make more changes and commit
   21: demo.description = "Git is fun and easy, and very powerful.";
   22: demo.displayDescription();
   23:
   24: // Make another change
   25: demo.description = "Changes for rebase";
   26: demo.displayDescription();
   ```

   and then commit.

   ```
   git commit -am "changes to feature for rebase"
   ```

3. Make some more changes by adding lines 27 to 30.

   ```
   24:     // Make another change
   25:     demo.description = "Change1 for rebase";
   26:     demo.displayDescription();
   27:
   28:     // And yet another change
   29:     demo.description = "Change2 for rebase";
   30:     demo.displayDescription();
   31:}
   ```

   and then commit:

   ```
   git commit -am "more changes to feature for rebase"
   ```

4. Switch back to `refactoring3`:

```
git switch refactoring3
```

5. Make some commits to the `refactoring3` branch, and add lines 17 to 19.

```
14: public static void main(String[] args) {
15:     GitDemo demo = new GitDemo("Hello, Git!");
16:
17:     demo.description = "Continuing on branch";
18:     demo.displayDescription();
19:
```

and then commit:

```
git commit -am "more changes to refactoring3"
```

> **TIP** *If you don't include a* `-m` *commit message, then a VI editor window will appear and prompt you for a commit message. If that happens, hit* `i` *to enter edit mode, and type your message; then hit Enter to start a new line. When done, hit Esc to exit edit mode, type* **`:w`** *to write your message to the commit, and type* **`:q`** *to quit. That's basic VI editing, which Unix/Linux users are intimately familiar with.*

6. Copy branch `refactoring3` to `refactoring3a`.

```
git branch -c refactoring3a
```

7. Merge `feature` into `refactoring3a` (as with the last merge, a Git window may appear with a default commit message; you can leave that message and type **`:q`** as earlier).

```
git merge feature
```

8. Switch to `refactoring3`.

```
git switch refactoring3
```

9. Rebase the feature into `refactoring3`.

```
git rebase feature
```

10. Compare the logs for `refactoring3a` on the top (merge) and *refactoring3* on the bottom (rebase). You can see that *rebase* moved the commit history to the end of the target branch, whereas merge created a new *merge* commit.

```
git log --graph --oneline refactoring3
```

This includes the following:

```
* 019f4f7 (HEAD -> refactoring3) more changes to refactoring3
* 4954034 (feature) more changes to feature for rebase
* 607d6bb changes to feature for rebase
* 502f3b3 resolved conflict
```

```
git log --graph --oneline refactoring3a
```

which includes the following:

```
*   7f5c82c (refactoring3a) Merge branch 'feature' into refactoring3a
|\
| * 4954034 (feature) more changes to feature for rebase
| * 607d6bb changes to feature for rebase
* | 4821d9c more changes to refactoring3
|/
* 502f3b3 resolved conflict
```

Either way the code is identical, but the rebase produces a much cleaner history. So what's the downside? Why would we ever use merge and not rebase?

The answer is that rebase rewrites your commit history. Remember, we said that a commit ID includes the previous version. Well, since we are moving the commit history to the end of the branch, the previous version is different, and therefore the commit ID is different. Why is that bad? Well, it is not bad if you are working on the branch alone and if you have not merged your work into any other branch. But if you are collaborating or if you have merged this branch into any other shared branch, then anyone sharing that work will have trouble merging that work back into their own code.

As you can see in Figure 3.6, both branches `refactoring3` and `refactoring3a` have the same exact version of the code, but `refactoring3a` (the merged branch) consists of two parallel branches that are merged into a single commit, whereas `refactoring3` (the rebased branch) is one straight branch.

Branch	Commit Message	Branch Name	User	Commit ID
	Merge branch 'feature' into refactoring3a	refactoring3a	vgrazi	7f5c82cb
	more changes to refactoring3		vgrazi	4821d9cb
	more changes to feature for rebase	feature	vgrazi	4954034c
	changes to feature for rebase		vgrazi	607d6bb4
	resolved conflict		vgrazi	502f3b3f
	added conflicting code		vgrazi	5666eab6

Branch	Commit Message	Branch Name	User	Commit ID
	more changes to refactoring3	refactoring3	vgrazi	019f4f7b
	more changes to feature for rebase	feature	vgrazi	4954034c
	changes to feature for rebase		vgrazi	607d6bb4
	resolved conflict		vgrazi	502f3b3f
	added conflicting code		vgrazi	5666eab6

FIGURE 3.6: Merge versus rebase

THE GOLDEN RULE OF REBASING

The golden rule of rebasing says to never rebase a branch that is shared with other developers or has been pushed or merged to a remote repository. Rather, you should only ever rebase local or private branches to your own repository.

What this means in practice is, don't rebase anything that has already been pushed to the remote, or anything that has been merged into another branch that will be pushed in the future.

Cherry-Picking

You have learned about developing your changes on a branch and then merging or rebasing those changes into other branches. But what happens if you would like to selectively integrate some but not all changes from one branch to another?

Git provides a solution to this problem in the form of *cherry-picking*. Cherry-picking is the capability to apply specific commits from one branch to another. To do this, switch to the target branch, locate the commit ID of the commit you want to cherry-pick, and then call the `git cherry-pick` command. You don't need to specify the entire commit ID; just the first few characters that identify the commit uniquely are sufficient. For example, to cherry-pick commit ID 4954034c. . . into branch *refactoring1*, do this:

```
git switch refactoring1
git cherry-pick 4954
```

Remember that you will have different commit IDs if you are following along, so use `git log` to find one to cherry-pick. Beware: in many cases cherry-picking will lead to a merge-conflict that you will need to resolve, so exercise caution. In this case, we get a conflict; resolve it manually as before, and to continue, call this:

```
git commit -am "Cherry picked and then resolved conflict"
```

Git graciously responds with this:

```
1 file changed, 8 insertions(+)
```

Reverting and Resetting

How do you undo a commit? There are two ways: `git revert` and `git reset`.

`git revert <commit id>` creates a new commit to change the files to the state they were in at the time of that commit ID.

`git reset <commit id>` is more intrusive; it actually changes history and throws out the commits that followed the commit id. This command comes in three flavors:

`git reset --soft <commit id>` resets the pointer for the current branch to point to the specified commit. However, it keeps any changes you have made in the working directory and staging area. This has the effect of "uncommitting" your changes.

`git reset -hard <commit id>` also resets the branch pointer to point to the specified commit. However, it discards all changes in both the working directory and the staging area, resetting the branch to the specified commit. With a hard reset all of your changes are lost.

`git reset <commit id>` without specifying `--soft` or `--hard` is a "mixed reset." As with all resets, it resets the branch pointer to the specified commit. Like a soft reset, it preserves your changes, but it unstages them. This is useful when you want to start your staging all over and reevaluate what to stage and what not to stage for the next commit.

Rather than specifying a commit, you can specify the number of commits to back out of by using the HEAD~ syntax. For example, `git reset HEAD~1` will do a mixed reset, setting the branch pointer to one commit before the latest. `HEAD~2` will set it to two commits before the latest, and so on. Any positive integer can be used after `HEAD~`.

To better understand the semantic differences, see the comparison in Table 3.1.

TABLE 3.1: Revert and Reset

COMMAND	CREATES NEW COMMIT	DISCARDS HISTORY	KEEPS LOCAL CHANGES
git revert <commit id>	Yes	No	No
git reset --soft <commit id>	No	Yes	Yes
git reset --hard <commit id>	No	Yes	No
git reset <commit id>	No	Yes	Yes, but unstaged

Optimizing with IDE Support

All of the major IDEs provide world-class support for Git. In this section we will cover IntelliJ IDEA support.

An untracked file will show up in a maroon color. IntelliJ will offer to start tracking it for you, as in Figure 3.7.

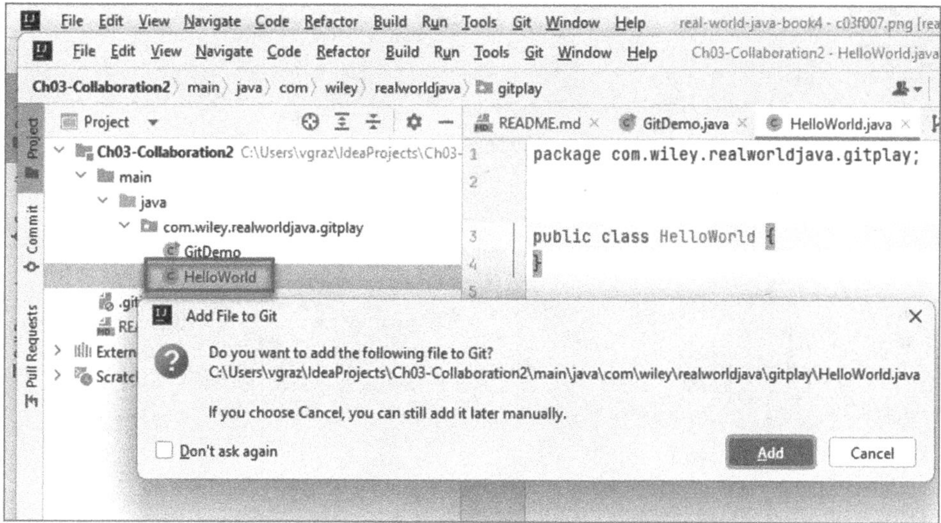

FIGURE 3.7: Tracking a new file

The first time a file is tracked, it will be colored green to indicate a newly tracked file that has never been committed per Figure 3.8. (The `HelloWorld` class that is circled is colored in a green font.)

If a file was already created externally (perhaps it was moved into the project from the file system), you can still track it; just right-click the file and select Git and then Add. This will add it to the staging area, as shown in Figure 3.9.

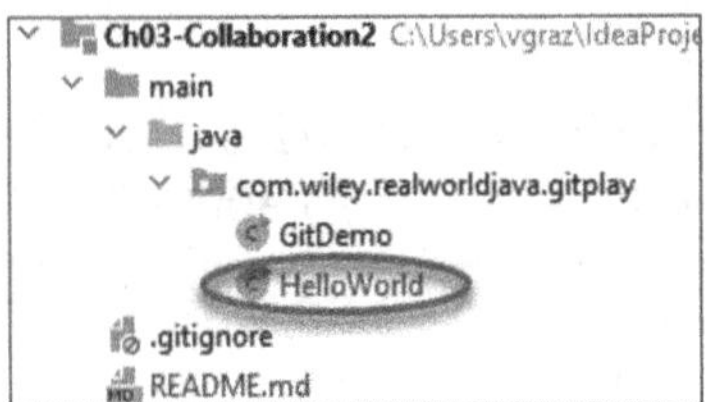

FIGURE 3.8: Color coding for a newly tracked file

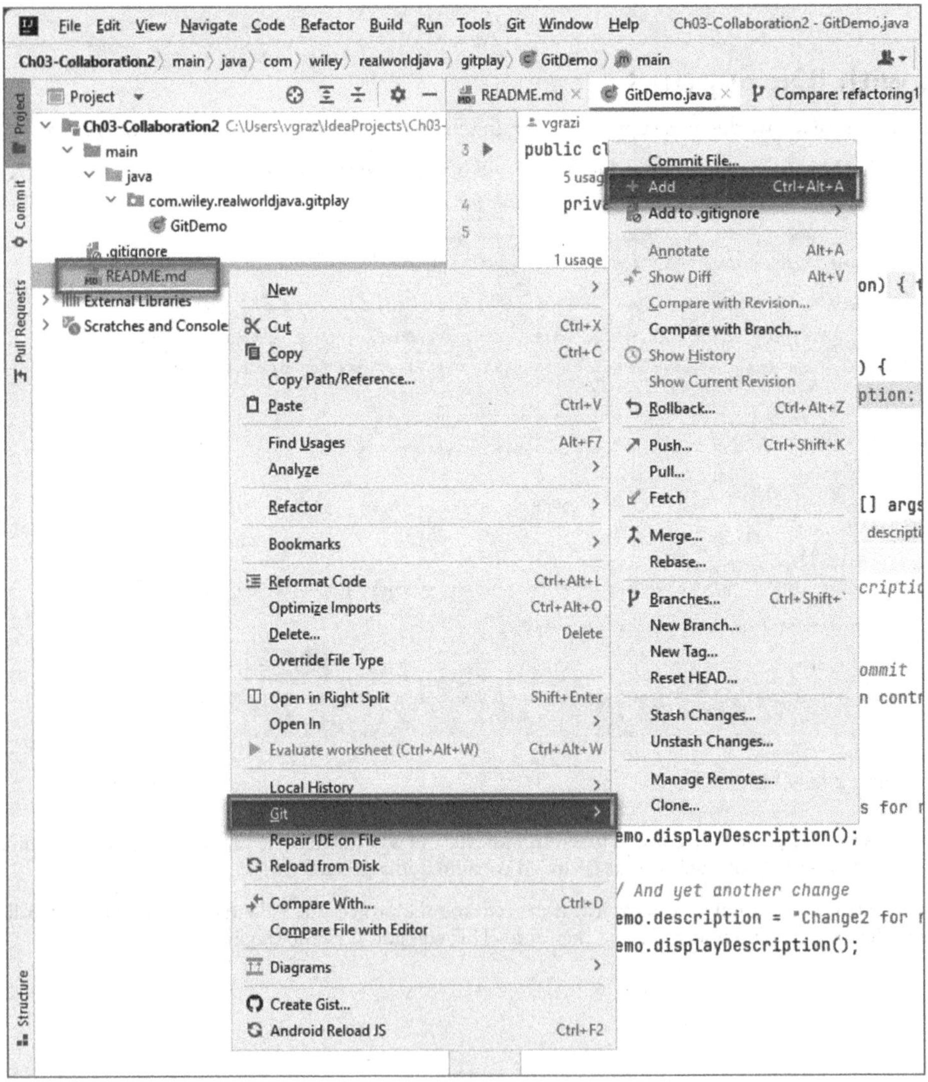

FIGURE 3.9: Tracking an external file

Looking at the Commit Window

Staging changes is a common operation, so for convenience we set Ctrl+Alt+A as the Windows Key Map shortcut for this operation. Refer to Chapter 2 for creating Key Map shortcuts.

To commit your changes, choose the menu option Git/Commit (the Windows shortcut is Ctrl+K; the Mac shortcut is Cmd+K). This will bring up the *commit* window where you can see all your staged files.

> **TIP** *Ctrl+K (or Cmd+K) is also useful when you just want to see what has changed. It opens the commit window, which displays all of your changes. Use F7 and Shift+F7 to navigate forward and backward through all your changes.*

Changes to tracked files are automatically staged and will appear in the commit window, but if you are not ready to commit yet, you can unstage them by unclearing the check box next to the filename in the commit window.

Right-clicking in the commit window will bring up a context window. Most of the choices there are self-explanatory, but draw your attention to the New Changelist option (see Figure 3.10). IntelliJ ensures that you can commit only one changelist at a time, so if you want to keep some files out of your commit for now, you can create a new changelist and move those files to that changelist to separate your commits.

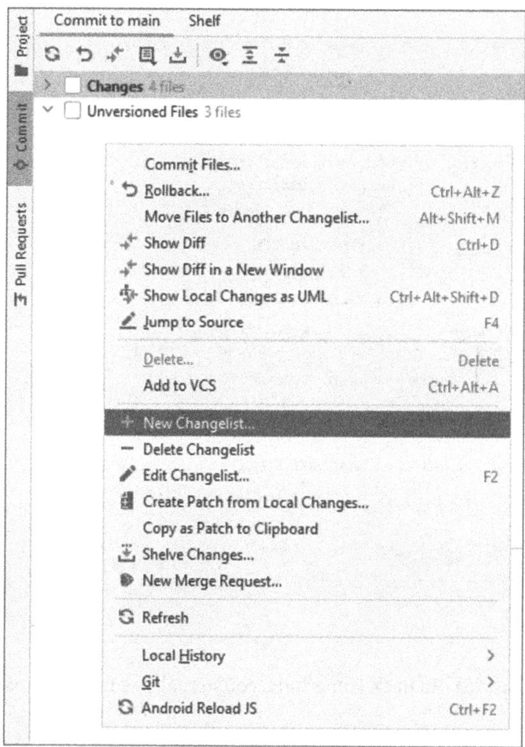

FIGURE 3.10: Commit context window

Using the Diff-Viewer Window

If you double-click files in the commit window, that will bring up the diff-viewer window, where the previous and current versions are displayed side-by-side. You can make edits directly in the diff-viewer window. You can choose from the selector at the top of the diff-viewer window, if you want to ignore whitespace changes, blank line changes, etc.

> **TIP** *It is a good practice to double-click the files in the commit window to open the diff-viewer window, where you can review your changes. This provides you with one last look before you commit your code. When doing so, you will invariably locate opportunities to remove duplicate code, correct typos, and perform similar cleanups.*

F7 is a convenient shortcut for navigating from one change to the next. Shift+F7 will navigate back to the previous change. When you get to the end of the file and click F7 again, IntelliJ will prompt you to move to the next file.

Changed lines will appear in the diff-viewer window, as shown in Figure 3.11, with a light blue highlight and a check box in the margin. You can choose which changes to commit by checking or unchecking the check box next to each change in the diff-viewer window. Only the selected changes will be committed. If you right-click a change, you can choose to send that change to another changelist so that commits to that file will not include those changes.

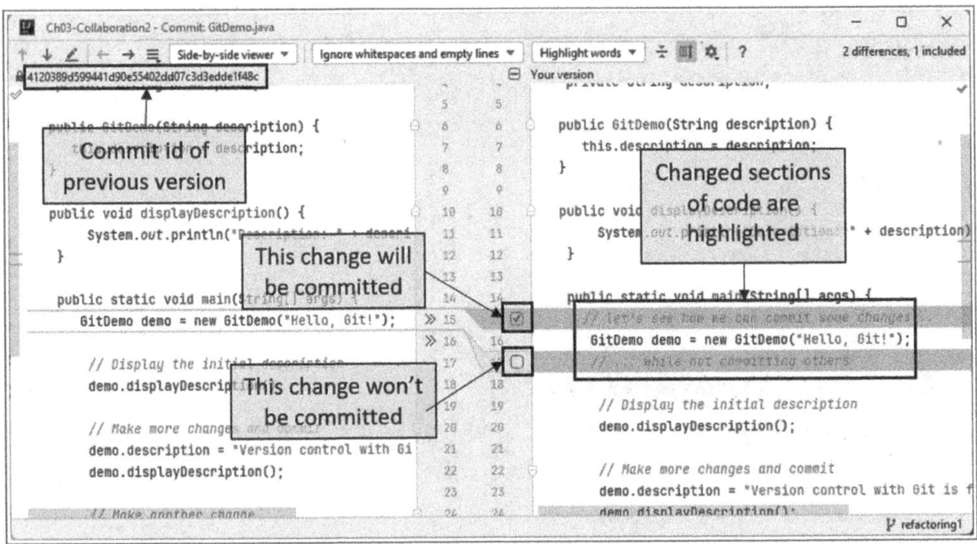

FIGURE 3.11: Diff-viewer window

To be safe, if you have a large number of changes, it is easy to uncheck something you actually wanted to commit or check something you didn't.

When you have code you don't want to commit, it is good to surround it with something very conspicuous, like the following. This will make it hard to commit by accident!

```
///////// Don't Commit //////////
someCodeToNotCommit();
someMoreCodeToNotCommit();
///////// Don't Commit //////////
```

The Git menu provides all the commands described and more, as you can see in Figure 3.12.

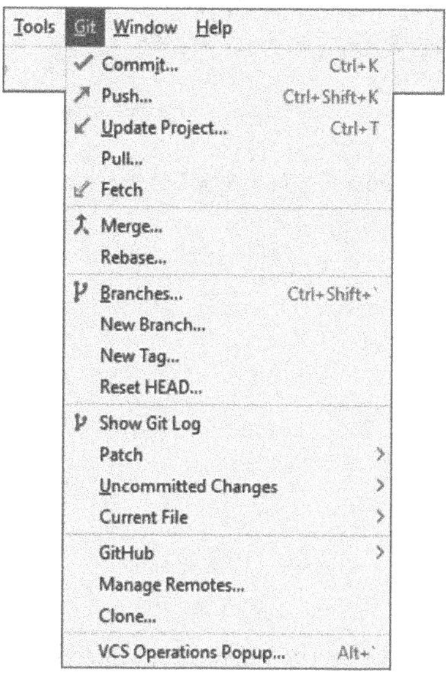

FIGURE 3.12: IntelliJ Git menu

- **Commit:** Commits changes in all tracked files to the local repository.
- **Push:** Pushes changes to the remote server.
- **Update Project:** Gets from the remote server the latest versions of all files in the currently checked-out branch; use Git ➪ Update Project or Ctrl+T (Cmd+T on Mac).
- **Pull:** Updates a specific branch from the selected remote.
- **Fetch:** Updates a specific branch from the server without actually checking it out. In case there is a conflict that the IDE cannot resolve, it will abort the fetch. In this case, you can shelve or stash your changes, do the fetch, and then unshelve your changes and manually resolve the conflicts. (More on shelving changes later in the chapter.)
- **Merge:** Merges the specified branch into the current branch.
- **Rebase:** Rebases the specified branch onto the current branch.
- **Branches:** A submenu for all branching operations, including creating a new branch or switching to another branch.
- **New Branch:** A dedicated menu for creating branches.
- **New Tag:** Creates new tag on the current branch.
- **Reset HEAD:** Allows you to roll back to a previous version, using Hard, Soft, or Mixed resets.
- **Show Git Log:** Gives a graphical representation of the git commit log and branches.
- **Patch:** Tools for creating a *patch*, which can be applied later to reproduce a certain state.

> **TIP** *A patch is a file that contains the differences between sets of changed files and the original version. You can apply a patch to a set of source files to produce a target version containing the changes captured in the patch file. You can also share patch files with others to have them produce the target state of changes.*

- **Uncommitted Changes:** This one deserves digging into to all its submenus; Figure 3.13 shows the options on the Uncommitted Changes submenu.

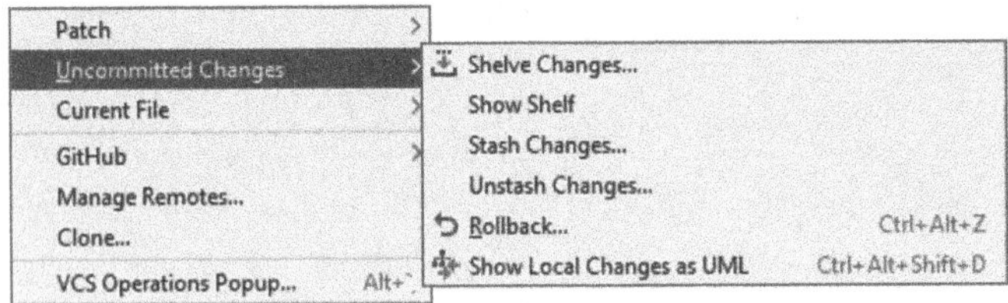

FIGURE 3.13: IntelliJ Uncommitted Changes submenu

  - **Shelve Changes:** Lets you temporarily set aside or *shelve* the current changes in IntelliJ's repo, where you can inspect and retrieve them later.
  - **Show Shelf:** Displays all of the shelved changes and provides selection tools for recovering some or all of the lines of change.
  - **Stash Changes:** Like shelving, but uses Git tooling under the covers. If you're using the IDE, IntelliJ's shelf feature is convenient, but if you prefer to run things from the command line, you might prefer stashing.
  - **Unstash changes:** Allows you to re-apply the stashed changes.
  - **Rollback:** Selects files to restore to the original state.
  - **Show Local Changes as UML:** Draws a UML class diagram containing the classes and methods containing local changes.
- **Current File:** This one also deserves an exploration of its submenus; see Figure 3.14.

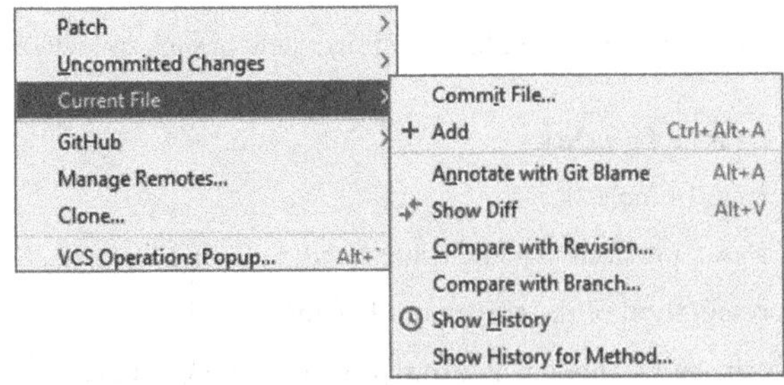

FIGURE 3.14: IntelliJ Current File submenu

- **Commit File:** Brings up the commit window, where you can select changes to commit.
- **Add:** Tells Git to track a new file.
- **Annotate with Git Blame:** Displays in the margin the name of the person who last updated each line of the current file.
- **Show Diff:** Shows side-by-side the diff-viewer window of the current file as it is now versus how it was when it was pulled.
- **Compare with Revision:** Provides a list of recent commits for you to compare with the local state.
- **Compare with Branch:** Provides a list of branches for you to compare with the local state.
- **Show History:** Displays a list of all commits for this file and allows you to compare against previous states.
- **Show History for Method:** Displays a list of all commits for the current method and allows you to compare against previous states.
- **Show History for Selection:** Appears only when you have something selected. This menu item displays a list of all commits for that selection and allows you to compare them against previous states.

You can get a broader list of Git options by right-clicking a file in the editor and choosing Git, as shown in Figure 3.15.

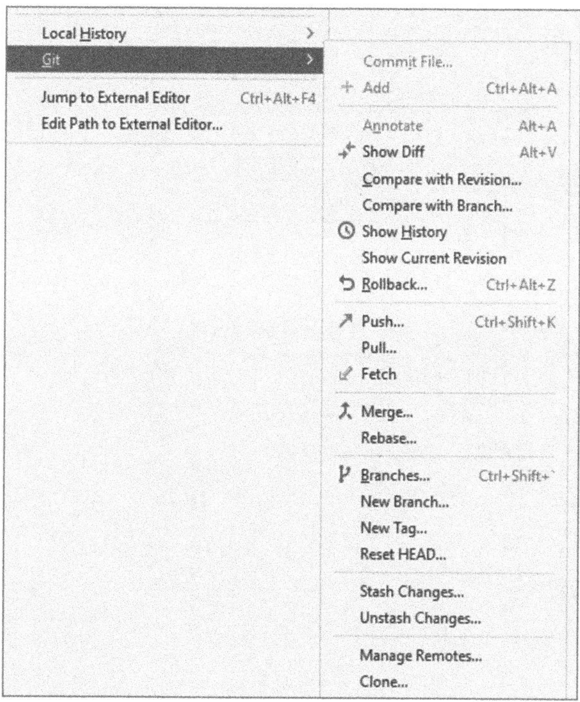

FIGURE 3.15: Git context menu

IntelliJ has a Git Log window that you can open by clicking the Git icon on the lower-left side. It includes a graphical log display that lets you select a branch, commit ID, and so on, and displays a tree illustrating your branches. This is much easier to use than typing log commands, as you can see in Figure 3.16.

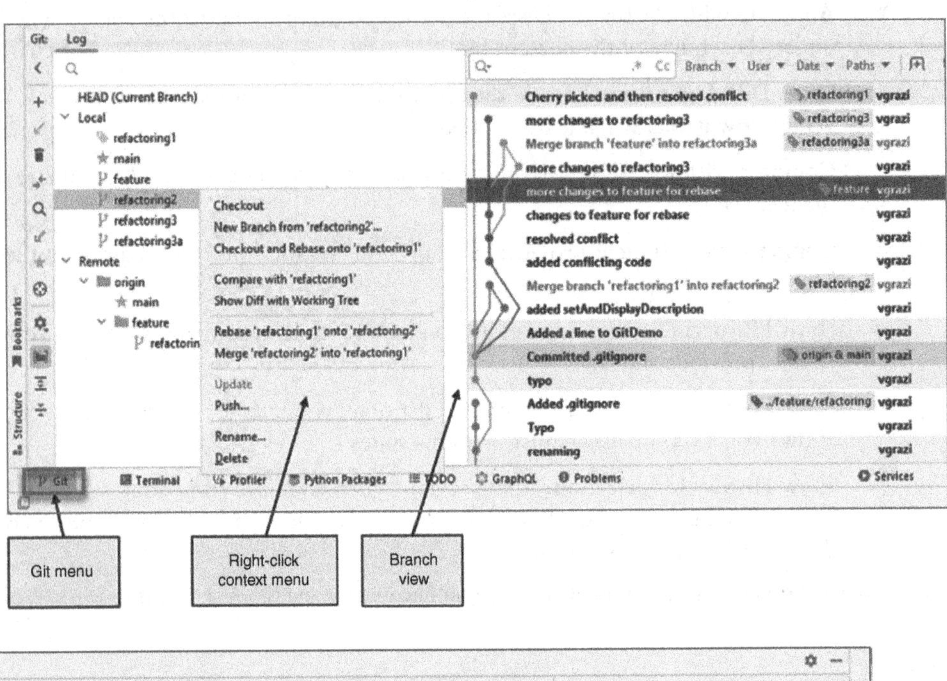

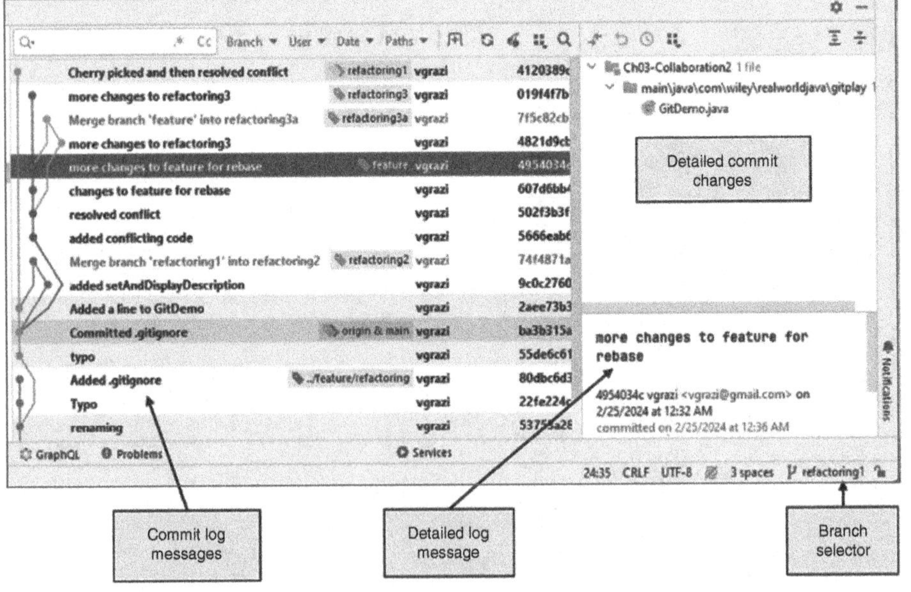

FIGURE 3.16: IntelliJ Git log window

You can select local or remote branches, but beware the list of branches and the contents of the branches will be as of your most recent update. Select Git ➪ Update to see a fresh list of branches and to refresh the currently checked-out branch from the server. To refresh other branches, you can select them individually from the Git ➪ Pull menu.

One more feature you should know is the Git ➪ History feature. You can right-click in any managed file and choose Git ➪ History to get a listing of all versions of that file. It is a life-saver when you discover something is broken and you want to locate a last known good version. You can get the history for an entire file, or you can make a selection and see the history for just that selection.

In related news, IntelliJ also offers a *local history* feature, where you can get a fast version history without Git, and even for files that are not tracked by Git.

Creating README Files with Markdown Language

When you browse to the home page of a Git project in GitHub or one of the other Git providers, you will generally see a description of the project, perhaps some usage instructions and useful links. As an example, head over to the chapter repository for this chapter at `https://github.com/realworldjava/Ch03-Collaboration`. You can create such documentation in your own projects by including a file called `README.md` in your project root. The `.md` extension stands for Markdown, a lightweight markup language used in Git documentation.

> **TIP** *While any* `.md` *file will be considered Markdown in GitHub, only the* `README.md` *file is automatically shown on the repository home page.*

Markdown supports straight text, as well as headings, emphasis, lists, links, and code blocks. The language is pretty simple, and there are just a few syntax elements you will need to learn. IntelliJ and VS Code are nice enough to show you a side-by-side view of your markup code and the visual rendering of it, so we encourage you to experiment with the `README.doc` in this chapter repo. Eclipse doesn't have a side-by-side view but it does have a preview tab.

Text can be entered directly. Contiguous lines of text will be merged into a single line, unless they are followed by a blank line, in which case a new paragraph will start. If you want to override this behavior and start a new line, just add two spaces to the end of the line, which will cause the next line to start on a new line.

Markdown supports six levels of headings. To designate a level-one heading, start the line with # followed by a space. A level-two heading starts with ## and a space, and so on.

To add italics, surround the text with `*`. Here's an example:

```
*This is italicized*
```

Be sure not to include a space after the first asterisk.

To bold selected text, surround the text with `**`. Here's an example:

```
**This is bold**
```

Again, there are no spaces after the first `**`.

Lists come in ordered and unordered flavors. To create an unordered list, place a `*` as the first character on the line, followed by a space. Here's an example:

```
* This is the first item
* This is the second item
* Etc.
```

To create an ordered list, start the line with an item number, followed by a period and a space. Here's an example:

```
1. This is the first item
2. This is the second item
3. Etc.
```

Regardless of what numbers you type, Markdown will display them in the natural order. We like to number every list item with `1.` so that if we switch things around, Markdown deals with the proper numbering so that we don't have to.

To specify a link, just start with `http://` or `https://` and Markdown will render it as a link. If you want to supply text for the link, use this syntax:

```
[This is the text](https://www.some-link.com)
```

The text in the square brackets will be displayed, and the text in the round brackets will be the link.

To specify code, you can specify the language and the code using the "triple backtick" syntax. Markdown recognizes the many language tags, including the following:

- `java`
- `python`
- `javascript`
- `html`
- `css`
- `markdown` (for nested code blocks)
- `bash`
- `sql`

Here's an example:

````
```java
public class HelloMarkdown {
    public static void main(String[] args) {
        System.out.println("Hello, Markdown!");
    }
}
```
````

Again, we encourage you to play with all of these to get the feel of using Markdown.

Using Gitflow for Collaboration

As you have seen, Git is a great tool for maintaining evolving versions of your software codebase. But this chapter is about *collaboration*! How can we leverage the powers of Git to collaborate in a dynamic, constantly changing dynamic environment?

There are a few popular methodologies. For example, *trunk-based* development is a process where code is frequently merged to the *main* (aka trunk) branch, and automated unit tests run on every commit. If the trunk builds, it is ready for release. In some cases, developers commit directly to *main*. In others, they use short lived branches and a pull request when the branch is ready to be merged into *main*.

In large, highly regulated environments such as banks and other financial institutions, releases must be much more controlled. For those requirements, Gitflow is a common methodology.

In a few words, Gitflow is a process that allows a team of developers to divide into smaller groups of one or more developers. Each group works on some feature, and the whole team shares a mutual codebase.

Using this strategy, every feature gets a *feature branch*, which is committed periodically, built and tested, and when done, the *feature* branch is merged into the common branch, typically called *develop*. Finally, when a release is planned, feature branches are merged into a new *release branch*, which is built, tested, and prepared for release. This strategy allows everyone to collaborate and to back out features that might have been prematurely staged for release.

Figure 3.17 shows the steps.

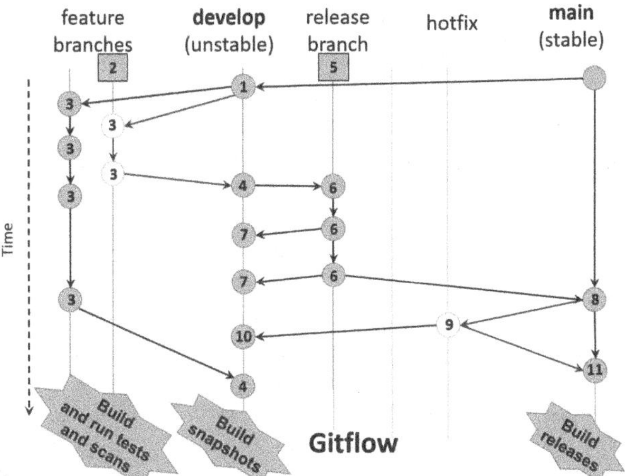

FIGURE 3.17: Gitflow workflow

1. The first step is to create a new branch called *develop* from the *main* branch. This is a one-time task. The *develop* branch is a collect-all branch, but nothing gets directly committed to *develop*. The *develop* branch only gets merges from other branches. Once *develop* is created, it remains for the lifetime of the project.
2. When a feature is agreed upon, a *feature* branch is created for that feature. Typically, the business will define a requirement for that feature and track it in some tracking system like *Jira* (which we will cover in the next section). The tracking system will assign a key to this requirement, and although the naming for the feature branch is flexible, it is common to give it a name that begins with *feature/* followed by the key and an extremely short but explanatory description (no spaces allowed, so use hyphens). An example feature branch name might be something like *feature/RWJ-1234-add-ui-login*, where *RWJ-1234* is the Jira key for this new "add a UI login" feature.
3. As the teams work on their feature branches, they continue to develop code and commit. The build server runs a build on every commit. See Chapter 4, "Automating Your CI/CD Builds with Maven, Gradle, and Jenkins," for more details.
4. When a feature is deemed complete, it is merged back into the *develop* branch. Remember that the `develop` branch has been evolving in parallel while you were working since other team members were writing their own code. Therefore, it will look different than when you originally branched the feature branch. Therefore, a new build and test cycle is again required, and that is exactly what the build server does.
5. The *develop* branch is ready for release. Create a new *release* branch from *develop* named *release/* followed by a release version. But the process does not end here. Now that the release branch has been cut, development can continue to evolve on the *develop* branch for future releases, and only this release is maintained on the *release* branch.
6. The *release* branch is now tested, possibly by a quality assurance (QA) team.
7. Bugs are reported, fixed, and merged back to develop.
8. When the release branch is certified as ready for release, it is merged to the *main* branch, and a release *tag* is cut on the *main* branch. The *main* branch tracks all the historical releases, and it is easy to reproduce a prior release by checking out the release tag for any release.

9. We have released the code to production, but we are still not done! Someone discovers a bug in production, a hotfix branch is created, work is done to swat the bug, and we repeat from step 5.
10. As with changes to any branch, changes made to the hotfix branch must be merged back to *develop*.
11. When ready the hotfix branch is merged to *main* and tagged for release.

Some of the benefits of Gitflow:

- Features are isolated, which makes it easy to manage your own feature changes in isolation.
- Easy to maintain different versions.
- Features are separated, allowing you to decide which features to include in release.

> **TIP** *One downside: if you are downloading the snapshot builds, you can find version conflicts when different teams build their features. When that happens, the generated binaries will all have the same* `-SNAPSHOT` *version number for entirely different feature sets. This is not a showstopper, because if you are deploying snapshots, teams can coordinate with each other to decide what to release.*

USING JIRA FOR ENTERPRISE PROCESS COLLABORATION

In the olden days, software was developed using a waterfall approach. This was a phased, sequential approach, where progress flowed downward, like a waterfall.

First functional requirements were prepared and approved. Then came the design phase followed by implementation, which would proceed for some time. Finally, it would be tested, deployed, and delivered to the customer. The full process could take months or years, and at the end the customer may or may not have been happy, and it was difficult to allocate resources because the phases were sequential, requiring business analysts (BAs) at the start, architects and developers in the middle, and testers and release staff at the end.

In 2001, the Agile Manifesto was born, introducing the world to a layered approach to software development. You will hear agile processes with names like *Scrum* and *Extreme Programming*. A new *sprint* would begin every two or three weeks, tasked with the delivery of a completed subset of requirements. Tasks would be assigned to the sprint and would progress through a workflow. Every role was involved in every sprint, including the business, the designers, the developers, QA, and so on. Requirements were dynamic, potentially evolving with every sprint, and every few cycles some product was delivered to the business. Another agile approach called *Kanban* observed that jobs are not always time-bound, and even if they were, they were not necessarily the same time windows. Kanban did away with sprints and instead asked teams to analyze their process and divide it into a sequence of columns such as design, develop, test, release. They would put work-in-process (WIP) limits on each column and used a *pull* system where work tickets would start on the left and get pulled to the right as they progressed. As developers finished work in their column, they would pull more work from the previous column.

Atlassian Jira is one of the most popular software tools for managing all things agile. You can select a Scrum board where work is divided into configurable-sized sprints or a Kanban board with WIP limits.

Jira has integration with GitHub and many other version-control systems, so when you make commits, you can include an issue key, and then you can see the commits associated with any Jira ticket.

Getting Started with Jira

Most enterprises will already have Jira installed, but we recommend you try it on your own. You can use the free cloud version of Jira at `https://www.atlassian.com/software/jira`. The local installation used in the enterprise may have a slightly different look and feel, but the concepts are identical.

Jira is a web-based UI that has evolved greatly over the years, starting life as a clunky ticket management program and evolving to become a full-featured tool for sprint planning and maintenance, issue-creation and editing, search, user administration, reporting, and so on.

Whichever type of board your project uses, Jira tickets represent a piece of work. Jira started life as a bug-tracking system; thus, the tickets are called *issues*, but many people affectionately refer to them simply as *jiras*. Issues come in many flavors, such as *epic*, *story*, *bug*, *task*, *subtask*, and so on. You can also create your own issue types.

Generally, epics are used as a *parent* for a group of smaller, related stories, bugs, and tasks.

These smaller issues themselves can contain their own issues, which are called subtasks. These may be created in any order, but in enterprise development a common practice is to attach most issues to an epic. Further, every subtask belongs to a parent issue, as in Figure 3.18.

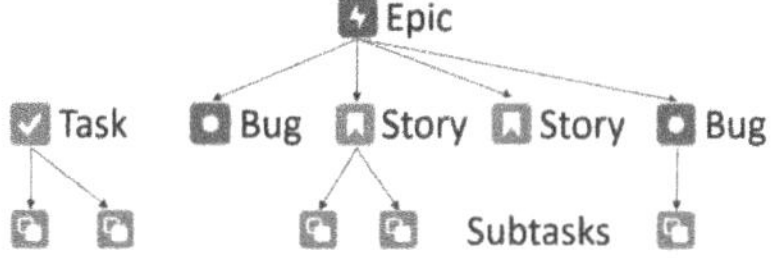

FIGURE 3.18: Jira issue hierarchy

Jira uses this hierarchy to provide a top-down view to management, which might be interested in only the larger epics, and a bottom-up view to individual contributors, who care more about the implementation details. While it is fine to have a small percentage of "loose" tasks or bugs not in an epic, these aren't the ones management is most interested in.

Creating a Project

Issues are assigned to projects. If you are coming into an existing team, there will usually be one or more projects set up. If you need to create a new project, go to the Projects tab and select Create Project, select an appropriate template, and follow the instructions there, as in Figure 3.19.

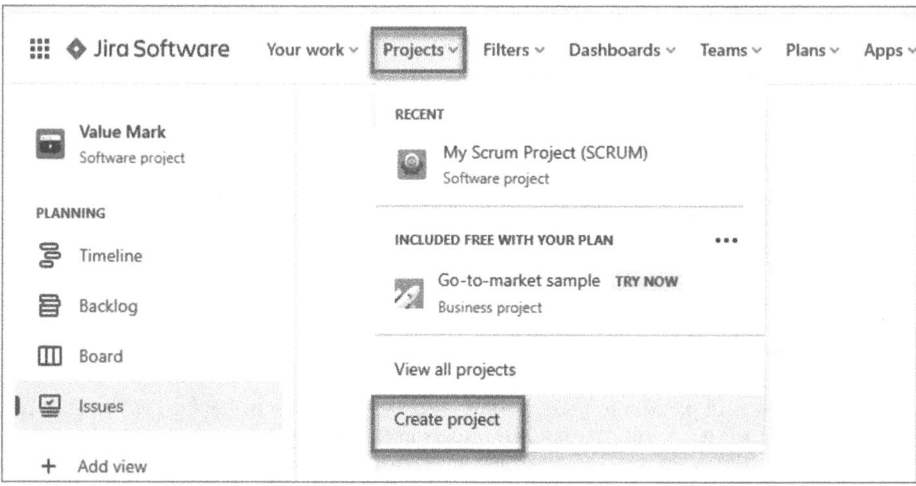

FIGURE 3.19: Creating a new project

There are stock board types for each template. For example, for software development, you can select Kanban, Scrum, and so on. We will choose Scrum for our example project. Scrum allows you to manage your deliveries in time-boxed sprints, which are two weeks long by default. Kanban has no time-boxing, but it divides the board into columns, representing general tasks or teams, and there is a WIP limit for each column on the board, as in Figure 3.20.

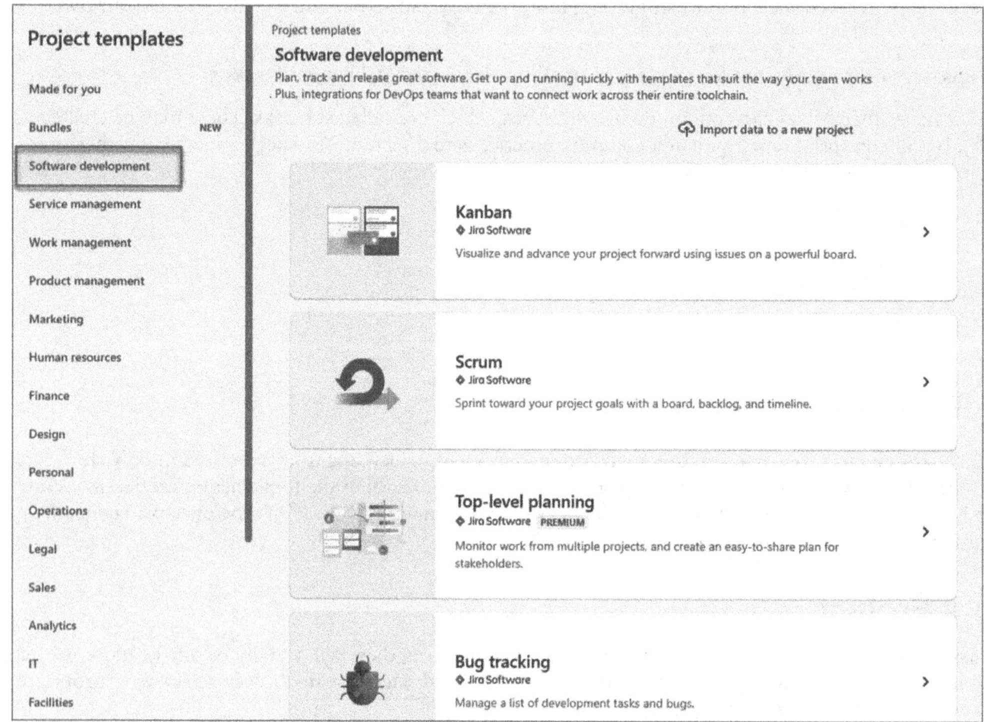

FIGURE 3.20: Selecting a project template

Creating an Issue

You create a new issue in Jira by clicking the Create button, as in Figure 3.21.

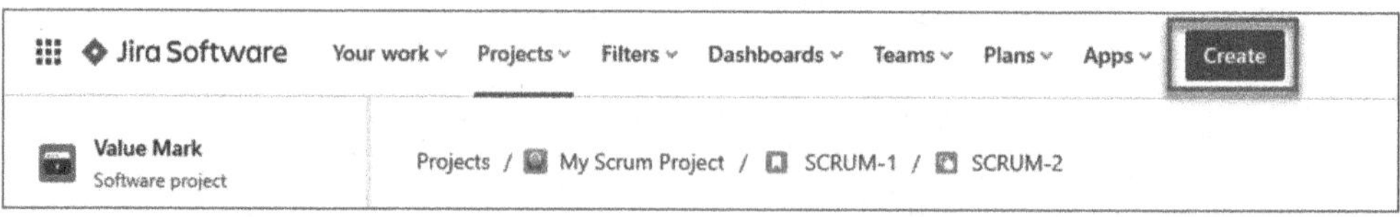

FIGURE 3.21: Creating a new issue

Select the issue type and complete all the details. Like all things Jira, the screen can be (and usually is) customized, so yours might look different. Each team will have its own fields, some mandatory. In the late 1990s an early agile methodology called the Extreme Programming (XP) was introduced to provide a user-friendly way of managing requirements in an agile way. Many organizations have adopted the XP practice of expressing issues of type Story in the form "As a <role> user, I want to perform <some activity> so that I can achieve <some benefit>."

Enter a summary, description, assignee (if known), and other fields as mandated by your team, as in Figure 3.22.

Fix error in search component
Required fields are marked with an asterisk *
Project *
Value Mark (VM)
Issue type *
Bug
Status
TO DO
Learn about issue types
Summary *
Fix error in search component
Description
Search component generally works, but if you hit
Create another issue
Create

FIGURE 3.22: Filling out the new issue

Linking to an Epic

As a best practice, most teams will have a policy of assigning most issues to a parent epic. You can link an issue to an epic when you create the issue, or you can add or change the epic link later. You can then get a high-level view of the whole project by viewing the epics on the project board as in Figure 3.23.

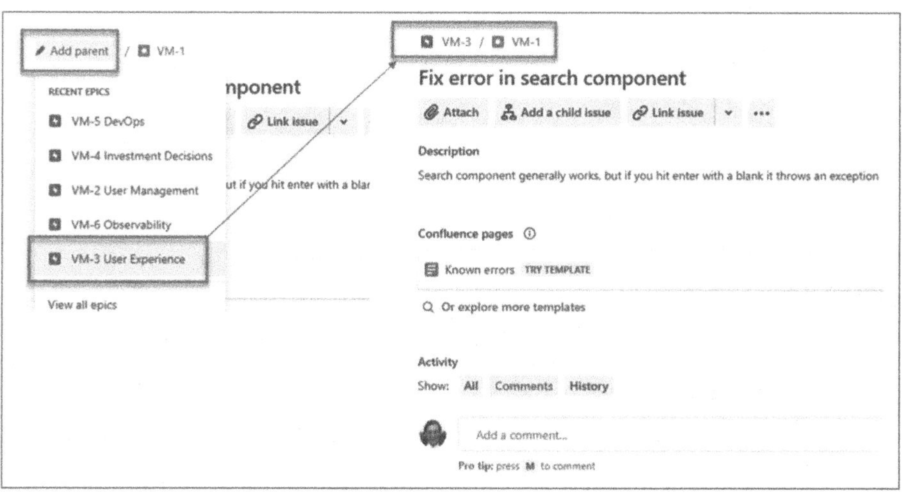

FIGURE 3.23: Assigning an epic to an issue

Working with Boards

The real benefit of Jira starts with the *board*. Our sample project is a microservice-based website called Value Mark, which guides users in choosing companies to invest in. A user logs in, the back end authenticates the user, and the browser displays UI frames relevant to their role.

By default, Jira launches a Scrum board with three default columns: *To Do*, *In Progress*, and *Done*. There is also *backlog* area (which can be displayed as the first column) where work is collected and can then be assigned to an appropriate sprint. You drag jiras from one column to another, to provide a visualization of the current state of the project and all its issues. Every column is mapped to a status, and every Jira has a field called Status. Whenever you transition a jira to a new column, the Status field of that Jira is updated with the status of the target column.

There is a role known as Board Administrator. Board Administrators have the ability to add, remove, and sequence columns, in conformity with the *project workflow*.

The project workflow, as shown in Figure 3.24, defines all the status choices for the project and their transitions. You can see by the flow of arrows that an OPEN issue can transition to IN PROGRESS, RESOLVED, or CLOSED

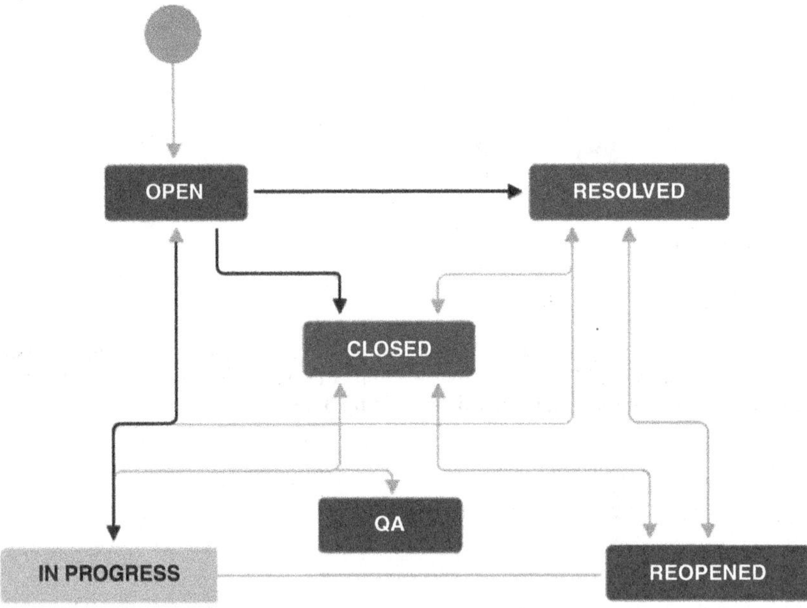

FIGURE 3.24: Design of a workflow

Creating a Sprint

Now that you have created some Jira issues, it is time to allocate the work. The work that the team needs to perform is divided into sprints. A sprint is a named (e.g.,VM Sprint 4 Aug 12-Aug 23), time-boxed (e.g., two weeks) period, where work is assigned to the team.

Starting from the backlog tab in Figure 3.25, you will find all your issues at the bottom of the page, in the Backlog section. Your first sprint will appear with a default name and no dates, but you can click the Add Dates icon to manage the sprint. You can create future sprints as well, using the same method per Figure 3.26.

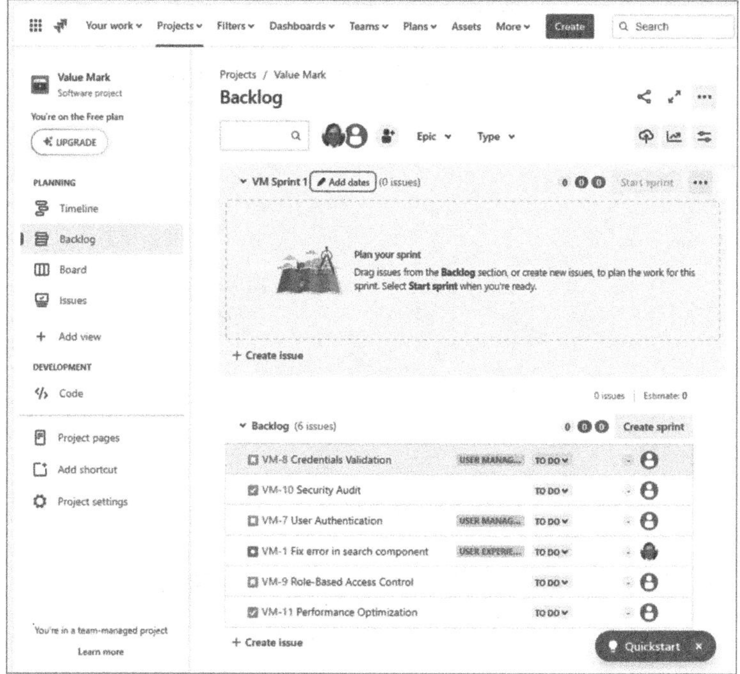

FIGURE 3.25: Backlog tab

FIGURE 3.26: Creating a sprint

Now that one or more sprints are created, you can drag and drop issues into the appropriate sprint, as in Figure 3.27.

Once the sprint is allocated, it can be started by clicking the Start Sprint button at the top left.

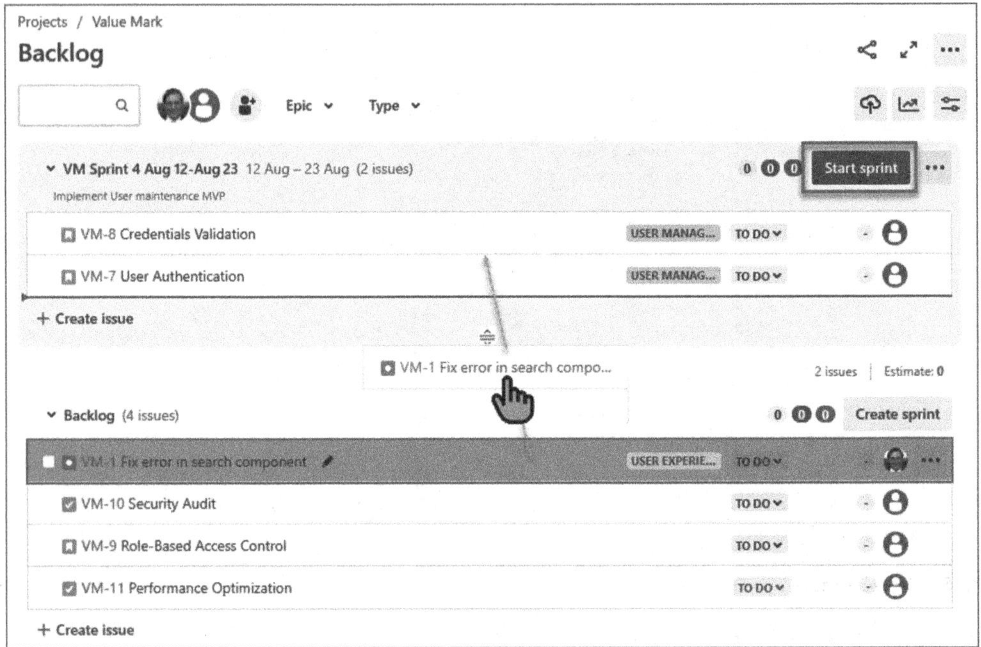

FIGURE 3.27: Assigning jiras to a sprint

Adding Users

A project administrator can add and maintain users and assign roles. Click the gear icon at the bottom left and click Access. Add your users and assign a role.

Once users are added to the project, click Back To Project on the left. Now you can assign users to issues, as shown in Figure 3.28.

Adding Columns

To add, remove, or re-sequence columns, a board administrator must click Columns And Statuses on the left side to launch the column maintenance screen.

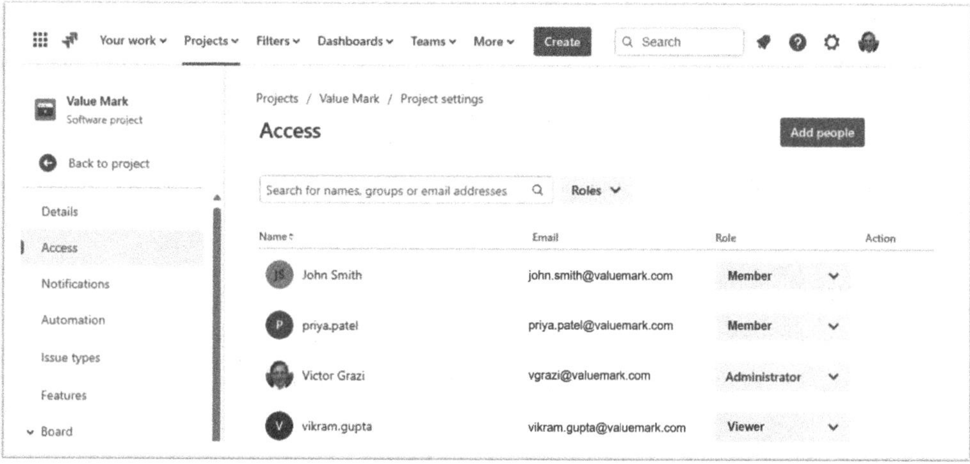

FIGURE 3.28: Adding users

Click the Create Column + sign button on the right side to add columns, as in Figure 3.29.

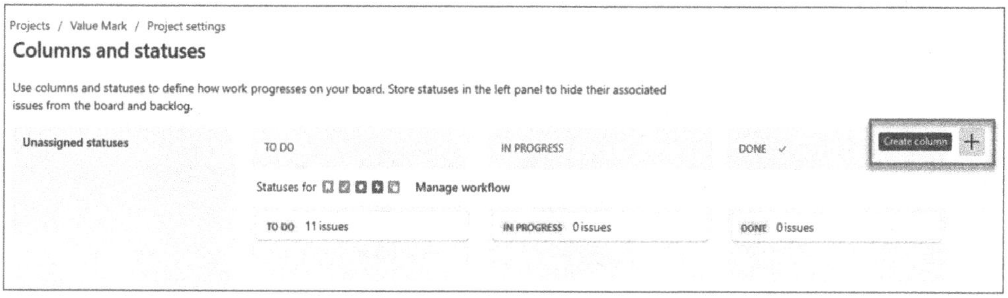

Projects / Value Mark / Project settings

Columns and statuses

Use columns and statuses to define how work progresses on your board. Store statuses in the left panel to hide their associated issues from the board and backlog.

Unassigned statuses | TO DO | IN PROGRESS | DONE | Create column +

Statuses for Manage workflow

TO DO 11 issues | IN PROGRESS 0 issues | DONE 0 issues

FIGURE 3.29: Adding new columns

Now the board administrator can add new columns, rename existing ones, re-sequence them, and assign a status from the workflow to each column, as in Figure 3.30.

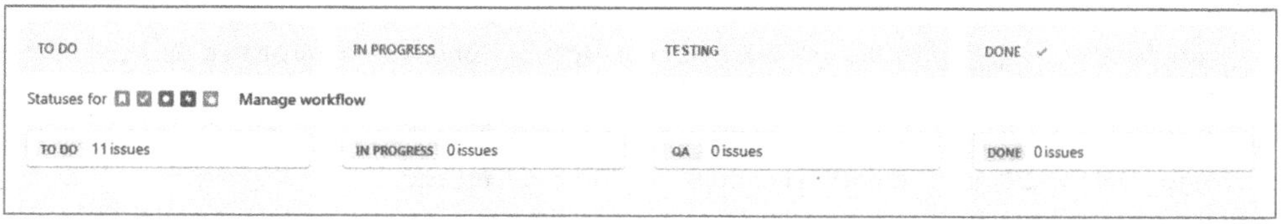

TO DO | IN PROGRESS | TESTING | DONE

Statuses for Manage workflow

TO DO 11 issues | IN PROGRESS 0 issues | QA 0 issues | DONE 0 issues

FIGURE 3.30: Column maintenance

Using Filters

As more and more jiras fill the board, it can become difficult to separate issues. For example, during stand-up meetings, teams may move from person to person to ask what you accomplished yesterday, what you will be working on today, and if there are any blockers. When your turn comes, wouldn't it be convenient to display the board with just your jiras and hide all the others? That is the purpose of filters.

Filters can be configured to filter by users or in fact by any other property or properties of your jiras, using JQL, as we will see in the following sections.

Seeing My Issues

You can see all your issues, across all boards and backlog, by selecting Filters/My Open Issues per Figure 3.31.

From the same screen, you can enter queries in *JQL* by clicking Switch To JQL.

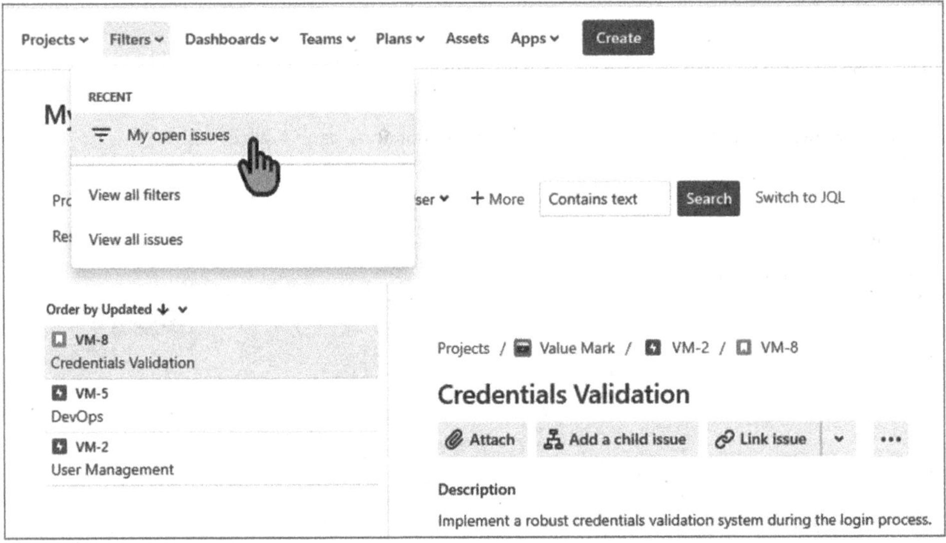

FIGURE 3.31: Viewing My Issues

Querying with JQL

The *Jira Query Language* (*JQL*) provides any user with the capability of selecting jiras based on select criteria. It is a simple language; you specify one or more fields and values for those fields and an `order by` clause.

A JQL query consists of one or more field selection clauses followed by an `order by` clause. The field selection clauses are separated by `AND` or `OR` and can be grouped by using parentheses.

A field selection clause consists of a field followed by an operator and a value. Tables 3.2, 3.3, and 3.4 show the valid operators.

TABLE 3.2: Comparison Operators

OPERATOR	DESCRIPTION
=	Field value equals the specified value
!=	Not equals
<	Less than
>	Greater than
<=	Less than or equal to
>=	Greater than or equal to
`IN`	In a list of values
`NOT IN`	Not in a list of values
`IS`	Is a specified value
`IS NOT`	Is not a specified value
`WAS`	Had a specified value in the past
`WAS IN`	Was in a list of values in the past
`WAS NOT IN`	Was not in a list of values in the past
`CHANGED`	Field was changed to a specified value
`BY`	Field was changed by a specified user
`AFTER`	Date field fell after a specified date or time
`BEFORE`	Date field fell before a specified date or time
`DURING`	Date field occurred during a specific date range

TABLE 3.3: Logical Operators

OPERATOR	DESCRIPTION
`AND`	Logical AND
`OR`	Logical OR
`NOT`	Logical NOT

Clauses can be separated by the keywords `AND`, `OR`, and `NOT`. To order by one or more fields, you can end the query with `ORDER BY` and a field name. You can control the sort order with `ASC` (default) or `DESC`.

TABLE 3.4: Special Operators

OPERATOR	DESCRIPTION
`EMPTY`	Field value is empty.
`NOT EMPTY`	Field value is not empty.
`NULL`	Field has a null value.
`NOT NULL`	Field is not null.
`~`	Matches a regular expression.
`~*`	Matches a regular expression, case insensitive.
`!~`	Does not match a regular expression.
`!~*`	Does not match a regular expression, case insensitive.
`CURRENTUSER`	Current user.
`currentUser`	Same as `CURRENTUSER` but case-insensitive.

You can also use wildcard characters (`*`) for partial matches. For example, this query finds all jiras with a summary that starts with `improvement`:

```
summary ~* "improvement*
```

You can use the special characters of `d` for days, `h` for hours, and so on, as shown in this query to find all jiras resolved in the last three days:

```
status = resolved AND resolved >= -3d
```

Parentheses can be used for grouping clauses to control what the logical operators apply to. This query finds jiras in the project Value Mark that are in the Unresolved state, assigned to the currently logged in user, with priority High or Critical:

```
project = "Value Mark" and assignee = currentUser() AND resolution = Unresolved AND
priority in (High , Critical) order by updated DESC
```

Making Bulk Changes

You can modify a selection of jiras based on a JQL query. From the JQL screen, you can click the Bulk Change button and then click the check box next to each issue you want to change, as in Figure 3.32.

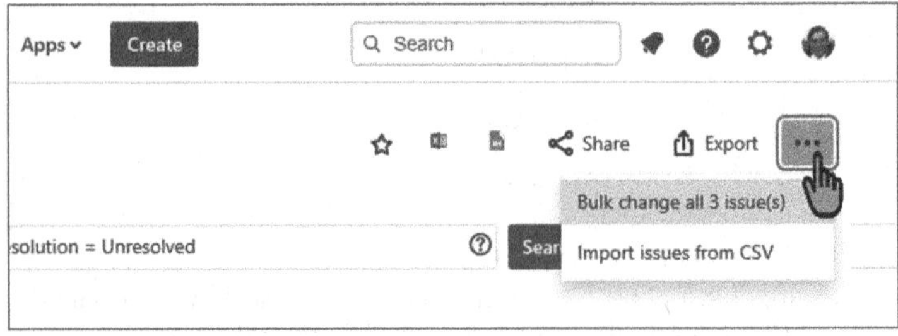

FIGURE 3.32: Bulk editing

You can then choose to edit the selected issues, move them to a new project, transition them, and so on, as in Figure 3.33 and Figure 3.34.

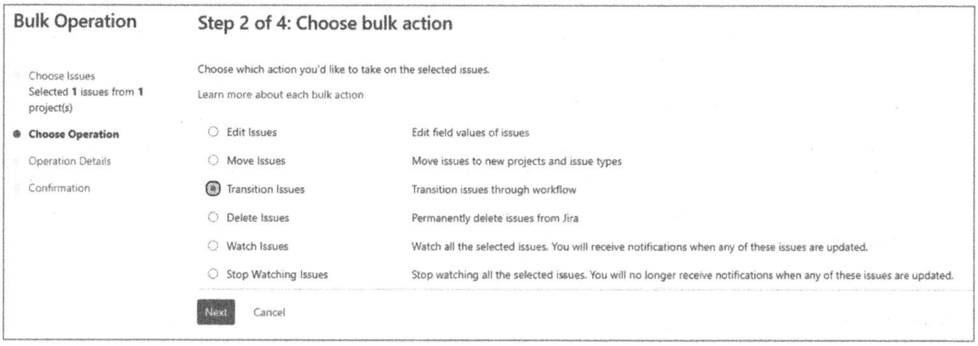

FIGURE 3.33: Bulk editing, Choose bulk action

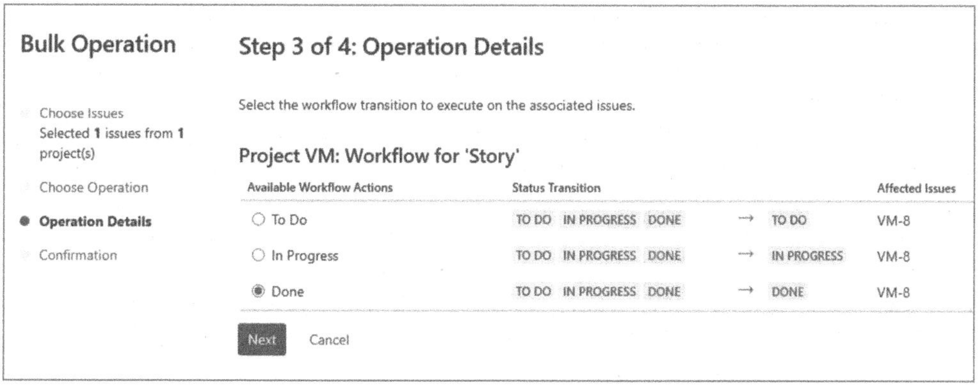

FIGURE 3.34: Bulk editing, Operation details

Connecting to Git

Your Jira admin can connect your Jira project to your Git provider. Once the Git provider is connected, include the Jira key in your commit messages to attach your commit to the associated Jira.

Here's an example:

```
git commit -m "Implemented credentials validation. VM-8"
```

You can then see a list of commits associated with any jira within the Jira ticket itself.

WORKING WITH CONFLUENCE, THE ENTERPRISE KNOWLEDGE MANAGEMENT SYSTEM

We have discussed collaborating with code using Git and how to collaborate on process using Jira. We will end our collaboration chapter with a discussion of Atlassian Confluence, the popular documentation tool.

Confluence is a ubiquitous incarnation of the wiki concept, a generic tool for sharing knowledge. Although there are other brands of wiki that are also popular in the enterprise, they are similar, and we chose Confluence, being one of the most pervasive.

Every team has a stated mission, which can include its purpose, the underlying technologies and processes, how the teams are structured, general knowledge sharing, and so on.

Confluence represents the culmination of the evolution of wiki tools over the years. It includes standard wiki features such as multiple people editing at the same time, viewing version history, and an impressive collection of macros for features such as tables and images.

These are some of the page types supported by Confluence out of the box:

- **Documentation Page:** Used to create documentation. Like all pages, it can include headings, bullet points, numbered lists, tables, and other styles you would expect to find in technical documentation.
- **Meeting Notes:** Specifically designed for capturing meeting minutes and things like action items, as well as other information discussed during meetings.
- **Blog Post:** Generally used for contributing informal insights in a blog-like format.
- **Blank Page:** An empty page where you can create content using Confluence's editing tools.

To create your own cloud version of Confluence, head to `https://www.atlassian.com/software/confluence`.

Confluence is divided into *spaces*, representing the teams. Spaces can have permissions for who can view, edit, and create pages within a space. Within a space, individual pages can be more granularly restricted, so for example if you are collaborating on a page but not ready to share it yet, you can permission just the page's working group and restrict everyone else.

You create a new page by clicking the Create button and selecting an appropriate template. Give the page a title, and then tab over or click into the content frame below the title.

You can now type freely into the content frame, or you can hit the / key to select from the many choices like Image, Table, or Code snippet. If someone else is editing at the same time as you are, Confluence will display a little flag with their initials, demarking their location.

To insert an image, you can drag and drop an image file from the file system onto your Confluence page, or you can copy and paste images from the clipboard, or you can click / and select Image, Video, Or File, and then select the image file.

You can resize the image by dragging and dropping the borders. When you click the image, additional editing options appear below the image, for borders, image alignment, and so on. Figure 3.35 shows how to insert an image.

Select Table to insert a new table. You can select a cell, several cells, whole rows, whole columns, or the entire table. When you make a selection, a little arrow appears at the top right of a cell. Click the arrow to expose a context menu with options for changing the background, or adding or deleting rows or columns. Figure 3.36 shows how to insert a table.

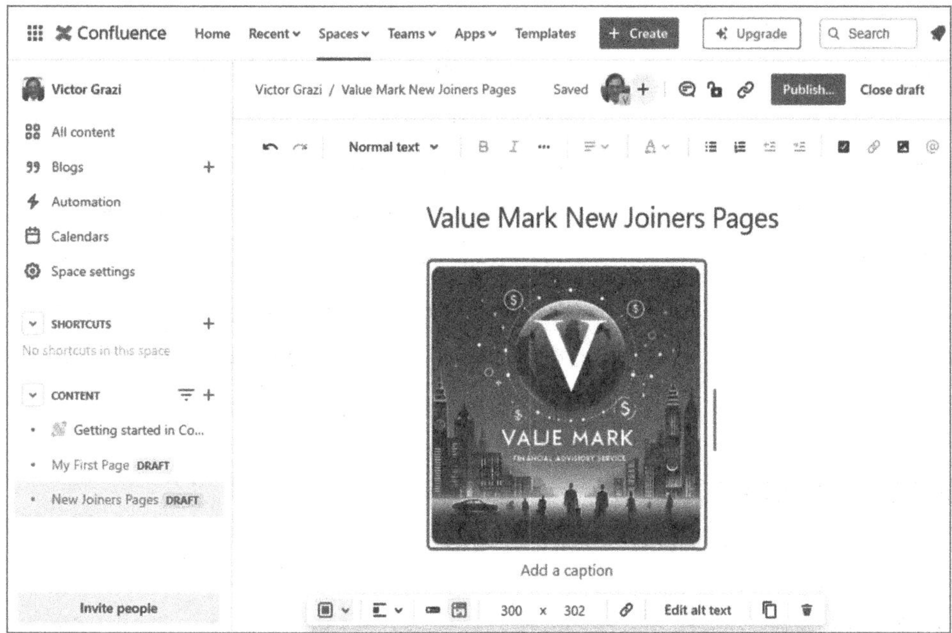

FIGURE 3.35: Inserting an image

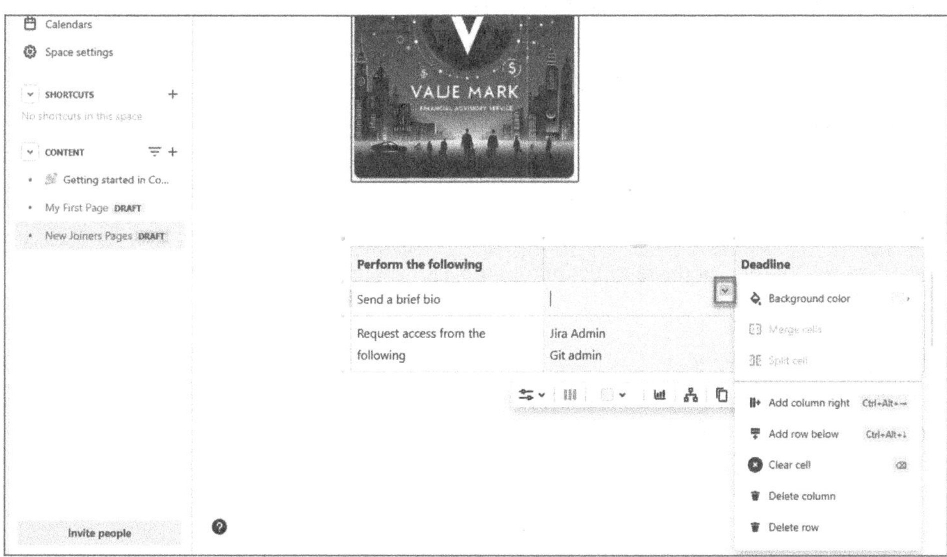

FIGURE 3.36: Inserting a table

Table 3.5 shows some useful macros so you can get a feel for the functionality. Feel free to experiment with them at your leisure.

As you use Confluence, you'll learn fun optimizations like typing *{note}* to create a note box or pasting in a Jira URL to automatically connect the ticket to the page including the status at the time of page rendering!

TABLE 3.5: Selected Confluence Macros

OPERATOR	DESCRIPTION
Table	Creates a table
Code Snippet	Creates formatted code
Note/Tip/Success/Warning/Error Panel	Creates text with an appropriate icon to flag attention
Heading 1, 2, 3, etc.	Creates an outline
Table of Contents	Shows the headings in a table of contents for navigation
Expand	Displays a link that can be expanded to show more detail
Excel	Embeds a spreadsheet tab

FURTHER REFERENCES

- `https://git-scm.com/docs`
  Complete Git Reference documentation
- `https://nvie.com/posts/a-successful-git-branching-model`
  Original Gitflow article by Vincent Driessen
- `https://www.atlassian.com/software/jira`
  Jira documentation
- `https://www.atlassian.com/software/confluence`
  Confluence documentation

SUMMARY

In this chapter, we looked at some of the most ubiquitous tools for enterprise collaboration.

- Git for code collaboration
- Jira for process collaboration
- Confluence for enterprise knowledge management

Automating Your CI/CD Builds with Maven, Gradle, and Jenkins

WHAT'S IN THIS CHAPTER?

- Building with Maven
- Building with Gradle
- Finding a Dependency
- Integrating with Jenkins
- Scanning with Sonar
- Explaining CI/CD Practices

So far, you have seen how to write code on your machine in Chapter 2, "Getting to Know your IDE: The Secret to Success," and share it with others in Chapter 3, "Collaborating Across the Enterprise with Git, Jira, and Confluence." In this chapter, you'll see how to build and package the code using Maven and Gradle.

While it is possible to run Jenkins on your own computer, companies run it on a remote server, just as they run their version control systems on a remote server. This ensures the build is clean and not reliant on a single developer's environment. It also allows Jenkins to run faster by not competing with a developer for computer resources. Plus, the build server never needs to sleep or go on vacation!

Jenkins performs *continuous integration*, which is the name for an automated build process that retrieves the latest code from the version control repository, builds it, runs tests and quality checks on it, and then packages it up and optionally deploys it. Despite the name, continuous integration does not run continuously. It is typically configured to run after each push to the repository. Running continuously would just waste resources if the code has not changed.

As we said, Jenkins continuous integration can be configured to deploy the software as well. *Continuous delivery* goes one step further than continuous integration and ensures the software is ready to deploy to production. With continuous delivery, the software is typically deployed to a preproduction environment. With continuous delivery, the deployment to production requires a manual step.

The most advanced practice is *continuous deployment*, which automatically deploys to production without any manual intervention. This requires a lot of automation and process maturity to avoid introducing problems into production.

There are many continuous integration tools used in the enterprise, for example GitLab CI and GitHub Actions. In this chapter, we cover Jenkins, but the concepts are similar across technologies.

CODE DOWNLOADS FOR THIS CHAPTER

The source code for this chapter is available on the book page at `www.wiley.com`. Click the Downloads link. The code can also be found at `https://github.com/realworldjava/Ch04-CICD`. See the `README.md` file in that repository for details.

BUILDING WITH MAVEN

Build servers don't really build anything, at least not without some help. Rather, they coordinate tools like Maven or Gradle for building, testing, and deploying your code. While Maven can, and often does, manage a project's build, reporting, and documentation needs, it is often called a *build tool* as shorthand.

One of the principles of Maven is "convention over configuration." This means that many configuration properties are assumed (although you can override them if need be). This approach of applying reasonable defaults has the advantage of making it easy for developers to switch between projects as they are typically set up with the same defaults.

For example, most Maven projects use the directory structure in Figure 4.1 with a `src` directory under your project root containing a `main` directory for the code that will be packaged, alongside a `test` directory for test-related code that won't be deployed. Chapter 7, "Testing Your Code with Automated Testing Tools," will cover how to use the `test` directory. The `java` subdirectory unsurprisingly contains Java source code, and the `resources` subdirectory is for text-based files such as database configuration and other application properties. The `target` directory is where the results of the build go.

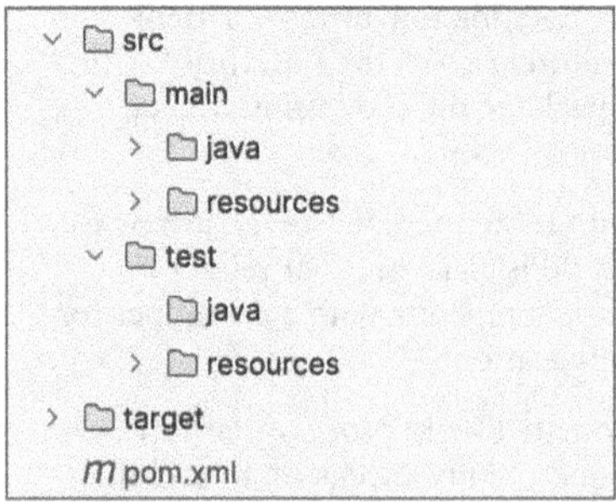

FIGURE 4.1: Directory structure in Maven

Building a Basic Maven Project

Let's start by building a simple Maven project and then dive into some features of Maven. Every Maven project has a pom.xml file. POM stands for Project Object Model and is an XML file that contains build information for our project. For more on XML, see the appendix, "XML and JSON." The shortest possible pom.xml file looks like this:

```
1:  <?xml version="1.0" encoding="UTF-8"?>
2:
3:  <project xmlns="http://maven.apache.org/POM/4.0.0"
4:     xmlns:xsi="http://www.w3.org/2001/XMLSchema-instance"
5:     xsi:schemaLocation="http://maven.apache.org/POM/4.0.0
6:     https://maven.apache.org/xsd/maven-4.0.0.xsd">
7:
8:     <modelVersion>4.0.0</modelVersion>
9:
10:    <groupId>com.wiley.realworldjava.maven</groupId>
11:    <artifactId>basic-pom</artifactId>
12:    <version>1.0.0-SNAPSHOT</version>
13: </project>
```

Lines 1–8 are boilerplate code, which you'll put in every POM file. They state that this XML file is intended to be parsed as a Maven POM. Typically, your IDE will generate this code for you when you create a new project. Alternatively, you can copy/paste this boilerplate from another Maven project.

Lines 10–12 are where you specify your Maven project coordinates. The group id usually maps to the package name, or a prefix of the package name. It creates a namespace to avoid conflicts with other Maven artifacts. The artifact id represents the specific project name within your group id. Finally, the version tag allows you to assign a version number to each build so that you can review and refer to past versions over time. Before your code is released, you would assign a SNAPSHOT suffix to the version, which tells Maven that this is not a final "release" version. (You'll learn more about versions in the next sections.) Taken together, these three tags are referred to as the GAV (group id, artifact id, version) coordinates of your project.

To run a build at the command line, you can execute mvn verify from the directory that contains the pom.xml file, which will do all of the following:

1. Download any dependencies needed for the build and store them in your Maven cache.
2. Copy any files found in src/main/resources into target/classes.
3. Compile any code from src/main/java storing the results in target/classes.
4. Copy any files found in src/test/resources into target/test-classes.
5. Compile any code from src/test/java storing the results in target/test-classes.
6. Run checks in the form of unit tests to verify that the build is valid and meets certain quality standards.
7. Create a JAR file named <artifactId>-<version>.jar (in this case basic-pom-1.0.0-SNAPSHOT.jar) with the files now found in target/classes and store it in target.

That's a lot of work for a POM with 13 lines, most of them boilerplate. This is the power of convention over configuration. Since we didn't state otherwise, Maven assumes the defaults: that we want to compile and test the code, storing the results in a JAR file!

MAVEN 3 VS. MAVEN 4

This book uses Maven 3 since that was the latest version at the time of writing. Maven 4 has a high degree of backward compatibility, so everything you learn will still apply. Note that the boilerplate and `modelVersion` will switch to 4.1.0 when you are ready to use Maven 4.

Understanding the Maven Repository and Dependencies

The first thing the Maven build did was look for *dependencies*. These are libraries the build needs to download in order to run. There are two types of dependencies. Some are needed specifically for your project and specified in the POM. You'll see those shortly. Others are needed for Maven itself. Just like the IDEs you saw in Chapter 2, Maven uses plugins to provide functionality. The first time you run a Maven build, it downloads these plugins. This may take some time; in fact, there is a joke that Maven needs to "download the Internet."

By default, Maven downloads everything it needs from a repository called Maven Central. Unlike GitHub, which is a source code repository as you saw in Chapter 3, Maven Central is a binary repository. Its primary purpose is to hold artifacts you can't open in a text editor, like JAR files!

The following shows the output of Maven downloading just one plugin:

```
Downloading from central: https://repo.maven.apache.org/maven2/
org/apache/maven/plugins/maven-compiler-plugin/3.11.0/
maven-compiler-plugin-3.11.0.pom
Downloaded from central: https://repo.maven.apache.org/maven2/
org/apache/maven/plugins/maven-compiler-plugin/3.11.0/
maven-compiler-plugin-3.11.0.pom (9.8 kB at 28 kB/s)
Downloading from central: https://repo.maven.apache.org/maven2/
org/apache/maven/plugins/maven-compiler-plugin/3.11.0/
maven-compiler-plugin-3.11.0.jar
Downloaded from central: https://repo.maven.apache.org/maven2/
org/apache/maven/plugins/maven-compiler-plugin/3.11.0/
maven-compiler-plugin-3.11.0.jar (66 kB at 1.2 MB/s)
```

As you can see, there are two pairs of messages: one when Maven starts downloading and one when it completes. First, Maven looks for the POM of each artifact, which tells Maven whether the artifact needs other dependencies, also known as *transitive dependencies*, in order to run. If so, Maven looks for these and downloads them as well, and so on. After taking care of the POM, Maven downloads the actual JAR requested.

Luckily, the artifact for each GAV is downloaded only once and stored in your local repository for future use. In your home directory, there is an `.m2` subdirectory. On Windows, this is `C:\Users\<your id>\.m2`. On Mac, it is `/Users/<your id>/.m2`.

Inside the `.m2` folder is a folder named `repository`, which contains subdirectories for each group id. The artifacts and versions are stored in subdirectories underneath them. For example, the files downloaded for the compiler plugin are in this directory:

```
.m2/repository/org/apache/maven/plugins/maven-compiler-plugin/3.11.0
```

The directory includes the POM and downloaded JAR files, along with `.sha1` files, which contains a hash that Maven uses to confirm the file was downloaded successfully.

Each time you run a build, Maven reads whatever it can from your local repository. Anything that is missing, Maven will download from Maven Central or from your corporate binary repository. This ensures that Maven's local build cache avoids the need to download files repeatedly for each build.

As mentioned earlier, the same technique works for dependencies you explicitly specify in the Maven POM. This example shows a POM that specifies a dependency on the `eclipse-collections` library.

```
<?xml version="1.0" encoding="UTF-8"?>

<project xmlns="http://maven.apache.org/POM/4.0.0"
   xmlns:xsi="http://www.w3.org/2001/XMLSchema-instance"
   xsi:schemaLocation="http://maven.apache.org/POM/4.0.0
   https://maven.apache.org/xsd/maven-4.0.0.xsd">

   <modelVersion>4.0.0</modelVersion>

   <groupId>com.wiley.realworldjava.maven</groupId>
   <artifactId>with-dependency</artifactId>
   <version>1.0.0-SNAPSHOT</version>

   <dependencies>
       <dependency>
           <groupId>org.eclipse.collections</groupId>
           <artifactId>eclipse-collections</artifactId>
           <version>11.1.0</version>
       </dependency>
    </dependencies>
</project>
```

You can specify as many dependencies as you'd like simply by adding more `<dependency>` tags inside the `<dependencies>` tag.

> **NOTE** *Eclipse Collections is not related to the Eclipse IDE. It gets its name from the Eclipse Foundation and goes beyond the collections framework included in the Java development kit (JDK).*

Now that you've seen two examples of a POM, we are going to omit the boilerplate and start examples with the `<groupId>` tag.

MORE ON MAVEN DEPENDENCIES

Often the GAV is sufficient to specify a dependency. However, there is more information that can be included in a `<dependency>` tag.

One optional tag is the classifier. This is used when there are multiple artifacts published using the same artifactId. For example, a classifier could be used to differentiate between JAR files for different versions of the JDK or different operating systems.

```
<classifier>jdk21</classifier>
```

Another optional tag is the `type` tag, which is typically used when the packaging type is something besides `jar`, such as a `war` (web archive).

```
<type>war</type>
```

You should also be familiar with the optional `scope` tag.

continues

(continued)

Maven supports the following scopes:

`compile`: Dependency is available to both the `src/main/java` and `src/test/java` directories on compilation. This is the default scope for all dependencies that don't specify a scope.

`test`: Dependencies are available to `src/test/java` only. This is the most common scope to specify.

`provided`: Dependencies are required for the build but will not be packaged because they are expected to be provided at runtime.

`runtime`: Dependencies are not required for compilation but will be needed for execution.

`system`: This is like `provided` scope, but you have to explicitly provide the JAR.

`import`: This is used within a `<dependencyManagement>` section to import potential dependencies from another POM file (for example, a bill of materials [BOM] POM, which we describe later in the chapter).

Differentiating Life-Cycle Phases

To kick off the previous Maven build, we ran `mvn verify`. The `verify` command is one of the Maven life-cycle phases. Each phase executes the previous phase in the life cycle before executing. Table 4.1 shows the most common phases in the default Maven life cycle.

TABLE 4.1: Maven Default Life-Cycle Phases

PHASE	DESCRIPTION
`validate`	Check that the POM file is correctly formatted and all the necessary information is provided.
`compile`	`validate` + compile code in `src/main/java`.
`test`	`compile` + run unit tests (see Chapter 7).
`package`	`test` + create JAR file.
`integration-test`	`package` + run any integration tests (see Chapter 7).
`verify`	`integration-test` + confirm package is valid.
`install`	`verify` + install the package into your local Maven repository for use by other builds.
`deploy`	`install` + publish the package outside your machine.

Become best friends with `verify` as it is the most common Maven phase to run on your machine. If you are working on multiple projects that interrelate, you'll need `install`, but that shouldn't be your "go to" since it takes longer to run and isn't usually needed.

WHAT ABOUT CLEAN?

The `clean` phase deletes anything generated from prior runs ensuring a, well, clean build. It doesn't run by default with the previously mentioned phases, because builds run faster when they don't have to recompile everything from scratch. When you are running on a build server like Jenkins, it can be useful to run a clean build. But you generally only have to run `clean` on your own machine when having problems.

Also note that you can run more than one phase in the same command, making it common to write this:

```
mvn clean verify
```

Exploring the POM

In this section, you'll learn about many of the capabilities available to you in the POM.

Working with Properties

In Java code, it's not a good idea to hard-code "magic numbers" (values without context) in your classes. Instead, it is better to use a named constant. Similarly, in a POM, it is common to place version numbers and other configuration data in properties, which you would normally include at the top of the POM file. It also allows you to share version numbers across multiple dependencies that need to stay on the same version. The following is equivalent to the previous POM except that it extracts the version number into a property:

```
<groupId>com.wiley.realworldjava.maven</groupId>
<artifactId>with-properties</artifactId>
<version>1.0.0-SNAPSHOT</version>

<properties>
   <eclipse.collections.version>11.1.0</eclipse.collections.version>
</properties>

<dependencies>
   <dependency>
      <groupId>org.eclipse.collections</groupId>
      <artifactId>eclipse-collections</artifactId>
      <version>${eclipse.collections.version}</version>
   </dependency>
</dependencies>
```

You can define as many properties as you want in a `<properties>` tag. In this case, there is one with the name `eclipse.collections.version` and the value `11.1.0`. To use the property, refer to the variable name inside the `${}` placeholder and Maven will automatically replace the placeholder with the property value.

Specifying Project Information

As mentioned earlier, Maven aspires to manage as much of your project information as possible. While not exhaustive, this example gives you an idea of the type of information that can be included.

```
<groupId>com.wiley.realworldjava.maven</groupId>
<artifactId>project-info</artifactId>
<version>1.0.0-SNAPSHOT</version>
<name>Project Info Test</name>
<description>This project shows using more tags
```

```
16:    than just the GAV to describe the project</description>
17: <url>https://www.wiley.com/en-us/Real+World+Java%3A+Helping+
18:    You+Navigate+the+Java+Ecosystem-p-9781394275724</url>
19: <inceptionYear>2024</inceptionYear>
20:
21: <properties>
22:    <git.url>https://github.com/realworldjava/Ch04-CICD</git.url>
23: </properties>
24:
25: <scm>
26:    <connection>scm:git:h${git.url}.git</connection>
27:    <developerConnection>scm:git:${git.url}.git</developerConnection>
28:    <url>${git.url}</url>
29:    <tag>HEAD></tag>
30: </scm>
```

Lines 14–15 provide a display name and details about the project, which can be used by other tools. Line 17 lists the URL for further details about the project, or in this case the book URL. Line 19 shows the year the project was started.

Some plugins require additional information. For example, lines 25–30 show a format for specifying a GitHub URL that is used when doing releases. It also conveniently shows the benefit of defining a property; this one is used three different times!

Other information that can be included in a POM include a link to the Jira project and the contact information for all the developers on the project.

Understanding Version Numbers

When working on code, you use a `SNAPSHOT` version like `1.0.0-SNAPSHOT`. Once you are ready for release, the `SNAPSHOT` suffix is dropped, and it becomes `1.0.0`.

You might have noticed the version numbers have all had three parts separated by dots. Maven artifacts typically follow *semantic versioning*. The first number is incremented for major versions, which might introduce new application programming interfaces (APIs) or breaking functionality. The second number is used for minor versions, generally compatible, perhaps improved versions. The third part is generally incremented for bug fixes.

Not all projects follow this naming convention, but most follow variants of it, like adding `.beta` or `.release` at the end of a name for more information.

Additionally, numbers lower than 1.0.0 often mean prerelease. Therefore, 0.2.6 might signify the project isn't ready for full initial release.

This is important to understand, so consider the sequence of events indicated in Table 4.2.

Using Common Plugins

As you saw earlier, plugins give Maven its functionality. They also provide the mechanism to customize behavior. Maven plugins are well documented, and understanding how to use the docs is just as important as knowing how to write code that uses the plugin.

In the following sections, you'll see how to use a common plugin and understand the documentation. Then you'll learn how to avoid repeating configurations followed by an overview of a number of other plugins.

Configuring a Plugin

Let's take a look at the compiler plugin. Using your favorite search engine, look for "maven compiler plugin," which will take you to `https://maven.apache.org/plugins/maven-compiler-plugin`, as shown in Figure 4.2. Most plugins are easy to find with a simple search. Conveniently, the common plugins also have a shared format for the documentation, so once you understand the compiler plugin, you know what you need for others!

TABLE 4.2: Version Number Example

VERSION	EXAMPLE OF MEANING
`0.0.1-SNAPSHOT`	Start initial work.
`0.0.1`	Ready for testers.
`0.0.2-SNAPSHOT`	Oops. We found a bug. Work on bug.
`0.0.2`	Bug fixed. Ready for testers again.
`1.0.0-SNAPSHOT`	Ready for prime time. Prepare for 1.0.0 release.
`1.0.0`	Ready to distribute 1.0.0.
`1.0.1-SNAPSHOT`	Oops. Another bug. Work on bug.
`1.0.1`	Bug fixed. We got it this time.
`1.1.1-SNAPSHOT`	Time to work on a minor enhancement.
`1.1.1`	Ready to distribute minor enhancement.
`2.0.0-SNAPSHOT`	Working on next major release

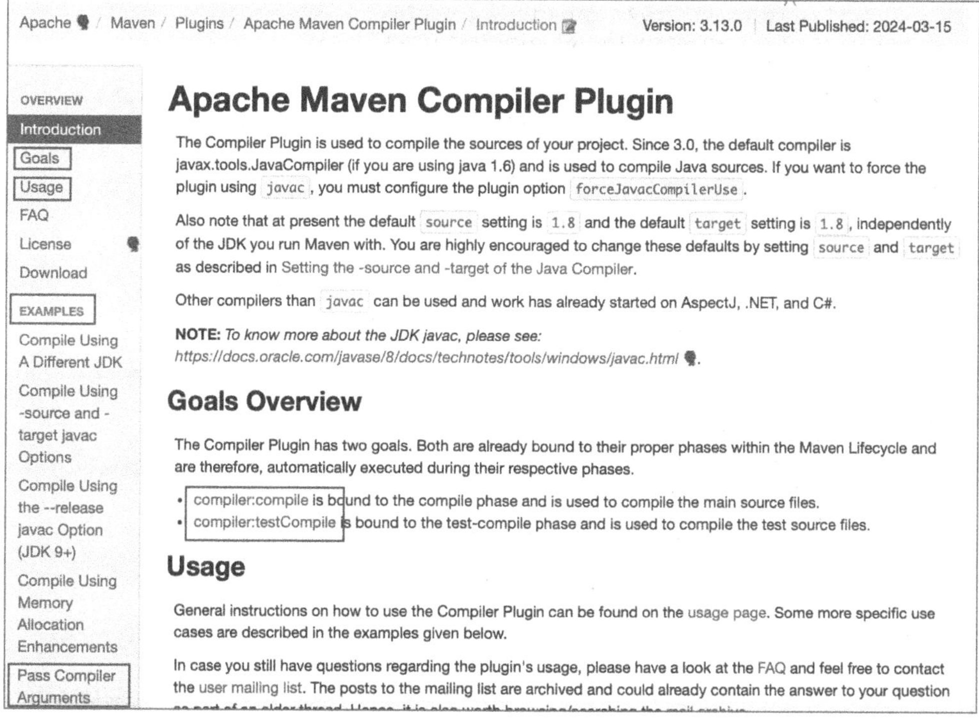

FIGURE 4.2: Maven compiler documentation home page

The plugin documentation page lists any goals that are part of the plugin, in this case `compiler:compile` and `compiler:testCompile`. It also tells you what phase in the life cycle they are automatically bound to if any. These goals are bound to the `compile` and `test-compile` phases, respectively. Plugins don't need to be bound to a specific phase, and you can just call them explicitly. However, in this chapter all plugins are bound. Chapter 7 shows an example of using code to bind `integration-tests` to a life-cycle phase so that they will be automatically run during the build.

The left navigation of the documentation page includes menu options for the following:

- **Goals:** Details on any plugins included with a focus on the required and optional parameters
- **Usage:** Shows how to include the plugin in your POM
- **Examples:** One or more links showing how to configure common scenarios

This example shows how to configure the compiler plugin to use Java 21:

```
<groupId>com.wiley.realworldjava.maven</groupId>
<artifactId>compile</artifactId>
<version>1.0.0-SNAPSHOT</version>

<properties>
   <java.version>21</java.version>
</properties>

<build>
   <plugins>
      <plugin>
         <groupId>org.apache.maven.plugins</groupId>
         <artifactId>maven-compiler-plugin</artifactId>
         <version>3.13.0</version>
         <configuration>
            <source>${java.version}</source>
            <target>${java.version}</target>
         </configuration>
      </plugin>
   </plugins>
</build>
```

Pay attention to the `configuration` tag. That's where the parameters in the "goals" documentation go. In this case, it specifies that you want to use Java 21 both to compile and to produce the bytecode.

> **TIP** *If you get* `error: invalid target release: 21`*, this means you have an older version of Java on your path.*

One of the examples in the documentation is how to "Pass Compiler Arguments" and is as follows:

```
<project>
   [...]
   <build>
      [...]
      <plugins>
         <plugin>
            <groupId>org.apache.maven.plugins</groupId>
            <artifactId>maven-compiler-plugin</artifactId>
```

```
                <version>3.13.0</version>
                <configuration>
                    <compilerArgs>
                        <arg>-verbose</arg>
                        <arg>-Xlint:all,-options,-path</arg>
                    </compilerArgs>
                </configuration>
            </plugin>
        </plugins>
        [...]
    </build>
    [...]
</project>
```

Comparing this example to the previous one, you can see the `configuration` section contains compiler arguments. The documentation uses `[...]` to indicate that there may be other code in your POM in those spots.

Recognizing Common Plugins

Now that you understand how to read the documentation for a plugin, we can introduce other common plugins. Each has custom configuration options that you can read about as you use them on your projects. The following common plugins are in group id `org.apache.maven.plugins`:

- `maven-assembly-plugin`: Create zip files for combinations of files. Useful when deploying to multiple environments with different settings.
- `maven-compiler-plugin`: Compile your code.
- `maven-dependency-plugin`: Various goals for working with dependencies like listing them or unpacking them.
- `maven-deploy-plugin`: Uploads the created artifact to a binary repository.
- `maven-enforcer-plugin`: Fail the build if your POM does not follow specified rules.
- `maven-failsafe-plugin`: Runs integration tests. See Chapter 7 for details.
- `maven-install-plugin`: Updates your local repository with the created artifact.
- `maven-jar-plugin`: Creates a JAR file artifact.
- `maven-javadoc-plugin`: Create Javadoc HTML pages for your project.
- `maven-release-plugin`: Various goals for releasing your software including tagging the repository and updating the POM version number.
- `maven-resources-plugin`: Copies source and test resources to the output directory.
- `maven-shade-plugin`: Create an uber-jar containing your classes along with the classes of all dependencies.
- `maven-site-plugin`: Generates HTML pages with information about the current project like Javadoc and release notes.
- `maven-source-plugin`: Create JAR file containing source code of the project.
- `maven-surefire-plugin`: Runs unit tests. See Chapter 7 for details.

Not all plugins are in the same group id. Some are supplied by other organizations. For example, Sonar, a static analysis tool, supplies a plugin. It is in group id `org.sonarsource.scanner.maven` and artifact id `sonar-maven-plugin`. You can see from the group id that it is supplied by SonarSource rather than Apache.

Working with a Parent POM

As you know in Java, every class has a superclass. Similarly, in Maven, every POM has a *parent POM*. In Java the common ancestor is `java.lang.Object` even if there is no `extends` specified. Similarly, Maven has a super POM that is inherited if no parent is specified. This super POM is where the convention over configuration defaults such as the `src/main/java` directory are actually specified. You can find a link to the super POM in "Further References." Alternatively, you can run `mvn help:effective-pom` from your project directory to see the effective POM, which includes your configuration along with everything it inherits from the super POM.

Creating Your Own Parent POM

In the enterprise, it is common to have a custom POM at the company, department, and/or team level. This allows local standards to be in one place.

A parent POM uses the packaging type pom. This tells Maven not to expect Java code and instead publish just the POM file. Here's an example:

```
<groupId>com.wiley.realworldjava.maven</groupId>
<artifactId>parent</artifactId>
<version>1.0.0-SNAPSHOT</version>
<packaging>pom</packaging>
```

There are different values you can put in the packaging tag. For example, `jar` is the default, which says to build a JAR. By contrast, pom is specified when you are building a parent POM. A parent POM can contain properties and plugins just like any other POM.

> **TIP** *Once you have created a parent POM, remember to run* `mvn install` *instead of* `mvn verify` *for the parent POM, as that places it in your local Maven repository and makes it available to all potential children.*

A child POM specifies the parent it would like to use by using the GAV:

```
<artifactId>child</artifactId>
<version>1.0.0-SNAPSHOT</version>

<parent>
   <groupId>com.wiley.realworldjava.maven</groupId>
   <artifactId>parent</artifactId>
   <version>1.0.0-SNAPSHOT</version>
</parent>
```

Notice that the child does not specify a `groupId`. This tag is optional if the parent and child have the same `groupId`.

Inheriting from the Parent

A parent POM is useful only if it has content! Take a look at this example parent POM, which introduces two new sections, `dependencyManagement` and `pluginManagement`:

```
<groupId>com.wiley.realworldjava.maven</groupId>
<artifactId>parent</artifactId>
<version>1.0.0-SNAPSHOT</version>
<packaging>pom</packaging>

<properties>
    <java.version>21</java.version>
```

```
        <eclipse.collections.version>11.1.0</eclipse.collections.version>
        <compiler.plugin.version>3.13.0</compiler.plugin.version>
    </properties>

    <dependencyManagement>
        <dependencies>
            <dependency>
                <groupId>org.eclipse.collections</groupId>
                <artifactId>eclipse-collections</artifactId>
                <version>${eclipse.collections.version}</version>
            </dependency>
        </dependencies>
    </dependencyManagement>

    <build>
        <pluginManagement>
            <plugins>
                <plugin>
                    <groupId>org.apache.maven.plugins</groupId>
                    <artifactId>maven-compiler-plugin</artifactId>
                    <version>${compiler.plugin.version}</version>
                    <configuration>
                        <source>${java.version}</source>
                        <target>${java.version}</target>
                    </configuration>
                </plugin>
            </plugins>
        </pluginManagement>
    </build>
```

First notice that in the `properties` section several properties are defined so that they can be used rather than hard-coding numbers in the other parts of the POM. This technique allows child POMs to use standard defaults but also lets them override any of the properties. This is like having a `protected` variable in a superclass in Java. It is helpful to be able to change any of these values independently without having to change to a different parent POM or rely on a different project to make a change.

Next comes the `dependencyManagement` section. The contents should look like `dependencies` in a regular POM. The key difference is that the artifacts in `dependencyManagement` are not actually loaded until they are referred to in a child POM. Similarly, `pluginManagement` configures the plugins in case the child POM uses that plugins.

How does a child specify it wants to use a dependency or plugin? Take a look at a child POM that uses this parent:

```
    <artifactId>child</artifactId>
    <version>1.0.0-SNAPSHOT</version>

    <parent>
        <groupId>com.wiley.realworldjava.maven</groupId>
        <artifactId>parent</artifactId>
        <version>1.0.0-SNAPSHOT</version>
    </parent>

    <dependencies>
        <dependency>
            <groupId>org.eclipse.collections</groupId>
            <artifactId>eclipse-collections</artifactId>
```

```
      </dependency>
   </dependencies>

   <build>
      <plugins>
         <plugin>
            <groupId>org.apache.maven.plugins</groupId>
            <artifactId>maven-compiler-plugin</artifactId>
         </plugin>
      </plugins>
   </build>
```

Notice how the configuration is minimal. Version numbers and configuration don't need to be specified; all of that comes from the parent POM.

Suppose you didn't want the `eclipse-collections` dependency from the parent POM. No problem—in the child POM just omit the dependency and it will be ignored:

```
<artifactId>child-without-dependency</artifactId>
<version>1.0.0-SNAPSHOT</version>

<parent>
   <groupId>com.wiley.realworldjava.maven</groupId>
   <artifactId>parent</artifactId>
   <version>1.0.0-SNAPSHOT</version>
 </parent>

<build>
   <plugins>
      <plugin>
         <groupId>org.apache.maven.plugins</groupId>
         <artifactId>maven-compiler-plugin</artifactId>
      </plugin>
   </plugins>
</build>
```

Other changes are also easy. If you want a different version of `eclipse-collections` or the `maven-compiler-plugin`, override the version property in the child POM, which will override the one from the parent. Alternatively, you can add an explicit version tag rather than inherit it.

Working with a Multimodule Project

So far in this chapter, each time we ran a Maven build, it ran one `pom.xml`. Sometimes you have a group of related projects. When this happens, you can create a multimodule project. There is still a parent POM, but with a multimodule project, all children are in subdirectories. For example, the directory structure would look like this:

```
module-parent
|- pom.xml
|- module-services
|   |- pom.xml
|  -module-util
     |- pom.xml
```

First let's look at the parent POM:

```
<groupId>com.wiley.realworldjava.maven</groupId>
<artifactId>module-parent</artifactId>
<version>1.0.0-SNAPSHOT</version>
<packaging>pom</packaging>
```

```
<modules>
   <module>module-services</module>
   <module>module-util</module>
</modules>
```

The POM contains a new `modules` section, which contains a list of the modules from the project subdirectories that should be included in the build. The order the modules are listed in is not necessarily the order they will be built.

One child can optionally contain another in its list of dependencies. In our example, `module-services` will depend on `module-util`. Maven is smart enough to figure out the proper order to build the children based on their dependencies.

> **TIP** *If* `module-services` *depends on* `module-util`*, then* `module-util` *cannot depend on* `module-services`*. This would create a cyclic dependency and cause the Maven build to fail.*

Next, we'll look at the `module-util` POM, which is nice and simple, only referencing the parent:

```
<artifactId>module-util</artifactId>
<version>1.0.0-SNAPSHOT</version>

<parent>
   <groupId>com.wiley.realworldjava.maven</groupId>
   <artifactId>module-parent</artifactId>
   <version>1.0.0-SNAPSHOT</version>
 </parent>
```

The `module-service` POM does the same but also specifies a dependency:

```
<artifactId>module-services</artifactId>
<version>1.0.0-SNAPSHOT</version>

<parent>
   <groupId>com.wiley.realworldjava.maven</groupId>
   <artifactId>module-parent</artifactId>
   <version>1.0.0-SNAPSHOT</version>
</parent>

<dependencies>
   <dependency>
      <groupId>com.wiley.realworldjava.maven</groupId>
      <artifactId>module-util</artifactId>
      <version>1.0.0-SNAPSHOT</version>
   </dependency>
</dependencies>
```

Since in this example everything is contained in a single project, you can run `mvn clean verify` on the `module-parent` level. The output contains the list of modules built and whether they were successful.

```
[INFO] ------------------------------------------------------
[INFO] Reactor Summary for module-parent 1.0.0-SNAPSHOT:
[INFO]
[INFO] module-parent ..................... SUCCESS [  0.077 s]
[INFO] module-util ....................... SUCCESS [  0.571 s]
[INFO] module-services ................... SUCCESS [  0.040 s]
[INFO] ------------------------------------------------------
```

Notice that Maven ran `module-services` last since it depended on `module-util`.

Using Other Maven Features

While there are many Maven features, this section covers a few you are likely to come across, including setting system properties, using a bill of materials, and releasing your project.

Setting System Properties

Java system properties are optional command-line arguments that change the build behavior. You can pass them in when calling Maven using `-D` on the command line, for example:

```
mvn -Dproject.build.sourceEncoding=UTF-8 clean verify
```

You can tell it is a system property because it begins with `-D`. Other system properties can be specified in the POM, in the configuration section of a plugin. For example, when writing unit tests, you can specify the following:

```
<configuration>
   <systemPropertyVariables>
       <myPropertyName>myPropertyValue</myPropertyName>
   </systemPropertyVariables>
</configuration>
```

Refer to the documentation of your plugin for the exact details. Be sure to follow the documentation as to whether to pass the system property to Maven itself or to a plugin within the POM.

Using a Bill of Materials

A bill of materials is a special POM file that specifies optional dependencies. It is useful when you are pulling in a lot of dependencies and they relate to each other.

A BOM uses dependency management like you saw in the parent POM section. The provider of the BOM certifies that the versions of dependencies included in the BOM are compatible with each other.

The most common way to use a BOM is to specify it in a `dependencyManagement` section of your POM as follows:

```
<groupId>com.wiley.realworldjava.maven</groupId>
<artifactId>using-bom</artifactId>
<version>1.0.0-SNAPSHOT</version>

<properties>
   <jackson.bom.version>2.17.0</jackson.bom.version>
</properties>

<dependencyManagement>
   <dependencies>
      <dependency>
         <groupId>com.fasterxml.jackson</groupId>
         <artifactId>jackson-bom</artifactId>
         <version>${jackson.bom.version}</version>
         <scope>import</scope>
         <type>pom</type>
      </dependency>
   </dependencies>
</dependencyManagement>
```

Notice that the `scope` is `import`, which is allowed only when `type` is `pom`. This scope expands the value of the imported POM dependencies as if you had included them directly in `dependencyManagement`. It is much easier to read than if you typed them all in. For example, `jackson-bom` has more than 60 dependencies specified. And you have only one number (`jackson.bom.version`) to keep up-to-date instead of all the dependencies individually!

Releasing Your Project

At some point, you are done with the initial work on your project and you are ready to release it. The `maven-release-plugin` has a number of goals. You run them from the Maven command just like `mvn verify`. The four most useful are the following:

- `release-clean`: Clean up any interim files from previous releases.
- `release-prepare`: Check that the project is in a state to be released. For example, the POM cannot reference `SNAPSHOT` dependencies since that would not create a repeatable release (remember, `SNAPSHOT` versions are subject to change). `release-prepare` also updates the version number in the POM.
- `release-perform`: Tag the code in version control and store the artifact in a binary repository.
- `release-rollback`: Restore the POM files from a failed `prepare`.

Getting to Know Maven in the IDE

As you saw in Chapter 2, using the integrated development environment (IDE) can be much more efficient than running things from the command line. Since running a build is such a basic operation, we show it in all three of the major IDEs.

Using IntelliJ

When you have a Maven project, there is a lowercase "m" icon representing Maven in the right sidebar. Click it to expand the Maven window. Expand the Lifecycle option as in Figure 4.3. You can double-click your desired goal (for example `verify`) to run a build or right-click for more options.

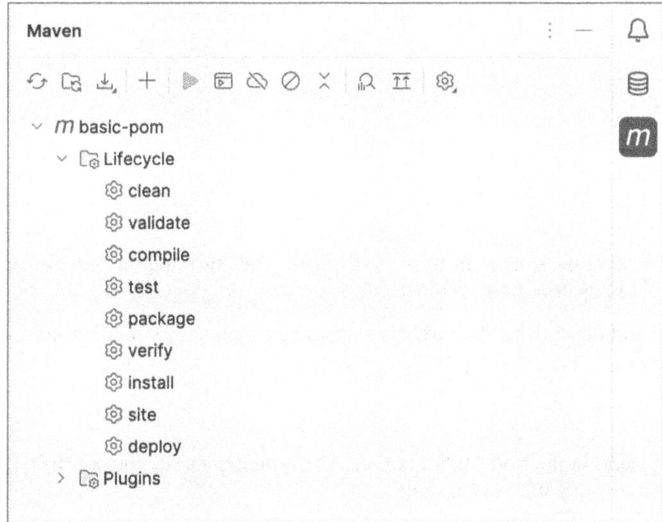

FIGURE 4.3: Running Maven from IntelliJ

IntelliJ provides other options for Maven. For example, the effective POM is useful for seeing what your POM looks like after all the inherited settings have been applied. Figure 4.4 shows that you can find this option by right-clicking the project and choosing the Maven menu.

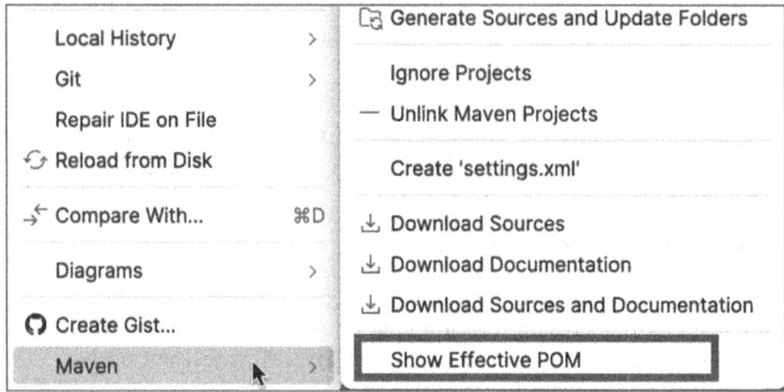

FIGURE 4.4: Viewing the effective POM in IntelliJ

If your project has a lot of dependencies, you may find it useful to right-click the project in the Maven sidebar and choose Analyze Dependencies. In this list you can click any dependency and see where it came from, even if it is a transitive dependency.

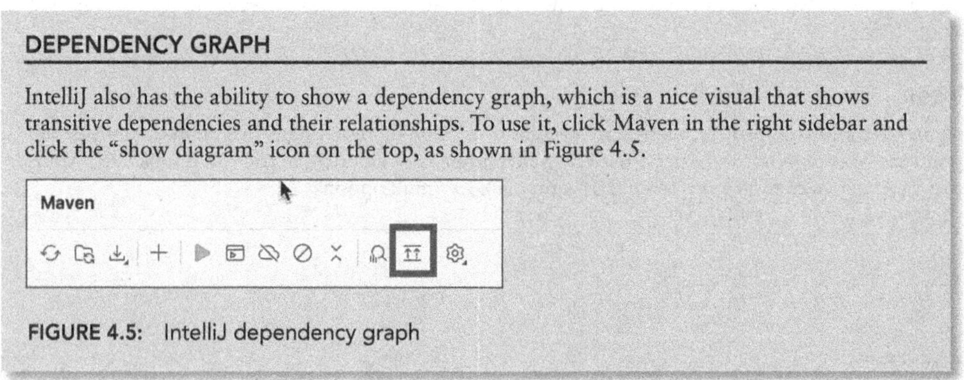

DEPENDENCY GRAPH

IntelliJ also has the ability to show a dependency graph, which is a nice visual that shows transitive dependencies and their relationships. To use it, click Maven in the right sidebar and click the "show diagram" icon on the top, as shown in Figure 4.5.

FIGURE 4.5: IntelliJ dependency graph

Using Eclipse

In Eclipse, you run a Maven build by right-clicking the project in Package Explorer and choosing the Run menu. Figure 4.6 shows this menu where you can click to choose a goal to run.

Eclipse also lets you view the effective POM and dependency hierarchy by opening the `pom.xml` file. The editor has tabs for both, as you can see in Figure 4.7.

Using VS Code

In VS Code, you have a "Maven" accordion menu in the bottom-left corner. After you expand it, you see the goals in Figure 4.8. You can right-click any of them to run your Maven build.

To see the effective POM, right-click the `pom.xml` file and choose Maven in the menu. Then click Show Effective POM, as in Figure 4.9.

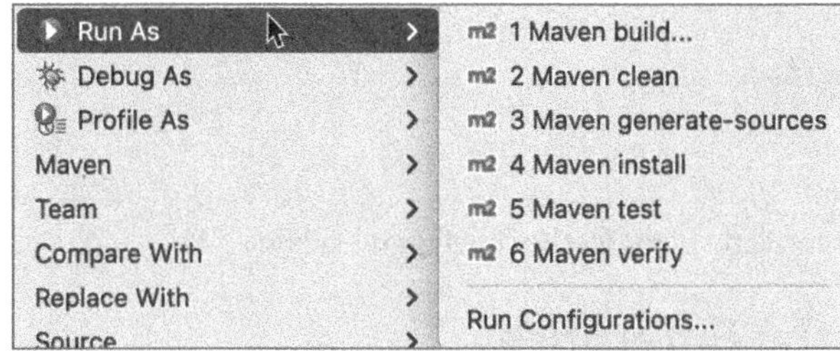

FIGURE 4.6: Running Maven from Eclipse

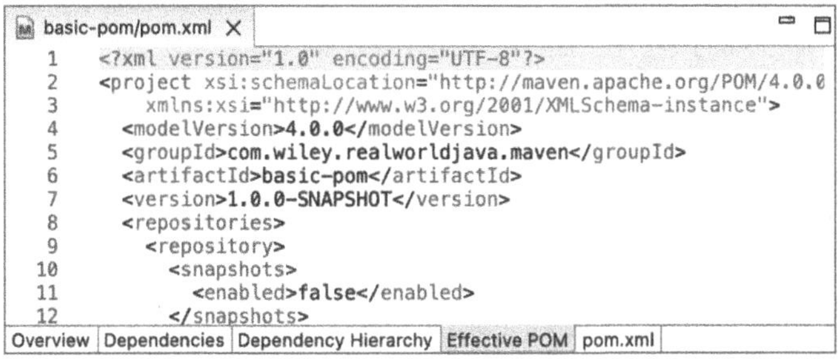

basic-pom/pom.xml

```
<?xml version="1.0" encoding="UTF-8"?>
<project xsi:schemaLocation="http://maven.apache.org/POM/4.0.0
    xmlns:xsi="http://www.w3.org/2001/XMLSchema-instance">
  <modelVersion>4.0.0</modelVersion>
  <groupId>com.wiley.realworldjava.maven</groupId>
  <artifactId>basic-pom</artifactId>
  <version>1.0.0-SNAPSHOT</version>
  <repositories>
    <repository>
      <snapshots>
        <enabled>false</enabled>
      </snapshots>
```

Overview | Dependencies | Dependency Hierarchy | Effective POM | pom.xml

FIGURE 4.7: Viewing the effective POM in Eclipse

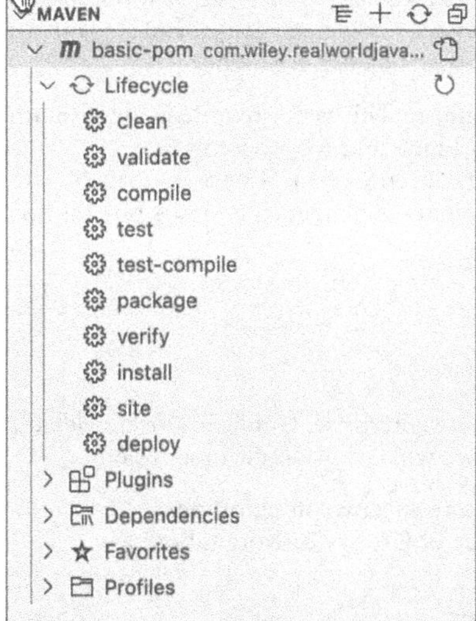

FIGURE 4.8: Running Maven from VS Code

FIGURE 4.9: Running Maven from VS Code

While there is a dependency list in VS Code, it isn't currently at the level of IntelliJ and Eclipse.

Configuring Maven Settings for the Enterprise

In the enterprise, Maven Central is rarely used directly as the binary repository. Instead, a binary repository like JFrog Artifactory or Sonatype Nexus is used as a proxy. This arrangement provides benefits including the following:

- **Performance:** Artifacts are downloaded from the Internet once and cached within the intranet for fast access.
- **Security:** It provides controls over who can access particular artifacts and can scan artifacts for security vulnerabilities before making them available to developers.
- **Anonymity:** Only one request from your organization goes out to the Internet, and then all other calls come from the cache. This prevents leaking how prevalent an artifact is used at your organization.
- **Audit:** Repositories generally require authentication, making it possible to see who downloaded which artifacts.
- **Custom repositories:** The enterprise binary repository can host internal libraries and third-party libraries that are not available in Maven Central.

All of the general Maven settings are configured in a file called `settings.xml`, including repository locations, authentication credentials, default profiles, and other configuration settings.

You can have the `settings.xml` files in one or two places. Global properties such as the URL of your binary repository are generally configured in `<maven install>/conf/settings.xml`. User-specific properties like token passwords (ideally encrypted) can be contained in `<user home>/.m2/settings.xml`. If both are specified, then they are merged, and if there are any duplicates, the user-specific ones are used.

The `settings.xml` files will generally be customized for your environment. This is not required, and if omitted, Maven will use the default local repository at `~/.m2/repository` on Linux and Mac systems or `C:\Users\<username>\.m2\repository` on Windows. It will use Maven Central (`https://repo.maven.apache.org/maven2`) as the default remote repository for binary dependencies. This is fine for home use, and you can ask your teammates how to set it up in your enterprise.

BUILDING WITH GRADLE

Maven and Gradle have many similarities, and both are widely used in the enterprise. Gradle is also the default build tool for Android applications. Since we covered Maven in detail, we will cover Gradle more briefly.

Where Maven uses `pom.xml`, Gradle uses a file named `build.gradle` to specify configurations like dependencies, plugins, and tasks. The build file is specified in your choice of Groovy or Kotlin. Both are languages that run on the Java Virtual Machine (JVM), just like Java.

Like Maven, Gradle relies on convention over configuration. The `src` directory structure is the same, but the output goes into a `build` directory instead of a `target` directory, as shown in Figure 4.10.

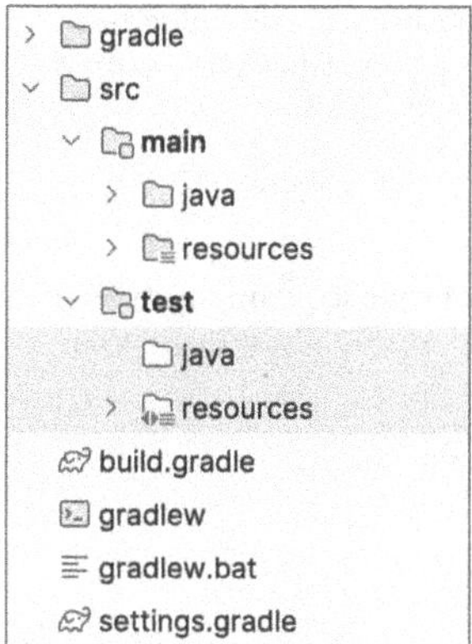

FIGURE 4.10: Directory structure in Maven

Where the `build.gradle` file contains project-specific configuration, the optional `settings.gradle` file can contain more information about your project.

Gradle will generate a file called `gradlew.bat` for running on Windows and a `gradlew` file for running on Linux and Mac. The `gradle` directory contains a `wrapper` subdirectory, which contains a JAR file with the code that actually runs Gradle.

> **NOTE** *Gradle syntax gets more involved as your build needs grow. This chapter only covers the basics.*

Building a Basic Gradle Project

Let's start by building a simple Gradle project before looking at some features. First, look at the `settings.gradle` file:

```
rootProject.name = 'basic-gradle'
```

That's the whole thing, which is pretty short! The simplest `settings.gradle` file just contains the name of the project, which is equivalent to the `artifactId` in Maven.

The `build.gradle` file is slightly longer:

```
1:  plugins {
2:     id 'java'
3:  }
4:
5:  group = 'com.wiley.realworldjava.gradle'
6:  version = '1.0.0-SNAPSHOT'
7:
8:  repositories {
9:     mavenCentral()
10: }
```

Lines 1–3 specify that this is a Java project. Lines 5–6 provide the group and version. Combined with the project name from `settings.gradle`, this is enough to define the project coordinates.

Finally, lines 8–10 say that this build will be using Maven Central as the default repository for downloading dependencies. Maven and Gradle generate the same format of artifacts, and therefore they can use the same remote binary repository.

To run a build at the command line, execute `./gradlew build` from the directory that contains `build.gradle`.

This will generate a lot of dynamic output on the screen. Instead of logging all the output sequentially as with Maven, Gradle dynamically updates the console output with the current build progress. Finally, it displays a summary of the results:

```
Starting a Gradle Daemon (subsequent builds will be faster)
> Task :compileJava
> Task :processResources
> Task :classes
> Task :jar
> Task :assemble
> Task :compileTestJava
> Task :processTestResources
> Task :testClasses
> Task :test NO-SOURCE
> Task :check UP-TO-DATE
> Task :build

BUILD SUCCESSFUL in 0s
5 actionable tasks: 5 executed
```

The tasks listed in this output will look similar to the Maven output. They compile the project, run any tests, and create an artifact. The files created are in the following locations:

- **`build/lib`**: Contains the `basic-gradle-1.0.0.jar` file.
- **`build/classes`**: Contains the class files generated from compiling. They are separated into `build/classes/java/main` and `build/classes/java/test`.
- **`build/resources`**: Contains copies of the resources separated into `build/resources/main` and `build/resources/test`.

GROOVY VS. KOTLIN

You have the option of using Kotlin for your `build.gradle` instead of Groovy. These two language choices are referred to as the domain-specific language (DSL) for Gradle. Kotlin support was added more recently, but the documentation has been fully updated to support both.

Basic Gradle examples look similar in Groovy and Kotlin. First is the `settings.gradle.kts` file:

```
rootProject.name = "basic-gradle"
```

The only difference is that Kotlin requires double quotes. In Groovy, single or double quotes are allowed, with single quotes being more common. Next is the `build.gradle.kts` file.

```
plugins {
    `java-library`
}

group = "com.wiley.realworldjava.gradle"
```

```
version = "1.0.0-SNAPSHOT"

repositories {
    mavenCentral()
}
```

In addition to the double quotes, note that in the Kotlin version java-library is in backticks. Finally, the Kotlin build filenames have a .kts extension.

In this chapter, we will show other differences between Groovy and Kotlin build files as we introduce each feature.

Understanding the Gradle Local Repository and Dependencies

Like Maven, Gradle stores downloaded artifacts locally. In your home directory, there is a .gradle subdirectory. On Windows, this is C:\Users\<your id>\.gradle. On Linux and Mac, it is /Users/<your id>/.gradle.

Gradle stores a lot more than just downloaded artifacts to make your builds faster. The downloaded dependencies are stored in the directory .gradle/caches/modules-2/files-2.1.

For example, the files downloaded for eclipse-collections are in this directory:

```
.gradle/caches/modules-2/files-2.1/org.eclipse.collections/
   eclipse-collections/11.1.0/
```

The directory has a subdirectory with a hash as the directory name, which confirms that the file was downloaded successfully. That subdirectory contains the actual JAR file within.

To specify this dependency in Groovy, add it to the dependency section in your build.gradle file.

```
dependencies {
   implementation group: 'org.eclipse.collections',
      name: 'eclipse-collections', version: '11.1.0'
}
```

These are the same coordinates you saw earlier in Maven. The implementation specifies it is the most common type of dependency—one that is used for compilation. Note that classifier is also allowed for when you need it to differentiate an artifact.

Gradle also supports a shorthand for specifying the full group, name, and version of a dependency using a single value:

```
dependencies {
   implementation 'org.eclipse.collections:eclipse-collections:11.1.0'
}
```

In this syntax, the coordinates are in one string separated by colons.

The corresponding Kotlin syntax would be included in the build.gradle.kts file as follows:

```
dependencies {
   implementation("org.eclipse.collections:eclipse-collections:11.1.0")
}
```

This time the implementation call looks like a method. All three of these approaches clearly specify the group, name, and version so Gradle knows what you are looking for.

TYPES OF GRADLE DEPENDENCIES

In the previous example, you saw `implementation` as the dependency configuration type. Some of the common dependency types include the following:

- `implementation`: Available at runtime to your application
- `testImplementation`: Available from `test/java` but not from `src/java`
- `compileOnly`: Available for compiling but not at runtime
- `runtimeOnly`: Available at runtime but not for compiling

Specifying Variables

Since a Gradle build file is actually Groovy or Kotlin code, you can specify variables in code. For example, this Groovy code declares a variable:

```
def collVersion = "11.1.0"

dependencies {
   implementation
   "org.eclipse.collections:eclipse-collections:${collVersion}"
}
```

Groovy uses `def` to declare a variable. The `${}` syntax tells Gradle to substitute the variable value. You need to use double quotes for that expansion to work. In Groovy, single quoted strings do not allow this feature.

By contrast, a Kotlin build file can also use a variable:

```
val collVersion = "11.1.0"

dependencies {
   implementation
   "org.eclipse.collections:eclipse-collections:${collVersion}"
}
```

The only difference between the two is that Groovy uses `def` to declare a variable, where Kotlin uses `val` for declaring immutable variables and `var` for mutable variables. Since the version is declared once and unchanged in the build file, this example uses `val`.

Using the Java Plugin

In Maven, you saw there were a number of plugins like `maven-compiler-plugin`, `maven-surefire-plugin`, and `maven-jar-plugin`. In Gradle, the Java plugin contains most of that functionality. The Java plugin documentation link is in the "Further References" section. It documents customizations you can make. For example, the following example sets the Java version to use:

```
java {
   toolchain {
      languageVersion = JavaLanguageVersion.of(21)
   }
}
```

You might have noticed we didn't say whether this was a Groovy or Kotlin example. It's both! This particular code has the same syntax in both languages.

> **TIP** *In addition to the Gradle* `java` *plugin, there is a* `java-library` *plugin that extends it. The* `java-library` *plugin adds extra functionality like an API configuration.*

The Java plugin page includes configuration for tests, Javadoc, and packaging. It also includes descriptions for configuring changes to any defaults such as source directories.

> **NOTE** *Gradle also supports multiproject builds like Maven's multimodule builds. You add an* `include` *statement in the* `settings.gradle` *file.*

Getting to Know Gradle in the IDE

Like Maven, it is easy to run a Gradle build in all three of the major IDEs.

In IntelliJ, there is an elephant icon in the right sidebar for Gradle projects. This is the Gradle logo. Once you've identified the logo, follow these steps to run a Gradle build:

1. Click the logo to expand the Gradle window.
2. Expand the Tasks option.
3. Expand Build. Figure 4.11 shows the UI at this point.
4. Right-click your desired task, like Build, and choose the run option.

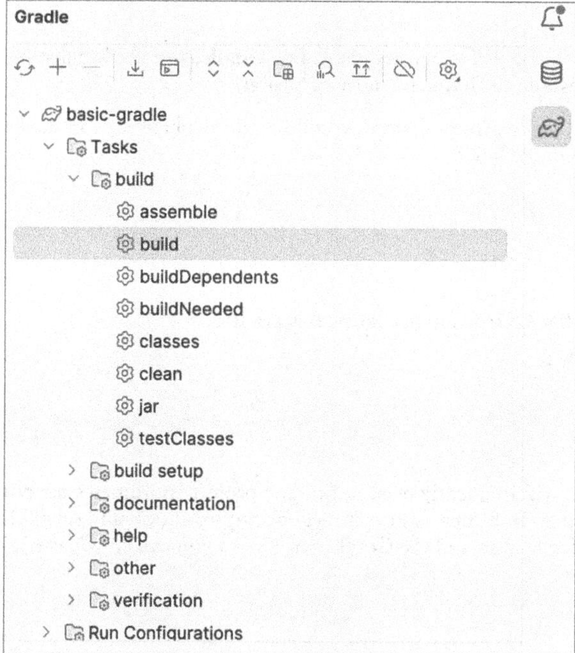

FIGURE 4.11: Running Gradle from IntelliJ

> **TIP** *The Analyze Dependencies menu is also available for Gradle projects, just like for Maven ones. Just open the Gradle sidebar, right-click the project, and choose Analyze Dependencies.*

In Eclipse, start with the Gradle Tasks view at the bottom of the screen. Then follow these steps to run a Gradle build:

1. Expand the project.
2. Expand Build. Figure 4.12 shows this view.
3. Right-click Build and choose Run Gradle Tasks.

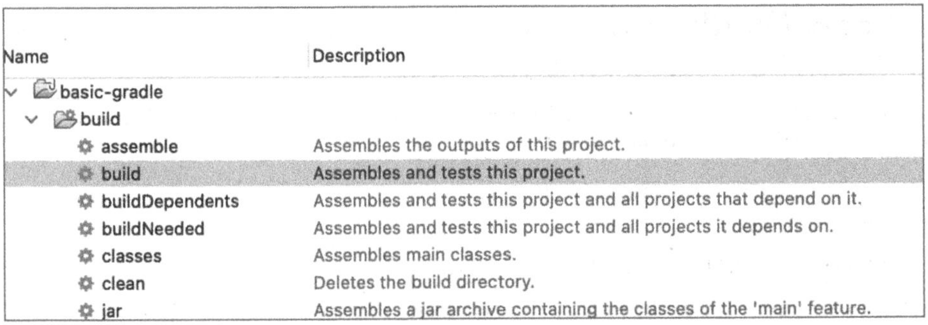

Name	Description
basic-gradle	
build	
assemble	Assembles the outputs of this project.
build	Assembles and tests this project.
buildDependents	Assembles and tests this project and all projects that depend on it.
buildNeeded	Assembles and tests this project and all projects it depends on.
classes	Assembles main classes.
clean	Deletes the build directory.
jar	Assembles a jar archive containing the classes of the 'main' feature.

FIGURE 4.12: Running Gradle from Eclipse

In VS Code, the Maven extension is included in the Java extension pack. For Gradle, you need to install the extension yourself. Go to Marketplace and install the Gradle for Java extension.

Once you have the extension installed and a Gradle project opened, you'll see the elephant logo in the left navigation. Then follow these steps to run a Gradle build:

1. Expand Gradle Projects.
2. Expand your project name.
3. Expand Tasks.
4. Expand Build. Figure 4.13 shows what VS Code looks like at this point.
5. Right-click Build and choose Run Task.

FINDING A DEPENDENCY

Whether you are using Maven or Gradle, you will frequently need to find the project coordinates for projects in Maven Central. One way to find them is to go to `https://central.sonatype.com` and search for your artifact. The resulting page has a pull-down for Maven and the Gradle variants so you can copy/paste it into your build.

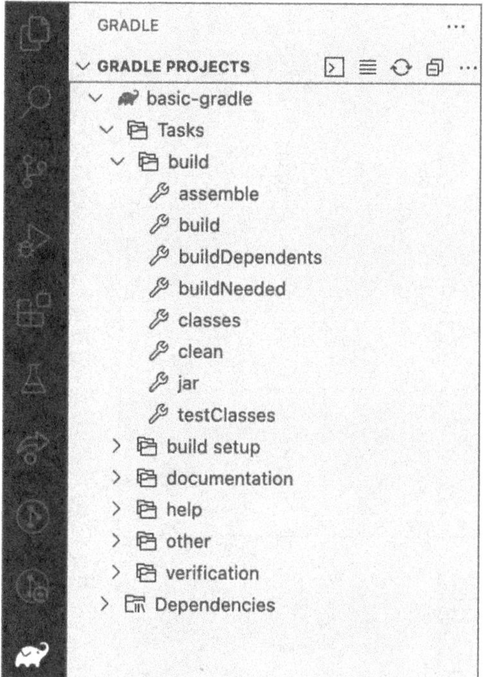

FIGURE 4.13: Running Gradle from VS Code

However, there is a faster way. If you search for "maven central" and the artifact name on your favorite search engine, the first hit is likely to be at `https://mvnrepository.com`. For example, searching for "maven central eclipse collections" takes you to `https://mvnrepository.com/artifact/org.eclipse.collections/eclipse-collections`. The Maven Repository site was built by a developer in Spain and has the same information as Maven Central. We use `mvnrepository.com` in this book when mentioning URLs due to its better search engine optimization.

Figure 4.14 shows the options available when you click a specific version of an artifact.

At the time of this writing, we chose Eclipse Collections version `11.1.0` for the example in this chapter. Notice that there is a later version, `12.0.0.M3`. The `M3` stands for "milestone 3." A milestone release is a publicly available release for testing new features and comes before the final version. Since it is not common to use milestone dependencies in production code, we chose the most recently released version.

In Figure 4.14, under the warning about the later version, there are tabs for many build systems. Select your build system, copy the dependency information, and paste that into your POM or Gradle build file.

> **TIP** *In the figure, the tabs SBT, Ivy, and Grape are other specialized build systems that are not covered in this book.*

Home » org.eclipse.collections » eclipse-collections » 11.1.0

Eclipse Collections Main Library » 11.1.0

Eclipse Collections Main Library

License	EDL 1.0 EPL 1.0
Categories	Collections
Tags	eclipse collections structures data
Date	Jul 05, 2022
Files	pom (5 KB) jar (10.0 MB) View All
Repositories	Central
Ranking	**#664 in MvnRepository (See Top Artifacts)** **#6 in Collections**
Used By	**729 artifacts**

Note: There is a new version for this artifact

New Version	12.0.0.M3

Maven | Gradle | Gradle (Short) | Gradle (Kotlin) | SBT | Ivy | Grape | Leiningen | Buildr

```
// https://mvnrepository.com/artifact/org.eclipse.collections/eclipse-collections
implementation group: 'org.eclipse.collections', name: 'eclipse-collections', version: '11.1.0'
```

FIGURE 4.14: Finding dependencies

INTEGRATING WITH JENKINS

Jenkins brands itself an "open-source automation server," and in fact Jenkins can automate pretty much everything. However, most people think of it as a continuous integration/continuous deployment (CI/CD) server, since its focus is build and deploy.

Jenkins is open-source and free to use. Cloudbees sells a version with proprietary content and support, but it's on the Cloudbees website, not the Jenkins website, so there's no risk of confusion.

In this section, you'll learn how to install Jenkins, which common plugins to install, and how to run a build.

Installing Jenkins

To install Jenkins, you can go to the download page in "Further References." You'll notice that there are many choices on that page.

First decide whether you want the stable version or the weekly release. The stable packages are released monthly, and Jenkins applies security and bug fixes to them for a period of time. Every three months, one of the stable releases becomes the long-term support (LTS) release. When running at home, any release is fine. Businesses will usually choose an LTS release or a vendor-supported version. We'll use the latest stable release in our example.

Next you must decide on the format for your Jenkins download. One option is to get it as a web archive (WAR) file to run on a web application server like Tomcat. Alternatively, you can get it as an operating system package to install as a binary or a Docker image. We'll use the Docker image in this chapter as an example. The link to download Docker is also in the "Further References" section. Any of these options is fine, though, when trying Jenkins on your personal machine.

For Docker, start by opening the "Docker Desktop" application to ensure Docker is running on your machine. Then open a command line and run the following command to download the latest stable Jenkins release:

```
docker pull jenkins/jenkins
```

The output will look something like this where each of the layers in the Docker image is downloaded:

```
Using default tag: latest
latest: Pulling from jenkins/jenkins
60bdaf986dbe: Pull complete
dfad4ee37376: Pull complete
206558d801c7: Pull complete
a5c2ffb5ffef: Pull complete
f0c0bc8bfcc6: Pull complete
064531224ab4: Pull complete
96aa304ced3c: Pull complete
056f1f47a471: Pull complete
ac5fc7f80726: Pull complete
8a59881e61b3: Pull complete
361281efe43a: Pull complete
aa0d9cfb3420: Pull complete
Digest: sha256:d4f805f9c225ee72c6ac8684d635eb8ec236569977f4cd6f9acd7c24a5d56985
Status: Downloaded newer image for jenkins/jenkins:latest
docker.io/jenkins/jenkins:latest
```

Next you run the Docker container:

```
docker run --name jenkins -p 8080:8080 jenkins/jenkins
```

This command gives your Docker container the name "jenkins" to make it easier to refer to later. It also exposes port 8080 so you can access it in a web browser. If that port is in use on your machine, feel free to use any available port.

> **NOTE** *You only use the* `run` *command the first time. After that, start Jenkins by calling* `docker start jenkins` *instead.*

The console output will include a message like this:

```
Jenkins initial setup is required.
An admin user has been created and a password generated.
Please use the following password to proceed to installation:

4ab39e58b99e4519b3edbf7e4df21d51

This may also be found at: /var/jenkins_home/secrets/initialAdminPassword
```

Make a note of this initial password so you can log in. Then open a browser and go to `http://localhost:8080`. Jenkins will ask you to enter the password you just noted. Paste in the password and click Continue.

Jenkins will ask you whether you want to "Install suggested plugins" or "Select plugins to install." Choose the suggested plugins so you can get started quickly. If you watch the screen during the plugin install, you'll notice that Jenkins downloads more than just the plugins on the screen. Just like Maven and Gradle dependencies, Jenkins plugins depend on other Jenkins plugins. Therefore, Jenkins will download those transitive plugin dependencies as well.

Next Jenkins asks you to set up your first admin user. Be sure to remember the username and password you pick as you'll need it to get back in. You no longer need the long initial password from the install anymore, though!

Finally, Jenkins asks you to confirm the URL. Using the default of `http://localhost:8080` is just fine. Jenkins will display the "Jenkins is ready!" screen. Just click Start Using Jenkins.

Learning Jenkins Terminology

Jenkins vocabulary includes words that may be unfamiliar to you. In this section, you'll learn this vocabulary to understand what is going on.

Jenkins has a *controller* that administers the *agents*. An agents is a process that actually runs Jenkins jobs. You can have one or more agents. The word *node* is used as a synonym of agent. By default, you get one agent on the same machine as the controller. You can set up additional agents on the same machine or across different machines. You can remove the agents on the controller machine to have more separation of concerns. In the past, the controller was called *master*, and the agent was called *slave*. You may see the older vocabulary in the documentation.

A Jenkins *job* refers to the configuration for what you would like to run. A *build* is a specific execution of that job. A *build step* is a single operation within a build. Jenkins limits the number of simultaneous jobs run on an agent at the same time by allowing you to specify the number of slots, or *executors*. Each agent can have one or more executors. This allows you to run many jobs at the same time on a single agent.

There are a few choices for configuring jobs. For example, jobs can be configured as *freestyle* jobs or *pipeline* jobs. A freestyle job uses a UI to specify configuration. A pipeline uses code to provide the details.

Jobs are initiated by *triggers*. One popular type of trigger is a source code commit. After all, continuous integration works only if you automate your builds to launch each time something changes. Or you can use time-based triggers, which launch based on a specified schedule. For example, you might want to run slow tests overnight. You can have one job trigger another, a useful strategy for chaining job types. Finally, you can have events outside Jenkins trigger a job via an API.

The *dashboard* lists all your jobs. You can organize them in *folders*. In fact, you can nest as many levels of folders as you want. You can also create *views* to control what you see.

Jenkins stores build files in a *workspace*. Examples of build files include the files checked out from Git and the target or build directory from your Maven or Gradle build. The items created by a build are called *artifacts*. Artifacts can be *archived* so you can see them in Jenkins even after the workspace is deleted.

Creating Jobs

In the following sections, you'll learn how to create three kinds of jobs.

- A simple freestyle job
- A job that runs Maven
- One that runs Gradle and a pipeline

Freestyle jobs require you to specify your build configuration using the Jenkins user interface. The freestyle approach has an easier learning curve than pipelines and will work for the majority of cases. Freestyle jobs let you see the workspace via a link in the left navigation.

Pipelines allow you to express your build using code. They also let you split your build into stages.

There are two types of pipelines: scripted and declarative. In this book, we use the scripted pipeline for Maven and the declarative pipeline for Gradle so you can see an example of each. Pipeline jobs provide a workspaces link on specific builds instead of on the job level.

Creating a Simple Freestyle Job

To create a job, follow these steps:

1. Click New Item in the left navigation.
2. Give it a name (freestyle-timer in our example).
3. Choose the job type Freestyle Project.
4. Click OK.

Jenkins will create the job and automatically take you to the configure screen. There are several configuration sections in a job, as shown in Figure 4.15.

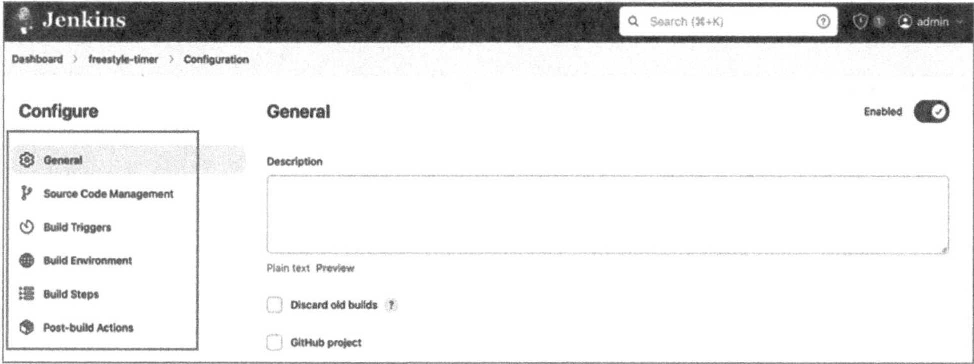

FIGURE 4.15: Jenkins freestyle sections

General contains checkboxes for you to select your options. For example, you can control how many old builds Jenkins saves or whether to run another build if the current one is currently running.

Source Code Management allows you to specify the version control system you are using. Git is included with the recommended plugins. If you are using a different VCS, you can install a plugin for it from Jenkins Plugin Manager page. There are also fields for the repository URL and any credentials needed to connect.

Build Triggers is where you choose what kicks off your build. In this example, we will use Build Periodically to show how a schedule is used. There are also options for a GitHub commit trigger and for polling the repository. The trigger for telling GitHub to initiate a build is called a *push*. By contrast, *polling* asks the repository to periodically check if there have been any changes, and if so, execute the build.

Build Environment lets you configure information about how Jenkins should behave. For example, you can have Jenkins add timestamps to each log entry, or you can set a strategy for when Jenkins should kill a long-running build.

Build Steps is the actual build, where you configure one or more build steps to run. For example, you can have Jenkins run a command from the command line or you can configure a Maven build here.

Post-build Actions allow you to deal with the result of a build. For example, you can send an email notification or publish a report.

Now that you understand what a freestyle job can do, let's create a simple one that prints hello every hour. First, you need to set the build trigger to build periodically. You can use a cron-like syntax (cron is the Unix built-in scheduler).

```
# MINUTE HOUR DOM MONTH DOW
* * * * *
```

Jenkins will advise you can use `H`, rather than specifying a precise time. `H` calculates a hash based on the job name to distribute jobs at different times, as shown here:

```
H * * * *
```

However, there is a better way. Jenkins provides an alias for each of the common frequencies, such as `@hourly`, `@daily`, `@weekly`, and `@monthly`. That means all you need to write is this:

```
@hourly
```

When you tab out of the schedule text area, Jenkins displays when the job would have last run and will next run. This is a convenient way of checking that your expression does what you expect.

Now it is time to add a build step. If you are on Linux/Mac, choose Execute Shell, and if you are on Windows, choose "Execute Windows Batch Command." Either way, enter the following command:

```
echo "hello"
```

Figure 4.16 shows the configuration for this job when run on Mac.

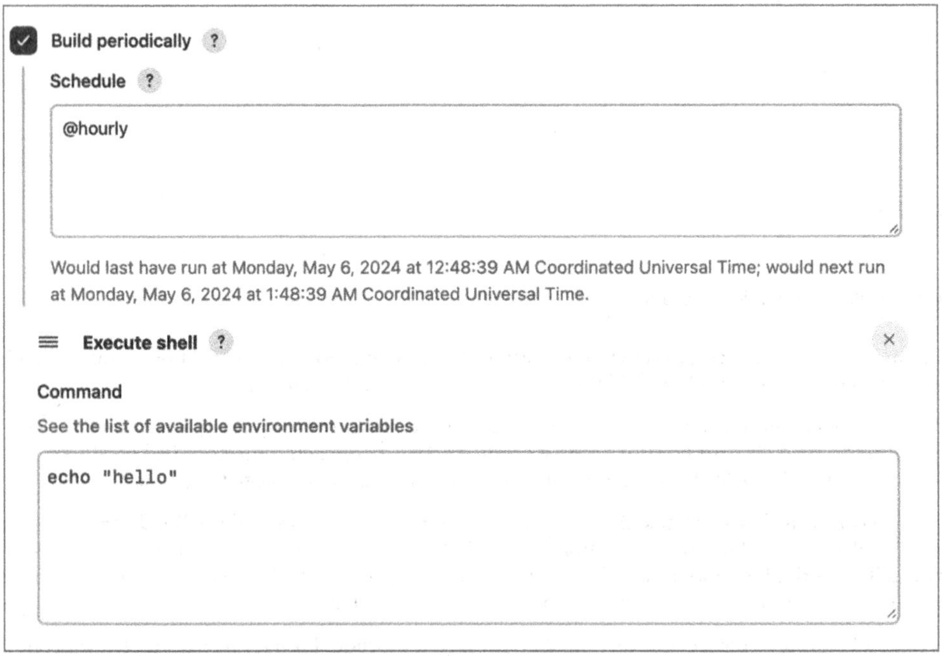

FIGURE 4.16: Freestyle timer job configuration

Now save your configuration. You can wait for the job's hourly run to have it run automatically. Or you can choose Build Now from the left navigation to trigger it to run right away. Figure 4.17 shows the build history after a few runs.

There is a green icon next to each run, since the build was successful. It will be yellow if the build is unstable or red if it failed. Clicking that icon takes you to the console output for your build. On a Mac, it shows the following:

```
Started by user admin
Running as SYSTEM
Building in workspace /var/jenkins_home/workspace/freestyle-timer
[freestyle-timer] $ /bin/sh -xe /tmp/jenkins14515196753987574989.sh
+ echo hello
hello
Finished: SUCCESS
```

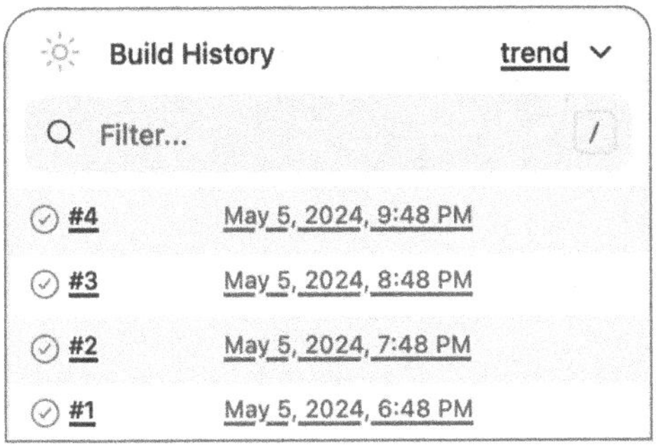

Build History	trend
Filter...	/
#4	May 5, 2024, 9:48 PM
#3	May 5, 2024, 8:48 PM
#2	May 5, 2024, 7:48 PM
#1	May 5, 2024, 6:48 PM

FIGURE 4.17: Jenkins build history

> **TIP** *You might have noticed the times are in Coordinated Universal Time (UTC). You can go to your user profile to change it for yourself. Or you can set the default by passing a parameter to Docker.*
>
> ```
> docker run --name jenkins -p 8080:8080 \
> -e JAVA_OPTS=-Duser.timezone=America/New_York jenkins/jenkins
> ```

Creating a Maven Freestyle Job

Before you create your first Maven job, you need to configure Maven to run on Jenkins. To do that, follow these steps:

1. Click Manage Jenkins in the left navigation.
2. Choose Tools.
3. Click Add Maven in the Maven Installations section.
4. Type a name like **Maven 3.9**.
5. Leave the default options, which will download the latest available Maven 3.9 from the Internet the first time you build with it. Figure 4.18 shows the configuration.
6. Click Save.

Now that Maven is configured, you can create a new freestyle job. The next step is to pull the code from GitHub. Jenkins has a Source Code Management section that provides a radio button for Git. Enter the repository URL for the code you want. For example, this chapter uses `https://github.com/realworldjava/Ch04-CICD`.

Since this repository is available on the Internet, Jenkins will be happy with the URL. If it were a private repository or if you had mistyped the URL, you would get a message like this:

```
Failed to connect to repository : Command "git ls-remote -h -
https://github.com/realworldjava/Ch04-CICD HEAD" returned status code 128:
```

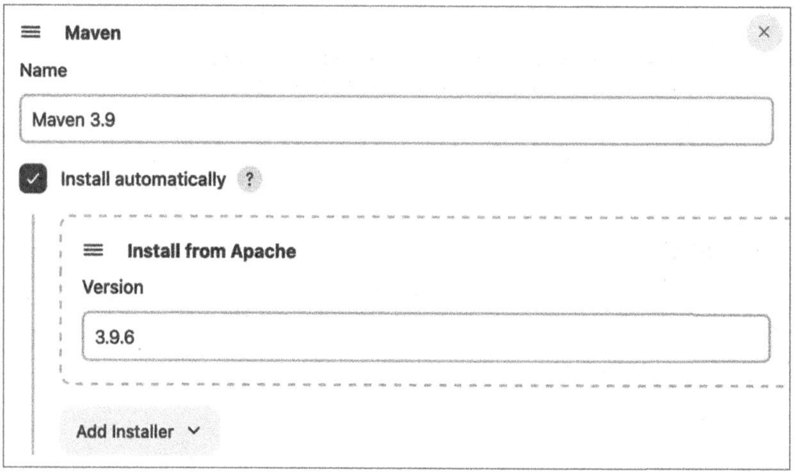

FIGURE 4.18: Maven tool configuration

Repositories in the enterprise will require authentication.

CONFIGURING CREDENTIALS IN JENKINS

In the enterprise, your repository will invariably require credentials. The Jenkins instance will use a token associated with a *service account* (that is, a nonhuman account) so that it will be clear that the activity resulted from an automated system. In this book, we will show you how to use a GitHub personal access token using your account.

GitHub may encourage you to use fine-grained tokens. You can see if their functionality has changed. We used classic tokens because at the time of this writing, only the repository owner can create fine-grained tokens and you are not always the owner of repositories you use.

To generate a token, follow these steps:

1. In GitHub, click your picture at the top right.
2. Click Settings.
3. In the left navigation, choose Developer settings.
4. Click Personal access tokens in the left navigation.
5. Click Tokens (classic) in the left navigation.
6. Click Generate new token in the top right and choose classic again.
7. Type a name for your token to remind you of the purpose. For example, Jenkins.
8. Choose the number of days for expiration. Many enterprises have rules on how long a token can exist before being cycled.
9. Generate the token.

Now that you have a token, you can set it up as a credential in Jenkins:

1. Click Manage Jenkins in the left navigation.
2. Choose Credentials.
3. Click (global) to make the credential available to all of Jenkins.

4. Click Add Credentials.
5. Enter your GitHub id as the user.
6. Enter the token as the password.
7. For the Id choose a descriptive name like GitHub.
8. Click Create.
9. Go to your Freestyle job and choose the credential you entered in the credentials pull-down under the repository URL.

In addition to specifying the repository, you need to specify the branch. The branch specifier field defaults to `*/master`, which is the name old versions of Git used for the default branch before they changed it to `main`. Change it to `*/main` or whatever your main branch name is.

The next step is to tell the freestyle job to run Maven. To do so, create a build step of type Invoke top-level Maven targets. Choose the Maven version you created earlier from the pull-down and type **`clean verify`** for the goals. This repository uses subfolders rather than having the `pom.xml` filename in the root; click Advanced, and enter **`maven/with-dependency/pom.xml`** for the POM. Figure 4.19 shows the configuration for this job.

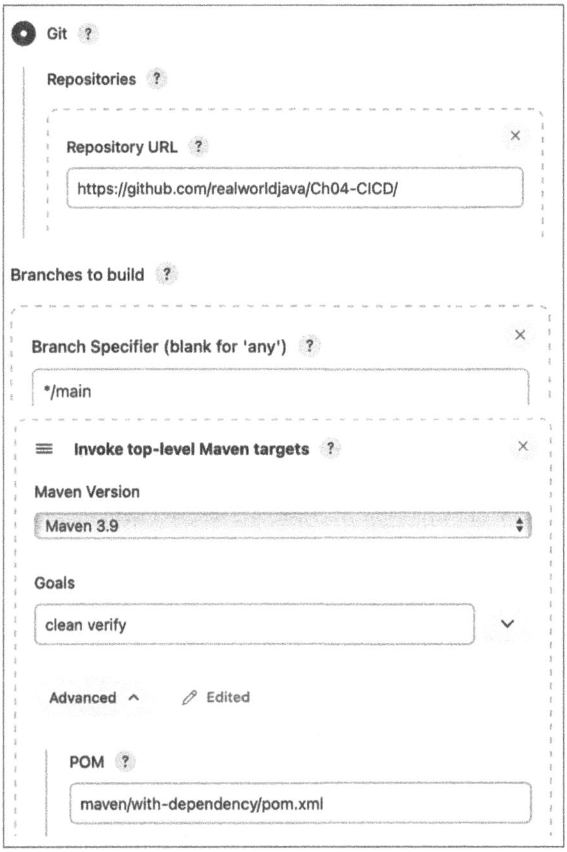

FIGURE 4.19: Maven freestyle job configuration

Creating a Gradle Freestyle Job

Unlike Maven, you don't need to set up a Gradle tool configuration to get started. The Gradle executable is already in your repository from your Gradle project.

Like Maven, you create a freestyle job and set up source code management. Use the same URL and branch as the Maven example. The next step is to tell the freestyle job to run Gradle. You create a build step of type Invoke Gradle script. Choose Gradle Wrapper and set the wrapper location to `gradle/groovy/with-dependency`.

Then enter **`build`** for the task. Finally, click Advanced and enter **`gradle/groovy/with-dependency`** for Root Build Script. Figure 4.20 shows the Gradle part of the configuration for this job.

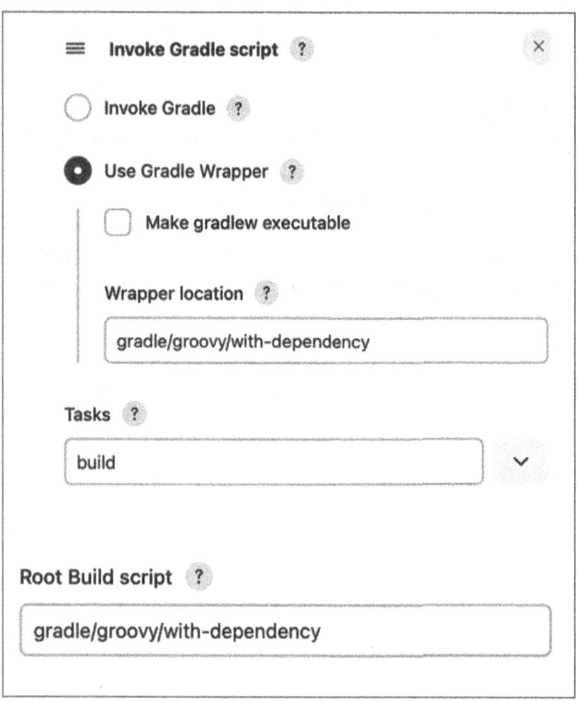

FIGURE 4.20: Gradle freestyle job configuration

Creating a Maven Pipeline

The Pipeline Maven Integration plugin makes it easier to write a pipeline that uses Maven, so install that before creating the pipeline:

1. Click Manage Jenkins in the left navigation.
2. Click Plugins.
3. Click Available Plugins in the left navigation.
4. Type **Pipeline Maven** in the search bar to filter the list of available plugins.
5. Click the checkbox to the left of that plugin name.
6. Click Install.
7. Click the checkbox to the left of Restart Jenkins When Installation Is Complete And No Jobs Are Running.

This will cause Jenkins to restart. Now that you have the plugin, you are ready to create a pipeline. Choose Pipeline instead of Freestyle Project when creating the job.

Pipeline jobs give you the choice of including the pipeline directly in the job configuration or getting it from a repository. For the former, choose Pipeline Script under the Definition label. Then in the text area beneath it, paste your pipeline as shown in Figure 4.21.

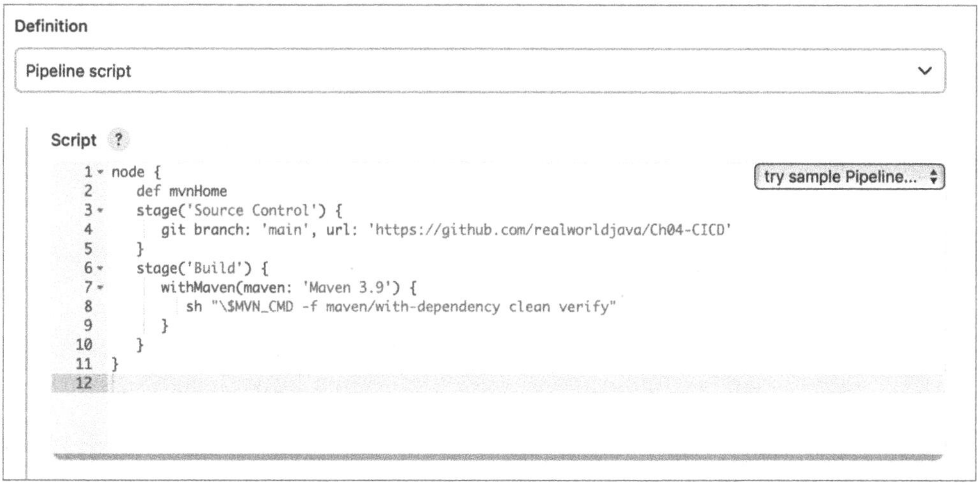

Definition

Pipeline script

Script ?

try sample Pipeline...

```
node {
    def mvnHome
    stage('Source Control') {
        git branch: 'main', url: 'https://github.com/realworldjava/Ch04-CICD'
    }
    stage('Build') {
        withMaven(maven: 'Maven 3.9') {
            sh "\$MVN_CMD -f maven/with-dependency clean verify"
        }
    }
}
```

FIGURE 4.21: Maven pipeline script

```
node {
   stage('Source Control') {
      git branch: 'main', url: 'https://github.com/realworldjava/Ch04-CICD'
   }
   stage('Build') {
      withMaven(maven: 'Maven 3.9') {
         sh "\$MVN_CMD -f maven/with-dependency clean verify"
      }
   }
}
```

This scripted pipeline has two stages, `Source Control` and `Build`. The first pulls the main branch of the repository. The latter uses functionality from `withMaven` to set up a Maven environment. Within that context it calls the Maven command at the operating system shell. If you are running on a Windows machine, use `bat` instead of `sh`.

Alternatively, you can store the pipeline itself in source control by following these steps, as shown in Figure 4.22:

1. Choose Pipeline script from SCM under the Definition label.
2. Choose Git for the SCM.
3. Enter a repository URL, for example, `https://github.com/realworldjava/Ch04-CICD`.
4. Change Branch Specifier to `*/main`.
5. Change Script Path to `maven/using-jenkinsfile/Jenkinsfile`.

WRITING PIPELINE CODE

When you open any pipeline job in Jenkins, there is a Pipeline Syntax link on the left navigation. This takes you to a wizard for generating code for both scripted and declarative pipelines. Fill in configuration values, and Jenkins will give you corresponding code. While this doesn't write your entire pipeline for you, it is an excellent starting point.

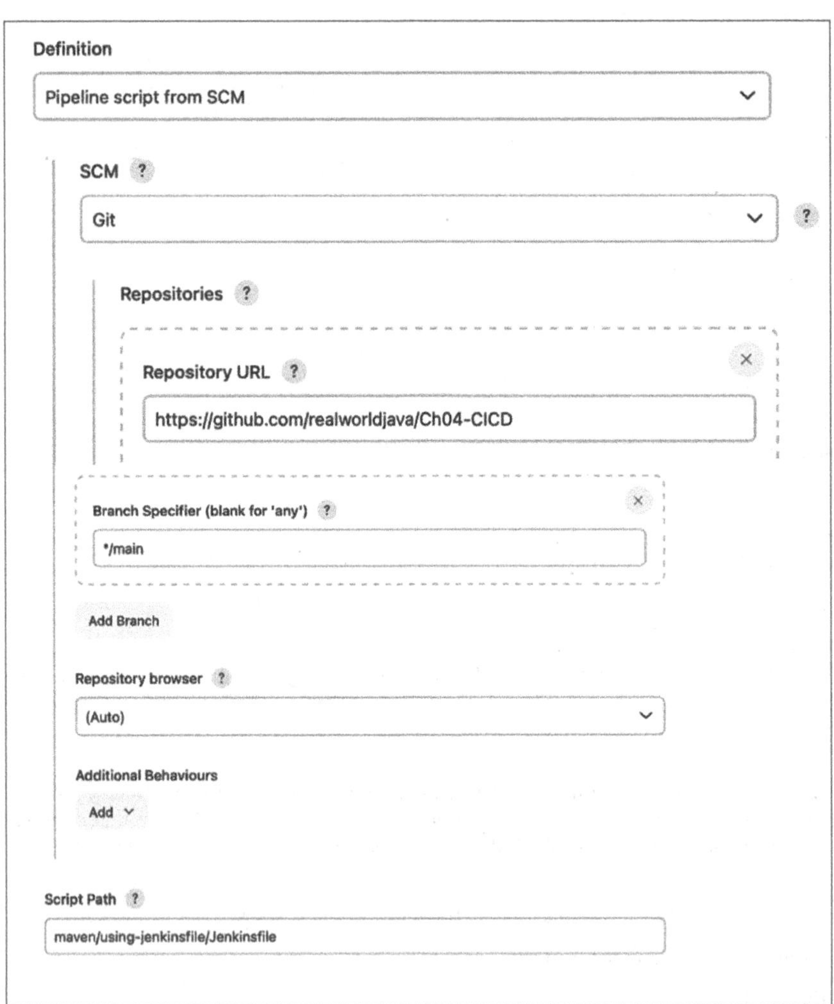

FIGURE 4.22: Maven pipeline from SCM

Creating a Gradle Pipeline

For Gradle, we are using the declarative pipeline syntax. The configuration in the job is the same as for Maven. The code in the text area is different, of course, since it uses Gradle syntax.

```
pipeline {
   agent any

   stages {
      stage('Source Control') {
         steps {
           git branch: 'main',
              url: 'https://github.com/realworldjava/Ch04-CICD'
         }
      }
      stage('Build') {
         steps {
           sh "gradle/groovy/with-dependency/gradlew "
              + "-p gradle/groovy/with-dependency build"
         }
      }
   }
}
```

This time, the `root` is `pipeline` instead of `node`. The `pipeline` keyword indicates that the code can be run on any agent. In this case, we have only one agent. There are also more levels, for example, the `steps` level. The ideas are the same across pipeline formats, and either pipeline format is fine to use. Just like the Gradle freestyle job, the `gradlew` from the repository is used to run the build.

> **TIP** *Pipelines have many advanced features including the ability to run steps in parallel, controlling when to fail the build, or even adding pauses.*

Learning About Common Plugins

Jenkins has a large selection of downloadable plugins. Some are specific to the task at hand such as the AWS plugins. Many are useful regardless of what you are building.

Jenkins has a plugin index at `https://plugins.jenkins.io` with more than 1,900 community plugins! The documentation pages for different plugins vary extensively in what they provide.

Searching for "Dark Theme" gives you an example of a popular plugin. The documentation page gives information on how to configure it and screenshots of what Jenkins looks like with the plugin. It also notes that 19.2% of controllers are using it. While this is an approximation since private enterprise installations aren't included, it suggests that many people find the plugin valuable. Useful plugins include the following:

- **Blue Ocean:** Offers features that make it easier to use pipelines, including a tabular UI for viewing results and durations of each stage
- **Build Failure Analyzer:** Highlights common reasons that you configure for build failures to make it easier to see the cause
- **Claim:** Offers users the ability to indicate they are working on fixing a failing job
- **Dashboard View:** Customizable views including summarization information
- **Javadoc:** Adds an option to publish Javadoc
- **Jira:** Includes links to Jira and options for generating release notes
- **Role-Based Authorization Strategy:** Provides the capability to define Jenkins roles and entitlements for users

Understanding Other Jenkins Capabilities

As you work with Jenkins, you'll find that there is a lot to explore. In this section, you'll get a brief overview of the types of things Jenkins can do.

Organizing Jobs

When you choose New Item, you aren't limited to jobs. You can also create a folder. Folders on Jenkins work like those on your computer. You can nest folders inside other folders to help keep your jobs organized.

You can also create *views* as an alternate way of looking at your jobs. Click the plus (+) above your jobs list to create a new view. By default, a configurable *list view* is available. You can manually select the jobs that go in a view, or you can provide a regular expression to specify a pattern. Chapter 10, "Pattern Matching with Regular Expressions," will cover how to use regular expressions in general. A list view also lets you control which columns appear. Views can also traverse into folders.

The Dashboard View plugin provides a much more powerful view type. It lets you select portlets to anchor to the top, bottom, left, and right of the Jenkins screen. You can have as many portlets in each area as you like, making for good layout control. The portlets include many statistics such as builds, jobs, and tests. You can even make your dashboard a full-screen view hiding the built-in Jenkins navigation.

Notifying Users

A failing job won't get fixed if nobody knows about it! By default, Jenkins provides email notifications on build failures. You can provide one or more email addresses and specify whether you want an email on every build that doesn't pass or just the first one. Additionally, you can include whoever made the commit that broke the build.

The editable email notification provides much more control. You can specify fields for email, subject, and content-template. You also have the option to attach the build log file. One of the powerful features of this plugin is that it provides you with fine-grained control over when emails are sent. You can choose any combination of success and failures, even sending different people the notifications for different cases.

Besides email notifications, Jenkins supports many other notification types via plugins. For example, the SMS plugin can send a text message when there is a failure. The Notify-Events plugin supports Skype, Telegram, voice call, and more. There are specialized notifiers for Slack or Amazon SNS topics.

If these active/push notifiers don't meet your needs, you can use a passive/pull approach. Jenkins supports RSS via the `/rssAll`, `/rssFailed`, and `/rssLatest` feeds.

Whichever notifier you choose, make sure it is one that will get someone's attention. After all, fixing a build is a high priority, and that won't happen unless someone knows that it is broken!

Reading Changes

Each Jenkins job has a Changes link in the left navigation. This tells you what has changed in the repository since your last build. Here's an example:

```
#8 (May 7, 2024, 9:36:22 PM)

add jenkinsfile – jeanne / githubweb
```

This message tells you that build 8 of this job was run on May 7. It provides the commit comment, the user ID, and a link to the Git commit where you can see the details. This feature is useful when your build fails so you can see exactly what changed.

SCANNING WITH SONAR

Jenkins is the hub of your CI/CD build, but a number of other tools will commonly integrate with it. The checkout/source control, build/compile, and unit test stages occur completely on Jenkins. In contrast, Jenkins performs quality checks, which often uses SonarQube, as described next. Other tools are used to check dependencies.

Let's look at SonarQube in more detail. SonarQube is made by a vendor called SonarSource. There is a commercial version and a free open-source version. It is a static analysis tool, which means SonarQube identifies problems in your code without running it. Additionally, a SonarQube static analysis scan becomes a step in your freestyle job.

SonarQube has many rules that come with the product for practically every programming language you can imagine. Even tools for verifying XML and JSON (see the appendix) are included! These rules check for all sorts of problems including common bugs, performance issues, and security problems.

SonarQube also allows you to configure a quality gate. If high-priority rules pass or tests fail, the quality gate will fail. You can also set up conditions on code coverage percentages and more. If you view the SonarQube reports generated during your Jenkins builds, you will find that your project code has improved substantially.

SonarQube performs static analysis and doesn't run your code. Nonetheless, it does ingest JUnit tests and code coverage reports from your Jenkins build, which allows SonarQube to have an excellent report showing code quality and code coverage.

> **TIP** *SonarLint is the IDE version of Sonar, so you can discover problems before even committing your code to version control.*

EXPLAINING CI/CD PRACTICES

Jenkins is a CI/CD tool, so you need to be aware of a number of CI/CD practices to use it effectively.

- **Version control:** Everyone on your team must be committing to the same repository and should commit regularly.
- **Automated build:** The build must be fully automated and reproducible. It is not sufficient to just work on one developer's machine.
- **Triggering:** Each commit must trigger a build and run the automated tests to quickly discover failures.
- **Fixing broken builds is the highest priority:** Broken builds must be fixed before committing more changes.
- **Incremental changes:** Make small changes and commit often.
- **Keep the CI build running fast:** The build should operate as fast as possible. Slower steps like Sonar can run in a pipeline that doesn't happen on every commit. For example, it might run overnight.
- **Visibility:** Everyone on the team and all the interested stakeholders must be able to see the status of the build.
- **Automated testing:** The tests must always pass to provide assurance the code is ready for deployment.
- **Automated deployment:** Deploying cannot require manual intervention.

FURTHER REFERENCES

Continuous Delivery: Reliable Software Releases through Build, Test, and Deployment Automation (Addison-Wesley, 2020)

- `https://maven.apache.org/guides/index.html`

  Maven documentation
- `https://maven.apache.org/download.cgi`

  Download Maven for use outside the IDE
- `https://maven.apache.org/ref/3.9.6/maven-model-builder/super-pom.html`

  Maven super POM
- `https:docs.gradle.org/current/userguide/userguide.html`

  Gradle documentation
- `https://docs.gradle.org/current/userguide/java_plugin.html`

  Gradle Java plugin
- `https://gradle.org/install`

  Download Gradle for use outside the IDE
- `https://docs.docker.com/engine/install`

  Download Docker
- `https://www.jenkins.io/download`

  Download Jenkins
- `https://www.jenkins.io/doc/book/pipeline`

  Jenkins Pipeline documentation
- `https://plugins.jenkins.io`

  Jenkins Plugins
- `https://www.sonarsource.com`

  SonarQube

SUMMARY

In this chapter, you learned about CI/CD. Key concepts included the following:

- Building with a Maven `pom.xml`
- Building with a Gradle `build.gradle` in Groovy
- Building with a Gradle `build.gradle.kts` in Kotlin
- Creating Jenkins freestyle and pipeline jobs
- The purpose of SonarQube, a static analysis tool
- Key CI/CD principles

5

Capturing Application State with Logging Frameworks

WHAT'S IN THIS CHAPTER?

- Needing to Move Beyond Print
- Using Java Util Logging
- Using Log4j
- Using SLF4J
- Using Logback
- Learning More About Logging
- Comparing Logging Frameworks

When you first started programming in Java, you probably used `System.out.println` to output information for use in troubleshooting why your code didn't work as expected. For example:

```
public void run(int count) {
   System.out.println("count=" + count);

   // run logic here
}
```

As you mature in your Java career, it becomes time to replace those `System.out.println` calls with a logging framework. In this chapter, you'll learn the benefits of logging frameworks, learn how to use the most common ones, and compare logging frameworks to choose the best one for you. Since many of the concepts are the same across logging frameworks, please read the "Using Java Util Logging" section first even if you intend to use a different logging framework in your work. Also, there are a lot of features in every logging framework. This chapter covers the most common ones, but do check the documentation if you have a more specialized need. For example, all the logging frameworks allow you to set the log configuration through Java code instead of via the more commonly used external file approach.

You may see people refer to "logging libraries" instead of "logging frameworks." This chapter uses the term *framework*, but we mean the same thing.

CODE DOWNLOADS FOR THIS CHAPTER

The source code for this chapter is available on the book page at `www.wiley.com`. Click the Downloads link. The code can also be found at `https://github.com/realworldjava/Ch05-Logging`. See the `README.md` file in that repository for details.

NEEDING TO MOVE BEYOND PRINT

There are a number of reasons that you should choose to use a logging framework instead of `println` method calls. One reason is you are able to control how much is logged. While you may want to output the value of `count` when troubleshooting, it would only clutter the logs once your application has many users! A logging framework lets you leave these logging statements in the code but allows you to specify a logging level, which only prints the messages you actually want to log in each environment.

Another reason to use a logging framework is to facilitate where the output goes. `System.out` and `System.err` get all mixed up in the console. If you use a logging framework, you can separate out your logging output, making it easier to understand. Further, you increase security because sometimes the people who operate the system will have access to `System.out` and are not the same people you want to have access to your most private log messages.

Additionally, you might need two sets of logs: troubleshooting logs and audit logs. Audit logs are used for seeing who did or accessed what and when they did it. This level of control is provided by the major logging frameworks.

Logging frameworks can make your application faster, by storing messages for asynchronous logging, rather than holding up your application waiting for the slow I/O output operation to happen in real time. Finally, log frameworks can take care of rotating log files so you have the latest ones available and not an ever increasing use of disk space.

USING JAVA UTIL LOGGING

Java Util Logging is built right into Java; there is no need for Maven or Gradle to pull in a dependency. In fact, Java Util Logging has been included since Java 1.4! The following shows a simple example of logging:

```
1:  package com.wiley.realworldjava.logging.jul;
2:  import java.util.logging.Logger;
3:
4:  public class BasicLogging {
5:     private static final Logger LOGGER =
6:        Logger.getLogger(BasicLogging.class.getName());
7:
8:     public static void main(String[] args) {
9:        LOGGER.severe("Something bad happened!");
10:    }
11: }
```

Lines 5 and 6 create the `Logger`. The `Logger.getLogger()` call is a factory. This design pattern is used to give more control to the API than it would have if you simply called a constructor.

In line 6, we could have called the equivalent:

```
Logger.getLogger("com.wiley.realworldjava.logging.jul.BasicLogging");
```

But that runs the risk of getting out-of-date if you refactor and change the class name. The better approach is to use `class.getName()`, which causes the logger name to automatically be renamed if the class gets renamed.

Line 9 is the logging statement. Java Util Logging, severe() tells the logger to use the highest priority level of logging. Running this code outputs something like this:

```
Feb 11, 2024 9:16:22 PM com.wiley.realworldjava.logging.jul.BasicLogging main
SEVERE: Something bad happened!
```

By default, this output contains the following information from where the logging occurred:

- Date and time
- Fully qualified class name
- Method name
- Logging level (SEVERE)
- Log message

LOGGER NAMES

While it is common to use the package/class name for a logger, you can choose any logger name. To do this, you can write the following:

```
private static final Logger LOGGER = Logger.getLogger(
   "CustomLogger");
```

Your choice of logger name does not impact what gets logged unless you specifically choose to include the logger name.

In the following sections, you'll see more details about using Java Util Logging.

Comparing Logging Levels

It is important to understand the concept of logging levels. The logging level can be set for your program as an environment variable or launch property. Suppose the program is set to use the WARNING logging level. (In the next section, you'll learn how to set the logging level.) Let's look at the output of the following three log statements:

```
private static final Logger LOGGER =
   Logger.getLogger(BasicConfig.class.getName());

public static void main(String[] args) {
   LOGGER.severe("this is bad");
   LOGGER.warning("be careful");
   LOGGER.info("just to let you know");
}
```

The output consists of just two log messages! What happened?

```
Feb 11, 2024 9:25:48 PM com.wiley.realworldjava.logging.jul.BasicConfig main
SEVERE: this is bad
Feb 11, 2024 9:25:48 PM com.wiley.realworldjava.logging.jul.BasicConfig main
WARNING: be careful
```

Notice how the severe() and warning() calls were logged, but the info() call was not. Java Util Logging only logs requests to the target logging level or higher.

Java Util Logging has seven logging levels along with two special options. Table 5.1 shows the logging levels and their intended purpose.

TABLE 5.1: Java Util Logging Levels

LOG LEVEL	INTENDED USE
`SEVERE`	Only log serious failures.
`WARNING`	Log potential problems or higher levels.
`INFO`	Log informational messages or higher levels.
`CONFIG`	Log configuration messages or higher levels.
`FINE`	Log tracing messages or higher levels.
`FINER`	Log more detailed tracing messages or higher levels.
`FINEST`	Log the most detailed tracing messages or higher levels.
`ALL`	Special option to log all messages.
`OFF`	Special option to specify no logging.

Suppose the logging level is set to INFO. Calls to `severe()`, `warning()`, and `info()` will be logged. To make sure you fully understand this, see Table 5.2.

TABLE 5.2: Method Calls for Logging

LOGGING LEVEL	`SEVERE()`	`WARNING()`	`INFO()`	`FINE()`	`FINER()`	`FINEST()`
`SEVERE`	Yes	Yes	Yes	Yes	Yes	Yes
`WARNING`	No	Yes	Yes	Yes	Yes	Yes
`INFO`	No	No	Yes	Yes	Yes	Yes
`FINE`	No	No	No	Yes	Yes	Yes
`FINER`	No	No	No	No	Yes	Yes
`FINEST`	No	No	No	No	No	Yes
`ALL`	Yes	Yes	Yes	Yes	Yes	Yes
`OFF`	No	No	No	No	No	No

Formatting Values

Often, you want to log variable values and not just static messages. The built-in `String.format` method formats values for Java Util Logging. For example:

```
LOGGER.severe(String.format("%s: %.1f is %d/%d", "Division", 1.5, 3, 2));
```

The message part of this output is as follows:

```
SEVERE: Division: 1.5 is 3/2
```

This example uses the most common formatter specifiers: `%s` (`String`), `%f` (floating-point number), and `%d` (integer number). These placeholder specifiers are replaced by the values that follow. They also show how to specify the number of digits you want after the decimal point for the floating-point number. This code doesn't call the `Formatter` class explicitly, but it is called under the covers by `String.format`. There are many other specifiers besides the ones mentioned earlier, refer to the Javadoc `Formatter` class.

Passing Basic Configuration

Java Util Logging comes with a default configuration so you can start logging without having to supply any external configuration at all. But you'll quickly want to customize this with your own.

The default configuration file is in your Java home directory in the `conf` folder in a file named `logging.properties`. For example, on Windows, this could be as follows:

```
c:\Program Files\Java\jdk21\conf\logging.properties
```

On Mac, the structure is deeper and looks like this:

```
/Library/Java/JavaVirtualMachines/jdk-21.jdk/Contents/
   Home/conf/logging.properties
```

Since this file is in the `Java` directory, you shouldn't change its contents. It is much better to specify a custom location for your logging properties. For example, `src/main/resources` in your project is a commonly used location, since that file is stored in version control along with your project. This location also causes the file to be automatically placed in the same location as the compiled source files by Maven or Gradle. Therefore, it is available as a classpath resource at runtime, so you don't have to do any extra work to access it.

First, set up a basic logging configuration file. This one shows the `WARNING` level used for Table 5.2:

```
.level= WARNING
handlers= java.util.logging.ConsoleHandler
```

To get Java to use this file, you set the `java.util.logging.config.file` system property. One way to do this is at the command line.

```
java -Djava.util.logging.config.file=src/main/resources/
   logging-warning.properties src/main/java/com/wiley/realworldjava/
   logging/jul/BasicConfigCommandLine.java
```

To learn how to set a system property using those tools, see Chapter 2, "Getting to Know Your IDE: The Secret to Success"; Chapter 4, "Automating Your CI/CD Builds with Maven, Gradle, and Jenkins"; and Chapter 6, "Getting to Know the Spring Framework."

> **NOTE** *In your applications, you are likely to set the system property as a launch parameter in whatever system is running your application. See Chapter 14, "Getting to Know More of the Ecosystem," for examples of such environments.*

Another way to set the system property is in code. This is not a common approach in real code. This approach is not normally recommended because it requires a recompile to change the location. However, the repository for this chapter uses this approach to facilitate using a variety of property files.

Since the property must be set before the `Logger` is instantiated, it is done in a `static` block.

```
import java.util.logging.Logger;

public class BasicConfig {

   static { System.setProperty("java.util.logging.config.file",
      "src/main/resources/logging-warning.properties"); };
   private static final Logger LOGGER =
      Logger.getLogger(BasicConfig.class.getName());

   public static void main(String[] args) {
      LOGGER.severe("this is bad");
      LOGGER.warning("be careful");
      LOGGER.info("just to let you know");
   }
}
```

Setting Logging Destinations

So far, the examples have used the `ConsoleHandler`. The following are the most common handlers:

- `ConsoleHandler`: Writes to `System.err`
- `FileHandler`: Writes to a file, optionally rotating them
- `SocketHandler`: Writes to a remote computer's port

> **NOTE** *Multiple handlers can be used by separating their types with commas:*
>
> ```
> handlers=java.util.logging.ConsoleHandler,
>   java.util.logging.FileHandler
> ```

The following configuration shows how to use the basic features of a `FileHandler`:

```
1: .level= WARNING
2: handlers=java.util.logging.FileHandler
3:
4: java.util.logging.FileHandler.pattern = java-log-%u.log
5: java.util.logging.FileHandler.limit = 100
6: java.util.logging.FileHandler.count = 2
```

Line 4 specifies the location for the log files to go. In this example, they are in the root directory of the code. In a real application, an absolute path is most common. The `%u` indicates to use a unique number. Each file gets a number to avoid naming conflicts.

Line 5 says how many bytes should be in each file. It is common for this to be a much larger number, like 100,000, but we used a smaller number for the purposes of our demonstration. Once this number is exceeded, a new file will automatically start. If you omit the `FileHandler.limit` property, there will be no upper bound to the file, potentially resulting in an unmanageably large file.

Line 6 specifies a maximum of two log files. Running this against a program that generates a lot of data creates two files:

```
java-log-0.log0
java-log-0.log1
```

The rest of the data is gone. That's what *log rotation* is; the older data gets rotated out and replaced by the latest data. Beware, if you leave out line 6, Java Util Logging will keep generating files potentially using up all the space on your disk! Typically you would keep a week's or month's worth of logs or so on disk, but that varies greatly depending on your team and your application.

Each file contains something like the following. This is a format called eXtensible Markup Language (XML). For more details about XML, see Appendix, "Reading and Writing XML, JSON, and YAML." Each handler has a default format. `ConsoleHandler` uses a text format. `FileHandler` uses XML.

```
<?xml version="1.0" encoding="UTF-8" standalone="no"?>
<!DOCTYPE log SYSTEM "logger.dtd">
<log>
<record>
   <date>2024-02-14T00:07:43.388849Z</date>
   <millis>1707869263388</millis>
   <nanos>849000</nanos>
   <sequence>999</sequence>
   <logger>com.wiley.realworldjava.logging.jul.FileRotationLogging</logger>
   <level>SEVERE</level>
   <class>java.util.stream.ForEachOps$ForEachOp$OfRef</class>
   <method>accept</method>
   <thread>1</thread>
   <message>Logging data: 0.707243274304531</message>
</record>
</log>
```

You can change the format from the default through configuration. The following example shows how to specify a custom format. Don't worry if the format seems complicated; you will want to keep the reference documentation open while you are configuring these things.

```
.level= WARNING
handlers=java.util.logging.FileHandler

java.util.logging.FileHandler.pattern = java-log.log
java.util.logging.FileHandler.limit = 100000

java.util.logging.FileHandler.formatter = java.util.logging.SimpleFormatter
java.util.logging.SimpleFormatter.format=DATE=%1$tc, MESSAGE=%5$s%n
```

This logs a single file up to 100 MB with lines like this:

```
DATE=Tue Feb 13 19:34:27 EST 2024, MESSAGE=Logging message
```

Some of the format is raw text like `DATE=` and `MESSAGE=`. The `%1` inserts the date, and `%5` inserts the message. The rest (for example, `$s%n`) are formatting characters.

The Javadoc for the `SimpleFormatter` class provides further detail.

Logging Lazily

So far, the output has been a simple `String`. Sometimes what you want to log is expensive to construct, and you want to avoid constructing it unless it will actually be logged. In such cases, you can use a lambda so that the message will be only constructed when the logging level is met:

```
public static void main(String[] args) {
   LOGGER.fine(() -> generateMessage());
}

private static String generateMessage() {
   return "This is an expensive message";
}
```

Inheriting Loggers

Up until now, the examples have used `.level` to specify the logging level. The `.` (dot) means the root logger. You can specify different levels of loggers, as in the following example. The logging level will apply to the specified logger and any children. If there are overlapping specifications, the most specific one will apply.

Suppose we have the following configuration, which sets three rules for logging levels:

```
.level= INFO
com.wiley.realworldjava.logging.jul.level= SEVERE
com.wiley.realworldjava.logging.jul.child.level= WARNING
handlers=java.util.logging.ConsoleHandler
```

Java Util Logging builds a logging hierarchy that looks like Figure 5.1. Therefore, the logger `com.wiley` inherits from the logger `com`. This is used to determine what logging configuration to use for a given logger.

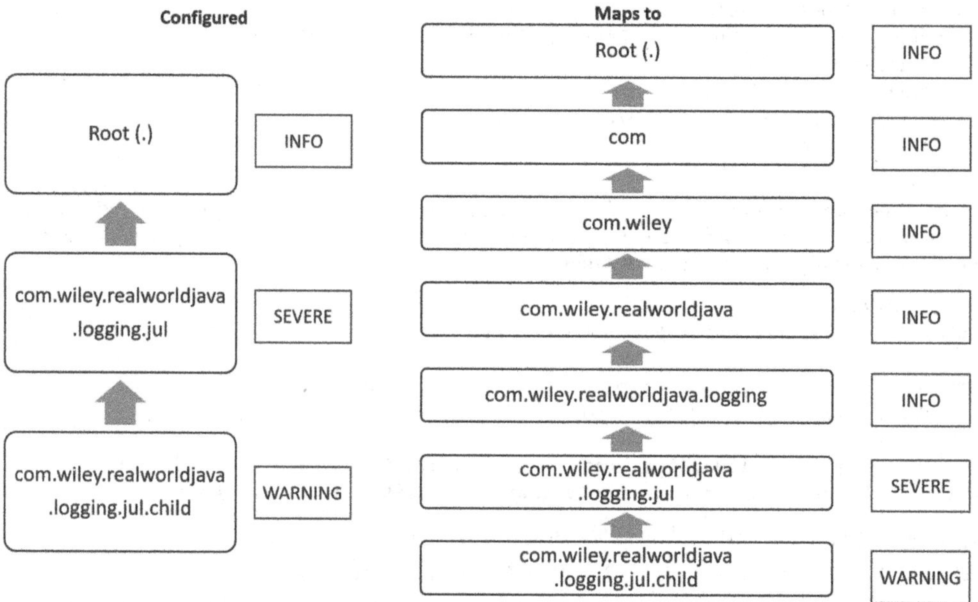

FIGURE 5.1: Logging hierarchy

The following example creates a logger that we appropriately named `com.wiley.realworldjava.logging .jul.MultipleLevelsLogging`:

```
package com.wiley.realworldjava.logging.jul;

import java.util.logging.Logger;
import com.wiley.realworldjava.logging.jul.child.ChildLogging;

public class MultipleLevelsLogging {

   private static final Logger LOGGER =
     Logger.getLogger(MultipleLevelsLogging.class.getName());
```

```
    public static void main(String[] args) {
        LOGGER.severe("Parent logging");
        LOGGER.warning("Parent logging");

        log();
    }
}
```

Java Util Logging looks for the most specific logger it can. In this case, it is the `com.wiley.realworldjava.logging.jul` logger, so `SEVERE` is used and `Parent logging` gets logged only once for `MultipleLevelsLogging`. By contrast, the following class uses the `com.wiley.realworldjava.logging.jul.child` logger, which we configured earlier to log at the `WARNING` level and which therefore causes `Child logging` to get printed twice, one for `SEVERE` and one for `WARNING`:

```
package com.wiley.realworldjava.logging.jul.child;

import java.util.logging.Logger;

public class ChildLogging {

    private static final Logger LOGGER = Logger
        .getLogger(ChildLogging.class.getName());

    public static void log() {
        LOGGER.severe("Child logging");
        LOGGER.warning("Child logging");
    }
}
```

The root logger is used when there are no other matching loggers. If we had a logger created with the name `com.wiley`, it would use the root logger at level `INFO`.

You can use inheritance with names for the logger that don't reflect the packages and classes for your application as well. In the following example, you can see three levels of loggers: the root logger, `custom`, and `custom.child`:

```
.level= INFO
custom.level= SEVERE
custom.child.level= WARNING
handlers=java.util.logging.ConsoleHandler
```

This time the loggers are created with the names of the logger (`custom` and `custom.child`) rather than the package and class name. The parent/child relationship still exists. In fact, both loggers are used in the same class!

```
public class MultipleLevelsLoggingWithManualHierarchy {
    public static void main(String[] args) {
        Logger parentLogger = Logger.getLogger("custom");
        Logger childLogger = Logger.getLogger("custom.child");

        parentLogger.severe("Parent logging");
        parentLogger.warning("Parent logging");
        childLogger.severe("Child logging");
        childLogger.warning("Child logging");
    }
}
```

All the logging frameworks have inheritance that works this way, so the section only appears in reference to Java Util Logging since it is covered first in the chapter.

USING LOG4J

Log4j is one of the oldest Java logging frameworks, even predating Java Util Logging. It has received many updates over the years and is in widespread use.

> **NOTE** *Log4j 2 was created as a replacement to Log4j 1 more than a decade ago. All references to Log4j in this chapter are to Log4j 2. If you are looking at code, you can tell you are on Log4j 2 if the import starts with* `org.apache.logging` *rather than Log4j 1's* `org.apache.log4j`.

You might have read about Log4j in the news. On December 9, 2021, a major security vulnerability known as Log4Shell was announced, which allowed bad actors to run arbitrary code in applications. Yikes! You don't have to worry about this as long as you are using a version of Log4j 2.17.2 or higher.

To use Log4j in your Maven or Gradle build, go to Maven Central `https://mvnrepository.com/artifact/org.apache.logging.log4j/log4j-core` and find the latest version number for your build tool. Table 5.3 shows what this looks like for each configuration at the time of this writing. Notice that you need both the API and Core dependencies. The API is the interface, and core is the implementation.

TABLE 5.3: Specifying Log4j as a Dependency

TOOL	SYNTAX

Maven	`<dependency>`
	`<groupId>org.apache.logging.log4j</groupId>`
	`<artifactId>log4j-api</artifactId>`
	`<version>2.22.1</version>`
	`</dependency>`
	`<dependency>`
	`<groupId>org.apache.logging.log4j</groupId>`
	`<artifactId>log4j-core</artifactId>`
	`<version>2.22.1</version>`
	`</dependency>`

Gradle (Groovy)	`implementation group: 'org.apache.logging.log4j',`
	`name: 'log4j-api, version: '2.22.1'`
	`implementation group: 'org.apache.logging.log4j',`
	`name: 'log4j-core', version: '2.22.1'`

Gradle (Kotlin)	`implementation("org.apache.logging.log4j:log4j-api:2.22.1")` `implementation("org.apache.logging.log4j:log4j-core:2.22.1")`

> **NOTE** `log4j-core` *pulls another library,* `log4j-api`*, as a transitive dependency. It is good practice to specify both since you'll be calling code from the API JAR directly.*

Grab the appropriate syntax for your build tool and include that in your dependencies. The following is a simple program that uses Log4j:

```
import org.apache.logging.log4j.LogManager;
import org.apache.logging.log4j.Logger;
```

```
public class BasicLogging {

   private static final Logger LOGGER = LogManager.getLogger();

   public static void main(String[] args) {
      LOGGER.fatal("this is bad");
   }
}
```

This example outputs the following:

```
21:18:55.826 [main] FATAL com.wiley.realworldjava.logging.log4j
   .BasicLogging - this is bad
```

Besides the package name difference, there are some other key differences between Java Util Logging and Log4j. First, the Log4j way of getting a logger is by calling the default `LogManager.getLogger()` method. Finally, Log4j uses the name `FATAL`, instead of `ERROR`, for the highest logging level.

Additionally, you might have noticed the default output is one line per message. (It shows on two lines in the previous example due to line length limits in a book.) This single line contains the following information from where the log call was made:

- Time
- Method name
- Logging level
- Fully qualified class name
- Log message

Finally, `LogManager.getLogger()` has three overloaded versions. The one without parameters derives a logger with the package/class name from the calling code. The other two take a specific name or the class reference itself. These three calls are all equivalent:

```
LogManager.getLogger();
LogManager.getLogger(GetLoggerEquivalents.class);
LogManager.getLogger(GetLoggerEquivalents.class.getName());
```

The first one is preferable because there is less code and you don't have to worry about copy/pasting it into a different class where you would have to remember to change the name of the logger!

In the following sections, you'll see more details about using Log4j.

Comparing Logging Levels

Log4j has six logging levels along with two special options. Table 5.4 shows the logging levels and their intended purpose. While the number of levels and names are different than Java Util Logging, you can see the ideas are the same. At the end of the chapter, there is a table so you can easily compare logging levels across logging frameworks. Note that log levels are case insensitive and are uppercase in this chapter for clarity.

TABLE 5.4: Log4j Logging Levels

LOG LEVEL	INTENDED USE
FATAL	Log problems that prevent the program from continuing.
ERROR	Log errors that might be recoverable.
WARN	Log events that might turn into errors.
INFO	Log informational events.
DEBUG	Log debugging information.
TRACE	Log fine-grained messages, typically showing the application flow.
ALL	Special option to log all events.
OFF	Special option to specify no logging.

Formatting Values

You have two options for formatting values in Log4j. The syntax varies depending on whether you obtain the logger by calling `getLogger()` or the alternative form `getFormattingLogger()`. Contrast the two versions in this example:

```
import org.apache.logging.log4j.LogManager;
import org.apache.logging.log4j.Logger;

public class LoggingWithParameters {

   private static final Logger LOGGER = LogManager.getLogger();
   private static final Logger FORMATTER_LOGGER =
      LogManager.getFormatterLogger();

   public static void main(String[] args) {
      LOGGER.fatal("{}: {} is {}/{}", "Division", 1.5, 3, 2);
      FORMATTER_LOGGER.fatal("%s: %.1f is %d/%d", "Division", 1.5, 3, 2);
   }
}
```

The message part of both of these log statements is as follows:

```
Division: 1.5 is 3/2
```

In the first version, you use {} as the placeholder for each value you want to include in the output. Log4j figures out the type automatically and uses a logical format. Notice how `1.5` is printed without having to specify how many digits you want after the decimal point. Log4j provides helpful logical defaults.

The second version uses a *formatter* logger, which uses the same syntax as `String.format`. It's more work to construct but gives a greater amount of control for the format.

In general, you should use `getLogger()` unless you require more granular formatting needs. If you find that `getLogger()` is useful most of the time and only need that fine-grained control on rare occasions, you can use `Logger.printf()` to use the formatted value syntax for just those calls, as shown here:

```
import org.apache.logging.log4j.Level;
import org.apache.logging.log4j.LogManager;
import org.apache.logging.log4j.Logger;
```

```
public class LoggingWithPrintf {

    private static final Logger LOGGER = LogManager.getLogger();

    public static void main(String[] args) {
        LOGGER.printf(Level.FATAL, "%s: %.1f is %d/%d", "Division", 1.5, 3, 2);
    }
}
```

The `printf()` method stands for "print formatted," the well-known construct borrowed from the C programming language. By calling `printf()` on your logger, you can pass formatting symbols without having to create a formatter logger first. The downside is that you have to specify the logging level as a parameter instead of calling a level-related method name like `fatal()`. Therefore, we recommend that you only use it when little or none of your logging needs formatting. Otherwise, the formatted logger will make your code more concise.

Passing Basic Configuration

Log4j recognizes various configuration file formats. If more than one is found, Log4j specifies a lookup order for which file it will use. First it looks for the system property `log4j.configurationFile`. For the purpose of this chapter, we use the system property approach for simplicity. In real applications, file configuration is more common.

If the `log4j.configurationFile` is not set, Log4j searches the classpath for the first configuration file it finds in the order specified in this list:

- `log4j2-test.properties`
- `log4j2-test.yaml`
- `log4j2-test.yml`
- `log4j2-test.json`
- `log4j2-test.jsn`
- `log4j2-test.xml`
- `log4j2.properties`
- `log4j2.yaml`
- `log4j2.yml`
- `log4j2.json`
- `log4j2.jsn`
- `log4j2.xml`

The configuration file approach is most common because having the file on your classpath (typically in `src/main/resources`) is sufficient.

The next section describes the difference in formats. Note that each of the format files listed have versions with and without "test" in the name. The "test" versions will be picked up by your JUnit tests if you place the file in `src/test/resources`, which allows your automated tests to easily use a different logging configuration than your application itself.

Finally, if no configuration is found, Log4j uses the default `ERROR` logging level, which sends *all* output to the console. To override that default, set the system property `org.apache.logging.log4j.level` to the desired level: `INFO`, `DEBUG`, etc.

Comparing Configuration File Formats

Each of the configuration file formats can be used to represent the same information. The following examples all show how to set the *root* (that is, default) level to `ERROR` while setting the logging for `com.wiley.realworldjava` and its subpackages to the `INFO` level. Since they have the same functionality, you can easily compare the formats. The first example uses `log4j2.xml`:

```
1:  <?xml version="1.0" encoding="UTF-8"?>
2:  <Configuration status="WARN">
3:     <Appenders>
4:        <Console name="Console" target="SYSTEM_OUT">
5:           <PatternLayout pattern="%m%n"/>
6:        </Console>
7:     </Appenders>
8:     <Loggers>
9:        <Logger name="com.wiley.realworldjava"
10:          level="info" additivity="false">
11:          <AppenderRef ref="Console"/>
12:       </Logger>
13:       <Root level="error">
14:          <AppenderRef ref="Console"/>
15:       </Root>
16:    </Loggers>
17: </Configuration>
```

On line 2, the file sets the log level to `WARN`, which is intended to log warnings about configuration errors. Lines 4–6 then create a single console appender with a pattern `"%m%n"` for including the message followed by a new line. Lines 8–16 create two loggers. The first, on lines 9–12, sets the `com.wiley.realworldjava` logger to the `INFO` level using the *console* logger. The second, on lines 13–15, sets the root logger to the `ERROR` level.

Remember from the "Using Java Util Logging" section that the root logger is the highest-level logger. It is used when there are no specific loggers configured to match a log request.

This is an example of code using this configuration:

```
import org.apache.logging.log4j.LogManager;
import org.apache.logging.log4j.Logger;

public class LoggingWithXmlConfig {

   static { System.setProperty("log4j2.configurationFile",
      "src/main/resources/log4j2-config.xml"); }

   private static final Logger LOGGER = LogManager.getLogger();

   public static void main(String[] args) {
      LOGGER.fatal("ending!");
      LOGGER.error("this is bad");
      LOGGER.warn("be careful");
      LOGGER.info("just to let you know");
      LOGGER.debug("let's find the problem");
   }
}
```

Since we log `INFO` or higher, there are four lines of output:

```
ending!
this is bad
```

```
be careful
just to let you know
```

None of this should be surprising as it matches the description of how we want logging to behave. There's one other attribute in the example, on line 10, `additivity`. By default, loggers inherit from each other in Log4j. Without setting additivity to false, the output would include duplicate rows because both the root logger and the `com.wiley.realworldjava` logger would be run for the same message.

XML was the original format supported by Log4j and so has the most examples online and is therefore often the best choice. Since it is the oldest, you may encounter Log4j 1.*x* examples on the Internet. If you see XML that contains `<log4j:configuration`, it is from Log4j 1.*x*, and you should find a newer example! Log4j2 examples have `<Configuration>` as the root XML tag.

Next, let's set the same configuration using a properties file, using name/value pairs. Similarly, if you see `log4j.rootLogger`, you are looking at Log4j 1.*x* documentation and should find a more modern example that doesn't have the `log4j` attribute prefix and simply has `rootLogger`.

```
appenders = console

rootLogger.level = error
rootLogger.appenderRefs = stdout
rootLogger.appenderRef.stdout.ref = STDOUT

logger.book.name=com.wiley.realworldjava
logger.book.level=INFO
logger.book.appenderRefs = stdout
logger.book.appenderRef.stdout.ref = STDOUT
logger.book.additivity = false

appender.console.type = Console
appender.console.name = STDOUT
appender.console.layout.type = PatternLayout
appender.console.layout.pattern = %m%n
```

The concepts are the same in the XML example. You see the root logger, appenders, console, logging levels, etc. A significant difference is that you must give each logger (other than the root logger) a reference that you use in the property file keys as a grouping. You can think of `book` as a variable name in this example. All of the rows that begin with `logger.book` are grouped together and define the settings that are applied to the `book` logger.

The `.json`/`.jsn` and `.yaml`/`.yml` versions of the configurations require you to add some additional dependencies in your project. Both use different APIs from the popular Jackson library for parsing. These APIs are not included as transitive dependencies of Log4j itself since they are optional dependencies, only required if you are using JSON or YAML, but not for the properties or XML flavors.

To use Log4j2, find the dependencies on Maven Central: `https://mvnrepository.com/artifact/com.fasterxml.jackson.core/jackson-databind` and `https://mvnrepository.com/artifact/com.fasterxml.jackson.dataformat/jackson-dataformat-yaml`. Find the latest version number for your build tool. See Tables 5.5 and 5.6 for the additional dependencies for JSON and YAML, respectively, using the latest version numbers at the time of this writing. Note that both pull in `jackson-core` as a transitive dependency of the one you specify.

> **NOTE** *If you omit the dependencies, Log4j silently ignores the JSON and YAML configuration files and will go on to the next file it can find in the lookup order or use the default. You will not get a failure message about the configuration file being ignored.*

TABLE 5.5: Specifying Log4j as the Jackson Dependency Needed for JSON

TOOL	SYNTAX

Maven	`<dependency>`
	`<groupId>com.fasterxml.jackson.core</groupId>`
	`<artifactId>jackson-databind</artifactId>`
	`<version>2.16.1</version>`
	`</dependency>`

Gradle (Groovy)	`implementation group: 'com.fasterxml.jackson.core',` `name: 'jackson-databind', version: '2.16.1'`
Gradle (Kotlin)	`implementation(` `"com.fasterxml.jackson.core:jackson-databind:2.16.1")`

TABLE 5.6: Specifying Log4j as the Jackson Dependency Needed for YAML

TOOL	SYNTAX

Maven	`<dependency>`
	`<groupId>com.fasterxml.jackson.dataformat</groupId>`
	`<artifactId>jackson-dataformat-yaml</artifactId>`
	`<version>2.16.1</version>`
	`</dependency>`

Gradle (Groovy)	`implementation group: 'com.fasterxml.jackson.dataformat',` `name: 'jackson-dataformat-yaml', version: '2.16.1'`
Gradle (Kotlin)	`implementation("com.fasterxml.jackson.dataformat:"` `+ "jackson-dataformat-yaml:2.16.1")`

The following shows the configuration from the previous examples represented in JSON. Log4j supports both the `.json` and `.jsn` file extensions. The content in the file is the same.

```
{
  "configuration": {
    "status": "warn",
    "appenders": {
      "Console": {
        "name": "STDOUT",
        "PatternLayout": {
          "pattern": "%m%n"
        }
      }
    },
    "loggers": {
      "logger": {
        "name": "com.wiley.realworldjava",
        "level": "info",
        "additivity": "false",
        "AppenderRef": {
          "ref": "STDOUT"
        }
      },
```

```
            "root": {
              "level": "error",
              "AppenderRef": {
                "ref": "STDOUT"
              }
            }
          }
        }
      }
```

Finally, the configuration in YAML is as follows. Log4j supports both the `.yaml` and `.yml` file extensions, which are both commonly accepted file types for YAML files.

```
Configuration:
  status: warn
  appenders:
    Console:
      name: STDOUT
      target: SYSTEM_OUT
      PatternLayout:
        Pattern: "%m%n"

  Loggers:
    logger:
      -
        name: com.wiley.realworldjava
        level: info
        additivity: false
        AppenderRef:
          ref: STDOUT
    Root:
      level: error
      AppenderRef:
        ref: STDOUT
```

Both the JSON and YAML examples use the same concepts as the XML example. The only difference is the syntax. Any of the formats is fine to use as the configuration. You can pick whichever one you or your team prefer.

Setting Logging Destinations

So far, the Log4j examples have used the console appender for logging all output to the system console. There are other appenders as well, the most common being the following:

- `Console`: Writes to `System.out` or `System.err`, depending on the configuration.
- `File`: Writes to a file.
- `RollingFile`: Writes to a file with file rotation.
- `RollingRandomAccessFile`: Writes to a file with file rotation and buffering.
- **And many more:** There are more than 25 appenders included with Log4j, including loggers for a database or queue.

In this section, you'll learn how to use `RollingFile`. (`RollingRandomAccessFile` works the same way.)

Each appender has its own set of attributes to control behavior. See the "Further References" section at the end of this chapter for a link to the full list.

For rolling files, you can control things like the name, formatting, how often to write to disk, and how to handle rotation. For example, you can rotate the file based on time, such as once a day, or size, such as when it gets to 25 MB.

This example rotates files after a day or 1 MB, whichever comes first:

```
1:  <?xml version="1.0" encoding="UTF-8"?>
2:  <Configuration status="warn" name="MyApp">
3:     <Appenders>
4:        <RollingFile name="RollingFile" fileName="java-log.log"
5:           filePattern="java-log-%d{yyyy-MM-dd}-%i.log.gz">
6:           <PatternLayout>
7:              <Pattern>%m%n</Pattern>
8:           </PatternLayout>
9:           <Policies>
10:             <TimeBasedTriggeringPolicy/>
11:             <SizeBasedTriggeringPolicy size="1 MB"/>
12:          </Policies>
13:          <DefaultRolloverStrategy max="3"/>
14:       </RollingFile>
15:    </Appenders>
16:    <Loggers>
17:       <Root level="error">
18:          <AppenderRef ref="RollingFile"/>
19:       </Root>
20:    </Loggers>
21: </Configuration>
```

On lines 4 and 5, the configuration specifies both the filename for the file actively being logged to (`java-log.log`), along with a naming convention for the rotated files (`java-log-%d{yyyy-MM-dd}-%i.log.gz`). The `.gz` extension means GNU Zip, which is a commonly used compression format.

Line 10 sets the time-based rotation option. The unit of measure is the most specific duration in the file pattern on line 5. In this case, that is day. By default, the interval is set to 1 since that is most common. You can set the attribute `interval` explicitly on the `TimeBasedTriggeringPolicy` tag in the XML to specify a different frequency.

The configuration allows at most three archive files as specified on line 13. After running a program that logs a million statements using this configuration, there will be four files: the active one and three archives:

```
java-log-2024-02-17-1.log.gz
java-log-2024-02-17-2.log.gz
java-log-2024-02-17-1.log.gz
java-log.log
```

Let's repeat the same configuration using a properties file. Notice how the information specified is the same; just the format changes:

```
appenders = rolling

rootLogger.level = error
rootLogger.appenderRefs = RollingFile
rootLogger.appenderRef.rolling.ref = RollingFile

appender.rolling.type = RollingFile
appender.rolling.name = RollingFile
appender.rolling.fileName = java-log.log
appender.rolling.filePattern = java-log-%d{yyyy-MM-dd}-%i.log.gz
appender.rolling.layout.type = PatternLayout
```

```
appender.rolling.layout.pattern = %m%n
appender.rolling.policies.type = Policies
appender.rolling.policies.time.type = TimeBasedTriggeringPolicy
appender.rolling.policies.size.type = SizeBasedTriggeringPolicy
appender.rolling.policies.size.size = 1MB
appender.rolling.strategy.type = DefaultRolloverStrategy
appender.rolling.strategy.max = 3
```

Contrast that with the comparable JSON version:

```
{
   "configuration": {
      "status": "warn",
      "appenders": {
         "RollingFile": {
            "name":"FILE",
            "fileName":"java-log.log",
            "filePattern":"java-log-%d{yyyy-MM-dd}-%i.log.gz",
            "PatternLayout": {
               "pattern":"%m%n"
            },
            "Policies": {
               "TimeBasedTriggeringPolicy" : {},
               "SizeBasedTriggeringPolicy": {
                  "size":"1 MB"
               }
            },
           "DefaultRolloverStrategy": {
             "max":"3"
            }
         }
      },
      "loggers": {
        "root": {
          "level": "error",
          "AppenderRef": {
            "ref": "FILE"
          }
        }
      }
   }
}
```

Finally, here's the YAML version:

```
Configuration:
   status: warn
   appenders:
      RollingFile:
         - name: FILE
           fileName: $java-log.log
           filePattern: java-log-%d{yyyy-MM-dd}-%i.log.gz
           PatternLayout:
              pattern: "%m%n"
           Policies:
              TimeBasedTriggeringPolicy:
              SizeBasedTriggeringPolicy:
                size: 1 MB
```

```
          DefaultRollOverStrategy:
            max: 3

    Loggers:
      Root:
        level: error
        AppenderRef:
          ref: FILE
```

Choosing Logging Output Formats

Many of the examples in this section have used the pattern `%m%n`, which simply indicates the message and a new line. In real-world logging, that is not usually sufficient; you will want to get more granular. First choose a layout for your log output. Common layouts include the following:

- **CSV:** Comma-separated values used for automated parsing or Excel analysis
- **JSON:** Java Standard Object Notation typically used for automated parsing
- **Pattern:** Text format that is used by default
- **XML:** Extensible Markup Language typically used for automated parsing
- **YAML:** Yet Another Markup Language typically used for automated parsing

Logs can be read into other systems or stored for later manual reading. If you are ingesting the logs into another system, choose the layout that is easiest for the consuming system. If you are reading them yourself, CSV or Pattern layout is best.

The Pattern layout has many special format characters. The following is a common example used in documentation:

```
%d %p %c{1.} [%t] %m%n
```

Here is what each part means:

- `%d`: Date using the default date format.
- `%p`: Logging level (for example, `INFO`).
- `%c{1.}` – How much of the fully qualified class name to show. The part in brackets provides the desired format. In this example, `%c` means the class name, and `{1.}` means one fully expanded item, which is the class name itself and the first letter of each part of the package name resulting in `c.w.r.l.l.LoggingWithPropertiesConfig`.
- `[%t]`: The method name in braces.
- `%m`: Log message.
- `%n`: A newline character.

Logging Lazily

Logging lazily for Log4j is similar to Java Util Logging. You use a lambda expression to compose the logging message. The lambda will be executed only if the logging level requires a message to be logged:

```
public static void main(String[] args) {
   LOGGER.error(() -> generateMessage());
}

private static String generateMessage() {
   return "This is an expensive message";
}
```

USING SLF4J

SLF4J stands for Simple Logging Façade for Java. You've already seen that each logging framework requires different API calls in your Java code. This makes it hard to switch logging libraries. SLF4J to the rescue! SLF4J is intended to be used as a wrapper so you can switch more easily.

Go to Maven Central at `https://mvnrepository.com/artifact/org.slf4j/slf4j-api` and find the latest version number for your build tool. Table 5.7 shows the dependencies, using the latest version numbers at the time of this writing.

TABLE 5.7: Specifying SLF4J as a Dependency

TOOL	SYNTAX

Maven	`<dependency>`
	`    <groupId>org.slf4j</groupId>`
	`    <artifactId>slf4j-api</artifactId>`
	`    <version>2.0.12</version>`
	`</dependency>`

Gradle (Groovy)	`implementation group: 'org.slf4j',` `   name: 'slf4j-api', version: '2.0.12'`
Gradle (Kotlin)	`implementation("org.slf4j:slf4j-api:2.0.12")`

In the following sections, we will look at the basics of using SLF4J and how to configure it to use different underlying logging frameworks.

Omitting a Logging Framework

In the following example, the only dependency specified is `slf4j-api`. That is enough to compile code and run, but not to do any actual logging:

```
import org.slf4j.Logger;
import org.slf4j.LoggerFactory;

public class NoUnderlyingImplementation {

   private static final Logger LOGGER = LoggerFactory
     .getLogger(NoUnderlyingImplementation.class);

   public static void main(String[] args) {
      LOGGER.info("just to let you know");
   }
}
```

This code resembles the earlier logging frameworks in this chapter. There is a factory to get the logger, this time called `LoggerFactory`. The logger name is passed into the factory to determine the appropriate logger. Unlike Log4j, you do need to pass it explicitly. The single log call to `info()` shows one of the logging levels.

However, actually running this code produces an error:

```
SLF4J(W): No SLF4J providers were found.
SLF4J(W): Defaulting to no-operation (NOP) logger implementation
SLF4J(W): See https://www.SLF4J.org/codes.html#noProviders for further details.
```

Since SLF4J doesn't know which logging framework to use, it doesn't do any logging and instead complains with the previous message. It uses a "no-operation" default, which does not do any logging. Clearly that is not your intent here!

Specifying SLF4J Simple

To fix this, you must specify a provider. First, we will use a simple logger, the provider built into SLF4J itself. By default, the simple logger logs all messages `INFO` or higher to `System.err`.

Go to Maven Central at `https://mvnrepository.com/artifact/org.slf4j/slf4j-simple` and find the latest version number for your build tool. Table 5.8 shows the dependencies for each build tool.

TABLE 5.8: Specifying SLF4J as a Dependency

TOOL	SYNTAX

Maven	`<dependency>`
	`    <groupId>org.slf4j</groupId>`
	`    <artifactId>slf4j-simple</artifactId>`
	`    <version>2.0.12</version>`
	`</dependency>`

Gradle (Groovy)	`implementation group: 'org.slf4j',` `   name: 'slf4j-simple', version: '2.0.12'`
Gradle (Kotlin)	`implementation("org.slf4j:slf4j-simple:2.0.12")`

`slf4j-simple` is the SLF4J default logging implementation. Re-running with the `slf4j-simple` as a dependency now gives the desired output:

```
[main] ERROR com.wiley.realworldjava.logging.SLF4J.Slf4jSimple
   - just to let you know
```

It is more common to use SLF4J with other logging frameworks rather than `slf4j-simple`, as you'll see later in the section. But first, let's cover how to use SLF4J itself.

Comparing Logging Levels

SLF4J has five logging levels. Table 5.9 shows the logging levels and their intended purpose. You can see the ideas are the same as the other logging frameworks you have seen so far. You might notice that there is no equivalent of `FATAL` or `SEVERE`. If you need to express a `FATAL` or `SEVERE` level, use `ERROR`.

TABLE 5.9: SLF4J Logging Levels

LOG LEVEL	INTENDED USE
`ERROR`	Log the worst errors.
`WARN`	Log events that might turn into errors.
`INFO`	Log informational events.
`DEBUG`	Log debugging information.
`TRACE`	Log fine-grained messages, typically showing the application flow.

Formatting Values

Like Log4j, SLF4J supports the {} syntax for placeholders with logical default formatting. If you need the more granular control of `String.format()`, you can call it directly. Both of the approaches are used here:

```
import org.slf4j.Logger;
import org.slf4j.LoggerFactory;

public class Slf4jWithParameters {

   private static final Logger LOGGER = LoggerFactory
      .getLogger(Slf4jWithParameters.class);

   public static void main(String[] args) {
      LOGGER.error("{}: {} is {}/{}", "Division", 1.5, 3, 2);
      LOGGER.error(String.format("%s: %.1f is %d/%d", "Division", 1.5, 3, 2));
   }
}
```

The message part of both of these log statements is as follows:

```
Division: 1.5 is 3/2
```

In general, you should use {} unless you find it doesn't meet your needs and then use `String.format()` for those specific calls that require more control.

Logging Lazily

Logging lazily gives you more control in SLF4J than Java Util Logging or Log4j. You still use a lambda that will only be executed if the logging level requires a message to be logged. However, there are separate methods for specifying the message and each argument to be logged.

```
public static void main(String[] args) {
   LOGGER.atDebug()
      .setMessage(() -> generateMessage())
      .addArgument(() -> generateParameterToFillInMessage())
      .log();
}

private static String generateMessage() {
   return "This is an expensive message with parameter: {}";
}

private static String generateParameterToFillInMessage() {
   return "This is an expensive parameter";
}
```

This approach of chaining calls is known as a *fluent API*. You chain the methods you want to call and then call `log()` at the end to indicate you are done. Remember to call `log()` at the end or nothing will be logged!

With the fluent API, you can choose to use lambdas for any expensive operations. For example:

```
LOGGER.atDebug()
   .setMessage("Message with expensive parameter {}")
   .addArgument(() -> generateParameterToFillInMessage())
   .log();
```

Since the message is not expensive to generate, there is no need to use a lambda for it. Any of the methods can choose independently whether to use a lazy operation or not. Similarly, each `addArgument()` call gets the same choice of whether to be lazy when you have more than one parameter.

Passing Basic Configuration

As we said earlier, `slf4j-simple` is not commonly used. However, it is possible to use `slf4j-simple` as a stand-alone logging framework if you have simple needs. The Javadoc for the `SimpleLogger` class has about a dozen system properties you can configure to control behavior. These are the most useful ones:

- `org.slf4j.simpleLogger.logFile`
- `org.slf4j.simpleLogger.defaultLogLevel`
- `org.slf4j.simpleLogger.dateTimeFormat`
- `org.slf4j.simpleLogger.showShortLogName`

It is much more common to configure SLF4J to use an external logging framework with more advanced features. The next section shows how to do this.

Using SLF4J with Other Logging Frameworks

SLF4J chooses the logging framework to use as a *provider* by inspecting the classpath for dependencies. That's why adding `slf4j-simple` as a dependency caused it to be used, even without any other configuration. In older versions of SLF4J, providers used to be called *bindings*, so you may see that in older documentation.

To show how easy it is to switch, we will create an example that uses Java Util Logging as the provider and then switch to Log4j. You need three JAR files:

- SLF4J itself
- Logging framework
- A provider to connect the logging framework to SLF4J

Each logging framework has its own SLF4J provider dependency. To find the Java Util Logging dependency, go to Maven Central at `https://mvnrepository.com/artifact/org.slf4j/slf4j-jdk14` and find the latest version number for your build tool. Table 5.10 lists the provider dependencies for the common build tools, along with the latest version numbers at the time of this writing. Note that `jdk14` is in the name because that's when Java Util Logging was introduced. This is still the artifact name even for modern versions of Java.

TABLE 5.10: Specifying Java Util Logging as SLF4J Provider as a Dependency

TOOL	SYNTAX

Maven	`<dependency>`
	`<groupId>org.slf4j</groupId>`
	`<artifactId>slf4j-jdk14</artifactId>`
	`<version>2.0.12</version>`
	`</dependency>`

Gradle (Groovy)	`implementation group: 'org.slf4j',` `name: 'slf4j-jdk14', version: '2.0.12'`
Gradle (Kotlin)	`implementation("org.slf4j:slf4j-jdk14:2.0.12")`

Next take a look at the structure of the Maven project, as shown in Figure 5.2. You can see only `slf4j-api` and `slf4j-jdk14` are set as dependencies.

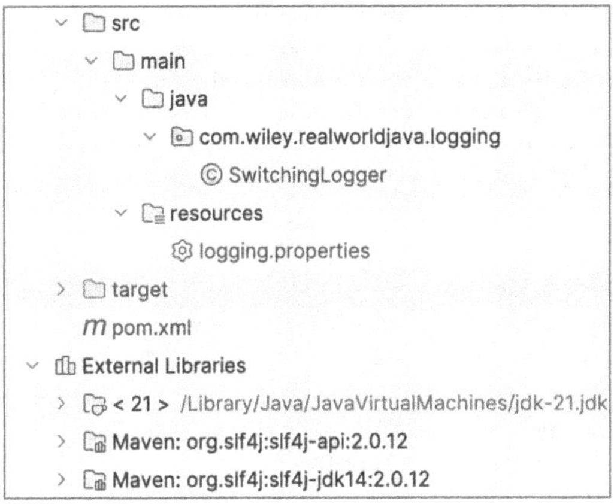

```
src
  main
    java
      com.wiley.realworldjava.logging
        SwitchingLogger
    resources
      logging.properties
target
pom.xml
External Libraries
  < 21 > /Library/Java/JavaVirtualMachines/jdk-21.jdk
  Maven: org.slf4j:slf4j-api:2.0.12
  Maven: org.slf4j:slf4j-jdk14:2.0.12
```

FIGURE 5.2: Maven structure for SLF4J

The logging configuration file tells Java Util Logging to log `WARNING` and higher to the console:

```
.level= WARNING
handlers= java.util.logging.ConsoleHandler
```

Finally, the actual Java code to log is as follows:

```
import org.slf4j.Logger;
import org.slf4j.LoggerFactory;

public class SwitchingLogger {

   static { System.setProperty ("java.util.logging.config.file",
      "src/main/resources/logging.properties");};
   private static final Logger LOGGER = LoggerFactory.
     getLogger(SwitchingLogger.class);

   public static void main(String[] args) {
      LOGGER.error("this is bad");
      LOGGER.warn("be careful");
      LOGGER.info("just to let you know");
   }
}
```

The only reference to Java Util Logging in the Java code is the system property, thus avoiding having to configure that in the IDE. Running the example does use Java Util Logging:

```
Feb 18, 2024 12:03:40 PM com.wiley.realworldjava.
   logging.SwitchingLogger main
SEVERE: this is bad
Feb 18, 2024 12:03:40 PM com.wiley.realworldjava.
   logging.SwitchingLogger main
WARNING: be careful
```

You might have noticed that the code uses the SLF4J method `error()`, whereas the output displays `SEVERE`. Since SLF4J is a façade over the underlying framework, it maps the logging call to an appropriate call on the underlying framework. The Java code uses SLF4J's naming, but since the underlying provider is Java Util Logging, the output uses Java Util Logging's names.

Now suppose you got a requirement to switch to Log4j since Java Util Logging didn't meet the project's needs. First you need to change the dependency from `slf4j-jdk14` to a Log4j 2 provider version, such as `log4j-slf4j2-impl` (see Table 5.11). Remember, the table uses the latest version number at the time of writing. To find the latest version number, go to `https://mvnrepository.com/artifact/org.apache.logging.log4j/log4j-slf4j2-impl`. The group ID is different from the previous example as the Log4j project maintains this integration, and the version number matches your version of Log4j rather than your version of SLF4J.

TABLE 5.11: Specifying Log4j as SLF4J Provider as a Dependency

TOOL	SYNTAX

Maven	`<dependency>`
	`<groupId>org.apache.logging.log4j</groupId>`
	`<artifactId>log4j-slf4j2-impl</artifactId>`
	`<version>2.22.1</version>`
	`</dependency>`

Gradle (Groovy)	`implementation group: 'org.apache.logging.log4j',` `name: 'log4j-slf4j2-impl', version: '2.22.1'`
Gradle (Kotlin)	`implementation("org.apache.logging.log4j:` `log4j-slf4j2-impl:2.22.1")`

After updating `pom.xml`, the next step is to create a log configuration for Log4j:

```
<?xml version="1.0" encoding="UTF-8"?>
<Configuration status="WARN">
   <Appenders>
      <Console name="Console" target="SYSTEM_OUT">
         <PatternLayout pattern="%d [%p] %m%n"/>
      </Console>
   </Appenders>
   <Loggers>
      <Logger name="com.wiley.realworldjava"
         level="warn" additivity="false">
         <AppenderRef ref="Console"/>
      </Logger>
      <Root level="error">
         <AppenderRef ref="Console"/>
      </Root>
   </Loggers>
</Configuration>
```

At this point, the project looks like Figure 5.3.

Notice how the configuration now has `warn` as used by Log4j instead of `WARNING` from Java Util Logging. The key is that all the changes are in the dependencies and config files rather than the Java code. Running the Java code without any changes now gives this:

```
2024-02-18 12:32:17,719 [ERROR] uh oh
2024-02-18 12:32:17,721 [WARN] be careful
```

You can see the format has changed and the log levels are now the ones Log4j uses.

As cleanup, you can remove the old property file and system property reference from the Java file. Or you can leave it there if you want to be able to quickly switch back and forth. Switching is easy; just change the dependencies to the one you want to use!

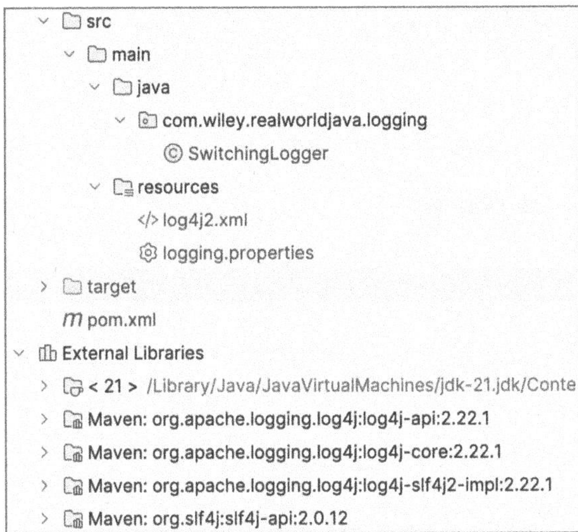

FIGURE 5.3: Maven structure for Log4J

USING LOGBACK

The final logging framework in this chapter is Logback. Both Log4j and Logback are popular choices in today's enterprises. Logback was designed to improve on Log4j, for example, to improve performance. Logback actually uses SLF4J natively rather than providing a separate API. In fact, the founder of Logback, Ceki Gülcü, is also the founder of SLF4J! That means everything you learned in the previous section will apply.

To get started, you need `slf4j-api` and two Logback-specific files. Go to Maven Central at `https://mvnrepository.com/artifact/ch.qos.logback/logback-classic` and `https://mvnrepository.com/artifact/ch.qos.logback/logback-core`. Find the latest version number for your build tool and substitute it into that what is shown in Table 5.12.

TABLE 5.12: Specifying Logback as a Dependency

TOOL	SYNTAX

Maven	`<dependency>`
	`  <groupId>ch.qos.logback</groupId>`
	`  <artifactId>logback-classic</artifactId>`
	`  <version>1.5.0</version>`
	`</dependency>`

Gradle (Groovy)	`implementation group: 'ch.qos.logback',`
	`    name: 'logback-classic', version: '1.5.0'`
	`implementation group: 'ch.qos.logback',`
	`    name: 'logback-core', version: '1.5.0'`

Gradle (Kotlin)	`implementation("ch.qos.logback:logback-core:1.5.0")` `implementation("ch.qos.logback:logback-classic:1.5.0")`

Note that `logback-core` is the main logging code. `logback-classic` adds additional features including being a SLF4J provider. You should always include both dependencies when using Logback. Since Logback uses the SLF4J API, you can refer to the SLF4J section for things that are exactly the same, such as formatting values.

A simple program that uses Logback looks just like the earlier SLF4J sample:

```
import org.slf4j.Logger;
import org.slf4j.LoggerFactory;

public class BasicLogging {

   private static final Logger LOGGER = LoggerFactory
     .getLogger(BasicLogging.class);

   public static void main(String[] args) {
      LOGGER.info("just to let you know");
   }
}
```

This example outputs the following:

```
13:05:05.034 [main] ERROR com.wiley.realworldjava.logging.log4j
   .BasicLogging - just to let you know
```

The output uses Logback defaults. In the following sections, you'll see more details about using Logback.

Comparing Logging Levels

Logback has the same logging levels as SLF4J along with two special options. Table 5.13 shows the logging levels and their intended purpose. By now, you should realize that logging levels are similar across frameworks, making this easy to understand.

TABLE 5.13: Logback Logging Levels

LOG LEVEL	INTENDED USE
ERROR	Log the worst errors.
WARN	Log events that might turn into errors.
INFO	Log informational events.
DEBUG	Log debugging information.
TRACE	Log fine-grained messages, typically showing the application flow.
ALL	Special option to log all messages.
OFF	Special option to specify no logging.

Passing Basic Configuration

Like Log4j, Logback specifies a lookup order for which file it will use. First it looks for the system property `logback.configurationFile`. That approach is used in the examples in this chapter to show a number of configuration files.

Next, Logback looks for the first configuration file it finds in the order specified in this list:

- `logback-test.xml`
- `logback.xml`

Logback iterates through the previous files in order, and when it finds one file, it stops iterating. Therefore, if `logback-test.xml` is in your `src/test/resources` folder, it will be loaded up first when executing unit tests, whereas `logback.xml` will be loaded for your standard program execution. Finally, if no configuration is found, Logback uses the default, which is `DEBUG`-level logging with all output written to the console.

Note that unlike Log4j, Logback only supports the XML configuration format. This makes finding examples online easier and reflects that XML is the most common configuration format for Log4j anyway.

In this example, the `logback.xml` file is used to log our package at `INFO` level and everything else at `ERROR` level with all the output logged to the console.

```
<?xml version="1.0" encoding="UTF-8"?>
<!DOCTYPE configuration>

<configuration>
   <import class="ch.qos.logback.classic.encoder.PatternLayoutEncoder" />
   <import class="ch.qos.logback.core.ConsoleAppender" />

   <appender name="STDOUT" class="ConsoleAppender">
      <encoder class="PatternLayoutEncoder">
         <pattern>%msg%n</pattern>
      </encoder>
   </appender>

   <logger name="com.wiley.realworldjava.logging" level="info" />

   <root level="error">
      <appender-ref ref="STDOUT" />
   </root>
</configuration>
```

Like Log4j, there is a configuration to write to the console, a root logger, and a custom logger.

Setting Logging Destinations

The previous examples used the console appender. The following are the most common appender classes:

- `ConsoleAppender`: Writes to `System.out` (can change to `System.err`).
- `FileAppender`: Writes to a file.
- `RollingFileAppender`: Writes to a file with file rotation.
- **And many more:** Many are to log to a database or queue. There are even email appenders for specific providers like Gmail.

Now you'll learn how to use the `RollingFileAppender` class.

Each appender has a number of attributes to control the behavior. See the end of the chapter for a link to the full list. For rolling files, this controls things such as the name, formatting, how to handle rotation, and when to clean up old files.

This example rotates files after one day (by default) or 10 KB, whichever comes first:

```
<configuration>
   <appender name="ROLLING"
      class="ch.qos.logback.core.rolling.RollingFileAppender">
      <file>java-log.log</file>
      <rollingPolicy
```

```
            class="ch.qos.logback.core.rolling.SizeAndTimeBasedRollingPolicy">
            <fileNamePattern>java-log-%d{yyyy-MM-dd}.%i.gz</fileNamePattern>
            <maxFileSize>10KB</maxFileSize>
            <maxHistory>3</maxHistory>
            <totalSizeCap>2GB</totalSizeCap>
         </rollingPolicy>
         <encoder>
            <pattern>%msg%n</pattern>
         </encoder>
      </appender>

      <root level="DEBUG">
          <appender-ref ref="ROLLING" />
      </root>

   </configuration>
```

Like Log4j, the configuration specifies both the filename for the file actively being logged to, and a naming convention for the rotated files. Since the `fileNamePattern` ends in `.gz`, it is automatically compressed.

We set the maximum file size here to 10 KB, which is lower than the 1 MB we set for Log4j. The reason is that Logback only checks to see if the file size limit has been exceeded every 60 seconds, whereas Log4j checks the file size more often. Therefore, we set the size lower in this example so that you get to see the files rotate without waiting a long time.

After running a program that logs 100 large statements using this configuration, there are two files: the active one and one archive:

```
java-log-2024-02-18.0.gz
java-log.log
```

Both files are larger than the 10 KB configured due to the heavy logging and short runtime of the test.

Choosing Logging Output Formats

The examples in this section have used `%msg%n`, which simply indicates the message and a new line. Luckily, Logback supports a variety of options. First you have to choose which layout you want to use. The following are common layout classes:

- `PatternLayout`: Plain-text format string like `%msg%n` to indicate what you want included
- `HTMLLayout`: HTML format using a pattern and CSS
- `XMLLayout`: Uses the Log4j XML format

Alternatively, you create a custom format.

`PatternLayout` is usually the best, because it has many special format characters. The following is a common example used in documentation:

```
%d{dd MMM yyyy:HH:mm:ss.SSS} [%method] %level - %msg%n
```

The following is what each part means:

- `%d`: Date/time followed by any formatting symbols
- `[%method]`: Method name in braces
- `%level`: Logging level
- `%msg`: Log message
- `%n`: A newline character

There are many other options in the documentation referenced at the end of the chapter. For example, you can log the number of milliseconds the application has been running.

LEARNING MORE ABOUT LOGGING

Regardless of which logging framework you use, there are some things you'll need to consider. This section covers five keys of them.

Deciding on Coding Standards

In this chapter, all the loggers we defined were `private static final` constants. Some people prefer to make loggers instance variables. You should check if your team has any rules or conventions and follow those.

Designing for Performance

Logging involves input/output (I/O), so it is slower than computations and other operations. You want to make sure that logging does not slow down your application! If you are logging to a remote source (for example, a database), you'll need to be even more careful.

The first thing to consider is the logging level. When you are first testing your application, you may want more verbose logging. Similarly, you may want to log more in your test or QA environment than your production environment. After all, the real application will have more usage, so the performance impact of granular logging is amplified.

Additionally, there are a number of settings you can choose when logging. Rotating the log file too often can produce a lot of files, making it harder to use them. Some logging frameworks allow you to control whether the output is buffered in memory, and some let you log asynchronously so your application can get on with functional behavior.

Choosing a Language for the Logs

When writing an application for users, you may read about internationalization and localization. Internationalization allows you to customize behavior such as whether the text appears in English or Spanish (or any other language). Localization lets you choose locale-specific behavior, for example whether to use dollars or pounds (or any other currency) even within English text. By contrast, logging occurs in one language: the one your team uses.

Preventing Log Tampering

Logs are important as they represent a record of what happened in your application. Some are used for problem-solving. Others are used for auditing activities. In both cases, you need them to be accurate.

However, hostile parties may want to mess up the logs. They could be internal employees who want to hide something bad they did. Or they could be outsiders who want to cause your company harm.

Log injection refers to hostile parties messing up your logs by including text you didn't expect. Consider this logging statement:

```
LOGGER.info("Invalid name: {}", name);
```

If `name` came from user input, it could contain anything. A malicious example of this is known as *log forging*, a penetration technique where a hacker injects special characters into the variable, to add forged data to your log.

Another example would be adding control characters, which could erase data from the log, thereby corrupting it. Bad data could even be used to trigger bad behavior if someone views the file in a browser.

You must always consider how much information to log. Sensitive date should not be logged for security reasons.

Aggregating and Forwarding Logs

Companies often store copies of the logs from multiple applications in one place for analysis, for example to more easily detect patterns, run queries, and provide support. They also want logs sent to specific places for ease in searching and monitoring alerts. The class of tools called *forwarders* exists especially for the purpose of moving local logs to a central location. Examples of such tools include Filebeat, Fluentd, LogBeat, and Splunk.

COMPARING LOGGING FRAMEWORKS

Table 5.14 is a quick comparison of the logging frameworks in this chapter.

TABLE 5.14: Comparing Logging Frameworks

FRAMEWORK	JAVA UTIL LOGGING	LOG4J	LOGBACK	SLF4J

Logging levels	`SEVERE`
	`WARNING`
	`INFO`
	`CONFIG`
	`FINE`
	`FINER`
	`FINEST`
	`ALL`
	`OFF`
		`FATAL`
		`ERROR`
		`WARN`
		`INFO`
		`DEBUG`
		`TRACE`
		`ALL`
		`OFF`
			`ERROR`
			`WARN`
			`INFO`
			`DEBUG`
			`TRACE`
				`ERROR`
				`WARN`
				`INFO`
				`DEBUG`
				`TRACE`

Output locations	`Console`
	`File`
	`Socket`
	`Memory`
		`Console`
		`File`
		`RollingFile`
		Many, many more
			`Console`
			`File`
			`RollingFile`
			Many more
				n/a; delegates to underlying logging provider

Output format	Text XML	CSV HTML JSON Pattern XML YAML etc.	HTML Pattern XML	n/a; delegates to underlying logging provider
Term for logging destination	Handler	Appender	Appender	n/a; delegates to underlying logging provider
Term for output format	Formatter	Layout	Layout	n/a; delegates to underlying logging provider

FURTHER REFERENCES

Each logging framework comes with useful references.

- Java Util Logging
  - `https://docs.oracle.com/en/java/javase/21/core/java-logging-overview.html`: Documentation for Java Util Logging
  - `https://docs.oracle.com/en/java/javase/21/docs/api/java.logging/java/util/logging/LogManager.html`: For customizing log configuration in Java Util Logging
  - `https://docs.oracle.com/en/java/javase/21/docs/api/java.logging/java/util/logging/FileHandler.html`: For configuring file logging
  - `https://docs.oracle.com/en/java/javase/21/docs/api/java.logging/java/util/logging/SimpleFormatter.html`: For customizing log message format
  - `https://docs.oracle.com/en/java/javase/21/docs/api/java.base/java/util/Formatter.html`: Formatter syntax
- Log4j
  - `https://logging.apache.org/log4j/2.x/javadoc/log4j-api/index.html`: Documentation for Log4j
  - `https://logging.apache.org/log4j/2.x/manual/appenders.html`: Full documentation of appenders
  - `https://logging.apache.org/log4j/2.x/manual/layouts.html`: Full documentation for layouts
- SLF4J
  - `https://www.SLF4J.org/manual.html`: Documentation for SLF4J
  - `https://www.SLF4J.org/api/org/slf4j/simple/SimpleLogger.html`: System properties if want to configure slf4j-simple
- Logback
  - `https://logback.qos.ch/manual`: Documentation for Logback
  - `https://logback.qos.ch/manual/appenders.html`: Full documentation for appenders
  - `https://logback.qos.ch/manual/layouts.html`: Full documentation for layouts

SUMMARY

- Java Util Logging is built into Java.
- Log4j and Logback are direct logging frameworks.
- SLF4J is a façade/wrapper for other logging frameworks like Java Util Logging, Log4j, and Logback.
- Logging frameworks provide file configuration options to specify the level of logging, format, destination, and more.

Getting to Know the Spring Framework

WHAT'S IN THIS CHAPTER?

- Configuring Spring
- Customizing Spring Applications with Properties
- Turbocharging Development with Spring Boot
- Working with Spring MVC
- Handling Errors in Spring
- Inspecting Your Application with Actuator
- Securing Your Application with Spring Security
- Exploring the Spring Projects

Spring, how do I love thee? Let me count the ways. Paraphrasing Elizabeth Barrett Browning's famous sonnet perfectly captures how we adore the Spring Framework. Born in 2003, the Spring Framework has become as important to the Java ecosystem as Java itself.

Spring is huge, and full coverage would require many voluminous tomes. In this chapter we cover the features you'll need to get up and running in everyday enterprise life.

Spring provides annotations where you configure *beans*, *components*, *services*, and *repositories*—all fancy names for "Spring managed instances."

ESSENTIAL SPRING CONCEPTS

Two design patterns are fundamental to Spring: *inversion of control (IoC)* and the related *dependency injection (DI)*.

IoC is a design pattern that *inverts* the normal pattern of control of objects. Traditionally an application might create objects in the program and then assign them for use. In IoC, however, the creation and assignment of new objects is managed by the framework rather than your program code. This pattern decouples object creation from object use, which simplifies program maintenance. The value of this is that class implementations can easily be snapped out and snapped in, interchanged in different environments, or mocked for testing.

DI is a specific form of IoC employed by Spring, where the dependencies are defined in the configuration, injected by the framework, and largely managed via annotations.

Spring has introduced some important improvements during its life, and all these paradigms are still heavily used, so let's study the evolution. Spring is built around the concept of a Spring *bean*. Beans are simply Java class instances that are managed by the Spring framework.

In the earlier days of Spring, you had to configure beans in an XML file that told Spring which classes and which properties to manage. Then Spring introduced `Configuration` classes, regular Java classes that are annotated with `@Configuration` or other specific annotations and that tell the Spring framework that these classes configure the Spring bean instances used in the application.

There is also a more succinct way of defining beans simply by annotating your configuration class with `@ComponentScan`, as we will see.

Later Spring introduced the game-changing Spring Boot framework. Where most frameworks come with some learning curve, Spring Boot actually has a negative learning curve! Spring Boot provides "opinionated" *starter dependencies*, each of which contains all of the required dependencies needed for a wealth of use cases, including web applications, relational and NoSQL databases, security, logging, and so much more. You just add the starter dependency to your Maven POM or Gradle build file, and Spring Boot loads up all the configuration and libraries required to support those use cases. Once you build your Spring Boot application, it automatically generates a self-executing JAR that you can just double-click to launch your application or to call:

```
java -jar <jar-name>.jar
```

Enterprises are migrating to Spring Boot in droves, but before we jump in, let's start with a good old-fashioned Spring example, where you can learn some basic Spring concepts including *component scanning* and DI. Then we will jump to Spring Boot and see how that simplifies things greatly.

CODE DOWNLOADS FOR THIS CHAPTER

The source code for this chapter is available on the book page at `www.wiley.com`. Click the Downloads link. You can also find the code at `https://github.com/realworldjava/Ch06-Spring`. See the `README.md` file in that repository for details.

CONFIGURING SPRING

In this section, you'll get a taste of Spring by building a basic project. First you'll see a sample application, and then you'll see how to configure it using both the XML and Java annotation approaches. Then you'll build on the Java approach using component scanning.

> **TIP** *The Spring Boot framework greatly simplifies the development and deployment of Spring-based applications, eliminating the need for configuring the explicit scaffolding.*

Our application is a mortgage calculator, where you can supply values for the principal, annual interest rate, and duration in years, and get back a monthly payment.

$$principal * rate * \frac{(1 + rate)^N}{(1 + rate)^N - 1}$$

FIGURE 6.1: Mortgage formula

Our calculator uses the mortgage formula as shown in Figure 6.1.

Payment is the monthly payment, principal is the amount of the mortgage, rate is the noncompounded monthly interest, and N is the number of months.

While the formula uses a monthly rate, traditionally the rate is expressed as a percentage of the annual rate, such as 4.5%, so our implementation class will divide the annual rate by 12 to get the monthly rate and then divide by 100 to convert the percentage to a decimal. Similarly, we multiply the number of years by 12 to get the total number of payments in months.

Best coding practices tell us to code to interfaces, so let's set up the `MortgageCalculatorService` interface defining our basic operation.

```
public interface MortgageCalculatorService {
    double payment(double principal,
        double annualInterestRate, int years);
}
```

Let's organize these into a "service" package to indicate that these classes perform the main application services. So, the corresponding implementation looks like this:

```
package com.wiley.realworldjava.service;

public class MortgageCalculatorServiceImpl
    implements MortgageCalculatorService {
    @Override
    public double payment(double principal,
        double annualInterestRate, int termInYears) {
        double monthlyInterestRate = annualInterestRate / 12 / 100;
        int numberOfPayments = termInYears * 12;

        // mortgage formula: P * R * [(1+R)^N] / [(1+R)^N - 1]
        return principal * (monthlyInterestRate
            * Math.pow(1 + monthlyInterestRate, numberOfPayments))
            / (Math.pow(1 + monthlyInterestRate, numberOfPayments) - 1);
    }
}
```

Using XML Configuration Files

Spring offers a few ways to define your beans. We will start with the traditional approach of using XML configuration. A more modern approach replaces the XML files with annotations and configuration classes, but the XML approach is still widely used in legacy applications, so we will start with that. As we progress through this chapter, you can find the various finished states committed to Git branches. We will mention the name of the branch at the start of each section so you can check out the branch and follow along with the working code. For the XML configuration, you can find the finished code in the Git branch `xml-config`.

Let's call our configuration file `applicationContext.xml`, the traditional name used by Spring. By convention, Spring expects this in the `src/main/resources` directory:

```
1:  <?xml version="1.0" encoding="UTF-8"?>
2:  <beans xmlns="http://www.springframework.org/schema/beans"
3:     xmlns:xsi="http://www.w3.org/2001/XMLSchema-instance"
4:     xsi:schemaLocation="
5:        http://www.springframework.org/schema/beans
6:        http://www.springframework.org/schema/beans/spring-beans.xsd">
7:
8:     <!-- Define the MortgageCalculatorService bean -->
9:     <bean id="mortgageCalculatorService"
10:       class="com.wiley.realworldjava.service.
             MortgageCalculatorServiceImpl"/>
11:
12:    <!-- Define the Main class bean -->
13:    <bean id="app" class="com.wiley.realworldjava.App">
14:       <constructor-arg ref="mortgageCalculatorService"/>
15:    </bean>
16: </beans>
```

This XML references two beans (remember, *bean* is Spring-speak for Spring-managed Java classes). Line 9 refers to the `MortgageCalculatorServiceImpl` declared in the previous section. Line 13 references a class named `App`, which we will introduce shortly. The `id` attributes of both are like variable names you can reference later. For example, line 14 uses `ref` to refer to one such `id`.

Spring exposes an *ApplicationContext* class instance, which contains references to all your beans, as well as other important Spring information, such as the *active profile*, which we will cover in short order.

To initialize the `ApplicationContext` instance and tell it to use the xml file, you call this:

```
ApplicationContext context
= new ClassPathXmlApplicationContext("applicationContext.xml");
```

We define an App class to initialize the context and kick off the process.

```
public class App {

   private final MortgageCalculatorService calculatorService;

   public App(MortgageCalculatorService calculatorService) {
      this.calculatorService = calculatorService;
   }

   public static void main(String[] args) {
      ApplicationContext context
         = new ClassPathXmlApplicationContext("applicationContext.xml");
// access the bean from its id specified in the applicationContext.xml
      App app = (App) context.getBean("app");
// alternatively, you can access it via its class type
//    App app = context.getBean(App.class);

      double principal = 250_000;
      double annualInterestRate = 6.5;
      int termInYears = 30;
      double payment = app.calculatorService.payment(principal,
         annualInterestRate, termInYears);
```

```
28:
29: // display result to 2 decimal places and commas
30: // for thousands separators
31:         System.out.printf("Monthly Payment: $%,.2f%n", payment);
32:     }
33: }
```

Lines 16 and17 create an `ApplicationContext`, which you can use to get your beans. You see in line 17 that it references the XML configuration file. Lines 19 and 20 show that you can look up a bean by name or by type.

Now let's try a thought experiment: suppose you request the same bean name (say `myBean`) in various places in your application. Will you get the same instance, or will Spring construct a new instance for each access?

The answer to that is it depends on the *scope*.

MANAGING BEAN LIFE CYCLES WITH SPRING SCOPES

By default, beans are created with *singleton* scope. That means every time you request an instance of bean `myBean`, Spring will return the same instance. However, you can change the scope to modify that behavior.

The most common scopes are:

- *singleton*: Returns the same instance for every access of a given bean name.
- *prototype*: Returns a new instance for every access of a given bean name.
- *request*: In a web application, Spring returns the same instance of the bean for every access of the given bean name during the processing of a single request. Surprisingly this is true even if you have multiple threads working on the same request; if they access the same bean name, they will get the same instance, so long as they are processing the same client request. But for each new client request, a new instance is created.
- *session*: In a web application, Spring will return the same instance for a given bean, even across multiple requests, as long as it is processing the same client HTTP session. A session is a series of associated requests and responses, which remains open until a timeout is reached or until the user logs out.

To specify a scope, modify the bean definition in `applicationContext.xml` by passing in the scope. For example, if you wanted to change the app bean in our example to be `prototype` scope, you would add the `scope` attribute to the XML as follows:

```
<bean id="mortgageCalculatorService"
    class="com.wiley.realworldjava.service
      .MortgageCalculatorServiceImpl"
    scope="prototype"/>
```

Using Java Configuration Classes

In more recent times, Spring introduced a new way to configure your application using Java "configuration" classes, a convenient alternative to XML config files. Let's try that approach—you can delete the XML file (or leave it there for comparison purposes, knowing that it won't be used). The finished code is in Git branch `configuration-class`.

Instead of the XML config files, you declare beans in one or more configuration classes. A configuration class is a standard Java class annotated with `@Configuration` above the class declaration. Inside the configuration class you can define one or more methods, each returning a bean instance. The name of the bean is just the method name, and the bean type is the return type of the method. You annotate those methods with `@Bean`, as follows:

```
9:  @Configuration
10: public class AppConfig {
11:     @Bean
12:     MortgageCalculatorService mortgageCalculatorService(){
13:        return new MortgageCalculatorServiceImpl();
14:     }
15:     @Bean
16:     App app(MortgageCalculatorService mortgageCalculatorService){
17:        return new App(mortgageCalculatorService);
18:     }
19: }
```

This code declares a configuration class named `AppConfig`, which declares a bean (in line 12) named `mortgageCalculatorService`, which returns an instance of the `MortgageCalculatorService` interface, with implementation class `MortgageCalculatorServiceImpl`.

> **TIP** *The configuration class name can be any legal class name, but it is good form to include* `Config` *in the name or keep it in a package named* `config`. *We do both, calling it* `com.wiley.realworldjava.config.AppConfig`.

The application grabs the `MortgageCalculatorService` bean from the `ApplicationContext`. We can see an example of that in the App class:

```
8:  @Component
9:  public class App {
10:     private final MortgageCalculatorService calculatorService;
11:
12:     public App(MortgageCalculatorService calculatorService) {
13:        this.calculatorService = calculatorService;
14:     }
15:
16:     public static void main(String[] args) {
17:        ApplicationContext context
18:           = new AnnotationConfigApplicationContext(AppConfig.class);
19:        App app = context.getBean(App.class);
20:
21:        double principal = 250_000;
22:        double annualInterestRate = 6.5;
23:        int termInYears = 30;
24:        double pmnt = app.calculatorService.payment(principal,
25:           annualInterestRate, termInYears);
26:
27:        // display result to 2 decimal places and commas
28:        // for thousands separators
29:        System.out.printf("Monthly Payment: $%,.2f%n", pmnt);
30:     }
31: }
```

Notice in line 19 how we grab an instance of App from the `ApplicationContext`. Even though the constructor of App requires an instance of `MortgageCalculatorService`, Spring supplies that instance for us by injecting the `MortgageCalculatorService` bean that was defined in the configuration class. That's dependency injection in action. Alternatively, we could remove the constructor parameter altogether and annotate the `calculatorService` with `@Autowired`. Using that approach, Spring would inject the bean automatically. The approaches are essentially equivalent, except that the constructor injection allows you to make the instance `final`. Here is the equivalent dependency injection using `@Autowired`:

```
@Autowired private final MortgageCalculatorService calculatorService;
```

If you choose to use `@Autowired`, then remember to remove the constructor parameter from the `App` bean constructor. If you use constructor injection, you don't need to annotate the constructor with `@Autowired`, but you may do so for emphasis if you like.

While the `@Autowired` annotation is still widely used for injection, the Good Housekeeping seal of approval is going to constructor injection rather than `@Autowired` for new code.

SPECIFYING SCOPE

To specify a scope using configuration classes, add an `@Scope` annotation above the `@Component` declaration, containing the scope name. For example, to change the `App` class to `prototype` scope, add an `@Scope` annotation containing the scope name (case insensitive) as follows:

```
@Scope(scopeName = "prototype")
@Component
public class App {
```

Using Component Scanning

Following Spring down the evolutionary chain, things were further simplified when the need to explicitly declare beans was replaced with "component scanning," a process where Spring inspects the file system for Spring annotated classes and automatically loads them as managed beans. Simply annotate your bean classes with one of the annotations that tell Spring to manage this class. Which annotation to use depends on the context, but they all have one thing in common: they tell Spring to manage this class. Here are the main annotations:

- **`@Configuration`**: Configuration class for defining Spring beans.
- **`@Component`**: Marks this class as a general Spring bean.
- **`@Service`**: Indicates that this class performs some service.
- **`@Repository`**: Indicates that this is a data access class.
- **`@Controller`**: This is an MVC controller, for handling web requests.
- **`@RestController`**: This is a RESTful web services controller, for handling HTTP requests.

The finished code for this example is in Git branch `component-scan`. Our application is a simple service, so we'll annotate our `MortgageCalculatorServiceImpl` class with `@Service` to indicate that our calculator is performing a service. We also annotated our `App` with `@Component` to tell Spring we want to access this class as a bean.

> **TIP** *We could have used the* `@Component` *annotation for our* `MortgageCalculatorServiceImpl` *class as well.* `@Component` *and* `@Service` *are essentially equivalent in how they work, but* `@Service` *expresses our intent more explicitly.*

Now we can remove the bean declarations from our `AppConfig` class and just add the packages to scan:

```
@Configuration
@ComponentScan(basePackages = "com.wiley.realworldjava")
public class AppConfig {
}
```

To use this approach, replace the `ApplicationContext` initializer in lines 17 and 18 of our `App` class with the following, passing in the config class name:

```
ApplicationContext context =
   new AnnotationConfigApplicationContext(AppConfig.class);
```

We can even remove the `Configuration` class entirely and simply pass the package name to scan into our `ApplicationContext` initializer:

```
ApplicationContext context
       = new AnnotationConfigApplicationContext("com.wiley.realworldjava");
```

> **TIP** *You can pass in a list of packages to scan by supplying multiple* `String` *parameters into the varargs* `AnnotationConfigApplicationContext` *constructor.*

CUSTOMIZING SPRING APPLICATIONS WITH PROPERTIES

You know that it is generally considered a bad practice to hard-code configuration parameters in your code, lest you need to modify your code every time configuration changes.

Spring lets you define properties in a resource file and introduce environment-specific modifications in profile-specific files. In standard Spring applications, this requires some simple scaffolding. In Spring Boot applications, that scaffolding all happens behind the curtains, so you needn't do anything. In the following sections, you'll see how to inject properties and then how to configure environment specific ones.

To see the finished product for this section, check out our branch called `profiles` in the repository.

Injecting Properties

To inject property values into your variables, create a file called `application.properties` in your `src/main/resources` folder, the default location where Spring expects your resource files to be defined. The file can contain your application-specific properties, expressed as key-value pairs. You can also use YAML files, which is an equivalent approach except using YAML, but in this book we use properties files. For more information on YAML, see the appendix of this book.

For the mortgage calculator, let's add the following properties:

```
default.interestRate=3.5
preferred.mortgage.holder=ABC Mortgage, Inc.
country=United States
```

In the `@Configuration` class (or in any Spring managed class), add the `@PropertySource` annotation above the class name, and pass in the name of the properties file. For example:

```
@Configuration
@PropertySource("classpath:application.properties")
public class AppConfig {
```

Now, all the properties specified in `application.properties` will be available to your application.

There are a few ways to *inject* those values into your Java application. One way is to annotate variables in your Java code with `@Value` and pass in a placeholder (in the form of `"${property.name}"`) with the property name. Spring will automatically inject the property with that name specified in your `application.properties` into that variable.

For example, to inject the `default.interestRate` from the previous `application.properties` into a variable of type double named `defaultInterestRate`, you can declare the variable as follows in any Spring managed class:

```
@Value("${default.interestRate}")
private double defaultInterestRate;
```

The variable can be any Java type, such as `String`, `int`, `Integer`, `double`, and so forth. Spring will do the String to type conversion for you, provided the value is legal for that data type. (In other words, don't try to assign an alphabetic value to a variable of type `double`!)

> **TIP** *Take note of the syntax for specifying the placeholder—you must include the property name inside* `${ }` *and all that inside quotes.*

Alternatively, you can include that placeholder as a constructor argument. For example, let's include the default interest rate placeholders as follows:

```
public MortgageCalculatorServiceImpl(
   @Value("${default.interestRate}")
   double defaultInterestRate) {
   this.defaultInterestRate = defaultInterestRate;
}
```

Configuring Environment-Specific Properties with Spring Profiles

In the previous section, we said that it is bad practice to hard-code values. So how can you inject values that are environment-specific, that is, that vary by environment? To accomplish that, Spring has a concept of profiles, which allow you to create environment-specific variables.

For example, let's say your application has different database properties, or calls different REST endpoint URLs, depending on the environment. You can create environment-specific property files. For example, to create a properties file for the dev environment, name it `application-dev.properties`. To create another for prod, name it `application-prod.properties`. Keep all these properties in your resources folder. Then add an `@PropertySource` annotation in your `@Configuration` class, specifying the profile placeholder, as follows:

```
@Configuration
@PropertySource("classpath:application.properties")
@PropertySource(
   "classpath:application-${spring.profiles.active}.properties")
public class AppConfig {
```

Now we have both properties specified, so Spring will use properties from both the `application.properties` file and the environment-specific properties file. If there is a conflict, the environment-specific one will win.

To tell Spring which profile to use, you can set the profile directly in IntelliJ as in Figure 6.2.

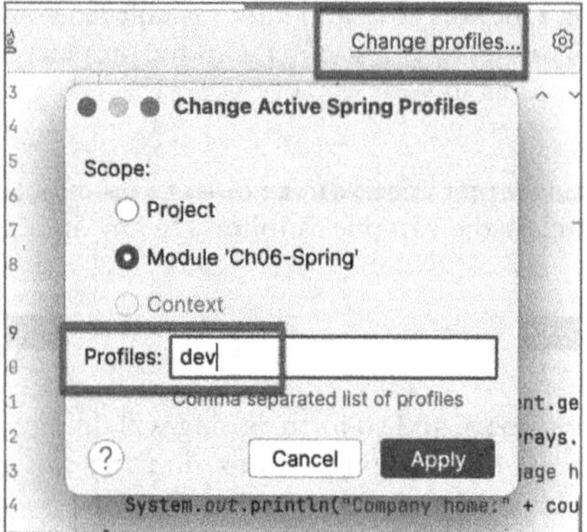

FIGURE 6.2: Setting the profile in IntelliJ with an option

Alternatively, you can edit the launch configuration to set the profile name as in Figure 6.3.

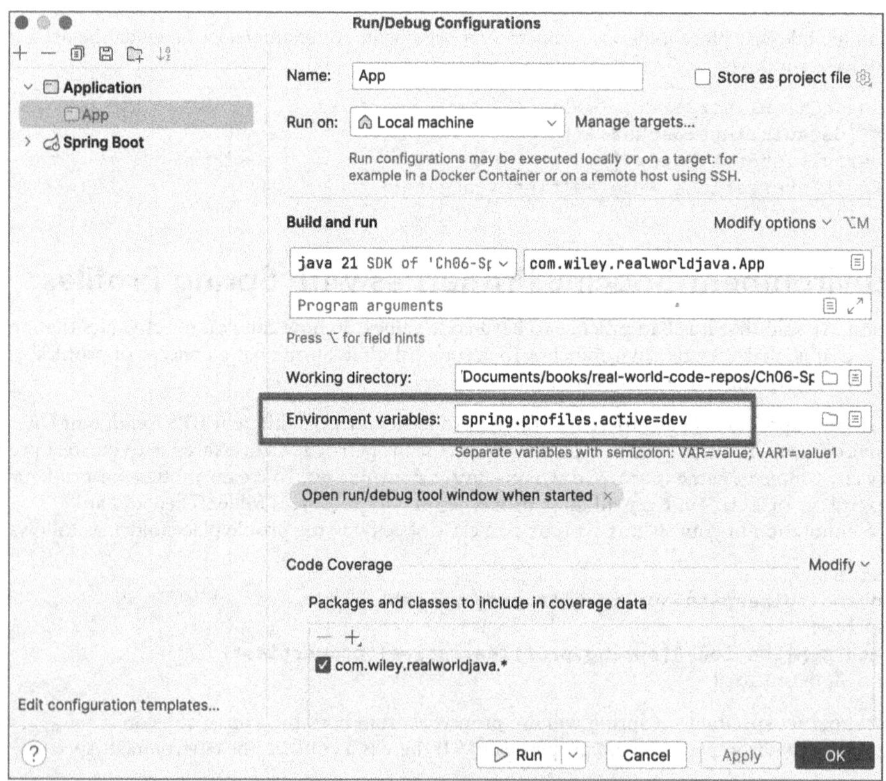

FIGURE 6.3: Setting the profile in IntelliJ with a launch configuration

Or you can simply pass in the profile name from the command line, as follows:

```
-Dspring.profiles.active=dev
```

For our current purposes, we'll specify the active profile to be `dev`, causing Spring to use the properties from `application-dev.properties`, in addition to the default properties from `application.properties`, which are always included regardless of profile.

Run that code and you'll see this output:

```
Profiles:[dev]
Preferred mortgage holder:ABC Mortgage, Inc.
Company home:United States
Loading Dev datasource
Monthly Payment: $1,122.61
```

Now change the active profile to `prod`, and run it again.

```
Profiles:[prod]
Preferred mortgage holder:ABC Mortgage, Inc.
Company home:UK
Loading Prod datasource
Monthly Payment: $1,531.17
```

The difference is that in dev, we did not specify a default interest rate in `application-dev.properties`, so the program picked up the default from `application.properties`.

```
default.interestRate=3.5
```

However, for the prod profile, the program saw the overridden property in `application-prod.properties` and so used that value for the calculation.

```
default.interestRate=6.2
```

Notice how when there is a conflict, the environment-specific version wins.

TURBOCHARGING DEVELOPMENT WITH SPRING BOOT

Spring Boot is a super-convenient framework that eliminates much of the scaffolding and setup required in Spring applications.

It uses the concept of "starter-dependencies," which are Maven/Gradle bill-of-material (BOM) dependencies, which means that they bring in all the required dependencies for their specific use cases. You can tell broadly what the starter is for by looking at its name, such as `spring-boot-starter-web` for building Spring MVC web applications, and `spring-starter-security` for applying security to your application with authentication and authorization.

An example is worth a thousand words, so let's take our mortgage calculator to the next level by exposing a web layer and adding some web URLs.

Initializing Spring Boot Projects with Spring Initializr

Spring provides a website called Initializr (their spelling!) where you select your dependencies and let Spring generate the full application skeleton, with everything in the right place, including a Maven POM or Gradle build file containing all the required properties and dependencies. Initializr is integrated into the major IDEs as well, and we will see how to use the Initializr website as well as the IDE integration.

To use the Initializr website, head over to `https://start.spring.io` from your favorite browser and select your build tool (in our case Maven), language (Java), Spring Boot version (3.3.3 is the latest stable release at the time of this writing; note that enterprises tend to avoid milestone release versions as they are still in progress), and enter your project metadata (Group, Artifact, Name, Description, and so forth) as in Figure 6.4.

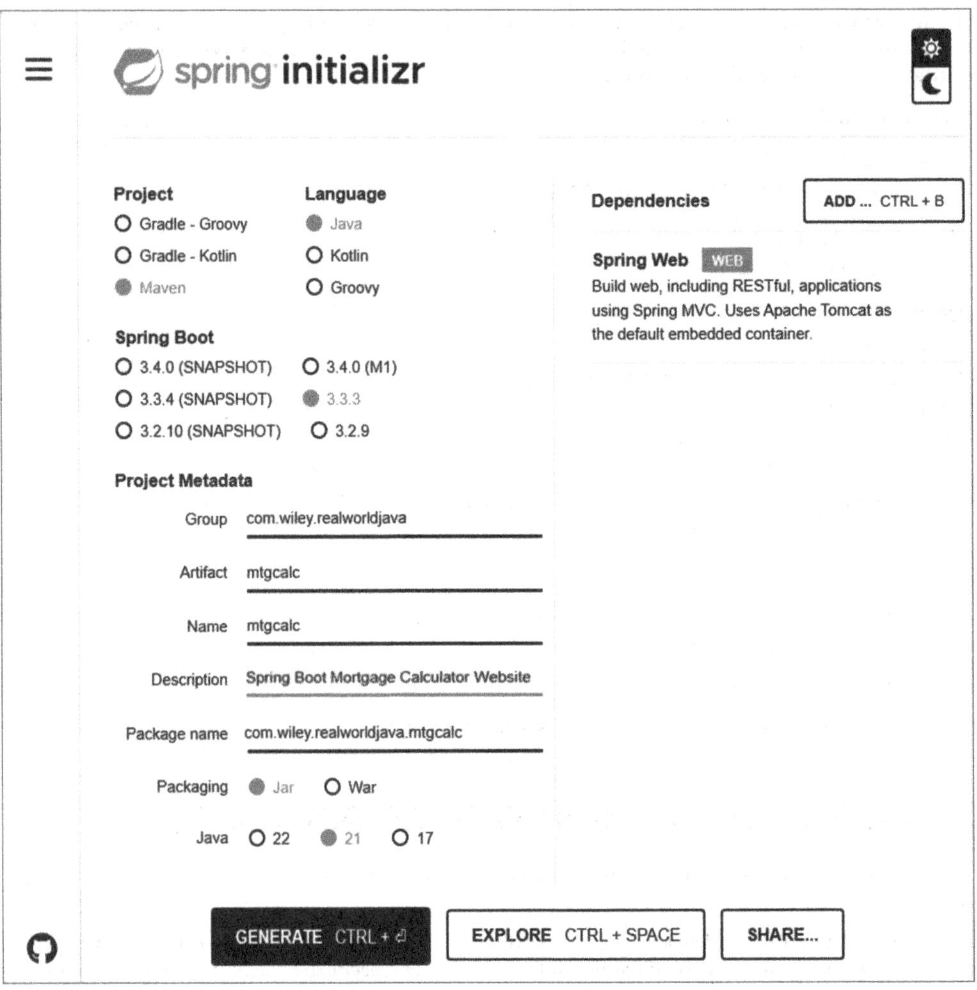

FIGURE 6.4: Configuring your project in Spring Initializr

Next, on the right side of the screen, click the Add dependencies button and select all dependencies you want included in your project. In our case, we will just use Spring Web for our web application. Finally, click the Generate button, which will produce a zip file (`mtgcalc.zip`) that you can unzip and open in your IDE.

Using IntelliJ Initializr Integration

You can also use the IDE to do all this for you, which is our preferred method. The completed code for this section is in the `spring-boot` branch.

Let's start a new project to see how to use Initializr support built into IntelliJ IDEA to generate a Spring Boot project. To generate a new Spring Boot project, choose File ➪ New ➪ Project and select Spring Boot. (Earlier versions of IntelliJ showed Spring Initializr instead of Spring Boot so you might still see that if you are using an earlier version.)

This opens a screen resembling the Initializr website, where you can enter your project details (see Figure 6.5.).

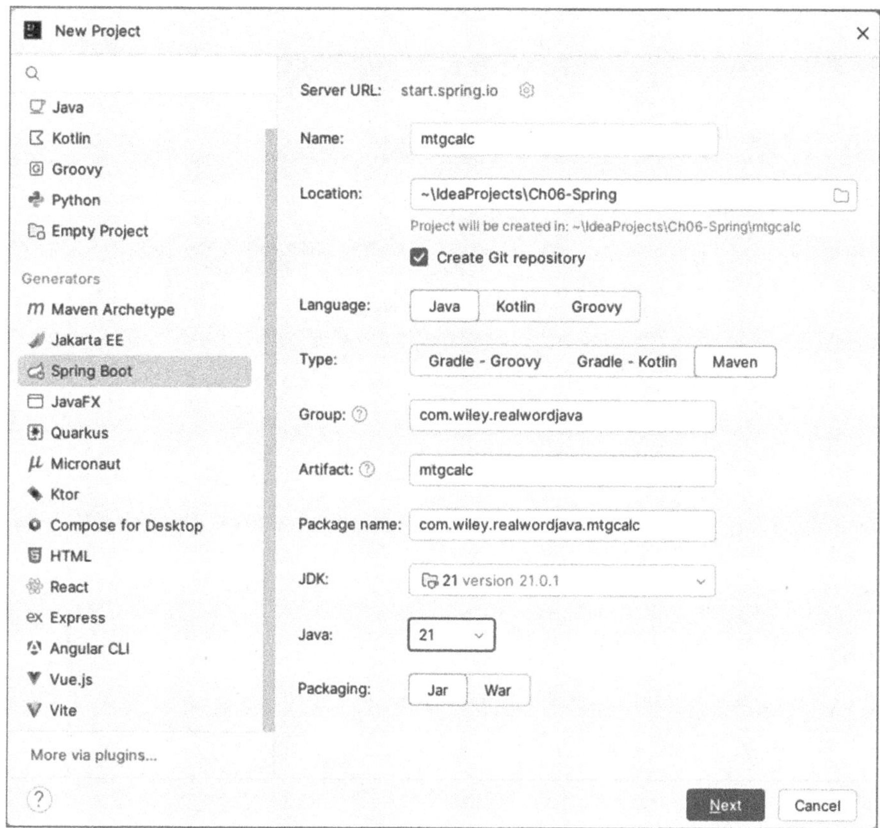

FIGURE 6.5: Configuring your Spring Boot project in IntelliJ

Click Next to select all your required dependencies. In our case, choose Spring Web, as in Figure 6.6.

Finally, click Create to generate the module. You can see the new module in your IDE. Open the `pom.xml` file, and you can see that Spring Boot generated a reference to the Spring Boot parent.

```
<parent>
    <groupId>org.springframework.boot</groupId>
    <artifactId>spring-boot-starter-parent</artifactId>
    <version>3.3.3</version>
    <relativePath/> <!-- lookup parent from repository -->
</parent>
```

The `spring-boot-starter-parent` is the parent of all Spring Boot projects, and it provides all of the default versions for the dependencies and plugins, under the tags `dependencyManagement` and `pluginManagement`, with references for every supported project. Maven looks at those `Management` references and only brings in the ones that are referenced as explicit dependencies in your POM. When you specify a dependency in the `dependencies` or `plugins` section, Spring pulls the versions from the parent POM `management` section, so you don't need to specify the version. That way when you upgrade your POM to the newest version, your project dependencies will also be automatically upgraded. If you specify an explicit version in your own POM, that will override the one in the parent.

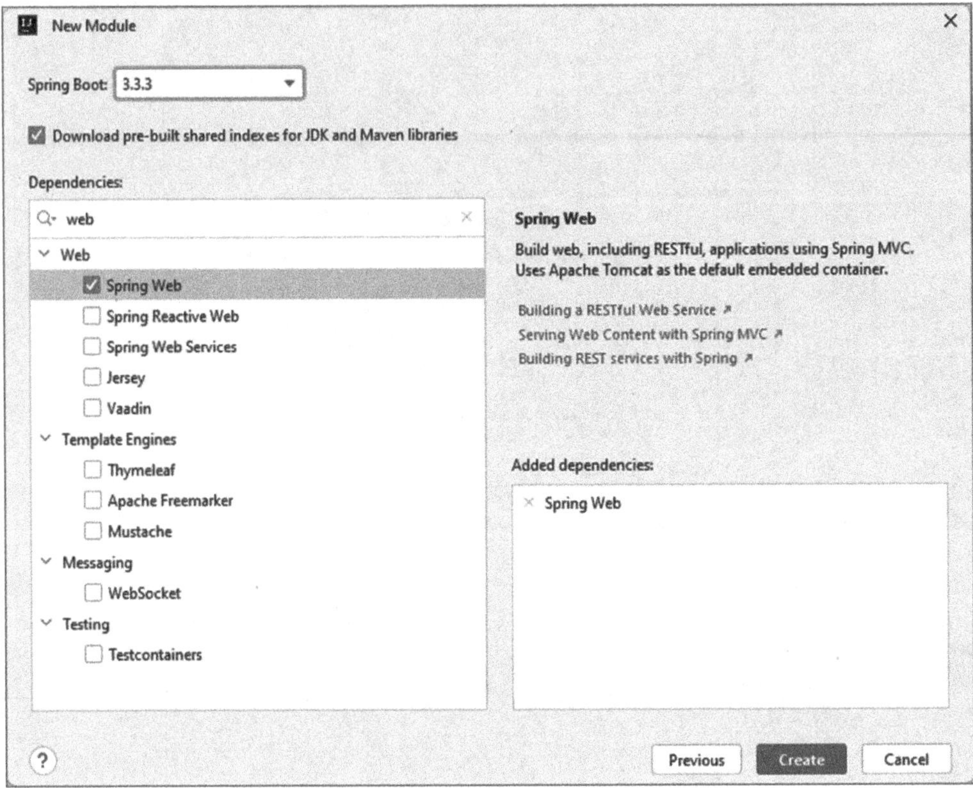

FIGURE 6.6: Selecting dependencies in IntelliJ

The POM also contains references to `spring-boot-starter-web` (since you selected Spring Web) and `spring-boot-starter-test`, which is always included.

You are going to want to add logging to your application, so add the following dependencies to your POM (no versions required; as usual Spring Boot provides the defaults):

```
<dependency>
    <groupId>org.slf4j</groupId>
    <artifactId>slf4j-api</artifactId>
</dependency>
<dependency>
    <groupId>ch.qos.logback</groupId>
    <artifactId>logback-classic</artifactId>
</dependency>
```

Open the file `application.properties` in your `src/main/resources` directory. Initializr was nice enough to insert a `spring.application.name=mtgcalc` entry for you, which you will see in your log messages and other applications. The `application.properties` file understands many default properties, for configuring every imaginable setting for your application. You can see the full list of recognized properties by clicking Ctrl+Space anywhere in that file.

Also, Initializr was generous enough to create a Spring Boot application class (named `MtgCalcApplication`) in the package root. A Spring Boot application class is required for all Spring Boot applications. It is a class in the root package that is annotated with `@SpringBootApplication` and is the entry point for the application. It is important to keep this at the package root, because Spring Boot automatically scans this package and everything under it by default, looking for Spring annotated classes.

For the fun of it, let's put our knowledge of logging, which you learned about in Chapter 5, "Capturing Application State with Logging Frameworks," and add a logger to print out the words "Hello, Mortgage Calculator" in the main method of `MtgCalcApplication` so that you can see that message when you run the application.

```
@SpringBootApplication
public class MtgCalcApplication {
   private final static Logger logger =
      LoggerFactory.getLogger(MtgCalcApplication.class);
   public static void main(String[] args) {
      SpringApplication.run(MtgCalcApplication.class, args);
      logger.info("Hello, Mortgage Calculator");
   }
}
```

Before we do any more work on our web application, let's launch the generated application to verify that everything is configured correctly.

There are several ways to run the application. The IDE should have created a run configuration for you, so you could just launch that by clicking the run button.

However, let's do it from the command line. Open a command prompt and `cd` to the project root; then build the code using the following (let's skip tests for now until we have implemented them):

```
mvn clean verify -DskipTests
```

That will generate a JAR file named `mtgcalc-0.0.1-SNAPSHOT.jar` in your `target` directory. Before running it, make sure the environment variable `JAVA_HOME` is set.

SETTING ENVIRONMENT VARIABLES

On Windows, you can run the following:

```
set JAVA_HOME=C:\Program Files\Java\jdk-21\
```

On Linux/Mac, it looks like the following:

```
export JAVA_HOME="/Library/Java/JavaVirtualMachines/jdk-21.jdk/
Contents/Home"
```

Launch the application by calling the following:

```
java -jar target/mtgcalc-0.0.1-SNAPSHOT.jar
```

If the default server port 8080 isn't free, you'll get an error. Let's change the server port from the default 8080 to 8081 by entering **server.port=8081** in `application.properties`, as in Figure 6.7. If you do this in IntelliJ, the type-ahead will show you the default value of 8080. Just type in **8081** in its place, which will set that as the port our web application will listen on. If 8081 is not free, choose one that is.

Re-build and launch the application, and you should see the output as in Figure 6.8. Notice how the application name is displayed in all of the logging output. Also observe the port displayed, as well as our "Hello, Mortgage Calculator" message.

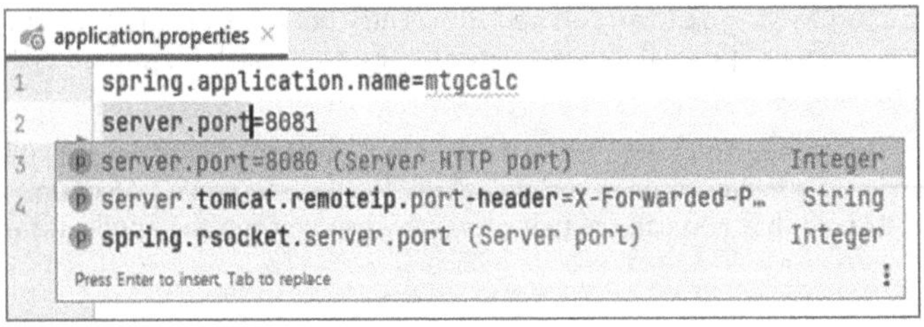

FIGURE 6.7: Specifying a server port

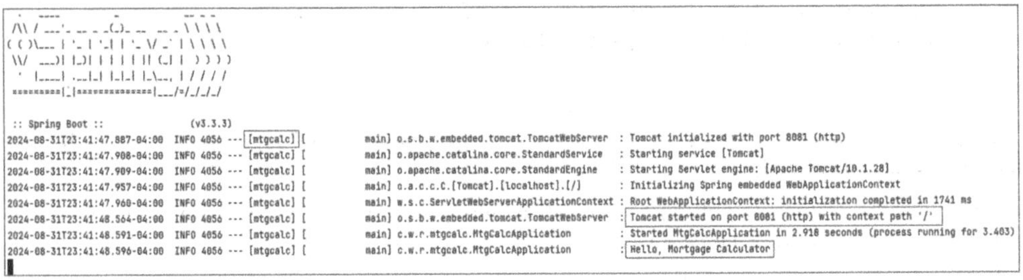

FIGURE 6.8: Output from Spring Boot launch

We saw earlier that Spring lets you specify an active profile, which you can use for creating environment-specific properties. For example, to specify that this is dev, pass in the JVM argument `-Dspring.profiles.active=dev`. This tells Spring to look for properties in `application-dev.properties`, in addition to the default `application.properties`. If there are overlapping properties, dev will win.

> **TIP** *Spring Boot lets you have many active profiles at the same time. You can specify additional profiles by listing their comma-separated names as in* `-Dspring.profiles.active=dev,cloud`. *If there is a conflict between property names,* `cloud` *would win in this case, since it appears later in the list.*

WORKING WITH SPRING MVC

Let's add some packages to our project. We will keep the calculation classes that do the grunt work under a `service` package. The web app endpoint is defined in a Spring *Controller* class (to be defined shortly), so we will keep that in the `controller` package. So, let's create packages `com.wiley.realworldjava.mtgcalc.service` and `com.wiley.realworldjava.mtgcalc.controller`. You can simply copy and paste the two classes `MortgageCalculatorService` and `MortgageCalculatorServiceImpl` from the original project into the new Spring Boot `mtgcalc` project.

To add web functionality, we need to add a controller class. This is a class that is annotated with `@RestController`. Create the class `MortgageController` in package `com.wiley.realworldjava.mtgcalc.controller`. Add methods to that class and annotate them with `@GetRequest("/my-endpoint")`; just rename `"/my-endpoint"` to the URL endpoint that you want to have referenced when that method is called. Let's give it a try by implementing a simple "Hello, World" endpoint:

```
@RestController
public class MortgageController {
```

```
        @GetMapping("/hello")
        public String hello(){
            return LocalDateTime.now() + ": Hello, World ";
        }
    }
```

Rebuild and launch, and from a browser hit the URL:

```
http://localhost:8081/hello
```

You should see the date, time, and a happy "Hello, World" in the browser! Now we are in a good position to implement our actual mortgage calculations. Let's autowire the `MortgageCalculator` into our controller class using *constructor injection*. When Spring sees a *bean* class like `MortgageCalculatorService` used as a constructor argument, it automatically creates an instance of that bean and injects it into the constructor.

```
@RestController
public class MortgageController {
    private final MortgageCalculatorService mortgageCalculator;
    public MortgageController(MortgageCalculatorService mortgageCalculator) {
        this.mortgageCalculator = mortgageCalculator;
    }
```

To tell Spring `MortgageCalculator` is a bean, annotate your implementation with one of the annotations `@Component`, `@Service`, and so forth, as we discussed in the earlier section "Using Component Scanning." Since this is a service class, we will use `@Service`.

```
@Service
public class MortgageCalculatorServiceImpl
implements MortgageCalculatorService {
```

For our calculator to be useful, we need to provide users with a way to pass in the required parameters, in this case the principal, years, and interest. We can do that by annotating the method arguments with `@RequestParam` in the `MortgageController`,

```
@GetMapping("payment")
public String calculateMonthlyPayment(
    @RequestParam double principal,
    @RequestParam int years,
    @RequestParam double interest) {

    double payment = mortgageCalculator.payment(principal, interest, years);
    String rval = String.format("Principal:%,.2f<br>Interest: %.2f<br>" +
        "Years: %d<br>Monthly Payment:%.2f", principal, interest, years, payment);
    return rval;
}
```

Notice that we inserted `<br>` in the output. This is the HTML syntax for inserting line feeds between the lines of output.

Now rebuild. Run and go to your browser and call the following:

```
http://localhost:8081/payment?principal=100000&years=30&interest=6.5
```

Our query string parameter names match the method argument variable names, so Spring MVC maps those to the method arguments and happily returns the nicely formatted result.

```
Principal:100,000.00
Interest: 6.50
Years: 30
Monthly Payment:632.07
```

USING @REQUESTPARAM

You can override the query string parameter names by supplying the desired name in the `@RequestParam` annotation. For example, changing the principal argument to `@RequestParam("amount") double principal` will alter the endpoint so that the call will become as follows:

```
http://localhost:8081/payment?amnt=100000&years=30&interest=6.5
```

Note that the calls we have so far implemented are HTTP GET requests, which is the default HTTP method when you call a URL from a browser. If you want to create endpoints for other HTTP methods such as POST or PUT, use the corresponding annotations `@PostMapping` or `@PutMapping`. There are annotations corresponding to all the possible HTTP methods including GET, POST, PUT, PATCH, DELETE, and so forth. These are all used in designing good resource-oriented architecture (ROA) RESTful web service applications. According to ROA principles, records are called *resources*. A GET request will query for a resource or list of resources. POST requests create a resource. PUT is used to replace an entire resource, PATCH updates fields of a resource. DELETE deletes the resource (or marks it for deletion). To learn more about RESTful web services, refer to the "Further References" section.

If your application exposes a complicated set of endpoints (which is typical in enterprise services), it is helpful to organize them into separate controllers, each with a common set of functionality. You can then assign a "context path," a prefix to all the endpoints in a given controller, by annotating the controller class itself with `@RequestMapping("/some-prefix")`, in which case every endpoint in that class would begin with `/some-prefix`. For example, in our case the class becomes the following:

```
@RestController
@RequestMapping("/mtg")
public class MortgageController {
```

Now all endpoints in this controller will need a `"/mtg/"` prefix. To use this new endpoint, restart the application and adjust your call to read as follows:

```
http://localhost:8081/mtg/payment?principal=100000&years=30&interest=6.5
```

This code is sufficient for serving browser pages, but for true resource-oriented RESTful web service APIs, you will often want to provide more information about the response, such as detailed response codes and response header messages.

A simple modification to your method signature lets you wrap your response in a generic `ResponseEntity`, a special Spring class that you can use to embed response metadata. For example, let's embed a header named `"Request time"` in our response, which will contain the time of the request.

```
@GetMapping("/payment")
public ResponseEntity<String> calculateMonthlyPayment(
   @RequestParam double principal,
   @RequestParam int years, @RequestParam double interest) {

   double payment = mortgageCalculator.payment(principal, interest, years);
   String rval = String.format("Principal:%,.2f<br>Interest: %.2f<br>" +
      "Years: %d<br>Monthly Payment:%.2f", principal, interest, years, payment);
   HttpHeaders headers = new HttpHeaders();
   headers.add("Request time", "Call for payment at " + LocalDateTime.now());
   return new ResponseEntity<>(rval, headers, HttpStatus.OK);
}
```

If you execute the call from the command line, you will see the response header. Use `curl -i` (`curl` to call the URL and `-i` to display the response body and headers), as shown in Figure 6.9.

```
curl -i "http://localhost:8081/mtg/payment?principal=100000&years=30&interest=6.7"
```

FIGURE 6.9: `curl` command to get response and headers

You should see the response:

```
HTTP/1.1 200
Request time: Call for payment at 2024-08-25T15:45:59.834954700
Content-Type: text/plain;charset=UTF-8
Content-Length: 77
Date: Sun, 25 Aug 2024 19:46:03 GMT

Principal:100,000.00<br>Interest: 6.70<br>Years: 30
   <br>Monthly Payment:645.28
```

That's how to do a GET request. Now orthodox resource-oriented architecture mandates using GET requests for read-only data access requests, and POST requests to update data. PUT requests are for operations that change data but are *idempotent*. Idempotent requests are calls that don't alter any underlying data after the initial request.

For read requests we'd like to use a GET; however, GET requests generally do not accept a body, and there are limitations to how much data you want to have in a URL query string. So, for querying a complex payload, such as an arbitrarily large list of data, enterprises will often use a POST request even for read-only queries.

A POST request supports a complex body, such as a JSON object. Let's learn some Spring magic and see how Spring automatically creates Java objects from JSON and vice versa.

We are going to create a POST request endpoint that will accept a JSON list composed of any number of mortgage calculations to be performed. We will then supply JSON object to the endpoint as a request body.

First let's create a new package called `com.wiley.realworld.java.mtgcalc.domain` and add to it three new classes: `User`, `Mortgage`, and `Response`:

```
public class User {
  private String name;
  private String location;
  // getters and setters go here
}

public class Mortgage {
  private double principal;
  private int years;
  private double interest;
  private User user;
  private double payment; // resulting monthly payment
  // getters and setters go here
}

public class Response {
  private final List<Mortgage> mortgages;
  private final LocalDateTime now;
  public Response(List<Mortgage> mortgages, LocalDateTime now) {
    this.mortgages = mortgages;
    this.now = now;
  }
  // getters go here
}
```

Here is the controller class:

```
28: @PostMapping("/payment")
29: public ResponseEntity<Response> calculateMonthlyPayment(
30:     // Spring converts the JSON list to a Java List
31:     @RequestBody List<Mortgage> mortgages) {
32:
33:     for(Mortgage mortgage:mortgages) {
34:        double principal = mortgage.getPrincipal();
35:        double rate = mortgage.getInterest();
36:        int years = mortgage.getYears();
37:        double payment = mortgageCalculator.payment(
38:           principal, rate, years);
39:        mortgage.setPayment(payment);
40:     }
41:     HttpHeaders headers = new HttpHeaders();
42:     headers.add("Total items", String.valueOf(mortgages.size()));
43:     return new ResponseEntity<>(new Response(mortgages,
44:        LocalDateTime.now()), headers, HttpStatus.OK);
45: }
```

Line 28 is declaring this method to be a POST request and binding it to the endpoint `/payment`. Note that is the same URL as our GET endpoint. When you call `/payment` as a POST call, it will call the new method, but when you call that same URL as a GET call, it will call the original method.

In line 31, the annotation `@RequestBody` tells Spring to convert a JSON payload to the argument type, in this case a Java `List` of `Mortgage` objects. Please see the appendix on JSON to learn more about how the deserializing from JSON into Java objects is done, under the covers.

Lines 33 to 40 iterate the list and perform the mortgage calculations for each element. Line 41 creates a response header, which is a convenient way of communicating metadata back to the caller.

Line 43 creates a new `ResponseEntity`, which accepts a `Response` body. In this case, the `Response` contains our list of solved mortgage calculations and current time.

The `ResponseEntity` also contains an `HttpHeaders` instance, a kind of `MultiValueMap` that Spring provides to let you return any response headers. It also contains an HTTP response status, in this case OK (which is HTTP code 200).

To execute this code, we need to compose a request consisting of a JSON payload. The server should be able to determine that you provided a JSON body, but it's a good practice to make this explicit by passing a `"Content-Type"` header into your request.

```
Content-Type: application/json
```

The request body is a list of requests. For example:

```
[
   {
      "user": {
         "name": "John Jones",
         "location": "Miami, Florida"
      },
      "principal": 250000,
      "years": 30,
      "interest": 6.5
   },
```

```
    {
        "user": {
            "name": "Mary Michaels",
            "location": "New York, NY"
        },
        "principal": 100000,
        "years": 30,
        "interest": 6.25
    }
]
```


You can find a copy of this JSON payload in the `request.json` file in the chapter Git repository, in the `mtgcalc/src/main/resources` directory of the `spring-boot` branch. Download that, then rebuild and launch your application, and call:

```
curl -X POST -H "Content-Type: application/json"
-d @request.json http://localhost:8081/mtg/payment
```

The result should be similar to the request body but populated with the resulting calculations, along with the date and time of the request (which is very helpful considering how mortgage rates change by the minute these days!).


```
{
    "mortgages": [
        {
            "principal": 250000.0,
            "years": 30,
            "interest": 6.5,
            "user": {
                "name": "John Jones",
                "location": "Miami, Florida"
            },
            "payment": 1580.170058732413
        },
        {
            "principal": 100000.0,
            "years": 30,
            "interest": 6.25,
            "user": {
                "name": "Mary Michaels",
                "location": "New York, NY"
            },
            "payment": 615.7172004263946
        }
    ],
    "now": "2024-09-03T17:42:07.017027"
}
```


HANDLING ERRORS IN SPRING

You can safeguard your application so that it handles all errors in a uniform way by introducing a controller advice. This is a class annotated with `@ControllerAdvice`, containing methods for handling any exceptions that you specify. The best way to do that is to create a special exception for your application that extends `RuntimeException` and throw that exception from your code. This section continues to use the `spring-boot` branch.

For example, let's create two classes in the `com.realworldjava.mtgcalc.exception` package. First, we create a `MortgageException`:

```
public class MortgageException extends RuntimeException{
  public MortgageException(String message) {
    super(message);
  }

  public MortgageException(String message, Throwable cause) {
    super(message, cause);
  }
}
```

Then create the global exception handler, by annotating a class with `@ControllerAdvice` and implementing methods for your exceptions; in this case we just implement one such method named `handleException`. The method must be annotated with `@ExceptionHandler` and must accept the exception to be handled as the lone method argument.

```
@ControllerAdvice
public class GlobalExceptionHandler {
   @ExceptionHandler
   public ResponseEntity<ErrorResponse> handleException(
      MortgageException exception) {
   ErrorResponse errorResponse =
      ErrorResponse.builder(exception, HttpStatusCode.valueOf(400),
      exception.getMessage()).build();
      return new ResponseEntity<>(errorResponse, HttpStatus.BAD_REQUEST);
  }
}
```

Finally modify the service implementation to throw a strategic exception:

```
@Override
public double payment(double principal,
                      double annualInterestRate, int termInYears) {
  if(termInYears <=0) {
    throw new MortgageException("Years must be positive");
  }
  double monthlyInterestRate = annualInterestRate / 12 / 100;
  int numberOfPayments = termInYears * 12;

  // mortgage formula: P * R * [(1+R)^N] / [(1+R)^N - 1]
  return principal * (monthlyInterestRate
     * Math.pow(1 + monthlyInterestRate, numberOfPayments))
     / (Math.pow(1 + monthlyInterestRate, numberOfPayments) - 1);
}
```

Rebuild and launch the code, and call the GET from the browser as before, and everything works fine. But then change the `years` to be `-30` by calling this:

```
http://localhost:8081/mtg/payment?principal=100000&years=-30&interest=6.7
```

That returns a response as in Figure 6.10.

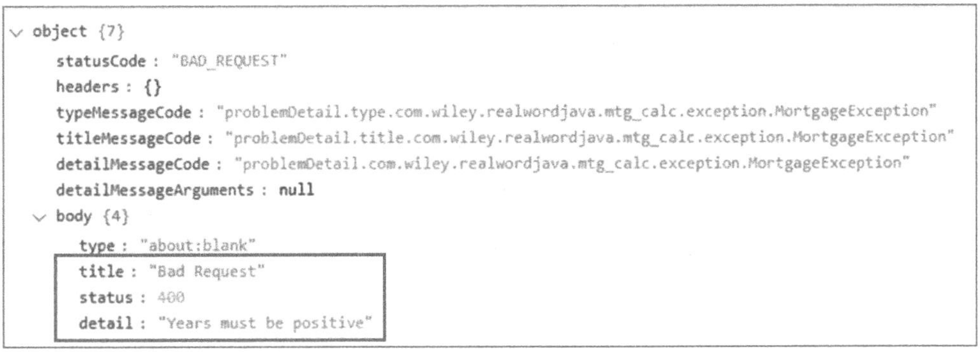

```
object {7}
    statusCode : "BAD_REQUEST"
    headers : {}
    typeMessageCode : "problemDetail.type.com.wiley.realwordjava.mtg_calc.exception.MortgageException"
    titleMessageCode : "problemDetail.title.com.wiley.realwordjava.mtg_calc.exception.MortgageException"
    detailMessageCode : "problemDetail.com.wiley.realwordjava.mtg_calc.exception.MortgageException"
    detailMessageArguments : null
  body {4}
      type : "about:blank"
      title : "Bad Request"
      status : 400
      detail : "Years must be positive"
```

FIGURE 6.10: Response from ControllerAdvice

INSPECTING YOUR APPLICATION WITH ACTUATOR

Actuator is a handy plugin you will want to use in your Spring-based applications. It exposes some standardized endpoints that can give you a wealth of information about your applications. The endpoints are used by tools such as Prometheus, Grafana, and other observability applications. (We cover observability in Chapter 12, "Monitoring Your Applications: Observability in the Java Ecosystem.") The code in this section is in branch `actuator`.

The following are some of the common endpoints you will see:

- **`/actuator`**: This displays a list of all actuator endpoints.
- **`/actuator/health`**: This useful endpoint provides health information about the application, in the form of a JSON response with the single property `{"status":"ok"}`. You can call this endpoint directly, but its main value is that it is used by monitoring tools to check on the health of your application.
- **`/actuator/info`**: This displays standard and bespoke (custom) application information.
- **`/actuator/metrics`**: This displays a list of names of metrics for the current application.
- **`/actuator/metrics/<metric name>`**: This displays the current value of the named metric. For example, `http://localhost:8081/actuator/metrics/disk.free` returns the usable disk space.
- **`/actuator/loggers`**: This displays the configuration of all loggers in the application.
- **`/actuator/env`**: This exposes properties from the Spring environment.
- **`/actuator/beans`**: This displays a list of every Spring bean in your application.

As an example, a GET call to `http://localhost:8081/actuator` returns a response that starts with this:

```
{
   "_links": {
      "self": {
         "href": "http://localhost:8081/actuator",
         "templated": false
      },
```

```
        "beans": {
            "href": "http://localhost:8081/actuator/beans",
            "templated": false
        },
        "caches-cache": {
            "href": "http://localhost:8081/actuator/caches/{cache}",
            "templated": true
        },
        "caches": {
            "href": "http://localhost:8081/actuator/caches",
            "templated": false
        },
        "health": {
            "href": "http://localhost:8081/actuator/health",
            "templated": false
        },
        "health-path": {
            "href": "http://localhost:8081/actuator/health/{*path}",
            },
        "metrics-requiredMetricName": {
            "href": "http://localhost:8081/actuator/metrics/{name}",
            "templated": true
        },
        "metrics": {
            "href": "http://localhost:8081/actuator/metrics",
            "templated": false
    },
```


Adding Actuator to an application is actually quite simple. First, add the actuator starter dependency.

```
<dependency>
    <groupId>org.springframework.boot</groupId>
    <artifactId>spring-boot-starter-actuator</artifactId>
</dependency>
```

The endpoint `actuator/health` is available by default, but the other endpoints need to be enabled explicitly. To do so, add the following property to your `application.properties` file, a comma-separated list of endpoints:

```
management.endpoints.web.exposure.include=info,metrics
```

To expose all endpoints, provide the value *:

```
management.endpoints.web.exposure.include=*
```

Now, if you call `http://localhost:8081/actuator/metrics`, it will return a list of metrics supported by actuator. There is also a *templated* URL `http://localhost:8081/actuator/metrics/{name}`.

> **TIP** *A templated URL means that it takes an additional parameter.*

Substitute one of the metric names to see the values for that metric. For example, a call to `http://localhost:8081/actuator/metrics/jvm.info` returns all you want to know about the current JVM:


```
{
    "name": "jvm.info",
    "description": "JVM version info",
```

```
        "measurements": [
            {
                "statistic": "VALUE",
                "value": 1.0
            }
        ],
        "availableTags": [
            {
                "tag": "vendor",
                "values": [
                    "Oracle Corporation"
                ]
            },
            {
                "tag": "runtime",
                "values": [
                    "Java(TM) SE Runtime Environment"
                ]
            },
            {
                "tag": "version",
                "values": [
                    "21.0.1+12-LTS-29"
                ]
            }
        ]
    }
```


SECURING YOUR APPLICATION WITH SPRING SECURITY

Security is going to be the most important nonfunctional requirement of any serious enterprise application. Spring provides first-class support for security. First, we'll introduce some terminology and then get into the Spring code.

Learning Security Terminology

First let's get familiar with some terminology.

- **Eavesdropper:** A person or program that surreptitiously gains access to data being transmitted across a network.
- **Encryption:** Process of encoding data to prevent unauthorized access.
    - **Symmetric Encryption:** The same key is used by the sender and receiver to encrypt/decrypt the data. Can be risky if the key is discovered by an eavesdropper.
    - **Asymmetric Encryption:** Data is encrypted using a *public key*, but can only be decrypted using a *private key*, known only to the server. This ensures that eavesdroppers cannot decrypt the data. Similarly, data can be encrypted using the private key and decrypted using the public key. This is done to ensure that the data was actually transmitted by the known sender.
- **Certificate:** A digital document that contains a public key and other information such as the name of the issuing certificate authority.
- **Certificate Authority:** A trusted organization that issues and maintains certificates.
- **Secure Sockets Layer (SSL):** A protocol for encrypting data for transmitting over the Internet. Uses certificates issued by a certificate authority.

- **Transport Layer Security (TLS):** A next-generation, more secure version of SSL.
- **Hypertext Transfer Protocol (HTTP):** An open protocol for transmitting data between a web client and web server. Uses port 80 by default but can easily be modified.
- **HTTPS:** A secure version of HTTP using SSL. Uses port 443 by default.
- **Authentication:** Verifies who you are. For example, you can enter a username and password, and the application checks those credentials in a secure manner.
- **Authorization:** Verifies that an authenticated user is authorized to see the resources they are attempting to access.

AUTHORIZATION

Spring Authorization framework supports all the important flavors of authentication:

- **Basic Authentication:** The username and password are transmitted in the `Authorization` header of the HTTP request using Base64 encoding. Base64 is a simple substitution algorithm that is easy to reverse, so when using basic authentication, be sure to provide a further layer of encryption, for example by using HTTPS, so eavesdroppers can't scrape secret information.
- **Form-Based Authentication:** Data is entered into a web form, which is transmitted to a server for verification. A *session cookie* is then assigned and used to verify the user during subsequent requests.
- **Digest Authentication:** Data is encrypted using a hashing algorithm. The receiver of the data applies the same algorithm to its database and compares the two hashed values.
- **OAuth2:** An authorization framework that allows users to sign into a website using credentials from another site.
- **OpenID Connect:** This authentication framework is frequently used with OAuth2.
- **JSON Web Token (JWT) Authentication:** This is a specially formatted and digitally signed token that contains "claims," which are standard or custom key-value pairs containing relevant information about the caller.
- **Lightweight Directory Access Protocol) Authentication (LDAP):** User information is maintained in an internal database, using a hierarchical structure that mimics the corporate organizational structure. Generally it uses TLS for secure transmission.
- **Custom Authentication:** This lets you implement custom logic for authenticating users.

Those are the general security-related terms you will hear in common security conversations. Now let's see how Spring puts it all together to secure your application.

Understanding Spring Security Processing

Spring Security uses *filters* (or more accurately "servlet filters") to handle authentication and authorization. Filters are small programs that intercept and enrich incoming requests or outgoing responses in a predefined order. Each filter performs its processing and then passes the result to the next filter in a chain of filters, until the request finally reaches the desired endpoint implementation.

This section starts using the `spring-boot-security-basic` branch. Following is the description of the authentication flow in a Spring MVC application. You can see this process illustrated in Figure 6.11.

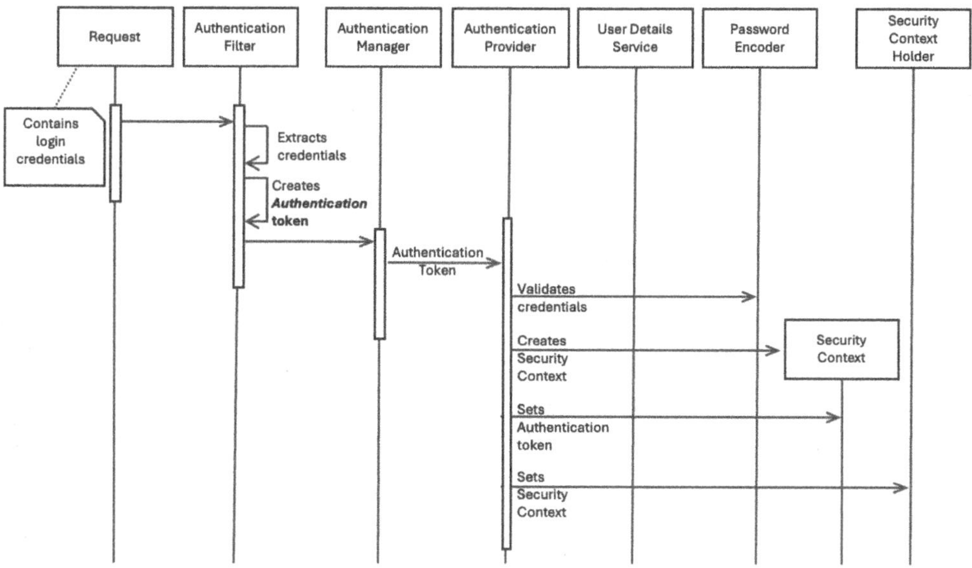

FIGURE 6.11: Spring Security filter interactions

The process starts when the user initiates a request. The servlet filters intercept the request and start processing. The first filter in the chain is the `AuthenticationFilter`, which extracts login credentials from the incoming request and passes them to the `AuthenticationManager`. The filter produces an `Authentication` token and passes that to the `AuthenticationManager`. The `AuthenticationManager` then passes the token to an `AuthenticationProvider`, which validates it using the `UserDetailsService` and `PasswordEncoder` interfaces. If the credentials are valid, it creates a SecurityContext to contain the token and stores that in the `SecurityContextHolder`, which is then accessible to subsequent filters. Applications can then access the `Authentication` token to check authorization.

After the request processing has completed, Spring Security clears the `SecurityContextHolder` to prevent reuse.

Spring Security by default uses *session-based authentication*. In that scheme, a session ID is preserved in a cookie and is sent with each request, allowing the server to retrieve the session and associated `SecurityContext`. In this way, the login remains valid until it times out or until the session ends, so there is no need to log in again for each request.

Applications can also choose to use *token-based authentication*. In that case a JWT token containing the user information is generated and passed in the request header for each request. Again, this allows the login to remain valid for the life of the token or until the session is terminated.

Let's implement Basic Authentication in our application. As a reminder, this will require a user ID and password to gain passage to our endpoint. Normally such credentials are stored in a database or in LDAP, and the `AuthenticationManager` and `AuthenticationProvider` work to validate logins. But for our application we will hard-code it in our application. A user will need to pass in a Base64-encoded username and password in the request headers, as we will soon see.

To get started, let's add the Spring Security dependencies to our POM. To determine what dependencies to add to an existing project, you can head back to the Spring Initialzr website at `https://start.spring.io` and pretend you are creating a new project. Type **Spring Security** to select dependency; then on the bottom of the screen select Explore. This will display the dependencies associated with Spring Security, which you can copy and paste into your POM (see Figure 6.12).

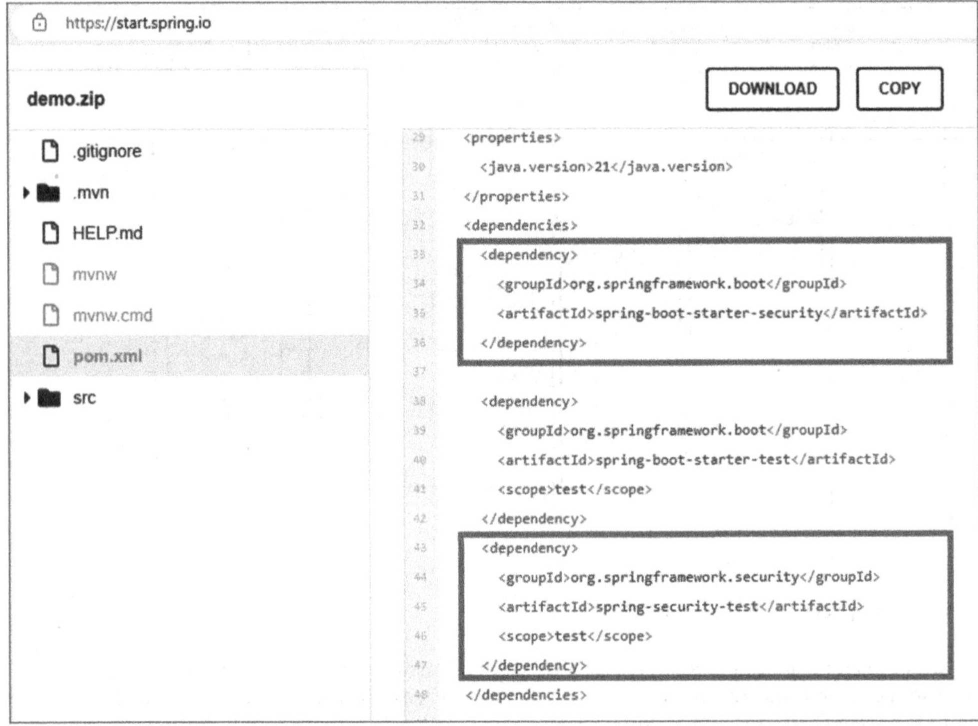

FIGURE 6.12: Using Initialzr to locate new dependencies

Copy the dependencies `spring-boot-starter-security` and `spring-security-test` into the dependencies section of your POM.

Or if you are using IntelliJ IDEA, you can click Edit Starters at the top of the `<dependencies>` section, and type **Spring Security** to enter the appropriate dependencies, as shown in Figure 6.13.

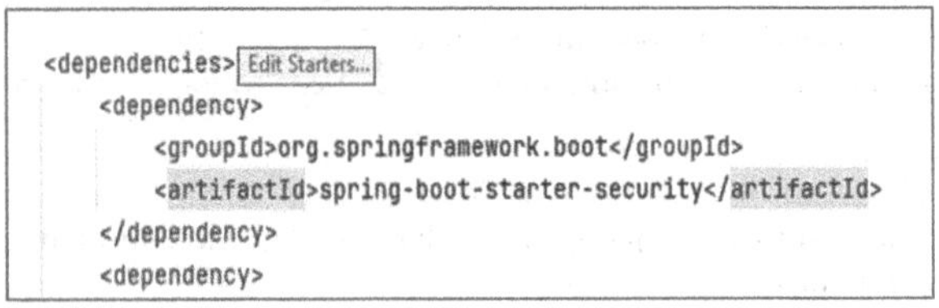

```
<dependencies> Edit Starters...
    <dependency>
        <groupId>org.springframework.boot</groupId>
        <artifactId>spring-boot-starter-security</artifactId>
    </dependency>
    <dependency>
```

FIGURE 6.13: Adding new dependencies using IntelliJ

Next, we have to create an `@Configuration` annotated class that enables Web Security.

```
@Configuration
@EnableWebSecurity
public class SecurityConfig {

    @Bean
```

```
23:     public SecurityFilterChain securityFilterChain(HttpSecurity http)
24:        throws Exception {
25:        http
26:           .csrf(csrf -> csrf
27:              .ignoringRequestMatchers(
28:                 new AntPathRequestMatcher("/mtg/payment",
29:                 HttpMethod.POST.name()))
30:           )
31:           .authorizeHttpRequests((authorize) -> authorize
32:           .requestMatchers(new AntPathRequestMatcher("/mtg/payment",
33:              HttpMethod.POST.name())).authenticated()
34:           .requestMatchers(new AntPathRequestMatcher("/mtg/payment",
35:              HttpMethod.GET.name())).authenticated()
36:           .anyRequest().authenticated()
37:           )
38:           // use basic authentication
39:           .httpBasic(Customizer.withDefaults());
40:        return http.build();
41:     }
42:
43:     @Bean
44:     public UserDetailsService userDetailsService() {
45:        PasswordEncoder encoder =
46:           PasswordEncoderFactories.createDelegatingPasswordEncoder();
47:        UserDetails user = User.builder()
48:           .username("user")
49:           .password(encoder.encode("password"))
50:           .roles("USER")
51:           .build();
52:        return new InMemoryUserDetailsManager(user);
53:     }
54: }
```

This uses the `@EnableWebSecurity` annotation (line 19).

We need to create a `SecurityFilterChain` bean to define the restrictions on each endpoint, using the `authorizeHttpRequests()` method (lines 31 to 36). Lines 30 to 33 specify that the POST flavor of the `/payment` endpoint requires authorization, and lines 34 to 35 specify the same about the GET flavor.

Line 39 tells Spring we are using Basic Authentication. Lines 44 to the end create a `UserDetailsService` to define the username (`"user"`) and the password, which in our case is the top-secret word "password." You could create additional users in the same way and supply them all as a varargs to the new `InMemoryUserDetailsManager()` constructor in line 52.

We glossed over the obscure CSRF code in lines 26 to 30. This tells the code to ignore Cross-Site Request Forgery checking for our POST call. Since POST calls are intended to modify data, Spring Security checks them for CSRF tokens. In a production system we want this protection to prevent hackers from impersonating a valid user, but for the sake of our demo, let's use this approach.

Now build and launch the application again and try to call the endpoint. In a browser, you'll be prompted for credentials. If you run this `curl` command, you will see the 401 HTTP return code, which means unauthorized.

```
curl -X POST -H "Content-Type: application/json" -d @request.json
--fail --silent --show-error  http://localhost:8081/mtg/payment
```

To solve this, we must add Basic Authentication to our request. This requires you to pass in a valid user and password in the Authorization header of the request. In a browser, this is easy. You type **`user`** and **`password`** when prompted, which are the values used in our example.

For the POST, you need to create a string composed of `user:password`, and then Base64 encode that whole string. You can do so easily by heading over to `https://www.base64encode.org` and paste in `user:password`, taking care not to leave any excess characters or spaces, and click the encode button. That should return `dXNlcjpwYXNzd29yZA==`, the keys to the castle. Create a new header named `"Authorization"` and provide the value as `Basic dXNlcjpwYXNzd29yZA==`, as follows:

```
Authorization: Basic dXNlcjpwYXNzd29yZA==
Content-Type: application/json
```

In curl, you can now run:

```
curl -X POST -H "Content-Type: application/json"
-H "Authorization: Basic dXNlcjpwYXNzd29yZA=="
-d @request.json http://localhost:8081/mtg/payment
```

This time you should get a happy response.

EXPLORING THE SPRING PROJECTS

This chapter gives you a taste of what Spring has to offer. Table 6.1 lists some examples. There are many more. If you are working with AI, GraphQL, or pretty much any technology, look to see if Spring has a project to make your life easier!

TABLE 6.1: Example Spring Projects

PROJECT	DESCRIPTION
Spring Framework	The core of Spring including dependency injection, web applications, messaging, and more. For more features of the Spring Framework, see Chapter 7, "Testing Your Code with Automated Testing Tools"; Chapter 9, "Parallelizing Your Application Using Java Concurrency"; and Chapter 11, "Coding the Aspect-Oriented Way."
Spring Batch	Used for batch processing applications.
Spring Boot	Gets your applications running quickly.
Spring Cloud	Supports cloud and microservices.
Spring Data	Used for working with databases.
Spring Integration	Supports popular enterprise integration patterns.
Spring Security	Adds authorization and authentication support.
Spring WebFlux	Provides reactive capabilities to web and REST endpoints (based on Project Reactor).

FURTHER REFERENCES

- `http://www.ics.uci.edu/~fielding/pubs/dissertation/rest_arch_style.htm`
  - Roy Fielding's original dissertation on REST
- `https://start.spring.io`
  - Initializr
- `https://docs.spring.io/spring-framework/reference/index.html`
  - Spring Framework Documentation
- `https://www.base64encode.org`
  - Base 64 encoder
- *RESTful Web Services* (O'Reilly 2007)
- *Spring in Action* (Manning, 2022)

SUMMARY

In this chapter, you learned much of what you will need to get comfortable with Spring. The Spring framework is huge, containing integrations with every conceivable framework. You learned about how to configure beans using XML and Java. Then you learned how to use the component scan to make the code even shorter. You learned to work with properties and profiles along with Spring Boot and Intitializr. Then you learned how to handle errors and deal with security. But most of all you learned that there is a lot to love about Spring. There is much, much more to learn, so if your enterprise uses specific features, you will want to read the documentation for those.

7 Testing Your Code with Automated Testing Tools

WHAT'S IN THIS CHAPTER?

- Understanding Testing Basics
- Learning JUnit
- Working with Common Testing Libraries
- Mocking Objects
- Measuring Test Coverage
- Optimizing Your Testing with IntelliJ
- Learning Other Testing Concepts

I am sure you have contemplated the great existential question of the century: how do you know your code works as expected? Early in your coding career, you probably attempted to answer that question by adding print statements or logging statements to see if the code was behaving as expected. Then you might have learned to use a debugger to step through your code. After a bunch of effort, you were fairly confident you had some working code. Now all you needed was a way to ensure that it stayed working!

In Chapter 4, "Automating Your CI/CD Builds with Maven, Gradle, Jenkins," you saw how to run builds every time a change is pushed to version control. By including automated tests in these builds, you benefit from *regression testing*, a kind of safety net that warns you when the behavior of your code differs from what you were expecting. This chapter covers automated testing and the related ecosystem.

The examples in this chapter use the JUnit 5 testing framework; however, there is a lot of JUnit 4 code in applications you may work on, so we will highlight common differences between JUnit 4 and 5. You may encounter another framework for unit testing in Java called TestNG. This chapter does not cover TestNG since JUnit is more popular. Before JUnit 5 was released, TestNG had some key features that JUnit was missing, but JUnit 5 has added these as well, and you are much more likely to need to know JUnit than TestNG. Regardless, once you know JUnit 5, you will find it much easier to pick up TestNG if needed.

> **CODE DOWNLOADS FOR THIS CHAPTER**
>
> The source code for this chapter is available on the book page at `www.wiley.com`. Click the Downloads link. You can also find the code at `https://github.com/realworldjava/Ch07-Testing`. See the `README.md` file in that repository for details.

UNDERSTANDING TESTING BASICS

In this section, you'll learn how to organize your tests and how to write a simple unit test using both Maven and Gradle. You'll also see an example of *Test-Driven Development* (TDD), where you write your unit tests before writing your code!

Staging Your Test Directory

Both Maven and Gradle use an opinionated approach to building. They expect a standard directory structure for staging your main and test code and artifacts. Fortunately, they share the same structure, which is very helpful since it enables you to quickly switch between build systems and expect the same structure.

Figure 7.1 shows how the directories are organized within that structure, which should look familiar from Chapter 4. The `src/main/java` directory contains the Java code that is part of your application, and the `src/main/resources` directory contains the non-Java artifacts such as XML and property files. All the code in the `src/main` directory structure is intended for production.

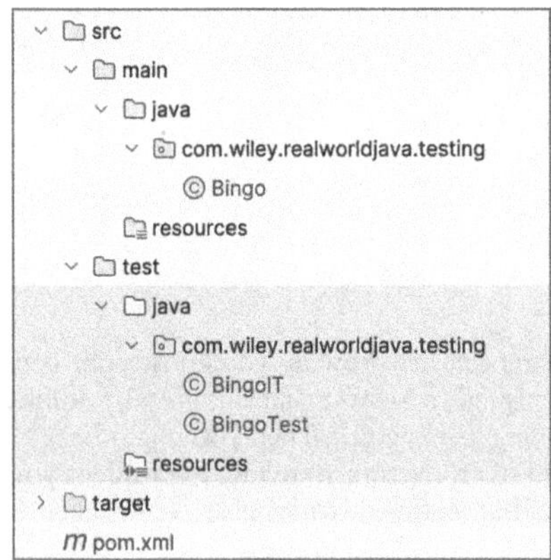

FIGURE 7.1: Test organization in Maven

By contrast, the `src/test` directory structure exists to ensure the code in `src/main` works as advertised. As with `src/test`, the `java` and `resources` subdirectories exist in `src/test` as well, to separate Java code from other files. This parallel directory structure becomes second nature very quickly.

> **MAIN VS TEST DIRECTORIES**
>
> Code under `src/test/java` can access both `src` and `test` subdirectories. Code under `src/main/java` can access `src` subdirectories but cannot access `test` subdirectories.

Our project contains a class called `Bingo`. You will notice that there are *two* test classes for `Bingo`. `BingoTest` is a unit test, and `BingoIT` is an integration test. Yes, `IT` stands for *integration test*, which tests the interactions between two or more parts of the system. It is common for an integration test to interact with a REST API or database or to make use of the file system, whereas unit tests abstract such details away with mocks, which you'll see later in the chapter.

Configuring JUnit in a Maven Build

You can look up the latest version of JUnit on Maven Central (`https://mvnrepository.com/artifact/org.junit/junit-bom`), which at the time of this writing was `5.10.2`. This is the version of both the bill of materials (BOM) and the `junit-jupiter` artifact itself. See Chapter 4 if you need a review of what a BOM is or how dependency management works.

```
<properties>
   <junit5.version>5.10.2</junit5.version>
</properties>

<dependencyManagement>
   <dependencies>
      <dependency>
         <groupId>org.junit</groupId>
         <artifactId>junit-bom</artifactId>
         <version>${junit5.version}</version>
         <type>pom</type>
         <scope>import</scope>
      </dependency>
    </dependencies>
</dependencyManagement>

<dependencies>
    <dependency>
       <groupId>org.junit.jupiter</groupId>
       <artifactId>junit-jupiter</artifactId>
       <scope>test</scope>
    </dependency>
</dependencies>
```

JUnit Jupiter is the English name for JUnit 5. The imports used in your JUnit tests have `jupiter` in the name as well. The BOM is an exception and uses `org.junit` (without `jupiter`) for the group ID. The `junit-jupiter` dependency is scoped as `test`, so it is available to the tests, but not the main code.

> **NOTE** *The group IDs are different for the JUnit 5 BOM and the* `junit-jupiter` *dependency. Be sure to use the right one in the right place.*

For actually running the tests, Maven uses the Surefire plugin for unit tests and the Failsafe plugin for integration tests. These plugins always keep their version numbers in sync, so you can look up the latest version of either one on Maven Central at `https://mvnrepository.com/artifact/org.apache.maven.plugins/maven-surefire-plugin`. This version number goes in the properties section of the POM:

```
<surefire.version>3.2.5</surefire.version>
```

To tell Maven to run the tests, you need to add the `maven-surefile-plugin` and the `maven-failsafe-plugin` to the `<build>` section of your Maven POM file. Here's an example:

```
<plugin>
   <groupId>org.apache.maven.plugins</groupId>
   <artifactId>maven-surefire-plugin</artifactId>
   <version>${surefire.version}</version>
</plugin>
<plugin>
   <groupId>org.apache.maven.plugins</groupId>
   <artifactId>maven-failsafe-plugin</artifactId>
   <!-- use same version as surefire -->
   <version>${surefire.version}</version>
   <executions>
      <execution>
         <goals>
            <goal>integration-test</goal>
            <goal>verify</goal>
         </goals>
      </execution>
   </executions>
</plugin>
```

> **NOTE** *You can remember which is which if you remember that unit tests will fail the build, but integration tests are* fail safe *unless you tell them to execute.*

The `maven-surefire-plugin` is configured by simply including it in the `build` section of `pom.xml`. That will ensure that unit tests are run automatically every time you run any Maven build that includes the `verify` life-cycle phase. As a review, the `verify`, `install`, and `deploy` phases are the most common ones that include tests.

By contrast, the `maven-failsafe-plugin` requires explicit configuration to run as part of `verify`. The execution registers the intent for integration tests to be mapped to `verify`. The difference exists because integration tests often require other resources to run, so Maven wants you to declare your intent that they will be available.

RUNNING INTEGRATION TESTS ONLY?

As an alternative, it is possible to run the `failsafe:integration-test` and `failsafe:verify` separately from the main build. You don't want to rely on your memory to run these!

Having separate unit and integration test steps is most useful if you have configured your CI/CD tool to have a build *pipeline* with multiple stages. For example, you might compile, run unit tests, and package the software in one stage and then deploy and start the application in another stage. Finally, you could run integration tests against deployed software in a final stage.

When running verify, the output will contain something like this:

```
[INFO] --- surefire:3.2.5:test (default-test) @ junit5-maven ---
[INFO] Using auto detected provider
org.apache.maven.surefire.junitplatform.JUnitPlatformProvider
[INFO]
[INFO] -------------------------------------------------------
[INFO]  T E S T S
[INFO] -------------------------------------------------------
[INFO] Running com.wiley.realworldjava.testing.BingoTest
[INFO] Tests run: 1, Failures: 0, Errors: 0, Skipped: 0, Time elapsed: 0.020 s
-- in com.wiley.realworldjava.testing.BingoTest
[INFO]
[INFO] Results:
[INFO]
[INFO] Tests run: 1, Failures: 0, Errors: 0, Skipped: 0
[INFO]
[INFO]
[INFO] --- jar:3.3.0:jar (default-jar) @ junit5-maven ---
[INFO] Building jar: /path/real-world-code-
repos/Ch07-Testing/junit5-maven/target/junit5-maven-0.0.1-SNAPSHOT.jar
[INFO]
[INFO] --- failsafe:3.2.5:integration-test (default) @ junit5-maven ---
[INFO] Using auto detected provider
org.apache.maven.surefire.junitplatform.JUnitPlatformProvider
[INFO]
[INFO] -------------------------------------------------------
[INFO]  T E S T S
[INFO] -------------------------------------------------------
[INFO] Running com.wiley.realworldjava.testing.BingoIT
[ERROR] Tests run: 2, Failures: 1, Errors: 0, Skipped: 0, Time elapsed: 1.048 s
<<< FAILURE! -- in com.wiley.realworldjava.testing.BingoIT
[ERROR] com.wiley.realworldjava.testing.BingoIT.connectivityTest -
Time elapsed: 0.006 s <<< FAILURE!
org.opentest4j.AssertionFailedError: database not available
   at org.junit.jupiter.api.AssertionUtils.fail(AssertionUtils.java:38)
   at org.junit.jupiter.api.Assertions.fail(Assertions.java:138)
   at com.wiley.realworldjava.testing.BingoIT.connectivityTest(BingoIT.java:26)
   at java.base/java.lang.reflect.Method.invoke(Method.java:580)
   at java.base/java.util.ArrayList.forEach(ArrayList.java:1596)
   at java.base/java.util.ArrayList.forEach(ArrayList.java:1596)
[INFO]
[INFO] Results:
[INFO]
[ERROR] Failures:
[ERROR]   BingoIT.connectivityTest:26 database not available
[INFO]
[ERROR] Tests run: 2, Failures: 1, Errors: 0, Skipped: 0
[INFO]
[INFO]
[INFO] --- failsafe:3.2.5:verify (default) @ junit5-maven ---
[INFO] ------------------------------------------------------------------------
[INFO] BUILD FAILURE
[INFO] ------------------------------------------------------------------------
```

The unit tests are run with Surefire. After that the integration tests are run with Failsafe. This separation allows the unit tests, which are faster, to run first. It also ensures that the slower integration tests are run only if the unit tests all succeed.

Both Surefire and Failsafe generate a report for each test class they execute. The report includes how many test-methods are present. When all tests complete, they each print a report on the total number of tests run, how many had issues or were skipped, and details about the issues. In the previous example, there was one unit test class containing one method that succeeded, and there was one integration test class containing two tests, one that passed and one that failed. The Maven console output displays the stack trace of the failure and also includes that stack trace in the summary results at the end of the Failsafe section. The single test failure automatically caused the Maven build to fail.

While the console shows just the highlights, the full tests results are available in the `target` directory. The unit test results are in `surefire-reports`, and the integration test results are in `failsafe-reports`. Each has XML files for automated systems to read and TXT files for developers to read, as you can see in Figure 7.2.

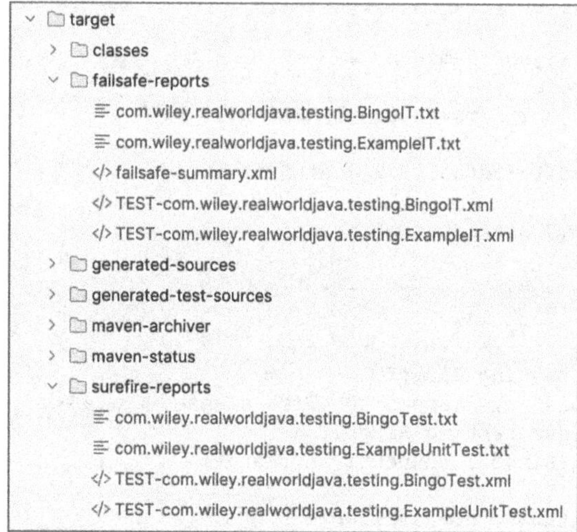

FIGURE 7.2: JUnit output in Maven

Maven provides many options to control the behavior of Surefire and Failsafe. For example, you can pass in system properties, control whether tests are run in parallel, include/exclude specific test patterns, decide if failing tests should fail the build, and more.

Configuring JUnit in a Gradle Build

In the previous section, you saw how to look up the latest version number for the `junit-bom`. That same number is used in Gradle. The following specifies how to set the dependencies in a `build.gradle` file using Groovy to run JUnit 5:

```
dependencies {
    testImplementation(platform('org.junit:junit-bom:5.10.2'))
    testImplementation('org.junit.jupiter:junit-jupiter')
    testRuntimeOnly('org.junit.platform:junit-platform-launcher')
}
```

As you can see, this example uses the same BOM as the Maven project. It also allows code in `test` to reference JUnit classes through the `junit-jupiter` dependency. The `junit-platform-launcher` dependency is new and is used by your build tool to hook into running JUnit. This dependency was optional in the past, so you may not see it in older documentation.

The following Gradle code uses Groovy syntax to tell Gradle to run all the JUnit unit and integration tests:

```
test {
    useJUnitPlatform()
    testLogging {
       events "passed", "skipped", "failed"
       exceptionFormat "full"
    }
}
```

The `useJUnitPlatform()` call has the Gradle built-in code kick off your tests. The `testLogging` code is how you tell Gradle to list more detail about the tests. By default, Gradle will list only the failing tests but will not include the failure message. But with this configuration, all the test methods get logged, whether they passed, were skipped, or failed, including any assertion failures. Using Groovy's Kotlin syntax, we can express the same thing as follows:

```
tasks.test {
   useJUnitPlatform()
   testLogging {
      events("passed", "skipped", "failed")
      exceptionFormat = org.gradle.api.tasks.testing.logging.
         TestExceptionFormat.FULL
   }
}
```

When running `build`, the output contains the following:

```
> Task :test FAILED

BingoIT > fromDatabase() PASSED

BingoIT > connectivityTest() FAILED
   org.opentest4j.AssertionFailedError: database not available
   at app//org.junit.jupiter.api.AssertionUtils.fail(AssertionUtils.java:38)
   at app//org.junit.jupiter.api.Assertions.fail(Assertions.java:138)
   at app//com.wiley.realworldjava.testing.BingoIT.connectivityTest(
      BingoIT.java:26)

BingoTest > math() PASSED

3 tests completed, 1 failed

FAILURE: Build failed with an exception.
```

That output shows the two test classes that were run: `BingoIT` and `BingoTest`. It also shows the details of why `connectivtyTest()` failed.

Like with Maven, the full Gradle test results are available on the file system, this time in the `builds` directory, as you can see in Figure 7.3. This time, the human-readable files are HTML and under `reports/tests`. The XML files are intended for a machine-readable audience under `test-results/test`. Also, like Maven, you can control the configuration of the tests in your build file.

```
v build
  > classes
  > generated
  > libs
  v reports
    v tests
      v test
        > classes
        > css
        > js
        > packages
          <> index.html
  v test-results
    v test
      > binary
        </> TEST-com.wiley.realworldjava.testing.BingoIT.xml
        </> TEST-com.wiley.realworldjava.testing.BingoTest.xml
```

FIGURE 7.3: JUnit output in Gradle

Using Test-Driven Development to Explore Tests

Now that you know how to organize tests and see the results, it is time to write a test. For this example, we will use Test-Driven Development.

> **TEST-DRIVEN DEVELOPMENT**
>
> Test-Driven Development is a software development approach that has its roots in the early days of agile development. Using TDD, tests are written *before* the actual implementation code. Since the test is written before the implementation, it is expected to fail. Once the implementation is added, the test passes and becomes part of your automated test suite.

In this example, we will create a simple test using Test-Driven Development. When coding using TDD, you write code in much smaller chunks than you might be used to, because you write the main code only when the test code you have written requires you to do so.

Using this approach ensures that all your code is tested. It also helps you think about the behavior of the code before writing each bit of it. Since you are writing the code one test case at a time, you will find that you need to refactor as you are writing. This is expected! The tests make refactoring safe because you are guaranteed to have full test coverage. The phrase *red-green-refactor* is used to sum up the TDD process.

1. **Red:** Write a test. At this early stage the test should fail (or the code should have compiler errors). We call this "red," but some IDEs show the failure in yellow instead of red. Nonetheless, it is still an error or failure, and the flow still applies.
2. **Green:** Make the test pass. Add all the code required to make the test pass.
3. **Refactor:** Make any changes needed to make the code cleaner and easier to understand.
4. Start over with a new test.

You can be more granular if needed by adding part of a test and making it compile before completing the test. Or you can add just an assertion instead of a whole test.

Let's get started. Imagine you are working on designing software for building robots that cannot weigh more than a certain amount. In this example, you'll design a class that provides information about a simple robot. The first step is to start writing the test by creating a class in `src/test/java`.

```
1:  package com.wiley.realworldjava.testing;
2:
3:  import org.junit.jupiter.api.BeforeEach;
4:  import org.junit.jupiter.api.Test;
5:  import static org.junit.jupiter.api.Assertions.assertEquals;
6:
7:  class FirstRobotTest {
8:
9:     private FirstRobot robot;         // DOES NOT COMPILE
10:
11:    @BeforeEach
12:    void setUp() {
13:       robot = new FirstRobot();     // DOES NOT COMPILE
14:    }
15:
16:    @Test
17:    void name() {
18:       robot.setName("Izzy");        // DOES NOT COMPILE
19:       assertEquals("Izzy", robot.toString());
20:    }
21: }
```

This code does not yet compile as the `FirstRobot` class does not yet exist. However, you can already see a few features of JUnit. Line 11 uses the `@BeforeEach` annotation to instruct JUnit to run the `setUp()` method before each test method in the class. Line 16 tells JUnit that the `name()` method is a test. Finally, line 19 tells JUnit to check that `robot.toString()` returns the expected value: `Izzy`.

> **NOTE** *In JUnit 5, the convention is to have package-private (aka default) access for the test class and methods.*

Now it is time to write the minimal code required to make this test pass. Your IDE can help with this. Click the word `FirstRobot` on line 9 and let the IDE create the class (using IntelliJ, this is Alt+Enter on Windows and Option+Enter on Mac). Be sure to select `src/main/java` as the destination directory. The minimal code to get this test to pass looks like this:

```
package com.wiley.realworldjava.testing;

public class FirstRobot {

   private String name;

   public void setName(String name) {
       this.name = name;
   }

   @Override
   public String toString() {
       return name;
   }
}
```

The `FirstRobot` class is called the *code under test* to differentiate it from the test code itself. Now that you have written a test and have gotten it to pass, the next step is usually to refactor, but in this case the code looks good as is, so there's nothing to refactor, so let's move on to the next test. This time you'll implement a requirement that states that the robot can add additional weight so long as the robot's total weight remains less than 125 pounds. One test you might start with is a 100-pound robot; add one component and test the current weight.

```
@Test
void singleComponent() {
   robot.setComponent(100);                      // DOES NOT COMPILE
   assertEquals(100, robot.getWeight());         // DOES NOT COMPILE
}
```

Again, the code does not yet compile. This is easy enough to fix by adding the following to the code under test:

```
private int weight;

public void setComponent(int weight) {
   this.weight = weight;
}

public int getWeight() {
   return weight;
}
```

This works for one component, and again it looks pretty good, so there's nothing to refactor. Now let's see if it works for a second component. It's time for a new test:

```
@Test
void twoComponents() {
   robot.setComponent(100);
   robot.setComponent(20);
   assertEquals(120, robot.getWeight());
}
```

This time the code compiles, but running the test gives a failure.

```
org.opentest4j.AssertionFailedError:
Expected :120
Actual   :20
```

Fixing this test requires a one-line fix to the code under test to `setComponent()`, as follows:

```
public void setComponent(int weight) {
   this.weight += weight;
}
```

It is time for the first refactoring opportunity. The name `setComponent()` doesn't tell the whole story. After all, a setter *replaces* the current value, whereas here we are adding to it. Using the Refactor menu, ask your IDE to rename the `setComponent()` method to the more appropriate `addComponent()`. Now let's write a test for the requirement to keep the weight to less than 120. To do so, let's import JUnit's convenient `assertThrows()` method and use it to write the test.

```
@Test
void overweight() {
   robot.addComponent(100);
   IllegalArgumentException ex =
      assertThrows(IllegalArgumentException.class,
      () -> robot.addComponent(50));
   assertEquals(
      "Cannot add component. Robot would be too heavy", e.getMessage());
}
```

The `assertThrows()` method confirms that the code does in fact throw the exception you said it would and returns the exception, which you can inspect for additional assertions. Running this test fails with the following:

```
org.opentest4j.AssertionFailedError: Expected
java.lang.IllegalArgumentException to be thrown, but nothing was thrown.
```

Since there is a failing test, the TDD methodology requires you to write the code to fix it.

```
public void addComponent(int weight) {
   int newWeight = this.weight + weight;
   if (newWeight > 125) {
      throw new IllegalArgumentException(
         "Cannot add component. Robot would be too heavy");
   }
   this.weight = newWeight;
}
```

While this code works, we can consider some more opportunities for refactoring. One such refactoring would be to extract the hard-coded value 125 to a constant, which we can call `MAX_WEIGHT`. Another refactoring opportunity would be to notice that the method argument and instance variable have the same name, so you might want to rename `weight` to `componentWeight`, leaving us with a final refactored method as follows:

```
public void addComponent(int componentWeight) {
   int newWeight = this.weight + componentWeight;
   if (newWeight > MAX_WEIGHT) {
      throw new IllegalArgumentException(
         "Cannot add component. Robot would be too heavy");
   }
   this.weight = newWeight;
}
```

In this section, we looked at TDD using a few features of JUnit 5. That concludes our coverage of TDD. The next sections cover many more JUnit 5 features.

LEARNING JUNIT

In the previous section, we started to explore JUnit 5, but it is important to get a more comprehensive understanding so you can efficiently read and write JUnit tests. In this section, we will cover many additional features, and where applicable we will mention the corresponding JUnit 4 syntax, in case you are working on an old codebase.

Looking at Test Flow

JUnit 5 provides annotations for designating methods that are to be executed before and after the individual tests, as well as annotations for methods to run before the first test and after the last test. The following code demonstrates all of these in action for a sample class with just two tests, named `test1` and `test2`:

```
class FlowTest {

   @BeforeAll
   static void first() {
     System.out.println("BeforeAll");
   }

   @BeforeEach
   void setUp() {
      System.out.println("BeforeEach");
   }
```

```
    @AfterAll
    static void last() {
       System.out.println("AfterAll");
    }

    @AfterEach
    void tearDown() {
       System.out.println("AfterEach");
    }

    @Test
    void test1() {
       System.out.println("Test");
    }

    @Test
    void test2() {
       System.out.println("Test");
    }
}
```

The `@BeforeAll` and `@AfterAll` annotated methods run once for the whole class before the first test and after the last test, respectively. Note that these two annotations must be applied to `static` methods since they do not correspond to any individual tests.

The `@BeforeEach` and `@AfterEach` annotated methods run right before and after each individual test. In earlier versions of JUnit, the methods that served this purpose were required to be named `setUp()` and `tearDown()`. While you can now name the methods anything, you might often see these traditional names due to their history.

The output of the previous code is as follows:

```
BeforeAll
BeforeEach
Test
AfterEach
BeforeEach
Test
AfterEach
AfterAll
```

As you can see, the `@BeforeEach` and `@AfterEach` annotated methods each ran twice since there are two test methods. In this example, we can see from the output that `test1` was executed before `test2`, but this is not always the case. JUnit uses an algorithm for determining the execution order that, although deterministic, is not always obvious. In any case, tests should be independent of each other, so never rely on the order the tests are written.

Table 7.1 reviews these annotations.

TABLE 7.1: Annotations for Test Flow

ANNOTATION	METHOD TYPE	DESCRIPTION
`@AfterAll`	Static	Runs once after all tests have completed
`@AfterEach`	Instance	Runs after each test has completed
`@BeforeAll`	Static	Runs once before any tests
`@BeforeEach`	Instance	Runs before each test

> **NOTE** *In JUnit4, these annotations were called* `@BeforeClass`, `@Before`, `@After`, *and* `@AfterClass`.

Skipping a Test

Sometimes you have a test that is partially written or has broken and needs more time to be fixed. But a failing test will fail your build, so what is a programmer to do? JUnit provides the `@Disabled` annotation that you can use to skip the test and report that it has been skipped in the JUnit result. Here's an example:

```
@Test @Disabled("need to finish implementation")
void notReadyYet() {
   assertEquals("dog", "cat");
}
```

As you can see, the `@Disabled` annotation accepts an optional parameter, which describes the reason the test is disabled. This is useful for people who are reading the code. It also appears in the test output if you look at the result in your IDE.

```
need to finish implementation
```

Running this test in Maven includes this output:

```
[INFO] Running com.wiley.realworldjava.testing.SkippingTest
[WARNING] Tests run: 1, Failures: 0, Errors: 0, Skipped: 1
...
[WARNING] Tests run: 7, Failures: 0, Errors: 0, Skipped: 1
```

And Gradle would include the following:

```
SkippingTest > notReadyYet() SKIPPED
```

> **NOTE** *In JUnit4, this annotation was called* `@Ignore`.

Asserting Logic

JUnit 5 provides a helper class called `org.junit.jupiter.api.Assertions`, which contains many static methods for asserting values.

The basic assertion checks whether two values are equal. Here's an example:

```
int expected = 3;
int actual = 1+2;
assertEquals(expected, actual);
```

The value you expect to receive is the first parameter. The actual value from the code under test is the second parameter.

There's an optional third parameter with a message to include if the assertion fails. It's good to include this message so you have clearer failures.

```
assertEquals(expected, actual, "numbers are not equal");
```

The `assertEquals()` method is overloaded so you can call it with any data type. There's even an `Object` overloaded version that calls the `equals()` method to determine whether the expected and actual values are the same.

> **NOTE** *In JUnit4, the message parameter is supplied first, unlike JUnit 5, where the message is supplied last on all the methods that use it.*

Using Common Assertions

Some common assertions are shown here:

```
assertNotEquals(4, 1+2, "not equals");
assertTrue(true, "true");
assertFalse(false, "false");
assertNull(null, "not null");
assertNotNull("cat", "not null");
```

These methods do as their names indicate, verifying that two values are not equal or that the actual value is true, false, null, or a value other than null. If the assertion fails, the test will throw an `AssertionFailedError` and report the error in the resulting report.

While the `assertEquals()` and `assertNotEquals()` methods check for object equality, they do not check if the references *refer to the same instance*. For that you need the `assertSame()` and `assertNotSame()` methods. In the following, all assertions pass:

```
List<Integer> expected = List.of(5);
List<Integer> actual = List.of(5);
assertSame(actual, actual, "same");
assertNotSame(expected, actual, "different");
assertEquals(expected, actual, "equality");
```

In the previous code, the two `List` objects pass `assertEquals()` since the contents are the same. They also pass `assertNotSame()` since they refer to different object instances.

Arrays are a special breed. Since they don't have an `equals()` method to check their contents, `Assertions` provides specialized methods for comparing them.

```
int[] expected = new int[] {5};
int[] actual = new int[] {5};
assertArrayEquals(expected, actual, "values");
assertNotEquals(expected, actual, "reference");
```

In the previous code, the values are the same, so `assertArrayEquals()` passes. Since they are different arrays, the `assertNotEquals()` method also passes.

Asserting Exceptions

Sometimes it is useful to check whether an exception is thrown and whether details about the exception are correct. Suppose you want to test this class:

```
public final class Validator {

   public static void validatePositive(int num) {
      if (num <= 0) {
         throw new IllegalArgumentException("Must be positive");
      }
   }
}
```

The shortest way is to check that the correct exception is thrown using `assertThrows()`:

```
assertThrows(IllegalArgumentException.class,
   () -> Validator.validatePositive(-1),
   "exception");
```

This method's first parameter is the type of exception you expect to be thrown. The second parameter is a lambda that takes no parameters and calls the code under test. Then there is an optional third parameter for a message to be included in the output if the test fails.

The `assertThrows()` method actually returns the thrown exception, which lets you control the details of what else is verified.

```
IllegalArgumentException actual =
   assertThrows(IllegalArgumentException.class,
      () -> Validator.validatePositive(-1),
      "exception");
assertEquals("Must be positive", actual.getMessage(), "Message");
```

Failing Programmatically

Sometimes you need to fail a test. For example, say you have an `if/else` clause, where the `else` clause should never happen. So, in the `else` clause, you can include this instruction:

```
fail("Fail here");
```

Like with the assertions, the message parameter in the `fail` instruction is optional, but it's useful to know why the developer wants the test to fail!

USE THE MOST SPECIFIC ASSERTION YOU CAN

Both of the following will check the value of `actual`:

```
assertEquals("dog", actual, "animal");
assertTrue(actual.equals("dog"), "animal");
```

However, the first one is better because it gives a clearer message on failure, as you can see from the following output for each of these assertions when run independently:

```
org.opentest4j.AssertionFailedError: animal ==>
Expected :dog
Actual   :cat

org.opentest4j.AssertionFailedError:
Expected :true
Actual   :false
```

The first one tells you what is actually wrong, which is much more useful when you have a failing test. Similarly, `assertNull()` is better because it tells you `cat` is not `null`, whereas `assertTrue()` merely tells you that it expected `true` but was `false`.

```
assertNull(actual, "not null");
assertTrue(actual == null, " not null");
```

Verifying Conditions Using Assume Logic

We have seen that when you want to skip a test you can annotate it with `@Disabled`. But there is a way to provide more granular control so that you can choose to execute a test only when specific conditions apply. To do so, you can use JUnit *assume* methods. Where assert methods will verify the results of a test, assume methods verify that some conditions are true before executing a test. The two assume methods are as follows:

```
assumeTrue(actual);
assumeFalse(actual);
```

Running this test gives a message like the following:

```
org.opentest4j.TestAbortedException:
   Assumption failed: assumption is not false
```

Additionally, the skipped test shows up in the output just like `@Disabled` tests do.

Parameterizing Tests

JUnit 5 provides a way to easily run the same test multiple times with different values using the `@ParameterizedTest` annotation.

```
@ParameterizedTest
@ValueSource(strings = { "cat", "dog" })
void values(String value) {
   assertEquals(3, value.length(), "# chars");
}
```

Figure 7.4 shows how running this code creates two tests that run independently.

> **NOTE** *You can list* `String` *and primitive values in the* `@ValueSource` *parameter list.*

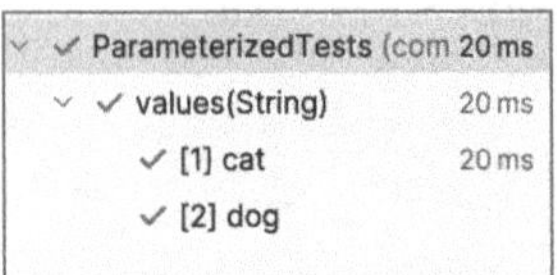

FIGURE 7.4: Parameterized test output

Beside `@ValueSource`, there are a few other types of sources. For example, `@CsvSource` reads from a file. `@MethodSource` is the most general-purpose one; it allows you to inject values returned from a static method into your test method signature. In the following example, we use `@MethodSource` to pass both test data and expected values:

```
static List<Object[]> fetchTestData() {
   return List.of(
      new Object[] { "cat", 3},
      new Object[] {"doggy", 5});
}

@ParameterizedTest
@MethodSource("fetchTestData ")
void values(String value, int expected) {
   assertEquals(expected, value.length(), "# chars");
}
```

In this case, JUnit calls the `fetchTestData()` method to discover the expected pairs of parameters for the parameterized test. If the method you want to call to get the parameterized data is in another class, you can use a longer form of `@MethodSource`.

```
@MethodSource(
   "com.wiley.realworldjava.testing.ParameterizedTests#fetchTestData")
```

Notice how the fully qualified class name is used this time. Additionally, the method to call in that class appears after a `#`. Regardless of the location of the target method, the method must be static to be called by `@MethodSource`.

WORKING WITH COMMON TESTING LIBRARIES

The JUnit ecosystem includes a number of open-source libraries. This section covers some useful ones.

Coding Using AssertJ

AssertJ is a library containing many "fluent" single-line assertions. To use AssertJ in your Maven or Gradle build, go to Maven Central (`https://mvnrepository.com/artifact/org.assertj/assertj-core`) and find the latest version number for your build tool. Table 7.2 shows what each one looks like at the time of this writing.

TABLE 7.2: Specifying AssertJ as a Dependency

TOOL	SYNTAX

Maven	`<dependency>`
	`<groupId>org.assertj</groupId>`
	`<artifactId>assertj-core</artifactId>`
	`<version>3.25.2</version>`
	`<scope>test</scope>`
	`</dependency>`

Gradle (Groovy)	`testImplementation group: 'org.assertj',` `name: 'assertj-core', version: '3.25.2'`
Gradle (Kotlin)	`testImplementation("org.assertj:assertj-core:3.25.2")`

The following shows how to write a single-line assertion for something that would otherwise require more logic:

```
package com.wiley.realworldjava.testing.assertj;

import org.junit.jupiter.api.Test;

import static org.assertj.core.api.Assertions.assertThat;

class AssertThatTest {

   @Test
   void spaces() {
      assertThat("cat").isEqualToIgnoringWhitespace("c a t");
   }
}
```

When using AssertJ, you start with `assertThat()` and supply a parameter to be tested. AssertJ allows chaining checks so you can write more succinct code such as this:

```
assertThat("cat")
   .startsWith("c")
   .endsWith("t");
```

AssertJ has lots of custom assertions for strings, lists, files, and more. Here are a few:

- `isSubstringOf()`
- `isUpperCase()`
- `matches()`

Most of the time, typing `assertThat()` and using autocomplete in your IDE will display all the assertion methods. The guide and Javadoc in the "Further References" section shows you where you can find more details.

And that's just in `assertj-core`! There are specific AssertJ libraries for more specialized needs.

In addition to custom assertions with `assertThat()`, AssertJ supplies soft assertions where you can easily collect multiple assert failures and list them all at once when the test fails. This is particularly useful for long end-to-end integration tests or monitoring tests so you can get a list of everything that is wrong at the same time.

This is the basic way of writing a soft assertion:

```
@Test
void callingAssertAll() {
   SoftAssertions softly = new SoftAssertions();
   softly.assertThat("robot").isEqualTo("izzy");
   softly.assertThat(126).isLessThanOrEqualTo(125);
   softly.assertAll();;
 }
```

This test has two failing conditions. If you use a simple assertion, the test will fail after the first assertion. Using soft assertions, the test fails with both issues rather than just the first one. The output contains the following:

```
org.assertj.core.error.AssertJMultipleFailuresError:
Multiple Failures (2 failures)
-- failure 1 -
expected: "izzy"
 but was: "robot"
at SoftAssertionsTest.callingAssertAll(SoftAssertionsTest.java:14)
-- failure 2 -
Expecting actual:
  126
to be less than or equal to:
  125
at SoftAssertionsTest.callingAssertAll(SoftAssertionsTest.java:15)
```

One caveat: you must call `assertAll()` at the end of the assertion chain, although there are a variety of ways to avoid having to remember to call `assertAll()`. See the `Selikoff.net` blog post in "Further References" for examples.

Coding with JUnit Pioneer Features

The JUnit Pioneer library contains many useful extensions to JUnit 5. Some of the functionality might even find its way into JUnit 5 one day.

To use the JUnit Pioneer library in your Maven or Gradle build, go to Maven Central (`https://mvnrepository.com/artifact/org.junit-pioneer/junit-pioneer`) and find the latest version number for your build tool. Table 7.3 shows what this looks like for each one at the time of this writing.

TABLE 7.3: Specifying JUnit Pioneer as a Dependency

TOOL	SYNTAX

Maven	`<dependency>`
	`    <groupId>org.junit-pioneer</groupId>`
	`    <artifactId>junit-pioneer</artifactId>`
	`    <version>2.2.0</version>`
	`    <scope>test</scope>`
	`</dependency>`

Gradle (Groovy)	`testImplementation group: 'org.junit-pioneer', name: 'junit-pioneer', version: '2.2.0'`
Gradle (Kotlin)	`testImplementation( "org.junit-pioneer:junit-pioneer:2.2.0")`

In this section, you'll see three of the features to get a feel for the functionality in this project.

Disabling Until a Date

The first feature addresses a limitation of `@Disabled`. A common problem when disabling a test is remembering to reenable it. JUnit Pioneer provides an annotation that lets you disable it until it expires.

If you forget about the test, it will automatically re-enable after the expiration date. You'll "suddenly" get a failure and remember the test exists, at which point you can decide whether to extend the expiration date or decide whether it is time to fix the test. Or perhaps the test passed without effort because you set the expiration to a time when some environment condition would be fixed. This code shows how to use the annotation:

```
@Test
@DisabledUntil(date="2030-01-01",
   reason = "Need our partner service to be ready")
void waitingForServiceAvailability() {
   // intentionally left blank
}
```

The reason is optional but recommended so you remember why the test was disabled. When the date is in the future, the test is skipped just like with `@Disabled`. If the date is in the past, the test will run, outputting a message that is no longer disabled.

```
timestamp = 2024-03-24T09:40:36.068881, DisabledUntilExtension = The `date`
2024-01-01 is before or on the current date 2024-03-24, so `@DisabledUntil`
no longer disabled test "[engine:junit-jupiter]/
[class:com.wiley.realworldjava.testing.pioneer.TemporarilyDisabledIT]
/[method:waitingForServiceAvailability()]". Please remove the annotation.
```

Retrying a Test

Sometimes you are dependent on an operation in another service that is unreliable. Or you need to run tests on an overloaded network. JUnit Pioneer provides an annotation to retry.

```
@RetryingTest(10)
void flakeyTest() {
   Random random = new Random();
   if (random.nextInt(1, 100) < 75) {
      fail("too high");
   }
}
```

The previous code retries the test up to 10 times and stops with a passing status if one succeeds. If all 10 attempts fail, the test fails. The skipped runs that failed will output a message like this:

```
org.opentest4j.TestAbortedException: too high
Test execution #1 (of up to 10) failed ~> will retry in 0 ms...
```

There are optional parameters for attributes like how long to wait and which exceptions to consider.

> **TIP** *This annotation works only for regular tests. If you need to retry a* `@ParameterizedTest`, *use* `https://github.com/artsok/rerunner-jupiter`.

Working with System Properties

Java has global system properties, which can be tricky to test. One approach is to call `System.setProperty()` with the value you want and then restore it at the end of the test. While this works, you have to code it carefully. You also have to ensure your build tool is set to run tests one at a time, which slows down your build.

JUnit Pioneer has two annotations that handle setting the system properties to some desired state just while the test runs. The following two tests show how to tell JUnit to temporarily clear a system property or to set a property to a specific value:

```
@Test
@ClearSystemProperty(key = "JAVA_HOME")
void clearProperty() {
   assertNull(System.getProperty("JAVA_HOME"), "path");
}

@Test
@SetSystemProperty(key = "JAVA_HOME", value = "c:/java/java21")
void maskProperty() {
   assertEquals("c:/java/java21", System.getProperty("JAVA_HOME"));
}
```

JUnit provides an option to speed up tests by running multiple tests at the same time. Since system properties are global, you don't want to run such tests in parallel. After all, `JAVA_HOME` can't be set to a specific value in one test and be empty in another at the same time. If you use JUnit Pioneer's annotations when using system properties in your test, Pioneer ensures that methods with conflicting system property annotations are not run at the same time.

Using Cartesian Test

The `CartesianTest` annotation allows you to specify multiple parameters that are combined to generate test cases. Two or more lists are supplied using `@CartesianValueSource`, and then all combinations of those lists will be supplied to the test for each execution. Here's an example:

```
class SomeCartesianTest {

    @CartesianTest
    void cartesianTest(
       @Values(ints = {1, 2}) int time,
       @Values (ints = {3, 4}) int tide) {
        // Your test implementation
    }
}
```

In this example, the `cartesianTest` method will be executed for every combination of `time` and `tide` values. That is, it will run with `(1, 3)`, `(1, 4)`, `(2, 3)`, and `(2, 4)`.

Learning About Other Features

In addition to the features in this section, some other useful JUnit 5 Pioneer pack features include the following:

- **`@JsonSource`**: Passes a JSON string for use in a `@ParameterizedTest`.
- **`@JsonClasspathSource`**: Passes the name of a JSON file for use in a `@ParameterizedTest`.
- **`@IntRangeSource`**: Passes a range of numbers to a parameterized test. You can specify the minimum and maximum values in addition to the increment value. Equivalents exist for the other numeric primitives.
- **`@DefaultLocale`**: Lets you run a test in a specific locale (such as a country or language) rather than relying on the system default.
- **`@DefaultTimeZone`**: Lets you run a test in a specific time zone rather than relying on the system default.

MOCKING OBJECTS

Needless to say, you want your unit tests to be fast and independent so you can provide fast feedback and ensure you are testing logic in isolation. But what can you do when your code needs to access a database, a REST API call, or another network call? Any of these might be slow or unavailable, and the results may vary. Or what if you want to call an interface for which the implementation hasn't even been written yet? *Mock objects* allow you to stub such calls by providing default implementations that you control from within the test.

A mock is a type of *test double* where an object other than the real class is used. Mock objects come in different flavors.

- **Dummy:** Objects that are passed into a method signature but never used. They are just supplied to satisfy a method signature.
- **Fake:** Objects that have some working implementation but are much simpler than the service they are mimicking.
- **Stubs:** Objects that provide contrived responses to expected calls.
- **Spy:** Objects that merge real-world behavior and mock behavior and/or verify information about the number of calls.
- **Mocks:** Objects that are preprogrammed to verify some expectations, for example that a certain method was called *n* number of times.

Mocking frameworks provide APIs for creating all of these. In this chapter, we will cover some of the most popular mocking frameworks: Mockito, EasyMock, and Spring MockMvc.

Mocking with Mockito

Mockito is a popular mocking framework used in many applications. Mockito rolls many of the mock flavors into a single *mock* annotation. It also has the concept of a *spy*, which is a kind of hybrid that uses the real class implementation by default but allows you to stub select methods.

To use Mockito in your Maven or Gradle build, you need to include two dependencies. The first dependency is the library itself, which is `mockito-core`. Additionally, `mockito-junit-jupiter` supplies the integration. Go to Maven Central (`https://mvnrepository.com/artifact/org.mockito/mockito-core`) and (`https://mvnrepository.com/artifact/org.mockito/mockito-junit-jupiter`) and find the latest version number for your build tool. Table 7.4 shows what this looks like for each one at the time of this writing.

TABLE 7.4: Specifying Mockito as a Dependency

TOOL	SYNTAX

Maven	`<dependency>`
	`    <groupId>org.mockito</groupId>`
	`    <artifactId>mockito-core</artifactId>`
	`    <version>5.11.0</version>`
	`    <scope>test</scope>`
	`</dependency>`
	
	`<dependency>`
	`    <groupId>org.mockito</groupId>`
	`    <artifactId>mockito-junit-jupiter</artifactId>`
	`    <version>5.11.0</version>`
	`    <scope>test</scope>`
	`</dependency>`

continues

TABLE 7.4: *(continued)*

Gradle (Groovy)	`testImplementation group: 'org.mockito', name: 'mockito-core', version: '5.11.0'`
	
	`testImplementation group: 'org.mockito', name: 'mockito-junit-jupiter', version: '5.11.0'`

Gradle (Kotlin)	`testImplementation("org.mockito:mockito-core:5.11.0")`
	
	`testImplementation( "org.mockito:mockito-junit-jupiter:5.11.0")`

Now let's look at an example to understand how Mockito works. Suppose you have an interface that retrieves scores.

```
public interface ScoreService {
   int retrieveScore(int matchNumber);
}
```

Now, you want to unit test a class called `Dashboard`, which uses an interface called `ScoreService`.

```
Public class Dashboard {

   private ScoreService service;

   public Dashboard(ScoreService service) {
      this.service = service;
   }

   public List<Integer> getScores(int maxMatch) {
      return IntStream.range(1, maxMatch + 1)
         .mapToObj(n -> service.retrieveScore(n))
         .toList();
   }
}
```

Pay attention to the fact that the constructor receives an interface as a parameter. The `Dashboard` class doesn't know or care what implementation of `ScoreService` it uses. This is a good practice, as it makes the code testable, because it allows you to mock the implementation.

```
@ExtendWith(MockitoExtension.class)
public class DashboardTest {

   private Dashboard dashboard;

   @Mock
   private ScoreService scoreServiceMock;

   @BeforeEach
   void setUp() {
      dashboard = new Dashboard(scoreServiceMock);
   }

   @Test
   void getScores() {
```

```
16:         when(scoreServiceMock.retrieveScore(1)).thenReturn(76);
17:         when(scoreServiceMock.retrieveScore(2)).thenReturn(91);
18:
19:         List<Integer> expected = List.of(76, 91);
20:         List<Integer> actual = dashboard.getScores(2);
21:         assertEquals(expected, actual, "scores");
22:
23:         verify(scoreServiceMock, times(2)).retrieveScore(anyInt());
24:     }
25: }
```

Line 1 of our test class tells JUnit this is a Mockito test. The `@Mock` annotation in line 6 tells JUnit to inject a mock instance of `ScoreService` into the variable `scoreServiceMock` on line 7. The mock object allows you to specify behavior without having a real instance of the class or even without such an implementation class even existing.

Lines 16 and 17 register the desired behavior with the mock (which technically makes it a *stub*). When the `dashboard` asks the mock to retrieve the score, the mock returns 76 or 91 depending on the parameter. Line 23 confirms the `retrieveScore()` method was called exactly twice with any values (which in this sense makes it a true *mock*).

The `@Mock` annotation works only for mocking instance variables. An alternative syntax for creating mocks is shown here:

```
ScoreService scoreServiceMock = mock(ScoreService.class);
```

This alternative syntax allows you to create mocked local variables.

MULTIPLE CONSTRUCTORS

If your class under test already has a constructor that accepts the required arguments, that's great as the mock can call it. Otherwise, just create a no-argument constructor and use `this()` to pass an instance of the real object to the constructor that requires one.

```
private Competition competition;

public TripPlanner() {
   this(new Champs());
}

public TripPlanner(Competition competition) {
   this.competition = competition;
}
```

The first constructor is used by the real code and the second by the tests. This allows full testing of the code without making life harder for the other callers of the class.

Since mock objects can be tricky to understand, let's look at the flow of the code in another way:

1. Lines 6–7 of the test have Mockito inject a mock `ScoreService`.
2. Line 11 of the test passes that mock to the constructor of `Dashboard`, which stores the mock in the `service` instance variable.
3. Line 16 of the test tells the mock what to do if and when `retrieveScore(1)` is called.
4. Line 17 of the test tells the mock what to do if and when `retrieveScore(2)` is called.

5. Line 20 of the test calls `Dashboard`, which is the code under test.
6. The `dashboard.getScores(2)` call in line 20 creates a range from 1 to 2 on the stream, ostensibly to retrieve a score for each element of the range.
7. The first call in the stream is `service .retrieveScore(1)`.
8. The mock consults the initial setup expectations and returns the requested 76.
9. Next is the `service.retrieveScore(2)`.
10. The mock consults the initial setup expectations again and returns the requested 91.
11. The `getScore()` method completes returning control to the test.
12. Line 21 of the test asserts the list values.
13. Line 23 is the `verify()` call where the mock thinks "You said you were planning on making two calls; let me check whether that happened. Yes, you did make two calls. All good!"

Now that you understand the flow, it is time to cover the most important Mockito features in the next sections.

TESTING A PRIVATE METHOD

There are generally three ways to test private methods.

1. Rely on tests of public methods that call the private method.
2. Make it package-private.
3. Refactor it to a public utility class.

Ideally, you can test all your code, even the private methods, by testing your public API. When you absolutely must test private methods explicitly, the first thing to do is to see if you can refactor to make the method you want to test public, perhaps by moving it to a helper class. But typically, you can test a private method by creating a tester to test nonprivate methods that call the private method. After all, private methods are ultimately called by nonprivate methods!

When these options are not feasible, another option is to make the method under test default (package-private) access. Some teams adopt the useful convention of only using *default* access for testing, which makes it clear that the method should not be called by any code other than the tests. This approach exposes the method for testing, while still preventing the code from being in the public API and called by others since it is limited to the same package. Also, you can refactor more easily in the future since you know there are no external callers. If you indeed end up having to do this, it is an indication that your code might not be as clean as it could be, and you might want to explore some opportunities for refactoring.

Configuring When/Then

To tell Mockito what to do when a specified call is made, start with `Mockito.when()`. It is common to use a static import so you don't have to type the `Mockito` class name part. The `when()` method takes as a parameter the method you are going to call. You can pass in either the parameter that you expect or a matcher like `anyInt()`. Finally, you specify one or more return values. The `thenReturn()` method takes a varargs parameter so you can specify unique values to be returned on subsequent calls.

```
when(scoreServiceMock.retrieveScore(1)).thenReturn(76);
when(scoreServiceMock.retrieveScore(anyInt())).thenReturn(76);
when(scoreServiceMock.retrieveScore(anyInt())).thenReturn(76, 82);
```

If you want to have the mock throw an exception instead of returning a value, you do that by calling `thenThrow()`, as shown here:

```
when(scoreServiceMock.retrieveScore(anyInt()))
   .thenThrow(new IllegalStateException());
```

STUBBING MULTIPLE PARAMETERS

When stubbing calls with multiple parameters, if you use one matcher (ex: `anyInt()`), then all of the parameters must be matchers. You cannot mix and match. If you want to mix and match, you can use the `eq()` method to wrap the specific value. For example:

```
when(myMock.myMethod(anyInt(), eq(1))).thenReturn(76)
```

There are lots of matchers you can pass instead of the direct primitive or object reference. For example:

- **Any value of a certain type:** `any(Class<T>)` or `anyXXX()` matches primitives, List, Set, Map, or Collection.
- **Equality:** `eq(X)` matches the primitive or object X.
- **Null checking:** `isNull()` or `isNotNull()` matches depending on whether `null`.
- **String operations:** `contains(String)`, `matches(Pattern)`, `startsWith(String)`, or `endsWith(String)` matches if `String` operation returns `true`.

> **TIP** *If you supply a null value, Mockito may not find the matching method. Therefore, if you know that a null value might be passed, you should specify* `nullable(MyClass .class)` *instead of* `any(MyClass.class)`.

Verifying Calls

It is often useful to check that the methods you expected were actually called. If you stub a mock call and never make that call on the code under test, Mockito will fail that by default. You can tell Mockito not to fail in such cases with the following:

```
@Mock(strictness = Mock.Strictness.LENIENT)
```

Independently, you can explicitly verify any or all of the calls in code. Here are some examples:

```
verify(scoreServiceMock).retrieveScore(1);
verify(scoreServiceMock, times(1)).retrieveScore(1);
verify(scoreServiceMock, atLeast(1)).retrieveScore(1);
verify(scoreServiceMock, atMost(1)).retrieveScore(1);
verify(scoreServiceMock, atMostOnce()).retrieveScore(1);
verify(scoreServiceMock, never()).retrieveScore(9);
```

The first and second lines of code in the previous block are equivalent ways of telling Mockito to verify that the call to `retrieveScore()` was made exactly once. (Since verifying that something happened exactly once is most common, it is the default.) The optional verification modes allow you to easily specify how many times a mock call should happen with given parameters. Additionally, you can use the matchers from the previous section. For example, the following code says to verify that exactly one call with any `int` parameter was made:

```
verify(scoreServiceMock, times(1)).retrieveScore(anyInt());
```

Mocking Concrete Classes

The previous example used an interface. However, not all classes have interfaces, and you shouldn't have to add interfaces just for the tests.

This time you have a new class, `DashboardViewer`. It uses the `Dashboard` class.

```
public class DashboardViewer {

   private Dashboard dashboard;

   public DashboardViewer(Dashboard dashboard) {
      this.dashboard = dashboard;
   }

   public String getFormattedData(int maxMatch) {
      List<Integer> scores = dashboard.getScores(maxMatch);
      return scores.stream()
         .map(s -> "-> " + s)
         .collect(Collectors.joining("\n"));
   }
}
```

To unit test this, you shouldn't have to go into the `Dashboard` implementation and worry about the `ScoreService`. Luckily, you don't have to. By mocking the concrete `Dashboard` class, you can unit test `DashboardViewer` in isolation.

```
1:  @ExtendWith(MockitoExtension.class)
2:  public class DashboardViewerTest {
3:
4:     private DashboardViewer viewer;
5:
6:     @Mock
7:     private Dashboard dashboardMock;
8:
9:     @BeforeEach
10:    void setUp() {
11:       viewer = new DashboardViewer(dashboardMock);
12:    }
13:
14:    @Test
15:    void scores() {
16:       when(dashboardMock.getScores(3)).thenReturn(List.of(69, 23, 106));
17:       String expected = """
18:          -> 69
19:          -> 23
20:          -> 106""";
21:       String actual = viewer.getFormattedData(3);
22:
23:       assertEquals(expected, actual, "data");
24:    }
25: }
```

The flow through Mockito is similar to the earlier example of mocking an interface. Lines 6–7 inject a mock, this time of a concrete class instead of an interface. Line 16 declares the expected calls and associated return value. Line 21 calls the code under test. The `DashboardViewer` class asks the mock to retrieve the scores. The class concludes by asserting the data is formatted correctly. The optional call to `verify()` to verify that the logic is correct is not required here. After all, if the mock wasn't called, line 21 would not have the right data. Notice how

ScoreService is not mentioned. Neither DashboardViewer nor DashboardViewerTest knows anything about the real implementation of Dashboard!

Mocking Statics

Injecting mocks works well for instance variables or method parameters, but what if you want to mock a static method call? Since the static is directly in the code under test, you can't simply inject an object. Luckily, you can still mock it out with Mockito!

Suppose DashboardViewer has a new method you need to test.

```
public String header() {
   return "%s Competition"
       .formatted(LocalDate.now().toString());
}
```

Testing this requires requesting a mock for the LocalDate.now() static method.

```
@Test
void header() {
   LocalDate testDate = LocalDate.of(2024, Month.NOVEMBER, 15);
   try (MockedStatic<LocalDate> localDateMock =
      Mockito.mockStatic(LocalDate.class)) {

      localDateMock.when(LocalDate::now).thenReturn(testDate);

      String expected = "2024-11-15 Competition";
      String actual = viewer.header();
      assertEquals(expected, actual, "header");
   }
}
```

The mockStatic() method creates a mock that is available within the try with resources block. The when/thenReturn structure is the same as for a nonstatic mock so it should look familiar by now.

Mocking with EasyMock

The concepts between Mockito and EasyMock are similar. Being able to read both will put you well on your way to reading any mocking code.

To use EasyMock in your Maven or Gradle build, go to Maven Central (https://mvnrepository.com/artifact/org.easymock/easymock) and find the latest version number for your build tool. Table 7.5 shows what this looks like for each one at the time of this writing.

TABLE 7.5: Specifying EasyMock as a Dependency

TOOL	SYNTAX

Maven	`<dependency>`
	`<groupId>org.easymock</groupId>`
	`<artifactId>easymock</artifactId>`
	`<version>5.2.0</version>`
	`<scope>test</scope>`
	`</dependency>`

Gradle (Groovy)	`testImplementation group: 'org.easymock', name: 'easymock', version: '5.2.0'`
Gradle (Kotlin)	`testImplementation("org.easymock:easymock:5.2.0")`

Looking at the unit test for `Dashboard` using EasyMock, you should see some familiar concepts.

```
1:  @ExtendWith(EasyMockExtension.class)
2:  public class DashboardTest {
3:
4:     private Dashboard dashboard;
5:
6:     @Mock
7:     private ScoreService scoreServiceMock;
8:
9:     @BeforeEach
10:    void setUp() {
11:       dashboard = new Dashboard(scoreServiceMock);
12:    }
13:
14:    @Test
15:    void getScores() {
16:       expect(scoreServiceMock.retrieveScore(1)).andReturn(76);
17:       expect(scoreServiceMock.retrieveScore(2)).andReturn(91);
18:
19:       replay(scoreServiceMock);
20:
21:       List<Integer> expected = List.of(76, 91);
22:       List<Integer> actual = dashboard.getScores(2);
23:       assertEquals(expected, actual, "scores");
24:
25:       verify(scoreServiceMock);
26:    }
27: }
```

Just like Mockito, line 1 has an `@ExtendWith` annotation to give the mocking framework control over the test execution flow. Line 6 has an `@Mock` annotation to inject a mock object. Lines 16 and 17 set the expected return values for when the `retrieveScore()` method is called. While the method names are different than Mockito, the concept is the same.

EasyMock has many more features. As you can see from the similarities with Mockito, it is easy to learn another mock framework once you know one!

Mocking with Spring MockMvc

You learned about Spring in Chapter 6, "Getting to Know the Spring Framework." Spring provides a library to facilitate testing. One of its key features is the ability to test your Spring controllers without having a server. This is a higher level of mocking than in the previous sections.

Spring's MockMvc is in Spring Test. The easiest way to install it into your Spring project is to specify the `spring-boot-starter` dependency, which will download all the required dependencies. To add this to your Maven or Gradle build, go to Maven Central (`https://mvnrepository.com/artifact/org.springframework.boot/spring-boot-starter-test`) and find the latest version number for your build tool. Table 7.6 shows what this looks for each one at the time of this writing.

TABLE 7.6: Specifying Spring Boot Starter Test as a Dependency

Tool	Syntax

Maven	`<dependency>`
	`<groupId>org.springframework.boot</groupId>`
	`<artifactId>spring-boot-starter-test</artifactId>`
	`<version>3.2.4</version>`
	`<scope>test</scope>`
	`</dependency>`

Gradle (Groovy)	`testImplementation group: 'org.springframework.boot', name: 'spring-boot-starter-test', version: '3.2.4'`
Gradle (Kotlin)	`testImplementation("org.springframework.boot" + ":spring-boot-starter-test:3.2.4")`

> **TIP** *The* `spring-boot-starter-test` *dependency pulls in a compatible version of JUnit, so do not include the JUnit BOM or dependency explicitly in your POM when using that dependency.*

To begin, we will create three example classes to show how to use MockMvc to test a controller. The example is a match-tracker service that retrieves the current match number at a competition. The first class is part of the application and exists only once, regardless of how many test classes you have.

```
@SpringBootApplication
public class DashboardApp {

    public static void main(String[] args) {
        SpringApplication.run(DashboardApp.class, args);
    }

}
```

The `SpringBootApplication` would start the app for real if we were running it. Even though this is only a test, it needs to exist for MockMvc to be able to tell if your Spring application will work. Next is the `MatchTrackerService` the controller will reference:

```
@Service
public class MatchTrackerService {

   private int matchNumber = 0;

   public void startMatch() {
      matchNumber++;
   }

   public int getCurrentMatchNumber() {
      return matchNumber;
   }
}
```

The implementation of this service is pretty basic, but that doesn't matter as you'll soon be mocking it out!

Finally comes the controller that uses the service.

```
@RestController
public class DashboardController {

   private MatchTrackerService tracker;

   public DashboardController(MatchTrackerService tracker) {
      this.tracker = tracker;
   }

   @GetMapping("/match")
   public @ResponseBody String displayCurrentMatch() {
      return "In match %s".formatted(tracker.getCurrentMatchNumber());
   }
}
```

This simple controller uses dependency injection (as you learned in Chapter 6 to get the `MatchTrackerService`). It uses the data returned from the service to format a nice display. You might be thinking that you could test the `DashboardController` class using Mockito or EasyMock directly, and you would be right! You can directly inject the dependency and test the `displayCurrentMatch()` logic. But what MockMvc adds is the ability to test your endpoints using REST calls and have Spring do all the dependency injection and testing that your annotations and Spring configuration are correct.

```
1:  @SpringBootTest
2:  @AutoConfigureMockMvc
3:  class DashboardControllerTest {
4:
5:     @Autowired
6:     MockMvc mockMvc;
7:
8:     @MockBean
9:     MatchTrackerService trackerMock;
10:
11:    @Test
12:    void matchNumber() throws Exception {
13:       when(trackerMock.getCurrentMatchNumber()).thenReturn(35);
14:
15:       mockMvc.perform(get("/match"))
16:          .andExpect(status().isOk())
17:          .andExpect(content().string(containsString("In match 35")));
18:
19:       verify(trackerMock, times(1)).getCurrentMatchNumber();
20:    }
21: }
```

Lines 1 and 2 take care of telling JUnit to use Spring MockMvc for testing. Lines 5 and 6 autowire the `MockMvc` object to make it available for the test. Lines 8 and 9 create a mock that uses Mockito under the covers. Line 13 sets up the Mockito mock's expected configuration.

Lines 15–17 use MockMvc to call the REST API `/match`. This simulates a call you could make in the browser as if the application were actually running! The call asserts the HTTP status code and expected return value. Finally, line 19 uses Mockito to verify the expected method was called on the mock.

MockMvc has many features such as methods to check the headers and content type.

MORE SPRING FEATURES

In addition to mocking, Spring has many other useful features for testing. For example, `WebTestClient` helps test HTTP calls.

Note that Spring is using servlets in the background, so servlet filter chaining is probably occurring, which could interfere with your tests, for example for checking Spring Security. To prevent the servlet chaining from occurring, you can inject a `OncePerRequestFilter`, which will bypass all of the filter chaining.

MEASURING TEST COVERAGE

OK, so you've had a great time writing your tests. But how do you know whether what you have written is meaningful? The first step is to ensure that a large percentage of your code is covered by tests!

Now that is not a foolproof gauge, because it is certainly possible to write bad tests that cover a lot of code, such as if you omit or write bad assertions. But assuming you've done a good job on those assertions, then coverage is the next thing you want to check.

The most common coverage tool is the open-source JaCoCo, which stands for Java Code Coverage. It was originally called EclEmma, so you will still see that name in documentation and URLs. JaCoCo reports on the percentage of the bytecode in your `.class` files covered by tests.

NOTE *Other code coverage tools in use are Clover and Cobertura. Clover started as a commercial tool from Atlassian and was open-sourced in 2017. Cobertura has always been open-source but is less popular than JaCoCo.*

JaCoCo works with Maven and Gradle for building and also integrates with SonarQube. Table 7.7 shows JaCoCo's IDE integration.

TABLE 7.7: JaCoCo IDE Integration

IDE	INTEGRATION
IntelliJ	Change in coverage settings pull down from IntelliJ coverage to JaCoCo.
Eclipse	Used by default.
VS Code	Java extensions or Code Gutters plugins display results generated from Maven/Gradle.

Calculating Code Coverage

In this section, you'll see how to calculate code coverage using an example. First look at the class under test, shown here:

```
public final class Match {

    private int number;
```

```
 4:     public int points;
 5:
 6:     public Match(int number) {
 7:        this.number = number;
 8:     }
 9:
10:     public void setWin() {
11:        points+=2;
12:     }
13:
14:     public void setTie() {
15:        points+=1;
16:     }
17:
18:     public String getFormatted() {
19:        String result = "";
20:        if (number == 0) {
21:           result = "n/a";
22:        } else {
23:           result = "Match %d, Score: %d".formatted(number, points);
24:        }
25:        return result;
26:     }
27: }
```

The test class for that is as follows. Notice how it is not very thorough, omitting several methods!

```
class MatchTest {

   private Match match;

   @BeforeEach
   void setUp() {
      match = new Match(4);
   }

   @Test
   void win() {
      match.setWin();

      assertEquals("Match 4, Score: 2", match.getFormatted());
   }
}
```

The `Match` constructor is fully executed as is the `setWin()` method, giving both 100% test coverage. The `setTie()` method is not executed at all, giving it 0% test coverage.

The `getFormatted()` method is more interesting because it is partially tested. In particular, the `else` block gets run by the test. This means line 21 is not covered by tests. Additionally, line 20 is partially covered. This means one of the paths is not tested, in this case the `if` branch.

Coverage tools report the coverage metrics under various categories. In our example, class coverage is 100%, since the class was touched, albeit partially. Method coverage is only 75%, since one of the four methods was not covered at all. Other categories of reporting might include line, branch, and statement coverage.

Seeing Code Coverage in the IDE

In IntelliJ or Eclipse, it is simple to see test coverage. Just run your JUnit tests in coverage mode. Figure 7.5 shows this option in IntelliJ, and Figure 7.6 shows it in Eclipse.

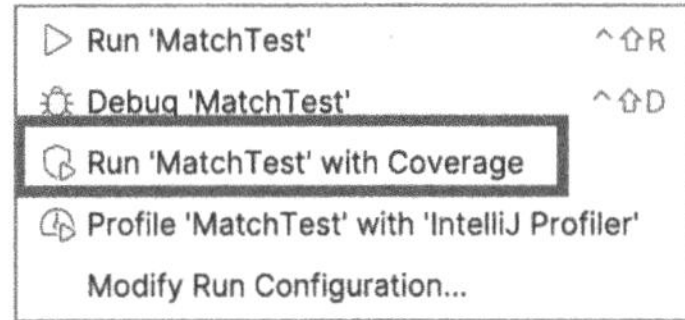

FIGURE 7.5: Running code coverage in IntelliJ

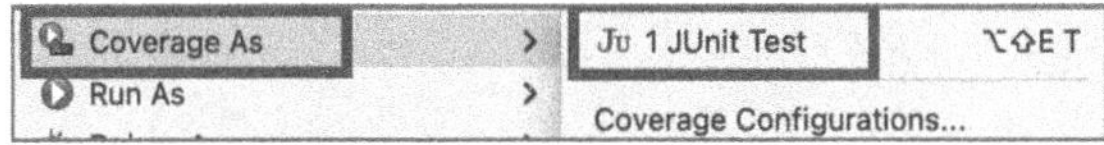

FIGURE 7.6: Running code coverage in Eclipse

Once you run one or more tests with coverage, you can see the results in two locations. First there is a coverage report. Figure 7.7 shows IntelliJ's JaCoCo report, and Figure 7.8 shows Eclipse's JaCoCo report. Notice how even when the underlying calculator is the same, the IDEs categorize the results in different ways.

Element	Class, %	Method, %	Line, %	Branch, %
com.wiley.realworldjava.testing	100% (1/1)	75% (3/4)	69% (9/13)	50% (1/2)
Match	100% (1/1)	75% (3/4)	69% (9/13)	50% (1/2)

FIGURE 7.7: Code coverage IntelliJ report

Element	Coverage	Covered Instructions	Missed Instructions	Total Instructions
junit5-jacoco	84.8 %	56	10	66
src/main/java	78.7 %	37	10	47
src/test/java	100.0 %	19	0	19

FIGURE 7.8: Code coverage Eclipse report

The other location where you can see the coverage is in the editor itself. Each line is annotated with a color so you can see the results directly while looking at the code and quickly identify untested code. The color legend is as follows:

- **Red:** The line is not tested at all.
- **Yellow:** The line is not tested for at least one branch.
- **Green:** The line is tested for all branches.

Running Coverage in the Build

For Maven, the first step in generating coverage reports is to find the plugin you need from Maven Central at `https://mvnrepository.com/artifact/org.jacoco/jacoco-maven-plugin`.

Then you add the plugin to the <build> section of your POM file.

```
<plugin>
   <groupId>org.jacoco</groupId>
   <artifactId>jacoco-maven-plugin</artifactId>
   <version>${jacoco.version}</version>
   <executions>
      <execution>
         <goals>
            <goal>prepare-agent</goal>
            <goal>report</goal>
         </goals>
      </execution>
   </executions>
</plugin>
```

Running the Maven build creates a `jacoco.exec` file in the target directory. The `.exec` file extension makes it easy to recognize the file is from JaCoCo. This contains the same data your IDE would generate if you ran all the tests in your project with coverage turned on. In fact, the `jacoco.exec` file can be read by your IDE to show the coverage directly on the class files or by Sonar to show the coverage results with your other Sonar reporting.

For Gradle, the setup is even shorter. Just add the ID `jacoco` to the `plugins` section. When you build, a `jacoco` directory will be created with a `test.exec` file in it.

OPTIMIZING YOUR TESTING WITH INTELLIJ

While all IDEs have features for working with tests, IntelliJ has the most comprehensive set. In the following sections, you'll get to explore these features.

Looking at Assert Messages

Suppose you have a failing test:

```
@Test
void diff() {
   String expected = """
      winter
      spring
      summer
      fall
      """;
   String actual = """
      winter
      spring
      summer
      autumn
      """;
   assertEquals(expected, actual, "seasons");
}
```

The output of this test in IntellIJ is as follows:

```
org.opentest4j.AssertionFailedError: seasons ==>
<Click to see difference>
```

Figure 7.9 shows what you see when you click to see the differences. The highlighted text is the difference between the expected and actual values. IntelliJ shows you the full text of each to make it easier to understand the context of the failure.

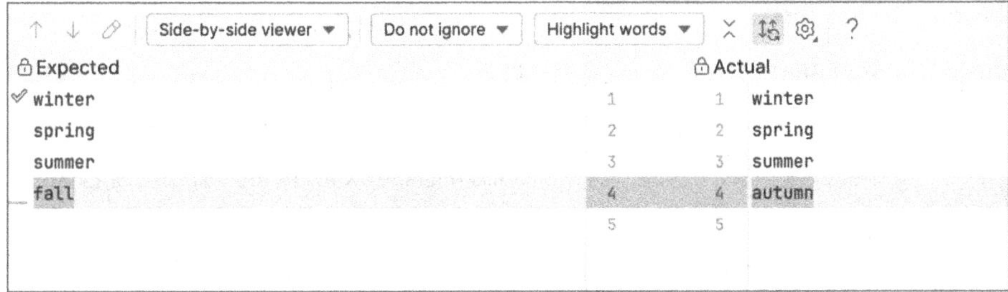

FIGURE 7.9: Comparing expected and actual in IntelliJ

Exploring Test Runs

When you run tests in IntelliJ, a window will appear providing options for viewing results, rerunning tests, dealing with failed tests, and more. (See Figure 7.10.)

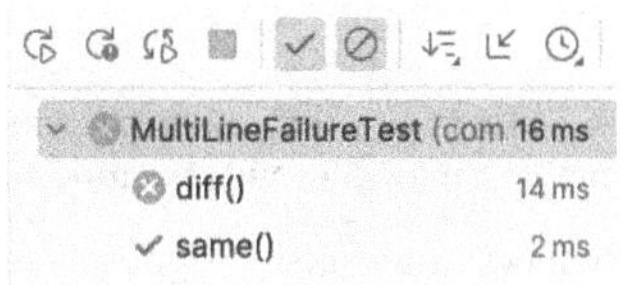

FIGURE 7.10: JUnit IntelliJ options

Using this window, there are a number of ways to rerun tests.

- Right-clicking a specific class gives an option to run all the tests in the class.
- Right-clicking a specific test method gives an option to run that test.
- Clicking the first icon in the top navigation runs all tests in the output.
- Clicking the second icon in the top navigation runs just the failing tests in the output.
- Clicking the third icon in the top navigation tells IntelliJ to automatically run tests when you change the code.

Additionally, you can change what tests show up in the view.

- Toggling the check icon in the top navigation changes whether the tests that passed are visible or hidden.
- Toggling the circle icon in the top navigation changes whether any disabled tests are visible or hidden.
- Clicking the down arrow in the top navigation provides sorting options such as alphabetical or by duration.

Finally, clicking the clock icon allows you to see test history and the results of each run.

Navigating to the Test

IntelliJ has a keyboard shortcut to switch between the code under test and the test itself. On Windows, use Ctrl+Shift+T, and on Mac use Command+Shift+T. Table 7.8 shows what happens when you use this shortcut in different scenarios for the `Match` class.

TABLE 7.8: Navigate to the Test

FILE WITH FOCUS	SCENARIO	RESULT
`Match`	Test class does not exist.	IntelliJ offers to create a new test class.
`Match`	Test class exists.	IntelliJ offers to switch to the test class or create another one.
`MatchTest`	Class under test exists.	IntelliJ automatically navigates to the class.
`MatchTest`	Class under test does not exist.	IntelliJ gets confused and offers to switch to itself or create a new test class.

Generating Test Boilerplate with TestMe

TestMe is a very useful third party-plugin. To install it, go to Settings in IntelliJ and install the TestMe plugin. (See Chapter 2, "Getting to Know Your IDE: The Secret to Success," for instructions on installing plugins.) Once that is installed, you can find the TestMe option in the Code menu.

Clicking the plugin lets you choose from a selection of testing frameworks you'd like to use. For example, you can choose JUnit 5 with Mockito if you don't need a mock in the test; the mock part of the option will be ignored.

The TestMe plugin will generate boilerplate code for your tests that you can then edit and finish. Suppose you want to test this class:

```
public class Weather {

   public static enum Season { WINTER, SPRING, SUMMER, FALL }

    public Season next(Season current) {
       return switch (current) {
          case WINTER ->  Season.SPRING;
          case SPRING ->  Season.SUMMER;
          case SUMMER ->  Season.FALL;
          case FALL ->  Season.WINTER;
       };
   }
}
```

TestMe generates the following:

```
class WeatherTest {
   Weather weather = new Weather();

   @Test
   void testNext() {
      Weather.Season result = weather.next(Weather.Season.WINTER);
      assertEquals(Weather.Season.WINTER, result);
   }
}

//Generated with love by TestMe :) Please raise issues &
 feature requests at: https://weirddev.com/forum#!/testme
```

This test fails because the assertion requires `SPRING` (not `WINTER`) as the expected value. However, it is a good start and lets you start focusing on logic right away.

LEARNING OTHER TESTING CONCEPTS

In this section, we will cover some useful concepts and patterns that are not necessarily associated with any particular library.

Using Behavior-Driven Development

Behavior-Driven Development (BDD) is a testing practice that uses a kind of natural language syntax communicated from your user base. Tests are structured using the following format:

```
Given that a customer wants to enable multi factor authentication
When the customer logs in
Then an option to call or text should appear.
```

The words *given*, *when* and *then* are standard for BDD. If you have more to say than comfortably fits in a phrase, you can use multiple *and* or *but* clauses to start a new line.

There are a number of testing libraries that support BDD.

- **Cucumber:** The most common BDD library, which uses Ruby
- **Cucumber-JVM:** An extension for Cucumber that uses Java
- **JBehave:** Uses Java and focuses on given/when/then stories as a series of steps

Testing Contracts

It is often useful to test the contracts of APIs, HTTP calls, or microservices. Consumer-driven contact (CDC) testing lets you test the components independently while ensuring that the components meet the contract requirements.

There are two parties to a contract. The *provider* supplies the API, and the *consumer* calls the API. Both need to respect the contract or the offending tests will fail.

To use CDC, you create a contract, which generates provider and client stubs. For example, you can specify an HTTP request and code the expected status, headers, and response. This represents the agreement, or "pact," between the consumer and provider.

Two popular frameworks for managing CDC are Spring Cloud Contract and Pact. Spring Cloud Contract uses Groovy or YAML to write the contracts and generates tests to validate the contract. Spring Cloud Contract can also integrate with Pact. In Chapter 6, we covered Spring Cloud Contract.

Understanding the Golden Master Pattern

Sometimes you want to ensure that the results from executing a program with a fixed set of inputs don't change over time. This is particularly useful when the program generates a file or long/complicated string. For example, suppose you want to test the following method, which accepts an array of string elements and produces a string containing each original string and its length.

```
public static String create(String... names) {
   return Arrays.stream(names)
      .map(s -> "%s,%d".formatted(s, s.length()))
      .collect(Collectors.joining("\n"));
}
```

One approach for the test is to use a bunch of asserts.

```
@Test
void testWithAssertions() {
   String actual = CsvGenerator.create("izzy", "sienna", "gabriel");
   String[] lines = actual.split("\n");
```

```
        assertEquals("izzy,4", lines[0], "first line");
        assertEquals("sienna,6", lines[1], "second line");
        assertEquals("gabriel,7", lines[2], "third line");
    }
```

While this works, it is harder to read than it needs to be. It is also brittle. If we make a change to the expected output to reorder the lines and another column, we have to change multiple pieces of code.

The *golden master* pattern provides an alternative to asserting granular details. The following example demonstrates the use of this pattern. Note that you store the expected result in a variable or file depending on how long it is and then compare to that:

```
@Test
void testWithGoldenMaster() {
    String expected = """
        izzy,4
        sienna,6
        gabriel,7""";
    String actual = CsvGenerator.create("izzy", "sienna", "gabriel");
    assertEquals(expected, actual, "data");
}
```

Now if the test fails, you can use your IDE's assertion comparison window to see all the differences and context in one place. Then you decide if the change is intentional. If not, you know the code is broken! If the change is on purpose, you can copy the entire new string from the comparison window and paste it into the text block or file. Now that string is the new golden master that future code will be compared to for deviations.

Testing Mutations

Earlier, you learned that code coverage is not necessarily sufficient to determine if tests are good. One way to ensure good tests is to conduct a code review. Another approach is *mutation testing*. When you run a mutation test, the mutation testing library inserts tiny changes and runs your tests. If the tests fail, that is good. It means the tests detected the change. If the tests still pass, they aren't thorough enough.

For example, a mutation test might get rid of an `if` statement, or perhaps it will change a < to a <=. Since there are a large number of possible mutations, a mutation testing library automatically takes care of this for you. In Java, the PIT (PITest) framework generates mutations and reports on the results. It can integrate with both your build and IDE. PIT used to stand for Parallel Isolated Test. As it evolved, or mutated, the acronym didn't apply anymore, but the name stuck.

Deciding Between DRY vs. DAMP

In development, we learn to write code that is DRY: "don't repeat yourself." The idea is that code should not have duplication, which might cause maintenance issues that lead your code to get out of sync when something gets changed in one place but not the other.

That is an important principle for code in general, but readability in tests is more important. So, for tests, "descriptive and meaningful phrases" (DAMP) often come into play. This doesn't mean you should ignore duplication in tests. It does mean that you should learn to recognize when duplication is OK.

Suppose you want to test this class:

```
public final class Shift {

    public static record Coords(int x, int y){ }

    public static Coords moveUp(Coords original) {
        return new Coords(original.x, original.y + 1);
    }
```

```
    public static Coords moveDown(Coords original) {
        return new Coords(original.x, original.y - 1);
    }
}
```

Testing it the DAMP way, you could write the following:

```
@Test
void moveUp() {
   Coords original = new Coords(4, 7);
   Coords actual = Shift.moveUp(original);

   assertEquals(4, actual.x(), "x");
   assertEquals(8, actual.y(), "y");
}

@Test
void moveDown() {
   Coords original = new Coords(4, 7);
   Coords actual = Shift.moveDown(original);

   assertEquals(4, actual.x(), "x");
   assertEquals(6, actual.y(), "y");
}
```

Notice how the code is very similar. However, all the logic is inline, and it is very easy to read. Refactoring this to DRY gives the following:

```
private static final int X = 4;

private void assertCoords(Coords actual, int expectedX, int expectedY) {
   assertEquals(expectedX, actual.x(), "x");
   assertEquals(expectedY, actual.y(), "y");
}
@Test
void moveUp() {
   Coords original = new Coords(X, 7);
   Coords actual = Shift.moveUp(original);
   assertCoords(actual, X, 8);
}

@Test
void moveDown() {
   Coords original = new Coords(X, 7);
   Coords actual = Shift.moveDown(original);
   assertCoords(actual, X, 6);
}
```

First, notice that the expected value 4 is no longer repeated in the test as it is a constant. Second, the duplication is abstracted into a common method called `assertCoords()`. Deciding which of these choices is the clearer one is subjective. The key in tests is to make sure you aren't avoiding repetition at the expense of readability. Some duplication is OK!

FURTHER REFERENCES

- `https://junit.org/junit5/docs/current/user-guide`

  JUnit 5 User Guide

- `https://github.com/junit-team/junit5-samples`

  Sample projects by build tool
- `https://assertj.github.io/doc`

  AssertJ documentation
- `https://www.javadoc.io/doc/org.assertj/assertj-core/latest/org/assertj/core/api/Assertions.html`

  AssertJ Assertion Javadoc
- `https://www.selikoff.net/2024/03/23/multiple-ways-of-using-soft-asserts-in-junit-5`

  Variety of ways to use Soft Assertions without calling `assertAll()`
- `https://junit-pioneer.org/docs`

  JUnit Pioneer documentation
- `https://javadoc.io/doc/org.mockito/mockito-core/latest/org/mockito/Mockito.html`

  Mockito documentation
- `https://easymock.org/user-guide.html`

  EasyMock documentation
- `https://docs.spring.io/spring-framework/reference/testing/spring-mvc-test-framework.html`

  Spring MockMvc documentation
- `www.eclemma.org/userdoc/index.html`

  JaCoCo documentation
- `https://openclover.org/documentation`

  Clover documentation
- `https://docs.pact.io`

  Pact Documentation
- `https://spring.io/projects/spring-cloud-contract`

  Spring Cloud Contract documentation
- `https://pitest.org/quickstart`

  PIT documentation

SUMMARY

In this chapter, you learned about how to write tests using Java. Key concepts included the following:

- Using JUnit for assertions and test flow
- Creating mock objects using Mockito, EasyMock, and Spring MockMvc
- Measuring test coverage to identify missing tests
- Types of testing

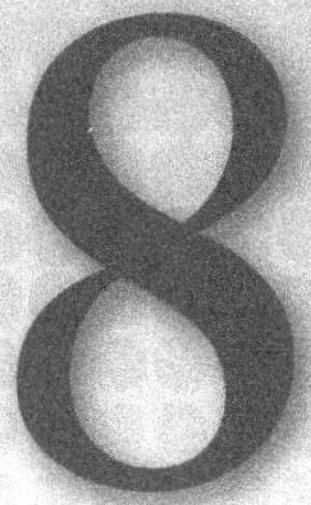

Annotation Driven Code with Project Lombok

WHAT'S IN THIS CHAPTER?

- Preparing Your Environment for Lombok
- Implementing Lombok
- Converting to the Lombok Way
- Delomboking Your Codebase

Project Lombok is one of life's little conveniences. Lombok uses simple annotations to eliminate a ton of boilerplate code, such as getters and setters, logging, `equals`, and `hashCode`, as well as other scaffolding that might otherwise obscure a Java codebase. Lombok does this through the magic of bytecode *reweaving*, a process that rewrites the `.class` files by adding the desired code, without modifying your source files.

You might worry that this will complicate debugging and logging since the source code line numbering won't match the modified class. But in fact, Lombok adjusts for that in the executing code, and the major Integrated Development Environments (IDEs) also handle it gracefully. Admittedly, there are times during intricate debugging sessions where stepping into generated code might be difficult, or cryptic logging messages might surface, for example if an exception is thrown from code that isn't in your codebase!

Some of this might sound like Java "records," introduced in Java 14. For cases where you need immutable data objects, records would usually be the way to go. But Lombok offers much broader capability, and many enterprise development teams are using it. For those that do, it adds great value.

You also might be thinking that you can use code generation to create getters, setters, equals, etc. The problem with code generation is that you have code that needs to be maintained and risks getting out of sync. Additionally, code coverage tools will show this generated code as having low coverage.

As a bit of trivia, Lombok was named after an island in Indonesia about a day's drive east of the great island of Java.

In this chapter, we will cover the most important parts of Project Lombok, including installing Project Lombok and using all of the major annotations, such as `@Data`, `@ToString`, `@Log`, etc.

> **CODE DOWNLOADS FOR THIS CHAPTER**
>
> The source code for this chapter is available on the book page at `www.wiley.com`. Click the Downloads link. The code can also be found at `https://github.com/realworldjava/Ch08-Lombok`. See the `README.md` file in that directory for details.

PREPARING YOUR ENVIRONMENT FOR LOMBOK

Before you use Lombok, you will want to tell your development environment what to expect. This means you need to install Lombok into your IDE as described in this section. You will also need to tell your build tool about it.

Installing in IntelliJ

As of IntelliJ version 2020.3, Lombok comes bundled, so there is not much to do. The first time you use Lombok, IntelliJ will prompt you to enable annotation processing, but you can be proactive inside IntelliJ by going to Settings ➪ Build, Execution, Deployment ➪ Compiler ➪ Annotation Processors, as shown in Figure 8.1.

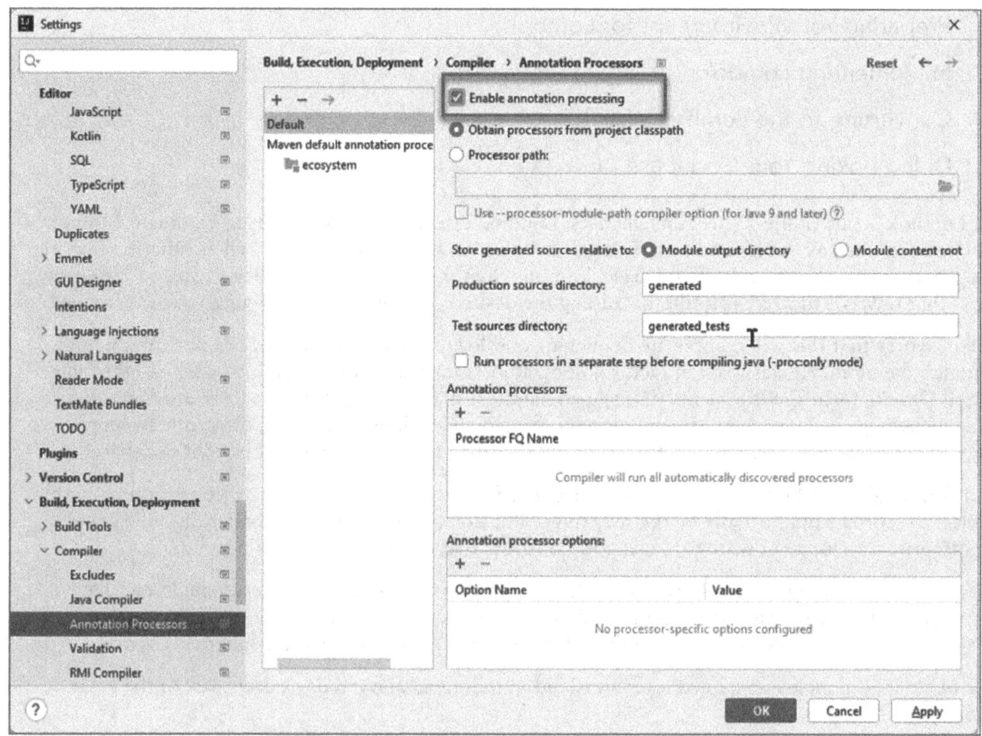

FIGURE 8.1: Select the Enable Annotation Processing checkbox.

To be sure, if you include the Lombok JAR in your build, the code will compile even without the plugin. But without the plugin, the IDE will think any calls to the Lombok-generated getters, setters, etc., are errors because the IDE will not see this code in the codebase. In earlier IntelliJ versions, developers would have needed to install the Lombok plugin. But nowadays, Lombok is included, so that is no longer required.

Installing in Eclipse

To install Lombok in Eclipse, follow these steps:

1. Head over to `https://projectlombok.org/download` and download the latest version of Lombok, naming it **lombok.jar**. Double-click `lombok.jar`, and in a few seconds it will locate your Eclipse installation (see Figure 8.2).

> **WARNING** *On a Mac, you may get the message "lombok.jar cannot be opened because it is from an undefined developer." If that happens, right-click the file and choose Open With and then Java Launcher. Then click Open on the subsequent pop-up that says "macOS cannot verify the developer of lombok.jar" confirming you want to open it.*

2. Click the Install/Update button to install Lombok in the selected versions.
3. Restart Eclipse, and you should be good to go.

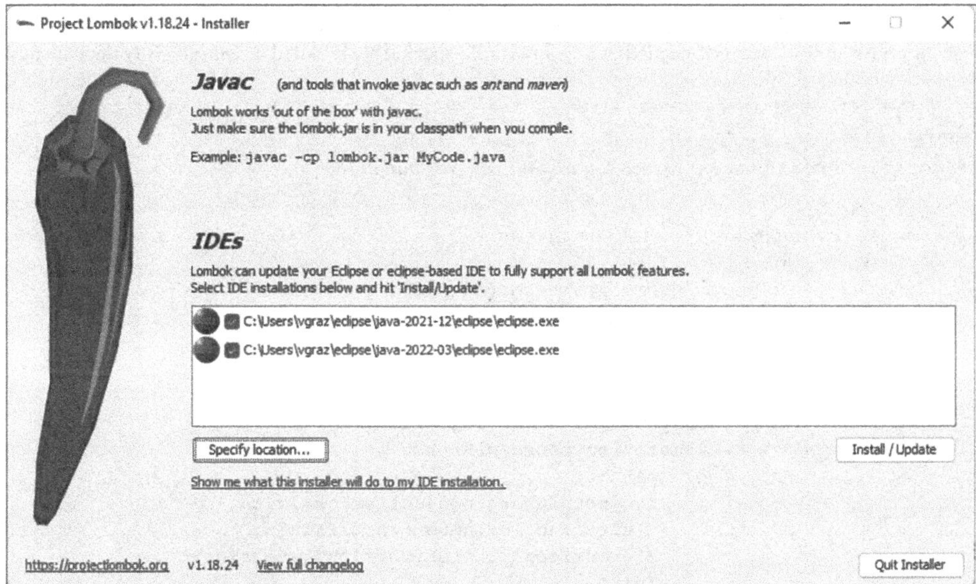

FIGURE 8.2: Installing Lombok in Eclipse

Installing in VS Code

The two major Java extensions for VS Code (Oracle and Microsoft) include Lombok support. There was an older extension from Microsoft called "Lombok's Annotation Support for VS Code." That is deprecated and only meant for people on old versions of the VS Code plugins.

Including in Maven or Gradle

To include Lombok in your Maven or Gradle build, you can go to Maven Central at `https://mvnrepository.com/artifact/org.projectlombok/lombok` and find the latest version number of "projectlombok" for your build tool. At the time of this writing, Table 8.1 shows what this looks for each configuration.

TABLE 8.1: Specifying Lombok as a Dependency

TOOL	SYNTAX

Maven	`<dependency>`
	`    <groupId>org.projectlombok</groupId>`
	`    <artifactId>lombok</artifactId>`
	`    <version>1.18.30</version>`
	`    <scope>provided</scope>`
	`</dependency>`

Gradle (Groovy)	`compileOnly group: 'org.projectlombok', name: 'lombok', version: '1.18.30'`
Gradle (Kotlin)	`compileOnly("org.projectlombok:lombok:1.18.30")`

Grab the dependency for your build tool and include that in your dependencies.

Please note that Lombok is only needed to compile your project. Once the project is compiled, you will no longer need it for executing your code. In Maven language, this is called a *provided* scope: the JAR is "provided" externally for execution (or in our case, not needed at all). In Gradle-speak, this is called a *compileOnly* dependency.

> **NOTE** *In Maven, you will get a warning if you don't add an* `annotationProcessorPaths` *section to your compile plugin like so:*

```
<build>
   <plugins>
      <plugin>
         <groupId>org.apache.maven.plugins</groupId>
         <artifactId>maven-compiler-plugin</artifactId>
         <version>3.12.1</version>
         <configuration>
             <source>${java.version}</source>
             <target>${java.version}</target>
             <annotationProcessorPaths>
                 <path>
                    <groupId>org.projectlombok</groupId>
                    <artifactId>lombok</artifactId>
                    <version>${lombok.version}</version>
                 </path>
             </annotationProcessorPaths>
         </configuration>
      </plugin>
   </plugins>
</build>
```

If you are not using Maven or Gradle, you will need to add Lombok to the classpath for your project. See the `README.md` file in the GitHub project folder for more details.

Compiling from javac

Finally, if you are building from the command line, you just need to include `lombok.jar` on your classpath, and Lombok will take care of the rest.

```
javac -cp lombok.jar etc.jar my-project
```

IMPLEMENTING LOMBOK

The best way to learn about Lombok annotations is to see them in action. Let's start with an example, a class called `User` that contains a user ID, name, address, and perhaps some other instance variables. First, we'll do it the old-fashioned way, without Lombok.

The class has three members: `userID`, `name`, and `address`.

```
public class User {
   // userID does not compile. We made it final to demo a constructor. Stay tuned!
   private final int userID;
   private String name;
   private String address;
}
```

But there is a lot of boilerplate code required to make this class useful. Adding getters, settings, `toString()`, and `hashCode()` turns the nice clean `User` class into this somewhat cluttered beast:

```
import java.util.Objects;
public class User {
   private final int userID;
   private String name;
   private String address;

   public int getUserID() {
      return userID;
   }

   public String getName() {
      return name;
   }

   public void setName(String name) {
      this.name = name;
   }

   public String getAddress() {
      return address;
   }

   public void setAddress(String address) {
      this.address = address;
   }

   public User(int userID, String name, String address) {
      this.userID = userID;
      this.name = name;
      this.address = address;
   }
```

```
    @Override
    public boolean equals(Object o) {
        if(this==o) return true;
        if(o==null) return false;
        return o instanceof User user
            && getUserID()==user.getUserID()
            && Objects.equals(getName(), user.getName())
            && Objects.equals(getAddress(), user.getAddress());
    }

    @Override
    public int hashCode() {
        return Objects.hash(getUserID(), getName(), getAddress());
    }

    @Override
    public String toString() {
        return "User{" +
        "userID=" + userID +
        ", name='" + name + '\'' +
        ", address='" + address + '\'' +
        '}';
    }
}
```

CONVERTING TO THE LOMBOK WAY

Annotations are the core of Lombok. In this section, we will introduce each annotation by rewriting the previous example with much less code!

Using @Data: the include-all Annotation

Start again from the basic class, but this time add the `@Data` annotation (remember to import the `lombok.Data` annotation).

```
import lombok.Data;
@Data
public class User {
    private final int userID;
    private String name;
    private String address;
}
```

This code looks similar to the original code! But if you were following along in your IDE, you would notice that the red underline on the final `userID` has disappeared since a constructor is now automatically generated. Lombok's `@Data` annotation automatically generates the bytecode into your class, for the following:

- `toString()`
- `equals()`
- `hashCode()`
- Getters on all fields
- Setters on all nonfinal fields

- A required-args constructor, containing the unassigned final, nonstatic, non-null instance variables
- `canEquals()`, which is used in special cases (if you need to redefine equality for inheritance, for example)

Lombok does not touch your source code; it just weaves the boilerplate code into your bytecode after compilation.

You will see soon that each of those methods can also be rewoven individually for more granular control, by the more specific annotations: `@ToString`, `@EqualsAndHashCode`, `@Getter`, `@Setter`, and `@RequiredArgsConstructor`.

Autogenerating Your @Getter and @Setter Methods

As you have already seen, you can annotate a class name with `@Data` to autogenerate a constructor and all getters, setters, and such. But there are times you want to override the autogenerated behavior; for example, you might want to change the access level from the default `public` to something more restrictive such as `protected`. Or perhaps you don't want your class to be a `Data` class, but you do want to generate some getters and setters. For that you can use `@Getter` and/or `@Setter` annotations.

For example, let's say we have a nonannotated class.

```
public class Automobile {
   private String model;
}
```

To autogenerate a getter and or setter for this, we can apply the annotations `@Getter` and `@Setter`.

```
import lombok.Getter;
import lombok.Setter;

public class Automobile {
   @Getter @Setter
   private String model;
}
```

This will weave the bytecode of the generated class to add methods.

```
public void setModel(String model)
public String getModel()
```

We can use the annotations independently. For example, if we want a getter and not a setter, we would use only `@Getter`. Java conventions are automatically followed. If the instance variable is a boolean, for example:

```
import lombok.Getter;

public class Automobile {
  @Getter
  private boolean used;
}
```

Then the generated getter will be as follows:

```
public boolean isUsed()
```

By default, autogenerated getters and setters will have public access, but you can change that by specifying an access method attribute. The following code says to generate a private `Setter`:

```
import lombok.AccessLevel;
import lombok.Getter;
import lombok.Setter;
```

```
public class Automobile {
   @Getter @Setter(AccessLevel.PRIVATE) private String model;
}
```

This will generate the following methods:

```
public String getModel();
private void setModel(String model);
```

You can also autogenerate getters and/or setters for the entire class by applying the `@Getter` and `@Setter` annotations to the class name. The class can be a standard outer class or even an inner class.

```
import lombok.Getter;
import lombok.Setter;

@Getter @Setter
public class Automobile {
   private String manufacturer;
   private String make;
   private String model;
}
```

This will generate public getters and setters for all your instance variables.

In case you want to change the access level for specific fields, you can annotate those individually, which will override the default behavior. You can also specify `AccessLevel.NONE` to prevent that accessor from being autogenerated at all.

```
import lombok.AccessLevel;
import lombok.Getter;
import lombok.Setter;

@Getter @Setter
public class Automobile {
   // Generate a protected setter for manufacturer
   // generates method: protected setManufacturer(String m)
   @Setter(AccessLevel.PROTECTED) private String manufacturer;

   // The class @Setter and @Getter annotations will generate
   // appropriate getter and setter for "make"
   private String make;

   // Don't generate a setter for variable "model"
   @Setter(AccessLevel.NONE) private String model;
}
```

The following are the supported access levels:

- `AccessLevel.NONE`: Do not generate the accessor method.
- `AccessLevel.PACKAGE`: Generate the default access method.
- `AccessLevel.PRIVATE`: Generate a `private` accessor method.
- `AccessLevel.PROTECTED`: Generate a `protected` accessor method.
- `AccessLevel.PUBLIC`: Generate a `public` access method. (This is the default and may be omitted.)

There is also an `AccessLevel.MODULE`, but this is no longer used.

Using @ToString

You can annotate any class with the @ToString annotation, which will generate a public String toString() method, containing all of the nonstatic fields.

Some optional switches let you format the String output, for example, how verbose to make it. We won't mention them all here; refer to the Lombok website at https://projectlombok.org/ for full documentation. However, one common feature we will mention is how to control which fields to include. By default, every nonstatic field is included. You can declaratively exclude fields by annotating them with @ToString.Exclude; for example in the following code, the address field is excluded. You can see in the printout from executing that code that the field is omitted in the output.

```
import lombok.AllArgsConstructor;
import lombok.ToString;

@AllArgsConstructor @ToString
public class User {
   private final int userID;
   private String name;
   @ToString.Exclude private String address;

   public static void main(String[] args) {
      User user = new User(123, "Joe", "123 Main");
      System.out.println(user);
   }
}
```

This prints the following:

```
User (userID=123, name=Joe)
```

For Collections, the @ToString annotation generates a deep rendering. For example, in the following code, the toString() method will include all members of list friends, as you can see in the printout of the toString() method after we execute that code.

```
import lombok.AllArgsConstructor;
import lombok.ToString;
import java.util.List;

@AllArgsConstructor @ToString
public class User {
   private final int userID;
   private String name;
   @ToString.Exclude private String address;
   private List<String> friends;

   public static void main(String[] args) {
      User user = new User(123, "John Jones", "123 Main",
         List.of("William", "Alok", "Heather"));
      System.out.println(user);
   }
}
```

This prints the following:

```
User (userID=123, name=John Jones, friends=[William, Alok, Heather]
```

Using @EqualsAndHashCode

One of the fundamental rules of Java programming is that the `equals()` and `hashCode()` methods must agree; i.e., any objects that are `equals()` must return the same `hashCode()`. In addition, we would prefer different instances to produce different hash codes.

We can achieve this by annotating classes with `@EqualsAndHashCode`, which applies a prime hash against all of the nonstatic, nontransient fields of the object instance.

You can specifically exclude fields from the `hashCode` and `equals`, by annotating the fields to exclude with `@EqualsAndHashCode.Exclude`, in a similar fashion to what we saw with `@ToString`.

```
import lombok.AllArgsConstructor;
import lombok.EqualsAndHashCode;

@AllArgsConstructor
@EqualsAndHashCode
public class Automobile {
   private String make;
   private String model;

   @EqualsAndHashCode.Exclude
   private String color;

   public static void main(String[] args) {
      Automobile car1 = new Automobile("Tesla", "Model 3", "Gray");
      Automobile car2 = new Automobile("Tesla", "Model 3", "Red");
      Automobile car3 = new Automobile("Tesla", "Model Y", "Red");

      System.out.println(car1.equals(car2)); // true
      System.out.println(car1.equals(car3)); // false
   }
}
```

You can see that `color` is excluded from the `equals` and `hashCode` methods. So, `car1` and `car2` are equal, since they differ only in color. However, `car2` and `car3` are not equal since they differ in `Model`.

Generating Constructors with @AllArgsConstructor, @RequiredArgsConstructor, and @NoArgsConstructor Annotations

Constructors are common boilerplate code, required in any class that is to be instantiated. If you have final, nonstatic instance fields in your class, they must be assigned in the constructor.

Annotate your class with `@AllArgsConstructor` to generate a constructor that will include assignments for all the nonstatic, nonfinal instance variables contained in the class.

Annotate your class with `@RequiredArgsConstructor` to generate a constructor that includes assignments for all the unassigned final instance variables contained in the class. Additionally, you can annotate instance variables with `@NonNull` to have them included in the `@RequiredArgsConstructor` annotation.

Annotate your class with `@NoArgsConstructor` to generate a no-args constructor. This would result in a compile error if there were any unassigned final instance variables. To work around this, use `@NoArgsConstructor(force=true)`. This will create a no-args constructor, whose implementation will assign null, zero, or false to any unassigned final instance variables.

You can annotate your class with any or all the constructor annotations. Here's an example:

```
import lombok.AllArgsConstructor;
import lombok.NoArgsConstructor;
import lombok.RequiredArgsConstructor;
import lombok.ToString;

@RequiredArgsConstructor @AllArgsConstructor @NoArgsConstructor(force = true)
@ToString
public class User {
   private final int userID;
   private String name;
   private String address;
}
```

This generates three constructors.

```
// from NoArgsConstructor
public User()
// from RequiredArgsConstructor
public User(int userID)
// from AllArgsConstructor
public User(int userID, String name, String address)
```

Weaving Loggers into Your Codebase with @Log and More

In Chapter 5, "Capturing Application State with Logging Frameworks," you saw some of the most common logging frameworks in the Java world. Thankfully, Project Lombok provides annotations for creating all of the common loggers, as well as many less common ones and even custom loggers, so that you can just start logging without cluttering your code with factory methods for creating loggers.

The loggers will be created automatically for you simply by annotating the class with one of the annotations in Table 8.2. In every case, the logger will be assigned to a variable named `log` by default. You do not need to explicitly import the logger, but you do need to include your logging library as a dependency in your project, and you do need to import the annotation. Here are two examples:

Using Java Util Logging:

```
import lombok.extern.java.Log;
```

Using Slf4j:

```
import lombok.extern.slf4j.Slf4j;
```

You don't need to memorize these; your IDE will insert the appropriate import for you automatically.

For example, the following snippet will write the appropriate log messages using Slf4j.

```
import lombok.extern.slf4j.Slf4j;
@Slf4j
public class LombokLogging {
   public static void main(String[] args) {
      log.debug("Starting");
      log.info("Hello, Words");
      log.debug("Goodbye");
   }
}
```

TABLE 8.2: Logging Annotations Supported by Project Lombok

ANNOTATION	GENERATED CODE
`@CommonsLog`	`private static final org.apache.commons.logging.Log log = org.apache.commons.logging.LogFactory.getLog(MyClass.class);`
`@Flogger`	`private static final com.google.common.flogger.FluentLogger log = com.google.common.flogger.FluentLogger.forEnclosingClass();`
`@JBossLog`	`private static final org.jboss.logging.Logger log = org.jboss.logging.Logger.getLogger(MyClass.class);`
`@Log`	`private static final java.util.logging.Logger log = java.util.logging.Logger.getLogger(MyClass.class.getName());`
`@Log4j`	`private static final org.apache.log4j.Logger log = org.apache.log4j.Logger.getLogger(MyClass.class);`
`@Log4j2`	`private static final org.apache.logging.log4j.Logger log = org.apache.logging.log4j.LogManager.getLogger(MyClass.class);`
`@Slf4j`	`private static final org.slf4j.Logger log = org.slf4j.LoggerFactory.getLogger(MyClass.class);`
`@XSlf4j`	`private static final org.slf4j.ext.XLogger log = org.slf4j.ext.XLoggerFactory.getXLogger(MyClass.class);`
`@CustomLog`	`private static final com.foo.your.Logger log = com.foo.your.LoggerFactory.createYourLogger(MyClass.class);` This option requires that you add a configuration to your `lombok.config` file to specify what `@CustomLog` should do.

Slf4j is a wrapper around any logging implementation. The default logger used by the Lombok `@Slf4j` annotation will be Logback, but you can override that by including a dependency to your preferred logging framework in your `pom.xml` or `build.gradle` file.

Additionally, there are many tweaks you can make in the `lombok.config` file to override the Lombok defaults. Just include `lombok.config` in or under your Java source root directory. The config file will apply to all source files in or under that directory.

As an example, let's say you want to change the default `log` variable name to `logger`. You would specify the following configuration in the `lombok.config` file:

```
lombok.log.fieldName=logger
```

Or consider the fact that the loggers are created to be static. But suppose you want to change these to be not static, say to avoid contention with various instances of the same class. Then you can include the following in `lombok.config`:

```
lombok.log.fieldIsStatic=false
```

To see the full list of `lombok.config` configuration keys with descriptions, use the following command:

```
java -jar lombok.jar config -g --verbose
```

Or see the Lombok online documentation at `https://projectlombok.org/features/configuration`.

DELOMBOKING YOUR CODEBASE

There might be times when you would like to see the code that Lombok has woven into your classes, for example, if things are going wrong, and you want to get a closer look at the problem code. Delombok is a tool that is included in `lombok.jar`, and it will recursively "delombok" every `.java` file in the source path you supply and will create a "delomboked" version in the directory you supply. For example, here is how you use it on Windows:

```
java -jar .\lombok.jar delombok .\src\ -d src-no-lombok
```

Here is how you use it on a Mac:

```
java -jar lombok.jar delombok src -d src-no-lombok
```

You can also install a Delomboking plugin for some IDEs. For example, IntelliJ offers the appropriately named Delombok plugin. Install this to add a "Delombok Project" option to the Build menu and create a `delombok` folder parallel to your `src` directory.

FURTHER REFERENCES

- `https://projectlombok.org`

  The complete guide to Lombok installation, features, and community

SUMMARY

In this chapter, you looked at the most important annotations provided by Project Lombok for getting rid of heaps of boilerplate code, you saw how to override default behavior, and you learned how to "Delombok" your code. There are more annotations, and there are configuration switches to modify the behavior of the ones you have seen, so refer to the excellent Project Lombok documentation at `projectlombok.org`.

Specifically, you learned about the following annotations:

- `@Data`: Injects into your bytecode ("weaves") `toString`, `equals`, and `hashCode`, as well as getters on all fields, setters on all nonfinal fields, and a required-args constructor.
- `@Getter` and `@Setter`: Weave getter and setter methods into your bytecode.
- `@ToString`: Weaves `toString` method based on some or all instance variable values.
- `@EqualsAndHashCode`: Weaves `equals` and `hashCode` methods based on some or all instance variable values as you like.
- `@NoArgsConstructor`, `@RequiredArgsConstructor`, and `@AllArgsConstructor`: Weave constructors into your bytecode.
- `@Log`, `@Slf4j`, `@Log4j2`, etc.: Create a static logger class variable.

Parallelizing Your Application Using Java Concurrency

WHAT'S IN THIS CHAPTER?

- Understanding Concurrency Basics
- Introducing Concurrent Collections
- Using Built-In Concurrency Support in Java Streams
- Using Concurrency Components to Reduce Complexity
- Learning Concurrency Support in the Spring Framework

Let's not pull any punches: concurrency is hard. We human beings are conditioned to think in a synchronous fashion. But if we want to have web servers that process zillions of requests, if we want to extract and transform tens of thousands of files per hour, or if we generally want to make our applications performant, we need to execute things concurrently. A thread is Java's unit of concurrency, and multiple threads can run at the same time. The challenge is that multiple threads can share common resources, and if some are writing and some are reading, there could be unexpected results. To make your applications thread-safe, you need to think about how two or more concurrent threads interact with each other and what happens when multiple threads try to access the same resource. Thankfully there are tools, rules, and frameworks that make things easier.

In this chapter we will review some low-level concurrency basics, followed by higher-level concurrency tools introduced to the Java language for synchronization, and in particular `CompletableFuture` and virtual threads.

Traditionally you would launch a thread by passing a `Runnable` to the `Thread` constructor and call `start()` on the newly created thread. Java 21 introduced some newer patterns for creating and starting threads, and we will see the new approach in this chapter. Finally, we will look at some of the concurrency tools included in Spring.

CODE DOWNLOADS FOR THIS CHAPTER

The source code for this chapter is available on the book page at `www.wiley.com`. Click the Downloads link. The code can also be found at `https://github.com/realworldjava/Ch09-Concurrency`. See the `README.md` file in that repository for details.

UNDERSTANDING CONCURRENCY BASICS

Java was one of the first languages to introduce concurrency as a native part of the language. Originally all Java threads were *platform* threads, managed by Java in coordination with the operating system.

Threads provide you with the ability to execute multiple operations concurrently. For example, let's say you have a website that processes user requests. It would not be acceptable to have each user wait for the previous user's request to be completed. For that reason, websites are a classic use case for concurrent threads. The complexity arises when threads contend for access to shared resources.

Also, when a thread is launched, you want your main application to continue working until a result is achieved. For example, imagine your application receives a request for some sort of client orders. To complete the request, you need to make a REST call to get the client name and address, a SQL call to a relational database to get the inventory, and a call to some NoSQL database to get the orders. You will learn more about these databases and their access languages, including Structured Query Language (SQL), in Chapter 14, "Getting to Know More of the Ecosystem." We could execute those requests sequentially, waiting for one to complete before executing the next. But for high-performance use cases, we want to execute those requests concurrently, wait until all of those requests have completed, and then return the merged result to the client. But if many threads are running in the background, how can they join up when done to form a unified result? One way would be for each thread to notify the main thread when it is done, but how can we do that?

One way of handling this is by providing a *callback method* to the thread. A callback method is a method that is to be executed by the thread when it completes. Callback methods are not bad when you have a small number of threads, but sometimes you have many threads running, which in turn call more threads, leading to an unreadable web of callbacks known in the vernacular as *callback hell*, but until Java 21 it was something Java developers had to learn to live with.

But then Java 21 introduced *virtual threads*, and the entire threading subsystem was rewritten to support them. Where a traditional platform thread is bound to an operating system, a virtual thread is mounted to and unmounted from a platform thread, which we will call a *carrier thread*, for execution. But when a virtual thread is waiting for any blocking operation, such as an I/O operation, Java *parks* it until it is ready and then unmounts it from its platform thread freeing it up to do more work for another process. When the virtual thread is ready to proceed, for example when the sleep operation has completed or when the I/O socket has returned its bytes, Java mounts that virtual thread back to an available platform thread, possibly different from the original thread. This arrangement greatly simplifies the creation and management of highly performant thread operations. Virtual threads handle the management of threads for you, allowing you to eliminate callback methods and program in a more comfortable, synchronous fashion.

There are a few ways to run a job in a thread. The least-used way is to override the `run` method in `Thread`:

```
new Thread() {
   @Override
   public void run() {
      doSomeWork();
   }
}.start();
```

A more common way is to provide a Runnable instance to a thread (in our case doSomeWork() is a method that will do some work):

```
// Create a Runnable that defines the work to be done:
Runnable someRunnable = new Runnable() {
   @Override
   public void run() {
      doSomeWork();
   }
};
// assign the Runnable to a thread and start it running:
new Thread(someRunnable).start();
```

You can get rid of some of the boilerplate code by defining your Runnable as a lambda. The following is equivalent to the previous code:

```
new Thread(()-> doSomeWork()).start();
```

A more modern and convenient way of creating and launching threads is to use one of the factory methods of the Thread class introduced in Java 21. These use a *fluent* builder pattern to configure, start, and return the thread.

```
Thread thread = Thread
   .ofPlatform()
   .start(() -> doSomeWork());
```

Using this syntax you can create a new thread, supply functionality in the form of a Runnable functional interface (coded as () -> doSomeWork()), and start it in one command.

You can optionally configure attributes such as the thread name, thread group, daemon, priority, and more using the builder syntax, as follows:

```
Thread thread = Thread.ofPlatform()
   .name("Some meaningful name")
   .priority(Thread.NORM_PRIORITY+1)
   .group(new ThreadGroup("Some thread group"))
   .daemon(false)
   .start(() -> doSomeWork());
```

To create a thread without starting it, use .unstarted() instead of .start().

```
Thread thread = Thread.ofPlatform()
   .name("Some meaningful name")
   .priority(Thread.NORM_PRIORITY+1)
   .group(new ThreadGroup("Some thread group"))
   .daemon(false)
   .unstarted(() -> doSomeWork());
```

DAEMON THREADS AND THREAD PRIORITY

By default, platform threads will prevent an application from exiting until they have all completed. Sometimes, however, we have support threads that just run in the background, but we don't want them to block the application from exiting. An example of this would be threads in a thread pool, where they are pooled in advance to execute anticipated work, but we don't want them to block the application from exiting. We can designate such a thread as a daemon thread by calling thread.setDaemon(true), or by calling .daemon(true) using the builder pattern. Daemon threads will not prevent an application from exiting, even though they are still in the runnable state.

Thread priority is used to hint to the thread scheduler which threads to dole out more time slices.

You can start that thread later using `.start()`.

```
thread.start();
```

You can use a similar syntax for starting virtual threads, which we will cover in the "Introducing Virtual Threads" section later in this chapter.

You will see other ways to create and launch threads in the following sections on `ExecutorService` and `CompletableFuture`. Each one provides features for handling common specialized use cases.

Dealing with Thread Contention

The challenge of dealing with contending threads is best illustrated with the classic problem of a Hit Counter. In this problem, you have a website with a hit counter that should be incremented by one every time a request comes in, as shown in Figure 9.1.

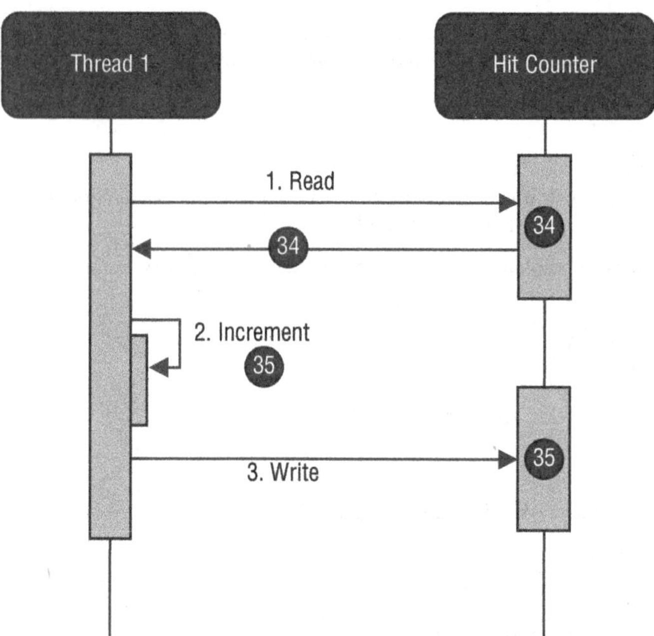

FIGURE 9.1: Hit counter happy path

In the happy path, a user request comes in on Thread 1 and we update the hit counter. Imagine the hit counter is up to hit #34 when the request comes in. It processes the request as follows:

- **Step 1:** User on Thread 1 reads the value of the hit counter and sees value = 34.
- **Step 2:** Thread 1 increments the value to 35.
- **Step 3:** Thread 1 writes back the incremented value to the hit counter, which now has a value of 35. And all is well.

But now let's look at the less fortunate path in Figure 9.2, where Thread 1 and Thread 2 are both trying to update the hit counter at the same time.

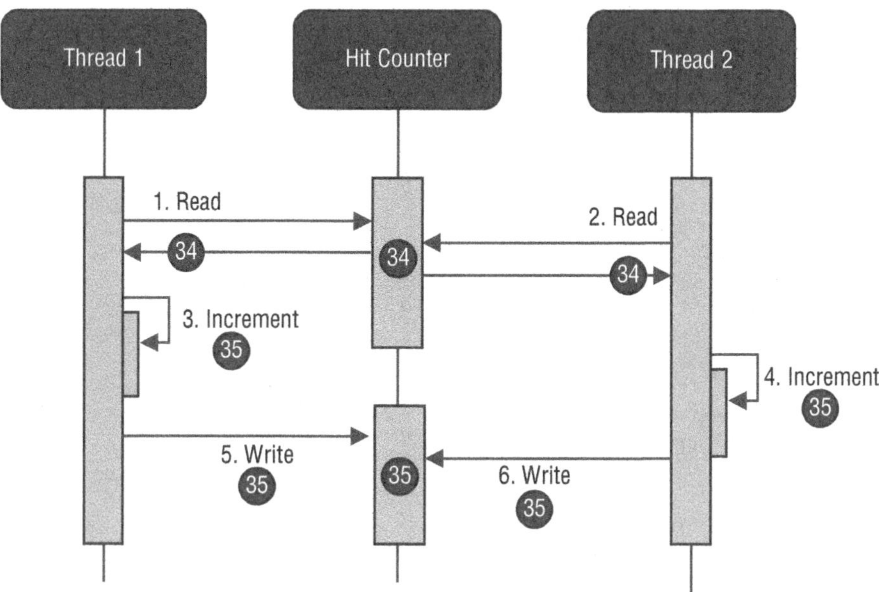

FIGURE 9.2: Hit counter with race condition

- **Step 1:** Thread 1 reads the Hit Counter and sees value = 34.
- **Step 2:** Before Thread 1 has a chance to update the Hit Counter to 35, Thread 2 reads the Hit Counter and sees 34 as well.
- **Step 3:** Thread 1, not knowing about Thread 2, increments its 34 to 35.
- **Step 4:** Just then, Thread 2 also increments its 34 to 35.
- **Step 5:** Thread 1 writes its 35 back to the Hit Counter.
- **Step 6:** Thread 2 writes its 35 back to the Hit Counter. Lo and behold, two threads updated the Hit Counter, but due to the unfortunate interweaving, only one hit was recorded. Not good. This is what is known as a *race condition*, and it is our job to protect against this in our multithreaded code.

We demonstrate this race condition:

```
public class HitCounter {
   public static final int HITS = 10_000;
   private static int hitCounter = 0;
   private static AtomicInteger atomicHitCounter = new AtomicInteger(0);
   public static void main(String[] args) throws InterruptedException {
      Runnable incrementTask = () -> {
         for(int i = 0; i < HITS; i++) {
            incrementHitCounter(i);
         }
      };
      Thread thread1 = Thread.ofPlatform().start(incrementTask);
      Thread thread2 = Thread.ofPlatform().start(incrementTask);
      thread1.join();
      thread2.join();

```

```
20:         System.out.println("Final hit counter value was: " + hitCounter
21:            + ". Expected " + (2*HITS));
22:         System.out.println("Final atomic hit counter value was: "
23:            + atomicHitCounter + ". Expected " + (2*HITS));
24:      }
25:
26:      private static void incrementHitCounter(int i) {
27:
28:         int temp = hitCounter;
29:         if(i % 1000==0) {
30:            System.out.println(Thread.currentThread() + " incrementing "
31:               + temp + ". Atomic hitCounter:" + atomicHitCounter);
32:         }
33:         // Simulate some delay
34:         try {
35:            Thread.sleep(0, 1);  // small delay in nanoseconds
36:         } catch(InterruptedException e) {
37:            Thread.currentThread().interrupt();
38:         }
39:         hitCounter = temp + 1;
40:         atomicHitCounter.incrementAndGet();
41:      }
42: }
```

In this code, we are launching two threads and asking each one to increment the hit counter 10,000 times. At the end we would expect the hit counter to be 20,000, which is the combined number of hits from both threads. However, if you run the program, you will see that the expected value is rarely achieved.

Lines 10–16 create and start two threads. Lines 17 and 18 use the thread *join()* method to wait for each other to complete; otherwise, the program would end immediately. Lines 20–23 display the actual hit count after both threads have completed. Lines 33–38 simulate some delay to emphasize the issue.

The challenge is to make the increment operation *atomic*, meaning that they must run as a complete step, without any chance of leaving the system in a partially complete state.

Java provides several atomic components that guarantee their operations will be atomic. One such component is `AtomicInteger`. Looking at the `atomicHitCounter` variable in the previous code, we see that the result on lines 30–31 shows the `atomicHitCounter` variable indeed achieves the expected 20,000.

To achieve atomicity in more specialized cases, Java provides the keywords *synchronized* and *volatile*, which we will soon discuss. Additionally, Java provides methods for telling a thread to *wait*, as well as methods to *notify* threads to stop waiting. Let's see how to ensure our own atomic code.

Coding Atomic Operations

Some ground rules—Java guarantees that all assignments and accesses to objects and primitives are atomic, except for *gets* and *sets* to long and double. This implies that when you get or set any object like Strings, Lists, or Arrays, as well as most primitives, the operations will be atomic, and there is no chance of some thread seeing a half-set result.

Longs and doubles are the exception and do not make such guarantees. These are 64-bit values, composed of two 32-bit words. It is entirely possible for long or double variables to return completely inconsistent data, as shown in Figure 9.3 where Thread 1 is setting a 64-bit value of AAAABBBB and Thread 2 is setting CCCCDDDD. The result is a half-set AAAA in the high word from Thread 1 and DDDD in the low word from Thread 2, producing a hybrid value that was not set by either thread.

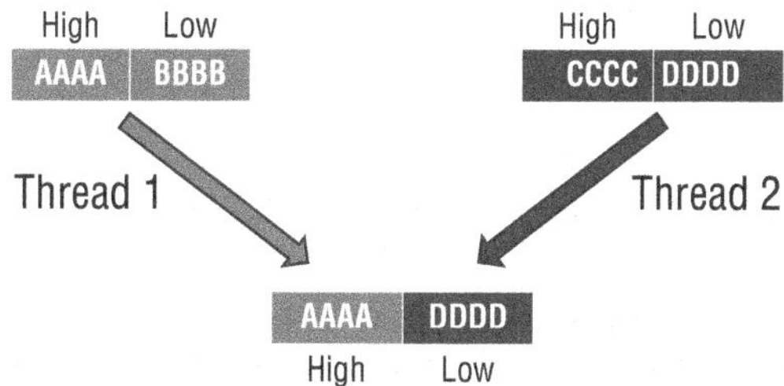

FIGURE 9.3: Each thread sets one-half of the variable producing an unexpected hybrid result.

> **TIP** *Even on a 64-bit machine, getting or setting* `long` *or* `double` *variables is not guaranteed to be atomic.*

Using the volatile Keyword

To ensure that a variable field's readers and writers are atomic, you can declare the field as `volatile`.

> **TIP** *Don't assume that means the ++ and -- operators are atomic; there are no such guarantees. Even if a variable is* `volatile`, *it would be entirely feasible for a reader to see a halfway set result of ++ or --.*

But `volatile` means more than just atomic operations.

You see, the operating system assigns each CPU core, and each thread its own area of memory. Accessing the memory registers in one core by another core could potentially slow your program down, so the designers of Java endowed each thread with the freedom to optimize things by reading a value from the golden source (that is, the official value) into its own local cache. The thread can then refer to the local value thereafter, even though another thread might have changed the golden source in the interim. This is a great optimization when you are not worried about shared access. However, when multiple threads are reading and writing to the same variable, you will want to ensure that all threads are seeing the same value from the same location. That is the job of *volatile*. The `volatile` keyword tells Java "This value is *volatile* (which means 'frequently changing'); please be sure to always access the latest value from the master location."

Whenever a variable is marked as volatile, any gets or sets to that variable will be from the main location and not from the CPU cache. Also (and concentrate here), if any `volatile` variable is visible to a thread at any time, then any gets or sets to even non-volatile variables will also be guaranteed to be refreshed from the golden source.

But there is more, and it has to do with the Java Memory Model.

In Java, both the compiler and the runtime have the option to *reorder* operations. For example, in the following code lines 11 and 12, `count` and `total` are independent, and so Java can optimize things by *reordering* their calculations and by executing them in parallel. However, line 13 depends on both, so line 13 must be executed in the order as defined. This is known as *happens-before* logic. Any given thread is guaranteed to see its variables in an order that is indistinguishable from the order in which they happen.

```
10: double value = 10.0;
11: double count = value + 1;
```

```
public void updateValue(double score) {
    double total = value + score;
    value = total / count;
}
```

However, another thread that is looking at those variables might see them in the order in which they are actually calculated, which could produce surprising results.

The `volatile` keyword helps in this regard as well. When you mark a variable as `volatile`, you are ensuring that all variables that are visible to that thread will be seen by all threads in the order they are specified. This is called *happens-before* semantics. Changing the previous code to the following ensures all threads see the variables in the order received:

```
volatile double value = 10.0;
volatile double count = value + 1;
public void updateValue(double score) {
    double total = value + score;
    value = total / count;
}
```

Transitioning Thread States

A thread is always associated with a thread state as described in the following sections. Figure 9.4 is a good reference as you are reading this section.

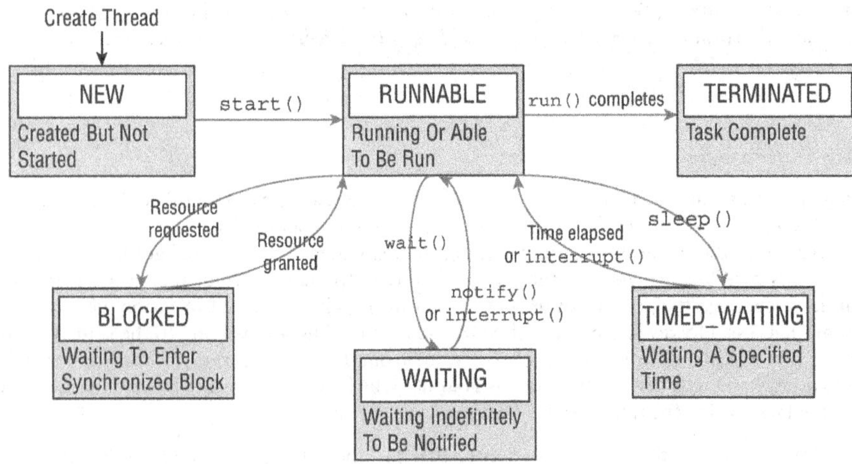

FIGURE 9.4: Thread states

NEW

`NEW` is for a thread that has been initialized but not yet started.

RUNNABLE

`RUNNABLE` is the thread state for a thread that is currently running or is able to run once a processor frees up. Threads transition from `NEW` to `RUNNABLE` when `start()` is called. Similarly, when a thread is no longer waiting or blocked, it changes back to `RUNNABLE` in preparation for its next turn to run.

BLOCKED

`BLOCKED` is the thread state for a thread waiting on a shared lock to enter or re-enter a `synchronized` block/ method, which you'll see in the next section.

WAITING

`WAITING` is the thread state for a thread waiting for a `notify()` or `notifyAll()` call from another thread that is locked on the same object. A thread will call `object.wait()` or `thread.join()` without a timeout to enter the `WAITING` state.

TIMED_WAITING

`TIMED_WAITING` is the thread state for when waiting for a specified amount of time to pass. A thread will call `Thread.sleep(long)`, `thread.join(long)`, or `object.wait(long)`, supplying a long timeout, to enter the `TIMED_WAITING` state.

TERMINATED

`TERMINATED` is the thread state for a thread that has completed execution.

Summarizing Thread States

To summarize, a thread is `NEW` if it has not started yet, and it is `RUNNABLE` once it has started. If it is trying to enter a synchronized block that is already owned by another thread, then it will enter the `BLOCKED` state; if it called `wait()`, it will enter the `WAITING` state; and if it called `wait(long)` or `sleep(long)`, it will enter the `TIMED_WAITING` state until the time passes (or if the waiting thread is notified).

Once a waiting thread is notified by another thread, it will transition to the `BLOCKED` state, until the thread owning the lock releases the lock by exiting the synchronized block, at which time the thread scheduler will randomly select another waiting thread to become `RUNNABLE` and enter the code block.

If you get a question in an interview "What is the difference between a blocked thread and a waiting thread?" one answer would be that there is no way to stop the blocked thread except by having another thread release the lock. Another answer would be that the waiting thread throws an `InterruptedException` that you must catch (or throw in the method signature), whereas a blocked thread does not declare that exception, simply because it cannot be interrupted.

Synchronizing

As an aid to preventing race conditions, Java allows you to call `synchronized(someObject)` before a block of code. That code block will then allow only one thread to grab a lock instance. In fact, any block of code that is locked in that way will be blocked from access by any thread except for the owning thread. Any waiting threads will be in the `BLOCKED` state and cannot proceed until the lock owner releases the lock by exiting the synchronized block.

There is one exception. When a thread is in a synchronized block, it can call `wait` on the lock. While that thread is in the `WAITING` (or `TIMED_WAITING` state, if it called `someObject.wait(long)`), then another thread can enter a synchronized block that is locked on the same lock instance. In this way, many threads can grab the same lock instance and call `wait` on the lock, and effectively all are waiting in the same lock. Finally, another thread can grab the `someObject` lock by calling `synchronized(someObject)` and then call `someObject.notify()` to wake up one random thread, or `someObject.notifyAll()` to wake up all of the waiting threads. Hmm, will there now be many threads owning the same lock? Not quite. The threads that are "awakened" will actually be transitioned to the `BLOCKED` state and will wait for the `RUNNING` thread to exit the synchronized block, thereby releasing the lock, at which point the thread scheduler will select one waiting thread and transition it to the `RUNNING` state.

In this way you can have one thread set some state and then call `notifyAll()` and exit the synchronized block. Then all waiting threads will have an opportunity to wake, check the state, and act accordingly, or go back to wait. First, suppose you have an object to use for locking:

```
final Object lock = new Object(); // can be any class type
```

Here is the syntax for entering the `WAITING` state:

```
synchronized(lock) {
   lock.wait();
}
```

Here is the syntax for a thread to notify one `WAITING` thread to wake up.

```
synchronized(lock){
   lock.notify();
}
```

Here is the syntax for a thread to notify all `WAITING` threads to wake up. Keep in mind that only one thread can be in the synchronized block in the `RUNNING` state, so the thread scheduler will wake up each waiting thread in random order.

```
synchronized(lock){
   lock.notifyAll();
}
```

There are two different syntaxes for synchronizing. First, we synchronize an entire method:

```
public synchronized void someMethod(){
   // ... do stuff ...
}
```

Next, we synchronize on an object:

```
private final Object LOCK = new Object();
public void someMethod(){
//      ... do stuff ...
   synchronized(LOCK){
      // ... do more stuff, this block is protected
   }
}
```

When you synchronize a method, you are synchronizing on the object instance containing that method.

> **TIP** *When you synchronize on a static method, you are synchronizing on the class object associated with that instance.*

Of course, the `Object` class is the ancestor of all other classes. These interthread communication methods are defined in the `Object` class:

- `wait(time)` where `time` is a `long`
- `wait(time,nanos)` where `time` is a `long` and `nanos` is an `int`
- `notify()`
- `notifyAll()`

One drawback with synchronized is that when a `RUNNABLE` thread owns a synchronized lock, any other thread that tries to grab the same lock will be blocked, that is, forced to wait, with no good way to cancel it. When we look at some of the higher-level concurrency components such as `ReentrantLock`, we will see ways to make locks that can be canceled.

Exploring Heap, Stack, and Metaspace

In Java, memory is divided into three main areas called the heap, the stack, and Metaspace.

The *heap* is one very large block of memory where all objects are allocated. In earlier versions of Java, Strings would be allocated in a "PermGen" area and would never be garbage collected. However, in modern versions of Java, Strings are allocated in the string pool, which resides on the heap, and they can be garbage collected when all references are removed.

GARBAGE COLLECTION

We won't go into garbage collection here, but suffice it to say that a garbage collector is invoked in the background to analyze the heap. It applies an algorithm to mark and *sweep* (remove) objects that are no longer referenced. It can then perform a compaction and reclaim valuable memory space. Depending on the garbage collector, the algorithm will vary, and later versions of Java will generally have faster and more predictable garbage collectors.

The *stack* is a last-in-first-out data structure associated with a thread. When a thread is executing a method, then every time a variable is assigned in that method, the variables in that method are pushed to the stack. If the method calls deeper and deeper methods, then the deeper method will push its variables to the stack. When the deeper method returns, the stack variable associated with that method will pop off the stack.

When a method is invoked, any non-primitive values created in the method are assigned on the heap, and the stack will contain a pointer to that object on the heap. When the method exits, the reference will be popped off the stack, but the instance it refers to will remain on the heap until it is garbage collected.

TIP *Primitive variables are not allocated to the heap and will disappear when the method exits.*

Metaspace is where things go if their lifetime is required to be the life of the VM. For example, class objects and static references are never garbage collected and so these are created in Metaspace.

INTRODUCING CONCURRENT COLLECTIONS

The standard data structures in Java, such as `HashMap`, `ArrayList`, and so forth, do not necessarily behave well under concurrent use. For example, if one thread is iterating a `HashMap` while another thread is updating it, the reader will throw a `ConcurrentModificationException`.

`ConcurrentHashMap` is a thread-safe `Map` implementation that allows for concurrent readers and writers. It implements the `ConcurrentMap` interface, which has the same methods as the `Map` interface, but the default method implementations differ. So you `put()`, `get()`, `computeIfAbsent()`, and so forth, exactly as you would with a `HashMap`, except that it plays nicely when there are many concurrent reader and writer threads.

`BlockingQueue` acts like any first-in-first-out queue, except that once its capacity is reached, putter threads will block, and if there are no entries in the queue, getter threads will block. To insert data into the queue, you can call add(data), which throws an IllegalStateException if the queue is full. Similarly, offer(data) will insert the data and returns true if there is space available, or if the queue is full returns false. The put(data) method will wait for space to become available. To get data from the queue, use the corresponding accessors: remove(), which throws an IllegalStateException if nothing is available; poll(long, TimeUnit), which removes and returns the head element, waiting for up to the specified time if necessary; and take(), which removes and returns the head, waiting indefinitely until data is available.

ConcurrentSkipListMap is another ConcurrentMap implementation that is backed by a Skip List data structure. A skip list uses an interesting algorithm to drill down to the desired data. (See the "Further References" section.)

CopyOnWriteArrayList is a concurrent List that works by ensuring that writers write to a fresh clone of the original backing array, which is not returned to readers until the write operation is complete, after which time the original is discarded. It implements the List interface, so you can add(data), get(), and so forth, just as you would do with any List implementation.

USING BUILT-IN CONCURRENCY SUPPORT IN JAVA STREAMS

For processing streams of data from a collection, Java provides the parallelStream() method. This is similar to the stream() method, except that it *forks* the backing collection into smaller and smaller chunks, processing them concurrently, which then will *join* the resulting threads to produce a single result.

For example, the following code uses a parallel stream to convert the words in the incoming List to uppercase. However, we are less interested in the resulting List and more interested in displaying the thread that is processing each piece.

```
List<String> words = List.of("It", "was", "the", "best", "of", "times",
    "it", "was", "the", "worst", "of", "times");
List<String> collect = words.parallelStream().peek(name -> {
    try {
       System.out.println("Thread: " + Thread.currentThread().getName()
       + " processing: " + name);
          Thread.sleep(100);
    } catch(InterruptedException e) {
       throw new RuntimeException(e);
    }
}).map(String::toUpperCase).toList();

System.out.println(collect);
```

This code displays the following:

```
Thread: main processing: was
Thread: ForkJoinPool.commonPool-worker-1 processing: best
Thread: ForkJoinPool.commonPool-worker-4 processing: it
Thread: ForkJoinPool.commonPool-worker-2 processing: of
Thread: ForkJoinPool.commonPool-worker-5 processing: times
Thread: ForkJoinPool.commonPool-worker-3 processing: was
Thread: ForkJoinPool.commonPool-worker-6 processing: of
Thread: ForkJoinPool.commonPool-worker-7 processing: It
Thread: main processing: the
Thread: ForkJoinPool.commonPool-worker-1 processing: worst
Thread: ForkJoinPool.commonPool-worker-2 processing: times
Thread: ForkJoinPool.commonPool-worker-3 processing: the
[IT, WAS, THE, BEST, OF, TIMES, IT, WAS, THE, WORST, OF, TIMES]
```

You can see from the listing that there were eight threads used to process this request: `worker-1` through `worker-7`, and the main thread. The eight threads correspond to the number of cores on this machine.

USING CONCURRENCY COMPONENTS TO REDUCE COMPLEXITY

Java provides high-level components for many common concurrency use cases, making concurrency much more accessible. In this section, we will cover several common ones, including:

- `ReentrantLock`
- `Phaser`
- `Runnable`, `Callable`, and `Future`
- `ExecutorService`
- `CompletableFuture`
- Virtual threads

We will first introduce the concepts and then see some code examples later in the chapter.

Locking with ReentrantLock

`ReentrantLock` provides a componentized answer to synchronization, which solves some of the associated challenges with synchronization. It is also critically important when using virtual threads, as you will see in the "Introducing Virtual Threads" section.

A `ReentrantLock` implements the `Lock` interface, which includes the following methods:

- **`void lock()`**: Requests a lock, if necessary waiting for it to become available.
- **`void lockInterruptibly()`**: Behaves like `lock()` except that if another thread interrupts the requesting thread as it waits, it will throw an `InterruptedException` and cancel its request for the lock.
- **`boolean tryLock()`**: Grabs the lock and returns `true` if lock is available. Otherwise returns `false`.
- **`tryLock(long, TimeUnit)`**: Behaves the same as `tryLock()` except that it will cancel its request for the lock after waiting the specified time.
- **`void unlock()`**: Releases the lock.
- **`Condition newCondition()`**: Allows for more granular control of thread communication.

`Condition` has its own APIs that work in coordination with `Lock`. The most common ones are:

- **`void await()`**: Waits for the current thread to be singled or interrupted.
- **`void signal()`**: Wakes up thread that is waiting on this lock. The thread will not actually awaken until the running thread releases the lock.
- **`void signalAll()`**: Wakes up all waiting threads. The threads will not actually awaken immediately; rather, they must wait until the running thread releases the lock, and even then they will wake up only one at a time, as each thread releases the lock.

You may recall that earlier we mentioned that if a thread tries to grab a synchronized lock that is being held by another thread, there is no way to get the blocked thread to back off. This is clear from the signature—it does not throw an `InterruptedException`, so there is no way to interrupt it!

ReentrantLock solves that by sporting the lockInterruptibly() method, which does throw an InterruptedException. If you call interrupt() on a thread that is waiting on a lockInterruptibly() call, it will be interrupted and back off.

ReentrantLock also solves another issue with synchronized blocks. If you have many threads waiting on the same synchronized lock, let's say you want to wake up one of them based on some condition (for example, collection is empty) and a different one based on some other condition (for example, collection is full). Using synchronized locks, you would need to call notifyAll() to wake up both threads and have each one check for their condition.

ReentrantLock provides a better solution, with the newCondition() method. When a thread locks a ReentrantLock, it can call newCondition() on that lock. Many threads can do the same.

Then when some detector observes a condition and wants to signal a particular thread to handle that condition, it just has to call condition.signal(), and just the thread awaiting that condition will wake up. We will see an example of this in the PingNetPong code later in this chapter.

Controlling Thread Access with Phaser

Before you learn about Phaser, we'll briefly mention two older APIs: CyclicBarrier and CountdownLatch.

CyclicBarrier was used when you had multiple threads that needed to perform a function and then wait until all of the other threads were ready. Like horses coming to the starting gate, the race can't start until all of the horses arrive.

CountdownLatch was similar, except that there is a set of one or more threads waiting for a different group of threads to finish before it starts. An example might be a website that can't serve requests until all of its caches are filled. Many threads are filling the caches, and the site has to wait for all of them so that it can start handling requests.

We won't go into those APIs, because Phaser combines those functions. You create a Phaser by supplying a number of permits in the constructor.

You could use Phaser instead of a CyclicBarrier by calling phaser.arriveAndAwaitAdvance(). All of the threads calling that will wait until the number of permits has been reached.

Phaser can alternatively act like a CountdownLatch. The waiting threads (for example, the web server) would call phaser.awaitAdvance(int) to wait until all of the other threads have performed their function (for example, loading the caches in our example). As each thread completes, it calls phaser.arrive(). When the number of permits has been reached, the Phaser signals the waiting thread to proceed. Note that the argument in awaitAdvance refers to the *phase*. The phaser can be reused, and each time it exhausts its permits, a new phase is started.

We will use the Phaser as a countdown latch in the PingNetPong code later in this chapter.

Using Runnable, Callable, and Future

There are three important interfaces you can use when building concurrency applications: Runnable, Callable, and Future.

We already discussed Runnable earlier in this chapter. Runnable was the original Java interface that you would implement a run method to define functionality for a thread to perform. The limitation with Runnable is that it does not return any result, and it does not declare any checked exceptions.

Callable was introduced later to remedy those deficiencies. Callable has a call method that returns a generic result and can throw a checked exception.

But if a thread executes asynchronously, how can the process that launches the thread obtain any results it produces? One clean way is via the Future interface.

`Future` has methods for checking if a computation was completed and for obtaining the result. It also has methods for forcing the future to complete with or without any exception.

> **TIP** *The* `Future` *interface would be more useful if it had methods for getting notified when a request is available or for performing follow-on actions when a request is complete. While* `Future` *does not offer these capabilities,* `CompletableFuture` *does, and we will see that a bit later.*

Table 9.1 summarizes these interfaces.

TABLE 9.1: Concurrency Interfaces

INTERFACE	METHOD	EXPLANATION

`Runnable`	`void run()`
	Can also be expressed as:
	`()-> doSomeWork()`
		A `Runnable` is supplied to a `Thread` or to an `ExecutorService` to define the functionality for the thread to perform asynchronously.

`Callable`	`V call()`
	`throws Exception`
	Can also be expressed as:
	`()-> doSomeWork()`
		A more capable interface than `Runnable`; returns a value and declares an exception.
		`Callable` cannot be supplied directly to a `Thread`, but you'll see how to use this shortly.

`Future`	`R get()`
	`R get (long timeout,`
	`TimeUnit unit)`
		Threads can be told to return their results to a `Future`, where other threads will wait for a result.

From what we have described, the `Future` seems like a useful construct, but how do we get one? One way is by *submitting* a `Runnable` or `Callable` to an `ExecutorService`.

Coordinating with ExecutorService

`ExecutorService` is an interface that is used to create and manage pools of threads. It extends the `Executor` interface, which has just an `execute()` command. There are various kinds of `ExecutorService`, most common being those for creating fixed sized thread pools, for creating scheduled thread pools, and for creating virtual threads. There are methods for retrieving results as a `Future`, for awaiting termination of all threads, and for forcing shutdown after (or even before) all threads have completed.

`ExecutorService` instances are usually created using a `static` factory method from the `Executors` class. Let's see how to use the most common `ExecutorService`, the fixed `ThreadPoolExecutor`. Then we will visit some of the other `ExecutorService` implementations, which have similar APIs but slightly different semantics.

Using Fixed-Count Thread Pools

Platform threads are relatively expensive to create, and they consume space on the heap, so it would be great if you could create them once and keep them around for reuse. Also, having too many threads can starve your system, so it would also be useful to limit the number of threads that an application creates. That is the purpose of a fixed `ThreadPoolExecutor`; it creates a fixed number of threads, which are then assigned to run your jobs. If all threads are busy, then subsequent calls to the `ExecutorService` will cause the caller to wait until a thread is freed up or the wait times out.

> **TIP** *Virtual threads are the exception; they are very light weight, as we will soon see, and so do not require pooling.*

To create a fixed `ThreadPoolExecutor`, pass in the number of threads such as:

```
ExecutorService executor = Executors.newFixedThreadPool(10);
```

There are essentially three ways to execute a thread using an `ExecutorService`. You can call `execute(Runnable)`, which returns `void`. Or you can call `submit(Runnable r)` or `submit (Callable c)`, which return a `Future`. Or you can call one of the `invoke` methods, which accept a collection of `Callable` instances. `invokeAll()` returns a `List` of `Future` instances, and `invokeAny()` waits until a value is available and then returns that value (not a Future).

The `ExecutorService` interface extends `AutoCloseable`, so you can create it using a try-with-resources block. Once all outstanding threads have been returned to the thread pool and there are no threads waiting for a thread to become available in the pool, then the `ExecutorService` will terminate, and the try-with-resources block will exit. So in effect, the try-with-resources ensures that all threads will complete before continuing.

`Executors.newSingleThreadExecutor()` returns a thread pool with exactly one thread. This is like calling `Executors.newThreadPoolExecutor(1)` with one thread. Why do we need a special executor for that rather than just creating a fixed `ThreadPoolExecutor` with just one thread? Because it guarantees the ordering, which is useful when you need to ensure tasks are performed in sequence, for example in a UI event dispatch thread, that controls things like button presses. Also, more importantly, if one of these threads terminates due to some exception during execution, a new thread will be created to take its place.

Scheduling with ExecutorService

`ScheduledExecutorService` is an extension of `ExecutorService`, which will schedule a job to be executed one or more times at a fixed interval. The `schedule()` method accepts a `Runnable` or a `Callable`, as well as an initial delay. The `scheduleAtFixedRate()` method accepts a `Runnable`, an initial delay (could be 0), a repeat delay period, and a `TimeUnit` instance. All of these methods return a `ScheduledFuture` instance. In the case of the `scheduleAtFixedRate()` method, the `ScheduledFuture` doesn't return anything useful, but you can call its `cancel()` method to cancel the scheduled task.

To create a `ScheduledThreadPoolExecutor` pass in a pool size such as:

```
ScheduledExecutorService executor = Executors.newScheduledThreadPool(10);
```

there is also a single-thread version:

```
ScheduledExecutorService executor =
   Executors.newSingleThreadScheduledExecutor();
```

Virtual thread-per-task executor is a special executor that runs its jobs on virtual threads. (For now think of virtual threads as ordinary threads, just much more light weight.)

Creating an `ExecutorService` for virtual threads is as easy as creating any other `ExecutorService`. Just call this:

```
ExecutorService executor = Executors. newVirtualThreadPerTaskExecutor();
```

The method doesn't take a pool size parameter, since as we said we never pool virtual threads.

There is no scheduled executor for virtual threads, but it is easy to hack one together by supplying a virtual `ThreadFactory` (an optional parameter) to the `newScheduledThreadPool()` method:

```
ThreadFactory factory = Thread.ofVirtual().factory();
ScheduledExecutorService x = Executors.newScheduledThreadPool(2, factory);
AtomicInteger counter = new AtomicInteger(0);
x.scheduleAtFixedRate(()-> logger.info(counter.incrementAndGet()),
   0, 1, TimeUnit.SECONDS);
```

You generally want to be careful about putting scheduled executers in a try-with-resources block, because the block will exit as soon as the job is kicked off, terminating the executor.

Building Reactive Code with CompletableFuture

`CompletableFuture` is a convenient concurrency tool that can be used to launch threads, combine results of threads, and launch follow on actions.

Functional Interfaces Used by CompletableFuture

`CompletableFuture` uses several functional interfaces that you will want to be familiar with. The names of these interfaces might not be intuitive, so let's review synchronous examples of each of those first, before diving into the `CompletableFuture` versions.

All the examples in this section have a corresponding tester in the `FunctionalInterfaceTests` class in the chapter repo. Note our use of Lambda expressions to define these implementations.

Interface: Runnable

Class name: `java.lang.Runnable`

Method: `void run()`

Accepts no arguments and returns no result; `Runnable` generally provides the functionality supplied to a `Thread`.

Interface: Supplier<T>

Class name: `java.util.function.Supplier`

Method: `T get()`

Accepts no arguments, performs some process, and produces a result. For example, this code defines a `Supplier` that produces a random integer between 100 and 200.

```
@Test
public void testSupplierGet(){
   Random random = new Random();
   // Create a Supplier that produces a random integer between 100 and 200
   Supplier<Integer> random100To200 = () -> random.nextInt(100,200);
   for(int i =0; i < 5; i++){
      Integer value = random100To200.get();
      System.out.println("Next random: " + value);
   }
}
```

When we ran the previous code, it printed the following (yours will differ since the generated values are random):

```
Next random:118
Next random:194
```

```
Next random:153
Next random:165
Next random:182
```

It is important to note here that our `Supplier` took no input parameters and returned a value.

Interface: Consumer<T>

Class name: `java.util.function.Consumer`

Method: `void accept(T t)`

Accepts a single argument; returns no result. For example, this code defines a `Consumer` that accepts a mutable List of Integer values and doubles each value in place:

```
@Test
public void testConsumerAccept(){
   // Define a Consumer that accepts a mutable List of
   // ints and replaces each value with twice its value
   Consumer<List<Integer>> twoTimes =
      list-> list.replaceAll(value -> value * 2);

   List<Integer> ints = new ArrayList<>(List.of(10, 20, 30, 40));
   twoTimes.accept(ints);
   System.out.println(ints);
}
```

The previous code will print this:

```
[20, 40, 60, 80]
```

It is important to note here that our `Consumer` accepted one input parameter but returned no value; it just modified the input in place. Other uses for consumer might be to print out the result of a computation or store a result to a database, without actually returning anything to the caller.

Sometimes you might want to chain more than one `Consumer` so that multiple actions are performed on the same input. `Consumer` supports the `andThen(Consumer after)` method, which produces a new `Consumer` that performs the first action and then performs the *after* action. For example:

```
@Test
public void testConsumerAndThen() {
   // printMessage Consumer prints the supplied value
   Consumer<String> printMessage = message ->
      System.out.println("Message: " + message);

   // upperCaseMessage Consumer converts the supplied value to uppercase
   Consumer<String> uppercaseMessage = message ->
      System.out.println("Uppercase: " + message.toUpperCase());

   // printAndUppercase uses andThen to chain two consumers
   // to produce a new consumer
   Consumer<String> printAndUppercase = printMessage.andThen(uppercaseMessage);

   // Apply the chained consumer to a message
   printAndUppercase.accept("Hello, World! ");
}
```

Running the previous code prints this:

```
Message: Hello, World!
Uppercase: HELLO, WORLD!
```

Interface: Function<T, R> (T Is the Argument Type; R Is the Return Type)

Package: `java.util.function.Function`

Combination `Supplier` and `Consumer`; accepts an input and returns a result. It contains additional methods for chaining more than one `Function` to produce a new `Function`. For example, let's define a function that accepts an Integer value and doubles it:

```
@Test
public void testFunctionApply() {
   // SquareIt function squares the supplied value
   Function<Integer, Integer> SquareIt = value -> value * value;
   for(int i = 1; i <= 5; i++) {
      System.out.println("2^" + i + " = " + SquareIt.apply(i));
   }
}
```

Executing the previous code prints this:

```
2^1 = 1
2^2 = 4
2^3 = 9
2^4 = 16
2^5 = 25
```

The method `andThen` is used for composing new functions based on two existing functions. In the following example we define a `Function` called `personToFullName`. Then we compose a new `Function` using `personToFullName` *andThen* String `toUpperCase()`. When that new composed function is called, it converts the person instance to the uppercase value of their full name.

```
@Test
public void testFunctionAndThen() {
   // Create a simple Person class. A record defines an
   // immutable class from the constructor parameters.
   record Person(String firstName, String lastName) { }

   // Function takes Person as input and produces a String
   // representing their full name
   Function<Person, String> personToFullName = (Person p) ->
      p.firstName + " " + p.lastName;

   // Combination Function, returns the person's full name as upper case
   Function<Person, String> personToUpperCaseFullName =
      personToFullName.andThen(String::toUpperCase);

   // Create a new Person object
   Person person = new Person("Mary", "Jones");

   // Apply the chained function
   String upperCaseFullName = personToUpperCaseFullName.apply(person);

   // Print the result
   System.out.println(upperCaseFullName);
}
```

Executing the previous code prints this:

```
MARY JONES
```

We just want to reemphasize that the function declaration that calls the `andThen` method (in this case `personToUpperCaseFullName`) does not perform any operation on the input parameters. Rather, it composes a new `Function` that, when applied to its input parameters, performs the base function (in our case personToFullName) and then supplies the result of that call to the andThen function (in our case the toUpperCase function of the String class).

Similar to andThen is the compose method, which works like andThen only in reverse; with compose, the function argument is applied first, followed by the base function. For example, we can rewrite the previous andThen code using compose as follows:

```
@Test
public void testFunctionCompose() {
   record Person(String firstName, String lastName) { }
   // Function takes Person as input and produces a String representing
   // their full name
   Function<Person, String> personToFullName = (Person p) ->
      p.firstName + " " + p.lastName;

   // Combination Function, returns the person's full name as upper case
   Function<String, String> toUpperCase = String::toUpperCase;
   Function<Person, String> personToUpperCaseFullName =
      toUpperCase.compose(personToFullName);

   // Create a new Person object
   Person person = new Person("John", "Smith");

   // Apply the chained function
   String upperCaseFullName = personToUpperCaseFullName.apply(person);

   // Print the result
   System.out.println(upperCaseFullName);
}
```

Interface: BiFunction<T,U,R> (T and U Are the Argument Types; R Is the Return Type)

Package: java.util.function.BiFunction

Accepts two inputs and returns a result. For example, let's define a BiFunction that accepts the lengths of two legs of a right triangle (a and b) and uses the Pythagorean theorem to calculate the length of the third side (c).

```
@Test
public void testBiFunctionApply(){
   BiFunction<Double, Double, Double> Hypotenuse = (a,b)-> Math.sqrt(a*a+b*b);
   Double c;
   c = Hypotenuse.apply(3d, 4d);
   System.out.println(c); // prints 5.0
                          // (since 3,4,5 is a Pythagorean triple.)
   c = Hypotenuse.apply(5d, 12d);
   System.out.println(c); // prints 13.0
                          // (since 5,12,13 is a Pythagorean triple.)
}
```

CompletionStage

CompletableFuture implements the CompletionStage interface, which contains the methods used for supplying and chaining asynchronous computations.

The methods in CompletionStage include the following:

- thenAccept(Consumer)
- thenApply(Function)

- `thenRun(Runnable)`
- `thenCompose(Function, CompletionStage)`
- `thenCombine(CompletionStage, BiFunction)`

Those are the synchronous forms, but each comes in asynchronous flavors as well, for example, `thenAcceptAsync()` and `thenApplyAsync()`.

Putting It All Together with CompletableFuture

`CompletableFuture` was Java's first native attempt at reactive code. Reactive code means code that runs asynchronously but immediately *reacts* by signaling another process that it has completed, thereby notifying the process to handle the result.

In the following code, line 15 is the standard way to launch a concurrent thread using the `CompletableFuture.supplyAsync()` method, which accepts a `Supplier` instance. Remember from the previous section on the `Supplier` interface, that `Supplier` accepts no parameters and produces a result. Using Java threads, there is no way to *ask* a thread to provide a result when it is done; rather, you must implement a signaling mechanism yourself. `CompletableFuture` solves that. As you can see in line 46, when a thread calls the `completableFuture.get()` method, the thread will *wait* until a result has been computed and then immediately will get the result.

You will notice that we did not have to create or start a `Thread` instance, and we did not have to supply an `ExecutorService`. Rather, the `CompletableFuture` does all that for us behind the scenes.

> **TIP** *The* `CompletableFuture.supplyAsync()` *method can also accept an* `Executor` *as an optional second parameter. That will cause the* `CompletableFuture` *to ask the* `Executor` *for threads.*

Next, we want to tell the `CompletableFuture` that as soon as it has computed the result, it should then accept (`thenAccept()`) a `Consumer`. Remember that a `Consumer` interface accepts one parameter, executes a process, and returns no result. That is perfect for our case, because we just want to print something out, and not return anything.

Now if we want to wait for `thenAccept()` to complete before proceeding, we can assign the `thenAccept()` to a new `CompletableFuture` instance. In the first `CompletableFuture` shown earlier, we called the `get()` method to wait for the result until it was ready. We can't call `get()` on the `thenAccept()` `CompletableFuture` because it is a `Consumer`, and so it does not produce any result. For such cases, you can call `completableFuture.join()`, which will wait until the consumer has completed processing without expecting any result.

```
7:  @Log4j2
8:  public class CompletableFutureTests {
9:     @Test
10:    public void testCompletableFutureThenAccept() {
11:       try {
12:          // Create a CompletableFuture that completes with a
13:          // result after a delay
14:          CompletableFuture<String> future1 =
15:             CompletableFuture.supplyAsync(() -> {
16:             try {
17:                log.info("supplyAsync called");
18:                // Simulate a long-running computation
19:                Thread.sleep(5_000);
20:                log.info("supplyAsync complete");
21:                return "Hello";
```

```
            } catch(InterruptedException e) {
               throw new RuntimeException(e);
            }
         });

         // Attach a thenAccept callback to the CompletableFuture
         CompletableFuture<Void> future2 = future1.thenAccept(result->{
            log.info("Computation complete. thenAccept sees result:" +
               " " + result);
            log.info("thenAccept performing another operation. " +
               "Result: " + (result + ", World"));
            try {
               log.info("thenAccept sleeping");
               Thread.sleep(5_000);
               log.info("thenAccept waking");
            } catch(InterruptedException e) {
               throw new RuntimeException(e);
            }
         });

         // Perform other work while the CompletableFuture is running
         log.info("Main thread continuing with other work...");

         // wait for the CompletableFuture to complete
         String result1 = future1.get();
         log.info("CompletableFuture #1 is complete. Result:"+result1);
         future2.join();
         log.info("CompletableFuture #2 is complete.");
      } catch(InterruptedException e) {
         Thread.currentThread().interrupt();
      } catch(ExecutionException e) {
         throw new RuntimeException(e);
      }
   }
}
```

Here is the output. Notice the timing of each call.

```
2024-07-23 17:35:31 [main]
   INFO  c.w.r.c.C - Main thread continuing with other work...
2024-07-23 17:35:31 [ForkJoinPool.commonPool-worker-1]
   INFO  c.w.r.c.C - supplyAsync called
2024-07-23 17:35:36 [ForkJoinPool.commonPool-worker-1]
   INFO  c.w.r.c.C - supplyAsync complete
2024-07-23 17:35:36 [main]
   INFO  c.w.r.c.C - CompletableFuture #1 is complete. Result:Hello
2024-07-23 17:35:36 [ForkJoinPool.commonPool-worker-1]
   INFO  c.w.r.c.C - Computation complete. thenAccept sees result: Hello
2024-07-23 17:35:36 [ForkJoinPool.commonPool-worker-1]
   INFO  c.w.r.c.C - thenAccept performing another operation.
   Result: Hello, World
2024-07-23 17:35:36 [ForkJoinPool.commonPool-worker-1]
   INFO  c.w.r.c.C - thenAccept sleeping
2024-07-23 17:35:41 [ForkJoinPool.commonPool-worker-1]
   INFO  c.w.r.c.C - thenAccept waking
2024-07-23 17:35:41 [main]
   INFO  c.w.r.c.C - CompletableFuture #2 is complete.
```

Line 28 shows how you can provide a `Consumer` to be executed only after a threaded task is complete, by saying `thenAccept(Consumer)`. That second task will execute in the original thread. You could also say `thenAcceptAsync(Consumer)`, which has the same semantics, except that it runs the consumer in a different thread. There can be many reasons for doing this. First, in a user-facing application, we might want to execute the `Consumer` in a separate thread to improve responsiveness. Or generally we might want to optimize performance by having these run in separate threads.

The `thenAccept(Consumer)` method is not the only way to chain a follow-on process. Alternatively, you can call any of the following to launch a process *after* the main process has completed:

- `thenAccept(Consumer)`: Launches a process to *consume* the result from the `CompletableFuture.supplyAsync()` method.
- `thenRun(Runnable)` : Launches a process that doesn't accept any parameter or return any result.
- `thenApply(Function)` : Launches a process that consumes the result of the original `CompletableFuture` and uses that to produce a new result.
- `thenCombine(CompletionStage, BiFunction)` : When the main thread and the supplied `CompletableFuture` both complete, the results will be applied to the `BiFunction` to compute a result.

There are also async versions of each of these:

- `thenAcceptAsync(Consumer)`
- `thenRunAsync(Runnable)`
- `thenApplyAsync(Function)`
- `thenCombineAsync(CompletionStage, BiFunction)`

Each of the async versions can accept an optional `ExecutorService` to provide you with more control over the number or schedule of threads.

Introducing Virtual Threads

Virtual threads are a new lightweight thread implementation created under the name "Project Loom" by the OpenJDK community and released in Java 21. Virtual threads are much cheaper to create and to run than the original "platform" threads. They also require less memory and stack space.

A virtual thread runs on a platform thread that carries it (thus we will call it a *carrier thread*), until it comes to a blocking operation such as an I/O operation or `Thread.sleep()`.

As of Java 21, the JDK implementations for all blocking operations have been reengineered so that when a blocking operation occurs, the virtual thread is *parked*, which means the thread scheduler unmounts the carrier thread, allowing it to be reused by another virtual thread. When the virtual thread is ready to run again the JVM dynamically assigns a new (possibly different) platform thread to *carry* the virtual thread.

You create a virtual thread using the same builder syntax as we saw for creating platform threads, except there is no priority, group, or daemon. If you try to change the priority of a virtual thread after it is created, that is a no-op operation and has no effect. If you try to change it to be a nondaemon, it will throw an `IllegalArgumentException`.

```
Thread thread = Thread.ofVirtual()
    .name("Some meaningful name")
    .start(() -> doSomeWork());
```

It's worth comparing the implementation of the blocking operations before and after Java 21. Before Java 21, the JDK implementation of `Thread.sleep()` was simply a native call to the operating system, as Figure 9.5 shows.

```
public static native void sleep(Duration duration)
    throws InterruptedException;
```

FIGURE 9.5: `Thread.sleep()` before Java 21

Post Java 21, that has been reengineered per Figure 9.6.

Causes the currently executing thread to sleep (temporarily cease execution) for the specified duration, subject to the precision and accuracy of system timers and schedulers. This method is a no-op if the duration is negative.

Params: `duration` – the duration to sleep

Throws: `InterruptedException` – if the current thread is interrupted while sleeping. The *interrupted status* of the current thread is cleared when this exception is thrown.

Since: 19

```
public static void sleep(Duration duration) throws InterruptedException {
    long nanos = NANOSECONDS.convert(duration);  // MAX_VALUE if > 292 years
    if (nanos < 0) {
        return;
    }

    ThreadSleepEvent event = beforeSleep(nanos);
    try {
        if (currentThread() instanceof VirtualThread vthread) {
            vthread.sleepNanos(nanos);
        } else {
            sleep0(nanos);
        }
    } finally {
        afterSleep(event);
    }
}
```

FIGURE 9.6: `Thread.sleep()` starting Java 21

When a virtual thread executes, behind the scenes it is assigned to a platform thread. You can see in Figure 9.6 line 590 that when it is parked `sleepNanos()` is called, which basically tells the thread scheduler to park it (that is, unmount it from the carrier) for the duration, and then unpark it; that is, assign it to an available platform thread in the JVM thread pool. Consequently, a single platform thread can execute many virtual threads.

It would be interesting to write some code that creates some threads, has them wake and sleep a few times, and capture their carrier threads each time, to see them change.

Let's write some example code to do exactly that.

```
@Slf4j
public class VirtualThreadStatesTests{
    private final Map<String, Set<String>> carrierMappings
        = new ConcurrentHashMap<>();

    @Test
    public void getCarriers(){
        // Launch a number of threads, get them to spin a million
        // times each, and collect the carriers in a map.
        // Then sleep for a bit to see the carrier unmount.
        // Do this a few times and capture the results.
```

```
24:       int threadCount = 4;
25:       // Increment an AtomicInteger, just so
26:       // the thread can complete some action
27:       AtomicInteger atomicInteger = new AtomicInteger();
28:       try(ExecutorService executorService
29:          = Executors.newVirtualThreadPerTaskExecutor()){
30:          for(int i = 0; i < threadCount; i++){
31:             executorService.submit(() -> {
32:                // Get the ID of this virtual thread for mapping
33:                Thread current = Thread.currentThread();
34:                String virtualID = ThreadUtils.getVirtual(current);
35:                // run and then sleep, several times
36:                for(int loopCount = 0; loopCount < 10; loopCount++){
37: // uncomment to synchronize, shows pinning
38: //                synchronized(this)
39:                   {
40:                      String carrierID = ThreadUtils.getCarrier(current);
41:                      Set<String> carriers =
42:                         carrierMappings.computeIfAbsent(
43:                          virtualID, x -> new HashSet<>());
44:                      carriers.add(carrierID);
45:                      for(int j = 0; j < 1_000_000; j++){
46:                         atomicInteger.incrementAndGet();
47:                      }
48:                      try{
49:                         // Briefly enter a blocking state,
50:                         // and see what happens when we awake
51:                         Thread.sleep(10);
52:                      } catch(InterruptedException e){
53:                         current.interrupt();
54:                      }
55:                   }
56:                }
57:             });
58:          }
59:       }
60:
61:       // print summary of all virtual threads and all carriers over time
62:       log.info("\n\nSummary");
63:       carrierMappings.forEach((key, value) -> {
64:          log.info(key + ": Carriers:");
65:          value.forEach(log::info);
66:          // put a blank line between the virtuals
67:          System.out.println();
68:       });
69:    }
70: }
```

In this example, we create four virtual threads (line 30). Each thread loops 10 times (line 36), each time adding an entry to the map, which captures the virtual thread to its carrier at that time (lines 40–44), and then does some work (lines 45–47) and then sleeps (line 51). Finally, when all threads have completed, the try-with-resourced block exits, and it displays the name of each virtual thread followed by the names of all the carrier threads that carried this virtual thread during the life of this program (lines 61–68).

The output of this program displays the ID of each virtual thread, followed by the list of each of the platform threads that carried it. You can see that there were four platform threads in the process, and each virtual thread was carried by three or four of them during its lifetime:

```
Summary
2024-07-23 18:14:59 [main]
   INFO  c.w.r.c.VTS - VirtualThread[#26]: Carriers:
2024-07-23 18:14:59 [main]
   INFO  c.w.r.c.VTS - ForkJoinPool-1-worker-1
2024-07-23 18:14:59 [main]
   INFO  c.w.r.c.VTS - ForkJoinPool-1-worker-4
2024-07-23 18:14:59 [main]
   INFO  c.w.r.c.VTS - ForkJoinPool-1-worker-2

2024-07-23 18:14:59 [main]
   INFO  c.w.r.c.VTS - VirtualThread[#25]: Carriers:
2024-07-23 18:14:59 [main]
   INFO  c.w.r.c.VTS - ForkJoinPool-1-worker-1
2024-07-23 18:14:59 [main]
   INFO  c.w.r.c.VTS - ForkJoinPool-1-worker-4
2024-07-23 18:14:59 [main]
   INFO  c.w.r.c.VTS - ForkJoinPool-1-worker-2
2024-07-23 18:14:59 [main]
   INFO  c.w.r.c.VTS - ForkJoinPool-1-worker-3

2024-07-23 18:14:59 [main]
   INFO  c.w.r.c.VTS - VirtualThread[#24]: Carriers:
2024-07-23 18:14:59 [main]
   INFO  c.w.r.c.VTS - ForkJoinPool-1-worker-4
2024-07-23 18:14:59 [main]
   INFO  c.w.r.c.VTS - ForkJoinPool-1-worker-2
2024-07-23 18:14:59 [main]
   INFO  c.w.r.c.VTS - ForkJoinPool-1-worker-3

2024-07-23 18:14:59 [main]
   INFO  c.w.r.c.VTS - VirtualThread[#22]: Carriers:
2024-07-23 18:14:59 [main]
   INFO  c.w.r.c.VTS - ForkJoinPool-1-worker-1
2024-07-23 18:14:59 [main]
   INFO  c.w.r.c.VTS - ForkJoinPool-1-worker-2
2024-07-23 18:14:59 [main]
   INFO  c.w.r.c.VTS - ForkJoinPool-1-worker-3
```

One programming note: a virtual thread is a subclass of `Thread`. You can convert the thread to a string by calling `thread.toString()`, and that string contains the ID of the virtual thread and of the carrier thread at that time. For example, it might produce a string like this:

```
VirtualThread[#22]/runnable@ForkJoinPool-1-worker-1
```

In this example, the virtual thread ID is `VirtualThread[#22]`, which in the thread string is everything from the beginning of the string up to and including the] character. The carrier thread is `ForkJoinPool-1-worker-1`, which is everything after the `@` up to the end of the string.

We use regular expressions to extract the virtual thread ID and carrier thread ID from that string. We revisit this example when we cover regular expressions in Chapter 10, "Pattern Matching with Regular Expressions." For now, take it on faith that our `getVirtual()` method will use regular expressions to extract the ID of the virtual thread, and `getCarrier()` will extract the ID of the platform thread.

There is one more important thing to know about virtual threads, and that is about *pinned threads*. A pinned thread is a virtual thread that is *pinned* to its carrier. Why would this ever happen? Let's consider an architectural issue that the designers of Java had to consider. When a thread enters a block that is synchronized on some lock, then no other thread can enter a block that is synchronized on the same lock. However, the same thread can! So now let's say virtual thread #V has carrier thread #P, and let's say #V grabs a synchronized lock and goes to sleep. Now #P goes to another virtual thread (or is used as a platform thread by the application), and it tries to grab the same lock. We expect that should block since it is a different thread. But the synchronized construct sees the same thread that grabbed the original lock and so allows it in! To prevent this the designers of Java designed virtual threads such that whenever they enter a synchronized block, they do not unmount from their carrier.

To see this, go back to the `getCarriers()` method and uncomment the synchronized block in line 39, and run the program again. This time we see that there is exactly one platform thread per virtual thread. When a virtual thread grabs a synchronized lock, it never unmounts as long as it retains that lock.

```
Summary
2024-07-23 18:20:41 [main]
   INFO  c.w.r.c.VTS - VirtualThread[#26]: Carriers:
2024-07-23 18:20:41 [main]
   INFO  c.w.r.c.VTS - ForkJoinPool-1-worker-7

2024-07-23 18:20:41 [main]
   INFO  c.w.r.c.VTS - VirtualThread[#25]: Carriers:
2024-07-23 18:20:41 [main]
   INFO  c.w.r.c.VTS - ForkJoinPool-1-worker-4

2024-07-23 18:20:41 [main]
   INFO  c.w.r.c.VTS - VirtualThread[#24]: Carriers:
2024-07-23 18:20:41 [main]
   INFO  c.w.r.c.VTS - ForkJoinPool-1-worker-3

2024-07-23 18:20:41 [main]
   INFO  c.w.r.c.VTS - VirtualThread[#22]: Carriers:
2024-07-23 18:20:41 [main]
   INFO  c.w.r.c.VTS - ForkJoinPool-1-worker-1
```

Pinning will not break your code; it will still execute. However, it will prevent you from getting the benefits of virtual threads. To prevent pinning, replace all synchronized locks with `ReentrantLock` instances.

This is important if you are migrating your application to virtual threads. The code will still work with synchronized lock, but it will not provide the performance benefits that you expect unless you make those changes.

There are many more components that we won't cover. But we recommend you become aware of them and learn how to use them when you need them. These include the following:

- `Semaphore`: Kind of a `Lock`, except you can specify the number of threads that can enter before it blocks.
- `ReadWriteLock`: To maintain data consistency in applications that have many reads and fewer writes, `ReadWriteLock` allows unlimited readers as long as there are no writers. Once a writer thread grabs the lock, all readers must wait until it is done, before admitting more readers. As long as there are writers waiting, readers will be blocked.
- `StampedLock`: Like `ReadWriteLock`, but also provides for optimistic locking scenarios.
- `TransferQueue`: An extension of `BlockingQueue`, used by producer threads to transfer their content to a consumer. Producer will wait until there is a consumer thread to accept its content, and likewise consumers will wait, if necessary, for data to become available.
- `CompletionService`: Useful component when you have many threads producing content, and we don't care about the order; we just want to process each result when it becomes available.

Interthread Communication

A common problem in concurrency is interthread communication, where each thread in a group must do some job and then signal the next thread to perform a follow-on action.

Java provides native support for interthread communication. Many threads can synchronize on the same lock and then wait.

A simple example will help drive home the concept. You are programming a ping-pong volley. You have three threads, one just says "Ping," the second says "Over the net," and the third just says "Pong." You want them to alternate so that the first thread prints `Ping` and then signals `Over the net` to print, which then signals `Pong`, and back to `Over the net` and then back to Mr. Ping thread, and so on, for a specified number of volleys. Let's prefix a volley number to the printout, so `1 Ping`, `1 Over the net`, `1 Pong`, `1 Over the net`, `2 Ping`, `2 Over the net`, `2 Pong`, `2 Over the net`, and so forth, continuing as such for N iterations.

The code is as follows:

```
public class PingNetPong{
   public static void main(String[] args){
      new PingNetPong().playPingPong(3);
   }

   public void playPingPong(int volleys){
      ReentrantLock lock = new ReentrantLock();
      Condition ping = lock.newCondition();
      Condition overTheNet = lock.newCondition();
      Condition pong = lock.newCondition();
      boolean[] pingOrPong = {true};
      try(ExecutorService executor
         = Executors.newVirtualThreadPerTaskExecutor()){
         Phaser phaser = new Phaser(3);

         executor.submit(() -> {
            lock.lock();
            IntStream.rangeClosed(1, volleys).forEach((i) -> {
               try{
                  phaser.arrive();
                  ping.await();
                  System.out.println(i + " Ping");
                  overTheNet.signal();
               } catch(InterruptedException e){
                  e.printStackTrace();
               }
            });
            lock.unlock();
         });

         executor.submit(() -> {
            lock.lock();
            IntStream.rangeClosed(1, volleys * 2)
               .forEach((i) -> {
               try{
                  phaser.arrive();
                  overTheNet.await();
                  System.out.println((i + 1) / 2 + " Over the net");
                  pingOrPong[0] = !pingOrPong[0];
```

```
49:                     if(pingOrPong[0]){
50:                        ping.signal();
51:                     }else{
52:                        pong.signal();
53:                     }
54:                  } catch(InterruptedException e){
55:                     e.printStackTrace();
56:                  }
57:               });
58:               lock.unlock();
59:            });
60:
61:            executor.submit(() -> {
62:               lock.lock();
63:               IntStream.rangeClosed(1, volleys)
64:                  .forEach((i) -> {
65:                  try{
66:                     phaser.arrive();
67:                     pong.await();
68:                     System.out.println(i + " Pong");
69:                     overTheNet.signal();
70:                  } catch(InterruptedException e){
71:                     e.printStackTrace();
72:                  }
73:               });
74:               lock.unlock();
75:            });
76:
77:            phaser.awaitAdvance(0);
78:            lock.lock();
79:            ping.signal();
80:            lock.unlock();
81:         }
82:      }
83: }
```

We start by creating a `ReentrantLock` in line 16 to manage our synchronization. Since we want to benefit from virtual threads, we want to avoid the synchronized keyword, so we use `ReentrantLock` instead.

Lines 17, 18, and 19 create new `Condition` objects for each of the communication states we want to signal.

Lines 21–22 use try-with-resources to create a `newVirtualThreadPerTaskExecutor` service, which is the `ExecutorService` used for creating and executing virtual threads. Unlike the fixed `ThreadPoolExecutor` the virtual thread executor does not pool, since we don't want to pool virtual threads.

Line 23 creates a Phaser with three permits, and in lines 29, 45, and 66, each of our three threads will signal its arrival when it is started. The `phaser.awaitAdvance()` in line 77 awaits all three threads to signal that they have started so that it can kick off the process by calling `ping.signal()` in line 79. Before it can call signal though, it must lock in line 78.

When all three signals arrive, the process begins.

Lines 25–37 configure the Ping runnable, 40–59 configure the "Over the net" thread, and 61–75 configure the Pong runnable. Let's drill down into those. The first thing we do is grab a lock. Each thread will hold the lock while it initializes itself, and when it is ready, it calls await on its `Condition` instance, allowing the next thread to configure itself.

Then each thread in turn wakes up, signals the next thread, and then awaits. The only other nuance is the `boolean[]` in line 20. The "Over the net" thread must alternate the next thread to signal, either Ping or Pong. We had to make it an array and not a plain old `boolean`, because it is being set inside our Lambdas, and therefore must be effectively final, so we carry the boolean value in one (effectively final) array instance.

LEARNING CONCURRENCY SUPPORT IN THE SPRING FRAMEWORK

If your project uses the Spring framework, there are components and annotations you can use to conveniently provide concurrency support. There are some things you need to keep in mind when using these or any other Spring annotations.

- The annotated class must be managed by Spring. That means the instance must be a bean, or a class annotated with `@Component`, `@Service`, and so forth.
- It must be injected using `@Autowired` or constructor injection, and so forth.
- The `@Async` annotated method will not execute in a separate thread if it is called directly from another method inside the same class. This is because if you call the method from inside the same class, you are not calling a Spring managed method.

> **TIP** *We recently encountered a bug in our code, where a class that was annotated as* `@Component` *was not respecting the annotations we describe in the following sections. The reason turned out to be that the program was calling the constructor of that class, rather than having it autowired. Rule of thumb: if Spring is not managing the class, it will not recognize Spring annotations!*

Now, let's look at the main Spring concurrency annotations.

Using @Async/@EnableAsync

Spring provides the `@Async` annotation, which can be applied above the signature of any method so that when that method is invoked, it will return immediately and process its functionality in a separate thread. To use the `@Async` annotation, you must tell Spring to enable async processing. You can do this by annotating any Spring managed class (usually the Spring Boot Application class, or perhaps some `@Configuration` class, or the class containing the `@Async`) with the `@EnableAsync` annotation.

Within any Spring-managed class you can annotate methods with `@Async` to have them execute asynchronously.

Such methods can return void to have them "fire-and-forget," in which case they will return immediately while the job executes in the background. Or they can return a `Future` or `CompletableFuture`, and these can wrap a serializable value. For Spring MVC endpoints, you can return `void` to fire and forget, or return a `CompletableFuture<ResponseEntity>`, to have the caller wait for the result of the call to be computed and returned.

Note that if the `@Async` method returns anything besides a `void` or a Future, the method may not execute asynchronously and will result in unexpected behavior.

In our `AsyncDemo` class, we annotate the following methods as `@Async`: `void performHeads(String message)` and `void performTails(String message)`. These will display `message + " Heads"` and `message+" Tails"`, respectively, three times each. We will have all these threads running concurrently, so the message helps us identify which thread is which.

First let's do it the wrong way. Can you see what is wrong with this code in the `AsyncDemo` class?

```
public void incorrectAsync(){
  performHeads("Incorrect");
  performTails("Incorrect");
}
```

The output looks something like this:

```
2024-07-1 12:07:28 [restartedMain]
   INFO  c.w.r.concurrency.AD - Incorrect Heads
2024-07-1 12:07:29 [restartedMain]
   INFO  c.w.r.concurrency.AD - Incorrect Heads
2024-07-1 12:07:30 [restartedMain]
   INFO  c.w.r.concurrency.AD - Incorrect Heads
2024-07-1 12:07:31 [restartedMain]
   INFO  c.w.r.concurrency.AD - Incorrect Tails
2024-07-1 12:07:32 [restartedMain]
   INFO  c.w.r.concurrency.AD - Incorrect Tails
2024-07-1 12:07:33 [restartedMain]
   INFO  c.w.r.concurrency.AD - Incorrect Tails
```

Judging from the output, we see the heads all execute before the tails can begin, and we see they are all executed in the same `restartedMain` thread. Obviously these two calls are running in sequence and not in parallel, but why?

The answer is that the async methods are being called from the class itself. As we said the async methods must be called in a Spring managed way, and not as a direct method invocation.

To fix this, let's call these from our `@SpringBootApplication` class, which in our case is `ConcurrencyApplication`. Run this application and notice that the `AsyncDemo` instance is injected into the variable `asyncDemo`. The run method then makes the following calls:

```
log.info("Starting perform heads and perform tails");
asyncDemo.performHeads("Correct");
ayncDemo.performTails("Correct");
```

Since these methods are called on a Spring managed class, it produces the expected interleaved output rather than sequential, and we see the two threads `taskExecutor-1` and `taskExecutor-2`, indicating that the two methods are executing concurrently.

```
2024-07-21 12:07:34 [taskExecutor-2]
   INFO  c.w.r.concurrency.AD - Correct Tails
2024-07-21 12:07:34 [taskExecutor-1]
   INFO  c.w.r.concurrency.AD - Correct Heads
2024-07-21 12:07:35 [taskExecutor-2]
   INFO  c.w.r.concurrency.AD  - Correct Tails
2024-07-21 12:07:35 [taskExecutor-1]
   INFO  c.w.r.concurrency.AD - Correct Heads
2024-07-21 12:07:36 [taskExecutor-1]
   INFO  c.w.r.concurrency.AD - Correct Heads
2024-07-21 12:07:36 [taskExecutor-2]
   INFO  c.w.r.concurrency.AD - Correct Tails
```

To see the result of returning a `CompletableFuture`, look at the method `callGetLongAfterDelay()`. This returns a `CompletableFuture`, and we log the time when we get the return. Then it waits five seconds and returns the result, which we log again. You can see the delay in the log, showing how we received a `Future`, and waited five seconds for the result.

```
private void callGetLongAfterDelay()
   throws InterruptedException, ExecutionException {
```

```
        CompletableFuture<Long> aLong = asyncDemo.getLongAfterDelay();
        log.info("Getting result");
        log.info("Got long:" + aLong.get());
    }
```

This displays the following:

```
2024-07-21 13:27:19 [restartedMain]
    INFO  c.w.r.c.ConcurrencyApplication - Getting result
2024-07-21 13:27:24 [restartedMain]
    INFO  c.w.r.c.ConcurrencyApplication - Got long:5
```

The `getLongAfterDelay()` method itself returns a `CompletableFuture`, which returns a result after a five-second delay:

```
// Returns a CompletableFuture, that contains a results after a few seconds
@Async
public CompletableFuture<Long> getLongAfterDelay(){
  return CompletableFuture.supplyAsync(()-> {
    try{
       Thread.sleep(5_000);
    }catch(InterruptedException e){
       e.printStackTrace();
    }
    return 5L;
  });
}
```

Scheduling with @Scheduled/@EnableScheduling

You can also tell Spring to *schedule* a job, beginning at a specified time (which by default is now) and running every specified number of milliseconds.

An example of this is also in our `AsyncDemo` class, method `fixedRateTest()`, which is defined as follows:

```
@Scheduled(initialDelay = 20000, fixedRate = 1000)
public void fixedRateTest(){
   log.info("Fixed rate");
}
```

The `initialDelay` argument is optional, and in our case indicates that it should start 20 seconds after the application is launched (giving our other tests to display their output), and then run every 1000 MS (every second). The useful functionality displays the words `Fixed rate` once per second. A more useful use case would be a file transform operation that must read files at a fixed interval, say market data files or sales reporting files, and process them into some control system. You need to tell Spring that your application uses scheduling by annotating any Spring managed class (usually the Spring Boot Application class, or perhaps some `@Configuration` class, or the class containing the `@Scheduled` annotation) with the `@EnableScheduling` annotation.

Launching Threads with ThreadPoolTaskExecutor

You can get more granular control over which executor Spring uses and provide more granular configuration by injecting a `TaskExecutor`.

Our `AsyncDemo` class autowires a `TaskExecutor` instance, which is used in the `useTaskExecutor()` method to execute the `performHeads()` and `performTails()` methods in parallel.

```
@Autowired TaskExecutor taskExecutor;
       . . .
public void useTaskExecutor(){
```

```
        taskExecutor.execute(() -> performHeads("using TaskExecutor"));
        taskExecutor.execute(() -> performTails("using TaskExecutor"));
    }
```

You can see from the alternating output and the two thread names in the logs that these two methods are being called in parallel:

```
2024-07-21 12:44:05 [task-1]
    INFO  c.w.r.concurrency.AD - using TaskExecutor Heads
2024-07-21 12:44:05 [task-2]
   INFO  c.w.r.concurrency.AD - using TaskExecutor Tails
2024-07-21 12:44:06 [task-1]
    INFO  c.w.r.concurrency.AD - using TaskExecutor Heads
2024-07-21 12:44:06 [task-2]
   INFO  c.w.r.concurrency.AD - using TaskExecutor Tails
2024-07-21 12:44:07 [task-1]
   INFO  c.w.r.concurrency.AD - using TaskExecutor Heads
2024-07-21 12:44:08 [task-2]
   INFO  c.w.r.concurrency.AD - using TaskExecutor Tails
```

Understanding @Transactional

While `@Transactional` is not specifically a concurrency annotation, it is crucial in our microservices-driven world for managing transactions and ensuring data consistency, and we should at least mention it. In the programming world, when we say that a multipart call is a transaction, we mean that that those parts either all complete or all roll back.

For example, let's say you have an order-entry application that adds an item to the cart, depletes from inventory, and charges a credit card. Now what happens if each of these steps is invoked in parallel? What if the card is declined or the cart exceeds our limit or the inventory is not available, and the other methods were all invoked? The entire transaction must be rolled back. The `@Transactional` annotation accepts a `rollbackFor` argument that indicates the compensating method that must be called in the event of a transaction exception.

FURTHER REFERENCES

- *Java Concurrency in Practice* (Addison-Wesley, 2006)
- *Concurrent Programming in Java* (Addison-Wesley, 1999)
- Java Concurrent Animated, a Swing application that demonstrates most of the concurrency utilities built into Java

  `https://github.com/vgrazi/JavaConcurrentAnimatedReboot.git`
- Explanation of Skip List algorithm

  `https://en.wikipedia.org/wiki/Skip_list`

SUMMARY

In this chapter, you learned that Java was one of the first languages to introduce concurrency as a native feature, and you learned how it has evolved to manage the complexity of multithreaded programming. You learned about fundamental concepts like atomicity and synchronization, thread states, and interthread communication. You saw the concurrent collections and data structures used for managing concurrency. You learned how `CompletableFuture` helps you build reactive programs and how virtual threads allow your multithreaded applications to scale. Finally, you learned about the concurrency support available in the Spring framework.

10

Pattern Matching with Regular Expressions

WHAT'S IN THIS CHAPTER?

- Introducing Regular Expressions
- Learning Basic Regular Expression Syntax
- Using Regular Expressions with Java APIs
- Exploring Advanced Regular Expression Syntax
- Identifying Common Mistakes
- Coding with Regular Expressions
- Using with Frameworks and Tools

Regular expressions are a powerful tool for searching text strings. They are also known as *regex* for short and processed by a regular expression engine.

You already probably have some experience with pattern matching. For example, when you are searching for a file, you might type `dir R*.pdf` or `ls R*.pdf` to get a listing of any file starting with `R` of type `pdf`. Regex is a more powerful matching system, with a completely different syntax.

Imagine you have a sequence of URIs, for example:

```
http://spring.io/projects/spring-cloud-contract
https://www.infoq.com/articles/Living-Matrix-Bytecode-Manipulation/
file:///C:/Documents/happy_birthday_sis.pdf
```

And imagine that for each URI you want to parse out the protocol (`http`, `https`, `file`), the website or directory, and the specific path.

You could do it the hard way, using `string.indexOf()` to search for a non-empty string followed by a colon and sequence of two or more slashes, followed by a bunch of characters until a slash, followed by everything else, and then using `string.substring()` to parse out the relevant text. Regular expressions make this far easier, and you'll see this example again later in the chapter.

Regular expression syntax has a reputation for being terse and hard to read, but in fact it is a powerful tool that you want in your arsenal. In this chapter you will learn how to build regular expressions and how to work with them in Java to handle most of the parsing requirements you will encounter in enterprise development. We will also review some tools and frameworks where you are likely to benefit from regular expressions.

> **CODE DOWNLOADS FOR THIS CHAPTER**
>
> The source code for this chapter is available on the book page at `www.wiley.com`. Click the Downloads link. The code can also be found at `https://github.com/realworldjava/Ch10-Regex`. See the `README.md` file in that repository for details.

INTRODUCING REGULAR EXPRESSIONS

Suppose you are reading an ebook or blog post and you come across a nice code example with ASCII art to create a computer. You copy and paste it into your IDE. Unfortunately, the line numbers are included in the copied text. Now you have to remove all 20 line numbers. That sounds tedious. If you're lazy, you could edit the text and remove the digits and colons, but that's a lot of work to remove 20 lines, and what if it's many more than that? Regular expressions to the rescue!

Suppose you have the following `.txt` file. If you are following along, it is `src/main/resources/TextBlock.txt` in the repository.

```
1:  public class TextBlock {
2:
3:      public static void main(String[] args) {
4:         String computer = """
5:                     +--------------+
6:                     |.------------.|
7:                     ||            ||
8:                     ||            ||
9:                     ||            ||
10:                    |+------------+|
11:                    +-..--------..-+
12:                    .--------------.
13:                   / /============\\ \\
14:                  / /==============\\ \\
15:                  /____________________\\
16:                  \\____________________/
17:            """;
18:            System.out.println(computer);
19:     }
20: }
```

In IntelliJ, here's how you can get rid of the line numbers:

1. Press Ctrl+R/Cmd+R to open search and replace on top of the editor.
2. Hit Alt+X/Option+X to turn on Regular Expressions search mode.
3. In the search box, type **`\d+:`** in the before box, leaving the replacement box blank. Be sure to include the colon!
4. Click Replace All.

Figure 10.1 shows the before and after of this regular expression replacement.

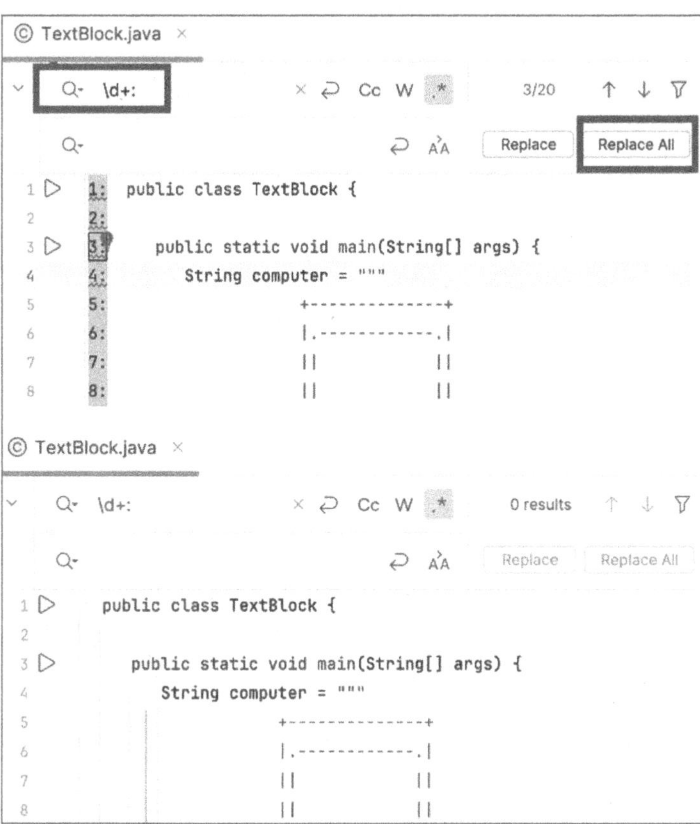

FIGURE 10.1: Replacing using a regular expression

Wait. What's this `\d+:` magic? This is the first regular expression we will see in the chapter. `\d` means "match any digit." + means match one or more occurrences of `\d`. Therefore, `\d+` means "match one or more digits." The colon is literally the colon (`:`) character. You are telling IntelliJ to remove any sequence of one or more digits followed immediately by a colon. The fun begins! You'll learn how to write many more regular expressions in this chapter.

Search (and replace) is a common use of regular expressions. Validating data and parsing data are also common use cases. What do all of these have in common? They involve processing text data and matching against a general pattern.

If you haven't used regular expressions before, the syntax takes a little getting used to. But once you master it, you will be able to perform searches and string processing tasks very efficiently.

LEARNING BASIC REGULAR EXPRESSION SYNTAX

You will want to become familiar with regular expression syntax before adding it to your Java code. To develop your regular expressions, keep a regular expressions tester handy. There are many available online. We like `https://regex101.com`, which provides full support for all regex features.

Regular expressions are similar across the different programming languages and environments, but they may not always be exactly the same. On the Regex101 site, you can select the Java flavor in the left navigation to get the exact syntax and options for Java. Figure 10.2 shows the `\d+:` example on this website.

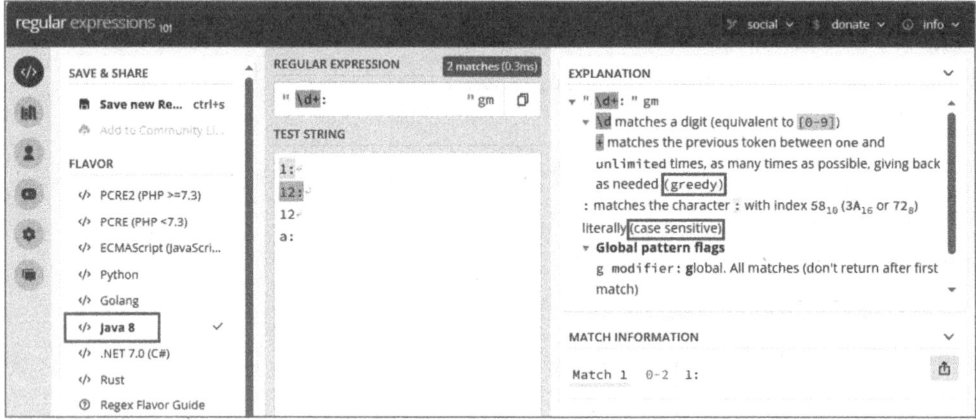

FIGURE 10.2: Regex101

Let's review the layout of Regex101. In the top text field, you will enter the regular expression pattern. You will notice a little `gm` to the right of the regular expression. The `g` (global) and `m` (multiline) are flags that you can turn off and that tell the regex parser to treat each line in your "test string" as an independent input string, rather than one long string. We'll cover these and other flags later in the chapter. Below the regular expression is where you enter one or more lines that you'd like to test for matches against the regular expression pattern.

At the top right, the website explains your regular expression. It tells you the mode is *greedy*, which we will also explain later in the chapter. It also reminds you that regular expressions are case sensitive (unless you specify otherwise).

Below the explanation area are the match results, and the corresponding matches are highlighted in the Test String area. In our example, the first two lines match our pattern because they are digits followed by a colon. The third line is missing a colon, and the fourth line is missing a number, so those two lines don't match.

In the following sections, you'll learn how to write basic regular expressions, and we will cover more advanced cases as the chapter progresses.

> **TIP** *The Javadoc for the* `Pattern` *class is an excellent reference when you need to look up regular expression syntax.*

Specifying Common Quantifiers

The simplest regex is nothing more than a literal sequence of one or more characters representing an exact match. So, the pattern `org` will be found in **`org`**`anization`, `f`**`org`**`ive`, and `cyb`**`org`**.

A quantifier is an operator that is placed after a text pattern, to specify how many times something should be matched. Table 10.1 shows you the most common quantifier operators. You will see more later in the chapter when we talk about reluctant and possessive quantifiers.

TABLE 10.1: Common Quantifiers

CODE	HOW MANY MATCH?	EXPLANATION
`R?`	Zero or one occurrence of the letter `R`.	The pattern `BR?AKE` will match `BRAKE` or `BAKE`.
`L*`	Zero or more occurrences of the letter `L`.	The pattern `JOL*Y` matches both `JOLLY` and `JOY`.
`L+`	One or more occurrences of the letter `L`.	The pattern `MARVEL+ED` matches `MARVELED` or `MARVELLED`.
`!{3}`	Exactly three occurrences of `!`.	The pattern `TERRIFIC!{3}` matches `TERRIFIC!!!` but not `TERRIFIC!!`.
`!{3,}`	Three or more occurrences of `!`.	The pattern `TERRIFIC!{3,}` matches `TERRIFIC!!!` and `TERRIFIC!!!!!`.
`!{3,5}`	Three, four, or five occurrences of `!`.	The pattern `TERRIFIC!{2,4}` matches `TERRIFIC!!` and `TERRIFIC!!!` and `TERRIFIC!!!!`.

When you are composing a regular expression, you might find there are multiple ways to express the same thing, so strive for clarity. All of the following are regex patterns for finding one or more occurrences of `x`. Think about which one you find clearest.

```
x+
x{1,}
xx?x*
x{1}x*
x{1,1}x*
xx{0,}
```

We hope you said `x+` is the clearest! What about this set?

```
xx+
x{2,}
xxx*
x{1}x+
x{2,}x*
xxx{0,}
```

All of these match two or more occurrences of the letter `x`. We think you'll agree `xx+` (`x` followed by one or more `x`) is the clearest.

Do take a moment to understand why each one in the set is equivalent. That exercise will help you remember the syntax for all the quantifiers. While you don't want to use them all in the same regular expression, they are all useful to know.

Matching Basic Boundaries

In addition to matching characters, you can match the area between characters. To understand what these mean, suppose you have the string `A GEEK` and want to find the boundaries. In Figure 10.3, the numbers before, between, and after the characters are the boundary positions.

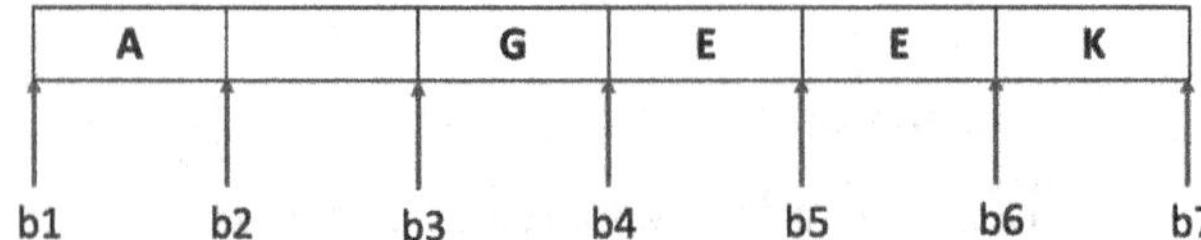

FIGURE 10.3: Identifying boundaries

Table 10.2 lists the four main boundary characters. First are the ^ and `$`, which match the beginning and end of the line, respectively. These are also known as *anchors* as they demark the start and end of a line.

TABLE 10.2: Boundaries

CODE	DESCRIPTION	POSITIONS MATCHED IN FIGURE 10.3
^	Beginning of a line	b1
$	End of a line	b7
\b	A word boundary	b1, b2, b3, b7
\B	Anything that is not a word boundary	b4, b5, b6

Next is `\b`, which matches a word boundary. A word boundary is the first and last characters of a *word*. By *word* we mean a sequence of one or more alphanumeric characters plus the underscore. This is useful for finding matches at the start and/or end of a word.

Finally, `\B` matches anything except for a word boundary. In regular expressions, an uppercase letter is used to negate the meaning of a special escape sequence. Every = position matches either `\b` or `\B`.

Working with Common Character Classes

Did you remember from the beginning of the chapter that `\d` means digit? It represents a single digit. This is an example of a *character class*. We will see more examples of character classes available out of the box. In addition, you can easily create your own character classes by listing the characters you want to include inside brackets. Both of the following character classes are equivalent to `\d`:

```
[0123456789]
[0-9]
```

These both match any character from 0–9, which happen to be all the digits. You can negate a character class by placing a caret (^) as the first character inside the brackets. For example, these all match anything that is not a digit:

```
[^0123456789]
[^0-9]
```

These use the ^ to negate a list of characters and a range of a characters.

To negate a built-in character class, capitalize it. So, a third way to say "any character except a digit" would be like this:

```
\D
```

This negates `\d` by making it uppercase.

WRITING UNREADABLE CHARACTER CLASSES

To combine character classes, use the `&&` syntax. For example:

```
[a-z0-9&&[^m-p45]]
```

These hieroglyphics represent a single character that is a lowercase letter or digit, but not ones in the range m–p or a number that is not 4 or 5. This could be written more clearly as follows:

```
[a-lq-z0-36-9]
```

The latter is certainly clearer. This difference helps show the importance of keeping your regular expressions readable. Just because syntax is legal doesn't mean you should use it. Keeping your character classes as simple as possible makes it easier to understand what they do.

Java predefines some character classes that make it easier to write a regular expression. You already saw `\d` and `\D`. Remember that the uppercase version is the inverse of the lowercase version; it matches everything the lowercase one does not. Table 10.3 shows the most useful predefined character classes and what they match.

> **TIP** *To remember the character classes,* `\d` *is for digit,* `\w` *is for word, and* `\s` *is for space.*

TABLE 10.3: Predefined Character Classes

CODE	DESCRIPTION	MATCHES LETTER K	MATCHES NUMBER 1	MATCHES A SPACE	MATCHES SYMBOL !
.	Any character	Yes	Yes	Yes	Yes
`\d`	Digit	No	Yes	No	No
`\D`	Not a digit	Yes	No	Yes	Yes
`\s`	Whitespace	No	No	Yes	No
`\S`	Not whitespace	Yes	Yes	No	Yes
`\w`	Word character (letter, number, or underscore)	Yes	Yes	No	No
`\W`	Not a word character	No	No	Yes	Yes

MORE ON THE DOT (.)

The dot (`.`) is a special character class that matches any character. You will often see code to match zero or more of any characters expressed as follows:

```
.*
```

or code to match one or more of any characters:

```
.+
```

Note that the characters matched do not need to be the same. For example, `.+` will match any of the following:

```
123
abcde
ZZZZ
OK.
```

Choosing Options

A character class works if you want to pick a sequence of zero or more characters from a predefined set of characters. But what if you want to match either one sequence of characters or another sequence of characters? You can use the | (pipe) character to provide choices. For example, you can decide what you want for lunch with this:

```
tuna|turkey
```

As you might imagine, this will match `tuna` or `turkey`. What happens if you want to add the word *sandwich* after. This works:

```
tuna sandwich|turkey sandwich
```

and so does this:

```
(tuna|turkey) sandwich
```

The latter version uses parentheses to specify the alternatives. Then it unconditionally matches `sandwich` after. This approach can make the regular expression clearer because it avoids the repetition of `sandwich` and shows that only the type of sandwich (in the parentheses) varies.

Escaping Characters

You should be familiar with the concept of escaping characters from working with strings. For example, if you want to include a double quote in a string, you must *escape it* with a backslash such as the following:

```
String escapeQuote = "\"Java is Great\"";
```

Similarly, you use another backslash to escape a backslash:

```
String escapeBackslash = "\\";
```

In regular expressions, you use a backslash to indicate that the character following it should be matched as a literal, rather than apply a regular expression meaning. For example, suppose you want to write a regular expression that matches a pattern of two single digit numbers being added together. One way to write it is like this:

```
String addition = "\\d \\+ \\d";
```

That may seem like a lot of backslashes, so let's take a moment to unpack this. The regular expression syntax for a digit is `\d`. However, a backslash already has a meaning in Java, so you need to add an extra backslash, making it \\d. Next comes a single space. That's straightforward; it matches a space.

After that, we want to match the literal plus sign (+). You can't just write +, though, because as we saw, that represents a quantifier, meaning one or more of the previous character. To match a literal plus sign, you have to add a backslash to escape the +. But guess what? To include a backslash in a Java string, you need to backslash it, so the backslash needs to be escaped, giving you `\\+`. To finish up our regular expression, we need another space and then another `\\d` combo.

If you want to avoid the backslashes, you can put the character in a character class. For example, both of the following match a single literal period (`.`):

```
String escapePeriod1 = "[.]"
String escapePeriod2 = "\\.";
```

> **NOTE** *While* `"\\"` *gives you a backlash when defining a string, it will not match a backslash for a regular expression in Java. That's because if we want to express* `"\d"`, *we need to write that as \\d. As a result, if you want to match a literal backslash character in Java, you need four backslashes (*`"\\\\"`*). Luckily, this doesn't come up often!*

USING REGULAR EXPRESSIONS WITH JAVA APIS

At this point, you know enough about regular expression syntax to start using them in Java. Some methods can be called directly on a `String` object, whereas others require the `Pattern` class, a special Java class used for creating reusable regex patterns.

Calling *String* Methods

In this section, you will see how to match, replace, and split a string using a regular expression. All of these methods are called directly on the `String` class just like the more common methods like `contains()` and `length()`.

Finding Matches

The `matches()` method takes a regular expression as a parameter and returns whether the regular expression is a *complete* match for the `String` instance. We intentionally used the phrase *complete match*. If there are extra characters in the text, even though the regex might match some portion of the text, nonetheless `matches()` will return `false`. Let's look at a few examples:

```
System.out.println("java book".matches("[aeiou]")); // false
```

The previous regular expression tries to match a single vowel. While there are vowels in the text, there are also other characters, so it is not a complete match. To fix this, you need to specify that any characters can be before or after the vowel.

```
String text = "java book";
System.out.println(text.matches(".*[aeiou].*")); // true
```

To make it clearer that the whole regular expression needs to match, you can optionally include the beginning (`^`) and end (`$`) anchors.

```
String text = "java book";
System.out.println(text.matches("^.*[aeiou].*$")); // true
```

For one more example, do you understand why the following matches?

```
String text = "java book";
System.out.println(text.matches("\\w+\\s\\w+")); // true
```

This pattern has three segments. `\\w+` matches "one or more" word characters. `\\s` matches a single whitespace character. Finally, the `\\w+` matches "one or more" word characters again. Many people find this hard to read. Luckily, it can be written in a clearer way.

```
String text = "java book";
String word = "\\w+";
String space = "\\s";
String regex = word + space + word;
System.out.println(text.matches(regex)); // true
```

Notice how the regular expression is defined in plain English. Clearly, the regular expression matches two words separated by a space. The `word` and `space` variables are also easier to understand because they have a clear name. For example, it should make sense that one or more word characters make up a word. Suppose you made a typo and wrote the pattern for "zero or more word characters" instead of "one or more":

```
String word = "\\w*"; // INCORRECT
```

By expressing the regex using named variables as we have done, then your intent is clear, and when doing a code review, a teammate is more likely to ask you why your word can have zero characters in it. The shortest words we know have one character, not zero, after all.

Replacing Values

There are two methods for replacing parts of a `String` that match a regular expression. The `replaceAll()` method replaces each substring that matches a supplied regular expression with a supplied value. The `replaceFirst()` method replaces only the first substring to match, as you might have gathered from the name.

```
String text = "java book";
System.out.println(text.replaceAll("[aeiou]", "_"));    // j_v_ b__k
System.out.println(text.replaceFirst("[aeiou]", "_")); // j_va book
```

Notice how `replaceAll()` replaced all the vowels with underscores, whereas `replaceFirst()` replaces only the first vowel. Now let's try matching more than one character at a time.

```
String text = "java book";
System.out.println(text.replaceAll("\\w+", "[word]")); // [word] [word]
```

\\w+ looks for "one or more" word characters. The replacement is the six-character string `[word]`.

Finally, you can use matched portions from the original text in your replacement using the `$` symbol, as follows:

```
String text = "java book";
System.out.println(text.replaceAll(  // book java
   "(\\w+)\\s(\\w+)", "$2 $1"));
```

The parentheses in the pattern create *capture groups*, which you can then reference in your replacement pattern as `$1`, `$2`, etc. In this case, there are two sets of parentheses, so there are two reference groups available. By reversing them in the replacement pattern, the code reverses their order in the replacement string, resulting in the output `book java`.

WHAT ABOUT *REPLACE()*?

Be sure not to mix up the regular `replace()` method with the regular expression ones.

```
String text = "java book";
// does not use a regular expression
System.out.println(    // java book
 text.replace("\\w+", "[word]"));
```

Nothing was replaced because the `replace()` does not recognize regex patterns. Rather it matches a literal string. Since the `\\w+` text does not appear in the text `java book`, nothing is replaced.

Splitting

The final regular expression operation you can do on the `String` class is splitting into a `String[]`. The most common way to use `split()` is to have a regular expression that represents a single separator character like a space.

```
String text = "java book";
String[] words = text.split(" ");
System.out.println(words.length);             // 2
System.out.println(Arrays.asList(words));     // [java, book]
```

The separator character, a space in this case, is called a *delimiter*. Of course, you can use a more involved regular expression like this:

```
String text = "123 - 456 - 789";
String[] words = text.split("[- ]+");
System.out.println(words.length);            // 3
System.out.println(Arrays.asList(words)); // [123, 456, 789]
```

This pattern matches separators consisting of one or more adjacent dashes and spaces. When using the `split()` method, take care that your delimiter doesn't match a zero character string, or you will get a sequence of single characters, as in this example:

```
String text = "123 - 456 - 789";
String[] words = text.split("[- ]*"); // matches zero or more characters
System.out.println(words.length);            // 11
System.out.println(Arrays.asList(words)); // [1, 2, 3, , 4, 5, 6, , 7, 8, 9]
```

"What happened there?" you ask. The regular expression matches the position between each character, so they all get separated out into the array, even the spaces. Unless that is your intent, be careful that the regular expression doesn't match an empty string!

You might be surprised what happens if the regular expression matches the beginning or end of your text. In this example, it matches both:

```
String text = "- 123 - 456 - 789 -";
String[] words = text.split("[- ]+");
System.out.println(words.length);            // 4
System.out.println(Arrays.asList(words)); // [, 123, 456, 789]
```

Notice how the first entry in the array is an empty string, but the last is not. This discrepancy is the way Java has chosen to implement the `split()` method.

> **TIP** *You might be thinking that* `split()` *is an easy way to parse a comma-separated value (CSV) file. This might produce undesired results because CSV files can use quotes to surround fields that may contain commas to indicate that the commas were not intended as field separators. The Apache Common CSV and Open CSV libraries are easy to use and handle this case. See "Further References" for links to these libraries.*

While `split()` is most commonly called with just the one regular expression parameter, there is a variant that accepts two parameters. The second is a number called `limit`, which is used to customize the behavior of `split()`. While this second parameter version is less commonly used, it is good to be aware of it. The following examples show these differences:

```
String text = "- 123 - 456 - 789 -";
String[] limit0 = text.split("[- ]+", 0);
System.out.println(limit0.length); // 4
System.out.println(Arrays.asList(limit0)); // [, 123, 456, 789]

String[] limit3 = text.split("[- ]+", 3);
System.out.println(limit3.length); // 3
System.out.println(Arrays.asList(limit3)); // [, 123, 456 - 789 -]

String[] limitNegative = text.split("[- ]+", -1);
System.out.println(limitNegative.length); // 5
System.out.println(Arrays.asList(limitNegative)); // [, 123, 456, 789, ]
```

As you can see from the first call, with a limit of 0, the output is the same as calling `split()` without passing a limit. In fact, behind the scenes the `split(regex)` method calls `split(regex, 0)`.

Passing a positive number as the limit is more interesting; it limits the result array to a maximum size of that number of elements. If there would have been more matches, only the first n-1 (where n is the limit value) would be split, and anything beyond that is combined as the last item. In the second call, we provide a limit of 3. Since the first element is the empty string due to starting with the delimiter, the second element is `123`, and the third is the entire rest of the string.

Passing any negative `int` returns the same result as passing a limit of zero, except that if there is a trailing empty match, it is included. That gives you an extra element in the array in this example.

Finally, Java 21 added another method called `splitWithDelimiters()`. It behaves the same way as `split()` with a positive limit value, except it also includes the matched delimiters as elements of the returned array. These delimiter elements don't count toward the limit count. For example:

```
String text = "- 123 - 456 - 789 -";
String[] limit3 = text.splitWithDelimiters("[- ]+", 3);
System.out.println(limit3.length); // 3
System.out.println(Arrays.asList(limit3)); // [, - , 123,  - , 456 - 789 -]
```

If you had called `split()`, this would have returned a three-element array instead. Notice how a single dash is at `limit3[1]` and `limit3[3]`. These are the delimiters.

Working with Patterns

All the methods from the `String` class that we saw in the previous section use the classes `Pattern` and `Matcher` behind the scenes. These classes are also available to you directly and provide additional methods for more power and improved performance.

Finding Matches

The `matches()` method on the `String` class tells you whether the regular expression matches the entire target. Oftentimes, however, you will want to match not the whole target, but rather you want to scan text to find all the sections that match a particular regular expression. You can do that using the `matcher.find()` method, as follows:

```
11: String text = "java book";
12: Pattern pattern = Pattern.compile("\\w+");
13: Matcher matcher = pattern.matcher(text);
14: while (matcher.find()) {
15:     System.out.println(matcher.group());
16: }
```

This code outputs the following:

```
java
book
```

Let's explore this code in more detail. Line 12 creates a `Pattern` instance that represents the compiled regular expression. If you are going to use this regular expression in other methods or classes, save it as an instance variable or static variable for future use.

Line 13 uses that `Pattern` to create a `Matcher` for the text you want to search or parse. Line 14 loops through each match for the regular expressions. You must call `matcher.find()` before calling `group()` to access the matched text. Line 15 uses the `group()` method to print out those matches, one at a time.

The `group()` method without any parameters returns the entire match. You can also supply an optional `int` parameter to access the specific groups from the match:

```
String text = "Real World Java";
String twoAdjacentWordChars = "(\\w)(\\w)";
Pattern pattern = Pattern.compile(twoAdjacentWordChars);
Matcher matcher = pattern.matcher(text);
while (matcher.find()) {
   String chars = "%s %s".formatted(matcher.group(1), matcher.group(2));
   System.out.println(chars);
}
```

This time our code matches the input text two characters at a time and outputs the following:

```
Re
al
Wo
rl
Ja
va
```

Note how the `d` in `world` was omitted, since it is not part of a pair of word characters (the character following the `d` is a space, not a word character). The group indexes are numbered according to the parentheses in the regular expression. Wait? Why are we starting the count from one? Isn't this Java, where indexes are always zero-based? The answer is that `group(0)` is used to return the entire match, so to access specific groups, you must start the counting from one.

Rather than referring to groups by number, you can assign names to the groups and refer to them by name. This is especially useful if you have a large number of groups. To name a group, add a group-name specifier as the first entry in the group. A group-name specifier consists of a question mark followed by the name in angled brackets, and then to grab the matching text associated with that group, use `matcher.group(name)`, as in this example:

```
String text = "Real World Java";
Pattern pattern = Pattern.compile("(?<first>\\w)(?<second>\\w)");
```

```
Matcher matcher = pattern.matcher(text);
while (matcher.find()) {
   String chars = "%s %s".formatted(matcher.group("first"),
      matcher.group("second"));
   System.out.println(chars);
}
```

Whether you find numbered or named groups clearer is a combination of personal preference and the code you are writing.

> **TIP** *To find the start and end indexes within the target string, of the latest match, call* `matcher.start()` *and* `matcher.end()`.

Replacing Values

The `String` methods `replaceFirst()` and `replaceAll()` are great when you want to replace the first match or all matches. But what if you want more specific replacement logic; for example, let's say you want to replace every other match. Luckily, you can do this with a `Pattern` and `Matcher` as well. This fun method makes every other word (of one or more letters) uppercase:

```
20: String text = "-->The---quick---brown---fox---jumped!!";
21: StringBuffer buffer = new StringBuffer();
22: Pattern pattern = Pattern.compile("\\w+");
23: Matcher matcher = pattern.matcher(text);
24: boolean flip = false;
25: for(int i = 0; matcher.find(); i++) {
26:    String group = matcher.group();
27:    flip = !flip;
28:    if(flip) {
29:       group = group.toUpperCase();
30:    }
31:    matcher.appendReplacement(buffer, group);
32:    System.out.println(i + "." + buffer);
33: }
34: matcher.appendTail(buffer);
35: System.out.println(buffer);
```

The output is as follows:

```
0.-->THE
1.-->THE---quick
2.-->THE---quick---BROWN
3.-->THE---quick---BROWN---fox
4.-->THE---quick---BROWN---fox---JUMPED
-->THE---quick---BROWN---fox---JUMPED!!
```

Lines 20 to 30 should mostly look familiar; we are simply looping through the matches of the regular expression. The `StringBuffer` in line 21 works like `StringBuilder`, except that it is thread-safe. While you don't need thread safety here, `StringBuilder` didn't exist when regular expressions were added to Java, so `StringBuffer` was used in the API.

The `appendReplacement()` and `appendTail()` methods are new; they append the replacement text to the `StringBuffer`. The `appendReplacement()` appends any characters after the previous match and before the current match, followed by the replacement itself (in this case the uppercase version of the match). The appendTail() method appends any remaining characters from after the last match until the end of the input string. To make sure you understand this, let's go through the flow of our sample:

1. On the first iteration of the loop, group contains The.
2. appendReplacement() starts by appending the text from before the match (in this case -->) to buffer and then appends the replacement text (THE) to buffer.
3. On the second iteration of the loop, group contains quick.
4. The appendReplacement() method appends the text from before the match (--) to buffer and then appends the replacement text (quick) to buffer.
5. It continues to find and capitalize every other word until, finally, appendTail() appends the remaining text after the match (!!) to buffer.

Trying another one, what do you think this does?

```
String text = "java book";
StringBuffer buffer = new StringBuffer();
Pattern pattern = Pattern.compile("(\\w)(\\w)(\\w)(\\w)");
Matcher matcher = pattern.matcher(text);
while (matcher.find()) {
   matcher.appendReplacement(buffer, "$1 $2 $3 $4\n");
}
matcher.appendTail(buffer);
System.out.println(buffer);
```

It outputs the following:

```
j a v a
 b o o k
```

The regular expression matches four consecutive word characters, each in a capture group. The appendReplacement() method supplies those same four characters, adding spaces between the characters. The b is indented one character due to the space in the original string.

What if you want to include a literal value of some regex command character, such as a backslash or dollar sign, in the replacement? The method quoteReplacement() tells Java to use the literal values and not their special meanings. For example:

```
String text = "java book";
StringBuffer buffer = new StringBuffer();
Pattern pattern = Pattern.compile("(\\w)(\\w)(\\w)(\\w)");
Matcher matcher = pattern.matcher(text);
while (matcher.find()) {
   // include a literal \ and $
   String replacement = Matcher.quoteReplacement("\\$1.00");
   matcher.appendReplacement(buffer, replacement);
}
matcher.appendTail(buffer);
System.out.println(buffer);
```

This time the output is as follows:

```
\$1.00 \$1.00
```

Notice how the $ is understood to be literal text, not the normal regex meaning of $ (which normally is an anchor that matches the start of the input). Similarly, the backslash is treated as a literal backslash instead of escaping the $.

Splitting as a *Stream*

`Pattern` provides one useful splitting method that is not available directly on `String`. With a `Pattern`, you can create a `Stream<String>` instead of a `String[]`. For example:

```
String text = "- 123 - 456 - 789 -";
Pattern pattern = Pattern.compile("[- ]+");
Stream<String> stream = pattern.splitAsStream(text);
stream.forEach(a -> System.out.println("*" + a + "*"));
```

This code outputs the following:

```
**
*123*
*456*
*789*
```

This produces the same four matches as `string.split()`, except that it returns the split results as a `Stream` of `Srings` rather than an array.

Controlling Behavior with Flags

When compiling a `Pattern`, you can optionally pass flags to the compile method to tweak the behavior of the regular expression. These same flags can be embedded into the regular expression itself. Table 10.4 shows the most common flags.

TABLE 10.4: Flags

CONSTANT NAME	EMBEDDED FLAG VALUE	DESCRIPTION
`CASE_INSENSITIVE`	`(?i)`	Ignores case when considering matches.
`DOTALL`	`(?s)`	Enables *single-line mode* by having the . instruction match even the line terminator.
`MULTILINE`	`(?m)`	Enables multiline mode by having ^ and $ match the beginning and end of each line, instead of the beginning and end of the entire string.
`UNICODE_CASE`	`(?u)`	Uses Unicode characters for case-sensitivity check instead of US-ASCII. Valid only if case-insensitive flag is on.
`UNICODE_CHARACTER_CLASS`	`(?U)`	Includes Unicode characters in the predefined character classes instead of limiting to US-ASCII.

The following example uses the first two flags at the same time:

```
String text = """
   Real-World Java: Helping You Navigate the Java Ecosystem
   Victor Grazi
   Jeanne Boyarsky""";

Pattern pattern = Pattern.compile("real.*sky",
   Pattern.CASE_INSENSITIVE | Pattern.DOTALL);
```

```
Matcher matcher = pattern.matcher(text);

if (matcher.find()) {
   System.out.println("I got this book!");
}
else {
   System.out.println("I should have gotten this book!");
}
```

The pattern will match any string containing `real` followed by any characters (including line feeds), followed by `sky`. Since there is a match, the output is as follows:

```
I got this book!
```

In the previous code, the bitwise operator (`|`) combines the two flags. The `CASE_INSENSITIVE` flag matches the lowercase `r` in the regular expression to the capital `R` in the input. The `DOTALL` treats the newlines in the strings as any other character, allowing `.*` to match them. If either of these flags were removed, there would be no match.

Rather than passing these flags to the compile method as parameters, you can embed them directly into your regex pattern. This is especially useful when you are supplying the regex to the `String.matches()` method, which does not have a version that accepts separate flag parameters.

The previous example could be written with embedded flags as follows:

```
String text = """
   Real-World Java: Helping You Navigate the Java Ecosystem
   Victor Grazi
   Jeanne Boyarsky""";
if (text.matches("(?i)(?s)real.*sky")) {
   System.out.println("I got this book!");
}
else {
   System.out.println("I should have gotten this book!");
}
```

While it is shorter and more expressive with the embedded flags, it is not necessarily clearer, so choose wisely.

The other flag we will show here is `MULTILINE`.

```
String text = """
   Real-World Java: Helping You Navigate the Java Ecosystem
   Victor Grazi
   Jeanne Boyarsky""";
Pattern pattern = Pattern.compile(".*[iy]$", Pattern.MULTILINE);
Matcher matcher = pattern.matcher(text);
while (matcher.find()) {
   System.out.println(matcher.group());
}
```

The regex matches anything that ends in an *i* or a *y*. Since it is in `MULTILINE` mode, it will find all lines that end in an *i* or a *y*. This code outputs the following:

```
Victor Grazi
Jeanne Boyarsky
```

The `MULTILINE` flag matches each line break with `$`. Since Victor Grazi and Jeanne Boyarsky end with `i` and `y`, both lines are output. Without the flag, only Jeanne's line would be output because then `$` would match only the end of the `String`.

EXPLORING ADVANCED REGULAR EXPRESSION SYNTAX

What you have seen until now is the basic regular expression syntax. Now let's advance that a level by looking at syntax for some more granular controls.

First, we will look at positive and negative look-ahead and look-behind. These let you change what you match based on neighboring text. After that, you'll see how to specify greedy, reluctant, and possessive quantifiers.

Looking at Neighboring Text

So far, the regular expressions in this chapter directly match the input text. But what if you want to find matches in relation to other text in the input? There are four types of constructs for this scenario. Suppose you have the text `dev.java/playground` and want to match `java`. However, you want to match only if certain things are true around its context. The four ways are as follows:

- **Positive look-ahead:** Checks that a certain pattern follows immediately after. For example, "match the letter `g` only if it immediately follows the word `play`."
- **Negative look-ahead:** Checks that a certain pattern is not immediately following. For example, "match only if a letter does not follow the word `java`."
- **Positive look-behind:** Checks that a certain pattern is immediately before. For example, "match only if a dot precedes `java`."
- **Negative look-behind:** Checks that a certain pattern is not immediately before. For example, "match only if a number does not precede `java`."

Positive look-ahead uses the syntax `(?=X)` where `X` is the regular expression to use in the look-ahead. Positive look-behind adds a `<` to the syntax, making it `(?<=X)`. You can remember this since the less-than symbol points to the left, which is the direction of "before." Negative look-ahead and look-behind use a `!` after the `?` instead of an `=` to indicate negation.

Table 10.5 reviews the syntax for each of these constructs. For look-behind, notice that `java` is in parentheses. This indicates that we want to look behind the whole word `java` and not just behind the last `a`.

TABLE 10.5: Positive/Negative Look-Ahead/Behind Patterns

NAME	SYNTAX	EXAMPLE	DESCRIPTION
Positive look-ahead	`(?=X)`	`play(?=g)`	Match the word `play` if immediately followed by a `g`.
Negative look-ahead	`(?!X)`	`java(?![a-z])`	Match the word `java` if not immediately followed by a lowercase letter.
Positive look-behind	`(?<=X)`	`(?<=[.])(java)`	Match the word `java` if immediately preceded by the literal period.
Negative look-behind	`(?<!X)`	`(?<![0-9])(java)`	Match the word `java` if not immediately preceded by a number.

Let's look at another example. Suppose you have the following text:

```
once upon a time
```

Let's see how some patterns match:

- **on**: This example (without look-ahead or look-behind) matches the letters on with no further constraints, which matches two instances of two letters each: **on**ce up**on** a time.
- **on(?=ce)**: This positive look-ahead example matches the letters on followed by the letters ce, which results in two letters matched **on**ce upon a time.
- **on(?!ce)**: This negative look-ahead example matches the letters on *not* followed by the letters ce, which results in two letters matched once up**on** a time.
- **(?<=up)on**: This positive look-behind matches the letters on only if they come right after the letters up, which results in two letters matched once up**on** a time.
- **(?<!up)on**: This negative look-behind matches the letters on unless they come right after the letters up, which results in two letters matched **on**ce upon a time.

Differentiating Quantifiers

Early in the chapter you learned about quantifiers. Table 10.1 listed the most common ones. But there are many more, and Table 10.6 provides the complete list. Note that a reluctant quantifier adds a ?, while possessive adds a +. Let's understand what those mean.

TABLE 10.6: All Quantifiers

DESCRIPTION	GREEDY	RELUCTANT	POSSESSIVE
Zero or one	J?	J??	J?+
Zero or more	J*	J*?	J*+
One or more	J+	J+?	J++
Exactly three	J{3}	J{3}?	J{3}+
Three or more	J{3,}	J{3,}?	J{3,}+
Three, four, or five	J{3,5}	J{3,5}?	J{3,5}+

Suppose you have the following text and want to match any characters that are followed by row your boat. How many matches would you expect there to be?

```
Poem:
Row, row, row your boat,
Gently down the stream,
Merrily, merrily, merrily, merrily
Life is but a dream.
Row, row, row your boat ... dream
```

The correct answer depends on which quantifier you use! Understanding how each of them processes data will make this clear. These examples use DOTALL mode since the newline characters need to match.

First look at a greedy quantifier:

```
.*row your boat
```

With a greedy quantifier, the regular expression engine reads the entire input at once and checks if there is a match. Unfortunately here the full text does not match so the engine uses a process called *backtracking*.

WHAT IS BACKTRACKING?

With backtracking, the regular expression engine realizes it has reached a dead end and cannot match. It then releases one character from the end and tries again. If there is still no match, the engine releases yet another character from the end, and so on, until either there is a match or the engine runs out of text. For example, suppose we are trying to match `.*abc` in the text `abcdefg`. With a greedy quantifier, the process looks like this:

- Does `abcdefg` match `.*abc`? No. Backtrack!
- Does `abcdef` match `.*abc`? No. Backtrack!
- Does `abcde` match `.*abc`? No. Backtrack!
- Does `abcd` match `.*abc`? No. Backtrack!
- Does `abc` match `.*abc`? Yes. There is a match, and the engine can stop looking.

After backtracking through the entire input in this case, you can see from the match (bolded in the following text) that it found the result to include everything from the beginning and up until the final `boat`. This is because `.*` matches everything up to the last occurrence of `row your boat`.

```
Poem:
Row, row, row your boat,
Gently down the stream,
Merrily, merrily, merrily, merrily
Life is but a dream.
Row, row, row your boat ... dream
```

Now compare that to a reluctant quantifier.

```
.*?row your boat
```

With a reluctant quantifier, the algorithm is reversed. The engine starts at the beginning, adding one character at a time until it finds a match. This gives a match of `Row, row, row your boat` from the first line, as highlighted in the following:

```
Poem:
Row, row, row your boat,
Gently down the stream,
Merrily, merrily, merrily, merrily
Life is but a dream.
Row, row, row your boat ... dream
```

After this first match, the reluctant quantifier picks up from where it left off and sees there is more text remaining in the input, so it tries again, revealing a second match.

```
Poem:
Row, row, row your boat,
Gently down the stream,
Merrily, merrily, merrily, merrily
Life is but a dream.
Row, row, row your boat ... dream
```

There are still characters of input that are unmatched at the end. The engine tries one more time and does not find another match, so it quits.

Finally, compare all that to a possessive quantifier.

```
.*+row your boat
```

With a possessive quantifier, the engine reads the entire input once. However, unlike a greedy quantifier, there is no backtracking. There are no matches for this regular expression since `.*` uses up the entire string. Notice how the three quantifiers gave completely different output!

Now take a look at an example where a possessive quantifier does find a match. Suppose you have the following text:

```
row row your boat
```

Using the pattern `.*+your boat` would not work for the same reason described in the previous example. However, you can make the regular expression more specific and still use a possessive quantifier. First consider the following:

```
(row )*+your boat
```

This example matches zero or more of the word `row` followed by a space. After it runs out, it matches `your boat`, which matches the entire text in this example:

```
row row your boat
```

It gets more interesting if you move the space to form this pattern:

```
(row)*+ your boat
```

The possessive quantifier first grabs the first three letters of the text: `row`. Since the fourth character of the input is a space that is not followed by `your boat`, that can't be a match, so those three characters are ignored. Then the next word `row` is considered. This time it is followed by a space and `your boat`. Eureka! The possessive quantifier version found a match.

row **row your boat**

DEBUGGING YOUR REGULAR EXPRESSION

If your regular expression isn't behaving the way you want it to, there are two good techniques for debugging it. One is to create a smaller regular expression that matches only part of what you are looking for. Once that works, add on slowly until something breaks, so you know where things went wrong.

The other is to use an online debugger. https:/regex101.com has a debugger, but only if you have PCRE2 mode selected. The syntax is often the same as Java, though, and it is a great visualization tool. The debugger lets you step through and see what part of the regular expression is being handled and what part of the input is being tested. See Figure 10.4 for an example.

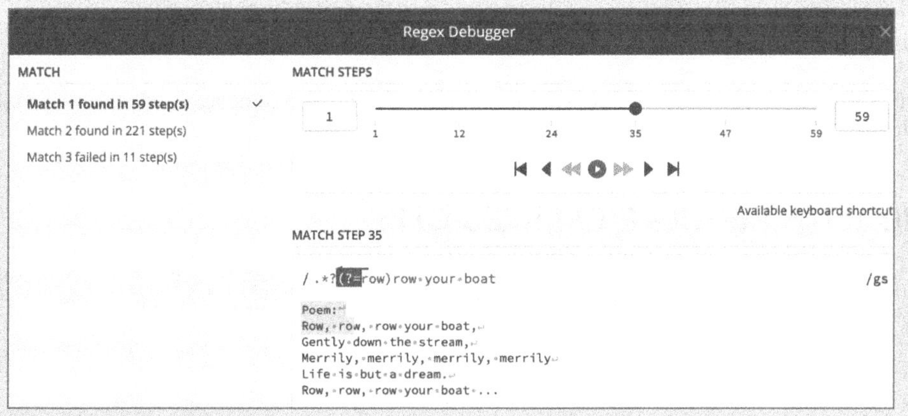

FIGURE 10.4: Debugging a regular expression

IDENTIFYING COMMON MISTAKES

In Chapter 4, "Automating Your CI/CD Builds with Maven, Gradle, and Jenkins," you learned that SonarQube is a common static analysis tool. It also has an IDE plugin called SonarLint. Sonar is excellent at identifying common problems with regular expressions, as well as the Java code itself.

Table 10.7 shows some of the highlights. Understanding these common mistakes will also help you better understand how to write regular expressions.

TABLE 10.7: Examples of Regular Expression Mistakes

<table>
<tr><th>CODE</th><th>WHAT'S WRONG</th></tr>
<tr><td>[ab]|a</td><td>The a is redundant; [ab] accomplishes the same thing.</td></tr>
<tr><td>x = x
.replaceAll("\\.\\.\\.", ";")</td><td>There's no need for a regular expression at all. This does the same thing and is easier to read:
x = x
.replace("...", "");</td></tr>
<tr><td><.+?></td><td>This backtracks needlessly. A more specific regular expression avoids such backtracking:
<[^>]+></td></tr>
<tr><td>$[a-z]^</td><td>The anchors are backwards. It should be:
^[a-z]$
As a memory aid, the ^ points up, to the start. The $ represents money, the bottom line.</td></tr>
<tr><td>(?=a)b</td><td>This is impossible. You already know the next character is b, so a positive lookahead of a is always false. Therefore, b alone would match the same result.</td></tr>
<tr><td>a++abc</td><td>This is impossible. Since a++ is possessive, it uses up all consecutive instances of a, so there can't be another after.</td></tr>
</table>

SonarQube also has a rule on ensuring your regular expression is not too complicated. Regular expressions are a tool to have in your toolbox, not the tool to use for every job!

CODING WITH REGULAR EXPRESSIONS

At the beginning of this chapter, you saw three URIs and a statement that regular expressions could easily separate the protocol, website or directory, and specific path. Now is the time to learn how! Consider the following code:

```
String uris = """
   http://spring.io/projects/spring-cloud-contract
   https://www.infoq.com/articles/Living-Matrix-Bytecode-Manipulation/
   file:///C:/Documents/happy_birthday_sis.pdf
""";

```

```
16: String twoOrMoreSlashes = "/{2,}";
17: String matchAny = "(.+)";
18: String matchAnythingButSlash = "([^/]+)";
19: String regex = matchAny + ":" + twoOrMoreSlashes
20:    + matchAnythingButSlash + "/" + matchAny;
21:
22: Pattern pattern = Pattern.compile(regex, Pattern.MULTILINE);
23: Matcher matcher = pattern.matcher(uris);
24: while (matcher.find()) {
25:    String protocol = matcher.group(1);
26:    String websiteOrDirectory = matcher.group(2);
27:    String specificPath = matcher.group(3);
28:    String formatted = "%s\t%s\t%s".formatted(protocol,
29:       websiteOrDirectory, specificPath);
30:    System.out.println(formatted);
31: }
```

The output of this program is just what the requirements specify.

```
http    spring.io      projects/spring-cloud-contract
https   www.infoq.com  articles/Living-Matrix-Bytecode-Manipulation/
file    C:      Documents/happy_birthday_sis.pdf
```

Lines 10–14 create a text block with the URIs we want to test. Lines 16–19 use self-documenting variables to clearly explain what we want to match. Line 16 gives an English description to matching two or more slash characters. Line 17 matches one or more characters, capturing the result for matching later. Line 18 matches one or more characters other than a slash, also capturing the result.

Lines 19–20 combine these subexpressions into the final regular expression. Lines 22–23 create a `Pattern` and `Matcher`. Finally, lines 24–27 loop through each of the three matching URIs and get the matching groups for the information we require.

As another example, in the previous chapter, you needed to parse information about a virtual thread. There are two good ways of implementing this using regular expressions. One is to use a similar approach to the previous example with a `Pattern` and `Matcher`.

```
String text = "VirtualThread[#22]/runnable@ForkJoinPool-1-worker-1";

String regex = "(.+]).*@(.+)";
Pattern pattern = Pattern.compile(regex);
Matcher matcher = pattern.matcher(text);
while (matcher.find()) {
   String virtualThread = matcher.group(1);
   String pooledThread = matcher.group(2);

   System.out.println(virtualThread);
   System.out.println(pooledThread);
}
```

The regular expression starts by capturing any sequence of characters ending in `]`. It then matches any characters up to and including an `@`. Finally, it looks for a capturing group of any characters. This could have been split up into variables for the three pieces if you preferred. The loop is similar to the previous example where the code gets the capturing group values.

Since you are matching only a single value, an alternative is to use `replaceFirst()` as shown here:

```
String text = "VirtualThread[#22]/runnable@ForkJoinPool-1-worker-1";

String virtualThread = text.replaceFirst("].*$", "]");
```

```
String pooledThread = text.replaceFirst("^.*@", "");

System.out.println(virtualThread);
System.out.println(pooledThread);
```

In this example, you use `replaceFirst()` to get rid of the part you don't want to match. For the `virtualThread` one, it replaces the `]` and everything after it with a `]`. For the pooled thread, it removes everything up to the `@`, Either way, you get the same output.

```
VirtualThread[#22]
ForkJoinPool-1-worker-1
```

USING WITH FRAMEWORKS AND TOOLS

Besides the regular expressions you write for your code or that you use for searching in your IDE, regular expressions are used in a number of libraries. In this section, you'll get a taste of how regular expressions are used to interact with these libraries.

Coding Regular Expressions for Apache Commons Validator

Apache Commons Validator is a framework you can use in your programs to verify that the program input complies with rules that you specify. One of the validators allows you to specify your own regular expression.

```
String regex = "^\\d{4}$"; // match 4 consecutive digits
RegexValidator validator = new RegexValidator(regex);
System.out.println(validator.isValid("2034")); // true
System.out.println(validator.isValid("5")); // false
```

Further, a number of the built-in validators use regular expressions behind the scenes. Some examples include `CreditCardValidator`, `EmailValidator`, and `ISBNValidator`. This is convenient because you don't have to write the regular expression yourself; you can just reuse the work of others.

Coding Regular Expressions for JUnit

JUnit 5 has some annotations that support using regular expressions to control behavior. For example, you can control which values in an enum are included in a parameterized test using a regular expression. This example allows only `PRE_PROD` and `PROD` to be included.

```
enum Env { DEV, TEST, PRE_PROD, PROD};

@ParameterizedTest
@EnumSource(mode = EnumSource.Mode.MATCH_ALL, names = "^.*PROD$")
void monitoring(Env env) {
   // assert env up
}
```

As you saw in the Chapter 7, "Testing Your Code with Automated Testing Tools," AssertJ provides custom matchers that you can use in writing assertions. One of them allows you to match on a regular expression. For example:

```
@Test
void chess() {
   String chessNotationRegex = "[a-hA-H][1-8]";
   String actual = "A5";
   assertThat("A5").matches(chessNotationRegex);
}
```

The JUnit Pioneer library also supports regular expressions. For example, you can disable a test based on the display name. In this case, the code disables the tests for any months with long names:

```
static List<String> months() {
   return List.of("January", "February", "March", "April", "May",
      "June", "July", "August", "September", "October",
      "November", "December");
   }

@DisableIfDisplayName(matches = "^Month: \\w{6,}$")
@ParameterizedTest(name = "Month: {0}")
@MethodSource("months")
void shortMonths(String reason) {
    // test short month name
}
```

Coding Regular Expressions for Log4j

Sometimes you need to go beyond logging level and restrict what Log4J logs. A capability called *filters* allows you to customize what gets logged, based on the value in the message. Suppose your audit department says you are not allowed to log the word `secret`. You can set up a filter on your appender to omit the entire line as follows:

```
<RegexFilter regex=".* secret .*" onMatch="DENY" onMismatch="ACCEPT"/>
```

The previous tells Log4J to skip logging any messages that contain `secret` with a space on both sides.

Coding Regular Expressions for Bean Validation

The bean validation framework provides a number of validators to check whether a JavaBean has the expected values.

One of these validators is `@Pattern`, which uses a regular expression:

```
import jakarta.validation.constraints.Pattern;

public class Bean {

    @Pattern(regexp = "[A-Z]+")
    private String uppercaseLetters;

    public String getUppercaseLetters() {
        return uppercaseLetters;
    }

    public void setUppercaseLetters(String uppercaseLetters) {
        this.uppercaseLetters = uppercaseLetters;
    }
}
```

In this example, validation will fail if `uppercaseLetters` contains lowercase letters or anything that is not a letter.

> **NOTE** *You might have noticed the import starts with* `jakarta`. *A number of standards were introduced in Java Enterprise Edition (JEE). To avoid trademark infringement, the JEE was rebranded to mean Jakarta Enterprise Edition. Conveniently, the acronym remains the same.*

Coding Regular Expressions for Spring

Spring uses regular expressions in Spring MVC to help obtain a portion of the URL and turn it into a variable. For example, in this controller, a sequence of digits is matched and assigned to the variable `bookId`:

```
import org.springframework.web.bind.annotation.PathVariable;
import org.springframework.web.bind.annotation.RequestMapping;
import org.springframework.web.bind.annotation.RestController;

@RestController
public class TheController {

   @RequestMapping("/book/{bookId: [0-9]+}")
   public String getBookById(@PathVariable("bookId") String bookId) {
      String result = // build return value
      return result;
   }
}
```

In the previous code, Spring takes a URL like `/books/469` and stores 469 in the `bookId` parameter. Using a regular expression gives you a lot of flexibility in specifying the format that should match.

NOT A REGULAR EXPRESSION

Now that you are used to seeing regular expressions, it is a good time to talk about other pieces of code that might look similar on first glance but are not regular expressions.

Do you think this is a regular expression?

```
try (DirectoryStream<Path> dStream = Files.newDirectoryStream(
   path, "**/*.{properties,txt}")) {
}
```

You probably aren't surprised, given the title of this section, that it is not a regular expression. There are a few clues. First, notice the `**`, which would never be a valid regex. Here it means traverse into any number of levels or directories. Also, notice how there is a `*` rather than a `.*` to match any characters. This is a big clue that you are not dealing with a regular expression. The syntax is called a *glob*. It matches any files ending in `.properties` or `.txt`.

Similarly, Ant (an older build tool than Maven and Gradle) uses patterns like `**/*.txt` to match text files in any directory. It is important not to mix up patterns like these with regular expressions.

FURTHER REFERENCES

- `https://www.pluralsight.com/courses/playbook-regular-expressions-java-fundamentals`
  - Victor's Pluralsight Course on Regular Expressions
- `https://docs.oracle.com/en/java/javase/21/docs/api/java.base/java/util/regex/Pattern.html`
  - Java Pattern Documentation

- `https://regex101.com`
  - Regular Expression Tester
- `https://commons.apache.org/proper/commons-csv`
  - Apache Commons CSV
- `https://opencsv.sourceforge.net`
  - Open CSV
- `https://commons.apache.org/proper/commons-validator`
  - Apache Commons Validator
- `https://regexcrossword.com`
  - Regular Expression crossword puzzles for learning them better.
- *Introducing Regular Expressions* (O'Reilly, 2012)
- *Regular Expressions Cookbook* (O'Reilly, 2012)

SUMMARY

In this chapter, you learned about how to write regular expressions. Key takeaways included the following:

- Character classes are a shorthand so you don't have to list every character you are interested in individually.
- Greedy, lazy, and reluctant quantifiers allow you to change matching behavior.
- Positive and negative look-ahead and look-behind allow you to constrain matches based on surrounding text.
- Built-in Java APIs support regular expressions.
- Regular expressions are also used in libraries.

11

Coding the Aspect-Oriented Way

WHAT'S IN THIS CHAPTER?

- Understanding the Need for Aspects
- Creating Our First Example
- Exploring the Pointcut Expression Language

Not all your Java code is coded in your Java code. While that paradox may sound like some Zen koan, it effectively sets the stage for this chapter on coding with *aspects*, which are orthogonal functions that can be triggered to execute when certain conditions are met. We will show the benefit of aspects and how to write your own.

> **CODE DOWNLOADS FOR THIS CHAPTER**
>
> The source code for this chapter is available on the book page at `www.wiley.com`. Click the Downloads link. The code can also be found at `https://github.com/realworldjava/Ch11-Aspects`. See the `README.md` file in that directory for details on how to run the examples using Postman and curl.

UNDERSTANDING THE NEED FOR ASPECTS

Imagine the following scenario—you get a new requirement to modify every REST endpoint so that it starts by capturing the start time and logging a message and ends with logging the call time.

```
public void someEndpoint(){
   long start = System.currentTimeMillis();
   log.info("Starting someEndpoint");

   // do stuff

   long duration = System.currentTimeMillis() - start;
   log.info("Completed someEndpoint. Execution duration:{}ms", duration);
}
```

Now, you can copy and paste that code into every endpoint, but nobody ever won a clean-coding award for copy-and-paste coding. Can you do it in one place? Yes! You can enforce the requirement and still achieve nirvana using aspect-oriented programming (AOP). In this chapter, we will cover Spring AOP. AspectJ is more powerful, but Spring AOP is perfect for most enterprise use cases.

The idea is to create some configuration that defines a *pointcut*, that is, a pattern describing which members will be modified.

Before we go any further, let's cover some vocabulary.

- **Advice:** Defines the action to take when a join point is reached
- **Join point:** The actual point in the code where the aspect is inserted
- **Pointcut:** An expression that defines a pattern that matches where the advice should be applied

The following are the types of advice:

- `@Before`: Invoked before the method starts
- `@AfterReturning`: Invoked after the method completes successfully
- `@AfterThrowing`: Invoked only after the method throws an exception
- `@After`: Invoked after the method completes, successfully or with an exception
- `@Around`: Invocation that gives full control of when to call the method and what to return to the advice

An example is worth a thousand words. Let's create a Spring Boot MVC project with a couple of endpoints. We will make it a product catalog.

CREATING OUR FIRST EXAMPLE

The boss comes to our desk with a new requirement: "You know that product controller we've been working on? Well, we want to log a message every time someone calls the `addProduct` method." Now that is a simple enough requirement, but he also tells us that there is going to be a similar requirement for all our endpoints. Then we learn that the logging is going to get a bit complicated, so copy-and-pasting is not going to be a solution. And anyway, we want clean code, so we definitely don't want to just copy and paste the logging at every method.

The original code looks like this:

```
@RestController
public class ProductController {

   private final Map<String, Product> productMap = new HashMap<>();

   @PostMapping("/product")
   public void addProduct(@RequestBody Product product) {
      productMap.put(product.getStyleNum(), product);
   }

   @DeleteMapping("/product")
   public Product removeProduct(String styleNumber){
      return productMap.remove(styleNumber);
   }

   @GetMapping("/product")
   public Collection<Product> listProducts(){
      return productMap.values();
   }
}
```

Let's add our boss's required logging using the magic of Spring AOP. The first step is to create an *aspect* component, which defines the pointcut patterns describing the methods to intercept, as well as the advice implementations providing the code to invoke when the pointcut is hit. An aspect class is just a standard Java class, annotated with both `@Aspect` and `@Component`. Remember to import these in your class:

```
import org.aspectj.lang.JoinPoint;
import org.aspectj.lang.annotation.Aspect;
import org.aspectj.lang.annotation.Before;
import org.springframework.stereotype.Component;
```

Then we have this class:

LISTING 11-1:

```
@Aspect
@Component
public class LoggingAspect1 {
   private final Logger logger = LoggerFactory.getLogger(LoggingAspect1.class);
   @Before("execution(public * com.wiley.realworldjava.aop.product."
      + "ProductController.addProduct(..))")
   public void logAddOperations(JoinPoint joinPoint) {
      logger.info("===============> called {}", joinPoint.getSignature().getName());
   }
}
```

To run the application, let's use Postman or `curl`. (Remember to see the full instructions in the `README.md` file.) Make the `POST` call with the parameters shown here.

Endpoint:

```
POST localhost:8081/product
```

Body (`Application/Json`):

```
{
    "styleNum": "123",
    "description": "IPhone"
}
```

Run the application and fire that endpoint to add a product; you will see the following output that includes the log message:

```
===============> called addProduct
```

This is a simple example, but it demonstrates the beauty of aspects. You can intercept calls to your code and take action, without ever touching the code being instrumented!

What happened here? Let's look at the sequence diagram in Figure 11.1.

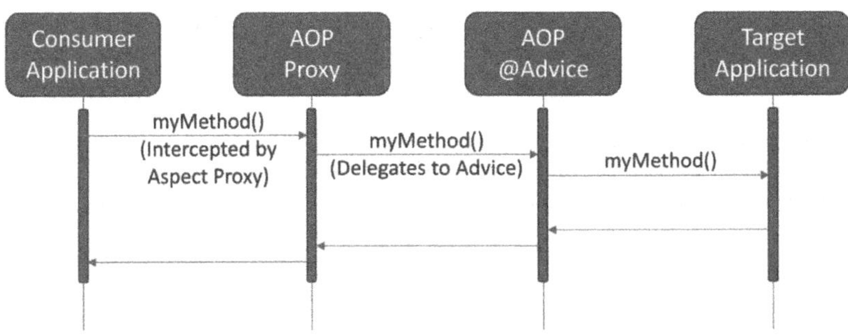

FIGURE 11.1: Sequence diagram

Spring saw your `@Aspect` annotation and introduced an invisible AOP proxy class.

This proxy evaluated the join point and delegated to an appropriate advice. The advice was invoked and, in its course, invoked the target method.

In addition, there are some important points to observe about the previous aspect in Listing 11.1.

- The `@Before` annotation tells the runtime to call this code *before* the method is called.
- The method body to be invoked, `logAddOperations()`, is called the *advice*.
- The part beginning with `execution` defines the pointcut: the pattern to match to methods (the matched method is called a *join point*) to apply this *advice*.

That's the general flow with AOP. Let's take a closer look at the APIs. You will notice that the `JoinPoint` class has several useful accessors. The one shown here is `getSignature().getName()`. Let's look at the rest of the APIs.

- **`getArgs()`**: Returns an `Object[]` containing all the arguments. For example:

  `Product{styleNum='123', description='IPhone'}]`

- **`getKind()`**: Returns a `String` representation of the kind of call. For example:

  `method-execution`

- **`getThis()`** and **`getTarget()`**: Return the instance `toString()` of the class containing the instrumented method. For example:

  ```
  com.wiley.realworldjava.aop.product.ProductController@29b5747
  - The instrumented instance
  ```

- **`toLongString()`**: Returns a long representation of the pointcut. For example:

  ```
  execution(public com.wiley.realworldjava.aop.product.Product com.wiley
  .realworldjava.aop.product.ProductController.addProduct(com.wiley
  .realworldjava.aop.product.Product))
  ```

- **`toShortString()`**: Returns a short-form representation of the pointcut. For example:

  `execution(ProductController.addProduct(..))`

- **`toString()`**: Returns an intermediate `String` representation of the pointcut. For example:

  ```
  execution(Product com.wiley.realworldjava.aop.product.
  ProductController.addProduct(Product))
  ```

- **`getSignature()`**: `Signature` is a class containing more details about the call. For example:

  ```
  Product com.wiley.realworldjava.aop.product.ProductController
  .addProduct(Product)
  ```

- **`getStaticPart()`**: `StaticPart` contains just the static information about a join point. For example:

  ```
  execution(Product com.wiley.realworldjava.aop.product.
  ProductController.addProduct(Product))
  ```

One important gotcha is that Spring AOP will instrument only Spring-managed classes, for example, `Component`, `Bean`, `Service`, and so on. Your advice can reference other data that is not managed by Spring, if that data is an argument or a return value. You will see some examples shortly, but pointcuts must refer to Spring-managed methods.

EXPLORING THE POINTCUT EXPRESSION LANGUAGE

Now the pointcut expression in the example looks like a scary beast, but it is really quite a tame fellow once you get to know it.

Let's look at it more closely at it in Figure 11.2.

- `@Before("execution(`: Tells the aspect to call this advice *before* executing this method.
- `public`: Optional. Tells the aspect to match only public methods. (This is the only one supported by Spring and can be omitted without loss of clarity.)
- `*`: The return type. You can use `void` or any Java type (generic or not), or you can use `*` to match any return type.
- `com.wiley.realworldjava.aop.product.ProductController`: Optional. The fully qualified class name to apply the aspect.
- `.addProduct`: The method name to apply the aspect.
- `(..)`: This is the list of parameters. To match only methods with no parameters, just leave the parentheses empty like this: `( )`. To match zero or more parameters, use `(..)` as shown. To match precise parameter types, specify the fully qualified class name for the parameter types. For example, to match the method `addProduct Product product)`, you could say `.addProduct (com.wiley.realworldjava.aop.product)`.

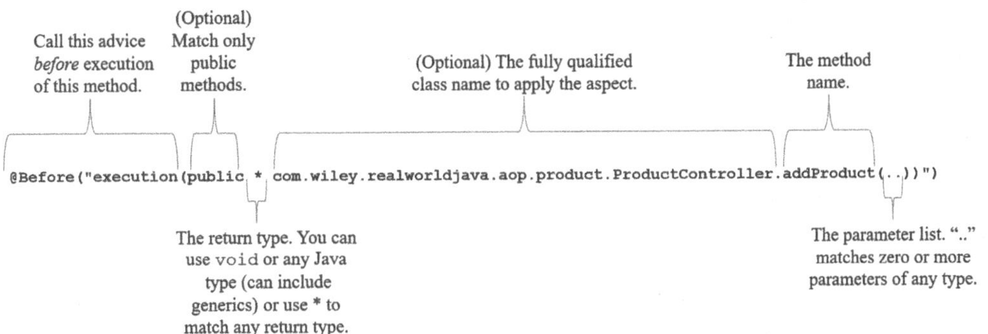

FIGURE 11.2: Pointcut expression

* Wildcards

You can use `*` as a wildcard to match a range of characters anywhere in the name of a method, class, or package. For example:

- **Method wildcard:** `execution(* add*(..))` matches any method starting with `add`.
- **Package wildcard:** `execution(* com.wiley.realworldjava..*.*(..))` matches any method in `com.wiley.realworldjava` or any of its subpackages.
- **Class name wildcard:** `execution(* your.package.name.*Controller*.*(..))` matches any method on any class with `Controller` in the class name.

Similarly, you can specify a `*` in a return type.

For example, the following will match any ProductController method named addProduct that returns any class starting with Pr and ending with ct. Therefore, it will match Product, Prospect, and Predict!

```
com.wiley.realworldjava.aop.product.Pr*ct com.wiley.realworldjava.aop.
product.ProductController.addProduct(..)
```

.. Wildcards

You saw how to use (..) to match one or more parameters in a method-call parameter list. You can also use that notation to match any method in a package or any of its subpackages. In general, .. indicates zero or more elements in the specified position.

For example, the following matches any zero-parameter method in the package com.wiley.realworldjava.aop.product or any of its subpackages:

```
execution(* com.wiley.realworldjava.aop.product..*Controller*.*())
```

Using @AfterReturning

The @AfterReturning type executes after a method returns successfully, that is, without throwing any exceptions. This can be useful for cases such as logging, but it is especially useful when you want to post-process data that was handled by the method.

Start with an execution pointcut exactly as you already learned, except annotate it with @AfterReturning.

```
@AfterReturning(pointcut =
  "execution(public * com.wiley.realworldjava.aop.product."
   +"ProductController.addProduct(com.wiley.realworldjava.aop.product.Product))")
public void logAfterReturning(JoinPoint joinPoint){
    logger.info("=====> called after returning {}",
        joinPoint.getSignature().getName());
}
```

A call to addProduct() shows in the log.

```
=====> called after returning addProduct
```

That will allow you to do things like logging, but what if you need the return value?

For that you can apply some signature magic to the pointcut to include the return value, as follows:

```
@AfterReturning("execution(public * com.wiley.realworldjava.aop.product."
  "+ "ProductController.addProduct(com.wiley.realworldjava.aop.product.Product))",
  returning = "product")
public void logAfterReturning(JoinPoint joinPoint, Product product){
    logger.info("===> called after returning {}  returned:{}",
        joinPoint.getSignature().getName(), product);
}
```

A call to addProduct() now displays in the log.

```
===> called after returning addProduct  returned:Product{styleNum='123',
  description='IPhone'}
```

The @AfterReturning advice lets you adjust the return value and return the adjusted value to the user. For example, let's say the requirement is to return uppercase descriptions. The advice can be written as follows:

```
@AfterReturning (value =
    "execution(public * com.wiley.realworldjava.aop.product."
    + "ProductController.addProduct(com.wiley.realworldjava.aop.product.Product))",
    returning = "product")
```

```
public void descriptionToUpperCase(JoinPoint joinPoint, Product product){
    logger.info("===> called after returning {}. Returned {}.",
        joinPoint.getSignature().getName(), product) ;
    product.setDescription(product.getDescription().toUpperCase());
}
```

Using @AfterThrowing

This is invoked only if the instrumented method ends abnormally by throwing an exception. You can capture the exception by adding it to the method call using a *throwing* parameter.

Let's add the following to our `ProductController` class to simulate an exception. A call to the `/products-exception` endpoint will always throw an `IOException`.

```
@GetMapping("/products-exception")
public Collection<Product> listProductsWithException() throws IOException {
    throw new IOException("An IOException to handle");
}
```

Now add the following pointcut to your `LoggingAspect1` class:

```
@AfterThrowing(value = "execution(public * com.wiley.realworldjava.aop.product."
    + "ProductController.listProductsWithException())", throwing = "cause")
public void logAfterReturning(JoinPoint joinPoint, Throwable cause){
    logger.info("===> called after throwing {}. Throwing:{}",
        joinPoint.getSignature().toShortString(),cause) ;
}
```

In this case, we captured the `Throwable` cause in the method. Using Postman, let's make a `GET` call to our new endpoint.

```
localhost:8081/products-exception
```

You will find the following in the logs, just before the stack trace:

```
===> called after throwing ProductController.listProductsWithException().
    Throwing: java.io.IOException: An IOException to handle
```

Using @After

`@After` is similar to the `@AfterReturning` and `@AfterThrowing`, except you won't have access to the result or any thrown exception. It is useful for things like general end of method cleanup, logging, or observability capture.

Using @Around

`@Around` provides more granular access to the instrumented method. With `@Around`, you can instrument before and after the method call, modify any results, handle or modify any exceptions, and even bypass the target call altogether.

A useful use case for this would be to provide caching for a method. Imagine we have a method whose results are lazy-loaded (which means the results are computed on the first invocation and are saved in a cache for future calls). An example would be an application that speaks to several databases, and we want to lazy-load the connection information, which doesn't change.

Let's add to our `ProductController` a new `POST` endpoint called `/connection`.

```
@PostMapping("/connection")
public Connection getDbConnection(@RequestBody Properties config)
   throws SQLException, ClassNotFoundException {

   Connection connection = createDBConnection(config.getProperty("driver"),
      config.getProperty("url"), config.getProperty("username"),
      config.getProperty("password"));

   return connection;
}
```

The idea is that we call this endpoint with a JSON payload like the following, containing connection information:

```
{
    "driver": "com.mysql.cj.jdbc.Driver",
    "url":"jdbc:mysql://localhost:3306/products",
    "username":"vgrazi",
    "password":"pa55w0rd"
}
```

The raw implementation would create a new connection for each call, which would be a resource-intensive design.

Let's correct that with AOP, using an `@Around` advice, to lazy-load the appropriate connection on the first invocation of this method for each set of `Properties` and then save it in a cache for subsequent calls.

```
 1: private final Map<String, Connection> connectionCache = new HashMap<>();
 2:
 3: @Around("execution(public java.sql.Connection com.wiley.realworldjava.aop."
 4:     +  "product.ProductController.getDbConnection(java.util.Properties))")
 5: public Connection cacheConnection(ProceedingJoinPoint joinPoint)
 6:    throws Throwable {
 7:    Object[] args = joinPoint.getArgs();
 8:    Properties properties = (Properties) args[0];
 9:    Connection connection = connectionCache.get(properties.
   getProperty("database"));
10:    if(connection==null) {
11:       logger.info("Nothing cached. Aspect proceeds with the original call!");
12:       try {
13:          connection = (Connection) joinPoint.proceed();
14:          logger.info("Aspect caches the connection for future calls");
15:          connectionCache.put(
16:                properties.getProperty("database"), connection);
17:       } catch(Throwable throwable) {
18:         logger.error("cacheConnection advice threw exception", throwable);
19:         throw throwable;
20:      }
21:   }
22:   else {
23:      logger.info("Aspect got connection from cache!");
24:   }
25:   return connection;
26: }
```

In line 1 we are creating a local cache to be used by our aspect. Note that this instance is unknown to our `ProductController`.

In line 3 we are creating a standard join point expression for our `getDBConnection` method. Note that we used the `@Around` advice. In the method signature on line 5, we return the same type as the target method call, in this case `Connection`. Also note that we replaced the usual `JoinPoint` instance with a `ProceedingJoinPoint`. This is always required for `@Around` so that we can call the `proceed` method to invoke the target method.

In line 8 we are intercepting the call arguments, which we will use to check for an instance in our cache, which we do in line 9.

In line 10 we found the cache was missing the connection, so in line 13 we call the target method by calling `ProceedingJoinPoint.proceed()`. This invokes the target method, which creates a new connection instance.

We cache that new instance in line 15. Note that any exceptions thrown by the target method call will be thrown by the `joinPoint.proceed()` call, which we catch in line 17 and throw back to the caller in line 19.

In line 23 we log a message that a connection was found, so we bypass the actual method call completely and just return that cached instance.

At this point a word of caution is in order. AOP is magical, and it's perfect for handling cases outside of the developers' area of concern, such as capturing observability metrics or logging to a distributed log.

But you should use it with care. If your development team is not aware of it, they could waste frustrating development cycles trying to understand why their product descriptions are being converted to uppercase, why their breakpoints are not being hit, or why their method calls are pulling from the cache rather than running their implementation!

Using @Pointcut

This would be a good time to talk about reuse. Imagine if you wanted to create a `@Before` advice for logging, an `@After` advice to capture time, and an `@Around` advice for caching. You would have to repeat the execution pointcut three times! And heaven forbid, if you want to make a slight change in the pointcut, you would need to remember all the places to make the change. Enter the `@Pointcut` annotation. `@Pointcut` allows you to give a short name to your pointcut expression and then use that name in place of the pointcut expression.

If you are following along in the code, you will notice we have been using the class `LoggingAspect1`. To continue the examples, comment out the `@Aspect` advice on line 16 of `LoggingAspect1`.

```
16: //@Aspect
17: @Component
18: public class LoggingAspect1 {
19:     private final Logger logger = LoggerFactory.getLogger(LoggingAspect1.class);
```

Then uncomment the `@Aspect` advice in line 15 of `LoggingAspect2`.

```
15: @Aspect
16: @Component
17: public class LoggingAspect2 {
```

This commenting/uncommenting will replace the AOP proxy from `LoggingAspect1` with the revised version in `LoggingAspect2` so you can continue to follow along. The following code lines refer to `LoggingAspect2`.

Let's revisit our pointcut expression from the earlier `@AfterReturning` section.

The expression was as follows:

```
@AfterReturning(value = "execution(public * com.wiley.realworldjava.aop.product."
"ProductController.addProduct(com.wiley.realworldjava.aop.product.Product))")
)
public void logAfterReturning(JoinPoint joinPoint, Product product){
   System.out.println("=============> called after returning " +
     joinPoint.getSignature().getName());
}
```

You can use the `@Pointcut` annotation to annotate a method that defines the execution and then refer to that method wherever it is needed, in place of the actual `execution` pointcut.

The paradigm is as follows: instead of specifying the execution in the advice annotation, specify the execution on an empty method. The method is not executed, but it is still important, because that method name can now be used instead of the explicit execution expression.

In the following example, the original `execution` expression is moved to the `addProductPointcut` method.

So, the previous snippet would be changed to the following equivalently named pointcut:

```
// Define an empty pointcut method named "addProductPointcut"
@Pointcut(value = "execution(public * com.wiley.realworldjava.aop.product."
   + "ProductController.addProduct(com.wiley.realworldjava.aop.product.Product))")
public void addProductPointcut() {}

// Our advice method (@AfterReturning) can now refer to the empty pointcut method,
// instead of inlining the execution
@AfterReturning(value = "addProductPointcut()", returning = "product")
public void logAfterReturning(JoinPoint joinPoint, Product product){
    . . .
}
```

The following REST endpoint will trigger the advice:

```
@PostMapping("/product")
public Product addProduct(@RequestBody Product product) {
   logger.info("Adding product {}", product);
   productMap.put(product.getStyleNum(), product);
   return product;
}
```

Now you can reuse that pointcut to redefine your `@AfterThrowing` and `@After` advice.

```
@AfterReturning(value = "addProductPointcut()", returning = "product")
public void logAfterReturningWithReturningValue(JoinPoint joinPoint,
   Product product) {

   logger.info("=====> called after returning {}  returned:{}",
     joinPoint.getSignature().getName(), product);
}

@AfterThrowing(value = "addProductPointcut()", throwing = "cause")
public void logAfterReturningWithException(JoinPoint joinPoint, Throwable cause) {
   logger.info("=====> called after throwing {}. Throwing:",
      joinPoint.getSignature().toShortString(), cause);
}
```

Combining Pointcuts

Now that you know that pointcuts can be named, you can do some interesting things by combining pointcuts using `&&` (AND), `||` (OR), and `!` (NOT) operators.

So, let's say you have defined the methods `pointcutA()` and `pointcutB()`. You are able to combine them into a single advice, which will be invoked if either `pointcutA()` or `pointcutB()` is matched by using the `||` (OR) operator.

For example:

```
@Pointcut(pointcutA() || pointcutB())
public void combinedOrPointcut() {
    // Invoked if either pointcutA() or pointcutB() are matched
}
```

Similarly, you can use the && (AND) operator to be invoked only when both pointcuts are matched.

```
@Pointcut(pointcutA() && pointcutB())
public void combinedAndPointcut() {
    // Invoked if both pointcutA() and pointcutB() are matched
}
```

Or you can invoke `pointcutA()` except when `pointcutB()` is matched.

```
@Pointcut(pointcutA() && !pointcutB())
public void NotPointcut() {
    // Invoked if both pointcutA() and pointcutB() are matched
}
```

Annotation-Based Pointcuts

Have you ever wondered how the Spring "automagic" configuration works? From what you have learned, you can surmise that products like Spring, Lombok, JCache, and many other frameworks are using AOP behind the scenes. Yet you never see such pointcut expressions in these applications. Instead, they use @ annotations of their own. How can we do that?

The answer is that you can create annotations using the `@annotation` pointcut.

For example, let's say we want to redo our caching advice to be reusable by any call that cares to be cached. Let's create a new annotation interface called `@Cache`. The first step is to create the annotation class.

```
import java.lang.annotation.ElementType;
import java.lang.annotation.Retention;
import java.lang.annotation.RetentionPolicy;
import java.lang.annotation.Target;

@Target(ElementType.METHOD)
@Retention(RetentionPolicy.RUNTIME)
public @interface Cache {
}
```

Next, associate the new `@Cache` annotation with a pointcut.

```
@Pointcut("@annotation(com.wiley.realworldjava.aop.Cache)")
public void cacheAnnotationMethod(){
}
```

Then, provide an advice to be invoked.

```
@Around("cacheAnnotationMethod()")
public Object cacheMethodResults(ProceedingJoinPoint joinPoint) throws Throwable {
   // Each unique combination of args will be cached separately.
   // Create a MultiKey representing the args
   // (MultiKey lets you define keys with arbitrary numbers of components):
   Object[] args = joinPoint.getArgs();
   Object[] argsLong = new Object[args.length + 1];
   System.arraycopy(args, 0, argsLong, 1, args.length);
```

```
        // we want to cache each different method separately,
        // so add the method and signature to the MultiKey as the first element of the array:
        argsLong[0] = joinPoint.toLongString();
        MultiKey key = new MultiKey(argsLong);

        Object result = methodCache.get(key);
        if(result==null) {
            logger.info("Nothing cached. Aspect proceeds with the original call!");
            try {
                result = joinPoint.proceed();
                logger.info("Aspect caches the connection for future calls");
                methodCache.put(key, result);
            } catch(Throwable throwable) {
                throw throwable;
            }
        }
        else {
            logger.info("Aspect got connection from cache!");
        }
        return result;
    }

    // and create the Map to capture cached results
    private final Map<String, Object> methodCache = new HashMap<>();
```

Finally, apply the new annotation anytime you want it invoked.

```
    @Cache
    @PostMapping("/connection")
    public Connection getDbConnection(@RequestBody Properties config)
        throws SQLException, ClassNotFoundException {
        Connection connection = createDBConnection(config.getProperty("driver"),
        config.getProperty("url"), config.getProperty("username"),
        config.getProperty("password"));
        return connection;
    }
```

Now calls to `getDbConnection()` will create a new connection on the first call and return the cached version in subsequent calls.

Try it using the following Postman `POST` body:

```
    {
        "driver": "com.mysql.cj.jdbc.Driver",
        "url":"jdbc:mysql://localhost:3306/products",
        "username":"vgrazi",
        "password":"pa55w0rd"
    }
```

Let's look at one more common example of `@Around`. We will define an annotation called `@Timing`, which will log the execution time of method calls that are annotated with `@Timing`.

```
    @Pointcut("@annotation(com.wiley.realworldjava.aop.aspects.Timing)")
    public void timingAnnotationMethod(){
    }
```

```
@Around("timingAnnotationMethod()")
public Object cacheTimingResults(ProceedingJoinPoint joinPoint) throws Throwable {
   // grab the start time
   long start = System.currentTimeMillis();
   // execute the target method...
   Object result = joinPoint.proceed();
   // grab the end time
   long end = System.currentTimeMillis();
   // log the timing
   logger.info(">>>> Call to {} took {} ms.", joinPoint.toString(), end-start);
   // return the call result
   return result;
}
```

Note that this method returns a result. What if it is applied to a `void` method? The answer is that the `joinPoint.proceed()` invocation will return `null`, and the final return result call will return `null`, which will be ignored by the caller since they are expecting a `void` return.

FURTHER REFERENCES

- `https://docs.spring.io/spring-framework/reference/core/aop.html`

  Complete documentation for Spring AOP
- `https://eclipse.dev/aspectj`

  Documentation for AspectJ, a broader aspects framework that works for even non-Spring projects

SUMMARY

The following are the key takeaways from the chapter:

- Aspects allow you to specify a pointcut that describes which methods to intercept and what action to take when intercepting method calls.
- A join point is where the code is inserted.
- Pointcuts can be named for reuse and can be combined using `&&`, `||`, and `!`.
- The major advice types are `@After`, `@AfterReturning`, `@AfterThrowing`, `@Around`, and `@Pointcut`.

12

Monitoring Your Applications: Observability in the Java Ecosystem

WHAT'S IN THIS CHAPTER?

- Introducing Observability
- Getting Started with Prometheus
- Adding Alert Manager
- Dashboarding with Grafana
- Logging and Tracing

In production systems, things go wrong. When they do, you want to know about it as early as possible. . .and even earlier! Monitoring your application is crucial for ensuring a pleasant and beneficial experience for your users. You need visibility into your application's inner workings to understand what's happening, and certain tools are designed to provide that visibility.

In this chapter, we'll explore some popular open-source tools in the observability space.

CODE DOWNLOADS FOR THIS CHAPTER

The source code for this chapter is available on the book page at `www.wiley.com`. Click the Downloads link. You can also find the code at `https://github.com/realworldjava/Ch12-Observability`. See the `README.md` file in that repository for details.

INTRODUCING OBSERVABILITY

Monitoring is just one component of "observability." What is observability? Ask 10 people and you'll get 12 different answers. To clarify, let's break it down. Observability involves the following key components:

- **Metrics:** Named units of data used to quantify events, monitor system performance, detect anomalies, and forecast future trends and issues
- **Alerting:** Automated notifications to the appropriate teams when predefined thresholds are breached, enabling rapid response to incidents
- **Dashboarding:** Real-time visualization of metrics, logs, and traces through customizable dashboards, allowing teams to monitor system health and make data-driven decisions quickly
- **Logging:** Centralized event snapshots in the form of detailed log messages, providing visibility and aiding in troubleshooting
- **Tracing:** Consolidated logging and responses using a unified "trace-id" to track the flow of a request across multiple services, enabling reliability engineers to identify failures, anomalies, or bottlenecks more effectively

For collecting metrics, there are two approaches: pushing and scraping. *Pushing* means that the applications you are monitoring are configured to send periodic metrics to a database, usually a time-series database such as Graphite. *Scraping* is a pull technique where the monitoring operation is configured to interrogate specific endpoints for metrics, which it saves in a database.

If you already have access to your enterprise Prometheus instance, you can run queries there, but we strongly recommend you install Prometheus yourself so that you can configure and experiment with it as you like.

GETTING STARTED WITH PROMETHEUS

In this chapter, we will cover Prometheus, which uses the scraping technique. Enterprise frameworks and infrastructure can be easily configured to provide Prometheus scrape endpoints. For example, Spring Boot applications will automatically expose a scrape endpoint, just by including the actuator and micrometer dependencies, which we will see. For applications and infrastructure that don't generate metrics, there are custom node exporters that will query the application and expose key metrics in the format required by Prometheus scrapers.

Starting the Test Application

The repository for this chapter contains a Spring Boot test application, `Ch12ObservabilityApplication`, which is similar to the application in Chapter 6, "Getting to Know the Spring Framework." To start the application, run the following:

```
mvn clean verify
java -jar target/observability-0.0.1-SNAPSHOT.jar
```

You can verify that it is running by going to this URL:

```
http://localhost:8081/mtg/payment?principal=100000&years=30&interest=6.5
```

The POM for this application has the `micrometer-registry-prometheus` dependency. This dependency automatically exposes the following endpoint:

```
http://localhost:8081/actuator/prometheus
```

Go to this URL to see the full list of metrics exposed to Prometheus from our application.

Installing the Exporter

Prometheus has various exporters, plugins that work with your applications, middleware, and infrastructure, to expose relevant metrics for Prometheus to scrape. Popular examples of this are Node Exporter for Linux/Mac systems, and Windows Exporter for Windows. When working on an enterprise application, you will want to run the exporter on the computer/server that you want to monitor, which will generally not be the same instance that is running Prometheus itself.

> **TIP** *Node exporters have no relation to the Node.js framework.* Node *is a Linux word that refers to the servers and containers that host your Linux-based applications.*

These exporters are configured to monitor nodes, from which they capture metrics and expose them in a format that Prometheus can scrape. There are hundreds of such metrics, including CPU utilization, disk usage, memory consumption, and so forth.

While you can install directly on your computer, we are using a Docker container in this chapter to ensure a consistent setup for readers. If you'd like a refresher on using Docker, see the Jenkins section of Chapter 4, "Automating Your CI/CD Builds with Maven, Gradle, and Jenkins."

In this section we will set up Node Exporter using Docker with a Linux image. After starting Docker Desktop, you can pull the image like so:

```
docker pull prom/node-exporter
```

That is not strictly required though. The `run` command will pull the image if it is not already there. To run the node exporter container, call the following:

```
docker run --name=node_exporter -p 9100:9100 prom/node-exporter
```

> **TIP** *Remember from Chapter 4 that you use the* `run` *command only once, to create the container. After the first time, you will start Prometheus by calling* `docker start node-exporter` *instead, to run the existing container instance.*

This command launches the node exporter using its defaults. (You can change these with flags. Find the full list of flags in the "Further References" section. Search for "Flags.")

Node Exporter runs by default on port 9100. To verify that the exporter is running, browse to `http://localhost:9100`. You'll see a web page that includes the version number, like this:

```
Version: (version=1.8.2, branch=HEAD,
revision=f1e0e8360aa60b6cb5e5cc1560bed348fc2c1895)
```

The URL `http://localhost:9100/metrics` exposes all the metrics being exported by the exporter. If this looks like a lot of gibberish, don't worry; that is Prometheus scrape format, and we will make sense of it shortly.

Installing Prometheus

The Prometheus binary keeps track of the metrics and includes a UI for queries.

First, run the following:

```
docker pull prom/prometheus
```

Copy the `prometheus.yml` file from the root of Chapter 12 repository into your working directory. We will explain this file in the next section. Run the following on Windows:

```
docker run --name prometheus -p 9090:9090
-v .\prometheus.yml:/etc/prometheus/prometheus.yml prom/prometheus
```

or the corresponding command for Mac/Linux:

```
docker run --name prometheus -p 9090:9090
-v ./prometheus.yml:/etc/prometheus/prometheus.yml prom/prometheus
```

> **TIP** *If you add the* `-d` *flag, Docker runs in the background.*

The Docker `-v` flag stands for volume. It allows you to map a Docker file or directory from your local computer into the Docker container. In this case, that allows you to supply your own `prometheus.yml` file. We copied this from the Prometheus distribution, with some modifications.

Prometheus runs by default on port 9090. You can browse to `http://localhost:9090` to confirm Prometheus started correctly. As you might imagine, after the initial start, you run `docker start prometheus` instead.

INSTALLING WITHOUT DOCKER

If you want to install directly, go to the Prometheus download site (`https://prometheus.io/download`). Be sure to choose the right OS and processor type, keeping in mind that Darwin is Mac.

When you run Node Exporter in Docker, you will primarily be exporting metrics from the container, not from the host operating system. That is sufficient for our demonstration purposes, but if you want to generate the actual host metrics, you will need to run it directly on the host. Node Exporter is available on the Prometheus download page mentioned earlier. Note that to monitor a Windows application, you need to use Windows Exporter instead of Node Exporter. That is available in the GitHub repository; see the "Further References" section.

Note that Windows Exporter uses port 9182 by default, while Node Exporter defaults to port 9100.

Configuring a Scrape

In the previous section, you referenced the YAML configuration file `prometheus.yml`. (For more about YAML, see the Appendix). The file configures your Prometheus to recognize your exporters and other applications so that it knows to scrape them.

Under `scrape_configs` in `prometheus.yml` you can see the following code, as supplied by Prometheus. We added the bold lines.

```
scrape_configs:
    # The job name is added as a label `job=<job_name>`
    # to any timeseries scraped from this config.
    - job_name: "prometheus"
```

```
25:
26:       # metrics_path defaults to '/metrics'
27:       # scheme defaults to 'http'.
28:
29:       static_configs:
30:         - targets: ["localhost:9090"]
31:
32:     - job_name: "node_exporter"
33:       static_configs:
34:         - targets: ["host.docker.internal:9100" ]
35:
36:
37:     - job_name: "mtg-calc"
38:       static_configs:
39:         - targets: ["host.docker.internal:8081" ]
40:       metrics_path: '/actuator/prometheus'
```

The first scrape config job on line 24 is named `prometheus`. Prometheus is self-aware, so it exports its own metrics, and this is where we configure Prometheus to scrape itself.

Lines 32–34 configure Prometheus to scrape the `node_exporter`, and lines 37–40 tell it to scrape the Spring Boot application. Lines 34 and 39 use `host.docker.internal`, which is how Docker refers to the host machine. Otherwise, it would look for the endpoint internally in the Prometheus container.

Let's explore the Prometheus interface. From a browser window launch the Prometheus web interface at `http://localhost:9090`. Choose Status ➪ Configuration to see all the scrapes configured in this instance, as shown in Figure 12.1. Notice both job names that we configured in the previous YAML are in this screenshot.

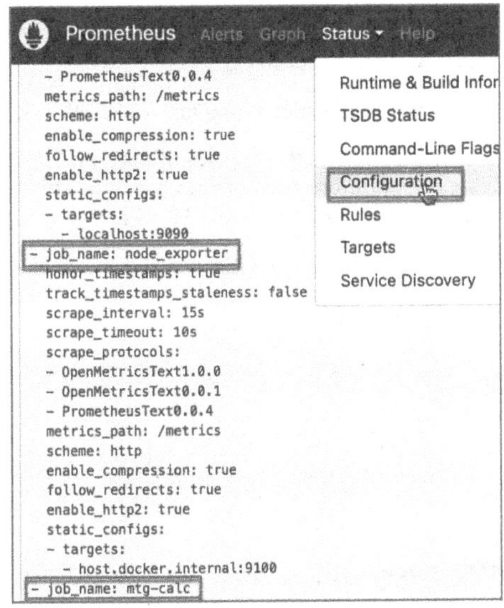

FIGURE 12.1: Prometheus configuration tab

Choose Status ➪ Targets to see the health of the scraped targets, as shown in Figure 12.2.

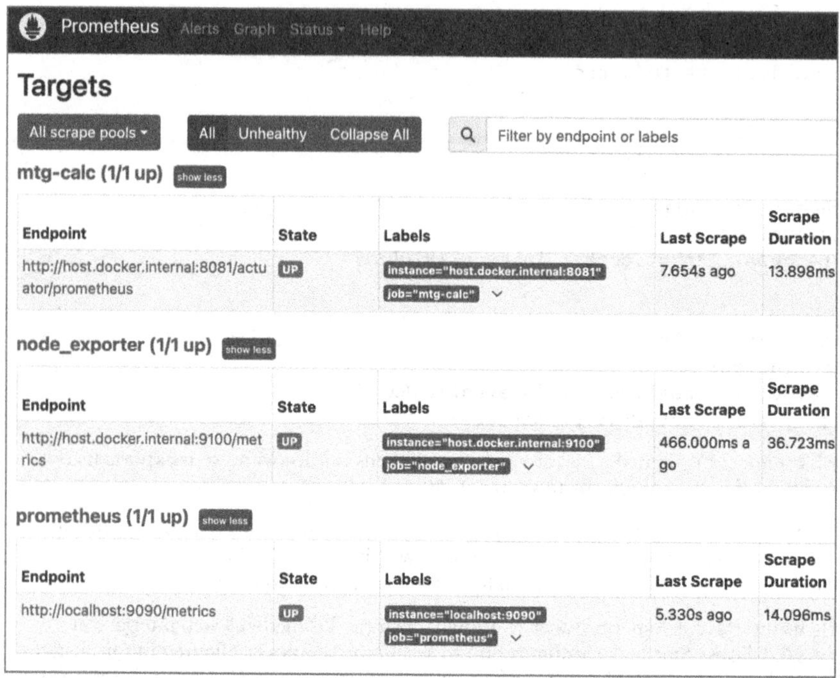

FIGURE 12.2: Prometheus targets' tab

Introducing PromQL: The Prometheus Query Language

The Prometheus persistence layer is a time-series database, which you can query using a language called PromQL.

The Prometheus Query Language (PromQL) lets users select, slice, and dice time-series metrics in real time. Results can be viewed as tabular data or as a graph in Prometheus's expression browser, or they can be displayed in a dashboarding tool like Grafana. They can also be queried by external systems via the HTTP API.

When you think about infrastructure metrics, several might come to mind, for example CPU utilization, *available* disk bytes, total disk bytes, and so forth. You might be surprised to learn that there are hundreds of such metrics, with a strange mix of exotic names, including the following:

- `node_cpu_seconds_total`
- `prometheus_engine_query_duration_seconds`
- `go_gc_cycles_total_gc_cycles_total`

The names generally conform to the following format:

- **Prefix:** Indicates the application or entity name, for example, `node`
- **Metric descriptive name:** For example, `cpu`, `gc` (garbage collections), and so forth
- **Suffix:** Unit of measure (in plural), for example `seconds`, `time`, `cycles`, and so forth
- **Aggregate metrics:** Will have an additional suffix, for example, `total`, `count`, and so forth

Let's get the feel by running some queries. Go back to the Prometheus query window, enter `node_cpu_seconds_total` in the search box, and hit Execute. You should see something like Figure 12.3.

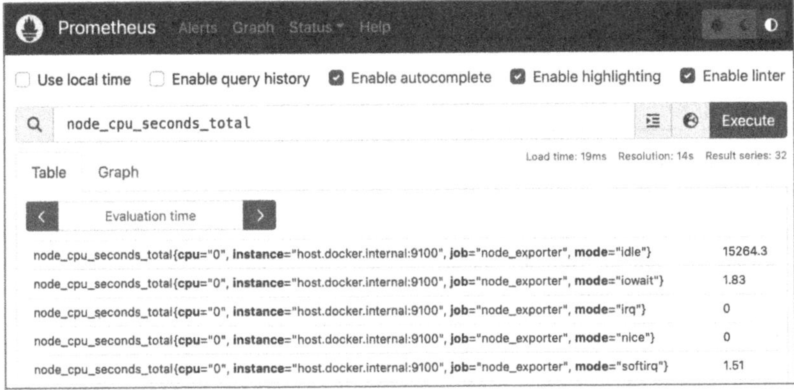

FIGURE 12.3: Querying for a single metric

The result set contains a new line for each mode associated with the query.

> **NOTE** *The metrics are operating system-specific. For example, Windows would use* `windows_cpu_time_total`. *Since the Docker container is a Linux one, you get to use* `node_cpu_seconds_total` *regardless of which operating system your machine happens to be.*

Notice that each metric is annotated with labels in brackets. You can query for specific labels by appending them to the metric name between brackets. To enter multiple labels, specify them as a comma-separated list of key="value" pairs between the squiggly brackets. For example, let's limit our query to just the "idle" CPU time, by adding the label `{mode="idle"}` to our metric. Click Add Panel to start a new query panel below the first one and enter the following:

```
node_cpu_seconds_total{mode="idle"}
```

The result is something like Figure 12.4. By comparing that to Figure 12.3, you can see how now we are just displaying the `mode="idle"` labels.

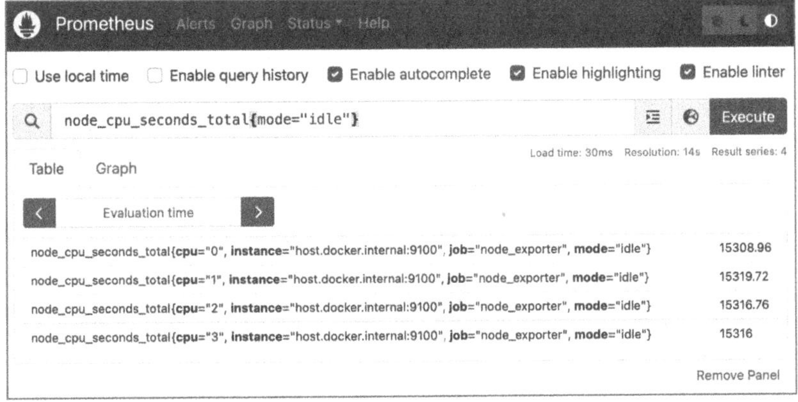

FIGURE 12.4: Specifying a label

This is how you can query any metric in Prometheus. If you need help, you can type a few characters and the auto-complete will guide you.

REMOVING LONG QUERIES

Every metric has an implicit label called `__name__` that contains the name of the metric. You can use this fact to get a full list of metric names by entering the query `{__name__=~".*_.*"}`. This will produce a very long list.

If you added multiple query panels to a single page, you'll notice Prometheus does not provide a way to remove a query panel, so we suggest you start a new Prometheus window for this query by starting a new browser tab and entering the URL `localhost:9090` again and entering the new query there.

Continuing from the `node_cpu_seconds_total{mode="idle"}` query in Figure 12.4, click the Graph button just below your query to see a graph of CPU idle time, as in Figure 12.5.

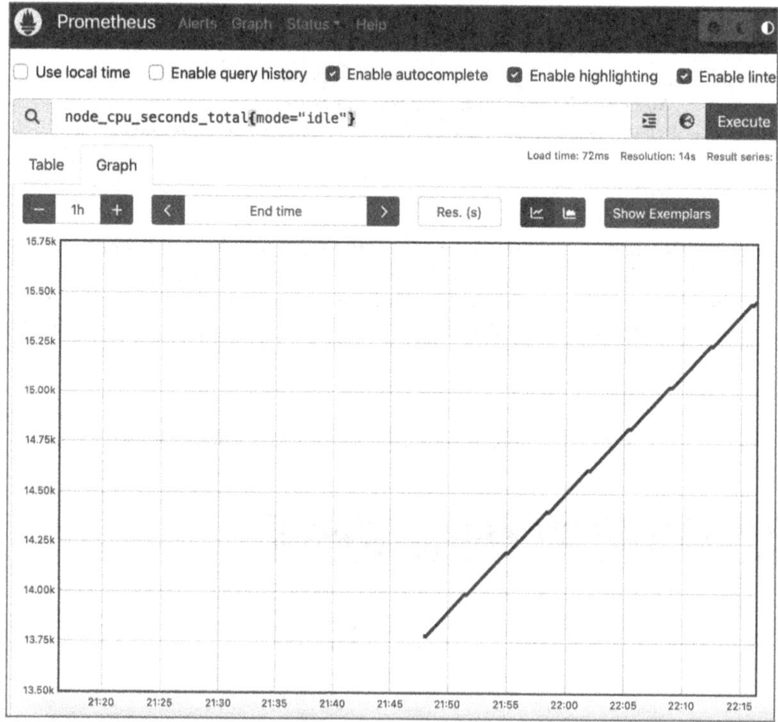

FIGURE 12.5: Displaying a graph of CPU idle time

An *instance vector* (a list of every label of the metric at a given time, in this case `node_cpu_seconds_total`) appears below the graph. You can deselect and reselect instances by clicking them in the list. By default, Prometheus graphs the last hour, but you can change that by clicking the – and + surrounding the time selector above the graph on the left side.

Prometheus supports a wide range of functions, including aggregation functions, rate calculations, value adjustments, and so forth.

For example, we can use the metric `node_cpu_seconds_total{mode="idle"}` to calculate CPU utilization. CPU utilization in a time window is defined as the percentage of time that the CPU is busy (aka not idle) in that time window.

The `rate` function calculates the per-second rate of change of a *range vector* within a specified time window. A range vector is essentially a sequence of instance vectors over a time range. In mathematical terms, it is a matrix. For example, `node_cpu_seconds_total{mode="idle"}[5m]` is a range vector that represents all the instance vectors within the last 5 minutes.

`rate(node_cpu_seconds_total{mode="idle"}[5m])` calculates the rate of change of idle time between the start and end of each five-minute window. This represents the idle time fraction, which can never be more than 1, indicating the CPU was completely idle. Subtracting that result from 1 returns the CPU utilization. Let's multiply that by 100 to convert to percent utilization, producing the following formula:

```
(1-rate(node_cpu_seconds_total{mode="idle"}[5m]))*100
```

WORKING WITH OFFSETS

You can use an offset to turn back the clock. For example, let's say we left our laptop off for five hours; we can set an offset of `5h` to tell Prometheus to run the query as if it were executed five hours ago:

```
(1-rate(node_cpu_seconds_total{mode="idle"}[5m] offset 5h))*100
```

This produces the graph of CPU utilization per logical core, as shown in Figure 12.6. This laptop has four cores, and you can see the utilization of each by clicking the ones you want to show and clicking off the rest.

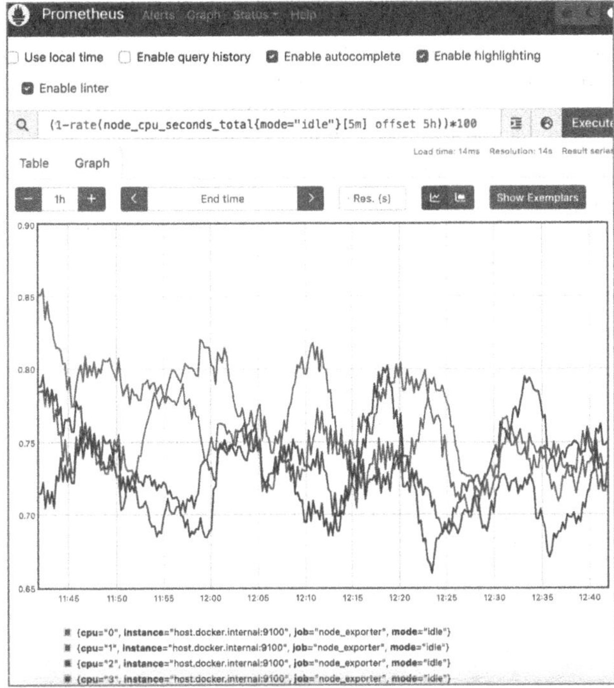

FIGURE 12.6: Graphing CPU utilization per core

To get an average across all CPUs, use the aggregate function `avg`. Aggregate functions aggregate all the instance vectors at each point in time. So, the `avg` function produces the average across all cores.

```
(1 - avg(rate(node_cpu_seconds_total{mode="idle"}[5m])))*100
```

You can see the graph in Figure 12.7 is similar to Figure 12.6, except that there is only one trendline, showing the average CPU utilization over all cores.

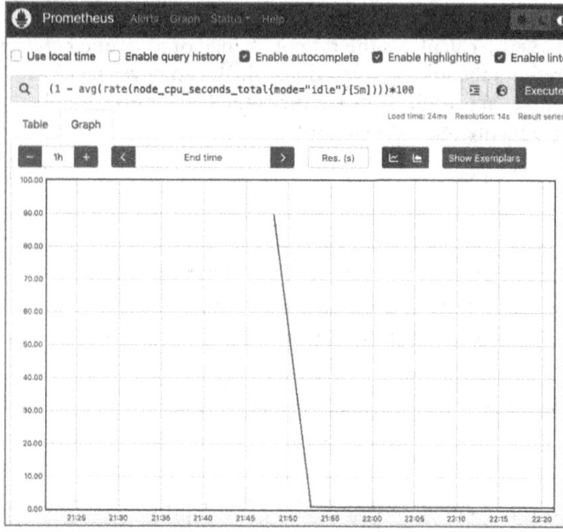

FIGURE 12.7: CPU utilization, average over all cores

In each of these cases, we showed a graph of an instance vector over time. If you come back to the Table tab, you will see the latest values for each instance in the vector. You can change that to a range vector by specifying the range, for example `node_cpu_seconds_total{mode="idle"}[5m]` displays the CPU idle time for each core, for every 15 seconds (Prometheus default) in the specified range, in this case five minutes, as shown in Figure 12.8.

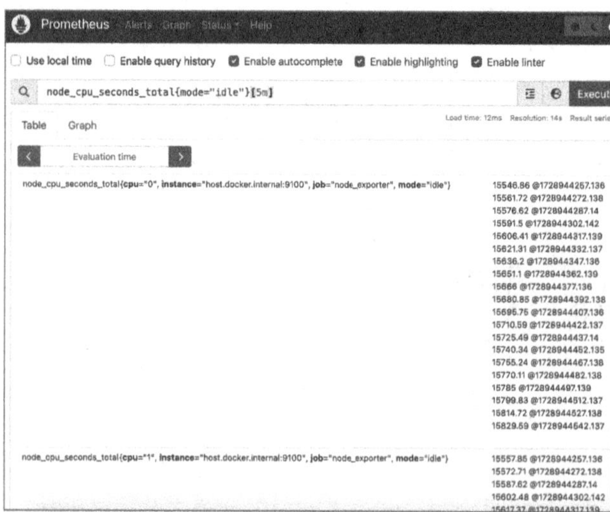

FIGURE 12.8: CPU range vector

We have already seen range vector units of m and h. The full set of range vector units is as follows:

- **ms:** Milliseconds
- **s:** Seconds
- **m:** Minutes
- **h:** Hours
- **d:** Days
- **w:** Weeks
- **y:** Years

Prometheus will display only a graph of instance vectors but not for range vectors. We have already seen some arithmetic operators such as `-` and `*`. The full list of arithmetic operators is as follows:

- +: Addition
- -: Subtraction
- *: Multiplication
- /: Division
- %: Modulus
- ^: Power

You can also use binary operators:

- `==`: Equal
- `!=`: Not equal
- `>`: Greater than
- `<`: Less than
- `>=`: Greater than or equal
- `<=`: Less than or equal

We saw the aggregation function `avg`. The following are the other aggregation functions:

- **avg:** The average over the values of an instance vector.
- **count:** The count of members of an instance vector.
- **max:** The maximum value of an instance vector.
- **min:** The minimum value of an instance vector.
- **sum:** The sum of all values of an instance vector.
- **count_values:** Counts the number of values for each value of the provided label. For example, `count_values("code", prometheus_http_requests_total)` provides the number of HTTP requests for each value of the label "code."

- **topk:** Specifies how many of the top values of an instance vector to retail. For example, to retain three: `topk(3, cpu_seconds_total)`.
- **bottomk:** Specifies how many of the values of an instance vector to retain. For example, to retain three: `bottomk(3, cpu_seconds_total)`.
- **stddev:** The standard deviation of the range vector.
- **stdvar:** The standard variance (or simply variance) of the range vector.

There is a lot more, but this should provide a flavor for the power of the PromQL language. We recommend you experiment and check the Prometheus documentation for more information.

Using Prometheus HTTP APIs

You can query Prometheus from your applications by calling the REST endpoints, all HTTP GET requests. We will provide examples of the most common ones, which you can call from your browser to hit your local Prometheus installation.

Doing a query returns the values for an instance vector. For example, to get the values of the up metric for all instances, enter `http://localhost:9090/api/v1/query?query=up`.

Like a query, a query range accepts a start and end date-time and returns all values within that range. For example: `http://localhost:9090/api/v1/query_range?query=up&start=2024-09-28T00:00:00Z&end=2024-09-30T00:00:00Z&step=60m`. Remember to change the start and end dates so the current date is included. Sample output starts with this:


```
{"status":"success","data":{"resultType":"matrix",
"result":[{"metric":{"__name__":"up","instance":
"host.docker.internal:8081","job":"mtg-calc"},"values":[[1728943200,"1"]]}
```


Notice that Prometheus returns the times as Unix timestamps (aka epoch time, or the number of milliseconds since January 1, 1970, until now). You can specify the time ranges in your queries using the same Unix format, or you can use ISO 8601 format (`yyyy-MM-ddThh:mm:ssZ`), as we have done. "Z" represents UTC. To use a different time zone, specify the offset. For example, for EDT you might use `2024-09-28T00:00:00-04:00`.

There are more advanced calls not just for querying metrics but for getting labels, targets, and so forth, so for more information. consult the documentation.

Micrometer and Actuator

In our sample project. we included Micrometer and Spring Boot Actuator, two dependencies for exporting standard metrics from an application. Let's understand the roles they play.

Micrometer is a library that collects and export metrics for various monitoring systems. Out of the box it provides dozens of standard metrics, but it is also customizable, and you can create your own metrics and export them to Prometheus.

Spring Boot Actuator exposes various endpoints to monitor your application, such as `/health`, `/metrics`, `/info`, and so forth. It also integrates with Micrometer to provide more detailed metrics.

By including these tools, you can monitor your application metrics to accumulate metrics and gather insights into your application's performance and health.

Dependencies for Micrometer and Actuator

As you can see in the sample application, these dependencies are included in the POM:

```
<dependency>
   <groupId>io.micrometer</groupId>
   <artifactId>micrometer-core</artifactId>
</dependency>
<dependency>
   <groupId>io.micrometer</groupId>
   <artifactId>micrometer-registry-prometheus</artifactId>
</dependency>
<dependency>
   <groupId>org.springframework.boot</groupId>
   <artifactId>spring-boot-starter-actuator</artifactId>
</dependency>
```

You also need to tell Spring to allow access to these management endpoints, by adding the following properties to `application.properties`:

```
management.endpoints.web.exposure.include=*
management.prometheus.metrics.export.enabled=true
```

Go to `http://localhost:9090`, enter the query **`{job="mtg-calc"}`** to see all the metrics exported by the application.

Creating Custom Metrics

As we have seen, you can simply add the Micrometer and Actuator dependencies to your project to export a wealth of application metrics. But there will be times when you want to capture custom metrics, such as specific hit counts, performance metrics, and so forth.

Let's implement a hit counter for our GET payment endpoint. First, you need the `micrometer-registry-prometheus` dependency we defined earlier.

There are four categories of metrics.

- **Counters:** An increasing metric; grows continuously unless and until it is reset
- **Gauges:** Freely varying metrics
- **Histograms:** Distribution ranges of a metric
- **Summaries:** Counts and totals of a metric

Counting Results with Micrometer Counter

To collect counts, Prometheus uses the Micrometer hit counter. Let's count the number of hits to our GET endpoint:

```
private Counter hitCounter;

public MortgageController(MeterRegistry meterRegistry) {
   this.hitCounter = Counter.builder("payments_get_counter")
      .description("GET payment counter")
      .register(meterRegistry);
                . . .
```

```
59: }

91: @GetMapping("/payment")
92: public ResponseEntity<String> calculateMonthlyPayment(
93:     @RequestParam double principal, @RequestParam int years,
94:     @RequestParam double interest) {
95:     hitCounter.increment();
96:     double payment = mortgageCalculator.payment(
97:         principal, interest, years);
98:     String rval = String.format("Principal:%,.2f<br>Interest: %.2f<br>" +
99:         "Years: %d<br>Monthly Payment:%.2f", principal, interest,
100:         years, payment);
101:     HttpHeaders headers = new HttpHeaders();
102:     headers.add("Request time", "Call for payment at "
103:         + LocalDateTime.now());
104:     return new ResponseEntity<>(rval, headers, HttpStatus.OK);
105: }
```

In lines 38–40 we create `hitCounter`, which is a Micrometer `Counter`. In line 54 we increment the counter.

Make a few calls to this `/payment` endpoint by calling `http://localhost:8081/mtg/payment?principal=100000&years=30&interest=6.1` from your browser (or from Postman or curl, as we did in Chapter 6). Then in Prometheus (`http://localhost:9090`), enter the metric `payments_get_counter_total` and hit Execute to see the growth. Try it in both the Prometheus Table tab and the Graph tab.

Capturing Fluctuating Values

A counter is great for capturing steadily increasing values, but it cannot be used to capture fluctuating values, such as performance metrics like query times, CPU utilization, and so forth. A Micrometer gauge is purpose-built for capturing such fluctuating metrics. Let's create a gauge to capture query time for our POST endpoint.

```
43: Gauge.builder("payments_query_duration_gauge", this::getDuration)
44:     .description("Duration of payment queries in seconds.")
45:     .register(meterRegistry);
```

Like we did with our counter, we call the `builder()` method and pass in the metric name, in this case `payments_query_duration_gauge`, and register it with the meter registry instance. Unlike counters, a gauge is bound to a getter method, in this case `getDuration()`.

When you create a gauge in Micrometer, you must provide a reference to a getter method that returns the current value of the metric. Then every time Prometheus scrapes the application endpoint, it calls this getter method to retrieve the current value.

We will show the full code in the next section, but when we call the `mtg/payments` POST endpoint a few times, it produces the graph in Figure 12.9.

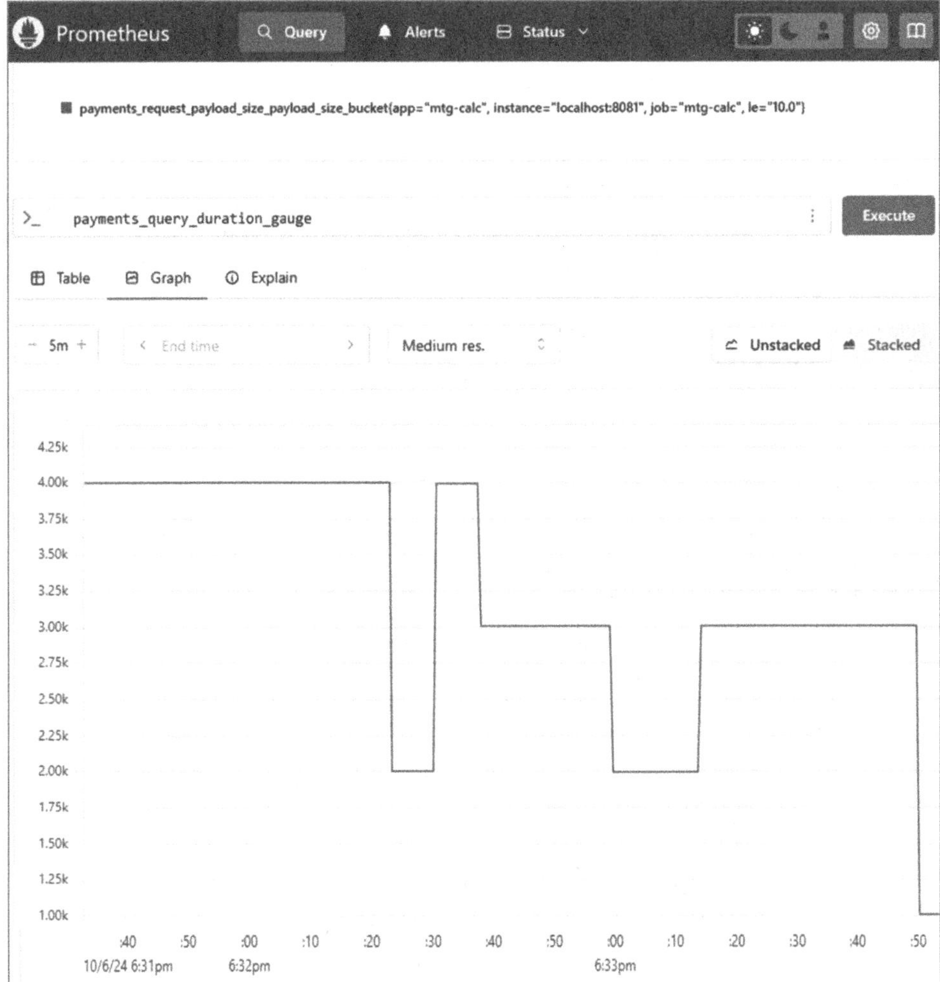

FIGURE 12.9: Graph of a gauge

Bucketing Values with Histograms and Summaries

You can also tell Prometheus to bucket values into ranges that can then be displayed as histograms in visualization tools such as Grafana. You will learn more about Grafana later in this chapter.

Let's use a Micrometer histogram to capture query times. We will use the `Timer` class, which is built for capturing timing histograms.

```
this.histogramTimer = Timer.builder("payments_query_duration_seconds")
    .serviceLevelObjectives(
        Duration.of(500, ChronoUnit.MILLIS),
        Duration.of(1000, ChronoUnit.MILLIS),
        Duration.of(1500, ChronoUnit.MILLIS),
        Duration.of(2000, ChronoUnit.MILLIS),
```

```
53:         Duration.of(3000, ChronoUnit.MILLIS),
54:         Duration.of(5000, ChronoUnit.MILLIS),
55:         Duration.of(10000, ChronoUnit.MILLIS)
56:     ) // Adjust your buckets as needed
57:     .publishPercentileHistogram()
58:     .register(meterRegistry);
```

As usual, we use the `builder()` method in line 47 to create and name our metric, in this case `payments_query_duration_seconds`. In lines 49–55 we set the buckets. Note that Prometheus buckets are cumulative. The first bucket (line 49) says capture everything less than or equal to 500 milliseconds. The second bucket says capture everything less than or equal to 1,000 milliseconds. So, if something takes 400 milliseconds, it will be captured in both buckets.

To record a value into the histogram, pass the value to the record method:

```
histogramTimer.record(delaySecs, TimeUnit.SECONDS);
```

Here is the code:

```
61: @PostMapping("/payment")
62: public ResponseEntity<Response> calculateMonthlyPayment(
63:     @RequestBody List<Mortgage> mortgages)
64:     throws InterruptedException {
65:     LocalDateTime start = LocalDateTime.now();
66:     long time = -1;
67:     try {
68:        logger.info("Called payment POST endpoint " + mortgages);
69:        for(Mortgage mortgage : mortgages) {
70:           double principal = mortgage.getPrincipal();
71:           double rate = mortgage.getInterest();
72:           int years = mortgage.getYears();
73:           double payment = mortgageCalculator.payment(
74:              principal, rate, years);
75:           mortgage.setPayment(payment);
76:        }
77:        long delaySecs = random.nextInt(1, 5);
78:        logger.info("Delay secs:" + delaySecs);
79:        Thread.sleep(Duration.ofSeconds(delaySecs));
80:        HttpHeaders headers = new HttpHeaders();
81:        LocalDateTime end = LocalDateTime.now();
82:        time = start.until(end, ChronoUnit.SECONDS);
83:        headers.add("Response time",  String.valueOf(duration));
84:        return new ResponseEntity<>(new Response(mortgages,
85:           LocalDateTime.now()), headers, HttpStatus.OK);
86:     } finally {
87:        histogramTimer.record(time, TimeUnit.SECONDS);
88:     }
89: }
```

This is the POST request from Chapter 6, with code added for capturing the metrics. In line 65 we get the start time, which we will use to calculate the call time. In lines 77 and 79, we add an artificial delay of 1 to 4 seconds so we can see the histogram in action. In line 82, we capture the call timing, and in line 87, we record it in Micrometer where it will be scraped by Prometheus. Notice that we created the buckets in milliseconds in lines 49–55. We used milliseconds instead of seconds so that we could capture fractions of a second (since the argument must be a whole long integer), but we recorded the metric in seconds (in line 87). Micrometer takes care of the conversions for us.

Call the `mtg/payments` POST endpoint a few times. Prometheus scrapes every 15 seconds by default, so leave that much time between calls. Your Prometheus graph of `payments_query_duration_seconds` should look something Figure 12.10.

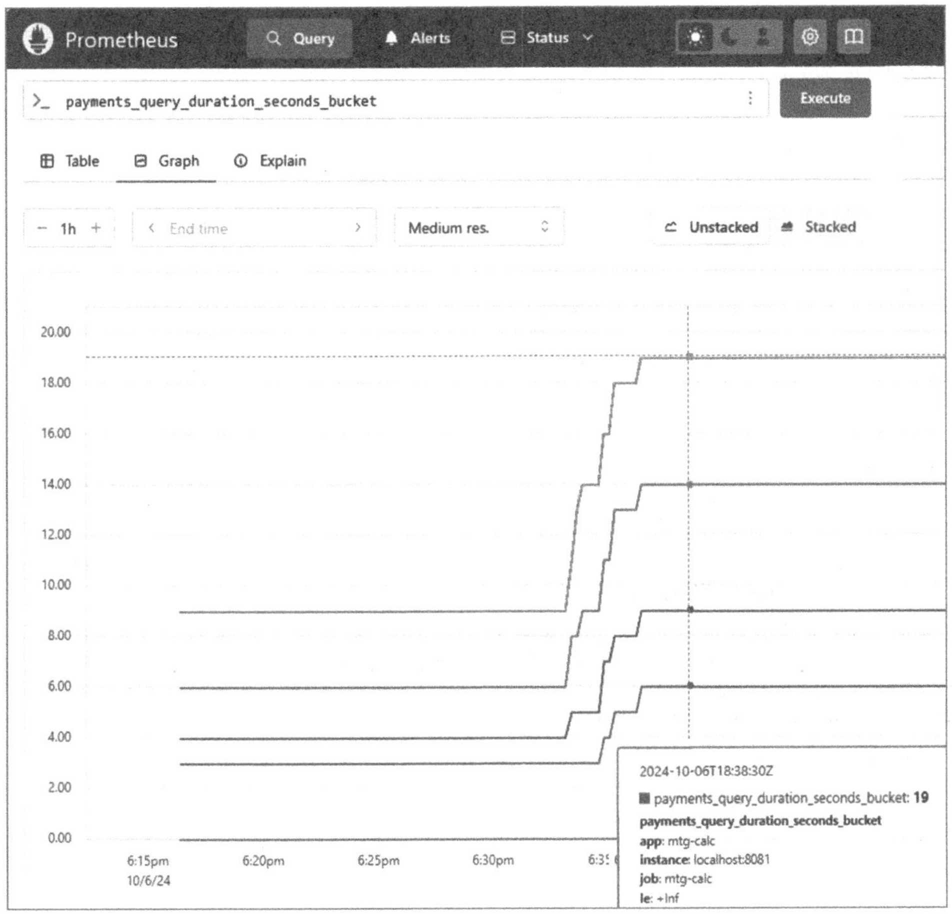

FIGURE 12.10: Graph of a histogram

ADDING ALERT MANAGER

Alert Manager is an independent installation from Prometheus. It integrates with Prometheus to allow you to configure rules for sending notifications when configured metrics breach some specified boundaries in a configurable time interval. Notifications can go via email and/or SMS and/or pretty much anything else using a Web Hook.

First run the following to pull Alert Manager. You'll run it later in the section.

```
docker pull quay.io/prometheus/alertmanager
```

Before you run Alert Manager, you must configure it. The root of the chapter repository has an `alertmanager.yml` file, which looks like the following. Substitute your SMTP server information if you have it.

```
global:
  smtp_smarthost: 'smtp server'              # Email SMTP server
  smtp_from: 'sender@my_company.com'         # Your Email address
  smtp_auth_username: 'username'             # Your username
  smtp_auth_password: 'pa55w0rd'             # SMTP password

route:
  # Default receiver (defined below) to send alerts
  receiver: 'email-receiver'

receivers:
  - name: 'email-receiver'
    email_configs:
      - to: 'notifications@my_company.com'

# Optionally add inhibit rules to prevent firing redundant alerts
inhibit_rules:
  - source_match:
      severity: 'critical'
    target_match:
      severity: 'warning'
    equal: ['instance', 'alertname']
```

The file contains the configuration for sending notifications. The previous example contains the SMTP configuration for the sender and the email address of the receiver.

Next let's create a rule. A realistic example would be when our average CPU utilization rate (across all cores) exceeds 80% for 5 minutes. Drawing on our knowledge of PromQL query, we can compose the query. If the idle CPU metric is `node_cpu_seconds_total{mode="idle"}`, then we need to capture the non-idle time when it is greater than 80%. That is expressed as follows:

```
1 - avg by (instance) (rate(node_cpu_seconds_total{mode="idle"}[5m])) > .8
```

The repository also contains a file called `alert.rules.yml` as follows:

```
groups:
  - name: windows-alerts
    rules:
     - alert: HighCpuUsage
       expr: 1-avg by (instance)(rate(node_cpu_seconds_total{mode="idle"}[5m]))>.8
       for: 5m
      labels:
         severity: critical
       annotations:
         summary: "High CPU usage detected on instance {{ $labels.instance }}"
         description: "CPU usage on instance {{ $labels.instance }} is over 80%"
```

Each rule gets a named alert, with an `expr` entry that defines the rule trigger, and a `for` entry that defines the required duration of the breach. The labels and annotations are used in composing the notification.

We need to tell Prometheus about our Alert Manager and rules, as well as how often to check for breaches. The `prometheus-with-alerts.yml` adds an `alerting` section just below and at the same indent level as `global`.

```
# Alertmanager configuration
global:
  # Set the scrape interval to 15 secs. Default is 1 minute.
  scrape_interval: 15s
  # Evaluate rules every 15 secs. Default is 1 minute.
  evaluation_interval: 15s

alerting:
  alertmanagers:
    - static_configs:
       - targets:
          - alertmanager:9093 # AlertManager IP/Port, 9093 by convention

# Load rules once and evaluate them every 'evaluation_interval'.
rule_files:
  - "alert.rules.yml"
```

CHANGING THE EVALUATION FREQUENCY

To override the global `evaluation_interval` for a given rule, open the rule file and specify an "interval" entry for that rule. For example:

```
- name: custom-interval-rule
  interval: 1m # Will be evaluated every 1 minute
```

If you have a SMTP server, you can start Alert Manager and point it to the `alertmanager.yml` configuration file we defined earlier by running the following:

```
docker run --name alertmanager -p 9093:9093
-v ./alert.rules.yml:/etc/alertmanager/alert.rules.yml
-v ./alertmanager.yml:/etc/alertmanager/alertmanager.yml
quay.io/prometheus/alertmanager
--config.file=/etc/alertmanager/alertmanager.yml
```

That should launch Alert Manager in your command shell.

Regardless of whether you configured SMTP, you can see the rule in Prometheus. In Docker Desktop, delete the existing Prometheus container and run the following:

```
docker run --name prometheus -p 9090:9090
-v ./prometheus-with-alerts.yml:/etc/prometheus/prometheus-with-alerts.yml
-v ./alert.rules.yml:/etc/prometheus/alert.rules.yml prometheus
--config.file=/etc/prometheus/prometheus-with-alerts.yml
```

Go to the URL `http://localhost:9090/alerts`. You should see the `HighCpuUsage` alert. Pop that open and you should see the alert, as in Figure 12.11.

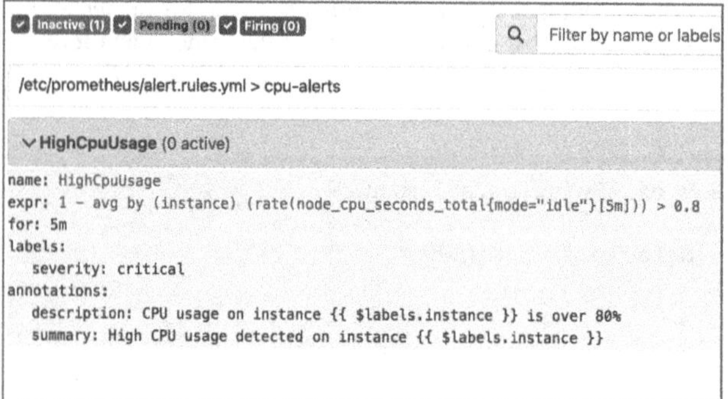
Inactive (1)
Pending (0)
Firing (0)
Filter by name or labels
/etc/prometheus/alert.rules.yml > cpu-alerts
HighCpuUsage (0 active)
name: HighCpuUsage
expr: 1 - avg by (instance) (rate(node_cpu_seconds_total{mode="idle"}[5m])) > 0.8
for: 5m
labels:
severity: critical
annotations:
description: CPU usage on instance {{ $labels.instance }} is over 80%
summary: High CPU usage detected on instance {{ $labels.instance }}

FIGURE 12.11: Prometheus alerts tab

DASHBOARDING WITH GRAFANA

Grafana is a fantastic visualization tool that provides connectors for many data sources, including Prometheus. Out of the box, Grafana provides a huge selection of graphs and tables to choose from.

Head over to the Grafana download site at `https://grafana.com/grafana/download`, and download and install the correct installation for your platform. Grafana is a browser application, which runs as a service on port 3000 by default. To start it, go to the `bin` directory and run the following:

```
grafana server
```

> **TIP** *If you are on Mac, go to Security and Privacy and approve if you get an unknown developer message. From your browser, navigate to* `http://localhost:3000` *to see the Grafana login page. Log in with username and password admin/admin. If you get prompted to change the password, you can either do so or click "skip."*

Once you have logged in, you'll need to add Prometheus integration. In the left navigation, click Data Sources and Add Data Source. Enter **`http://localhost:9090`** as the URL and then scroll all the way down to click Save & Test. Figure 12.12 shows this configuration.

prometheus
Type: Prometheus
Settings | Dashboards
Name: prometheus | Default
Before you can use the Prometheus data source, you must configure it below or in the config file.
*Fields marked with * are required*
Connection
Prometheus server URL *: http://localhost:9090

FIGURE 12.12: Integrating with Prometheus

Then click the option to add a new dashboard. A dashboard consists of rows, and rows consist of visualizations. Visualizations are the graphs, gauges, and tables that Grafana is known for.

Let's start a new dashboard, click the gear, set a title and description, and accept the remaining defaults, as shown in Figure 12.13.

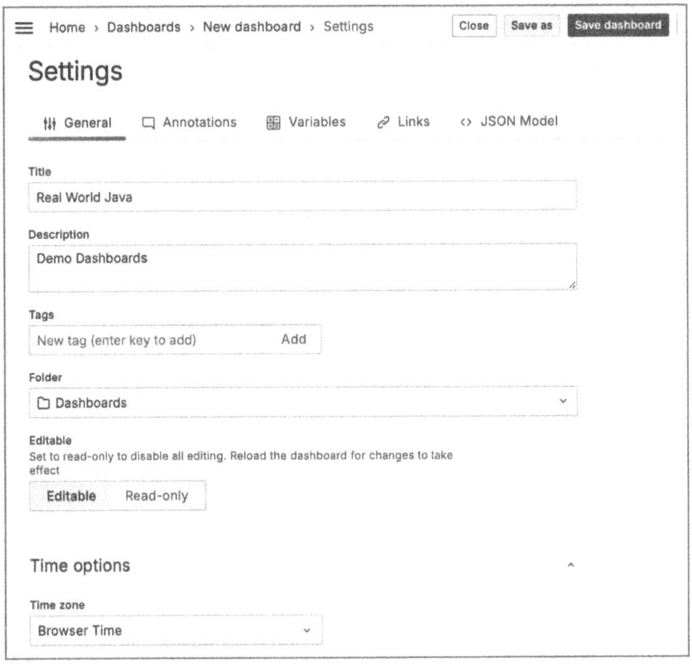

FIGURE 12.13: Configuring a Grafana dashboard

Save that to return to the page where you can add visualization. Click Add and add a row; call it **Infrastructure.** We will add visualizations to that row for displaying infrastructure performance metrics.

Hover over "Row title" to reveal a gear, which you can click to title your row, as in Figure 12.14.

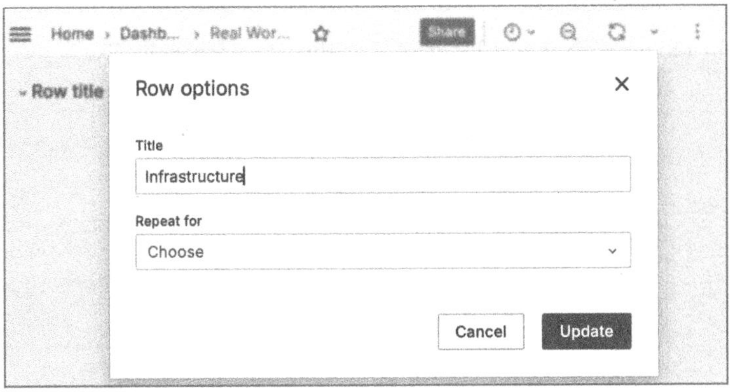

FIGURE 12.14: Adding a row title

Next choose Add ➪ Visualization. On the top right, you can select a visualization type. We will use the default time series and give the panel the title **CPU.** Below the graph is a place to enter your PromQL query. Click Code and use the following query:

```
100 - (avg by (instance) (rate(node_cpu_seconds_total{mode="idle"}[5m])) * 100)
```

which is the formula for CPU utilization. Then click Run Queries, just above the query expression. You should see a graph similar to the one in Figure 12.15.

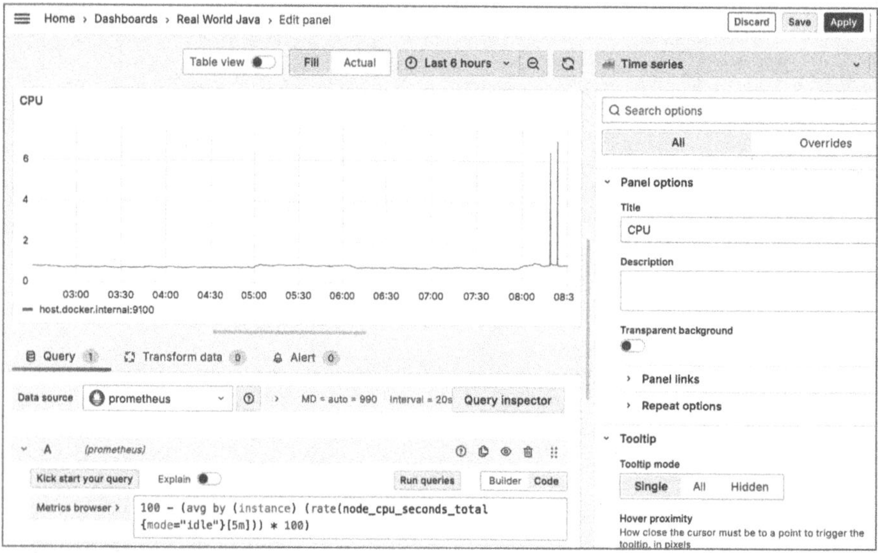

FIGURE 12.15: Adding a graph panel

Save that, and click Real World Java at the top to navigate back to the dashboard. Grab the graph from its title bar and drag it into the Infrastructure row.

In the same way, add a new visualization called **Memory,** and enter the following query:

```
100 - (avg by (instance) (rate(node_memory_MemAvailable_bytes [5m]))
/ avg by (instance) (node_memory_MemAvailable_bytes
) * 100)
```

Then save the panel and drag and drop it to the right of the CPU graph. You should see something like Figure 12.16.

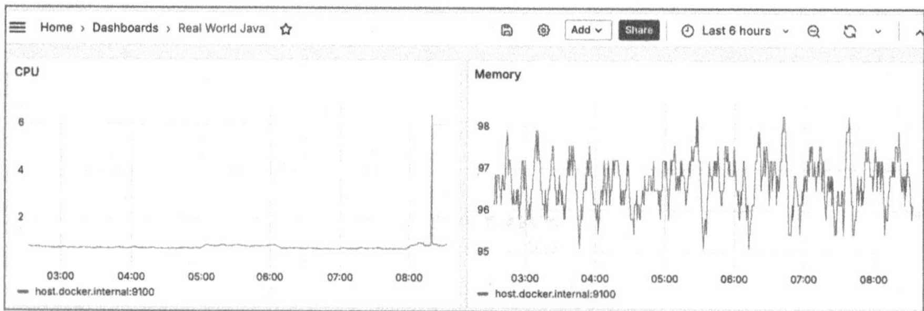

FIGURE 12.16: Adding a second graph panel

The time selector will default to six hours, but play around with that by selecting various time ranges.

Time series is just one of the many graph types available. We encourage you to play around with the others by editing a graph and selecting the various types. Then try different metrics and come up with your own.

LOGGING AND TRACING

Distributed logging and tracing are closely related and vastly popular in enterprise systems, especially with modern microservice-based architectures.

Distributed logging refers to having a common location for all your logs so that you can filter, aggregate, and extract metrics from the logs of all your applications in one place.

Distributed tracing at its simplest level refers to the ability to keep a common trace ID for all calls related to a single request and then including that trace ID in all of the distributed log messages, no matter which service performed the logging. There are also frameworks for allowing you to visualize the hops related to the call.

Introducing Logging

The key players in the distributed logging area are Elasticsearch (the "E" in the ELK stack), Splunk, and Loki. Splunk and Elastic Search are most popular, with Elastic Search more prevalent in smaller companies. Loki is the newest entry in this field and also enjoys a large following thanks to its seamless integration with Grafana and its LogQL language that is similar to Prometheus's PromQL.

Whichever flavor your enterprise uses, distributed logging is a critical component in any service-based enterprise. All the choices we mentioned are scalable and highly available.

Logstash is a forwarding service that can filter, transform, and transport strategic log messages to Elasticsearch. Kibana is Elasticsearch's analytics and visualization component, where you can seamlessly explore your data, and those (Elasticsearch, Kibana, Logstash) comprise the "ELK" stack.

Elasticsearch is a Java application, and the download distribution comes bundled with its own Java runtime.

Data is available in near real time. You can perform searches in Elasticsearch; the results are informed and relevant to the search query you supplied.

In Elasticsearch, an index is the fundamental unit of storage. It roughly corresponds to a table in a relational database, in that it stores related documents.

For collecting data, Elasticsearch provides the Logstash tool, the L in ELK. Logstash is an *ETL* tool used to collect, filter, and transform source data and forward it to Elasticsearch.

> **TIP** *Extract, transform, and load (ETL) refers to the fundamental steps in a data engineering pipeline, whereby data is* extracted *from some upstream source such as a database, REST call, files, messaging systems, and so forth, and then* transforms *that data by enriching it with missing fields, or deleting unneeded fields, and finally* loads *it into a downstream system, which for our purposes would be Elasticsearch.*

Logstash pipelines consist of three stages.

- **Input:** Data is collected from configured sources drawing from a wide range of available input plugins.
- **Filter:** This is the transform stage, where the data uses filter plugins to transform data by parsing, cleaning, and enriching it.
- **Output:** This is the forwarding stage, where data is moved to its destination. The destination is not limited to Elasticsearch; there are many plugins available for forwarding output to files, databases, REST endpoints, messaging systems, and so forth.

You can configure a data pipeline by specifying the appropriate input, filter, and output stages in a Logstash configuration file.

Elasticsearch provides its own analytics and dashboarding tool called Kibana, the "K" in ELK. By default, Kibana listens on port 5601, so is accessed at `localhost:5601` in a browser. We selected "Choose your own" for the integration and saw the screen in Figure 12.17. Kibana is now connected to Elasticsearch, which it found at the default port 9200.

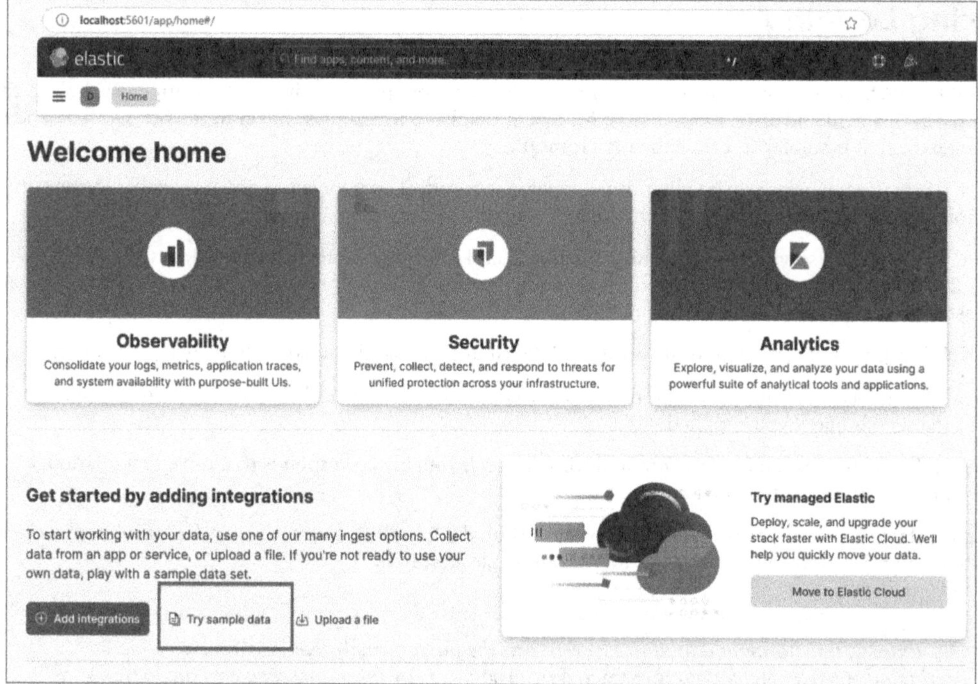

FIGURE 12.17: Kibana landing page

Kibana provides some sample data to play around with via "Try sample data" on the home page. The drop-down labeled "Other sample data sets" contains the data such as on the Sample eCommerce orders card.

Similar in concept to distributed logging, *distributed tracing* is a technique for following the path of requests through different components of a distributed system. In modern microservices, one request might be handled by many services, and if something goes wrong, we need a way to explore the logs across all calls related to a failed request. Tracing tools can provide real-time visualizations as requests flow through your system. They apply a unique "trace ID" to all calls associated with each request, helping you understand how services interact, and allowing you to diagnose issues and improve performance.

Key Concepts in Tracing

The basic unit of tracing, a *span* is a unique ID associated with a single request and a single service. Each span captures data associated with this request and service, such as service name and execution time. A *trace* is a collection of spans that comprise all processes managing a given request.

Coordinating this on your own would be tricky business, because your trace tooling would need to intercept each request and response to ensure that a common trace id is applied across hops. Additionally, logs need to be tagged and metrics labeled with the trace ID assigned by the tooling.

Tooling

OpenTelemetry is a widely adopted set of observability specifications, as well as an open-source reference implementation for managing metrics, logs, and traces with APIs in all popular languages. Other popular implementations include Jaeger and Zipkin, which collect, store, visualize, and analyze your logs and metrics.

Implementing Tracing in Spring Boot Applications

Micrometer Tracing is an open-source plugin you can add to Spring Boot applications that intercepts incoming and outgoing calls to ensure that a common trace ID is shared by all services managing a request.

Simply add the micrometer-tracing endpoint as a Maven or Gradle dependency. As of this writing, the dependency is `io.micrometer:micrometer-tracing:1.3.5`, which is compatible with Spring Boot 3 and on. Earlier versions of Spring Boot used Spring Cloud Sleuth to accomplish the same purpose. The magical beauty of these tools is that once you include the dependency, you don't need to change any of your code.

FURTHER REFERENCES

- Prometheus
    - `https://prometheus.io/docs/introduction/overview`: Prometheus documentation
    - `https://prometheus.io/download`: Prometheus and Linux Node Exporter
    - `https://github.com/prometheus-community/windows_exporter/releases`: Windows Exporter
    - `https://github.com/prometheus/node_exporter`: Node Exporter flags
    - `https://github.com/prometheus-community/windows_exporter/blob/master/README.md`: Windows Exporter flags
    - `https://prometheus.io/download/#alertmanager`: Alert Manager
- Other Tools
    - `https://docs.docker.com/engine/install`: Download Docker
    - `https://grafana.com/grafana/download`: Grafana
    - `https://www.elastic.co/downloads/elasticsearch`: Elastic Search

- `https://www.elastic.co/downloads/logstash`: Logstash
- `https://www.elastic.co/downloads/kibana`: Kibana
- `https://www.7-zip.org/download.html`: 7-Zip
- `https://opentelemetry.io`: OpenTelemetry Documentation
- `https://docs.micrometer.io/tracing/reference/index.html`: Micrometer tracing
- `https://www.jaegertracing.io`: Jaeger Documentation
- `https://zipkin.io`: Zipkin Documentation

SUMMARY

In this chapter, you learned about the major components of observability, including metrics, logs, alerts, dashboarding, and tracing. You learned how to instrument your applications, middleware, and infrastructure using Prometheus and how to visualize them using Grafana. You also got an introduction to the distributed logging and tracing landscape.

13

Performance Tuning Your Services

WHAT'S IN THIS CHAPTER?

- Learning the Concepts and Terminology
- Benchmarking
- Tuning JVM Settings
- Testing with JMeter
- Using JDK Tools
- Optimizing Your Application

Imagine you are shopping online or visiting your favorite news site or movie site. How long would you expect to wait for the web page to load? The answer is probably not more than a few seconds. Online vendors know that slow performance translates to lost customers. And that's not just on an average day, but websites must also make sure that they can handle large spikes in demand such as during the Super Bowl or on days like Black Friday or Cyber Monday, when United States retail sites expect massive volumes of online shopping.

When you are learning to program, performance is generally not your primary concern. But in the enterprise, performance is a critical component in customer retention and managing operational costs. After all, servers cost money, so maximizing server performance translates to fewer servers and therefore a bigger bottom line. Similarly, when you deploy to cloud environments like AWS, you are billed based on usage, so again we see that improving performance can reduce costs.

On the other hand, Donald Knuth, one of the pioneers of computer science, wrote in *The Art of Computer Programming* that "premature optimization is the root of all evil." Therefore, it is important to identify where the problem hot spots are and the severity of their impact so you can prioritize them and address the important issues first. We like to say "code for correctness and then correct for performance."

CODE DOWNLOADS FOR THIS CHAPTER

The source code for this chapter is available on the book page at `www.wiley.com`. Click the Downloads link. The code can also be found at `https://github.com/realworldjava/Ch13-Performance`. See the `README.md` file in that repository for details.

In this chapter, you'll learn basic performance concepts, how to write performant code in Java, and how to performance tune your application. You'll also learn about some popular tools that can help you produce performant code.

LEARNING THE CONCEPTS AND TERMINOLOGY

Let's start by introducing some general performance concepts and terminology and then advance to Java-specific concepts. Following that, you will learn how to write more performant code.

Let's start with some definitions: *performance* is defined as how fast and how efficiently a system operates under a given load. If you go to a website and it takes 10 seconds to load, you will complain that it is slow and not performant. *Scalability* measures how well the system can perform with added load. *Horizontal scalability* refers to the benefit realized by adding more resources (that is, machines) to a task. For example, if half the user requests are processed on one machine and the other half on another, you have horizontal scaling. By contrast, *vertical scalability* is the amount that the system benefits from adding more resources to the same machine. For example, if you upgrade the CPU or add more memory, you have vertically scaled.

The following are some important performance metrics:

- **Response time:** In our website example, this is the amount of time to get the result.
- **Throughput:** This measures the amount of work a system can perform in a specified time, usually operations per second.
- **Latency:** This is the time to perform a component of the total response time. For example, *network latency* measures the delay caused in transferring data between two machines. If you are communicating with a database or remote service, network latency would be the time it takes to reach that server or the time it takes for the response to travel from the server back to the caller.

The following are some other terms used when discussing performance:

- **Caching:** This means storing data in memory to speed up slow operations.
- **Bottleneck** or **hot spot:** This is the part of the system that causes unacceptable performance.
- **Profiler:** This is the class of tools used to identify potential hot spots in your application.
- **Memory leak:** This is a situation where the program consumes memory without releasing it.
- **Just-in-time (JIT) compilation:** This is a capability of the JVM that discovers patterns in your application usage and replaces bytecode with optimized native code.

BENCHMARKING

Suppose you identify a section of your code that is slow. Maybe it "pins" your CPU using so much CPU that your machine is maxed out. Or maybe it is doing operations sequentially when it could be running them in parallel. *Benchmarking* allows you to measure the time it takes to run specific portions of your code. Running a benchmark both before and after you make a change lets you see if you have made the program faster. You'll see examples of benchmarking using built-in Java APIs, and then you'll learn how to use a library for more accurate results.

Benchmarking with Built-In Java APIs

The Fibonacci sequence is a well-known sequence in nature and in computer science. It starts with 0,1, and then every term is the sum of the previous two terms: 0,1,1,2,3,5,8,. . . .

The following example shows an inefficient way of calculating the value at a certain position in the Fibonacci sequence. In this example, if you pass in 6, it returns 8 because that is the sixth entry in the sequence. Since each entry is calculated by adding the previous two numbers, the inefficient algorithm calculates the previous two numbers and adds them together. It does this recursively, which calculates the same information repeatedly.

```
public static void main(String[] args) {

   final int nanosPerSecond = 1_000_000_000;
   long start = System.nanoTime();
   long recursive = fibonacci(50);
   long end = System.nanoTime();

   System.out.println(recursive);
   System.out.printf("Took %d seconds", (end-start)/nanosPerSecond);
}

public static long fibonacci(int number) {
   if (number <= 1) return number;

   return fibonacci(number - 1) + fibonacci(number - 2);
}
```

One of our runs showed the output of this code as follows:

```
12586269025
Took 36 seconds
```

Thirty-six seconds is a long time to calculate the result. Luckily, recursion isn't needed to solve this problem. Let's rewrite this code without recursion and compare the performance:

```
public static void main(String[] args) {

   final int nanosPerSecond = 1_000_000_000;
   long start = System.nanoTime();
   long recursive = fibonacci(50);
   long end = System.nanoTime();

   System.out.println(recursive);
   System.out.printf("Took %d seconds", (end-start)/nanosPerSecond);
}

public static long fibonacci(int number) {
   long previous = 0, current = 1;
   long result = 0;

   for (int i = 1; i < number; i++) {
      result = previous + current;
      previous = current;
      current = result;
   }
   return result;
}
```

This time the output is less than a second. Much faster to accomplish the same task! We see from this example that although there can be many ways to accomplish a task, some ways may perform better than others.

Always think through your approach. Although recursion is appropriate for many situations, in this case it was the wrong approach because it was repeatedly recalculating the same intermediate results.

```
12586269025
Took 0 seconds
```

SYSTEM.NANOTIME() OR SYSTEM.CURRENTTIMEINMILLIS()?

`System.nanoTime()` is more precise than `System.currentTimeInMillis()` because under the covers it requests the time from the JVM rather than relying on the underlying operating system, which may not be accurate.

Microbenchmarking

The code in the previous example was so inefficient that we didn't need a detailed benchmark to see that the time was improved. But in real life we must often locate and tune portions of code with minor improvements. *Microbenchmarking* refers to the act of measuring the performance of small, isolated portions of code.

Writing good benchmarks with precision is hard. You must ensure that no competing tasks (like logging, garbage collection, and so forth) are happening at the same time that might affect the benchmark. You also must ensure that the JVM doesn't optimize the code in a way that makes your benchmark invalid. For example, the application might have portions of code that produce an unused result. The JVM may consider such portions as dead code and optimize it away so it doesn't run! Additionally, the JVM optimizes code where possible so it may be faster on later runs than earlier ones in a loop. Or the JIT compiler might convert bytecode to native code. All of these can greatly skew any benchmarks that were produced before the optimization kicked in.

Luckily, Java Microbenchmark Harness (JMH) exists so you don't have to worry about such optimizations and can just focus on measuring your code. The JMH maintainers recommend using the JMH archetype `jmh-java-benchmark-archetype` to generate a new project. You can add your project as a dependency to give it access to run your code:

```
mvn archetype:generate
   -DinteractiveMode=false
   -DarchetypeGroupId=org.openjdk.jmh
   -DarchetypeArtifactId=jmh-java-benchmark-archetype
   -DgroupId=com.wiley.realworldjava.jmh
   -DartifactId=jmh-benchmark
   -Dversion=1.0.0
```

This runs the `archetype:generate` goal to generate a new project using the specified Maven archetype. The first `-D` system property just says to not prompt for confirmation. The next two properties specify the JMH archetype. The last three you use to assign a GAV (group ID, artifact ID, and version) for your project.

The generated code is a Maven project. The archetype created one Java class named `MyBenchmark.java` with one empty method. Let's replace that with the following code containing a call to the sluggish `fibonacci()` implementation method signature from the previous example:

```
package com.wiley.realworldjava.jmh;

import org.openjdk.jmh.annotations.Benchmark;
import org.openjdk.jmh.infra.Blackhole;

public class MyBenchmark {

   @Benchmark
   public static void benchmark(Blackhole blackhole) {
```

```
        long result = fibonacci(50);
        blackhole.consume(result);
    }

    public static long fibonacci(int number) {
        // implementation omitted
    }
}
```

There are two features to highlight in this example. First, the `@Benchmark` annotation tells JMH that this is the method to measure. Second, we removed the code that printed the output, and instead we feed the result into a `Blackhole`. The reason for this is that we want to ensure that the output of the `fibonacci()` method is used so that the JVM doesn't optimize out the method implementation entirely. However, printing the output would skew the generated metrics since I/O is slower than CPU operations. The `Blackhole` class takes care of this by quickly and silently consuming the value.

Before you run the benchmark, run a Maven build to create the benchmark's JAR file:

```
mvn clean verify
```

This creates a file named `benchmarks.jar` in the `target` directory.

To run the benchmark, call this:

```
java -jar target/benchmarks.jar
```

By default, JMH runs five iterations of your benchmark. Each iteration has five warm-up iterations that don't count toward the total, and five iterations that do count. This means the method you annotated with `@Benchmark` runs 50 times by default. Part of the output from a sample run using the slow implementation of `fibonacci()` is shown here:

```
# Run progress: 80.00% complete, ETA 00:05:52
# Fork: 5 of 5
# Warmup Iteration   1: 0.028 ops/s
# Warmup Iteration   2: 0.026 ops/s
# Warmup Iteration   3: 0.025 ops/s
# Warmup Iteration   4: 0.026 ops/s
# Warmup Iteration   5: 0.028 ops/s
Iteration   1: 0.029 ops/s
Iteration   2: 0.029 ops/s
Iteration   3: 0.028 ops/s
Iteration   4: 0.029 ops/s
Iteration   5: 0.029 ops/s

Result "com.wiley.realworldjava.jmh.MyBenchmark.benchmark":
  0.028 ±(99.9%) 0.001 ops/s [Average]
  (min, avg, max) = (0.028, 0.028, 0.029), stdev = 0.001
  CI (99.9%): [0.028, 0.029] (assumes normal distribution)

# Run complete. Total time: 00:29:33

Benchmark                Mode  Cnt  Score    Error  Units
MyBenchmark.benchmark   thrpt   25  0.028 ±  0.001  ops/s
```

By default, JMH measures the throughput in operations per second. As you can see from the output, the number of operations per second is low. After all, the average of .028 operations/second is less than 2 operations per minute! Earlier in the chapter, it took 36 seconds, which is in the same ballpark. You can also see that the time per run doesn't vary much. The standard deviation (0.001) and +/-(99.9%) in the output shows that percentage-wise the time was almost the same for each run.

The time to run was slightly higher during the warm-up period where the JVM figured out how to optimize, but both before and after the warmup period, the performance was slow.

At the end of the output, you get a summary. It took almost 30 minutes to run the benchmark. That's time to drink a lot of coffee! The output also summarizes the result and variance. Rerunning using the faster `fibonacci()` implementation reports far more operations per second:

```
# Run progress: 80.00% complete, ETA 00:01:40
# Fork: 5 of 5
# Warmup Iteration   1: 3080887445.320 ops/s
# Warmup Iteration   2: 3086292064.630 ops/s
# Warmup Iteration   3: 3088137264.756 ops/s
# Warmup Iteration   4: 3089568664.300 ops/s
# Warmup Iteration   5: 3084161269.692 ops/s
Iteration   1: 3097137124.647 ops/s
Iteration   2: 3080164130.908 ops/s
Iteration   3: 3095501587.777 ops/s
Iteration   4: 3088198606.124 ops/s
Iteration   5: 3084219015.220 ops/s

Result "com.wiley.realworldjava.jmh.MyBenchmark.benchmark":
   3054970163.963 ±(99.9%) 129045935.961 ops/s [Average]
 (min, avg, max) = (2229602431.413, 3054970163.963, 3110210135.698),
   stdev = 172272632.473
  CI (99.9%): [2925924228.001, 3184016099.924] (assumes normal distribution)

# Run complete. Total time: 00:08:21

Benchmark                Mode  Cnt          Score           Error  Units
MyBenchmark.benchmark   thrpt   25  3054970163.963 ± 129045935.961  ops/s
```

First, notice that it took far less time for the benchmark to run, finishing in less than 9 minutes instead of 30. Additionally, you can see that there were many more operations per second using the faster code!

You might be wondering how much longer it took to run a single benchmark. After all, 3,054,970,163 operations per second is a lot but not the easiest number to work with. Luckily, you can configure JMH to give output that is easier to read. You can tweak the output by adding attributes to the `@Benchmark` annotation as follows:

```
@Benchmark @BenchmarkMode(Mode.AverageTime)
 @OutputTimeUnit(TimeUnit.MICROSECONDS)
```

This time you get output like the following for the slower and faster implementations, respectively:

```
Iteration   1: 35172416.167 µs/op
Iteration   1: ≈ 10⁻³ µs/op
```

The output is in µs/op, which means microseconds per operation. For the faster code, you can see the output uses scientific notation since the result was a lot smaller than a microsecond. For the slow code, you instead see a large number for the number of microseconds per operation.

As the developer, it is up to you to choose modes and units that make sense for the code you are measuring. Table 13.1 shows the options for `Mode`, and Table 13.2 shows the options for `TimeUnit`. If you don't specify, `Mode.Throughput` and `TimeUnit.SECONDS` are used.

TABLE 13.1: JMH Benchmark Modes

@BENCHMARKMODE	DESCRIPTION
`Mode.Throughput`	Number of operations per unit of time
`Mode.AverageTime`	Average time for a single operation

@BENCHMARKMODE	DESCRIPTION
`Mode.SampleTime`	Minimum, maximum, and average time
`Mode.SingleShotTime`	Time for one run with no warmup
`Mode.All`	Includes all of the above

TABLE 13.2: JMH Output Time Units

@OUTPUTTIMEUNIT	DESCRIPTION
`TimeUnit.NANOSECONDS`	Units of thousandths of a microsecond
`TimeUnit.MICROSECONDS`	Units of thousandths of a millisecond
`TimeUnit.MILLISECONDS`	Units of thousandths of a second
`TimeUnit.SECONDS`	Units in seconds
`TimeUnit.MINUTES`	Units in minutes
`TimeUnit.HOURS`	Units in hours
`TimeUnit.DAYS`	Units in days

TUNING JVM SETTINGS

We will now cover the JVM settings that you can control. Before applying these remember that "premature optimization is the root of all evil." With great power comes great responsibility, so don't change settings without a reason.

In this section, you'll learn how to control runtime memory and garbage collection settings.

Configuring Memory Settings

In Chapter 9, "Parallelizing your Application Using Java Concurrency," you learned that stack memory is used for parameters and local variables within a thread. Heap memory is the shared memory space that gets cleaned up with garbage collection. Metaspace is for data that needs to be available for the life of the VM, such as class objects and static references.

In large applications, the defaults for these will generally not be enough. Additionally, the default for some of these settings can vary across machines or Java releases, so there is an advantage to being explicit when your application performance depends on having sufficient memory.

`-Xms` sets the initial minimum size of the heap. This allows the space to be allocated up front, rather than having it dynamically allocated, possibly slowing down your application when it is trying to process user requests. By default, this setting is configured in bytes. However, for large values that is not easy to read. Luckily, you can include a suffix to specify a unit of measure. The following units are supported:

- **k or K**: Number of kilobytes
- **m or M**: Number of megabytes
- **g or G**: Number of gigabytes

Using the unit specifiers, all of the following represent the same configuration:

```
-Xms1g
-Xms1G
-Xms1024m
-Xms1024M
-Xms1048576k
-Xms1048576K
-Xms1073741824
```

The first two are the clearest since they don't require you to do math to determine the value is 1 gigabyte!

Table 13.3 shows the most common memory flags. It is more common to use the short form in configuration even though it is less explicit when reading.

TABLE 13.3: Three Common Memory Options

FLAG	ALIAS	DESCRIPTION
`-Xms`	`-XX:InitialHeapSize`	Initial and maximum size of the heap. It must be more than 1 megabyte and a multiple of 1024.
`-Xmx`	`-XX:MaxHeapSize`	Maximum heap size. It must be more than 2 megabytes and a multiple of 1024.
`-Xss`	`-XX:ThreadStackSize`	Size of the thread stack.

WHAT ARE X AND XX?

The use of `-X` and `-XX` might seem rather arbitrary, but how these designations evolved is interesting. `-X` was originally intended to be a nonstandard option, not guaranteed to work on all JVMs. `-XX`, on the other hand, represented more stable, more advanced, or more granular options. However, the `-X` options listed in Table 13.3 have become firm standards and are not likely to change anytime soon.

All of the options described in this book, including `-X` and `-XX` options, are in Oracle's JDK documentation and are widely supported.

Collecting the Garbage

You are probably familiar with the idea of garbage collection (GC). Java runs GC to reclaim memory when objects are no longer referenced. You can't control when GC is run or how long it takes, at least not directly. As you'll see, there are some memory settings you can configure that affect frequency and duration of garbage collection.

You might be wondering why we are talking about garbage collection in a chapter on performance. Quite simply, if your CPU is busy dealing with garbage collection, it isn't available for the work of processing user tasks!

When you create new objects, in general, they are not likely to be used after their initial allocation. Therefore, they can be dereferenced early so that they don't consume valuable memory. To minimize the impact of garbage collection, Java organizes memory into generations. The young generation consists of Eden space and two Survivor spaces (S0 and S1). Objects are initially allocated in Eden space. When Eden space fills up, a *Minor GC* is performed. During a minor GC, most objects are found to be unreferenced and are swept out. Survivors of the minor GC are moved to the active survivor space (say S0). During the next minor GC, unreferenced objects are removed from Eden, survivors are moved to the other survivor space (S1), and the survivors from S0 are also moved to S1. S0 is reclaimed, and S1 becomes the active survivor space, and so on. After a configurable number of movements between S0 and S1, surviving objects are promoted to Old Generation, also known as Tenured Space.

There is also a Metaspace for things like static data and class objects that must remain available for the entire life of the program. (Metaspace replaces the permanent generation space, also known as PermGen, from earlier versions of Java.)

This section explains the common types of garbage collectors provided in Java, as well as their settings. Before you configure a garbage collector, you want to check if the default meet your needs. The JDK will attempt to pick the best garbage collection algorithm based on your configuration, machine, and type of JVM available.

Setting Sizes for Garbage Collection

Regardless of which garbage collector you use, you can configure some sizes:

- **`-Xmn`**: Initial and maximum size of the young generation (Eden + Survivor spaces). If this number is too small, garbage collection may happen too often. If it is too large, garbage collection may be slow and infrequent. Oracle recommends a range of 25 percent–50 percent of heap size. Alternatively, you can use `-XX:NewSize` and `-XX:MaxNewSize` if you want to configure individual values for initial and maximum young generation sizes.
- **`-XX:MaxMetaspaceSize`**: Maximum size of the Metaspace that must remain available.
- **`-XX:MetaspaceSize`**: Initial size of the Metaspace. A garbage collection will run the first time it is full.
- **`-XX:MaxTenuringThreshold`**: Number of times an object switches between S0 and S1 before being promoted to tenured space.

The specific garbage collectors have custom settings you can tune. See the Java documentation page's advanced garbage collection section for details if you find yourself tuning your garbage collector.

> **TIP** *For settings that don't require multiples of 1024, it is good to use powers of two for the numbers, e.g., 2, 4, 8, 16, 32, 64, 128, 256, and 512. Why not 1024 you ask? Because 1024 kilobytes is one megabyte. You'd move up to the next unit of measure instead of typing a larger number.*

Using Serial Garbage Collection

Serial garbage collection is an older type that is rarely used in current practice. However, it is good to understand it before getting to the others.

With a serial garbage collector, your entire application stops while one thread performs garbage collection. This is known as *stop-the-world*. In some applications, this pause is fine. However, where performance is a requirement this is not going to be acceptable!

Oracle's documentation says the serial garbage collector is for small and simple applications. However, in these days of multicore machines, even small applications can use another type. If you do want to use a serial garbage collector, use the option `-XX:+UseSerialGC`.

Using Parallel Garbage Collection

The parallel garbage collector is also a stop-the-world garbage collector. However, it is faster than the serial garbage collector because it uses multiple threads for the garbage collection work.

Again, this stops all work while it does its garbage collection. If you do need to require the parallel garbage collector, use the option `-XX:+UseParallelGC`.

Using G1GC

Garbage First Garbage Collector (G1GC) is designed for multicore servers with a lot of available memory. It works by splitting the heap into logical sections, which allows G1GC to clean up all generations at the same time, section by section. As a result, pauses are rare, and stop-the-world is not a problem.

While there are still Eden, survivor, and tenured regions, they are located throughout the heap in different logical sections. The result is that G1GC is going to be a better algorithm for a large heap.

You might be thinking that this sounds great and wonder why G1GC doesn't get used all the time. The main reason is that it requires a lot of RAM. A heap size of 6GB or higher is recommended for G1GC. If you aren't working with a large memory space, parallel might be better for you.

Oracle/Open JDK defaults to G1GC. However, if you are relying on this garbage collector, you should still specify the option `-XX:+UseG1GC`.

> **TIP** *The Z Garbage Collector is a variant of G1GC for very large heaps. It uses the option* `-XX:+UseZGC`.

TESTING WITH JMETER

JMeter is a popular open-source load-testing tool. Load-testing means testing your application under a high volume of traffic. We created a basic sample application to show how to use JMeter. It is a single-page application that allows users to borrow and return sports equipment at a recreation center. As shown in Figure 13.1, there are four sports you can play. The basketball and pickleball paddles are currently out on loan, but the table tennis rackets and volleyball are available to borrow. In this section, we will test our application with JMeter to see how our small recreation center performs if it suddenly receives a high volume of requests in a short time!

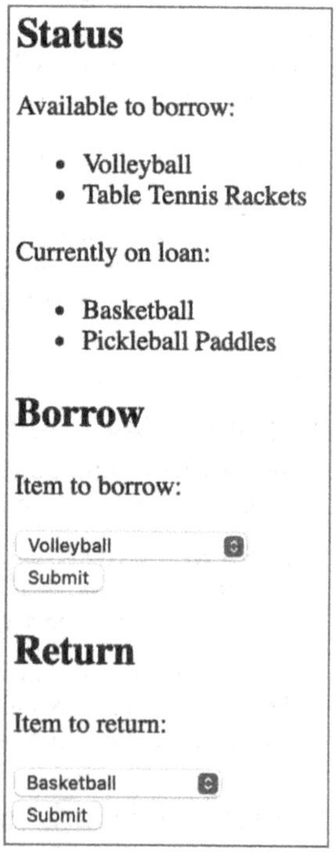

FIGURE 13.1: Sample application

In a nutshell, testing with JMeter is a three-step procedure. First you use the graphical UI to create a test plan. Then you run the tests at the command line or from directly within the tool. Finally, you analyze the results. The next sections show these steps.

Creating a Test Plan

The first step in using JMeter is to download the JMeter binaries. See the "Further References" section for the download link. The download contains everything you need to test a web application or REST API. If you are planning to test Java Database Connectivity (JDBC) or Java Messaging Service (JMS), you will need additional software. See Chapter 14, "Getting to Know More of the Ecosystem," for more on these technologies.

Once JMeter is downloaded and unzipped/untarred, you will have a directory named `apache-jmeter-x.y.z`. (We tested with JMeter version 5.6.3.) Open a command line and navigate to the `bin` directory. Then run `jmeter.bat` on Windows or `jmeter.sh` on Mac.

Give your test plan a name. You can see "Rec Center" is our test plan name. You can enter an optional comment to express the purpose of your test.

Next create a *thread group*, which defines the number of simulated users, how often they should send requests to your application, and how many requests they should send all together. Right-click your test plan and then select Add ➪ Threads (Users) ➪ Thread Group.

You can give the thread group a name and configuration options. For example, in Figure 13.2 you can see this thread group contains five users each with two requests. The ramp-up period is the default of one second, which tells JMeter how long to pause between starting each of the users.

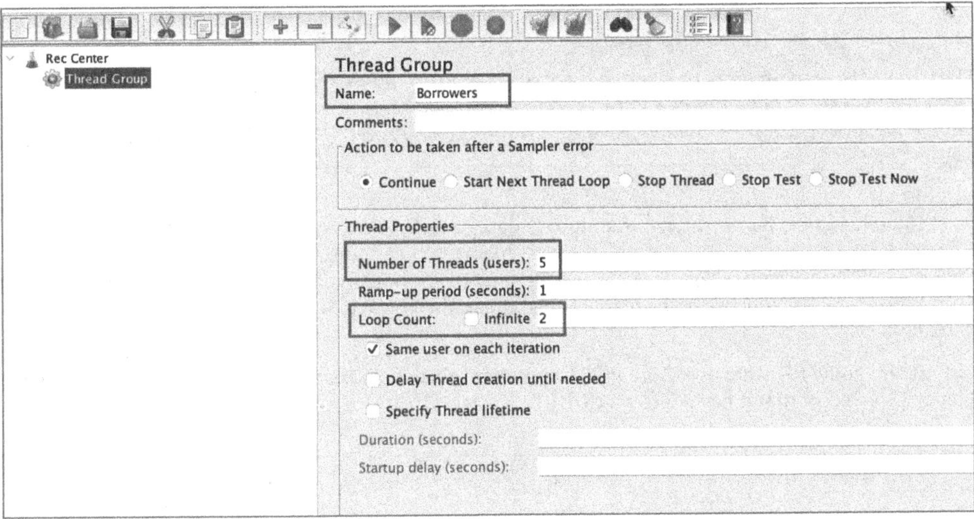

FIGURE 13.2: JMeter thread group

Now that there is a thread group, it is time to tell it what to do! Right-click the thread group and choose Add ➪ Sampler ➪ HTTP Request.

In Figure 13.3, you can see the following information changed from the defaults:

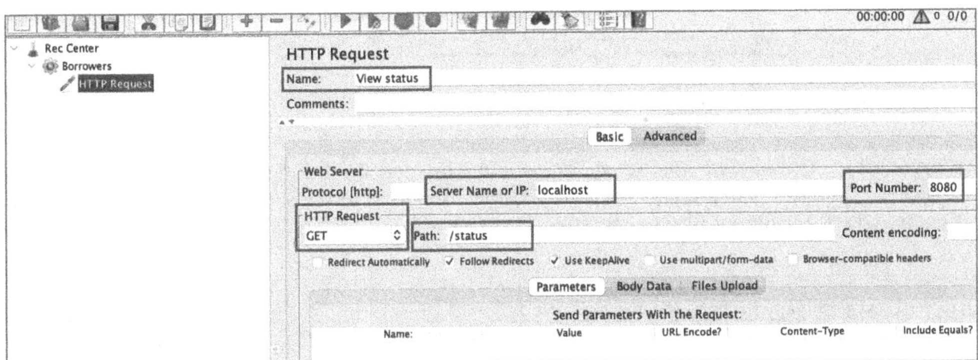

FIGURE 13.3: JMeter HTTP GET request

- **Name:** This is the display name of the request, in our case "View status."
- **Server name or IP:** We used localhost since this test is running on a laptop. You can use a server name or DNS alias here.
- **Port number:** We used 8080, corresponding to the default port used in our sample web application.
- **HTTP request:** We choose `GET`, the HTTP verb usually associated with a query that does not change data.
- **Path:** This is the remainder of the URL. Be sure to start with a leading slash such as `/status` in this case.

> **TIP** *If you have more than a few requests, it is easier to configure the server name/IP and port number as defaults so you don't have to specify them on each request. This is done by right-clicking the test plan and choosing Add ➪ Config Element ➪ HTTP Request Details.*

It is common to do load tests on operations that update data as well, so let's create another HTTP request, as shown in Figure 13.4. Like in the `GET` example, there is a name, server name, and port number. This time the HTTP request is `POST` since we are trying to change the state of the borrowed items. The URL again begins with a slash: `/borrowItem`. This time we provide the `itemId` parameter `basketball` at the bottom, as required by our POST request.

For this test, we are going to create one more POST endpoint called `/returnItem`. The configuration is the same as Figure 13.4 except that it has a different URL.

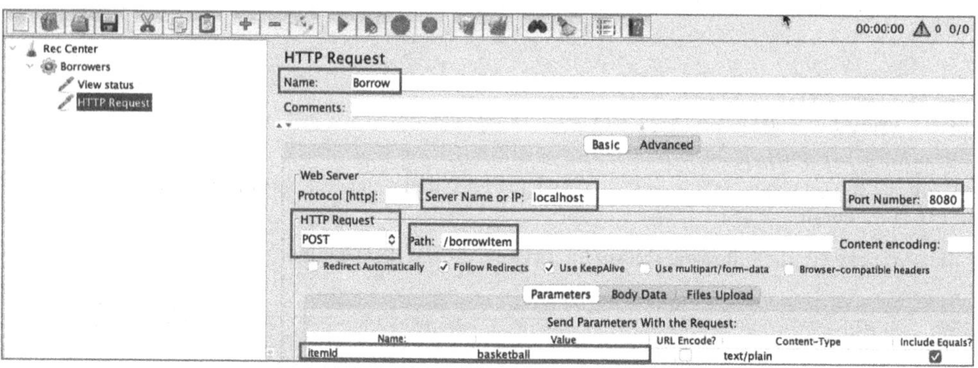

FIGURE 13.4: JMeter HTTP POST request

Since you want to view the results, we need to add one or more listeners by clicking the thread group and choosing Add ➪ Listener. This menu item presents you with a variety of output formats. For example, this example uses Summary Report and sets the output filename to `summary.csv`.

WHAT IF I HAVE MORE COMPLEX NEEDS?

No problem. JMeter has lots of settings, such as for passing login credentials or for working with cookies. Within your tests you can configure different orderings and combinations. You can add "think time" delays or have JMeter randomly select from a list of URLs. JMeter can do almost anything you could possibly need. This example is purposely simple so you can understand the basics. To go deeper, we encourage you to explore the truly excellent JMeter documentation. See "Further References" to learn what to do when you encounter more complex test scenarios.

For now, it is helpful to understand the most common elements of a test plan so you know what to look for in the documentation when the time comes:

- **Thread group:** Control the frequency of the threads being run. Each test plan has one or more thread groups.
- **Controller:** For sending requests. The sampler (HTTP request) you saw earlier is the simplest type of controller. There is also a variety of logic controllers to customize when requests are sent. For example, you can add randomization for the order of the requests, add the length of time tests should run, or even delegate to another test plan.
- **Listener:** For accessing information such as the results you saw earlier.
- **Timer:** Allows adding delays.
- **Assertion:** For adding data-validation tests to your JMeter tests, such as for checking values in the UI.

Now that you have a test plan, you can save it as a Java Management Extensions (JMX) file by going to File ➪ Save Test Plan As, and enter your desired filename and location before saving.

The `.jmx` file is saved in `src/main/resources` in the repository. You can open the JMeter UI and choose File ➪ Open to view it with all the settings used in this book.

A JMX file is an XML file. You'll learn about XML in the Appendix, "Reading and Writing XML, JSON, and YAML." For now, know that XML is a structured text format, and you can open the file in a text editor if you are curious about what is inside.

Running the Load Test

Be sure your application (in this case, the `RecCenterApplication` Spring Boot application) is running before executing the load test. Click the green arrow to run the tests. Once you are comfortable that they work, set up the tests to be able to run from the command-line interface.

Before launching JMeter, remember to add the JMeter `bin` directory to your path and run this:

```
jmeter -n -t RecCenter.jmx
```

The `-n` option means non-GUI, which is CLI mode (otherwise JMeter will launch its UI). The `-t` option means test file, which should be followed by the name of your JMX file. There are many additional options; for example, `-l` specifies the log file name, and `-o` specifies an output directory. If you need a proxy server to access the Internet, `-H` specifies the proxy host and `-P` the proxy port. There are many others, so review the documentation.

JMeter automatically creates a `jmeter.log` file. The output includes information about each thread, including the name (`Borrowers`), thread group, and number (`1-2`, and so forth). In this case, there is only one thread group making all the numbers begin with `1-`. There are five threads, so the second number ranges from one to five:

```
INFO o.a.j.t.JMeterThread: Thread started: Borrowers 1-1
INFO o.a.j.t.JMeterThread: Thread started: Borrowers 1-2
INFO o.a.j.t.JMeterThread: Thread is done: Borrowers 1-1
INFO o.a.j.t.JMeterThread: Thread finished: Borrowers 1-1
```

```
INFO o.a.j.t.JMeterThread: Thread started: Borrowers 1-3
INFO o.a.j.t.JMeterThread: Thread is done: Borrowers 1-3
INFO o.a.j.t.JMeterThread: Thread finished: Borrowers 1-3
INFO o.a.j.t.JMeterThread: Thread started: Borrowers 1-4
INFO o.a.j.t.JMeterThread: Thread is done: Borrowers 1-4
INFO o.a.j.t.JMeterThread: Thread finished: Borrowers 1-4
INFO o.a.j.t.JMeterThread: Thread started: Borrowers 1-5
INFO o.a.j.t.JMeterThread: Thread is done: Borrowers 1-5
INFO o.a.j.t.JMeterThread: Thread finished: Borrowers 1-5
INFO o.a.j.t.JMeterThread: Thread is done: Borrowers 1-2
INFO o.a.j.t.JMeterThread: Thread finished: Borrowers 1-2
INFO o.a.j.e.StandardJMeterEngine: Notifying test listeners of end of test
INFO o.a.j.r.Summariser: summary =     30 in 00:00:01 =   23.0/s
   Avg:    46 Min:     2 Max:  1014 Err:      0 (0.00%)
```

In this example, the test plan said to use five threads. Seeing that some threads managed to complete before others were started, we can conclude that they weren't started at the same time. You might notice that there are pairs of "done" and "finished." In JMeter, "done" means successful. By contrast, "finished" means the thread has stopped. Done threads are always finished, but not all finished ones go through done; some end in failure.

Additionally, the output ends with a summary of how long the request took, with the maximum, minimum, and average included.

Analyzing the Results

The `summary.csv` file contains many columns by default. You can customize it in the JMeter UI when creating the JMX file if you want a specific format. The first few columns are as follows:

- **Timestamp:** The start time of the request represented in "epoch time," which is the number of milliseconds since January 1, 1970.
- **Elapsed:** How long it took to complete the request.
- **Label:** The name of the request. In this case, they are View Status, Borrow, or Return.
- **Response Code:** This is 200 if the request was successful. For failures, the HTTP response code is useful in knowing what type of problem occurred. There's also a response message in the event of failure, which we omitted here since it was always blank.
- **Thread name:** In this example, it's Borrowers 1-1, Borrowers 1-2, and so forth. This is the thread group and the number you saw in the log file for the thread.

There are also columns for the number of byes in the request/response, and metrics on idle time and latency. The following is the beginning of the report for these initial columns with the elapsed time column in bold:

```
timeStamp,elapsed,label,responseCode,threadName
1.72279E+12,202,View status,200,Borrowers 1-1
1.72279E+12,37,View status,200,Borrowers 1-2
1.72279E+12,9,View status,200,Borrowers 1-3
1.72279E+12,10,View status,200,Borrowers 1-4
1.72279E+12,11,View status,200,Borrowers 1-5
1.72279E+12,1024,Borrow,200,Borrowers 1-1
1.72279E+12,10,Return,200,Borrowers 1-1
1.72279E+12,9,View status,200,Borrowers 1-1
1.72279E+12,1015,Borrow,200,Borrowers 1-1
1.72279E+12,13,Return,200,Borrowers 1-1
1.72279E+12,5025,Borrow,200,Borrowers 1-2
1.72279E+12,10,Return,200,Borrowers 1-2
```

```
1.72279E+12,8,View status,200,Borrowers 1-2
1.72279E+12,5014,Borrow,200,Borrowers 1-3
1.72279E+12,7,Return,200,Borrowers 1-3
```

Looking at this output, you can see that the `View status` operation is always fast. It took significantly longer the first two times, which is normal. When an application first starts, the JVM is figuring out the optimal way to run the code for performance. In fact, most people run the application outside of JMeter before doing a performance test in order to exclude this starting-up data.

Similarly, the `Return` operation is also fast. In contrast, however, the `Borrow` operation has quite the range. It is either just over a second or just over five seconds. Now it's time to let you in on a secret. This is the implementation of `borrowItem()`:

```
50: @PostMapping("/borrowItem")
51: public String borrowItem(@RequestParam(name="itemId", required=true)
52:    String itemId, Model model) {
53:    if (itemAvailability.getOrDefault(itemId, Boolean.FALSE)) {
54:       itemAvailability.put(itemId, Boolean.FALSE);
55:       sleep(1_000);
56:    } else {
57:       model.addAttribute("message", "Sorry, item not available");
58:       // if not available, wait five seconds
59:       sleep(5_000);
60:    }
61:    return sendToStatusPage(model);
62: }
```

Well, no wonder. The code waits one or five seconds. That's a poor implementation choice, and the load test highlighted it. The developer who wrote this code could benefit from a code review. However, there's a worse problem here. Lines 53 and 54 are not thread-safe. Seeing this, the developer decided to "fix" the code by making `borrowItem()` and `returnItem()` synchronized and then ran JMeter again to see the impact:

```
timeStamp,elapsed,label,responseCode,threadName
1.7228E+12,196,View status,200,Borrowers 1-1
1.7228E+12,29,View status,200,Borrowers 1-2
1.7228E+12,8,View status,200,Borrowers 1-3
1.7228E+12,16,View status,200,Borrowers 1-4
1.7228E+12,12,View status,200,Borrowers 1-5
1.7228E+12,1018,Borrow,200,Borrowers 1-1
1.7228E+12,5445,Borrow,200,Borrowers 1-5
1.7228E+12,10641,Borrow,200,Borrowers 1-4
1.7228E+12,15858,Borrow,200,Borrowers 1-3
1.7228E+12,10006,Return,200,Borrowers 1-4
1.7228E+12,21030,Borrow,200,Borrowers 1-2
1.7228E+12,20013,Return,200,Borrowers 1-1
1.7228E+12,5003,Return,200,Borrowers 1-3
1.7228E+12,15010,Return,200,Borrowers 1-5
```

The developer quickly realized this was not a good change. The `Borrow` operation is now far slower, and the performance problem has spread to the `Return` operation as well. We recommend the author of this code reread Chapter 9 to better understand concurrency! Nonetheless, this was a good demonstration of JMeter.

USING JDK TOOLS

The JDK install comes with a number of tools that help locate performance hotspots. We will look at these in the following sections. You can use them in combination with JMeter when testing under load or run them directly against your application to locate the source of known problems.

> **TIP** *Add the JDK* `bin` *directory to your path to run the commands in this section so that you don't have to type the fully qualified path at the command line.*

The examples in this section show how the application behaves when hitting the URL `http://localhost:8080/emailSummary` in our recreation center application. This endpoint produces a report of how many emails were received each month. Figure 13.5 shows the output from loading this page. Judging from this report we can assume that June (month 6) had an inordinate amount of spam! We have purposely coded this endpoint to use a very inefficient algorithm, which is invoked every time the page is hit. The algorithm reads a file and compares it to the previously loaded file. The code takes less than a second to run the first time and about 19 seconds on subsequent runs. To make matters worse, it also wastes memory. The last section in this chapter will show how to improve the situation. For now, let's take a look at the tools themselves.

Calls by Month

Month	Number of Calls
1	4073
2	4011
3	4254
4	4269
5	4236
6	54129
7	4214
8	4167
9	4054
10	4272
11	4158
12	4163

FIGURE 13.5: Email summary page

Now let's look at some tools for investigating performance problems.

Using Java Flight Recorder

Java Flight Recorder (JFR) is a monitoring tool for the JVM. JFR is primarily concerned with measuring three types of events:

- **Instant:** Logged as soon as some specified activity occurs
- **Duration:** Logged if activity exceeds a specified length
- **Sample:** Periodically captures activity

Java Flight Recorder logs events to a file named `flight.jfr`. You can generate a text report by executing the `jfr` command from the command line, or you can see the results in a visual format directly in Java Mission Control. The next section covers Java Mission Control.

Java doesn't automatically run Java Flight Recorder; you have to turn it on. There are several ways to turn it on. One option is to pass the `-XX:StartFlightRecording` option when starting your application. You can also configure additional options. For example, `-XX:StartFlightRecording=delay=5s,maxSize=1G` means ignore any data from the first five seconds of the program and limit the file size to one gigabyte, after which the file rolls over. The `java` tool documentation page has the full list of options.

Alternatively, you can use the `jcmd` program to tell a running JVM application to start profiling it with Java Flight Recorder. This approach accepts either a process ID (PID) or Java program name as input. So, for example, if our application is running as process ID 14020, then the following two commands would be equivalent ways of profiling it under JFR:

```
jcmd RecCenterApplication JFR.start filename=flight.jfr
jcmd 14020 JFR.start filename=flight.jfr
```

When you start Flight Recorder from the command line, it kindly displays a command that you can run later to dump all of the output to a file. You can launch that dump command at any time to get the full dump. Regardless of whether you ran the command using a process ID or Java program name, the dump command uses a process ID. For example, it could output the following:

```
Use jcmd 14020 JFR.dump name=1 to copy recording data to file.
```

Running that command tells you the size of the Flight Recorder file and where it was written to on disk:

```
Dumped recording "1", 519.1 kB written to:

/Users/<full path omitted>/rec-center/flight.jfr
```

The program was running for only a few seconds and generated 500KB of output. As you might imagine, this file gets large quickly!

> **HOW DO I FIND THE PID?**
>
> Typing `jps` lists the Java processes. For example:
>
> ```
> 14020 RecCenterApplication
> ```
>
> The `jps` docs say it is experimental and unsupported. It has been stable for more than two decades and is safe to use. Alternatively, you can use operating system commands. In Windows, open Task Manager and choose the process you want. On Linux/Mac, run the `ps` command and filter it (`grep`) by the name of the application.
>
> ```
> ps -ef | grep RecCenter
> ```

The output of a summary begins with the following:

```
jfr summary flight.jfr

 Version: 2.1
 Chunks: 2
 Start: 2024-08-10 14:14:27 (UTC)
 Duration: 103 s

 Event Type                              Count  Size (bytes)
=============================================================
 jdk.NativeMethodSample                   4485         48353
 jdk.ModuleExport                         1852         20076
 jdk.SystemProcess                        1512        155051
 jdk.NativeLibrary                        1332        116086
 jdk.ActiveSetting                        1077         31846
 jdk.BooleanFlag                           978         30255
 jdk.GCPhaseParallel                       438         10814
```

This on its own isn't terribly helpful, but JFR provides some templated "views," which can be more useful if you have an idea of where your problem might lie or if you want to test if some tweaks can improve some specific metrics. For example, the following shows the output of the thread-allocation view:

```
jfr view thread-allocation flight.jfr

                          Thread Allocation Statistics

Thread                                  Allocated Percentage
--------------------------------------- --------- ----------
http-nio-8080-exec-2                    25.0 MB     47.12%
Attach Listener                         18.8 MB     35.41%
http-nio-8080-exec-1                      7.5 MB     14.10%
RMI TCP Connection(1)-192.168.1.153     822.2 kB      1.52%
```

You can get the list of views by running the following command. Figure 13.6 shows the output.

```
jfr --help view
```

```
Java virtual machine views:
 class-modifications        gc-concurrent-phases longest-compilations
 compiler-configuration     gc-configuration     native-memory-committed
 compiler-phases            gc-cpu-time          native-memory-reserved
 compiler-statistics        gc-pause-phases      safepoints
 deoptimizations-by-reason gc-pauses            tlabs
 deoptimizations-by-site    gc-references        vm-operations
 gc                         heap-configuration

Environment views:
 active-recordings          cpu-information        jvm-flags
 active-settings            cpu-load               native-libraries
 container-configuration    cpu-load-samples       network-utilization
 container-cpu-throttling cpu-tsc                recording
 container-cpu-usage        environment-variables system-information
 container-io-usage         events-by-count        system-processes
 container-memory-usage     events-by-name         system-properties

Application views:
 allocation-by-class     exception-count       native-methods
 allocation-by-site      file-reads-by-path    object-statistics
 allocation-by-thread    file-writes-by-path   pinned-threads
 class-loaders           finalizers            socket-reads-by-host
 contention-by-address hot-methods           socket-writes-by-host
 contention-by-class     latencies-by-type     thread-allocation
 contention-by-site      longest-class-loading thread-count
 contention-by-thread    memory-leaks-by-class thread-cpu-load
 exception-by-message    memory-leaks-by-site  thread-start
 exception-by-site       modules
```

FIGURE 13.6: JFR views

Finally, if you want to search for something in particular, you can use the `print` option to list the results in XML or JSON format. However, if you don't know what specifically you are looking for or you just want to explore, omit the `print` option and just use Java Mission Control to open the file.

Visualizing in Java Mission Control

Java Mission Control is a UI meant for viewing information from Java Flight Recorder. In the past, Java Mission Control was in the JDK, but these days it is licensed separately as an independent download. It remains free for learning and experimentation, but if you plan to use it in production, check the license.

After following the download link in the "Further References" section, you should untar or unzip the downloaded file. Then launch Java Mission Control from the command line. Next go to File ⇨ Open and select the `.jfr` file from the previous section. Figure 13.7 shows some sample JFR memory output, which is a snapshot of how much memory is allocated to each class, sorted in order from most to least.

In the left navigation you can see other things mission control reports such as the following:

- **File I/O:** Lists time spent on input/output operations
- **Lock Instances:** Lists processes waiting on monitor locks
- **Method Profiling:** Shows stack trace for calls using the most CPU
- **Thread Dumps:** Shows what threads were running at various points in time
- **Garbage Collection:** Includes which garbage collector is used along with a graph showing pauses and available heap memory
- **Processes:** Shows CPU and other processes using significant CPU outside of the JVM

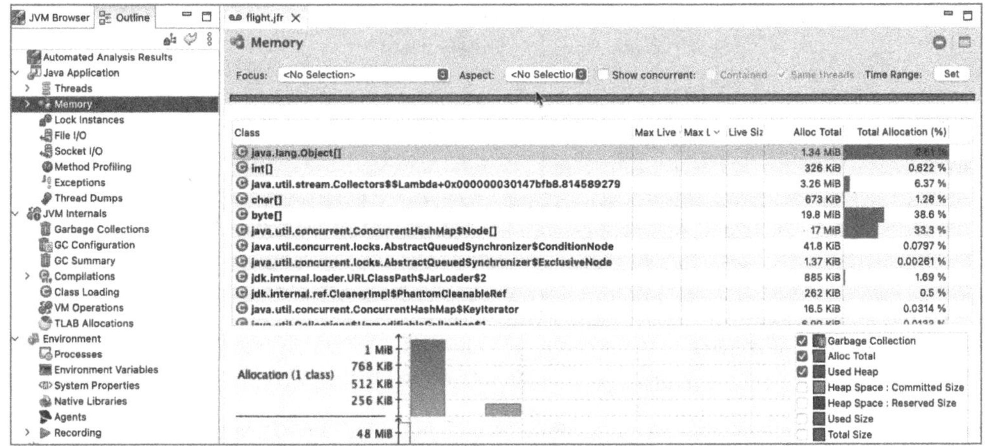

FIGURE 13.7: Java Mission Control

Monitoring with JConsole

Mission Control gives you data on an application after you've loaded the Java Flight Recorder file. In contrast, `jconsole` lets you see real-time metrics from your running application.

> **TIP** *JConsole will introduce some performance overhead on the application it is profiling, so it is not recommended to run it in production.*

To launch JConsole, just pass the process ID.

```
jconsole 5045
```

Figure 13.8 shows the overview tab of JConsole. You can see this application uses a lot of heap memory and it keeps increasing, which is not a pattern you want to see. By contrast, the CPU spikes when work is being done and then goes back down after the operations complete. That is a good thing as it means the CPU is doing its job!

The memory tab lets you look at a graph of each generation on the heap and displays the effects on garbage collection. The threads tab is helpful in detecting deadlocks. The VM Summary tab gives you statistics like the number of threads in use and the size of the heap including maximums for each. It also shows you which garbage collector is running. The classes and MBeans tabs are not as commonly used.

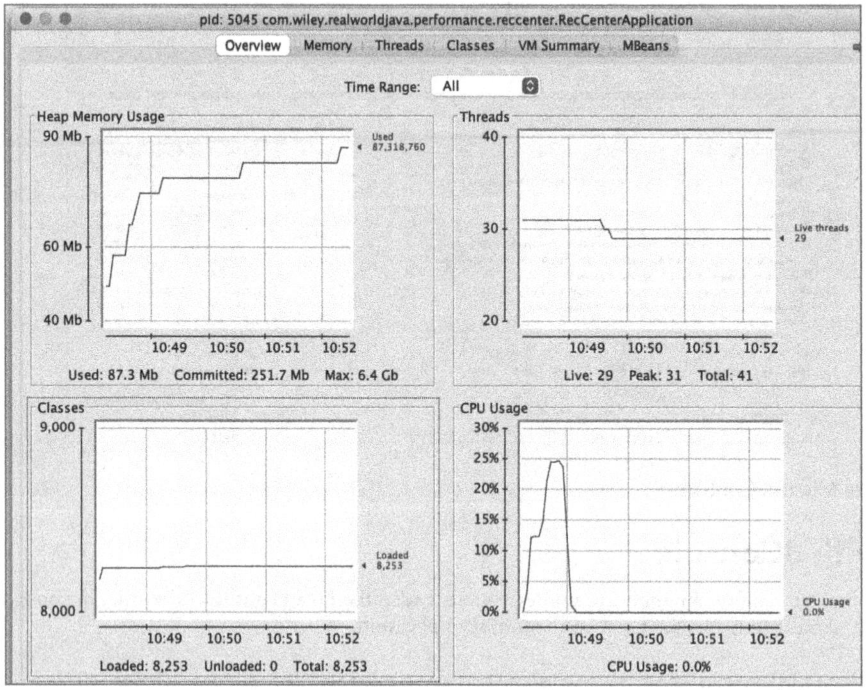

FIGURE 13.8: JConsole

Using VisualVM

Like Java Mission Control, VisualVM was originally distributed with the JDK. Originally named `jvisualvm`, it is now available as a stand-alone tool that you can download from the link in "Further References."

> **TIP** *IntelliJ, Eclipse, and VS Code all have plugins/extensions for using VisualVM straight from the IDE.*

To launch VisualVM, call `visualvm.exe` on Windows or `visualvm` on Linux/Mac. Notice that you don't pass in a process ID; VisualVM automatically provides all the Java processes it can find in the left navigation. Just double-click the one you want information on.

Like JConsole, VisualVM can provide real-time monitoring of your process, as shown in Figure 13.9. You can toggle between the heap and Metaspace graphs on this Monitoring tab. Clicking Heap Dump shows you which classes are using the most memory with a single click.

The Threads tab provides information on CPU use and wait time. The Sampler tab shows you CPU and memory usage details in real time. The Profiler tab allows you to gain insight into your application. Besides profiling a running app, you can also load JFR files or dump files that you generated at the command line.

You might have noticed some of the tools in this chapter overlap. VisualVM is commonly used for initial or quick profiling and is the fastest to get started with. If that isn't enough to find the problem, you will generally find that moving on to Java Flight Recorder/Java Mission Control or an alternate profiler is worth the time.

> **OTHER PROFILERS**
>
> There are many free and commercial profilers. Like VisualVM, they let you dive into the CPU, memory, I/O, garbage collection, and any other parts of your application likely to cause a performance problem. Each works differently, but the ideas are the same. Other common profilers include JProfiler, YourKit Profiler, Dynatrace, and AppDynamics.
>
> IntelliJ comes with a built-in profiler as well. IDE tools are great for improving performance in development or against a test server. The more powerful profilers are useful for testing in upper environments such as QA where you have production-like conditions, or even in production itself.

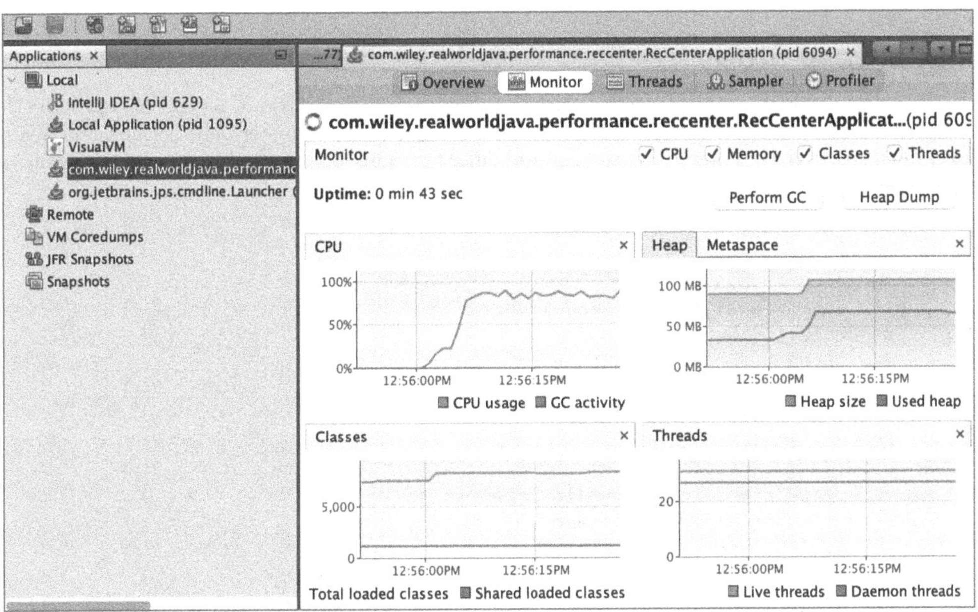

FIGURE 13.9: VisualVM

Reporting with JStat

While `jconsole` provides a graph of garbage collection, the `jstat` command gives you this information in text form. For example, the following command passes the process ID to monitor memory use and garbage collection. It prints a line twice every second (that is, every 500 milliseconds) and continues 20 times.

```
jstat -gcutil 5045 500 20
  S0      S1      E
     - 100.00   8.57
     - 100.00   8.57
     - 100.00  11.43
     - 100.00  11.43
     - 100.00  11.43
```

The previous example shows the output of the first three (of many) columns of output for garbage collection statistics. The first two columns are the survivor space from garbage collection. The first column is blank while an application is starting. The third column is the size of Eden, which is where objects are initially allocated. You can see this increase as the program runs.

GCUtil also displays information about how long it took to run garbage collection, along with information about Metaspace use. The `jstat` command has many options about the classloader, heap, and garbage collection. If you find yourself needing real-time information, the `jstat` documentation page covers all the options.

OPTIMIZING YOUR APPLICATION

Whether you have identified the performance problem using the tools described in this chapter or if you are just thinking about making your code under development more performant, this section will help you design and write more performant code. First, we will use the `emailSummary` operation as a case study to show that performance shouldn't be an afterthought. While "premature optimization is the root of all evil," designing and writing performant code in the first place is not! Then, you'll see how SonarQube can help you avoid performance problems at the coding level. Finally, we'll provide a checklist of things to consider.

Exploring a Case Study

Let's start by coding the implementation of the `/emailSummary` endpoint that runs when a user calls the URL to request an email summary. The code reads from a file containing a list of numbers, one per line, representing the number of emails received. It has a variety of performance problems. See how many you can find while reading the code!

```
private List<String> numberOfEmails;

@GetMapping("/emailSummary")
public String emailSummary(Model model) {
   readFile();
   Map<Integer, Long> byMonth = calculateTotals();

   model.addAttribute("byMonth", byMonth);
   return "emailSummary";
}
private Map<Integer, Long> calculateTotals() {
   return numberOfEmails.stream()
      .map(Integer::parseInt)
      .collect(Collectors.groupingBy(Function.identity(),
      TreeMap::new, Collectors.counting()));
}
private void readFile() {
   Path path = Path.of("src/main/resources/lastYear.txt");
   List<String> fileData;
   try {
      fileData = Files.readAllLines(path);
   } catch (IOException e) {
      throw new UncheckedIOException(e);
   }
   if (numberOfEmails == null ||
         numberOfEmailsChangedSinceLastRead(numberOfEmails, fileData)) {
      numberOfEmails = fileData;
   }
}
private boolean numberOfEmailsChangedSinceLastRead(
   List<String> numberOfEmails, List<String> fileData) {
   if (numberOfEmails.size() != fileData.size()) {
      return false;
   }
```

```
44:     for (int i = 0; i < numberOfEmails.size(); i++) {
45:        for (int j = 0; j < fileData.size(); j++) {
46:           if (i == j &&
47:              ! numberOfEmails.get(i).equals(fileData.get(j))) {
48:              return false;
49:           }
50:        }
51:     }
52:     return true;
53: }
```

The first problem starts in line 14, where we read the file every time a user requests the report. This file contains data from the previous year. It isn't changing. I/O and network operations are often the most expensive parts of an application. Considering whether you can cache data or batch operations will often help your performance. In this case, the file needs to be read only once. If the file was changing, you could check on the timestamp or have another process invalidate the cache to avoid reading every time.

Even if we did have a requirement to compare the file contents, the implementation of `numberOfEmailsChangedSinceLastRead()` is a terrible way to do it, because it is comparing way too much. The entire method could be written as follows:

```
return numberOfEmails.equals(fileData);
```

Using a built-in method instead of writing your own is likely to be faster since library providers spend time optimizing them. In this case, `numberOfEmailsChangedSinceLastRead()` has nested loops, which is much slower than needed.

BIG O NOTATION

Big O notation is used to describe the asymptotic growth pattern of an algorithm as a function of the input size. Asymptotic means what happens as the data gets larger and larger, approaching infinity.

The idea is that if doubling the input sizes causes the execution time to grow from 10 seconds to 100 seconds, then that is way more significant than if it grew to only 20 seconds. Big O notation provides a shorthand to discuss these scenarios. If performance grows linearly with the input size n, then we say the complexity is $O(n)$. If the performance varies as the square of the input, then we say the complexity is $O(n^2)$.

You should be able to recognize these common ones in increasing cost:

- **O(1) – constant time:** The time doesn't depend on the size of the input. Reading a single item from an `ArrayList` is an example.
- **O(log *n*) – logarithmic time:** The time increases much more slowly than the input. Searching to find a value in a sorted list is an example.
- **O(*n*) – linear time:** The time is proportional to the size of the input. Searching to find a value in a random list is an example.
- **$O(n^2)$ – quadratic time:** The time increases quadratically. The nested loops in `fileChangedSinceLastRead()` are an example.
- **$O(2^n)$ – exponential time:** The time doubles with each additional item in the input. The Fibonacci recursion in the benchmarking section is an example.

The next problem is that this program wastes memory. There are a million rows in the file. Yet the algorithm needs only a summary. It would be better to store the results of the calculation rather than the original data since it is used for only this one purpose.

Finally, `calculateTotals()` converts the `String` to an `int` and then boxes it to an `Integer`. This isn't a problem on its own. However, the result is only used for counting, so it might as well have stayed a `String`. Many compilers are smart enough to optimize this type of inefficiency out of existence. However, it is better if you can avoid unnecessary work in the first place.

The following is the more efficient version of the code:

```
private Map<String, Long> emailSummary = getEmailSummary();

@GetMapping("/emailSummary")
public String emailSummary(Model model) {
   model.addAttribute("byMonth", emailSummary);
   return "emailSummary";
}
private Map<String, Long> getEmailSummary() {
   Path path = Path.of("src/main/resources/lastYear.txt");
   List<String> fileData;
   try {
      fileData = Files.readAllLines(path);
   } catch (IOException e) {
      throw new UncheckedIOException(e);
   }
   return fileData.stream()
      .collect(Collectors.groupingBy(Function.identity(),
      TreeMap::new, Collectors.counting()));
}
```

In addition to being faster, the code is also shorter and clearer!

Using SonarQube

As you learned in Chapter 4, "Automating Your CI/CD Builds with Maven, Gradle, and Jenkins," you can run SonarLint in your IDE or SonarQube in your build. Both provide a set of rules tagged as `performance`. Table 13.4 shows examples of rules that it can detect.

TABLE 13.4: Examples of Sonar Performance Rules

RULES	REASON
Strings should not be concatenated using + in a loop.	`StringBuilder` is more efficient.
`entrySet()` should be iterated when both the key and value are needed.	It is slightly faster to use `entrySet()` than continually call `get()`.
Synchronized classes `Vector`, `Hashtable`, `Stack`, and `StringBuffer` should not be used.	These APIs lock the entire collection during any access. These were replaced with more efficient versions long ago.
`wait(...)` should be used instead of `Thread.sleep(...)` when a lock is held.	Could cause scalability issues and potential deadlocks. The reactive `wait()` is preferred because it wakes up as soon as it is notified, whereas `sleep()` must finish its sleep time.

Considering Performance

When you work on performance tuning, you are likely to find the problem lies in one of a few areas. This section provides a checklist you can use for ideas on what to consider for each one being the bottleneck after using a profiler to determine the cause.

Network/Bandwidth

- Batch/reduce the number of network calls
- Avoid returning unnecessary data
- Cache data

CPU

- Use more efficient algorithm
- Use parallelization (see Chapter 9)
- Do work asynchronously where possible

Memory

- Use more efficient data structures
- Only save data when you need it
- Increase allocated memory

I/O

- Cache data
- Use a logger instead of `printlns` (see Chapter 5, "Capturing Application State with Logging Frameworks")
- If using a database, use a connection pool

FURTHER REFERENCES

- Java Performance (O'Reilly, 2020)
- `https://github.com/openjdk/jmh`

  JMH
- `https://docs.oracle.com/en/java/javase/21/docs/specs/man/java.html`

  `java` configuration options
- `https://docs.oracle.com/en/java/javase/21/docs/specs/man/jstat.html`

  `jstat` configuration options
- `https://speakerdeck.com/cguntur/java-garbage-collection-a-journey-until-java-13-darkbg`

  Detailed presentation on garbage collection
- `https://jmeter.apache.org/download_jmeter.cgi`

  Download JMeter

- `https://jmeter.apache.org/usermanual/index.html`

  JMeter documentation
- `https://www.oracle.com/java/technologies/jdk-mission-control.html`

  Download Java Mission Control
- `https://visualvm.github.io/download.html`

  Download Java VisualVM

SUMMARY

In this chapter, you learned about performance concepts and tuning. You saw how to create a microbenchmark and perform low-level comparison. Then you learned about garbage collection and how to configure the JVM for your application. JMeter is used for running load tests, and a variety of tools are used to gather data about running applications and identifying performance problems. Finally, you saw how to improve applications once a problem is identified.

14

Getting to Know More of the Ecosystem

WHAT'S IN THIS CHAPTER?

- Writing Javadoc
- Comparing JVM Languages
- Exploring Jakarta EE
- Comparing Database Types
- Learning About Integrations
- Deploying Java
- Building REST APIs
- Picking a Virtual Machine
- Exploring Libraries
- Securing Your Applications
- Staying Informed About Changes

As we mentioned in the introduction, this book introduced you to many of the most common technologies that you will encounter as you grow in your career as a Java engineer. The Java ecosystem is vast, and it isn't possible to cover everything, or learn everything, in one go!

This chapter gives a high-level overview of many other technologies that you'll hear about or work with at some point. Understanding what they are for will help you follow conversations and know when to come back to the further references if you are about to work with them.

CODE DOWNLOADS FOR THIS CHAPTER

The source code for this chapter is available on the book page at `www.wiley.com`. Click the Downloads link. You can also find the code at `https://github.com/realworldjava/Ch14-More-Ecosystem`. See the `README.md` file in that repository for details.

WRITING JAVADOC

When you are learning about a Java API, for example `Executors` in Chapter 9, "Parallelizing your Application Using Java Concurrency," you would check the Javadoc for information about available methods, parameters, and more. You might be wondering how that document got created.

In the following example, the code is annotated with special Javadoc comments as shown:

```
4:  /**
5:    * An object that contains information about
6:    * topics the reader may want to learn.
7:    *
8: * <p><b> There is a lot more to learn!</b>
9:    * To use:
10:   * {@snippet lang = java:
11:   *       Learning learning = new Learning();
12:   *       learning.addTopic("Docker");
13:   * }</p>
14:   */
15: public class Learning {
16:    private Set<String> topics;
17:    /**
18:      * Creates a new Learning object
19:      */
20:    public Learning() {
21:       topics = new HashSet<>();
22:    }
23:    /**
24:      * Stores a topic the reader wishes to learn.
25:      *
26:      * @param topic the name of the topic to learn
27:      * @return {@code true} if this topic was not already stored
28:      */
29:    public boolean addTopic(String topic) {
30:       return topics.add(topic);
31:    }
32: }
```

Lines 4–14, 17–19, and 23–28 show three Javadoc comments. As you can see from line 8, Javadoc comments can contain a limited set of HTML tags. Lines 10–13 show a feature added in Java 18 that allows your IDE and other generated documentation to format sections of your Javadoc with Java and other language-specific code examples. Lines 26 and 27 show the `@param` and `@return` annotations, which provide information about the method parameter and return types. Javadoc has many more features such as additional package-level documentation. See "Further References" for more on writing Javadoc.

You can generate Javadoc as part of your build. For example, using the maven-javadoc-plugin in a <reporting> tag causes Javadoc to be created when you run maven site.

COMPARING JVM LANGUAGES

This book has focused on Java, as it is the most popular language used on the JVM, as you might infer, given that the letters stand for "Java Virtual Machine." There are many other languages that run on the JVM. In the following sections, you'll get a taste of three JVM languages: Kotlin, Groovy, and Scala. There are many more including Clojure, for pure functional programming, JRuby, which allows Ruby applications to run on the JVM, and Jython, which provides a Python implementation for the JVM.

Sampling Kotlin

Kotlin is a popular language used for writing Android applications and is becoming a popular alternative to Java. Java code can call Kotlin code and vice versa. Kotlin allows you to write more concise code and offers handy features such as catching null pointer errors at compile time instead of runtime. The following example shows some Kotlin features:

```
1:  package com.wiley.realworldjava.more
2:
3:  class Destination(val city: String, val state: String)
4:
5:  fun countCitiesInCalifornia(cities: List<Destination>): Int {
6:     return cities.count { it.state == "California" }
7:  }
8:
9:  fun main() {
10:    val cities = listOf(Destination("Atlanta", "Georgia"),
11:       Destination("San Jose", "California"),
12:       Destination("Denver", "Colorado"),
13:       Destination("San Diego", "California"))
14:
15:    val californiaCityCount = countCitiesInCalifornia(cities)
16:    print("Visited ${cities.size} cities " +
17:       "starting with ${cities.first().city}");
18:    println(" including $californiaCityCount in California")
19: }
```

Like in Java, the package statement on line 1 is optional. Line 3 shows how to create a data class. These are similar to Java records, being a one-liner to create a simple data structure. The val in the parameter declarations means the data type is immutable, in contrast to var, which would be mutable. Unlike Java, the type declaration String comes after the parameter name.

Lines 5–6 show how to create a function in Kotlin; this one takes a single List parameter named cities and returns an Int. The implementation uses a concise functional programming statement to count the number of Destination values that have a state of California. Like Java, a lambda expression is used to encapsulate the logic for matching. However, it is more concise than Java. There is no lambda variable required, since it is provided by default.

Line 9 declares a main method, which is much shorter than the public static void main(String[] args) familiar to all Java programmers. The args parameter is optional, and we omit it since it is not used. Lines 10–13 create an immutable list using the listOf() function. Notice that the new keyword is not used when instantiating the Destination objects.

Lines 16–18 show concise code for output. `System.out` is omitted when printing. Additionally, *string interpolation* is used, which means variables are evaluated when declared in the string with a `$` such as `$californiaCityCount`. Additionally, code can be configured inside a `${}` allowing methods to be called directly inside the string. Finally, note that `size` is used instead of `size()` since Kotlin provides `size` as a property to allow for more concise code than Java.

Another thing that makes the code more concise is the lack of semicolons to end statements. If you noticed the word "concise" used a lot in the explanation, you understand a key benefit of Kotlin: more concise code!

Sampling Groovy

Groovy is a scripting language, which means you do not have to compile it. As with many other scripting languages, Groovy does not require types to be specified. The following shows the Kotlin example code translated to Groovy:

```
1:  class Destination {
2:     String city
3:     String state
4:
5:     Destination(String city, String state) {
6:        this.city = city
7:        this.state = state
8:     }
9:  }
10:
11: private static int countCitiesInCalifornia(List<Destination> cities) {
12:     cities.count { it.state == "California" }
13: }
14:
15: def cities = [
16:     new Destination("Atlanta", "Georgia"),
17:     new Destination("San Jose", "California"),
18:     new Destination("Denver", "Colorado"),
19:     new Destination("San Diego", "California")
20: ]
21:
22: def californiaCityCount = countCitiesInCalifornia(cities)
23: print "Visited ${cities.size()} cities " +
24:     "starting with ${cities.first().city}"
25: println " including $californiaCityCount in California"
```

In Groovy the package declaration is also optional. Lines 1–9 create a class. While properties are available based on the instance variables, a constructor must be coded to be called.

Lines 11–13 declare a function using a signature that should look familiar from Java. The implementation matches the Kotlin version except the `return` keyword is missing, even though the method has a return value. If you omit the return, Groovy automatically returns the value produced in the last statement in the function.

Notice how there is no main method required! Lines 15–20 create a mutable list using brackets (`[]`) around the contents. Unlike Kotlin, note that new is required to create an instance of an object.

Line 22 shows that Groovy uses `def` when you don't want to code the type of a variable. Lines 23–25 are the same as Kotlin except for `size()`, which must use the method name since a shorthand property is not available.

Sampling Scala

Scala is a compiled language that was designed to process large amounts of data efficiently as well as for working with distributed systems. Additionally, Scala has built-in support for many functional programming patterns. To get a feel for the syntax, here's the example you saw in Kotlin and Groovy rewritten for Scala:

```
1:  package com.wiley.realworldjava.more
2:
3:  case class Destination(city: String, state: String)
4:
5:  object Travel {
6:
7:     private def countCitiesInCalifornia(
8:        cities: List[Destination]): Int = {
9:        cities.count(_.state == "California")
10:    }
11:
12:    def main(args: Array[String]): Unit = {
13:       val cities = List(
14:          Destination("Atlanta", "Georgia"),
15:          Destination("San Jose", "California"),
16:          Destination("Denver", "Colorado"),
17:          Destination("San Diego", "California")
18:       )
19:
20:       val californiaCityCount = countCitiesInCalifornia(cities)
21:       print(s"Visited ${cities.size} cities" +
22:          s"starting with ${cities.head.city}")
23:       println(s" including $californiaCityCount in California")
24:    }
25: }
```

You can see different JVM languages have some elements in common. Scala uses `def` when creating functions like Groovy. The `val` declaration and a return value of `Int` are like Kotlin.

There are unique elements as well. Line 3 shows `case` classes, a breed of class used to produce immutable data structures. Generics are available but where Java uses < and >, Scala uses brackets, as you can see in the type declaration of `List[Destination]` in line 8. The implementation should look familiar from Groovy except _ is used as the default lambda variable.

Line 12 uses `Unit`, the Scala equivalent of `void` in Java. On lines 21–23, you can see that `s` precedes a string to tell the runtime to use string interpolation. Line 22 also shows `head` is provided instead of using `first()` to get the first element.

EXPLORING JAKARTA EE

As we mentioned in Chapter 1, "How We Got Here: History of Java in a Nutshell," Jakarta EE (Enterprise Edition) is an alternative to Spring for enterprise applications. Jakarta EE was previously called Java EE before it was open-sourced.

Some of the concepts you see in Spring depend on Jakarta EE. For example, in Chapter 6, "Getting to Know the Spring Framework," you learned that filters are also known as servlet filters. A *servlet* is a subclass that processes a request and returns a response. The most common type is `jakarta.servlet.http.HttpServlet`, which is for web requests and responses.

Jakarta EE is organized into specifications, and you can use just the parts you want. For example, the core profile is meant for microservices while the web profile is meant for web applications.

Table 14.1 gives you a feel for what is available in Jakarta EE. You might notice this table has more rows than the Spring projects listed in Table 6.1. That's because Jakarta EE projects are more granular. Jakarta EE and Spring are excellent competitors and provide most of the common functionality that you'd expect. The organization you work for is likely to have a preference, so you should use that one!

TABLE 14.1: Example Jakarta EE Projects

PROJECT	DESCRIPTION
Jakarta EE Platform	Umbrella project for the most common parts of Jakarta EE including the core profile and web profile
Jakarta Batch	Used for batch processing applications
Jakarta Enterprise Java Beans	Architecture for enterprise components
Jakarta Faces	Supplies a MVC framework
Jakarta Mail	For sending emails
Jakarta Messaging	For using Java Messaging Service (JMS)
Jakarta Persistence	Supports object-relational mapping
Jakarta RESTful Web Services	Used for creating REST web services
Jakarta Security	Adds authorization and authentication support
Jakarta Transactions	Supports transactions across multiple data stores
Jakarta XML Binding	Map Java objects and XML (a competitor of Jackson that was used in the Appendix, "Reading and Writing XML, JSON, and YAML")

COMPARING DATABASE TYPES

The applications in this book either did everything in memory or read from a file. In the real world, you will want to deal with more organized sources of information in a *database*.

Understanding Relational Databases

Relational databases store data in rows and columns. Figure 14.1 shows a sample database named `Zoo`. It has two tables: `exhibits` and `names`. The `exhibits` table has two rows and three columns. A *primary key* is one or more columns that uniquely identify a row, in this case `id`. Different databases have different types. A common one is *varchar*, which stands for "varying character." Unlike with a Java `String`, you have to specify the maximum length of your `varchar` column, so the database knows how much space to allocate.

Some of the most common relational databases are MySQL, PostgreSQL, MariaDB, Oracle, and Microsoft SQL Server. Figure 14.1 shows how a zoo would be structured in a relational database such as PostgreSQL.

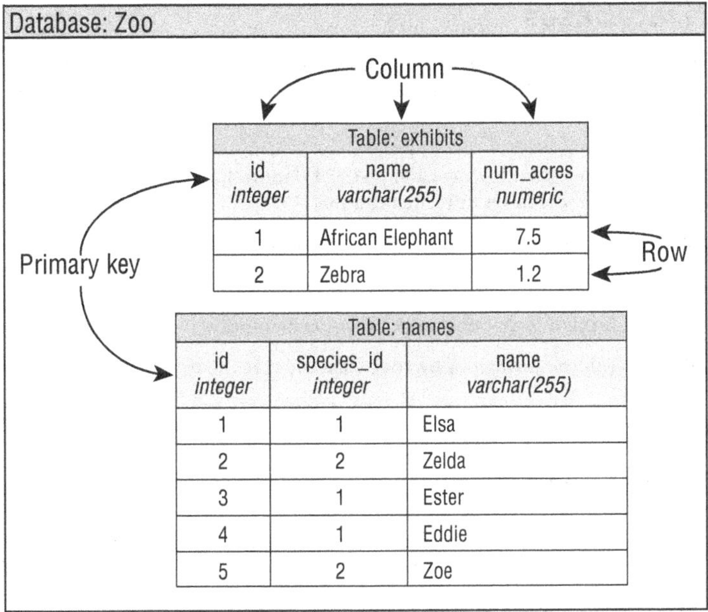

FIGURE 14.1: Relational database

Relational databases use a language called Structured Query Language (SQL) to work with the data. There are four main database operations, which comprise the popular acronym known as CRUD (Create, Read, Update, Delete). Table 14.2 gives you a feel for what SQL looks like using each of the major types of operations.

TABLE 14.2: SQL Keywords

SQL EXAMPLE	EXPLANATION
`INSERT INTO exhibits VALUES (3, 'Asian Elephant', 7.5);`	Adds a new row with the provides values. Defaults to the order in which the columns were defined in the table.
`SELECT * FROM exhibits WHERE ID = 3;`	Reads data from the table with an optional `WHERE` clause to limit the data returned. In the `SELECT`, can use `*` to return all columns, list specific ones to return, or even call functions like `COUNT(*)` to return the number of matching rows.
`UPDATE exhibits SET num_acres = num_acres + .5 WHERE name = 'Asian Elephant';`	Sets a column's value with an optional `WHERE` clause to limit the rows update.
`DELETE FROM exhibits WHERE name = 'Asian Elephant';`	Deletes rows with an optional `WHERE` clause to limit the rows deleted.

An alternative to using SQL would be to use an object-relational mapping (ORM) framework, which maps the database to Java objects for you behind the scenes. Hibernate, Spring, and Java Persistence Architecture (JPA) are options for ORM.

Understanding NoSQL Databases

NoSQL databases are used for storing unstructured or partially structured data, where rows and columns might not be the best storage choice. As you might imagine from the name, they do not use SQL for queries. The following are popular NoSQL database types:

- **Document:** Stores data as JSON documents, allowing each piece of data to have different attributes. Couchbase and MongoDB are the most common implementations.
- **Graph:** Stores data as a graph of nodes and relations. Neo4J is the most popular implementation.
- **Key/value:** Stores data as key/value pairs like in a map. Redis is the most popular implementation.
- **Time series:** Stores data by time. InfluxDB is the most popular implementation.
- **Wide column store:** Stores data by column instead of by row. Cassandra is the most popular implementation.

LEARNING ABOUT INTEGRATIONS

In addition to databases, there are a number of common technologies that Java applications integrate with. This section explains how JMS, LDAP, and EJBs fit into the Java world.

Java Message Service (JMS) is used for asynchronous communication between systems and processes. A message is placed on a queue. A single recipient can pick up the message later for processing using a *point-to-point* model. Alternatively, you can set up a *publish-subscribe* system to have the message delivered to many recipients.

Lightweight Directory Access Protocol (LDAP) is used for looking up user information. It is commonly used to determine what groups someone is in and what they have access to. Additionally, information about the user can be available, such as a department ID or start date.

Enterprise Java Beans represent components in Jakarta EE that can have services like transactions and security added to them. They represent an alternative to Spring, which provides the same functionality with more flexibility. The following are the types of EJBs:

- **Stateless session beans:** For providing a service without having to remember user info between visits.
- **Stateful session beans:** For providing a service with the requirement to remember user data. This type is less common since user data is typically stored in other layers of the application.
- **Singleton session beans:** For data that can be shared by the entire application.
- **Message-driven beans:** For processing JMS messages.

In the past, entity beans were used for working with data. The industry has moved on to JPA and other object-relational mapping frameworks.

DEPLOYING JAVA

In this book, all development happened on your computer, and you started up some applications at the command line. Contrast that to enterprise software, where the software runs in a location where your users can access it, and that is most certainly not your computer. This section describes the main categories available for hosting your applications.

Differentiating Web and Application Servers

You are most likely to encounter a *web server* when providing static content, such as HTML, CSS, and JavaScript to your users. While web servers can also serve dynamic languages, they are limited to running scripting languages like Python and Ruby. The most common web servers are Apache HTTP Server and ngnix.

> **TIP** *A content delivery network (CDN) can also serve static content. CDNs are frequently used for caching static content, like images and open-source JavaScript libraries, to save bandwidth costs and provide a faster response.*

An *application server* is able to run Java code packaged as a WAR (web archive) or EAR (enterprise archive). A WAR consists of JAR files along with a web directory structure with the specifics of how to process web requests. An EAR file can include a WAR file, JAR files, and Enterprise Java Beans (EJBs).

Common application servers include Apache Tomcat, Glassfish, JBoss, Papaya, and IBM WebSphere. Spring Boot MVC applications run an embedded Apache Tomcat.

> **TIP** *Notice there is both an Apache HTTP Server, which is a web server, and an Apache Tomcat, which is an application server. Developers often reference "Apache" for the web server and "Tomcat" for the application server. However, make sure you know which "Apache" is under discussion from the context; otherwise, ask.*

Using Containers

Whatever application you are running, whether a simple stand-alone application, some Spring Boot application, or a high-traffic web server, you need a machine with an operating system to run it on. In large organizations, another team is responsible for the maintenance and patching of that operating system. To avoid surprises, many teams use a *container* like Docker. Containers are executable packages containing not only your application but the operating system and any software it depends on. The container image is packaged up and hosted, and you just need to download it and run it, no installation or configuration required.

When distributing software for others to run, vendors have more control of the environment, thereby reducing support costs. For example, in Chapter 4, "Automating Your CI/CD Builds with Maven, Gradle, and Jenkins," installing Jenkins was as simple as running two commands:

```
docker pull jenkins/jenkins
docker run --name jenkins -p 8080:8080 jenkins/jenkins
```

The `pull` command downloaded the images, and the `run` command set up the initial configuration. Subsequent installs were even easier with the following:

```
docker start jenkins
```

Since the name and port were already set up, all you had to do was `start`.

Similar to Maven Central for Java artifacts, Docker uses a repository called DockerHub, which is at `https://hub.docker.com`. The configuration is in a file called `Dockerfile`. The beginning of the Jenkins `Dockerfile` for Alpine Linux looks like this:

```
ARG ALPINE_TAG=3.20.3

```

```
FROM alpine:"${ALPINE_TAG}" AS jre-build

ARG JAVA_VERSION=17.0.12_7

SHELL ["/bin/ash", "-o", "pipefail", "-c"]

COPY jdk-download-url.sh /usr/bin/jdk-download-url.sh
COPY jdk-download.sh /usr/bin/jdk-download.sh

RUN apk add --no-cache \
    ca-certificates \
    jq \
    curl \
    && rm -fr /var/cache/apk/* \
    && /usr/bin/jdk-download.sh alpine

ENV PATH="/opt/jdk-${JAVA_VERSION}/bin:${PATH}"
```

The bold words in this `Dockerfile` are the instructions. The ones used in this example are as follows:

- **`ARG`**: Defines a local variable that is available only in the `Dockerfile` but cannot be referenced in the image.
- **`FROM`**: Builds a new image from the base image, in this case Alpine Linux. The base image can be an operating system or another `Dockerfile` that you want to add to.
- **`SHELL`**: On Linux/Mac, you can choose which shell to use for operations at the command line.
- **`COPY`**: Copies a file from the machine running the build into the image.
- **`RUN`**: Runs an operating system command. It is common to run multiple commands connected with `&&` to reduce the number of layers in the image. Each layer takes up extra space and is slower to download. In this example, `apk` installs `ca-certificates`, `jq`, and `curl`. It then removes the cached files and downloads the JDK.
- **`ENV`**: Sets an environment variable in the image.

WHAT IS KUBERNETES?

Kubernetes is sometimes shortened to K8s with the 8 representing the number of letters between the first and last. It is used to deploy, scale, and manage containers. This means you can deploy Docker images directly not just with Docker but with Kubernetes as well.

Kubernetes is particularly useful if you have complex needs or relationships among your containers. For example, Kubernetes can restart your application as needed and helps with fault tolerance.

Launching to the Cloud

While the servers and containers discussed so far can be deployed to a server that your organization owns, a common alternative is to deploy them to the *cloud* instead. Cloud computing is where the data center is owned by someone else. Amazon Web Services (AWS), Microsoft Azure, and Google Cloud are the three most common cloud environments.

Each cloud provider uses different terminology, as shown in Table 14.3.

TABLE 14.3: Sample Cloud Technologies

TECHNOLOGY	AWS	AZURE	GOOGLE CLOUD
Server—provides operating system to application	Elastic Compute Cloud (EC2)	Azure Virtual Machine	Google Compute Engine (GCE)
Kubernetes support	Elastic Kubernetes Service (EKS)	Azure Kubernetes Service (AKS)	Google Kubernetes Engine (GKE)
Serverless computing—for short-running applications	Lambda	Azure Functions Serverless Compute	Google Cloud Functions
Platform as a service—for web applications	Elastic Beanstalk	Azure App Services	Google Application Engine (GAE)
SQL database	Relational Database Service (RDS) Aurora—serverless alternative	Azure SQL Database	Cloud SQL
Serving static content	Simple Storage Service (S3)	Azure Blob Storage	Google Cloud Storage (GCS)
Content Delivery Network (CDN)—for caching data	CloudFront	Azure CDN	Cloud CDN
Networking	Virtual Private Cloud (VPC)	AWS Virtual Private Network (VPN)	Google Cloud Networking Services
Email/text alerts	Simple Networking Service (SNS)	Azure Notification Hubs	Firebase Cloud Messaging
Messaging queues	Simple Queue Services (SQS)	Azure Service Bus Azure Storage Queues	Google Cloud Pub/Sub
Access management	Identity and Access Management (IAM)	Azure AD	Cloud Identity

BUILDING REST APIs

Representational State Transfer (REST) is the most common API for creating web services in Java. The following are the most common actions:

- **`GET`**: Retrieves resource(s)
- **`DELETE`**: Deletes a resource
- **`POST`**: Creates a resource
- **`PUT`**: Updates a resource
- **`PATCH`**: Partially updates a resource

It is common for APIs to implement one of PUT or PATCH but not both, depending on the functionality of the API.

> **WHAT IS A MICROSERVICE?**
>
> Microservices represent an architectural style where the application is a collection of small services. REST APIs are often used to communicate in a microservices application but are often used without microservices.

Creating Web Services

Spring makes it easy to make a REST API as you saw in Chapter 6. The following shows a @RestController with two GET, one POST, and one DELETE action:

```
1:  @RestController
2:  @RequestMapping("/api")
3:  public class CitiesController {
4:
5:     private List<Destination> cities = new ArrayList<>();
6:
7:     @GetMapping("/cities")
8:     public List<Destination> cities() {
9:        return cities;
10:    }
11:    @GetMapping("/citiesByState/{state}")
12:    public List<Destination> citiesByState(
13:       @PathVariable("state") String state) {
14:       return cities.stream()
15:          .filter(c -> c.state().equals(state))
16:          .toList();
17:    }
18:    @PostMapping("/add")
19:    public void add(@RequestParam(name="city") String city,
20:       @RequestParam(name="state") String state) {
21:       cities.add(new Destination(city, state));
22:
23:    }
24:    @DeleteMapping("/delete")
25:    public void delete(@RequestParam(name="city") String city,
26:       @RequestParam(name="state") String state) {
27:       Destination dest = new Destination(city, state);
28:       cities.remove(dest);
29:    }
30: }
```

Lines 7–10 define a method to GET all the defined cities. It can be called as follows:

```
curl http://localhost:8080/api/cities
```

Since Jackson is a dependency in the POM, Spring automatically converts the Java application to JSON. When the application is first started up, the result is [] since the list is empty. See the Appendix if you'd like a description of the JSON syntax. After adding a city, it can look like this:

```
[{"city":"New York","state":"NY"}]
```

Lines 11–17 show another GET. This time a URL parameter is used so the state name can be passed in. For example:

```
curl http://localhost:8080/api/citiesByState/NY
```

Lines 18–29 declare the POST and DELETE method. Each receives the parameters as JSON in the request body and are called as follows:

```
curl -d city='New York&state=NY' http://localhost:8080/api/add
curl -X "DELETE" -d city='New York&state=NY'
   http://localhost:8080/api/delete
```

Documenting APIs

Swagger combines documentation and the ability to actually run the REST APIs in a browser. It's easy to add to a Spring application using a dependency with the group ID `org.springdoc` and artifact ID `-openapi-starter-webmvc-ui`. While you could use `curl` to access the REST APIs, without running a build, Swagger does require building and launching. Run the following from the `rest-apis` directory:

```
mvn clean verify
java -jar target/rest-api-0.0.1-SNAPSHOT.jar
```

Once the application is started, going to `http://localhost:8080/swagger-ui/index.html` in a browser pulls up Swagger. As you can see in Figure 14.2, all four REST APIs are automatically shown without any extra work.

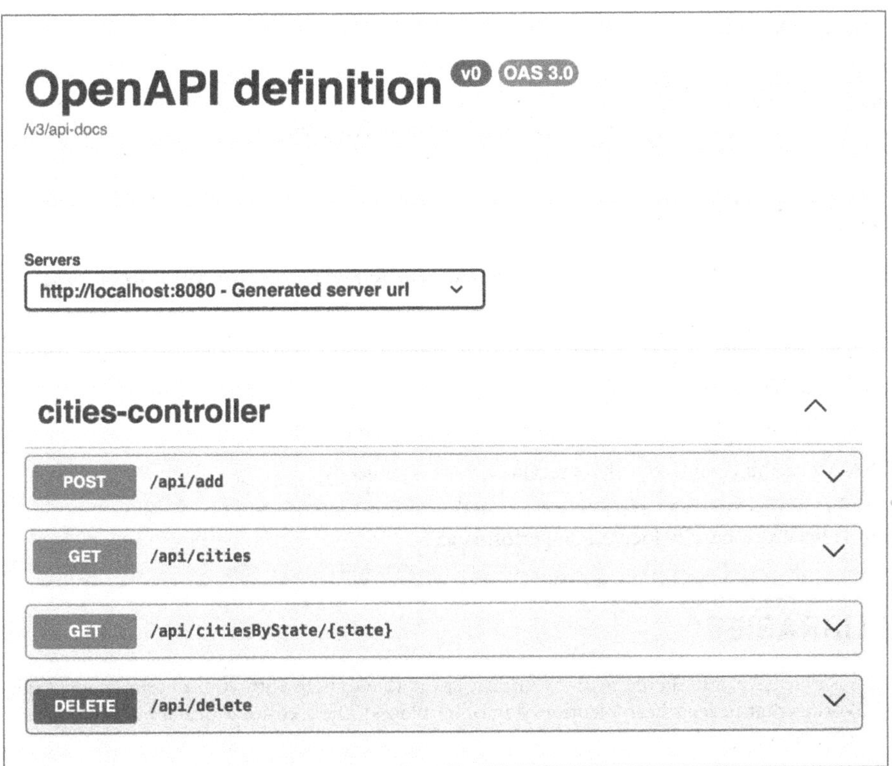

FIGURE 14.2: Swagger REST APIs

To run an API, expand the one you are interested in and click "Try it out." After adding any required parameters, click "Execute." As you can see in Figure 14.3, there are input fields for the city and state parameters generated as well.

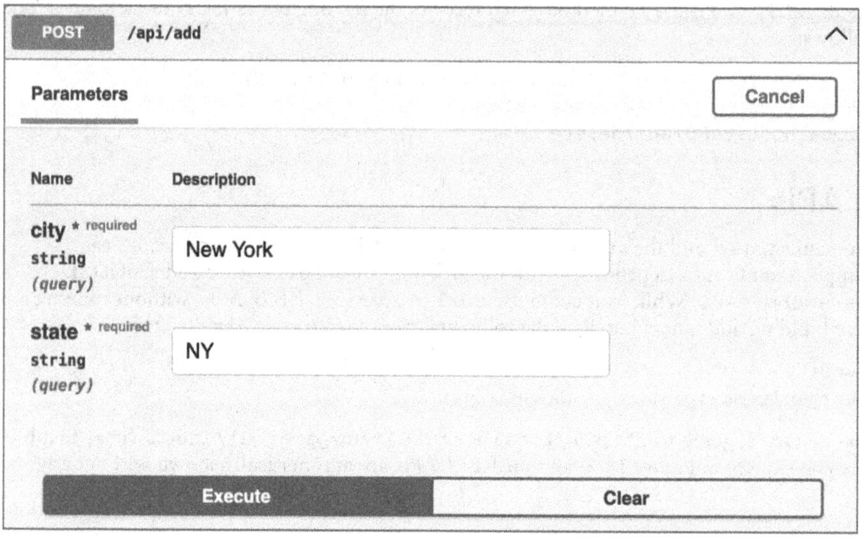

FIGURE 14.3: Executing an API

A `curl` command gets automatically generated, which is helpful if you want to test at the command line. Additionally, a 200 response code is returned since the REST API call is successful.

PICKING A VIRTUAL MACHINE

There are many Java Virtual Machines available for download. The following list gives you a feel for the options:

- **Open JDK:** Oracle's free JDK worked on with a collection of other parties. A number of vendors distribute builds based on Open JDK including Amazon Corretto, Eclipse Temurin (Adoptium), Microsoft Open JDK, and Red Hat Open JDK.
- **Oracle JDK:** Oracle's commercial JDK, which includes fixes and support.
- **Azul:** Makes free and commercial JDKs serving a variety of needs.
- **Graal VM:** A commercial JVM made by Oracle that supports both just-in-time and ahead-of-time optimization. This JVM is heavily focused on performance.

EXPLORING LIBRARIES

The Java ecosystem is extensive, and there are many libraries available to help with your development. Table 14.4 lists some of our favorites that haven't been mentioned in other places! The website for each one is in the "Further References" section.

TABLE 14.4: Example Java Libraries

LIBRARY	DESCRIPTION	FREE?
Akka	Library for concurrent and distributed systems.	Free and commercial options
Apache Commons	Parent project for many libraries supporting functionality such as CSV reading/writing, CLI argument parsing, I/O, and more.	Free and commercial options
Apache Kafka	Distributed event streaming framework often used for real-time data.	Free
Apache PDF Box	Read and write PDFs.	Free
Apache POI	Read and write Word and Excel formats. POI originally stood for Poor Obfuscation Implementation as a joke.	Free
Eclipse Collections	Many extensions to the Collections interface including more types and methods. The library allows you to write code faster and with more readability. Also, very memory efficient data structures.	Free
Google Guava Collections	Another popular collection library.	Free
iText	Read and write PDFs.	Free (under limited conditions) and commercial options
RxJava	Library for asynchronous and event-based programs.	Free

SECURING YOUR APPLICATIONS

Security is important in any project you do at work. When building your application, you as a developer should find inspiration from the OWASP Top 10.

Exploring the OWASP Top 10

The Open Worldwide Application Security Project (OWASP) Top 10 is a list of critical security guidelines you should consider when building applications. In this section, you'll see the web and mobile top 10 and understand why they matter.

While the OWASP Top 10 is updated every few years; the most recent version at the time of this publication was 2021. (The next update is projected for the first half of 2025.) There is also a mobile version that we won't be covering in this book.

The following is a summary of each. The OWASP website (see "Further References") supplies a lot of detail on each.

1. **Broken Access Control:** Users should only be allowed to see data or perform actions that their permissions allow.

2. **Cryptographic Problems:** Data should be protected at rest (for example in a database) and in transit.
3. **Injection:** All data must be sanitized (ideally against an "allow" list) to ensure that user-supplied data conforms to its expected type and does not change the meaning of any queries or output.
4. **Insecure Design:** This item pertains to the lack of security controls in the design and architecture.
5. **Security Misconfiguration:** All framework defaults should be considered and should be changed where more appropriate values are required. All settings should be configured securely.
6. **Vulnerable and Outdated Components:** Vulnerable libraries should be upgraded where possible and unused libraries should be removed. Several years ago, there was a security vulnerability in the news concerning the popular Log4J logging framework. And now, years later, there are still applications on that version!
7. **Identification and Authorization Failures:** Users should not be allowed to impersonate other users or intercept/reuse their credentials.
8. **Security and Data Integrity Failures:** All downloads should be verified to ensure they are legitimate.
9. **Security Logging and Monitoring Failures:** Data should be logged and monitored to detect attacks early.
10. **Server-Side Request Forgery (SSRF):** Applications should not be able to send data to unexpected destinations.

CVEs AND Log4J

The Common Vulnerabilities and Exposures (CVE) database is run by the U.S. government and operated by the MITRE Corporation. When a security issue is discovered, it gets a CVE number and appears on the website.

For example, Figure 14.4 shows the Log4J issue. What you may not have known was that there were four separate CVEs for Log4J within that month. The sequence of events was:

- 12/10/21 - CVE-2021-44228: The original finding where the fix was to upgrade to 2.15.0.
- 12/14/21 - CVE-2021-45046: Turns out 2.15.0 did not cover all cases.
- 12/18/21 - CVE-2021-45105: A new problem was found in all Log4J 2 versions.
- 12/28/21 - CVE-2021-44832: Yet another new problem was found.

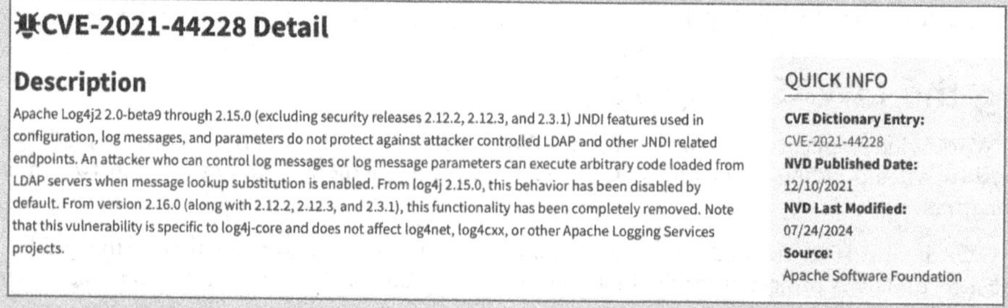

CVE-2021-44228 Detail

Description

Apache Log4j2 2.0-beta9 through 2.15.0 (excluding security releases 2.12.2, 2.12.3, and 2.3.1) JNDI features used in configuration, log messages, and parameters do not protect against attacker controlled LDAP and other JNDI related endpoints. An attacker who can control log messages or log message parameters can execute arbitrary code loaded from LDAP servers when message lookup substitution is enabled. From log4j 2.15.0, this behavior has been disabled by default. From version 2.16.0 (along with 2.12.2, 2.12.3, and 2.3.1), this functionality has been completely removed. Note that this vulnerability is specific to log4j-core and does not affect log4net, log4cxx, or other Apache Logging Services projects.

QUICK INFO

CVE Dictionary Entry:
CVE-2021-44228
NVD Published Date:
12/10/2021
NVD Last Modified:
07/24/2024
Source:
Apache Software Foundation

FIGURE 14.4: Log4J CVE

Comparing Types of Security Tools

There are a number of categories of tools to secure your application. The following are good acronyms to know:

- **Static Application Security Testing (SAST):** Tools that look at the source code to try to find vulnerabilities. SonarQube from Chapter 4 is a SAST tool.
- **Dynamic Application Security Testing (DAST):** Tools that try to inject vulnerabilities into an application while it is running.
- **Interactive Application Security Testing (IAST):** Tools placing an agent inside the running application to test in a non-production environment.
- **Runtime Application Security Protection (RASP):** Tools placing an agent inside an application running in production that looks for attacks.

STAYING INFORMED ABOUT CHANGES

Technology is fun because it changes frequently. This means it is important to read and remain up-to-date. This section suggests places to read to keep up.

If you are on social media, `https://javabubble.org` is an excellent place to find people to follow on Twitter/X, Mastodon, and LinkedIn along with a smaller number on other platforms.

For articles and blog posts, the following sites are good:

- `https://dev.java`
- `https://www.infoq.com`
- `https://foojay.io`
- `https://dzone.com`

FURTHER REFERENCES

- Javadoc
  - `https://docs.oracle.com/en/java/javase/21/docs/api/index.html`: Java 21 Javadoc
  - `https://docs.oracle.com/en/java/javase/21/javadoc/javadoc.html`: Javadoc Guide including new snippets feature
  - `https://www.oracle.com/technical-resources/articles/java/javadoc-tool.html`: How to write Javadoc
- JVM Languages
  - `https://dev.java/playground`: To run Java code online
  - `https://kotlinlang.org/docs/getting-started.html`: Kotlin documentation
  - `https://play.kotlinlang.org`: To run Kotlin code online
  - `https://groovy-lang.org/documentation.html`: Groovy documentation
  - `https://groovyide.com/playground`: To run Groovy code online

    - `https://docs.scala-lang.org`: Scala documentation
    - `https://scastie.scala-lang.org`: To run Scala code online
- Jakarta EE
    - `https://projects.eclipse.org/projects/ee4j.jakartaee-platform`: Umbrella project for the main parts of Jakarta EE
    - `https://jakarta.ee/projects`: Full list of projects
    - `https://javadoc.io`: Search for the group ID *Jakarta* to see Javadoc for each project
- Containers
    - `https://hub.docker.com`: DockerHub
    - `https://kubernetes.io/docs/home`: Kubernetes
- Cloud
    - `https://docs.aws.amazon.com`: AWS
    - `https://learn.microsoft.com/en-us/azure`: Azure
    - `https://cloud.google.com/docs`: Google Cloud
- Libraries
    - `https://akka.io`: Akka
    - `https://commons.apache.org`: Apache Commons
    - `https://pdfbox.apache.org`: Apache PDF Box
    - `https://poi.apache.org`: Apache POI
    - `https://eclipse.dev/collections`: Eclipse Collections
    - `https://guava.dev`: Google Guava Collections
    - `https://itextpdf.com`: iText
    - `https://github.com/ReactiveX/RxJava`: RxJava
- Security
    - `https://owasp.org/www-project-top-ten`: OWASP Top 10 for Web Applications
    - `https://owasp.org/www-project-mobile-top-10`: OWASP Top 10 for Mobile Applications
    - `https://nvd.nist.gov/vuln/search`: Search CVEs
    - `https://nvd.nist.gov/vuln/detail/CVE-2021-44228`: Log4J CVE

SUMMARY

In this chapter, you learned about various technologies in the Java ecosystem. Javadoc is used to document Java APIs, and Swagger documents REST APIs. Kotlin, Groovy, and Scala are just a few of the many JVM languages. Jakarta EE is a competitor of Spring with many specialized projects to meet your needs. In fact, Java has extensive libraries that you can download from Maven Central. Many technologies integrate with Java including databases, queues, and LDAP. Java applications can be deployed to an application server, made part of a Docker image, or be deployed to the cloud. Finally, you learned about some security principles and how to keep current on the Java ecosystem.

APPENDIX

Reading and Writing XML, JSON, and YAML

WHAT'S IN THIS CHAPTER?

- Working with XML
- Working with JSON
- Working with YAML

When you think about it, a Java object consists of data and functionality. If you could somehow extract the data, save it, and then marry it back to its functionality later, then you have effectively achieved a form of serialization, allowing you to persist the object's state and restore it when needed.

In this book, we use XML, JSON, and YAML in many of our examples. All three are text formats that can contain configuration data, or can be used to *serialize* data, which means converting Java instances to a format that can be easily saved on disk or transmitted. Conversely, *deserialization* is the process of rehydrating these text files back to Java instances. It is important to understand these formats since they come up frequently in the Java ecosystem.

This appendix will help you learn the basics of these formats and some ways to read and write these files from your programs. Note that the libraries we cover will have many features. These examples give you the basics, and we encourage you to explore the excellent documentation supplied with these libraries online.

CODE DOWNLOADS FOR THIS CHAPTER

The source code for this chapter is available on the book page at `www.wiley.com`. Click the Downloads link. The code can also be found at `https://github.com/realworldjava/Appendix`. See the `README.md` file in that repository for details.

WORKING WITH XML

XML stands for eXtensible Markup Language. XML files use `.xml` as a file extension. Almost all the chapters in this book have XML files in their repository, since we use Maven heavily and Maven uses a `pom.xml` file to configure a project build. REST APIs and RSS feeds also use XML.

A *markup language* is a text-based syntax that expresses relationships between tags in a document. HTML and GitHub's Markdown language are other types of markup languages. For example, in HTML, you can put bold text within a paragraph, and in Markdown you can make a bulleted list.

Learning the XML Format

Unlike HTML and Markdown, XML does not have a fixed set of elements, but you can make up your own to suit the use case at hand. That's why it's called "extensible": while the syntax is well-defined, you can extend it with your own tags and attributes in a tree structure. For example:

```
<book title="Real World Java">
   <edition>1</edition>
   <!-- multiple authors -->
   <authors>
      <author>Victor Grazi</author>
      <author>Jeanne Boyarsky</author>
   </authors>
   <paperback />
</book>
```

An XML *element* is a section that is surrounded by an opening *tag* and corresponding closing tag. An opening tag is a name surrounded by < and >. A closing tag is the same name surrounded by </ and >. Elements in XML must be nested so that opening and closing tags are all balanced. Every XML document starts with a root tag, in this case, `book`. Tags can be enriched with one or more *attributes*; quoted labels included are inside the opening tag. The `book` tag in this example has one attribute named `title`.

The third line is a comment, surrounded with `<!--` and `-->`. Comments are allowed to span multiple lines.

Most of an XML document is structured as a series of nested elements. In this example, the element names are `book`, `edition`, `authors`, `author`, and `paperback`. Notice that every element has an open and closing tag except `paperback`, which uses a shorthand. For a tag without any content, these two formats are equivalent:

```
<paperback />
<paperback></paperback>
```

The first is known as an empty element. The second has opening and closing tags without any content in between.

XML files must be *well formed*, which means they follow all of these rules:

- Tags and attribute names are case sensitive. `<paperback>` and `<Paperback>` are not the same.
- Unless using the empty tag, both an opening and closing tag are required.
- All of the tags except the root element must be nested under a parent tag.
- Tags must be nested properly, which means a child must be closed before its parent.

> **TIP** *Your integrated development environment (IDE) will give you an error if your XML file isn't well formed. Additionally, there are many online validators such as* `https://onlinexmltools.com/validate-xml`.

If you saw any of our Maven POM files, you might have noticed that the `pom.xml` files start with this:

```
<?xml version="1.0" encoding="UTF-8"?>
```

This is an optional feature called an *XML prolog*, which is used to specify the character encoding. For example, UTF-8 is most common in the United States.

You also may have noticed more code at the beginning of each `pom.xml` file.

```
<project xmlns="http://maven.apache.org/POM/4.0.0"
   xmlns:xsi=http://www.w3.org/2001/XMLSchema-instance
   xsi:schemaLocation="http://maven.apache.org/POM/4.0.0
   https://maven.apache.org/xsd/maven-4.0.0.xsd">
```

The `xmlns` attribute stands for "XML namespace." Namespaces are a standard way of listing what elements are allowed to be in the XML file. Further, namespaces allow specifying a version number.

The rest specifies the location of the XML schema definition, which in this case is the actual file location with this data. If you need to use an XML namespace or schema definition, the authors of that data would supply it to you. For common ones, like the Maven POM, it is automatically generated.

XML-RELATED TECHNOLOGIES

You may come across some other terms related to XML.

- **XML Schema Definition (XSD):** A standard format for describing the expected elements and other structure of an XML file
- **Document Type Definition (DTD):** An older format for describing the expected structure of an XML file. XML schema are now the preferred approach for this functionality
- **eXtensible Stylesheet Language Transformations (XSLT):** A stylesheet language that is applied to an XML file to produce a transformed file, such as an HTML web page
- **XML Path Language (XPath):** An expression language for concisely working with XML files
- **STreaming API for XML (StAX):** An API that parses an XML file by processing as the parser reads the file and not storing the entire file in memory
- **XML Query (XQuery):** A query and functional programming language for working with XML files

Reading XML with Jackson

Jackson is a popular library for programmatically reading (deserializing) and writing (serializing) XML. Jackson started as a JSON library, so you will see references to JSON in the code. As you might imagine, you'll see Jackson again in the JSON section!

> **TIP** *The original Jackson was made by Codehaus but is no longer supported. The current version by FasterXML is the current version, and it supports XML, JSON, and YAML.*

To use Jackson in your Maven or Gradle build, go to Maven Central at `https://mvnrepository.com/artifact/com.fasterxml.jackson.dataformat/jackson-dataformat-xml` and find the latest version number for your build tool. Table A.1 shows what this looks like for each configuration at the time of this writing.

TABLE A.1: Specifying Jackson as a Dependency

TOOL	SYNTAX

Maven	`<dependency>`
	`<groupId>com.fasterxml.jackson.dataformat</groupId>`
	`<artifactId>jackson-dataformat-xml</artifactId>`
	`<version>2.17.2</version>`
	`</dependency>`

Gradle (Groovy)	`implementation group: 'com.fasterxml.jackson.dataformat',` `name: 'jackson-dataformat-xml', version: '2.17.2'`
Gradle (Kotlin)	`implementation("com.fasterxml.jackson.dataformat:jackson-` `dataformat-xml:2.17.2")`

To include Jackson in your project, grab the appropriate syntax for your build tool and include that in your dependencies. (We cover build tools in Chapter 4, "Automating Your CI/CD Builds with Maven, Gradle, and Jenkins.")

To read a file, create an `ObjectMapper` and use it to navigate the tree structure.

```
10: File file = Path.of("src/main/resources/book.xml").toFile();
11: ObjectMapper mapper = new XmlMapper();
12: JsonNode root = mapper.readTree(file);
13:
14: System.out.println("Title: " + root.get("title").asText());
15: System.out.println("Edition: " + root.get("edition").asInt());
16: System.out.println("Paperback? " + (root.get("paperback") != null));
17:
18: JsonNode authors = root.findValues("author");
19: for (JsonNode chars : authors) {
20:    System.out.println(chars.asText());
21: }
```

This code outputs the following:

```
Title: Real World Java
Edition: 1
Paperback? true
Victor Grazi
Jeanne Boyarsky
```

Line 11 starts the XML parsing, and line 12 reads the file into a `JsonNode` instance, a Java object that encapsulates the XML tree structure and returns the root node. Lines 14 and 15 read a tag or attribute as a node along with specifying the type of the data returned. Line 16 checks if the `paperback` tag is present.

In line 18, the `findValues()` method returns a `JsonNode` containing all the author tags. Lines 19–21 loop through them outputting the text inside the tags. The `findValues()` method includes both direct children and descendants, while the `get()` method looks only at direct children.

The previous code is a brute-force approach for parsing XML, but this approach can get cumbersome for a complex XML file. Luckily, Jackson can do this much more concisely using annotations.

First you create an object that represents the XML format.

```
public class Book {
   private String title;
   private int edition;
   private Object paperback;

   @JacksonXmlElementWrapper(localName = "authors")
   @JacksonXmlProperty(localName = "author")
   private List<String> authors;

   public boolean isPaperbackBook() {
       return paperback != null;
   }
   // remaining getters and setters omitted to save space
}
```

Notice how few references there are to Jackson. If the field names match the element names precisely, you can omit those annotations, and Jackson will infer those relationships for you. The `@JacksonXmlProperty` annotation is used to tell Jackson which class fields correspond to which XML elements. `@JacksonXmlElementWrapper` tells Jackson to create a `List` of the author elements.

> **TIP** *The* `localName` *attribute is useful if you want to use a different instance variable name than what is specified in the XML. An XML element may contain characters that are not allowed in Java variables (such as hyphens) or do not follow Java naming conventions.*

Once you have a Java object, the code to populate it and read the values is easy.

```
File file = Path.of("src/main/resources/book.xml").toFile();
ObjectMapper mapper = new XmlMapper();
Book book = mapper.readValue(file, Book.class);
System.out.println(book.getTitle());           // Real World Java
System.out.println(book.getEdition());         // 1
System.out.println(book.isPaperbackBook());    // true
System.out.println(book.getAuthors());   // [Victor Grazi, Jeanne Boyarsky]
```

This object-mapping approach does precisely the same thing as the previous example, but much more concisely. Where the `readTree()` method returned a `JsonNode` instance, the `readValue()` method does all the work of parsing and converting the XML file to the supplied class type (`Book.class`) behind the scenes.

Writing XML with Jackson

If you choose the object-mapping approach, writing XML is easy. Jackson will use the getter methods that begin with `get` and `is` to generate the XML. But be careful to ensure that the methods that start with `get` and `is` are actually getter methods. In the `Book` example, there is an `is` method with business logic. To tell Jackson to ignore such a method, add the `@JsonIgnore` annotation to omit it from the XML:

```
@JsonIgnore
public boolean isPaperbackBook() {
   return paperback != null;
}
```

The `@JsonIgnore` annotation tells Jackson not to include it. Even though this is an XML parser, it uses the word JSON in the annotation. Remember that the library handles both XML and JSON, so much of the code is shared.

Additionally, you can tell Jackson to make the `book` tag in lowercase in the generated XML file with this:

```
@JacksonXmlRootElement(localName = "book")
public class Book {
```

Now that the mapping is complete, let's write code that uses the default values for all tags except for the authors.

```
Book book = new Book();
book.setAuthors(List.of("Victor & Jeanne"));

ObjectMapper mapper = new XmlMapper();

String xml = mapper
   .writer()
   .withDefaultPrettyPrinter()
   .writeValueAsString(book);
System.out.println(xml);
```

The code starts by creating a mapper as did the previous examples. It then uses the mapper `writer()` method to tell Jackson it wants to write. `withDefaultPrettyPrinter()` says to use a "pretty" format for the output. If you don't use the pretty printer, all the XML will be generated on one line. The code then writes out the XML and stores it in the variable named `xml`. The output is:

```
<book>
   <title/>
   <edition>0</edition>
   <paperback/>
   <authors>
      <author>Victor &amp; Jeanne</author>
   </authors>
</book>
```

Notice that the empty tag is used for the text fields without set values since they are `null`. By contrast, `edition` is an `int` and since we didn't provide a value in our class instance, it assigns the default `int` value of `0`. Also notice that `&` was escaped to `&` since `&` is a reserved XML escape character, it makes a best-effort to avoid using it.

> **TIP** *Important escape sequences to know for XML are `<` (<), `>` (>), and `&` (&).*

You can also write an XML file programmatically without a mapper object. It is generally more complicated and not as flexible. For example, you can't add attributes using this approach. But you will come across this kind of code:

```
ObjectMapper mapper = new XmlMapper();

ObjectNode root = mapper.createObjectNode();
root.put("edition", "1");

String xml = mapper
    .writer()
    .withRootName("book")
    .writeValueAsString(root);
System.out.println(xml);
```

Line 20 creates the usual mapper. Line 22 creates a new unnamed XML node. It gets named in line 27, which will be used when written out. In line 23 the `put` method creates a child XML node named `edition`. In this example, we omitted the pretty print so you can see how the output looks on a single line.

```
<book><edition>1</edition></book>
```

Reading and Writing XML with DOM

The Document Object Model (DOM) is an alternative to Jackson that is part of the Java for XML Processing (JAXP) APIs that are available directly in the JDK. The classes are in the package `javax.xml.parsers`.

The DOM APIs provide methods to directly navigate the XML tree. It's more verbose than Jackson, so you'll find yourself creating convenience methods if you use it. This example reads the same XML file as our previous Jackson example:

```
File file = Path.of("src/main/resources/book.xml").toFile();

// To start parsing, DOM requires a DocumentBuilder. Steps to get that:
DocumentBuilderFactory factory = DocumentBuilderFactory.newInstance();
DocumentBuilder builder = factory.newDocumentBuilder();
Document doc = builder.parse(file);

Node root = doc.getElementsByTagName("book").item(0);
System.out.println(
   root.getAttributes().getNamedItem("title").getNodeValue());
System.out.println(
   doc.getElementsByTagName("edition").item(0).getTextContent());

System.out.println("Paperback? " + (doc.getElementsByTagName(
   "paperback").getLength() != 0));

NodeList authors = doc.getElementsByTagName("author");
for (int i = 0; i < authors.getLength(); i++) {
   System.out.println(authors.item(i).getTextContent());
}
```

As you can see, there is an API to get all the elements with a specific tag. From an element, you can get attributes or the text data between tags. You can also loop through all the children of a node.

Writing a file via the DOM contains a good amount of boilerplate code.

```
DocumentBuilderFactory factory = DocumentBuilderFactory.newInstance();
DocumentBuilder builder = factory.newDocumentBuilder();
Document doc = builder.newDocument();

Element root = doc.createElement("book");
doc.appendChild(root);

Element edition = doc.createElement("edition");
edition.appendChild(doc.createTextNode("1"));
root.appendChild(edition);

DOMSource source = new DOMSource(doc);
StreamResult result = new StreamResult(System.out);

TransformerFactory transformerFactory = TransformerFactory.newInstance();
Transformer transformer = transformerFactory.newTransformer();
```

```
transformer.setOutputProperty(OutputKeys.INDENT, "yes");
transformer.setOutputProperty(OutputKeys.OMIT_XML_DECLARATION, "yes");
transformer.transform(source, result);
```

Here you can see that `createElement()` is used to create a tag and `createTextNode()` is used to add the text inside a tag. A `Transformer` is used to control the output settings, in this case, adding indentation and removing the XML prologue. Finally, the `transform()` method actually writes the XML.

Reading XML with SAX

JAXP also includes the Simple API for XML (SAX), which is an event-driven approach for reading an XML file. Since SAX processes data as it is read, the whole file does not need to be loaded into memory at once, making it a good choice for large files. Note that SAX is only for reading; you cannot write a file using SAX.

The first step for parsing an XML file using SAX is to create a *handler*. For simple use cases, a handler can be fairly short. For more complex ones, it can be harder to understand.

```
12: public class BookSaxHandler extends DefaultHandler {
13:
14:    private boolean inTagWithText = false;
15:    private boolean paperback;
16:
17:    @Override
18:    public void startElement(String uri, String localName,
19:       String qualifiedName, Attributes attributes) {
20:       switch (qualifiedName) {
21:          case "edition", "author" -> inTagWithText = true;
22:          case "paperback" -> paperback = true;
23:          case "authors" ->
24:             System.out.println("Paperback? " + paperback);
25:          case "book" ->
26:             System.out.println(attributes.getValue("title"));
27:       }
28:    }
29:    @Override
30:    public void endElement(String uri, String localName,
31:          String qualifiedName) {
32:       inTagWithText = false;
33:    }
34:    @Override
35:    public void characters(char[] chars, int start, int length) {
36:       if (inTagWithText) {
37:          String text = new String(chars, start, length);
38:          System.out.println(text);
39:       }
40:    }
41: }
```

In SAX, you extend a handler as shown on line 12. As the parser encounters elements, it calls methods like `startElement`, `endElement`, and `characters`, which you override for your use case.

The `characters()` method starting in line 35 prints the text inside the tag. You might be thinking that `edition` and `author` are the only tags that even have data. However, the other tags have empty strings, so we still need this logic. SAX passes more data than we care about, so we build a `String` of just the part of the array that goes with these tags.

The endElement() method override simply updates a boolean to say we are no longer in a tag. While it could check to see if it is a tag we care about, the operation is redundant if already false. Therefore, the method is as simple as possible.

Then there is the startElement() method override, which uses a switch to perform a different operation based on the tag. Note that localName is relevant only if working with namespaces, so this code uses qualifiedName. Line 21 sets a boolean if the tag is edition or author. This is the boolean used in characters(). Line 22 notes if the paperback tag is seen, and lines 23–24 print whether paperback was seen when getting to the authors tag. Lines 25–26 print the attribute title if on the book tag.

Now that you have the handler, actually reading is easy.

```
File file = Path.of("src/main/resources/book.xml").toFile();

SAXParserFactory factory = SAXParserFactory.newInstance();
SAXParser parser = factory.newSAXParser();
BookSaxHandler handler = new BookSaxHandler();

parser.parse(file, handler);
```

The only things happening here are creating the objects and calling parse(). All the logic is in the handler class.

Comparing XML Libraries

There are many XML libraries. The following lists some of the more popular ones:

- **Faster XML Jackson:** This library provides multiple ways of reading and writing data as shown earlier in the chapter. The code is similar for XML and JSON, which often makes it a good choice.
- **Java API for XML Processing (JAXP):** The DOM and SAX examples you saw previously were JAXP. These libraries are good for straightforward uses or if you have existing code using them. They come built-in with the JDK.
- **Document Object Model for Java (DOM4J):** This library is less verbose than DOM from JAXP. It is also faster and more memory efficient for large XML files.
- **Xerces:** This library provides alternate, and faster, DOM and SAX implementations than JAXP. Many open-source and commercial products use Xerces under the covers.

DO I NEED A LIBRARY?

Technically, you could read the XML as text and parse it using indexOf() or a regular expression. Please don't. The resulting code is very difficult to read compared to the XML parsing libraries.

Writing XML should also use a library if doing anything of reasonable complexity. However, for short XML, it is viable to write it directly as follows:

```
String xml = """
   <book>
      <edition>%d</edition>
   </book>""";
System.out.format(xml, 1)
```

WORKING WITH JSON

JSON (pronounced "jay-sawn" or "jay-sahn") stands for JavaScript Object Notation. Like XML, it is a way of specifying data. Examples of JSON include working with REST APIs and configuring libraries, such as logging. JSON files most commonly use the extension `.json`, but can also use `.jsn`.

Learning the JSON Format

Let's consider how to transform our book XML file to JSON format:

```
{
  "title": "Real World Java",
  "edition" : 1,
  "authors" : [ "Victor Grazi", "Jeanne Boyarsky"],
  "paperback" : true
}
```

The data consists of key/value pairs. In our example there are four keys, `title`, `edition`, `authors`, and `paperback`, which represent the four elements in the XML example.

The code shows that the values can be any of a variety of data types including string, number, array, and boolean. It is possible to nest JSON, so for example, to add more detail to each author, the `authors` array could be expanded to this:

```
"authors": [
    {
      "name": "Victor Grazi",
      "first": true
    },
    {
      "name": "Jeanne Boyarsky",
      "first": false
    }
  ],
```

A JSON file must comply with the rules in order to be valid. In particular:

- Keys are case sensitive.
- Keys must be in double quotes.
- Strings must be in double quotes.
- If nesting is used, it must be well formed.
- Data is separated by commas.
- There is no comma after the last key/value pair.

> **TIP** *Like XML, your IDE will give you an error if your JSON file isn't valid. There are also many online validators such as* `https://jsonlint.com`.

Unlike XML, JSON does not support comments.

The JSON schema is an optional way of describing the expected shape of your JSON data. There are a number of tools for processing and querying JSON including `jq`.

Reading JSON with Jackson

Remember Jackson from the previous section? Using Jackson with JSON is similar to using it with XML, which means this code will look familiar. We'll highlight the differences after each piece of code rather than explaining it from scratch.

If you are following along, you don't need to add a dependency, as `jackson-databind` is a transitive dependency of `jackson-dataformat-xml`. If you are starting from scratch and want to use Jackson for JSON in your Maven or Gradle build, go to Maven Central at `https://mvnrepository.com/artifact/com.fasterxml.jackson.core/jackson-databind` and find the latest version number for your build tool. Table A.2 shows what this looks like for each configuration at the time of this writing.

TABLE A.2: Specifying Jackson as a Dependency

TOOL	SYNTAX

Maven	`<dependency>`
	`<groupId>com.fasterxml.jackson.core</groupId>`
	`<artifactId>jackson-databind</artifactId>`
	`<version>2.17.2</version>`
	`</dependency>`

Gradle (Groovy)	`implementation group: 'com.fasterxml.jackson.core, name: 'jackson-databind', version: '2.17.2'`
Gradle (Kotlin)	`implementation("com.fasterxml.jackson.core:jackson-databind:2.17.2")`

Grab the appropriate syntax for your build tool and include that in your dependencies.

Our first example will navigate the tree structure.

```
11: File file = Path.of("src/main/resources/book.json").toFile();
12: ObjectMapper mapper = new JsonMapper();
13: JsonNode root = mapper.readTree(file);
14:
15: System.out.println(root.get("title").asText());
16: System.out.println(root.get("edition").asInt());
17: System.out.println("Paperback? " + root.get("paperback"));
18:
19: JsonNode authors = root.findValue("authors");
20: for (JsonNode chars : authors) {
21:    System.out.println(chars.asText());
22: }
```

To parse JSON, we use a `JsonMapper` in line 12. Contrast this to the `XmlMapper` we used for parsing XML. Additionally, the `null` check for `paperback` is gone since the JSON example is using a `boolean` rather than an empty tag.

Like XML, you can map the JSON to a Java object such as this:

```
public class Book {
   private String title;
   private int edition;
```

```
        @JsonProperty("paperback")
        private boolean paperbackBook;
        private List<String> authors;
        public boolean isPaperbackBook() {
            return paperbackBook;
        }
        // remaining getters and setters omitted to save space
    }
```

The annotations that were required for our XML parser for mapping nested `author` tags into a `List` are gone, since JSON is using an array, which automatically maps to `List`. The `@JsonProperty` is new and is used to map the field using a different instance variable name than the JSON file. Finally, notice that `isPaperbackBook()` is now a normal getter as the specialized logic for the empty XML tag is gone.

Now that you have a Java object, the code to populate it and read the values should look familiar:

```
File file = Path.of("src/main/resources/book.json").toFile();
ObjectMapper mapper = new JsonMapper();
Book book = mapper.readValue(file, Book.class);
System.out.println(book.getTitle());
System.out.println(book.getEdition());
System.out.println(book.isPaperbackBook());
System.out.println(book.getAuthors());
```

The only difference in this code besides the filename is that `JsonMapper` is used instead of `XmlMapper`.

Writing JSON with Jackson

Writing JSON is just as easy as writing XML. No changes are needed to the `Book` class.

```
Book book = new Book();
book.setAuthors(List.of("Victor & Jeanne"));

ObjectMapper mapper = new JsonMapper();

String json = mapper
   .writer()
   .withDefaultPrettyPrinter()
   .writeValueAsString(book);
System.out.println(json);
```

The only material change here is the mapper class name `JsonMapper`. Additionally, we changed the name of the `json` variable for clarity. The output is as follows:

```
{
   "title" : null,
   "edition" : 0,
   "paperback" : false,
   "authors" : [ "Victor & Jeanne" ]
}
```

As with XML, all defaults are used except the `authors` array. Note that `&` is not escaped as JSON doesn't view it as a special character.

Writing JSON programmatically is also similar to the XML version.

```
ObjectMapper mapper = new JsonMapper();

ObjectNode root = mapper.createObjectNode();
```

```
root.put("edition", "1");

String json = mapper
   .writer()
   .writeValueAsString(root);
System.out.println(json);
```

Again, the mapper and variable names now refer to JSON. Additionally, the method call to set the root name is gone since JSON does not have the concept of a named root node. The output is as follows:

```
{"edition":"1"}
```

Reading and Writing JSON with Gson

Gson is Google's lightweight JSON library. While we recommend Jackson for new projects, Gson is widely used. It is also helpful to see how similar basic operations are. This will help you learn other libraries faster as you encounter them.

To use Gson in your Maven or Gradle build, go to Maven Central at `https://mvnrepository.com/artifact/com.google.code.gson/gson` and find the latest version number for your build tool. Table A.3 shows what this looks like for each configuration at the time of this writing.

TABLE A.3: Specifying Gson as a Dependency

TOOL	SYNTAX

Maven	`<dependency>`
	`<groupId>com.google.code.gson</groupId>`
	`<artifactId>gson</artifactId>`
	`<version>2.11.0</version>`
	`</dependency>`

Gradle (Groovy)	`implementation group: 'com.google.code.gson',` `name: 'gson', version: '2.11.0'`
Gradle (Kotlin)	`implementation("com.google.code.gson:gson:2.11.0")`

Grab the appropriate syntax for your build tool and include that in your dependencies.

First you create the `Book` class.

```
public class Book {
   private String title;
   private int edition;

   @SerializedName("paperback")
   private boolean paperbackBook;
   private List<String> authors;
   // getters and setters omitted to save space
}
```

Notice how the only difference from Jackson is that Gson uses `@SerializedName`, which is used to map the JSON field name to a different Java field name. The Gson idiom for creating an instance of `Book` is as follows:

```
Gson gson = new Gson();
Book book = gson.fromJson(new FileReader(file), Book.class);
```

The idea is similar to Jackson. Create a class to do the work and call an API, this time `fromJson()`, to create the `Book` instance. The following is the equivalent code for writing:

```
Book book = new Book();
book.setAuthors(List.of("Victor & Jeanne"));

Gson gson = new Gson();
System.out.println(gson.toJson(book));
```

This code calls `toJson()` since it is writing JSON, as opposed to `fromJson()` that was used for reading. The output yields the following:

```
{"edition":0,"authors":["Victor \u0026 Jeanne"]}
```

But what's that `\u0026`? That is a Unicode escape sequence; by default, Gson makes the output HTML safe. While this is legal JSON, it might not be what you were expecting. You can use `GsonBuilder` to turn off this behavior:

```
Gson gson = new GsonBuilder().disableHtmlEscaping().create();
```

Comparing JSON Libraries

There are many JSON libraries. The following lists some of the more popular ones:

- **Jackson:** This library provides multiple ways of reading and writing data as shown earlier in the chapter. The code is similar for XML and JSON, which often makes it a good choice.
- **Gson:** This is Google's lightweight library, which is also used in this chapter.
- **JSON.Java:** This library is also known as org.json and was built as a reference implementation but is still being updated.
- **JSON-P and JSON-B:** These are the Jakarta parsing and binding specifications.

WORKING WITH YAML

YAML (rhymes with camel) originally stood for Yet Another Markup Language, but was renamed to YAML Ain't Markup Language. Without quibbling about the definition of a markup language, YAML replaces tags and brackets with indentations and is a succinct way of specifying data and configuration.

Examples of YAML include configuring Spring Cloud Security or libraries such as logging frameworks. Many CI/CD systems even let you use YAML to specify your build pipeline. YAML files can use the extension `.yaml` or `.yml`.

Learning the YAML Format

Let's revisit our book file, this time using YAML:

```
---
title: "Real World Java"
edition: 1
# multiple authors
authors:
  - Victor Grazi
  - Jeanne Boyarsky
paperback: true
```

Unlike XML and JSON, indentation matters in YAML. Spaces are used to show levels of indentation. It doesn't matter how many spaces you use for each level of indentation, provided that you always use the same number of spaces for each level. Tabs are not allowed to be used since IDEs handled them differently, and they would throw off the white space count.

The three dashes at the top start the document and are optional. YAML allows you to put multiple YAML documents in the same file, so the three dashes show the start.

Like JSON, the file consists largely of key/value pairs. There are four keys, `title`, `edition`, `authors`, and `paperback`, which represent the four pieces of data in the XML and JSON examples.

Also, like JSON, there can be string, number, and boolean types. In our example, the authors are specified with both indentation and hyphens to show they are part of a sequence, or ordered list. You can have multiple levels of indentation for more involved data structures.

YAML supports single-line comments anywhere in the document. Comments begin with the # character and continue to the end of the line.

A YAML file must comply with the rules to be valid. In particular:

- Keys are case sensitive.
- Indentation must be consistent and use spaces, not tabs.
- Hyphens are used for sequences.

> **TIP** *Like XML and JSON, your IDE will give you an error if your YAML file isn't valid. There are also many online validators such as* `https://www.yamllint.com`.

Reading YAML with Jackson

While you used Jackson earlier in the chapter, another dependency is needed for YAML. To use Jackson for YAML in your Maven or Gradle build, go to Maven Central at `https://mvnrepository.com/artifact/com.fasterxml.jackson.dataformat/jackson-dataformat-yaml` and find the latest version number for your build tool. Table A.4 shows what this looks like for each configuration at the time of this writing.

TABLE A.4: Specifying Jackson YAML as a Dependency

TOOL	SYNTAX

Maven	`<dependency>`
	`   <groupId>com.fasterxml.jackson.dataformat</groupId>`
	`   <artifactId>jackson-dataformat-yaml</artifactId>`
	`   <version>2.17.2</version>`
	`</dependency>`

Gradle (Groovy)	`implementation group: 'com.fasterxml.jackson.dataformat', name: 'jackson-dataformat-yaml', version: '2.17.2'`
Gradle (Kotlin)	`implementation("com.fasterxml.jackson.dataformat:jackson-dataformat-yaml:2.17.2")`

Grab the appropriate syntax for your build tool and include that in your dependencies.

The Book class is exactly the same as we defined it when we used Jackson to parse JSON. This time the code to read our YAML file uses a YAMLMapper:

```
File file = Path.of("src/main/resources/book.yaml").toFile();
ObjectMapper mapper = new YAMLMapper();
```

Yes, that is all. You read the YAML file using the YAMLMapper. Other than that, it works the same as the JSON version. Even the @JsonProperty is the same since the Jackson parser shares code.

Writing YAML with Jackson

The code to write YAML is similar to the JSON code.

```
Book book = new Book();
book.setAuthors(List.of("Victor & Jeanne"));

ObjectMapper mapper = new YAMLMapper();

String yaml = mapper
   .writer()
   .withDefaultPrettyPrinter()
   .writeValueAsString(book);
 System.out.println(yaml);
```

The changes are the usual, just the mapper and variable name. The output uses all the type defaults for any values that aren't explicitly set. It also includes quotes around the authors string value:

```
---
title: null
edition: 0
authors:
- "Victor & Jeanne"
paperback: false
```

Similarly, writing a specific field uses the put method, as we saw earlier in our XML and JSON examples.

```
ObjectMapper mapper = new YAMLMapper();

ObjectNode root = mapper.createObjectNode();
root.put("edition", 1);

String yaml = mapper
   .writer()
   .writeValueAsString(root);
System.out.println(yaml);
```

The output shows only one field since that is the only one set.

```
---
edition: 1
```

Reading and Writing with SnakeYAML

SnakeYAML is a popular library for working with YAML. It is easy to use for simple operations and offers powerful customizations for advanced users. To use it in your Maven or Gradle build, go to Maven Central at https://mvnrepository.com/artifact/org.yaml/snakeyaml and find the latest version number for your build tool. Table A.5 shows what this looks like for each configuration at the time of this writing.

TABLE A.5: Specifying SnakeYAML as a Dependency

TOOL	SYNTAX

Maven	`<dependency>`
	`<groupId>org.yaml</groupId>`
	`<artifactId>snakeyaml</artifactId>`
	`<version>2.3</version>`
	`</dependency>`

Gradle (Groovy)	`implementation group: 'org.yaml',` `name: 'snakeyaml', version: '2.3'`
Gradle (Kotlin)	`implementation("org.yaml:snakeyaml:2.3")`

Grab the appropriate syntax for your build tool and include that in your dependencies.

First, you'll see the code for navigating the YAML.

```
File file = Path.of("src/main/resources/book.yaml").toFile();
Yaml yaml = new Yaml();
Map<String, Object> map = yaml.load(new FileReader(file));

System.out.println(map.get("title"));
System.out.println(map.get("edition"));
System.out.println("Paperback? " + map.get("paperback"));

List<String> authors = (List<String>) map.get("authors");
for (String author : authors) {
   System.out.println(author);
}
```

As you can see, a `Yaml` object is constructed and used to load the data. An advantage of SnakeYAML is that the data is loaded into a `Map`, which you can print out to see what was read. A disadvantage is that casts are necessary for any data you want to assign to a variable like `authors` being a `List<String>`.

```
File file = Path.of("src/main/resources/book.yaml").toFile();
Constructor constructor = new Constructor(Book.class, new LoaderOptions());
Yaml yaml = new Yaml(constructor);

Book book = yaml.load(new FileReader(file));

System.out.println(book.getTitle());
System.out.println(book.getEdition());
System.out.println(book.isPaperback());
System.out.println(book.getAuthors());
```

To load data into a Java object, you create a `Constructor` class and then a `Yaml` object. While this works for basic classes, it is difficult if you want to change the names from the YAML or specify generic types.

Writing YAML created from a `Map` is straightforward.

```
Map<String, String> map = new HashMap<>();
map.put("edition", "1");

DumperOptions options = new DumperOptions();
options.setDefaultFlowStyle(DumperOptions.FlowStyle.BLOCK);
```

```
Yaml yaml = new Yaml(options);

String output = yaml.dump(map);
System.out.println(output);
```

Calling `dump()` creates YAML with the one value specified:

```
edition: '1'
```

By contrast, writing a YAML file from an object is more complicated because the defaults might not be intuitive.

```
11: Book book = new Book();
12: book.setAuthors(List.of("Victor & Jeanne"));
13:
14: DumperOptions options = new DumperOptions();
15: options.setDefaultFlowStyle(DumperOptions.FlowStyle.BLOCK);
16:
17: Representer representer = new Representer(options);
18: representer.addClassTag(Book.class, Tag.MAP);
19:
20: Yaml yaml = new Yaml(representer, options);
21:
22: String output = yaml.dump(book);
23: System.out.println(output);
```

On lines 11 and 12, we create a `Book` instance. Next, we create an instance of `DumperOptions` to configure the YAML. In this example, the flow style is set to `BLOCK`, which causes `Victor & Jeanne` to be displayed after a hyphen since it is a `List`. YAML has a more concise alternate style that is output if you don't specify `BLOCK`.

Lines 17 and 18 define the `Representer`. Since SnakeYAML automatically outputs a tag for the class name, the `Representer` is configured so that is not included. If you don't do this, special code that lists the name of the class gets output in the JSON preceded by `!!`.

Finally, the YAML object is created, and the output is dumped, giving you the following:

```
authors:
- Victor & Jeanne
edition: 0
paperback: false
title: null
```

Comparing YAML Libraries

As you might expect, there are many YAML libraries. The following lists some of the more popular ones:

- **Jackson:** YAML support works like the XML and JSON support making it an excellent choice when supporting multiple data formats.
- **SnakeYAML:** This library is popular and used in this chapter. It is simple to use for loading/dumping from a `Map` and has powerful customizations.
- **YAMLBeans:** This is a lightweight framework for YAML.

FURTHER REFERENCES

- XML
    - `https://www.w3.org/TR/xml`: XML specification
    - `https://onlinexmltools.com/validate-xml`: Online validator

    - `https://javadoc.io/doc/com.fasterxml.jackson.core/jackson-databind/latest/index.html`: Jackson Javadoc
    - `https://dom4j.github.io`: DOM4J
    - `https://xerces.apache.org`: Xerces
- JSON
    - `https://datatracker.ietf.org/doc/html/rfc8259`: JSON specification
    - `https://jsonlint.com`: Online validator
    - `https://json-schema.org`: JSON schema
    - `https://jqlang.github.io/jq/`: JSON query language and processor
    - `https://javadoc.io/doc/com.google.code.gson/gson/`: Gson Javadoc
    - `https://github.com/stleary/JSON-java`: `JSON.java`: (also known as org.json)
    - `https://javaee.github.io/jsonp/`: JSON-P
    - `https://javaee.github.io/jsonb-spec/`: JSON-B
- YAML
    - `https://yaml.org/spec/`: YAML specification
    - `https://www.yamllint.com`: YAML validator
    - `https://bitbucket.org/snakeyaml/snakeyaml/wiki/Documentation`: SnakeYAML
    - `https://javadoc.io/doc/org.yaml/snakeyaml/latest/index.html`: SnakeYAML Javadoc
    - `https://github.com/EsotericSoftware/yamlbeans`: YAMLBeans

SUMMARY

XML, JSON, and YAML are common formats for specifying configuration and data. The Jackson library works with all three formats. JAXP, via DOM and SAX, works with XML. The Gson library works with JSON. Finally, the SnakeYAML library is used for YAML.

INDEX

A

B

C

D

E

F

G

H

I

J

M

Q

R

S

T

U

V

W

X

Y

Z